P9-CEF-749

HITLER'S WARRIOR

HITLER'S WARRIOR

The Life and Wars of SS Colonel Jochen Peiper

DANNY S. PARKER

Da Capo Press
A Member of the Perseus Books Group

 Printed in the United States of America. For information, address Da Capo Press, 44 Farnsworth Street, Third Floor, Boston, MA 02210.

Maps were created by Gene Thorp; all photos are from the author's collection unless otherwise noted.

Editorial production by Lori Hobkirk at the Book Factory.

Set in 10 point Adobe Garamond Pro

Cataloging-in-Publication data for this book is available from the Library of Congress.
ISBN: 978-0-306-82154-7 (hardcover)
ISBN: 978-0-306-82354-1 (e-book)

Published by Da Capo Press
A Member of the Perseus Books Group
www.dacapopress.com

10 9 8 7 6 5 4 3 2 1

For two wonderful sisters,
Susan and Sharon,
and lovely days together

CONTENTS

List of Maps ix
Prologue: The Simple Life xiii

Part One Ascent

1 Dream of the Reich 3
2 Empire 13
3 The Inner Ring 23
4 With Himmler 36

Part Two Zenith

5 Hubris 53
6 Barbarossa 69
7 Letters from the War 84
8 Front and Fatherland 100

Part Three Fall

9 Oblivion 117
10 Endgame 130
11 Manhunt 137
12 On Trial 147
13 Ellis 159
14 Verdict 172

Part Four In Extremis

15 Landsberg 187
16 Steeplechase 200
17 "We All Have Our Crossroads" 213

18 Under Four Eyes 223
19 Old Hares 236

Part Five Requiem

20 The Old German Hero 245
21 Blow-Up 251
22 La Fête Nationale 262
23 Reckoning 270
24 Ghosts of the Past 286

Epilogue 305

Notes 309
Acknowledgments 422
Index 427

LIST OF MAPS

1. Peiper's World, 1915–1976   x–xi
2. Traves, France, Summer 1976   xvi
3. Approach to Peiper's House, Night of July 13–14, 1976   283
4. The Final Minutes   283

Peiper's World
1915-1976
NORWAY
Oslo
SWEDEN
North Sea
DENMARK
Copenhagen
IRELAND
GREAT BRITAIN
London
Kiel
Bad Doberan
Rostock
Hamburg
Neuengamme
Brückenthin
Stettin
Hagen
Elbe R.
Amsterdam
NETHERLANDS
Rahden
Ravensbrück
Birkenwa
Rotterdam
Nijmegen
Münster
Braunschweig
Berlin
Wormhoudt
Dixmude
GERMANY
Wilmersdorf
Wattenburg
Wewelsburg
Quedlinburg
Jüterbog
English Channel
Esquelbecq
BELGIUM
Weser R.
Abbeville
Brussels
Cologne
Kassel
Buchenwald
Arras
Dresden
Atlantic Ocean
Tilly
Caen
Wervicq
Koblenz
Oberursel
Karlsbad
Prague
Avranches
Falaise
Detail
Frankfurt
Garcelles
Paris
Schwäbisch Hall
Flossenberg
Verneuil sur Avre
Etrépilly
Metz
Zuffenhausen
Nuremberg
Sinzheim
Feuchtwangen
Seine R.
Stuttgart
Mauthausen
Vesoul
FRANCE
Traves
Reutlingen
Dachau
Munich
St. Pölt
Gray
Freiburg
Landsberg
Halfing
Dijon
Basel
Bad Tölz
Steyr
St. Pourçain
Besançon
SWITZERLAND
Berchtesgaden
St. Anton
Bad Gastein
Orador-sur-Glane
Tegernsee
AUSTRIA
Miesbach
Obersalzberg
Bordeaux
Savoie
Lago Maggiore
Rhône R.
Torino
Po R.
Milan
Dax
Alessandria
Cuneo
Boves
Borgo San Dalmazzo
Marseilles
Monaco
St. Tropez
Adriatic
Madrid
Montserrat
ITALY
SPAIN
Barcelona
Rome
Tyrrhenian Sea
Mediterranean Sea
SICILY
Map by Gene Thorp

100 0 200 miles
100 0 200 kilometers
International borders as of 1937
ESTONIA
LATVIA
Riga
Baltic Sea
Dünaberg
Krottingen
LITHUANIA
Kowno
Wilna
EAST PRUSSIA (GER.)
Danzig
Hochwald
Augustow
Grodno
Graudenz
Wolfsschanze
Bromberg
Soldau
Bialystok
Staren
Plock
Warsaw
POLAND
Kutno
Lodz
Tomassow
Bug R.
Lublin
Kielce
Oppeln
Vistula R.
Krakau
Przemysl
Jaroslaw
Minsk
Moscow
U . S . S . R .
Kursk
Prokhorovka
Teterewino
Belgorod
Alexandrowka
Ljubotin
Kharkov
Federowka
Smijew
Stanitschnoje
Staroverowka
Jefremowka
Donetsi R.
Pripyat
Krasnoborki
Sabolot
Radomyshl
Pekartschina
Kiev
Tortschin
Zhitomir
Dnieper R.
Pivd. Buh R.
Dniester R.
Taganrog
Rostov
Mariupol
Greigova
Cherson
Budapest
HUNGARY
ROMANIA
Black Sea
Danube R.
BULG.
ALBANIA
GREECE
Larissa
Athens
Ionian Sea
NETH.
Venlo
Düsseldorf
Antwerp
GERMANY
Rhine R.
Cologne
Hasselt
Brussels
Maastricht
Düren
Weilwerwist
Altenkirchen
Aachen
Bonn
BELGIUM
Meuse R.
Huy
Liege
Rheinbach
Bad Münstereifel
Charleroi
La Gleize
Malmedy
Blankenheim
Ligneuville
Koblenz
Losheim
Petit Thier
Thirimont
St. Vith
Prüm
Marienfels
Mosel R.
Bastogne
Lutrebois
LUX.
Osweiler
Colmar-Berg
Trier
FRANCE
Luxembourg City
0 40 miles
0 40 kilometers

"If only it were all so simple! If only there were evil people somewhere committing evil deeds, and it were necessary only to separate them from the rest of us and destroy them. But the dividing line between good and evil cuts through the heart of every human being. And who is willing to destroy a piece of their own heart?"

—Aleksandr Solzhenitsyn,
The Gulag Archipelago

PROLOGUE

The Simple Life

THE OLD MAN LIKED TO CHOP FIREWOOD FOR RELAXATION. HIS SKIN WAS sunburnt and leathery, and his forehead was etched deeply above his brow. His aging Romanesque profile was topped by wiry hair. It was white now, and his hairline was receding and his eyebrows bushy and unkempt, but his angular features remained handsome in old age. He liked to wear oversized plaid hunting shirts with the sleeves rolled up to his elbows, revealing long, sinewy arms. Although retired, the man often worked outdoors for long hours each day. He loved the gentle rolling green hills of Eastern France. Each sunrise promised the freedom of working with his hands under a broad blue sky. It was a simple life, but for him a satisfying one.

At sixty-one, he was slim and fit, although he had a few complaints. His right leg—an old war injury—bothered him from time to time. Yet each day he would spend an hour or two running his two big Deutsch Drahthaar hunting dogs. Fondly nicknamed Cuno von Grafengau, Timm was the father of the younger puppy, Tamm. "My lions," he called them affectionately.[1] His hounds had free rein of the forest ways that threaded along the river by his house and, as dogs were wont to do, would sometimes venture off. On May 28, 1976, they got to a flock of sheep in nearby Scey-sur-Saône—something had to be done.[2] Years before, the man had fabricated an enclosure to contain their wanderlust. Now he would double down—something more for the worklist.[3]

He rose early each morning to review the day's schedule over cups of steaming tea. Often the penciled list involved clearing the birch and firs that continuously threatened to reclaim his oasis in the woods. Sometimes it was the blackberry vines. Skilled with an axe and saw, he civilized the wilderness outside and stood against the growth. The task was unending. It was something of a sanguine vision of Camus's *Myth of Sisyphus*. In the afternoons he often worked a small flower garden he had arduously carved out of the brush. "Outside the weather is marvelous," he wrote his good friend. "The thermometer on my pigeon coop says 80 degrees. The Saône flows quietly, flowers wink everywhere. My dog Timm walks impatiently back and forth on the terrace as if looking for a forest ghost."[4]

Inside the home was a sanctuary. His wife kept that. Upon arriving at the doorstep, he was careful to clean his boots and leave them outside. Even strangers arriving at the door had to be properly dressed and muddy shoes cleaned before entering. Otherwise the German had to speak with them on the patio under the glass terrace. And even his beloved dogs had to stay outdoors unless she cleaned their paws.

On lazy summer afternoons he and his wife frequently rowed their small wooden boat on the quietly flowing River Saône. The river there was about twice as wide as the man could throw a stone. Each bank was covered by long hanging trees under which the muddy water curled and eddied slowly by, just like the languid pace of life in nearby Traves. A straw hat, fishing reels, and a box lunch could make for a relaxing afternoon among the lily pads. Some days he walked along the high banks of the Saône, watching the swans as he neared the bridge. On other mornings he could be heard tapping away at his typewriter in his study or on the veranda. In the heat of the afternoon he would swim across the Saône several times to relax and cool off, then perhaps some reading under the shade of the saplings he had planted. The vision was French pastorale.

Winter days were equally rustic. Against the cold he would retire to the comfort of his home and carry an armload of his carefully cut wood to the fireplace. A crackling fire provided heat and light as he read in an easy chair. A hot cup of tea would shed any remaining chill. The short days were quiet and uneventful. "Here, we have not only silence," he wrote a friend, "but also complete peace."[5]

At night he and his wife would share a simple meal. Rather than refined fare, he liked family cooking—hearty stews and the like. If it were a special occasion, they might share a bottle of red wine—a gift from their caring friend, Dr. Benno Müller.[6] To keep up with world events in his isolated abode, he would often read *Der Spiegel* from one cover to the next.[7] After dinner he would ease into his favorite chair, sip tea, perhaps indulge in good pipe tobacco, and spend an hour or so listening to classical music on the hi-fi. Pieces by Bach or Telemann were appropriate if the mood was light. If he were feeling serious, he might choose the rich pathos of Beethoven's *Eroica Symphony* or the *Pathétique*.

Reading was a passion. He enjoyed the works of Ernest Hemingway. *For Whom the Bell Tolls* was a favorite, but it was a book by Ernst Wiechert, *Das einfache Leben: The Simple Life*, which held a special place on his bookshelf—it was Benno's favorite book.[8] He had great empathy for the main character in Wiechert's book, a retired soldier who came to terms with the war through hard work and sacrifice. The old man liked to think his "lonely and secluded world" was something Wiechert would have approved.[9] His life was plain and ingenuous. "That was my world," Wiechert had said of his own experience.

To earn the little money they needed to live, he translated books from English into German. The man's wood-paneled study on the west end of the house was crowded with books and papers. The publisher, Motorbuch Verlag, specialized in volumes on varied topics: professional racing, the campaigns of Napoleon, Frederick the Great, or espionage thrillers set in World War II. One of the stories his publisher considered, featured an SS hero who bravely saved the day by crossing to Danzig in a ferry to undermine the Polish defenders. However, the old soldier, being personally familiar with the changed sentiments in postwar Germany, opined that the story would have to be altered to ever be published. Being a former Waffen SS man himself, he knew that no man in that condemned organization could be called a hero after the war![10] Besides, what good could come of revisiting those days? He found his task somehow depressing—he was glad to be away and living in the tranquillity of nature.

His home was a modest two-story, two-bedroom affair built by laborers from the nearby village. The rectangular structure had white stucco walls with the style of red-tile roof and wooden shutters typical of newer homes in the valley. On the ground floor was a family room, kitchen, bathroom, and library. There was a glassed-in terrace on the west side. Ascending the stairs one passed his book-lined study and the master bedroom that adjoined an open-railed balcony facing east.[11] Standing on the balcony, he could glimpse the lazy Saône through the dense tree boughs fifty yards off to the left. To the south he could see a worn walking trail from the local road that led beyond Traves to Cubry-lès-Soing. Beyond that he could watch as the local farmers on tractors tilled the clay soil and planted fields of green that contrasted sharply where the red earth met the horizon.

The house stood in the middle of dense woods hugging the Saône River. It was remote from the narrow farm road and almost invisible from the nearest dirt path a hundred meters away. Although its French design was typical, there was something reminiscent of the land to the East, a certain simplicity and neatness that spoke of order and things in their place. The villagers called it "*Le Ranfort*" for the woods in which it was nestled. However, for the old German soldier it was "*Le Renfort*," a play on words suggesting that the long stone wall next to the property made the hideaway his private bastion.[12] Although the place was hardly a fortress, it was private and nearly hidden from view of the casual passerby. The old German had reasons for monkish isolation. His fortune in adult life had been mostly bad. Like many from the time of the Third Reich, the past was off-limits: "Please, no talk of the war."At least to strangers.

The property was on the edge of the small village of Traves in Eastern France. This aging hamlet was about a kilometer away from his doorstep. Traves had no main road, and the rolling pastures of the region alternated with thick woods. It was a sleepy provincial place without substantial history or intrigue—sheep herding was the major occupation. Most of the 380 souls in the little French village knew of him, but only the mayor knew him well. It seemed a strange place for a German to settle. With the crumbling walls of its buildings, the clutter on its streets, and the general untidiness, the entire atmosphere in the village was an anathema to all things German. Except for Herr Erwin Ketelhut.

Strangely, the old man had another German neighbor who had moved in just 250 yards to the west. Ketelhut had refurbished the run-down mill into an expansive French estate. And although the men came from the same wartime unit and were first friends, they later grew apart. He was too flippant and unreliable, and even more, his proper wife from northern Germany didn't particularly like him. Too jolly, too casual! It was a typical clash of Prussian and Bavarian sensibilities.

Although polite, he mostly kept to himself. True, he did go by the town baker every week to get the *pain de seigle* (rye bread) he preferred, but he paid for everything in cash and said little more than hello and good-bye.[13] He almost always came

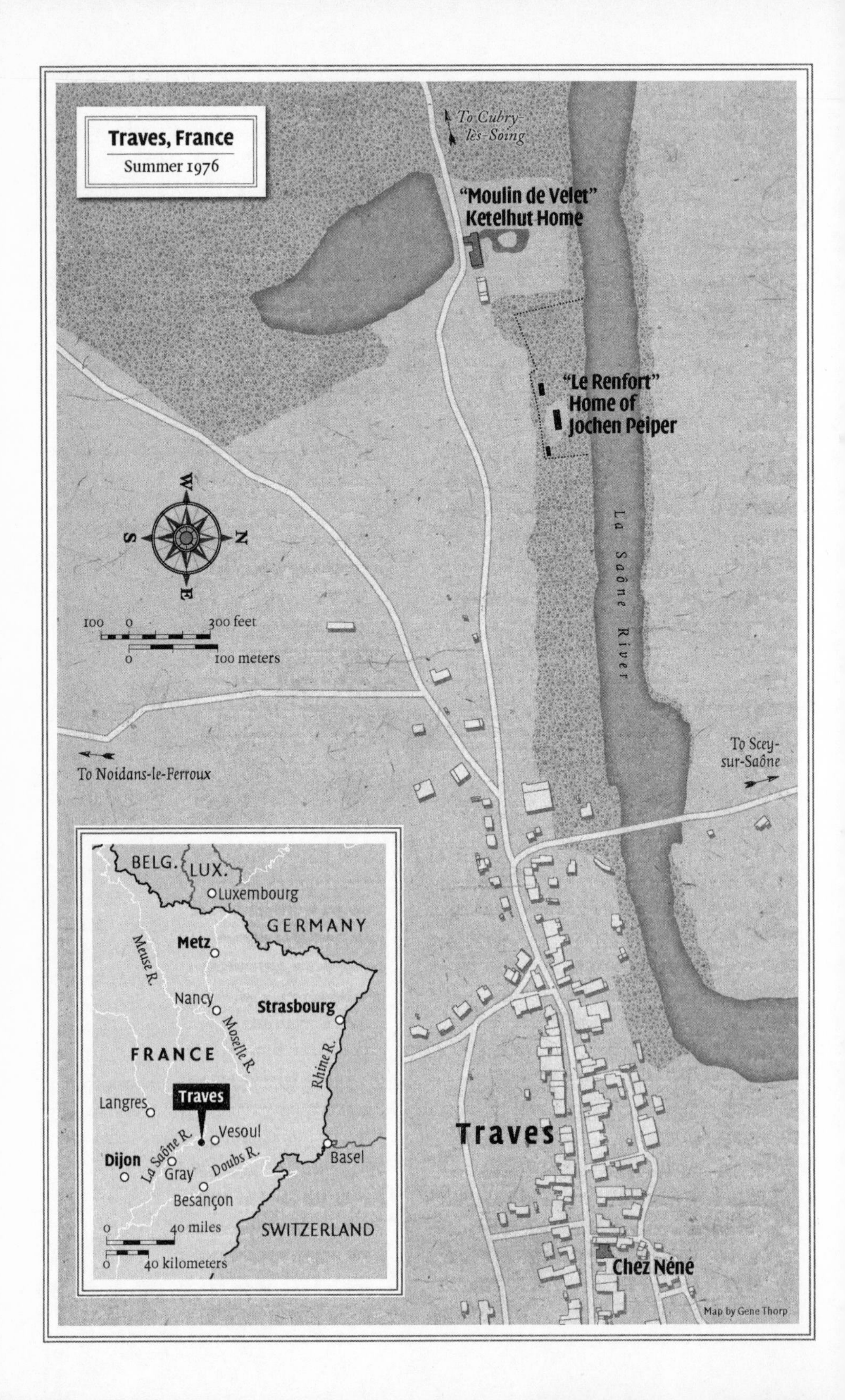

Traves, France
Summer 1976
To Cubry-lès-Soing
"Moulin de Velet"
Ketelhut Home
"Le Renfort"
Home of
Jochen Peiper
La Saône River
W
S
N
E
100 0 300 feet
0 100 meters
To Noidans-le-Ferroux
To Scey-sur-Saône
BELG.
LUX.
Luxembourg
GERMANY
Metz
Meuse R.
Nancy
Moselle R.
Strasbourg
Rhine R.
FRANCE
Traves
Langres
Vesoul
La Saône R.
Dijon
Gray
Doubs R.
Basel
Besançon
0 40 miles
0 40 kilometers
SWITZERLAND
Traves
Chez Néné
Map by Gene Thorp

with his two big dogs, which he tied out front. Even so, he was well liked; they called him "*Vieux Allemand*"—the old German. Most villagers had a bucolic image of the handsome old expatriate: the tranquil German, the honest warrior who was unlucky in war, the polite and pleasant old soldier who now sought his peace on the banks of the Saône.[14] Nothing was particularly strange in this; hermitage wasn't all that unusual in remote Eastern France.

The inhabitants reflected their isolation: many were descendants of the Druids, and visitors passing through noted signs of prolonged inbreeding and a lack of anything modern. The Scey-sur-Saône district was a backwater; there were few telephones, and Traves had only a single café and no hotels. The people were primitive French farmers, sometimes friendly yokels with bad teeth. The whole scene was something like a hillbilly Appalachian village, Eastern French style.[15] Certainly the settlement was remote; the nearest town of Vesoul was eighteen kilometers away, and better-known Dijon was four times that far. The German border was one hundred kilometers to the east. The village had no history in the glory that was France; most Frenchmen had no idea where it was.

Not that there was much to see in Traves. Driving into the hamlet from Vesoul, one first spied the bulbous onion dome of the church rising out of the cow pastures. As with many small French villages, its presence dominated the landscape, the only rival being the listless waters of the Saône discreetly paralleling the main street until it reached the bridge that crossed it. The old church had seen better days. The structure was built from stones from the Château de Humbert of Traves, but the interior was run down and dilapidated. The adjoining cemetery sheltered the crowded headstones of those passed on. Wilted flowers and faded ribbons from World War I decorated graves of one family member that often had other ancestors close by—stone signals from the past. The church bell sounded each hour as it had for centuries, the peals measuring time for sleepy Frenchmen, their brown-spotted cows, and fat sheep. No one particularly noticed; this small place was one that time forgot. Traves was a sleepy Eastern French farming village. There wasn't much else there—some houses, a service station, and a bakery. And Chez Néné.[16]

As with the smallest French village, the café was a central social fixture, even in Traves, where the social atmosphere was almost nonexistent. Like in an old Grade B Western, the mayor of the town, Ernest Rigoulot, wore several hats. Not only was he the chief village officer, but he also owned the only café, which also had a small grocery in the adjoining stone alley. Rigoulot's nickname was "Néné," so naturally the establishment became Chez Néné. Every day the locals stopped by at the appointed hour to have a drink and talk. And Chez Néné was the only game in town. In good weather the few cheap tables outside were always filled with people talking, often loudly. Inside the air was stale with cigarettes and the smell of spilled wine and beer. In the afternoon revelry the noisy laughter of wine flowed out of the door into the street. Hard-boiled eggs could be bought at the counter to appease the hunger of one long day of drinking. It was a pleasant thing to do when there was nothing to do.

The villagers seldom saw much of "*L'Allemand*." The man rarely appeared in Rigoulot's café. Even so, for those who frequented the place, anything foreign was grist for the gossip mill. Although most knew him as a "tranquil German"—both *trés tranquille* and *sehr korrekt*—the local priest found him cold and eyed him with suspicion.[17] However, the man's two daughters, his son, and the expanding circle of grandchildren who visited occasionally were always courteous.[18]

The man's French was good enough, but the accent was clearly Teutonic. One villager who brought him milk thought him friendly and appreciative of things French, but even to the farmer he made no attempt to hide his contempt for the Russians—he still called them Bolshevists.[19] The old man wasn't the only one calling names. Whispers in the café spoke of the "*Boche*"—a derogatory moniker for a German soldier. But in the summer of 1976, World War II was thirty years distant. And, true, the region of Burgundy-Franche-Compté in France had been something unusual during the German occupation: SS men had taken recreation there. Villagers sometimes wondered why.[20]

The only monument with names chiseled on it in Traves was from the Great War of 1914, a few meters from Chez Néné. There were two small French flags and a spouting stone fountain nearby, but the ancient thing was stained by time and poorly kept. "A Ses Enfants Pour la France," it said, mentioning sixteen names etched on its gray sides who were lost from the two wars.[21] The obelisk was a less than inspiring token of the local patriotism. That was okay. As the old man himself had said of the past, "Why do people want to think about that? The coffee is cold."[22]

THE PAST HAD BEEN A RECURRING PROBLEM FOR HIM IN HIS NATIVE LAND. The old German had been something of a war hero, but alas, a hero in the wrong war. There was no longer any peace for him in Germany, so France looked like a better proposition. In the 1960s, with two friends of the family, Max Moritz and Heinz-Ulrich Wieselmann, he began searching for a haven during holidays.

During the war, Moritz had commanded an auto repair unit stationed in France at Sochaux after being wounded in 1940.[23] The old German soldier had come to know Moritz well while working at Volkswagen.

Together, in 1961, they motored over to Midi in France, to the spectacular Alps of Haute Provence. Later they traveled to the beautiful Côte d'Azur to stay at the luxurious Saint Tropez spread of Hans Schwarz van Berk, an old comrade who had once written for Hitler's propaganda minister, Joseph Goebbels.

His other close friend, Uli Wieselmann, was the influential editor-in-chief of the popular magazine *Auto-Motor und Sport*. Wieselmann had befriended the man's entire family in 1957. For Wieselmann, there was always another new car to be taken out for road touring. While sharing such travels with Wieselmann, the old war hero seemed to reclaim some of his free-ranging soldier days. Together they journeyed to Brittany, on the island of Bréhat. France was beautiful. In particular, to him, Bréhat was gorgeous, but he realized there were too many people there and, even worse, "too many uniforms."[24] Some of his old comrades were being called to trial in one place or another. Safe haven in another country might prove illusory.

But it was in his westward travels that the old soldier had a contrary revelation. "I saw myself also coming to France," he said. And then he added with a characteristic hint of irony, "France, a country I had learned to appreciate during my campaigns."[25] From Moritz's secretary he learned of a property available on the Saône in Eastern France. During the fighting in 1940 Moritz had become acquainted with the region around the Langres Plateau and provided assistance to a French POW, a German-friendly fellow, Monsieur Albert Gauthier from Chancey, whom the German vet recommended be released to his family. Returning the wartime favor, Gauthier met his German comrade in Reutlingen and offered to sell him a small property in Eastern France.[26] Although the land was not worth much, as it was on steeply sloped ground that angled sharply down to the nearby river, the German decided it was just right. "I liked the size of the country," he said of Eastern France. "It is not as crowded as we are in Germany."[27] So, with savings from his more prosperous days selling automobiles, he was able to accumulate enough money to buy it under his wife's name in the summer of 1964.

He was so taken with the verdant forest that he pitched an army tent there with his son during a holiday in 1964. There was plenty of work that summer vacation on the banks of the Saône. The forest grew quickly in the wet regions of the valley; he and his son began to clear the land by hand with axe and saw. It was hard work, but the calluses of the hand softened the heart. Age, too, mellowed him. "One doesn't have time," the man would often say. "One makes time." For the many gaps in their relationship, made worse by a troubled past, the cutting and sawing drew father and son together, claiming something basic from the land. And around the campfire at night the two had long talks, not only of his days at war but also of his young son's aspirations. He had just completed his military service that year and would no longer be living at home. The son would never forget their summer discussions on the philosophical questions of life—"*Gott und die Welt*"—all under the stars. It was somehow very satisfying, so much so that the work was more a pleasure than a chore.[28]

At last the plot was cleared off—at least well enough for construction. With the help of Monsieur Michel Obriot, a mason from Traves, the concrete walls rose.[29] Over the next year the German oversaw the construction on weekends, and every so often old wartime friends came to lend him a hand.[30] The house was partly complete in 1965, but he continued to craft it to his needs—a wood shed, stronger roof framing, a guest room. There was always something to be done.

The aging soldier often returned to the property on weekends and each summer for a vacation, but he was still working in Germany. Circumstances there soured, however, when the Italian government tried to have him extradited to stand trial for an alleged war crime in Boves, Italy. "I once again became the object of a campaign lead by Simon Wiesenthal who claimed I was Eichmann Number 2."[31] He was interrogated twice and gave depositions and testimony. The investigation droned on for three years. Finally, in 1968, the investigation was dropped for lack of sufficient proof. Yet the damage was done. On one occasion, stirred up by members of the Italian resistance, inquisitive members of the press came by his home in Stuttgart. Work and professional activities became difficult, and the bad luck wasn't over.

In May of 1970 his longtime friend Uli Wieselmann died. The man took on Wieselmann's grief-stricken daughter, Bettina, as a sort of goddaughter. On top of this shock, without Wieselmann's strong influence in the publishing business, he found himself dismissed by his publisher. With that indignity, he resolved to abandon his native land. After all, another war crimes trial could not be long in coming. "I decided to avoid all new adventures of this type," he said.[32] "As a persecuted person of the Third Reich, for which there is no longer any place left in Germany," he was ready to leave.[33] His home in Traves became a haven; he was there with his son on his birthday, January 30, 1971:

> My son asked me for a walk together in the forest. During the day we cleared the forest and exchanged expert comments about birds, trees, and weather. At nightfall, we cooked and later we sat at the fireplace and silently puffed on our pipes, carefully probing each other's worlds. Considering that which is taking place around us—domestic and foreign policy, economics, ethics and morality, and the increasingly polluted air and growing landfills—I check off every completed year of my life with satisfaction, withdrawing to my interior lines without animosity. To do that, one must leave behind a lot of dead weight that before was dear and precious. Thank God, a person changes, as one grows older. One can smile about things, which formerly would have driven one onto the barricades, as distance grows from the idealism of the youth. Unfortunately, attempts at inner equilibrium and a peaceful acceptance of the past are repeatedly disturbed by opportunists and professional scab scratchers, who are active as body-strippers on old battlefields. . . . As things stand, I have no other choice than to prepare myself with stoicism and fatalism for the next war crimes trial, which for a change, looks to come from our new friends in the East.[34]

He was speaking of matters going on in East Germany. Although his wife was aghast at the idea of moving from the big city of Stuttgart for a forest villa in the French countryside, the economic reality of unemployment made it necessary. They would leave Germany for good. On February 20, 1972, the man applied for a five-year residence visa in Traves.

When he met Rigoulot, the little village's mayor who would enter a recommendation for the visa, he made no attempt to conceal his identity.

The silver-haired mayor vaguely knew of the man's past, but for whatever misgivings, he admired the sincerity of this man. He gave a favorable endorsement to the application. "He owns a house and wishes to retire and live in our village." On April 27 the request was approved.

During his war years the old soldier had a knack for locating his headquarters in a commanding, well-camouflaged vantage point, where the approach was from but a single discernible direction. He was no fool: he wanted to be left alone and to know when visitors were approaching, and "Le Renfort" fit the bill. The structure was sited on the reverse side of a hill in a dense copse of trees and could not be seen from town. Located on a high bank above the Saône, there was no access from the rear. The road provided the sole access, and it did not even lead directly to the house. Only the presence of a power line and an ivy-covered stone chimney poking out of the foliage betrayed its existence. And from the post of his upstairs balcony the man could look down upon the four points of the compass.

Yet privacy had a price; there was no direct automobile access to the property. His beige BMW CSi 3.0 was parked at Monsieur Raymond Obriot's rented garage in the village. To walk to his property, he had to cross another's land. He had an agreement with Raymond Louette, the local farmer who owned the pasture between his property and the road. That meant walking down a long path from the road across a pasture to the thick woods of "Le Renfort." There were two separate gates to be opened across barbed-wire fences to reach his home, and the final steps went past his two hunting dogs. And there the postman did not go. A yellow metal mailbox was hung discreetly on the barbed-wire fence by the road; it was there he would meet anyone scheduled to visit.[35] Le Renfort was remote.

But for the man's long-suffering wife, Sigurd, the Traves property was far too remote. Her husband became progressively more of a hermit and was fully content when she returned to Germany to visit family and friends: "We three dogs live here alone in the woods and indulge in our natural inclination to run wild," he joked in a letter to a friend one November. "This summer flooded us with guests, most who simply wanted to see how the old goblin lives."[36] He wrote his son:

> The more one sits on one's behind, the more and more things recede that once seemed important. One's children spoil you, dress you, and prepare you with practical things for the old chair. Yes, I am aware of being a grandfather. To be sure, in everyday life I cannot devote myself to such nostalgia. There simply is always something to be done and one is constantly challenged physically. It is of benefit that the work not only is ideally divided into physical and mental, but above all, that I can allocate it. I am *free*! Currently I am translating a book about the aerial war against Germany—which certainly is mentally more stressful for me than the English author. And in the *bois* with axe and motor saw, I create enormous devastation, botching up nature's labor. On those occasions, I miss you often, even though Timm is ever present and, with him, one does not feel alone even in the densest woods. We are inseparable. When in the evening he repeatedly wants to get on my lap, he is my brother. His trust reassures me.

Vaporous columns of roiling summer clouds grew in the Eastern sky as the aging German considered his summer idyll. He had hardly a care in the world—peaceful pleasure.

> A thunderstorm is getting ready. I must secure my laundry and my Jeans. . . . Now I sit with my favorite "Earl Grey" tea and feel like him. And I eat Mami's birthday cake and pick up my pipe. If you should see smoke signals, they come from "Lincoln" tobacco and not from the chimney.[37]

It seemed perfect—perhaps too perfect for an old man with a past like his. From that, there seemed no escape. His perfect sanctuary seemed fragile—or even unlikely.

Yet that summer there seemed little to argue with. Even if he were an old, outdated *Wehrbaurer*, an agricultural soldier peasant, he was a comfortable one—and mildly surprised to be living some fantasy that had emerged from a dreamlike time many years before.

BUT SOME NIGHTS, IN HIS DREAMS, HE WAS BACK THERE AGAIN, IN THOSE days during the war.

Part One
ASCENT

All men dream: but not equally.
Those who dream by night
in the dusty recesses of their minds,
wake in the day to find that it was vanity:
but the dreamers of the day
are dangerous men,
for they may act their dreams
with open eyes, to make it possible.

—T. E. Lawrence, *Seven Pillars of Wisdom*

Chapter 1

DREAM OF THE REICH

It was one hour before midnight on November 9, 1935, when Joachim Peiper swore absolute allegiance to Adolf Hitler.

A tolling bell from the baroque Theatinerkirche across the square signaled the event. The bell tones resonated through the cold foggy air, invisibly moving the witnesses to the solemn occasion. In the quiet of that Saturday evening, amid the towering marble columns of Munich's Feldherrnhalle, the torch flames bathed the hallowed war memorial in a fiery orange glow. Great red chalice-like torches—pylons fifteen feet high, adorned with menacing eagles—stood on the elevated marble stage above the huge central square of the Odeonsplatz. The cupped flames blazed brightly on each pedestal, spreading the faint odor of burning kerosene. To the rear a backdrop of red curtains, twenty meters high, hung from the curved ceiling, which loomed above. Two massive stone lions glowered from the altar onto a "sea of black steel helmets" in the great plaza. The mass of uniformed SS troopers, ordered in rows and columns, strangely reflected the blood-red glow of the torchlight.[1]

More than a thousand men stood outside the monument in precise lines on the crowded plaza floor. Great stone columns rose out above the stairs, spreading into huge arches above the memorial. The square glimmered in the dark, covered with the pine bough wreathes and ornate Teutonic decor. The quiet panorama was interrupted only by the measured tolling of church bells.

The appearance was completely fantastic—a surrealistic military spectacle so portentous, so moving, as to provoke emotion, emotion none of the young stony-faced candidates, helmets lashed onto their jaws, could be seen to acknowledge. Each wore the Großer Dienstanzug, the black uniform of the recently consecrated military branch of Hitler's fashionable Praetorian Guard, the Schutzstaffel, or SS.[2] A black tunic and trousers composed the basic dress uniform; the collars were embroidered in white with the victory sign of double S Sig-runes from the old Norse alphabet.[3] Placed together, the runes looked like lightning bolts. On the left arm of each man was the bold black swastika on an armband of red and white. Gleaming black boots, knee high, stood heel to heel in perfect symmetry. At the end of the hall a giant swastika adorned the huge red flag of National Socialism, hung symbolically from the highest tier facing the ocher-shaded Theatinerkirche across the street. Other diaphanous wafting ribbons of red, illuminated by spires of light hung from buildings on both sides of the plaza, reached back on the Ludwigstrasse as far as the eye could see. If anything could rouse the spirits of ancient Germanic warriors, this panoramic scene could. It all took on an orchestral military beauty, an incarnation of Siegfried's Funeral March and the Immolation of the Gods. It was like a specter of the *Götterdämmerung*!

Joachim Peiper was one of the officer candidates standing in the lined up formation among the multitudes and witnessing the fantastic choreography that night. He was a twenty-year-old staff sergeant—SS Scharführer—in the SS *Verfügungstruppe*—the VT or "Readiness Troops." A native of Berlin, he was being promoted to cadet on this day. He stood ramrod straight, shoulder to shoulder with the precisely ordered rows of other black-uniformed troopers all bathed in the eerie light. The impact was undeniable.[4] Peiper likely knew little of Hitler's artistic intention: the fiery ritual was a spiritual celebration, a Wagnerian homage to the blood of the Teutonic Knights. A central credo of Hitler's new SS was the Blood Myth, which evoked the twin visions of racial fastidiousness and combat on a cosmic stage. It was an idea familiar to all Germans from the ancient fable of the *Nibelungenlied*, in which Siegfried slays the dragon and bathes in its blood to remain invincible. Blood was the new holy water, the entire ceremony exuding medieval overtones of sacrifice and racial purity, central to the aims of National Socialism. Perhaps more importantly, however, the pageant elicited the SS oath of absolute devotion to Hitler as the *Führer*—the anointed leader of Germany.

It was ten o'clock when the Führer's gleaming Mercedes Benz arrived at the courtyard of the Wittelsbach Palace. And then Adolf Hitler himself, revealed in the brilliant torchlight, strode confidently onto the portico. The band struck up the German leader's signature musical entrance, the "Präsentiermarsch." Reaching the podium, the man stood historically positioned. To his right was a larger-than-life bronze statue of Tzerklas Graf von Tilly, the Teutonic hero of the Thirty Years War; on his left was another Germanic champion, a hulking metallic likeness of Karl Wrede, the famous Bavarian field marshal. And Adolf Hitler stood right in the middle!

He raised his hand in salute. "*Heil, SS Männer!*" the German leader barked. "Heil to you, SS men!" The microphones boomed Hitler's voice, echoing down the streets of Ludwigstrasse. The SS men roared back with an even louder unamplified response: "*Heil, mein Führer!*"

Then the unlikely looking leader of the Schutzstaffel raised his sword to signal a stop in the music. He moved up to the podium. This was Heinrich Himmler—the Reichsführer SS. Here was a thin, bespectacled man with a receding chin line, thin colorless lips, and a scant moustache that gave him a mousy appearance. His complexion looked pale and even unhealthy. This man, who some thought looked vaguely Asian, bade the assembled German youth at ease.[5] In unison all of those he commanded moved as one—hundreds of steel helmets removed. To set the new mood, the band moved onto a solemn number, "Wir treten zum Beten"—the Old Netherlands "Prayer of Thanks."[6]

Now came the oath. If not charismatic, Himmler dutifully uttered the binding oath as he looked out across a thousand raised arms. The men to be sworn in repeated Himmler's words line by line. The Reichsführer's commands echoed across the square as he presented the SS Leibstandarte (Bodyguard) formation to the leader:

I swear to you,
Adolf Hitler
Führer and Chancellor of the German Reich
Loyalty and valor.
I pledge to you
and the superiors appointed by you
Obedience until death,
So help me God.[7]

A crescendo of affirmations ended with helmets donned once more—the Führer would speak! The mustachioed leader of the Third Reich quietly stepped up to the podium.[8] His few words were measured, almost quiet, with their careful choice adding to the sanctimonious atmosphere. He concluded his short remarks with a rejoinder of oath: "I expect you to remain ever true to the motto of the Order to which you have the honor of belonging. Your honor must always and under all circumstances be loyalty." And then, in the final admonition, he reminded the cadets "of their duty to be prepared to die for him at all times."[9]

At this, Himmler, standing behind him, nodded, and the SS band took up an old German spiritual, "Wenn alle untreu werden," adopted as the SS song of loyalty. The SS men sang along in a resounding chorus:

When all become disloyal
We remain loyal
So that on earth a flag will wave for you . . .
We don't want to break our word,
Not become like boys,
And we want to preach and talk
Of the "Holy German Reich."[10]

Hitler, head held high, proudly descended the steps, moving down the long lines of men below to review his new recruits.[11] From right to left he passed by the assembled troops. When that was complete, the Führer re-ascended the steps to the Feldherrnhalle as the Reichsführer called everyone to attention: "Eyes right!" The band again stuck up the Präsentiermarsch.

An immaculately adorned SS honor guard presented arms before the stage in front of a red flag and the black flag marked with white SS runes. Two SS officers, swords in hand, crossed their blades by touching the poles of the dipped flags. At that, Hitler ceremoniously accepted the red *Blutfahne*—or blood flag—from the SS bearer. Nazi legend claimed that the colors of the flag were stained with the gore of men killed during the Munich Putsch, when, in 1923, Hitler led a contingent of about two thousand men in an attempt to seize control of Munich, only to be put down by police, who killed sixteen of the Nazis during the confrontation. Regardless of whether this legend was factual, the grim artifact had become the crucifix of the Nazi movement. Hitler dutifully accepted the blood oath from the bearer. "I vow to remain true to my Führer, Adolf Hitler. I bind myself to carry out all orders conscientiously and without reluctance."

The men of the Leibstandarte SS Adolf Hitler (LSSAH) were expected to be equally willing to give up their lives as the sixteen men who fell for Hitler at this site twelve years earlier. And only the men of the SS personally made this oath before Hitler. All volunteers and handpicked, each was expected to be mindful their decision bound them unconditionally to Hitler's will and fortunes.[12]

With this rite satisfied, Obergruppenführer Josef Dietrich, the paternal leader of the Leibstandarte, joined the Führer. Standing at Hitler's side with Himmler on the other, the three solemnly descended the steps of the Feldherrnhalle. With this, the accompaniment shifted to the holy anthem of National Socialism, the Horst Wessel song "*Die Fahne hoch, die Reihen fest geschlossen*"—"Flag high, ranks closed."[13] Over them wafted a euphoric mood as "millions, full of hope, look[ed] up to the swastika."

Hitler bid the men good-bye by raising his hand in salute. Himmler was at his side as they entered the car at the courtyard.

> For the struggle now, we all stand ready.
> Soon will fly Hitler flags over every street

The mood was ghostly, almost supernatural. "We had no personal aspirations," Peiper later remembered. Our "vision was always the Dream of the Reich!"

> *Denn heute da hört uns Deutschland und morgen die ganze Welt!*
> (Because today we are heard in Germany and tomorrow the whole world!)[14]

Later, the young soldier would meet Hitler face-to-face for the first time. During a review Hitler passed a group of officers with which Peiper was standing. Hitler then turned and looked directly at Peiper and faintly smiled. There were those *shining blue eyes*—the *Führerkontakt*. "This look changed my life," Peiper said of the first encounter, "He looked at me and I was ready to die for him."[15]

Joachim Peiper's father, Woldemar, had fought for Kaiser Wilhelm II in World War I. He had nearly given his life in the fighting in colonial Africa, where he was wounded. Beyond that the war clearly marked him.[16] Indeed, the Captain's third son, Joachim, was born at 3:30 a.m. on January 30, 1915, just as that war moved into a critical phase. Young Joachim had two brothers, Hans Hasso, five years his elder, and Horst, born in 1912. Peiper's father had wanted to name his youngest boy Dixmundieus after the village in Belgium that had been such a scene of climactic fighting in October 1914.[17] Yet even if the scene of battle forged an epiphany for Woldemar, Peiper's mother, Charlotte, prevailed—that was no name for a son!

Their third child would be branded with a full family name: Joachim Sigismund Albrecht Klaus Arved Detlev Peiper. He would go by Joachim—although his young friends soon called him Jochen. The boy would be baptized at the Kaiser Wilhelm memorial church on his sixth birthday. By that time his father was home from

Germany's capitulation after the First World War. It was an unhappy time all over Europe.

Living in the upscale Wilmersdorf district in Berlin, the Peiper flat at Zähringerstrasse 17 was only a few blocks from the famous Kurfürstendamm promenade. Raised by the stern retired captain, the sons grew up on stories from the Great War. The glorious adventures of fighting for the Fatherland in exotic Africa seemed far from the center of Berlin near Wilmersdorf. Yet his father's tales of wartime glory always came to the same ill end, for Germany had lost the war and, seemingly, its grip on global aspirations. During Peiper's early years a devastating depression swept Europe in the late 1920s, leading to widespread disillusionment and gloom within German society. Six million were unemployed. To become a soldier seemed appealing.[18]

Woldemar was a completely convinced devotee of Hitler's National Socialism, but that was not true for the larger family. The Peiper ancestors had originally come from Protestant Lutheran roots, fleeing Flanders in the mid-1500s. Yet Berlin, where the two arms of the family had coalesced, was hardly a natural spawning ground for the Nazis, with its left-wing traditions, a vibrant Jewish community, a gay subculture, and a cosmopolitan elite. Yet Peiper's father evolved (as did many others in the city) into not only a convinced National Socialist but, even more, an acerbic anti-Semite.[19]

Even so, one side of the family tree, under Dr. Herbert Peiper, had warily viewed the embrace of National Socialism by Woldemar's wing of the family. His branch of the family tree was peopled with doctors, the well educated, and artists—often the groups the Nazis targeted. Even worse was that Woldemar's sons were in the SS—Jochen with the Leibstandarte and Horst with the *Totenkopfverbände*—Death's Head units. Neither had a soothing reputation. Then, in 1938, it became widely known in family circles that Jochen Peiper was now adjutant to Heinrich Himmler. Herbert Peiper suggested his boys not associate too closely with Woldemar and his kin. "*Das wird ein böses Ende nehmen!*"—"This will end up badly!"[20]

In the early 1930s, liberal Berlin still seemed to embrace the freedom for which it was famous. The colorful *Wandervögel* (literally "Birds of Passage") generation had just passed, transforming the next propagation of young German males into fervent nature lovers.[21] Youth movements sprouted all over Deutschland. Typical German boys, Joachim and his brother Horst relished the outdoor life. In nature they could discuss ways to elude the stodgy social conditions of the day, organize treks to explore the beautiful German countryside, and toughen themselves in personal challenges. They hiked over the hills, with cookouts in the Prussian pinewoods, followed by sleeping under the stars.

It was the pure notion expounded by Hermann Löns, the German Thoreau. Löns extolled a simple life within nature—wild, unvarnished by modern trappings, and embracing hardship as a test of personal power and self-worth. And if not hiking in July, they enjoyed afternoons on a small family sailboat on the nearby dark waters of Lake Wannsee, where the mood was festive if understated: Coney Island, Berlin-style. Even though the waters were cold and somehow vaguely smelling of old leaves, the Peiper boys loved swimming there. Every outdoor challenge was welcome.

So it was not at all surprising that in 1926, after attending Halensee Elementary School, the eleven-year-old boy followed his brother Horst and became a German Boy

Scout. He later rose to squad leader during his time at the Goethe Technical High School in Wilmersdorf, although he found himself also interested in German history, foreign languages, music, and the humanities. With a student pass to the Schiller Theater, he and his classmates enjoyed many of the classical works of Goethe, Shakespeare, and Molière.

Yet, although absorbed by literature and the theater, he had become more intrigued with scouting and sports. Increasingly accomplished at swimming, fencing, and handball, his interest in academic subjects may have flagged—an affliction common to many boys his age. In any case, he did not achieve the *Abitur*, a required final exam taken at the end of secondary school, which would have allowed him to attend a university.[22] The Abi was easily within reach; he had only six months to go at school. Why? "From early youth it was obvious to me to become a soldier," the nineteen-year-old Peiper wrote when applying for consideration as an SS officer trainee just before Christmas in 1934.[23] Getting away from home may have been a motivation.

The Peiper household was often unsettled. Unlike his younger brothers, Hans Hasso was not interested in the outdoors, preferring literature and the arts. As an aesthete among manly egos, the eldest argued frequently, both with his brothers and his father. Indeed, although unsaid, it seemed that Hans Hasso was not only an aesthete or *Schöngeist* but also a likely homosexual—with all the condemnation that descended on that group within the new National Socialist regime.[24] Even young Jochen did not see eye to eye frequently with his demanding father, but the unrelenting criticism was too much for Hans Hasso, and his mental situation frayed. While in high school the eldest boy attempted to kill himself.

Even if the motives were not completely clear, the result was more certain. Although failing suicide, Hasso's oxygen-starved brain sustained irreparable damage. In 1931 the youth was placed into Berlin's St. Joseph's Hospital for Gentlemen with Emotional and Nervous Disorders, where his saddened mother frequently took him food for nourishment even though the long S-bahn and tram ride to the other side of Berlin often took more than an hour.[25] What the younger brothers thought of the tragic episode is not recorded, but each was close to their adoring mother.

Two years later, on January 30, 1933—Jochen Peiper's eighteenth birthday—Adolf Hitler took power.[26] The occasion became a state holiday: the *Machtergreifung*. At a time in history when the conjunction of events was often imbued with near-mystic relevance, for Jochen it may have seemed to portend an augury of life-long devotion. To the young man, as with many Germans of that time, the Fatherland at last had its spectral leader. Adolf Hitler, the inspiring and confident Führer, had emerged from obscurity in Austria to a vaunted position as Germany's anticipated head of state. One had only to listen to a song now being recited by young men of the *Jungvolk* at the *Sonnenwende* summer solstice celebration to sense his near-messianic influence:

> Adolf Hitler is our savior, our hero,
> He is the noblest being in the whole wide world
> For Hitler we live,
> For Hitler we die.

Our Hitler is our Lord,
Who rules a brave new world.[27]

As the SS taught it, through the ideology of their *Weltanschauung*—"world vision"—the German nation would claim its rightful inheritance as the racial superiors of the human species. And the SS men would be the unquestioning protectors of what Hitler already referred to as the Third Reich. As it evolved, the organization was to represent both an ideal police organization and one that would be armed to ensure obedience at home. There was to be no repetition of the Communist upheaval within the Fatherland like that of 1918, which, together with the Allied onslaught, doomed German fortunes at the end of World War I. Even more, the SS would eventually furnish a small elite combat force to assure success in any future armed conflict. After Himmler's SS had proved its worth in putting down an attempted revolt in 1931, Hitler delivered an accolade of praise to the embryonic organization. "Your honor is loyalty," he told them. It was a phrase soon embossed on every SS man's belt buckle.[28]

BEYOND A SUPERIOR POLICE AND ARMY, HIMMLER SAW THE SS AS A PRECISE embodiment of the hope of spawning a new European race to exemplify the highest standards of Aryan purity while also unflinchingly eliminating what he saw as mongrel human elements. These, National Socialism preached, were the great enemy. "We create an order which will spread the idea of Nordic blood," he would later inform his SS recruits, "so that we can attract to ourselves all the Nordic blood in the world, denying it to our adversaries, so that Nordic blood will not fight against us. We must get it and others cannot have it."[29]

Himmler further invoked the "blood and soil" ideal of his mentor, Richard Walther Darré. Both Darré and Himmler knew much about livestock breeding and planned that the SS would be used to genetically engineer an elite racial aristocracy. This would be accomplished through voluntary selective breeding, taking evolution of the National Socialist vision to its logical climax: the racial zenith of the pure Nordic man. So important was this task that Himmler saw to it that a special SS Race and Settlement Office was set up to supervise the planned human breeding transformation.[30]

The fate of what the SS saw as less desirable types of human beings in the Nazi machine was a problem yet to be resolved.[31] But what that meant took little imagination. Peiper and the rest of Germany could not avoid seeing the signs that sprouted all over the German road-scape in the 1930s: "*Juden sind hier unerwünscht!*"—"No Jews wanted here!"

Indeed, the SS Reichsführer endeavored to foster an esprit de corps among his SS by encouraging Jew-hatred. Accordingly, in 1934 the Leibstandarte received its own chief educational leader, SS Hstuf. Georg Weibgen. There were daily lectures with anti-Semitic themes (e.g., the dangers of Freemasonry and Bolshevism) as well as propaganda movies and a glorification of war in the style of Ernst Jünger. Many of the guest lecturers were men who would later lead killing squads or guard concentration camps.[32] In the monthly SS Leadership magazine such themes were accompanied by idealized photos of blonde-haired women and happy children living in the open air, with scattered poetry extolling the glory of the German warrior-father. Far from a side issue, Himmler intended SS ideology to permeate on all levels of the organization, of which the Leibstandarte stood at the forefront.[33]

Peiper would later admit that he was a fervent supporter of the National Socialist movement but claimed to be swept ahead by the promise of a military career. Still an avid member of the German Boy Scouts in the spring of 1933, Peiper followed when that organization was absorbed into the Hitler Youth.[34] In 1933 Germany was still in the clutches of a worldwide depression, and many discontented citizens turned to Hitler, who promised hope and glory for the nation.[35] Peiper likely saw things as most other Germans did. The new regime promised an effective remedy to the worrisome problems of unemployment and housing through public works and rearmament of the German Army.

To be sure, many saw Hitler's iron-fisted governing certainty as a welcome bromide to the seesaw political gang warfare dominating the streets of Berlin. "*Arbeit und Brot*"—"work and bread" was the German leader's slogan of the day. Yet perhaps the most important elixir of National Socialism was the transformation of the dented national image from the humiliating defeat of World War I and the Treaty of Versailles. Hitler spoke of plans to regain the nation's dignity and their rightful heritage to *Lebensraum*—space required for life and growth—for Germanic peoples. There was also the veiled promise to reunite all the German-speaking peoples of Europe.

At every opportunity National Socialism carted out its scapegoats for previous misfortune—a vitriolic blend of racial causality and anti-Semitism. It was the Jews and the Bolshevist communists who were responsible for 1918. In all this Peiper was a believer. By his own admission the youthful SS man was "idealistic and idealistic against Bolshevism," the Nazi categorization for Soviet communism during the 1920s.[36] And Peiper was not alone. "Everyone and I too, supported Hitler enthusiastically until the tide turned." As one citizen reflected, "Afterwards, you could not find anyone to say good."[37]

BEYOND POLITICS, YOUNG PEIPER WAS FASCINATED WITH HORSES AND THE mystique of the cavalry. He soon joined Berlin's prestigious Beerman Riding Academy. There, at the Tattersall Beermann, not far from the Tiergarten and the Kaiser Wilhelm Church, he trained most afternoons to become an accomplished horseman.[38] Even though Woldemar had wanted Jochen to be part of an elite Cavalry Regiment, the Machiavellian Prussian war horse and family friend, Col. Walther von Reichenau, seems to have convinced Woldemar the right decision was to join the volunteer SS cavalry.

The snob appeal was clear—those young men in the saddles of the SS Reitersturm in 1933 comprised Berlin's upper crust and even featured princes in its ranks.[39] And von Reichenau was fully behind Hitler and the National Socialists. That struck Peiper just right, for he took interest in more than the glamour of cavalry; he longed to be a part of Hitler's National Socialist movement, as the wildly popular German leader seemed to hold an exalted place. And so, by joining the SS Reitersturm in Berlin on October 16, he would have his cake and eat it too. The organization had been set up by Himmler to attract the more acceptable elements into his fledgling SS. Even so, the choices said much about Jochen and his family's emerging political views—at that time, one could have easily avoided membership in either the Hitler Youth or the SS. Jochen and his father decided that would be his best career move.

PEIPER WAS ASSIGNED TO THE 1. STURM OF THE SS REITER STANDARTE 7.[40] The regimental-sized, nonmilitary organization was essentially a ceremonial SS horse rider's club in Berlin. Its head was SS Hauptscharführer Gustav Lombard, a long-faced cavalry man who thoroughly trained his young riders in the equestrian arts, from dignified unit maneuvers to individual riding and even steeplechases. The SS cavalry quartered in Charlottenburg was already something of an elite, with their ranks joined by famed horsemen like the dashing Günther Temme, who, with his steed Nordland, would soon star at the Berlin Olympics. Lombard was training his best riders—including Peiper—in the "American drill" he had learned while in the United States during World War I.[41] Less well known about Lombard was that he was violently anti-Semitic.[42] During the typical week at the Berlin SS riding club not only would there be equestrian instruction but also Weltanschauung at a weekly *Stammtisch*—table meeting—with enthusiastic political discussion.

Like many young men of the day, young Jochen must have found great attraction in joining the black-uniformed SS, already an exclusive order within Hitler's National Socialist movement. As a fledgling candidate of the Allgemeine SS, the high school student had to submit proof of his family's racial purity going back to 1750—the so-called *Großer Ahnennachweis* (Great Family Tree). These evaluations were resolved favorably, and the following July Peiper took part in a monthly combat-sport course as a designated squad leader.

Political events swelled Peiper's personal achievements. On July 20 Hitler had a spoken in glowing terms of the SS for its key role in the "Night of the Long Knives," a series of political murders that established Hitler's place as supreme leader of Germany, three weeks before. "In consideration of the very meritorious service of the SS, especially in connection with the events of June 30, 1934, I elevate it to the standing of an independent organization within the NSDAP."[43]

On July 23, three days after Hitler issued his great endorsement, Jochen Peiper became SS Mann Number 132496. Peiper almost certainly relished his first taste of military life and newly acquired status; there was the undeniable bluster of being able to wear the smart black uniform while attending high school. Yet he still planned to graduate before entering the Reichswehr. All this changed, however, on the *Reichsparteitag*—Party Congress—on September 7, 1934, when the youth met Heinrich Himmler. The Party Day that year in Nuremberg was a fantastic Nazi spectacle, forever immortalized as the *Triumph of the Will* by avant-garde filmmaker Leni Riefenstahl.[44]

If the dashing Riefenstahl needed prototypical Aryan male beauty for film, she need not have looked further than young Peiper. For the top rung in Himmler's SS, the physical requirements were fashioned to skim the cream of Nordic manhood. Candidates for the Leibstandarte Adolf Hitler (LAH) had to be at least five feet eleven inches tall, with a strong muscular frame and no physical defects of any kind, not even a single filled tooth.[45] Although one inch short of the established height requirement and not so muscular and powerful as other recruits, the lanky Prussian youth made up for it in handsome features. His hair was always carefully groomed—a perfect *Seitenscheitel* (side part)—and his piercing blue eyes were accented by fine features and an aquiline nose. Moreover, the boy possessed almost irrepressible self-confidence.

Others were also impressed. Peiper, along with the other handsome riders of 1. Sturm, was chosen to serve as an escort on the train for foreign diplomats.[46] Peiper found himself close by Dr. Joseph Goebbels, Hitler's minister of propaganda, as well as many ambassadors including the Reichsführer SS himself. Even amid heady festivities with some eleven thousand SS men participating, the peevish Himmler noticed Peiper. In a portentous encounter, the SS leader paused to speak with the high school student. What were his aspirations? Learning that young Peiper intended to become an officer in the Reichswehr, Himmler issued a personal invitation to instead apply for the analogous position in his SS Verfügungstruppe.

Impetus to take the Reichsführer up on the offer came with his induction of Peiper as SS Sturmmann on September 7. Later that evening Peiper participated in the mass event where two hundred thousand party faithful with more than twenty thousand unfurled flags crowded into Zeppelin field, all lined in military precision. The theatrical effect—130 giant searchlights streaming skyward in a "cathedral of light"—was breathtaking. Hitler's amplified voice reflected rising national excitement: "We are strong!" he cried shrilly over loudspeakers, "and we will get stronger!"[47] To top it off, there was a glittering fireworks display, followed over the city by tolling church bells. The finale was a mass chorale of one hundred thousand faithful droning the Horst-Wessel song to end the night.

Peiper returned home, swept away by the emotional wave. He wanted to leave Goethe High School immediately to join the SS Verfügungstruppe. At first his father was opposed, as acceptance would mean not completing high school and obtaining the Abitur, which would be a social stigma, equivalent in the United States to not completing high school. Yet his youngest son was keen to follow this course, so Woldemar reluctantly gave his blessing. Although without the Abi he could not become an army officer or attend a university, there was no such requirement in Himmler's new SS organization.

This was the new Germany!

Chapter 2

EMPIRE

IN LATE 1934, AT THE SUGGESTION OF HEINRICH HIMMLER, YOUNG JOCHEN Peiper put in his application to become an SS officer candidate.

The head of Berlin's SS Senior District East was Josef "Sepp" Dietrich, the faithful bodyguard of Hitler during the days of beer-hall brawls in the streets of Munich. Acceptance of Peiper's application from Dietrich's office was not long in coming.

During the 1934 Christmas holidays, orders came for Peiper to report to the Officer's Candidate course at Jüterbog, south of Berlin. The place was an old army exercise field with a couple of barracks, designed for training with live ammunition for artillery. The course there was aimed to weed out less qualified SS recruits and identify those who might blossom.

The chief instructor at Jüterbog was SS Hauptsturmführer Emil Adolf Sator, a hard-boiled leader who, like Lombard, came primed with a vociferous anti-Semitic attitude. In a play on his last name, his men in the Totenkopf Standarte—the Death's Head Command—would later nickname him "Devil."[1] There were approximately sixty students with Peiper at Jüterbog, broken up into two classes under instructors Obscha. Michael Gerullis and Ustuf. Karl Künstler. Both were *Zwölfender*—former Reichswehr sergeants with twelve years military time—but also without training experience. Each had been out of active service for years—they were now office clerks! An old fighter, Gerullis was known for scowling loudly at recruits—he had little else to offer—whereas Künstler was an army washout and an alcoholic.[2]

The course began in October, but Peiper, with a personal exception card from Himmler, arrived late on January 6, 1935. Even so, in a short time Peiper made a positive impression on his squad leader, SS Unterscharführer Rudolf Lehmann. Lehmann himself did not have exemplary qualifications as an instructor; most of his reputation was based on a penchant for a perfect march drill and organizing a spotless office.[3] Nor did he have any military experience. Neither knew it at the time, but both men would later become lifelong friends. Another SS man Peiper met in his squad was a similarly ambitious lad, Max Wünsche. Coming from the SS Sports Academy at Wolfenbüttel, he was fiercely competitive.

Even if training was not always up to regular German army standards, the duty was hard. And although the course had already been in progress for two months, Peiper was determined not to be left behind. He arrived to find the cadets training on night drills—how to move and fire at night. To strengthen, there were marches of more than thirty kilometers, instruction on how to mount a close infantry assault with hand grenades, and even instruction on changing the barrel of a light machine gun. But there was the other stuff too: ideological training on "Soldier and National Socialism" and guard and parade drills to execute the perfect goose step.[4] After Peiper made his way through several weeks of basic training at Jüterbog, Sator evaluated him favorably:

> Officer Candidate Joachim Peiper, despite his youth, is a determined, energetic and self-confident person—very intelligent and approaches the assignments given to him with appropriate enthusiasm and seriousness. . . . He succeeded, despite his short presence at the course, not only to keep up with all exercises, but also to substantially outperform many of his comrades. . . . Definitely suitable to be an officer.

Yet in spite of all the glowing evaluations within the SS, the Reichswehr's own evaluation came to a very different judgment. An assessment on April 1 by team of doctors at a Wehrmacht Psychological Testing Station X in Braunschweig revealed some serious reservations about the SS officer candidates—not only for Peiper but for others too. Only 52 percent passed, and so miserable was the result that the SS decided to never have candidates so tested again—it was a bad reflection on the organization.[5]

For Peiper, the results were eerily accurate: "The test subject is intelligent and has willpower," began the evaluation, "but he tends to close himself off from other people and withdraw into a world of distrust and prejudices."[6]

FURTHER, THE HEADSTRONG YOUTH'S REPEATED BOAST OF HIS ENCOUNTER WITH Himmler did not curry favor: "At times he appears to be cunning—attempts to impress disguised with his 'good connections.'" The examiners also duly noted Peiper developing cynicism and an egocentric view: "Generally, he is very inclined to deprecating fault finding and a negative attitude" and "there exists the danger that one day he will become a difficult subordinate, an unbearably ironic comrade or an arrogant superior."[7] Even so, beyond any critical misgivings, the team "conditionally approved" the self-centered candidate. In any case, here was a potentially resourceful and certainly headstrong young SS man.

He was also ready to leave home. Weeks later, Charlotte and Woldemar Peiper escorted their son to the Berlin Bahnhof. There a man checked off Jochen Peiper's name as one of those to be sent to Braunschweig. Peiper boarded the coach, which whistled off to another future. On April 24, 1935, he became an SS officer candidate.

Life at *SS Junkerschule Braunschweig* was probably to Peiper's liking. The SS training center was accommodated within the pillars of the stately Welfen Castle. Accommodations for the 240 candidates were Spartan. Each room was furnished with a simple table, two bunk beds, and two white wooden lockers without locks. A portrait of Adolf Hitler, which hung conspicuously in the middle of the whitewashed walls, watched over the scene. Another sign in the barracks quoted Nietzsche: "Praise be that which toughens."

The head of instruction was SS Standartenführer Paul Hausser, a retired Reichswehr general who had completely embraced the tenets of National Socialism. Knowing the Leibstandarte was regarded for its emphasis on precision parade drill down Berlin's black-top streets—hence the derogatory name "asphalt soldiers"—Hausser made certain that his training at Braunschweig was more than for show. He wanted the atmosphere at Braunschweig to bear the trappings of an elite.[8]

If plain in decor, officers' quarters were always outfitted with round tables where superiors could meet under ornate chandeliers to discuss class progress. The day began at five, and a less-than-clean coffee pitcher or a failed bed crease could result in punishment push-ups upon inspection. Parade drill was seemingly endless. The midday meal came only after the 1st Sergeant conducted a careful fingernail inspection. A fifteen-minute nap after lunch was just before the whistle to assemble for singing—oddly, singing skills in the SS were important. Taps came at 2200.

When time was available the candidates could perhaps visit the music hall to listen to Mozart or Beethoven. Respect for private possessions and trust in one's comrades was held in highest esteem, and a premium was placed on social behavior, proper dress, and manners. Detailed regulations covered everything from the proper posture to the approved way to present flowers when calling on a lady.[9]

At Braunschweig Peiper made some close friends—one was Karl Heinz Brohl.[10] "Hardest were our instructors," remembered Günther Börchers, "but deep was a relationship to each other. . . . We were bound together into a tight brotherhood."[11] Beyond camaraderie, there were hours of ideological training each week, organized around Himmler's puerile fantasies and predicated on the *SS Leitheft*—guidance brochures—a sort of monthly digest of the movement. The gazette was full of stories of inspirational German historical figures, pictures of lovely Nordic maidens, and celebrations of the glories of agrarian life. They were also punctuated by heavy doses of anti-Semitism. These sessions were something that Peiper would later claim was seldom taken seriously. "Intensive ideological orientation is an 'old wives tale,'" he ventured, noting that the division ideological trainer, "the priest of Wotan" was chased out of the unit.[12]

Contrary to Peiper's postwar declaration, the SS Junkerschule in Braunschweig enthusiastically embraced National Socialist ideological instruction. For instance, during his time as a Junker, the subject of Weltanschauung was given an emphasis equal to performance in military subjects, with anti-Semitism being a central tenet. Rather than criticizing such instruction, those at the school asked for more of this type of instruction from their teacher, Hstuf. Otto Eysell.[13] And contrary to being an ancillary issue, those who failed at Weltanschauung failed the entire SS officer's training course! This seems to have come about due to focused efforts to form the Leibstandarte into an SS fighting force devoted to Hitler and Hitler alone.[14] And for his part, the German leader continued to refer to the troop as "his" Leibstandarte.

And what about military instruction at Braunschweig? There were a number of instructors, but most of these were Reichswehr has-beens, usually forty years or more and often old fighters with the Freikorps. Matthias Kleinheisterkamp taught tactics and was a favorite of Paul Hausser, but he was constantly in conflict with Himmler, as he was a raging alcoholic.[15] Younger ones included the likes of Franz Magill, the horse-riding instructor whom Peiper knew from Berlin with Lombard, or Erwin Tzschoppe, who taught weapons instruction and map reading. Both would later be deeply implicated in war crimes.[16] Still, to his previous accomplishments Peiper added the Rider's Medal in Bronze. Even so, a closer look at the instructors at Braunschweig during Peiper's time raises the question as to whether they were competent at all. Certainly most would not have been acceptable within Wehrmacht schools, where officers training was typically twice as long as that for the SS Junker.

According to popular accounts (championed by Richard Schulze-Kossens and Ernst-Günther Krätschmer) the SS leaders benefitted from a dawn-to-dusk emphasis on physical conditioning, sport, and realistic combat training. As they later told it, the SS men were forged into an elite by long cross-country marches, map exercises, river crossing under fire, use of smoke for daylight assaults, weapons instruction—it went on and on.[17] "The rules of German-ness were not read," Krätschmer related of experiences at the Junkerschule. "One learned them by leaps from 10-meter towers, a march of 30 kilometers in full pack and by the most severe training on the exercise grounds."[18] Although sport and intensive physical training had an emphasis at Braunschweig, there was, in fact, little if any training with live ammunition or heavy weapons at the school. And it becomes interesting to note that a final graduation exercise for the SS officer class was a strange one. A fully mounted *Fuchsjagd*—a fox hunt—as the final test for what was to be later touted as an elite military finishing school![19]

After the oath on November 9, 1935, Peiper received the rank of SS Standartenjunker, and just four months later, on March 3, 1936, he was promoted to Oberjunker. Although lanky, but somewhat shorter than some other candidates at Braunschweig's SS Officer school, Peiper showed himself to be driven and tenacious. Physically he excelled at sports: he was a first-class swimmer and still bore the marks of his boyish enthusiasm for hiking. In one competition, young Peiper marched doggedly more than twenty kilometers to take second place amongst a fiercely competitive group. "Tough on himself and others," SS Hstuf. Rolf Lochmüller proclaimed. "He is a born soldier."[20]

At Dachau the SS officers from both Braunschweig and Bad Tölz came together in February 1936 for six weeks for a "platoon leader course," which may have been intended to bring the 240 leaders from the two schools in seamless form. Although the actual teaching done at Dachau remains speculative, as no records exist, we do know that it was conducted by the SS Hauptamt (Main Office) and that at the end of the course the SS leaders were assigned to the various branches of SS operations.[21] This included the militarized *Verfügungstruppe* (VT), the *Totenkopfverbände* guarding and running the concentration camps, the Police, the General SS, SD, the security police, and the *Rasse and Siedlungshauptaunt* (RuSHA), handling racial affairs. This would indicate that the course actually functioned to assess the Junker's talents and qualifications. There, at Dachau, Peiper met a number of SS leaders who would later figure prominently in his life. One was an SS Lieutenant from Riga, Latvia, and recently transferred from Bad Tölz: Heinz von Westernhagen.[22]

The site with the SS barracks, shooting ranges, sports fields, classrooms, and riding grounds in Dachau 1936 was right next to the Dachau Concentration Camp (the first Nazi concentration camp, opened in 1933), separated only by a wire fence. Everyone could see what was going on there. In any case, at Dachau, the graduates were given a guided tour of Theodor Eicke's concentration camp system on the grounds, where approximately two thousand political prisoners were held under brutal conditions. Indeed, the KZ or *Konzentrationslager*, was separated from the Kaserne where Peiper and the others trained by only a barbed wire fence.[23] And Peiper and the others roomed at the barracks with the concentration camp guards. They saw it all.

After finishing the Junker school course Peiper was then assigned as a cadet in the Leibstandarte SS Adolf Hitler. He was at the top of the pyramid as one of Hitler's praetorian guardsmen. Not only had he made the cut into the elite of the elite of the militarized SS, but finally, on April 20, 1936—Hitler's birthday—Peiper received his commission as an officer. At twenty-one he became an SS Untersturmführer (2nd Lieutenant) of the Leibstandarte Adolf Hitler.[24] Even years later Peiper saw his assignment as the height of good fortune—an "elite regiment of the regime" where membership was "an honor at that time, which every German dreamed of."[25]

Young Peiper returned to his hometown of Berlin to spend leave with his family. There it seemed, life was looking up. Unemployment was down and downtown Berlin surged with newfound prosperity, with Berliners flocking to cinemas, restaurants, and the theater. The rejuvenated economy bustled with massive renovation and rebuilding—Germany would host the Olympic Games that summer. Once derided and feared, Adolf Hitler—the man on Peiper's sleeve—was now widely adored.

While home, Jochen Peiper also heard of the exploits of his older brother Horst, who, after having fancied a career as a Luftwaffe officer, had changed his mind to join the SS VT as well. His brother's stated reasons for the change made his political persuasion clear: "I took the opportunity to opt for the VT, which I then joined as an officer candidate," Horst explained, "as I believed that in the Luftwaffe, my strong political interests could come up short. Then too, one of my brothers had started down the path to become an SS officer, a course of action which greatly appealed to me."[26]

Even so embraced, it must have been intimately obvious to both brothers that National Socialism had at its heart a violence that was not only tolerated but also elevated to extreme virtue. Within its racial philosophy, a crude and specious amalgam between Nietzsche and social Darwinism, killing and brutality was not only preached as the preferred manner to achieve and maintain power, but it also formed a part of the SS man's very vision of the world—his Weltanschauung. At least officially it did.[27]

On Saturday, June 30, 1934, when Jochen was first impressing his superiors in the SS cavalry, a selected execution squad of the Leibstandarte Adolf Hitler had drawn the grim duty of annihilating Hitler's potential political rival of the Sturmabteilung (SA), Ernst Röhm.[28] During the Night of the Long Knives the head of the Leibstandarte himself, Josef "Sepp" Dietrich, presided over the firing squad at Stadelheim Prison in Munich. Although never denying responsibility, he later said the assignment made him "sick." Still, Dietrich tersely obeyed his Führer's bidding, and fourteen of the Brownshirts—a number of whom he had personally known—were shot dead in the prison courtyard at dawn.[29] On the following day the rotund commandant of the notorious Dachau Concentration Camp, SS leader Theodor Eicke, personally confronted Röhm and shot him with a pistol in his jail cell.

The SS participants of the operation were ordered to keep quiet about their murderous duty, but the *Night of the Long Knives* became common knowledge—even a matter of pride—within Hitler's Bodyguard. Indeed, although two companies had traveled by rail to Munich for the shootings with Dietrich, still another battalion of the Leibstandarte remained in Berlin to assist. Jochen was not involved in the actual shootings, as he was not a member of the Leibstandarte at the time; however, as all SS men in Berlin had to report to Lichterfelde Barracks where the executions took place, he would have witnessed the proceedings. The gangster-style killings went on for over two days in Berlin as Leibstandarte members in the city apprehended 170 key SA members and brought them to Lichterfelde to be dispatched by gunfire.[30]

Such deeds were at the heart of the SS credo: "Hard as steel, a community of men defying death—an order of men sworn to the Reich."[31] For National Socialism saw itself as the final realization of human evolution in the most unfeelingly raw and Darwinian form. "Everything in life is struggle," said Himmler. "Everything is selection. That which survives in the final analysis through the centuries is always the better and the stronger."[32] Glorification of the concept of *Härte* within the SS organization played a central role. Loosely translated as "harshness" or "toughness," Härte translated to a contemptuous treatment of antagonists or inferiors with a total suspension of established ethics and moral precepts when it came to the unquestioning pursuit of Hitler's will. An excerpt from an SS ideological training manual conveys the quasi-Nietzschean spirit and contempt for racial difference:

> Where equals meet
> Hatred compels
> Good will does not help.[33]

Härte in armed conflict would be elevated to a holy paradigm within the SS, whereas mercy was a sign of weakness—it was intolerable: "Here God wants no love," the verse concluded. Another article went further: "We have a right to be harsh against others," the author reasoned, "because we have been tough on ourselves as well." And there was the recurring admonition against lapses of pity: "The SS possesses this toughness that will break all weakness," the lesson ventured. The concluding thought? "Let our enemies fear and hate us."

And not only was there philosophical reasoning justifying an SS ethos, there was also a spiritual training for the inner SS man as well. Himmler sought to create an SS spiritual retreat in a renovated castle at Wewelsburg in the picturesque Westphalian countryside near Paderborn. The ancient castle was fabled to be the final refuge of ancient German knights from their enemies in the East. It was said that from its ruins a future breed could launch a new battle to reclaim the proud German heritage.

HIMMLER HAD A PENCHANT FOR PEASANT NORDIC MYSTICISM, SO MUCH SO that he referred to his charge as the "SS order." Indeed, he came to believe his own twaddle, eventually informing his Swedish masseur of his certainty that he was the reincarnation of Heinrich I, sent back to Germany to continue the holy war against the Slavs to the East.

And Himmler, the hopeless romantic, carefully harbored the aura of terror and dark mystery to envelop his mystic movement. With a serious face, he would enjoin the twelve high SS officers sitting at his SS castle round table to concentrate their thoughts in a telekinetic gaze. The mind of the Nordic mystic had the potential, he insisted, to influence others. Many officers, including Peiper, wore their awarded "Death's Head" rings and carried along the ceremonial daggers, and some of the SS trainers came to believe in their own preaching—the mystical power of the SS runes and rites.[34]

Himmler made his Black Knights the curators of this new order. And so there, at Wewelsburg, the SS elite could go to contemplate their Nordic line or seat themselves in high-backed leather armchairs to converse with the SS Reichsführer at a twelve-place Arthurian round table.[35] Himmler might lecture his "New Nobility" on everything from anti-Bolshevism, a constant theme, to the knightly virtues of a breakfast of leeks polished off with SS-sanctioned mineral water.

The doors and windows of the castle were adorned with blue granite and a banister of forged iron emblazoned with runic motifs covered a tremendous staircase. There was an imposing ninety thousand–volume library enclosed in oak wood and a large wing for use by pseudo-scientists in charge of the SS archaeological section. On the practical side Himmler ordered that a particularly large room in the castle would be dedicated to accumulated gold and silver loot that would surely be plundered in the Hitlerian conquests to come.[36] Other rooms were designated for King Heinrich the First (Himmler's room) as well as King Arthur and one for the Holy Grail—yet to be located.

And that was not all. Long fascinated by the cosmos, Himmler even maintained an astrologer on staff—the long-range plan called for an astronomical observatory. The cellar of the old castle was converted to a black marble crypt with murky mystical intentions. At the apex of its dome was an ornate extended Hakenkreuz rune set in stone. Himmler declared this spot—*Valhalla*, or the "Realm of the Dead"—was the center of the Nazi universe.[37]

Yet everyday life for Jochen Peiper, the new SS officer, was not in a castle but in metropolitan Berlin. There he joined the other Leibstandarte at their Lichterfelde Barracks, an academy rich in German military tradition. The grounds were impressive: huge oak trees, massive brick buildings in a Victorian style, and even a gorgeous pool. The place exuded martial pride, particularly when the men of the Leibstandarte took to the central square to endlessly practice parade drills with robotic precision.[38] On Hitler's birthday, April 20, 1936, Peiper was placed in charge of the third platoon of the 11th Company.

His commander was SS Capt. Carl Marks, a leader with such enthusiasm for night marches that the 11th was jokingly dubbed the "moonshine" company.[39] Peiper had quarters on the second floor of the red-bricked Hermann Göring building. The accommodations were agreeable, and because he was stationed in his hometown, he kept a motorcycle in the basement of the barracks so he could go off-site to sleep at home periodically or to get around on his own. The men assigned to Peiper were at first taken aback by his boyish demeanor—"a Hitler Youth," one surmised—yet soon learned that their leader was not only a stickler for discipline but also something of a do-gooder. Still, such moral fastidiousness probably fit Carl Marks just fine, particularly given Himmler's virtuous obsession within his SS. For before Peiper had joined the troop, on March 9, 1935, his company had participated in a Gestapo raid on the Weinmeister Klause in Berlin, where homosexuals were arrested and brought to the feared investigation Gestapo catacombs at Prinz Albrecht Straße.[40] What would Peiper have thought of that, with one brother already seemingly on that side of the fence?

Peiper seldom frequented the bars of risque-raucous Berlin along with the other carousing youths. Young SS troopers were like most other soldiers around the world in at least three respects: drinking, driving, and women. To conform, the men at Lichterfelde took full advantage of the vibrant atmosphere Berlin had to offer: they quaffed beer, got into trouble with cars, and chased skirts at the Café Olympia until it was placed "off limits."Usually, however, Peiper stayed home at the Lichterfelde apartments and read underneath their diamond-paned windows. There he indulged a love of literature or, at night, went to the barracks cinema to see *Madame Pompadour* or the like.

During the day there was the opportunity to take a dip in the large indoor pool, play handball, or sun oneself in the spring air.[41] Peiper, the accomplished swimmer, also often took a summer plunge in the nearby Teltow Canal. And for culture there was often someone playing music or the chance to meet with the traveling SS poet Hanns Johst.[42]

The *Landsknecht* personality of Sepp Dietrich was still in charge of the Leibstandarte, giving a distinctly ceremonial complexion to its assignments. As a self-proclaimed elite within the National Socialist system, the Leibstandarte not only provided marching columns for parades and visits by heads of state but also supplied honor guards for the Reich Chancellery in Berlin and Hitler's alpine retreat at the Berghof in Berchtesgaden. Careful appearances meant everything! Peiper was often assigned as officer of the day or assigned to take charge of the honor guard in the stoned courtyard of the Chancellery. Far from devotion to Hitler as an abstract concept, within the ranks of the Leibstandarte the person of the Führer was a concrete reality. Where else would members of a German troop refer to Hitler as "*der Alte*"—the old man?[43]

Membership to the officer corps of the Leibstandarte grew more intoxicating each month. During the summer of 1936 Hitler had Germany and National Socialism on their best behavior for hosting the 11th Olympics Games. The SS men at Lichterfelde nicknamed their domain Olympic Village. On August 1 Hitler opened the Games in an expansive new Berlin stadium built expressly for the event. Jochen Peiper drew the plum assignment of escorting honored guests during the proceedings over the next two weeks. From small talk with the Americans he was able to improve his English.[44] And courtesy of the *Bund Deutscher Mädel* (BDM), the female equivalent of the Hitler Youth, there were beautiful girls to enliven the scenery.

The men of the Leibstandarte were sporting their smart new parade uniforms and attending one ball and dance after another. Not only were these lads beautiful men, but they also excelled at sport, played music, and exuded culture. Why, they were discussing freethinkers of the day like the renegade poet Heinrich Heine![45] And all this against a backdrop of towering Germanic splendor. Everything during those sultry days was gargantuan in size and tempo.

On August 11 Peiper and a group of other select men at the Lichterfelde Barracks were assigned to serve as escorts during the evening for the German women's Olympic team. Their purpose was to serve as the finest gentlemen companions in Germany—but just in case, during the preceding week the group had received instruction on avoiding venereal disease.[46] Whether the advice was needed was not revealed, but the social calendar was full regardless. The following day Peiper was an honor guard at a huge evening reception for foreign guests at the Reich Chancellery followed by a gigantic military band concert in the Olympic Stadium in which over a thousand musicians took part. That summer, National Socialist pride gushed from every German pore.

A seminal point for young Peiper came in September 1936, when he was first personally presented to Adolf Hitler. The occasion was the Reich Party Day in Nuremberg. The graduate SS officers from the newly formed cadet schools were introduced to the German leader on the parapet of Nuremberg castle while a massive crowd of the party faithful called for Hitler outside.

In the opening ceremony Himmler personally handed him the gleaming black and silver ceremonial SS dagger in its ornate scabbard.[47] On the polished silver blade shone the engraved motto: *Meine Ehre heisst Treue!*—My honor is loyalty! Then Peiper, with other officers, was received by Hitler himself. They met in the hallowed Hall of the Hohenzollernburg. Hitler greeted Peiper and closed with a firm handshake.

After that heady moment Peiper knew he had made it. He was now an SS officer of the Leibstandarte Adolf Hitler and was welcomed to the elite brotherhood by the Führer himself! With Hitler's name on their coat sleeves, they

> must recognize no other ties than to the Führer and his orders. . . . We must and can so use the time . . . to weld the units of the Leibstandarte into a stout tool in the hand of the Führer.[48]

The year 1937 was spent at Lichterfelde with one assignment and another. In May and June his unit held assault training exercises at Lüneberge Heide. The weather was sunny and warm as Peiper and the others sweated their way through forced marches and terrain exercises in mock combat. By night they watched movies, such as *Daughter of the Samurai*, or listened to the radio. Peiper showed himself as becoming something of an officer aristocrat, extending his capabilities both in hard-wheeling automobiles as well as expertise at dressage and riding horses.

And on May 28 there was the big annual celebration of Sepp Dietrich's forty-fifth birthday in Hansfeld. The event in 1937 was an expansive *Fest* that degenerated into a wild party at which over fourteen thousand liters of beer were drunk. Hangovers and arrogant egos sunbathed the following day.[49] Peiper maintained his pull to receive the plum assignments: on September 25 the infantry leader with two battalions of the Leibstandarte were on display for the Munich reception by Hitler for the Italian dictator, Benito Mussolini.

To be sure, there also was military training—and not always without incident. On December 7, Peiper and his platoon were in the field near Berlin learning how to throw hand grenades. Unfortunately one of the men hesitated too long in throwing a "potato masher," which exploded close by. Peiper was wounded by fragments in the buttocks and was hurried off to the SS hospital in Berlin, where his wounds were dressed. From the hospital, Peiper called SS Scharführer Karl Hollander and asked him to bring a civilian suit at once: the battalion officer, Obersturmbannführer Trabandt, had invited Peiper to a party that evening and there were sure to be many young ladies. Peiper did not intend to miss the party. Although Peiper was there, he stood for the entire occasion.

On March 13, 1938, Peiper was present for the "wildly enthusiastic" reception for the men of the Leibstandarte during their march into Austria. It was the Anschluss, or annexation of Austria into the German Reich. Church bells rang out and hysterically enthusiastic crowds choked the Austrian roadsides. Women swooned and fainted along their path.[50] As Hitler led the way, Himmler and Sepp Dietrich stood just steps behind him, marching down the shiny, rain-soaked streets of Vienna. Just paces to the rear was a smartly uniformed Leibstandarte officer, Jochen Peiper. Himmler, seeing again the thoroughbred SS soldier he had picked out of a crowd once before perhaps saw him again in a new light. Here was his future aide–de-camp, his man servant, his blue-eyed, racially pure assistant.

Eventually the entourage made their way to the magnificent Heldenplatz in downtown Vienna. There, amid a 360-degree grandeur of buildings, trimmed gardens, and statues, Peiper and other SS officers watched as Hitler addressed an huge crowd of wildly cheering Austrians. It went on like that for days. Back home even Himmler's sharp-tongued wife seemed inspired: "The weather is wonderful. It is really spring," she said, following the event on the radio until two in the morning. "Austria is now part of the German Reich! H. [Heinrich] was the first to arrive in Vienna. The cheers of joy were indescribable when the Führer, on Saturday morning, arrived in Braunau." Then on March 27, her famous husband was back to their villa in Berlin. "H. just returned from his performance in Austria with great satisfaction, almost jubilant," she recorded. "The *human material* he has in the SS!"[51]

Peiper and other SS "human material" lingered in stylish Vienna for another six weeks. At one point he and the other officers of the Leibstandarte strode confidently into the local barracks. There they confronted old pot-bellied Austrian soldiers, now worried they would lose their jobs if merged into the German Wehrmacht. Yet Peiper and his ilk had more on their minds than old Austrian Landsers. For these youthful SS guys, only the best was good enough, so they seemed naturally smitten by the lithe and curvaceous female actors and dancers of the Vienna State opera house.[52]

It was a new world—a German world order. And as Jochen Peiper's station spun toward the inner ring, his star rose on the horizon of National Socialism itself.

Where would it end?

Chapter 3

THE INNER RING

RETURNING FROM JUBILANT AUSTRIA IN APRIL 1938, JOCHEN PEIPER WAS THE young man who would be adjutant to SS Reichsführer Heinrich Himmler.

Arriving in Berlin, he learned from his superiors at Lichterfelde that he would soon be assigned to the staff of the head of Himmler's SS, who was now creating a massive empire for that organization. Peiper and Himmler's stars would now be linked. Himmler's star at that time was on a sharply ascendant path. And along with that heady mark came a lot of fringe benefits.

Initially all looked great. Just back from a stay of SS glamour and glitz in Vienna, Peiper was given gratis tickets to the famously dangerous Avus Rennen race on May 22, 1938. The price of the tickets for the affair was equal to half a month's rent for a typical family in Berlin! And the entire affair was thrilling as the Germans in their sleek BMW 328s took all the top six spots in winning the race.[1] Then, in early July 1938, three months after being promoted to SS Obersturmführer (1st Lieutenant), Joachim Peiper was officially posted to Himmler's personal staff. The promise of the three-month assignment seemed real enough. For anyone less competitive the election to Himmler's staff might have been the apex of a young officer's career. Hardly. Peiper's unspoken rival, Max Wünsche, was now at the Reich Chancellery to serve Hitler himself.

Stunningly blonde, Wünsche was an equal SS prince to Jochen Peiper. Wünsche had done exceptionally well at officers training school at Bad Tölz before being assigned to the Leibstandarte.[2] Strangely, in Hitler's Third Reich, importance was attached to birthdays and their astrological conjunction with others in the organization. If Peiper had his birthday on the auspicious day of the *Machtergreifung* (January 30), Wünsche could do him one better. Fair Max had the exact birthday of the Führer! Indeed, young Wünsche soon commanded the ornate SS honor guards at Hitler's Bavarian mountain retreat, the Berghof. There he welcomed European dignitaries and ran about with Hitler in his resplendent summer-white SS uniform.[3] Like chosen fair-haired sons, he and Peiper had anointed positions. But did Wünsche have the better deal?[4]

Peiper may have been slightly surprised by his new assignment. After all, there had been problems. Peiper had been the duty officer the year before and had run afoul of Himmler's wife, Marga, at their fashionable Berlin villa in Dahlem at Nr. 8/10 Dohnenstieg. Typically Leibstandarte men were assigned to guard the homes of important people like the Reichsführer SS and his family. Yet when Peiper arrived he found the Leibstandarte men toiling away at the daily chores for Mrs. Himmler—moving laundry, cutting the grass. "No, this is not possible any longer," Peiper sternly informed Frau Himmler. "We forbid our men to do housekeeping work." That was that. Marga Himmler concluded that the Prussian officer was snooty and arrogant.[5] "I have not heard anything from Heini for two days," Marga wrote in her diary, "I don't dare ask the staff. They are not polite."[6] Peiper's confrontation with Himmler's shrewish wife seems not to have done any lasting damage to his prospects for selection. In any case, the arrangement for Peiper as Himmler's adjutant must have agreed with both men, as the adjutant's appointment would later be extended.

His standing with the Leibstandarte and Himmler's familiarity could not have hurt.[7] After all, the Reichsführer SS had personally chosen the youth out of the crowd at the Reichs Party Day in 1934. And Peiper's fresh good looks and cultured demeanor was a plus for Himmler, whose gawky appearance always sought its opposing pole. Indeed, in choosing men like Karl Wolff or Jochen Peiper for his officers, Himmler appeared to looking for respectability to set his SS organization apart from the thugs in the Sturmabteilung.

True to form, Peiper was one of those "double Aryan" type of Nordics at which regulars in the Waffen SS liked to poke fun: Jochen Peiper, "Reichsführer SS recommended edition."[8] And Himmler, who was obsessed with astrology, had natal charts cast for every member of his potential staff.[9] To see a young man, born on the very day of the inception of the National Socialist party—well, that was grand. Peiper was an Aquarian with Sagittarius rising and Jupiter ruling, to boot; this suggested a useful blend of loyalty with a willingness to take risks. Or at least that was what Himmler's astrologer told him.

What would Peiper's boss be like? The first assignment to meet the Reichsführer SS provided a strong clue. That was the annual summer visit to the old city of Quedlinburg and the burial site of King Heinrich the 1st, Henry the Fowler, who Himmler saw himself as his reincarnation.[10]

On the first day of July Himmler and his entourage greeted their new SS officer candidates at the Junkerschule in Braunschweig and dined with them at the Rathaus. Peiper himself was a graduate. Next the group made the pilgrimage down the half-timbered buildings of old Quedlinburg to the cathedral where two years before Himmler had organized a festival to celebrate the thousandth anniversary of the historical figure's death.[11] There, in the presence of dignitaries of his Black Order, Himmler descended to the domed crypt by the light of resin torches where the bones of König Heinrich were interred. Reaching the tomb, ceremonially guarded by SS men, Himmler laid wreathes and flowers. He vocally vowed before his audience to honor the lessons of the "most German of all Germans." He was Himmler's cult hero who had conquered the hallowed region of the Lorraine, unified the German tribes, and drove east of the Elbe River to stop the incursions of the Bohemians and the Slavs.

From correspondence it becomes clear that Himmler preferred his inner circle to refer to him as K. H.—a barely secret notation for *König Heinrich*. Thus, he sought to revive a web of ancient Teutonic and cosmological dogmas linking new SS recruits to their Germanic ancestors.[12] Like Henry the Fowler, Himmler viewed himself as the modern-day crusader for what he saw as the inevitable war against the Slavs to the East. The SS would be his Teutonic Knights, with himself the grand master, helping to breed a new *Herrenvolk* aristocracy. But most important was his envisioned modern-day experiment for racially engineering his SS privileged Nordic class come to dominate Europe. These Aryan warriors would be tall, with blue eyes and blond hair.[13]

Although Peiper was not towering, he had the other qualifications. Within a short time of his stint with Himmler, Peiper took over work as Second Adjutant, moving into the ornate five-story baroque palace at Prinz Albrecht Straße 8 in Berlin.[14] This was the headquarters of Himmler's SS, and the adjoining building was the headquarters of Reich Main Security Office Chief, Reinhard Heydrich, and the equally feared Gestapo. Designed by Prussia's most famous architect, Karl Friedrich Schinkel, that address was perhaps the most feared in Germany, for it was there that Himmler had his office. Having been transformed from the former Hotel Prinz Albrecht, the headquarters was elegant: a massive front staircase, with two additional wings enclosing a courtyard. Yet the Wilhelmine structure struck fear into the hearts of Berliners with anything to conceal, for the fabled Gestapo torture chambers were concealed in the bowels of the building's cellars.

But above ground its brilliant gleaming corridors, with its stylish cast-iron stairs, teemed with young men arrayed in the black and white SS uniform, all dapper and perfectly appointed. There everyone seemed to be rushing from one place to the next as if their every move was tremendously important.

Yet if he looked sharp and soldierly, Peiper found the work there hardly fit for the military mold to which he aspired; the young aide sat in small anteroom just outside Himmler's office. Most often the door was open and communication was casual, but there was no escaping that the Leibstandarte man who fancied himself a pure warrior was, in fact, a well-dressed desk clerk.[15] In the mornings Peiper opened mail for Himmler, who was then briefed on the contents by his office manager, Dr. Rudolf Brandt.[16] But word got out that young Peiper had connections. Soon wives of ostracized Waffen SS soldiers wrote to Peiper asking him to intercede, as they knew he was a conduit to the Reichsführer—perhaps errant decisions could be effectively reversed.[17]

Himmler arrived at the office at around 10 a.m. but performed his office duties with "unusual punctuality." Announcing the arrival of office visitors, Peiper had orders that anyone on the daily schedule who was more than a few minutes late would be turned away.

Lunch at the mess was at 1400 sharp and lasted thirty minutes: soup and main course with dessert. At lunch Himmler, Wolff, Peiper, secretaries, and staff gathered at the canteen for the noonday meal.[18] Office afternoons were a little more electric. Beyond taking telephone messages and telegrams and composing short letters, there were other odd tasks, including everything from delivering Himmler's treasured gift Yule candle holders from the Allach Porcelain Factory to preparing instructions on the proper production of mead, an ancient fermented honey drink that the Reichsführer SS claimed to possess important health benefits for Germanic men.

Himmler, who was fond of coffee, often brought it each day to the office. The workday went on until 8 p.m., at which time there was a short dinner, a hot meat dish and soup washed down with a single glass of red wine. During meals official business was not discussed, but neither was there much small talk. On these occasions Himmler would often recount his favorite topics—the kingdom of the Goths, the written works of Edwin Erich Dwinger, or the new SS state to be established in Burgundy. After Himmler's evening cigar, the prosaic tasks or literary discussions often stretched until one in the morning.[19]

Just before the office closed Peiper carefully arranged his boss's appointment calendar for the next day.

If hardly a flashy assignment, looking trim was important, for Peiper greeted guests for the SS Reichsführer and introduced each. When it came time to see the second-most powerful man in Germany, Peiper often closed the heavy lacquered wood door: the SS Reichsführer preferred most meetings *unter vier augen*—under four eyes. And for sensitive matters not even notes could be taken. The head of the SS conducted meetings like a mafia godfather.

But if one wanted to speak of sensitive matters only face to face, then travel across Hitler's growing empire was needed. Thus, much of Peiper's responsibilities entailed endless journeys with his new boss. Some of it was perfunctory: on July 8–10 in Munich for the Day of German Art and, in the last week of the month, the big Wagner music festival in Bavaria.[20] Hitler would be there on both occasions. What was Himmler thinking about that summer? Little in the way of soldiering. On the next to last day of July Peiper joined Himmler on one of the frequent of junkets, this time being surprised when the Reichsführer SS ordered the car to pull over by the road near Graublau. Why? The head of the SS wanted to speak with two blonde German children enjoying the warm afternoon. As Peiper looked on, Himmler, in full black uniform with polished riding boots and SS dagger, paused to pick flowers with little kids.[21] And that was not all.

Curiously, Peiper discovered that the second-most powerful man in the Reich was obsessed with "secrets"—did sorcerers and witches in the Finnish area around Karelia possess lost mystical knowledge that could hold the keys for future Nazi domination?[22] Then there was his fixation on threats to German racial purity and the "gypsy nuisance."[23] And now he was coordinating with his chief SS ceremonial designer Karl Diebitsch to obtain just the right wall stones and the mix of deciduous and conifer trees to create a lush Nordic outdoor metaphysical garden at Sachsenhain bei Verden. It was to be a macabre monument to the place by the Aller River where Charlemagne had supposedly executed forty-five hundred Saxons in the year 782.[24] But above all the place was to be peaceful, for Himmler's vision of the ideal Germanic SS man featured an adoration of the outdoors: *Heimat*—Homeland and a return to a simple life of self-sufficiency.

Peiper's early time on his staff met with Himmler's approval. In mid-October his superior extended Peiper's time on his personal staff by three months.[25] Days later, on October 18, he and Himmler traveled to Italy to take part in the annual celebrations with their counterparts in the fascist Italian police. There was a gala reception by Benito Mussolini in Rome with Himmler, the guest of honor for Police Chef Arturo Bocchini. Four days of Italian hospitality—pizza, pasta, prosecco! Along for the trip was the first adjutant, Hajo von Hadeln, SS interpreter, Hstuf. Eugen Dollmann, as well as three men who would later figure prominently in the Final Solution: Reinhard Heydrich, Kurt Daluege, and Karl Wolff.[26]

When Peiper returned to Berlin social life later that autumn the racial persecution had become obvious. Fired up by Hitler and his propaganda minister, Joseph Goebbels, the anti-Jewish sentiment in Germany boiled over. On November 7, 1938, a disgruntled teenaged Polish Jew, living in Paris, strode into the German embassy there, pulled out a pistol, and mortally wounded a German official. Although the young man had his reasons—the new National Socialist deportation program had forcibly evicted his parents from Germany to Poland—this hot spark was all that was needed to touch off a firestorm of anti-Semitism in Germany.

As this transpired, Hitler and Himmler were in Munich for the annual festivities commemorating the 1923 Beer Hall Putsch. Peiper, as 2nd adjutant, was with Himmler as events unfolded. On the night of November 9, as Hitler and Himmler welcomed the newest SS recruits at the Feldherrnhalle, the riotous storm troopers of the SA exploded in the streets of Germany, killing a hundred Jews, destroying synagogues and businesses, and sweeping thousands into concentration camps. Hitler and Himmler learned of the events at the Feldherrnhalle.[27] It came to be known as *Kristallnacht*; as Peiper stood with Himmler listening to "*Wir treten zum Beten*," in Munich's torch-lit streets, the night of broken glass raged across Germany.

At 11:20 p.m. a Gestapo operative informed Reinhard Heydrich, who was staying at the Hotel Vier Jahreszeiten, that the Munich synagogue next door was ablaze. Tumultuous riots erupted. Heydrich immediately phoned Himmler, then at Hitler's Munich apartment on the Prinzregentenplatz, with Peiper and Karl Wolff at his side. "Demonstrations against the Jews are to be expected in the course of the night 9 to 10 November 1938 in the entire Reich," went out orders from the Reichsführer SS. "The demonstrations are not to be hindered by the police."[28] As Peiper and Himmler returned from the midnight swearing-in of the SS cadets, the sky was red from the fire of the burning old synagogue on Herzog-Rudolf-Strasse.

Heinrich Himmler claimed to be aghast at Kristallnacht too, but his concerns had nothing to do with the inhumanity being waged against the Jews, only the damage done to foreign opinion of Germany abroad. Peiper's superior believed this move was simply not the way to proceed against the Jews—that should be done secretly. Further, it did not help that the insurrection might increase the vanquished SA's standing with Hitler. Later Karl Wolff would claim that the Reichsführer told Heydrich that his SS was not to take part.[29] In fact, Himmler strongly endorsed SS participation in the pogrom with elements of the SS Verfügungstruppe directly participating in some riots.

While Heydrich was ordering wealthy male Jews to be apprehended and sent off to concentration camps, Himmler warned that any SS men taking part in the "demonstrations" should do so only in civilian clothes. "There would come a time,"

Himmler railed, "when the world would have no place for the Jews." There were two mutually exclusive outcomes for the twentieth century, he told the assembled SS officers. With failure of the National Socialist movement, Germany would come to nothing and the dream of the Reich would fade. If the SS did its duty, however, Himmler boasted to his audience, Hitler would deliver the greatest empire in world history.[30]

But down on earth the "greatest empire in world history" posed some petty conflicts for Jochen Peiper in Himmler's bustling Berlin office in early 1939. At one point, early on, Himmler noticed that his underling did not wear the swastika tiepin of a National Socialist Party member. A bit taken aback, Himmler asked whether he was a party member. Peiper politely replied that there had been an application, but he had never received a card.[31]

On April 27, 1939, the Berlin Office sent a letter to the NSDAP office in Munich, stating that the "Reichsführer SS is very interested that a man, from his innermost circle be a party member." The eventual result: a National Socialist party number was provided to Peiper on 6 May 1939.[32] There was no date-of-rank listing, and Peiper would coyly deny that he ever possessed a party number.[33] But, in fact, two applications were made. As Peiper had claimed to Himmler that he had never received his membership card, a new one was sent.

Party member or not, in the beginning Peiper was mainly Himmler's messenger boy. That first summer of 1938 the adjutant traveled back and forth as courier over the long 650 kilometer distance between Berlin and Tegernsee south of Munich and near the Austrian border. On the shores of that beautiful alpine lake Himmler had set up a fashionable warm-weather home at St. Quirin, not far from the Austrian border and close by the SS training school at Bad Tölz. He even had a hunting lodge in the nearby Schliersee Mountains on the Austrian border.

When Peiper drove into Gmund am Tegernsee and turned down Kurstrasse, it wasn't difficult to find Himmler's house. It was big. The architecture was Upper Bavarian: a white-walled two-story affair with a big, timbered A-frame roof and dominated by a dark wood balcony and green shutters. Looking out on the majestic lake and Hirschberg beyond, it was surrounded by rustling linden trees in quiet splendor. *Der Lindenbaum*, Himmler was fond of reminding everyone, was the sacred tree of the ancient Burgundian German tribes—tribes he believed were the original Teutonic home of a tall Aryan race. Indeed, the Benedictine monastery in Tegernsee, one of the oldest in Europe, was founded by two brothers from Burgundian royalty of extraordinary height who were still buried there.[34] For Himmler, all was ode to the proper Nordic man. *Lindenfycht* in Tegernsee was the perfect place for him—a Nazi cosmic convergence.

It seemed appropriate then that during one of these visits to Lindenfycht, Peiper met a tall Nordic blonde woman with thin austere features. She was Sigurd Anna Hinrichsen, a secretary working closely for Himmler in his offices.[35] Hinrichsen was the daughter of a dentist from Kiel, Schleswig-Holstein, and a friend to Lina von Osten, more recently Lina Heydrich.[36]

The smiling, oval-faced frau was the politically ambitious wife of Reinhard Heydrich, the greatly feared head of the Sicherheitsdienst, or SD, the security service of the SS. Unimpressed with Himmler's pudgy, embittered wife, Lina Heydrich looked to bring some class to the SS entourage. Did she know that Himmler purposefully chose only secretaries with blonde hair and blue eyes? The intention was that they would be eventually married off to SS officers?[37] In any case, she recommended to Himmler her friend "Sigi," a blonde with emotional sympathies to match his own—an *herbe Schönheit.*

Indeed, Sigurd Hinrichsen had been friends with Lina's husband, Reinhard, *before* marriage. Himmler, ever aware of the limits of his own image, was happy to oblige—more strikingly tall Nordic men and women![38] Sigurd Hinrichsen joined the personal staff of the Reichsführer SS in October 1936, moving to an apartment in Wilmersdorf at Waitzstrasse 5.[39] There she met Hedwig Potthast, a sharp twenty-five-year-old clerical secretary from Cologne who had been there since the preceding January, living in Berlin's Steglitz district.[40]

The two women were the only secretaries present at Himmler's private birthday celebration on October 7, 1937. And at the marriage of SD man Richard Pruchtnow on January 29, 1937, Sigurd was photographed leaning chummily behind Himmler at the wedding ceremony.[41] As with most of his subordinates, they would claim that the Reichsführer told them only as much as they needed to know. However, the truth was quite different.[42] So important did Potthast—"HP"—become that she was frequently writing correspondence as Der Reichsführer-Privatsekretariat on a variety of matters. These covered the gamut, from the progress of SS artifact hunter, Otto Rahn, looking for the Holy Grail around Turin in Northern Italy to mundane correspondence with the SS school at Wewelsburg on genealogy records for SS men looking to marry.[43]

Still, from 1937 to 1939, it becomes obvious from the office correspondence that "HP" became progressively more important in the world of Heinrich Himmler. Whenever Himmler was in Tegernsee his staff often worked at the SS headquarters in nearby Gmund and stayed at the nearby Gasthof Glasl. Typically, the cast included Jochen Peiper—officially assigned to escort the Reichsführer SS to Lindenfycht—along with the traveling secretarial pool, Sigi and Hedwig Potthast.[44] The hotel proprietor was an SS officer too. Moreover, Ernst Glasl possessed an *early* NSDAP party number and had been an SA member for five years before transferring to the SS in 1937. Glasl even eventually became a member of the Leibstandarte Adolf Hitler.[45]

Glasl's hotel reflected its owner's political sympathies, with its checkered-tile dance floor and big wall hanging of Hitler over the fireplace in the Café Maximilian. Often populated by Himmler's staff during summer, the place became sort of a SS hangout for those in his inner circle. For secretaries and adjutants mixing at the fashionable spot it became something of a secret rendezvous haven for black-uniformed men at the apex of the SS ziggurat.[46]

Sigurd and Hedwig were favored within Himmler's inner circle at the top. Indeed, the SS Reichführer seemed sweet on Sigurd's officemate, gifting her a box of chocolates on her birthday on February 6. Later that year, near the close of 1938,

Hedwig accompanied Himmler to Tegernsee, where he flirted at the dinner table in conversation on mundane matters. The two discussed the travesty of how the lofty High German of Goethe was now watered down and in need of a linguistic renaissance. Shakespeare and the English were overtaking world literature. Then there was the good fortune of National Socialists to inherit the sympathetic reign of Pope Pius XI—chitchat with the secretary.[47]

But there were lusty sparks by then too, for by Christmas 1938 Hedwig Potthast and Heinrich Himmler had a heart-to-heart meeting during one of the sojourns. There, in Tegernsee, the two agreed that, even though he was married and eleven years her elder, they were hopelessly in love.[48] He now called her by her affectionate nickname, *Häschen*—little bunny. Over the holidays the Aryan flames glowed as Peiper, Himmler, and the others attended the required *Winter-Sonnwendfeier* replete with music—Wagner, Beethoven and Grieg: *Flamme empor!*[49]

A FEW WINTER WEEKS LATER, HOWEVER, HEDWIG WAS HAVING DOUBTS ABOUT their relationship. "About the bad question: your fear over whether I will have you again: I have already written you about that three days ago," Himmler penned from Berlin on February 4, 1939. "The rules you have are in your own mind. My good dear Little Bunny will know better. Come again soon to visit me. I am sure you will be completely happy."[50] The second-most powerful man in the Reich was having an affair. And that was not all.

At first Sigurd Hinrichsen was reticent to be courted by Jochen Peiper, the young adjutant upstart, but she soon dropped her guard. Häschen seemed smitten with Jochen as well. After all, how debonair was this dashing prince! To Sigurd, Jochen was the perfect *Edel Germane*. And besides noble Germanic looks, both Sigurd and Joachim had much more in common. Like Peiper's family, Sigurd also had two brothers in the SS Schutzstaffel.[51] Although she was two and a half years older than her interest, the acquaintance of Joachim and Sigurd within the headquarters of the Reichsführer slowly evolved into another cozy office love affair at the unlikely address of Prinz Albrecht Straße. Of this, Himmler approved completely; he constantly lectured his SS men of the need to bear children of good Nordic stock, either through marriage or even outside of wedlock. "My personal opinion," Himmler himself stated, "is that it would be a natural development for us to break with monogamy."[52] Yet, for now, matrimony would be a key requirement for a proper SS leader, he insisted.

After all, the women of his SS thoroughbreds had to be racially suitable to bear children and equally dedicated to the SS cause of loyalty and honor. "We stand or die with this leading blood of Germany," Himmler advised. "And if the good blood is not reproduced," he blustered without a hint of drama, "we will not be able to rule the world."[53]

As Peiper wooed his future bride, the threat of war drew near along with the augury of National Socialism's ominous plans for the unfavored races. On his twenty-fourth birthday, January 30, 1939, Peiper was present at the Reichstag to witness Hitler's infamous speech before the rostrum at the Kroll Opera. The Führer stood before the four microphones in his tidy brown uniform, clutching the wooden sides of the pulpit. The Nazi kismet seemed seismic, for as Hitler spoke underneath a giant golden eagle, menacing and clutching a swastika in its talons, Peiper, basked in his same-day promotion to the rank of Obersturmführer, or SS 1st Lieutenant. Peiper stood motionless behind Himmler, as the four-hour ear-numbing sermon called for the Western democracies to take on Germany's Jews—or else:

> We fight a truly gigantic struggle to which we have dedicated the entire force and energy of our people and we will win the struggle without reservations. . . . After all, German soldiers have never fought on American soil other than for the cause of America's independence and freedom. Yet American soldiers were shipped to Europe and contributed to the suppression of a great nation struggling to preserve its liberty. It was not Germany that attacked America; it was America that attacked Germany. . . . Nevertheless, let there be no doubt as to one point: all these attempts will not in the least sway Germany from its reckoning with Jewry. . . . Once again, I will be a prophet: should the international Jewry of finance succeed, both within and beyond Europe, in plunging mankind into yet another world war, then the result will not be the Bolshevization of the earth and with it the victory of Jewry, but the annihilation [Vernichtung] of the Jewish race in Europe.[54]

Against that apopolytic prospect, Peiper's star rose quickly with the rocket-like trajectory of the Reichsführer SS. Heinrich Himmler's organization had grown enormously since 1933; a big change came in 1936 with his post as head of the German order police and the formation of the Waffen—Weapons—SS from the SS Verfügungstruppe.

Meanwhile, at Himmler's side, Peiper became something of an SS everyman, meeting all the top dignitaries and personalities of the Third Reich. In September 1938 Peiper again attended the Reichsparteitag in Nuremberg, where he had been introduced to Himmler four years earlier. And in the following month he was part of the official entourage in the bloodless annexation of the Sudetenland to Germany. On October 3, women and children were once again screaming enthusiastically, throwing flowers in their path as the Führer's three-axle G-4 Mercedes touring car drove across the border. Improvised Nazi banners hung from the streets near Wildenau. In his wake, Himmler, Peiper, and military dignitaries followed Hitler, inspecting blasted fortifications along the Shober line, then gulping mineral water in Karlsbad. Everywhere there were eager crowds.

There was more press as well. On February 14, 1939, Peiper was present when Hitler and Himmler launched the brand-new forty-two-thousand-ton battleship, the *Bismarck*. The Leibstandarte band blared away as the champagne splattered across the hull in great fanfare. For Jochen and Sigurd Peiper, the *Bismarck* would later become of greater interest. After it became operational, the ship's tough-looking dentist was none other than Dr. Rolf Hinrichsen, Sigi's older brother.[55]

Close to the Führer, Peiper's boss was now famous the world over. In April, Himmler's profile even graced the covers of *Time* magazine in the United States.[56] On Sunday, March 12, 1939, Peiper stood in the back row behind the Führer and Himmler for the *Heldengedenktag*—Hero's Day—in Berlin at the majestic State

Opera House, Unter den Linden.[57] For Hitler the place was symbolic of the potential apogee of German culture. Had not the rococo interior been home to Frederick the Great's court opera house? Peiper was on the inner orbit of Hitler's Reich.

As if to affirm that fact, just days later Peiper accompanied Hitler on the planned invasion of the Czech Republic. "Our borders must stretch to the Carpathians," Hitler had confided to Joseph Goebbels, his propaganda minister, on March 11. The military invasion would launch with the Ides of March; Himmler and Wolff had donned their combat grays, with Peiper set to tag alongside. Yet Hitler's last-minute political extortion of the elderly Czech State president Emil Hácha produced a fantastic concession. "The Luftwaffe will be over Prague at dawn," Göring blustered. "Will we have to bomb?" Although Hácha fainted and had to be restored by Hitler's doctor, the Czech statesman consented. The German invasion would be a bloodless one. Hitler considered the coup the height of his glory. Bursting in on his secretaries, he asked for a kiss. "So children," he gushed, "this is the happiest day of my life!"[58]

As the German army crossed the Czech border that morning of March 15, Peiper sat alongside Himmler in his master's Mercedes. A wet snow fell in a thick blanket on the long columns of German soldiers and automobiles. As Peiper looked out he did not see the joyous crowds he had seen a year before in Austria. Now there were only sullen-looking, curious Czech Slovaks huddling to keep warm. But the cold did nothing to chill German spirits. Hitler hastened to Prague to march through its icy streets alongside Himmler, Wolff, and Peiper. All entered the ancient Hradschin Palace, the legendary home of the Bohemian Kings. The German leader gushed with bravado as he looked out of an upper-floor window upon the latest land of conquest. "Here I stand!" he said balling his fist, "and no power in the world can remove me from here!"[59]

That late winter and spring of 1939 Peiper accompanied Himmler on one excursion after another. One was to an infamous location. On April 25, 1939, Peiper went with Himmler and a galaxy of generals to Dachau Concentration Camp, where the SS invited dubious Wehrmacht representatives to show it off. Theodor Eicke and Oswald Pohl made introductions and proudly described the two hundred–building complex. There was a series of briefings and a description of a training course about the National Socialist Weltanschauungs to help set inmates on a proper course. Peiper himself was captured on film as the group moved from one camp inspection to another. The day ended with an expansive concert and torchlit dinner at the swanky Munich Hotel Vier Jahreszeiten held before a huge Teutonic wall tapestry in "real SS style."[60]

Appearances remained important. On May 5 there was a combined celebration with Hitler and Himmler greeting an adoring mass of Hitler Youth, followed that night by a formal dinner and stage play of *Hamlet* at the Dessau Theater.[61] In a later journey, Peiper was seen with Himmler and Hitler during a general inspection of the Westwall fortifications along the Belgian border that was to protect Germany's boundaries in the event of war.[62]

Later that month Peiper accompanied the Reichsführer and Reinhard Heydrich, ostensibly on a diplomatic mission to Italy to help strengthen their alliance. It seems Himmler had other aims. Staying at the Villa Madama in Rome, Himmler drove the Italians crazy insisting that they find the spot where Visigoth King Alaric met his end at the Busento River. His quest? To locate a big cache of buried loot that belonged to the Germanic people. And Bocchini, the Italian chief of police, was obliged to send his policemen traipsing through the hills of Southern Italy, looking for buried treasure. Himmler claimed to have special clues from SS specialists at Wewelsburg, but their guidance was fanciful at best.[63]

Quite apart from Himmler's archaeological fantasies, a big military demonstration came after they returned. On May 20, Himmler and Peiper joined Hitler at the Munster training grounds, where a group of assembled generals observed the first demonstration of the newly trained SS combat forces. On display was Felix Steiner's SS Regiment Deutschland. Steiner believed the future of the militarized SS lay with specially trained squad-level battle groups, a modernized version of the *Stosstruppen* that had shocked Allied forces at the end of World War I. The action was an astonishing display—a large-scale infantry attack on entrenched positions, complete with live machine gun and artillery fire. Hitler marveled as he, Himmler, and Peiper gazed across fields of exploding shells, with men rushing forward in precision, throwing hand grenades and fighting their way through tangles of barbed wire.[64] One "enemy" position after another fell to the swarming troops. The assembled generals were impressed, although two SS men were wounded in the demonstration. Himmler's reaction? "Every drop of blood spilled in peacetime," he said, "saves streams of blood in battle."[65]

Himmler remained more than pleased with Peiper as his aide-de-camp. At the beginning of June 1939 Peiper was officially promoted to the First Adjutant under Himmler. He now traveled for all official functions; he was along with his boss and Hitler to the *Reichskriegertag*—a special day for all veterans to meet—at Kassel on June 6, 1939.[66] Three weeks later, on June 26, 1939, Peiper helped orchestrate a portentous Himmler meeting in Berlin at the Haus der Flieger.[67] That place was just across the street from Peiper's Berlin office, a grand affair during which his boss gave the highest of the high officers and officials a detailed look into his far-reaching plans for the Schutzstaffel and his police.

After Himmler extended a short briefing on his Black Order, the head of the uniformed Order Police, SS Obgruf. Karl Daluege and Dr. Werner Bracht, delivered a lecture. More than anyone under Himmler, it would be Daluege, an able but dull bureaucrat, who would serve a key role in Himmler's pursuit of racial genocide.[68] For it would be his uniformed police battalions who would commit mass murder in Russia and Poland alongside the *Einsatzgruppen*—"action groups"—being deployed under Reinhard Heydrich. But during the three-day-long affair it was the economic promise of the concentration camp system that was on display.

After Daluege and Bracht spoke, the entire group traveled north of Berlin, thirty-five kilometers, to Oranienburg. There the fanatical anti-Semite, Theodor Eicke, and the SS industrial wizard, Oswald Pohl, gave the participants a tour of the Sachsenhausen Concentration Camp. On the second day of the SS gala Reinhard Heydrich spoke glowingly about the SD, and Arthur Nebe about the Kriminalpolizei. The evening was celebrated at Peiper's old digs, the officer's club of the Leibstandarte at Lichterfelde, where Sepp Dietrich showed the guests the expansive new barracks. More speakers were on tap for the final day. Werner Ohlendorf led off, detailing how the concentration camp system would produce an economic windfall for Germany.

Afterward, Paul Hausser discussed how the Verfügungstruppe—now in transition to the Waffen SS—would become the military enforcers of the policies of Hitler's Reich. Hausser argued that a dramatic expansion was needed for the organization to which Peiper belonged; the unspoken insinuation was that the German Army was not idealistic and tough enough for the coming challenges to the Third Reich. Nor was Himmler hiding the concentration camp system—it was an object of pride. Moreover, as plans were fleshed out, Himmler made it clear that the plans for expanding the soldierly section of the SS was to not be separate from the activities of the police and general SS and the concentration camp system; indeed, as Himmler saw it, they were *integral* to them.

Finally, Dr. Werner Best spoke about the RSHA and the effort to obtain a stringently pure race in the Reich. Himmler praised this mission, as if it were a holy task. Expanding the SS in all its aspects would require more Germanic children, because, as Himmler saw it, for Hitler to rule the world, they would likely need massive wars of expansion. Pure blood would be needed if Germany was to meet its destiny. Marriage was the critical requirement for the successful SS man. Even if he fell in battle, his genes could fight on in the distant Germanic future.

Peiper aimed to fulfill his part of that deal. The very next day, after the meetings were over, Peiper cemented his position into the greater SS family. The Peipers had been of the Lutheran faith for many generations. However, the young officer, like nearly all SS men, converted to Himmler's preferred *Gottgläubigkeit*—"believing in God."[69] At that time recurring rumors circulated in Berlin: new applicants to the Leibstandarte need only apply without denominational affiliation.[70]

"Believing in God," though religious in tone, did not divulge that Gottgläubigkeit was decidedly un-Christian. For Himmler's National Socialist God was loving and compassionate only to the preferred Nordic racial stock, while fiercely contemptuous of "inferiors." Himmler was clear: "I insist that members of the SS must believe in God," he would later insist. "I am not going to have men around me who refused to recognize any higher being or Providence."[71] The same was true of unmarried SS men—a decided negative in Himmler's book.

In any case, Peiper's single days were done. On March 6, 1939, Jochen made the official application to be married, with Nazi awards choreographer, Professor Karl Diebitsch serving as witness. Himmler himself personally signed the permission documents.[72] On Thursday, June 29, Jochen Peiper married Sigurd Hinrichsen. The stated religious preference on the legal record at the Wilmersdorf town office conformed perfectly: Gottgläubig.[73]

The marriage itself was at 9:30 a.m. at Margaretenstrasse 11 at the palatial mansion of Hitler's socialite friend, Frau Viktoria von Dirksen. The proceedings were in keeping with the SS Reichsführer's adapted ceremony, supposedly based on ancient Germanic ritual. A choir opened the ceremony with a chorus from Lohengrin.[74] The groom was dressed in the seldom-seen black SS officer's evening dress uniform with black silk-lapel waist coat, aluminum-corded adjutant's aiguillettes, and a large silver badge on the right breast.[75]

The couple took their vows before an altar draped with a red National Socialist flag and capped with a yellow sun disk made of flowers. The special guest of honor was Heinrich Himmler himself and his fleet of attendants.[76] The SS Reichsführer was invited to say a few words, a toast to the newlyweds. Behind the altar on the wall was a black banner stamped with the white Sig-runes of the SS, and on the table was a framed likeness of Adolf Hitler. At the close of the ceremony the couple was offered bread and salt before exchanging rings. The knot was tied.

As with other SS newlyweds, Jochen and Sigurd received an ornately carved wooden box marked with oak leaves, acorns, and Nordic runes. Nestled inside the case was a black-leather bound copy of *Mein Kampf*, embossed with a golden eagle gripping the swastika in its talons. Prominently displayed on the overleaf was a handwritten dedication to their marriage from Adolf Hitler himself—"on the occasion of your wedding day."[77]

THEIR RACIAL HERITAGE WAS STRONG AND PURE. NOW THEY COULD CREATE a perfect SS family.

Chapter 4

WITH HIMMLER

IN 1939 JOCHEN PEIPER WAS NO LONGER JUST AN OFFICER WITH THE Leibstandarte Adolf Hitler; he was now the experienced and dedicated twenty-four-year-old assistant to Heinrich Himmler. As aide-de-camp, Peiper assisted Himmler's every move. At the time he drew his assignment, few in Germany knew the powerful and feared head of the SS closely—a man whose small eyes squinted from behind the round spectacles with a mysterious half-smile. After the war, military types derisively referred to Himmler as *Reichsheini*. Yet such criticism would not come from his adjutant. Indeed, one of Jochen's closest comrades in battle later told how Peiper was one of the few SS officers who really *liked* the Reichsführer. They were intimates. Of course that had to be: an adjutant for Himmler was a man he found totally sympathetic with his new SS order.[1]

Himmler was the obsessive bureaucrat, energetic organizer, and the meddling political force behind the SS. He had no military experience but fancied lofty martial aspirations that made Peiper's appointment—an SS officer—effective office window dressing.

Himmler's other strong personality, König Heinrich, was a religious believer—a romantic obsessed with mysticism and symbols. Although he was son of a Bavarian school teacher of modest means, Himmler fervently admired Prussian austerity and hardness. And although physically uninspiring and almost clumsy, his innermost urge longed for the ancient Teuton kings. Indeed, he saw himself the reincarnated soul of King Heinrich the First, the famous German conqueror referred to as "the hammer of the Slavs." When Himmler joined the National Socialist party in 1925, some claimed he was already a member of the Thule Society, a cabalistic order extolling the greatness of German history stretching back to AD 9, when Teutonic tribes decimated the Roman army. The Thule society symbol became that for National Socialism—the Swastika.[2]

Even though constantly dabbling in philosophic esoterica, Himmler was scientifically unsophisticated.[3] True, Himmler was fascinated by astronomy, but at the same he time also embraced Hans Hörbiger's outlandish Cosmic Ice Theory, *Welteislehre*. In that far-fetched scheme the ice ages came when a string of moons crashed into the earth, resulting in a cold and dark time when human evolution reached an apex with the Nordic man.[4] The early ancestors of the Aryans had been frozen in ice until released by divine thunderbolts![5] The lost continent of Atlantis, Himmler believed, was, in fact, located near Greenland. It was the fountainhead of Caucasian races and the seat of German culture.[6] For Himmler, herbs and homeopathy trumped modern medicine, and weather forecasting could be replaced by a weird synthesis of astrology and sunspot study.[7]

Yet against his admiration of physical perfection and athletic skill he perpetually suffered from stomach cramps, once even collapsing in a running competition.[8] Even with a devoutly Catholic mother, Himmler relentlessly attacked Christianity while also espousing SS precepts based on spiritual exercises and the Jesuit principles of Ignatius Loyla. He admired mystics and seers and quoted the *Vedas* and arcane Buddhist precepts. Himmler embraced eugenics, clairvoyance, and reincarnation.[9] Although music seldom moved him, the head of the SS endorsed Gregorian chant.[10]

With little use for valuables, the Reichsführer expounded the virtues of a simple life in open air, Heimat, and the peasant farmer's existence.[11] Always preaching to his SS of the need for toughness, he, in fact, had a soft spot for children.[12] Himmler was a total contradiction. "He seemed like a man from another planet," said Gen. Heinz Guderian, who deemed Himmler a total nut case. Others, like Carl Burckhardt, the commissioner of Danzig, was even less sympathetic: "What made him sinister was his capacity to concentrate upon little things, his pettifogging conscientiousness and his inhuman methodology; he had the touch of the robot."[13]

His neighbor on the Tegernsee, Max Amann, said that although others might characterize him as a tyrant, Himmler, in fact, had a homely nature—he was a Nazi Robespierre.[14] But perhaps most important, Amann saw Himmler as steadfastly dedicated to the elimination of all enemies of the Reich, "and he did so calmly and without hate or sympathy." *Anständig*—decency—was Himmler's watchword. He believed that if killings were necessary for a higher Aryan mission, it must be done "decently," a perverse state of affairs he extended wholeheartedly into every corner of his SS—killing should be done *decently*.

Himmler's cool emotional exterior likely suited Peiper, who emerged from Western Berlin with a brusque Prussian streak. Sarcasm, irony, and cynicism were Peiper's prime antisentimental expressions. Himmler, his boss, drank little, and was circumspect. To Peiper, the proper SS officer, these were likely admirable traits. But fundamentally Himmler was propelled by obsessive organization. And he was fanatically devoted to the tenets of National Socialism and the natural hegemony of tall, blond Nordic men in all worldly things.

As Himmler's closest aide and someone always at his side, slender and blue-eyed Jochen Peiper seemed the perfect match. Some sarcastically referred to the young adjutant as an "SS poster boy." Peiper certainly looked the part. Like Karl Wolff, Peiper possessed those qualities that were lacking in the Reichsführer: good looks, charm, and airs of culture. If not so muscular as an Arno Breker sculpture, he was always correctly dressed, impeccably appointed, and "never sloppy."[15] Peiper was the incarnate vision of Himmler's SS warrior.

Within Himmler's mix of personalities—a twin obsession with toughness and decency, was a magnetic vision of the SS legions to which Peiper belonged. The first SS responsibility was a cold-hearted SS police to enforce Hitler's vision and banish enemies to concentration camps. As Himmler emphasized, even his later SS warriors would first and foremost embrace his image for the *Allgemeine* (General SS). And what of his newly armed SS, which would be set up in 1940? These he saw as modern-day black-clad Germanic knights, sporting tanks and cannon rather than horse and lance. They would be fearsome SS warriors, like Napoleon's Old Guard, to win the key battles that could give Hitler victory in the war.

But how would these twin goals be accomplished for Germany? Fast forward to Himmler's bizarre preoccupations with lost civilizations, Germanic archaeology, the Holy Grail, and Indo-Germanic tribes, all entangled with Darwinist racial theories that demanded the elimination of the unfit. By the time Peiper appeared at Himmler's Berlin office, both Hitler and the Reichsführer had become obsessed with the persona of Genghis Khan, the ruthless Mongolian ruler from the eleventh century. This came about through admiration of Michael Prawdin's *Genghis Khan: Storm out of Asia*, a book Himmler had passed on to the Führer with a glowing recommendation.[16]

So impressed was Himmler with this work that in 1938 he directed his training official, Gottlob Berger, to create a special SS edition that he then distributed to his officers at Christmas.[17] Peiper undoubtedly received a copy, although Genghis Khan was already a topic with which he was intimately familiar, having written a detailed paper on the subject during a political training assignment the year before.[18] That Himmler's fixation made a deep impression on his adjutant seems undeniable, for Peiper referred to the Mongol leader in his own writings after the war.[19] What was this kind of warfare? "The first attack, according to Genghis Khan's tactics, had to carry terror and panic to the remotest part of the country. The invaded country was to be paralyzed with fear; the inhabitants would be made to believe that resistance would be a futility."[20]

For Himmler, Genghis Khan epitomized the features he saw vital to solving the problems of twentieth-century Europe: launch huge battles of conquest led by elite legions who killed entire populations in invaded countries and took wives and daughters of the slain for siring new populations in the subjugated lands. That Prawdin's vision of the Mongol warrior affected Hitler's thinking was amply demonstrated by the secret address the German leader made to the high officials of the army on August 22, 1939, just before the outbreak of World War II. Foremost in Hitler's mind was his army's readiness for ideological battle in Poland:

> Our strength is our speed and our brutality. Genghis Khan led millions of women and children to slaughter with premeditation and a happy heart. History sees in him solely the founder of a state. It is a matter of indifference to me what a weak European civilization will say about me. . . . Accordingly, I have placed my death's head formations in readiness . . . with orders to send to death mercilessly and without compassion, men, women and children of Polish derivation and language. Only thus shall we gain the living space [Lebensraum] which we need. Who, after all, speaks today of the annihilation of the Armenians?[21]

War was coming. The glitzy zenith of Peiper's assignment at the Reichsführer SS headquarters was topped by an ominous lining. Himmler and his long-faced security police head, Reinhard Heydrich, had organized *Einsatzgruppen*—a euphemism for killing squads that were to eliminate Polish Jews and other undesirables in the rear of the army. Additional regiments were organized by the racial fanatic, Theodor Eicke, from Totenkopfverbände—Death's Head units and concentration camp staff. Eicke would later form these killing teams into a fighting division in the Waffen SS with a terrible reputation to match.[22]

The war broke out on the first day of September 1939 as Hitler's tanks rolled over Poland in a lopsided conquest. The first "lightning" war—the *Blitzkrieg*—lasted just eighteen days, although formal capitulation did not come until September 28. On Sunday, September 3, at 9 p.m., Hitler and Himmler, with a gaggle of adjutants, clerks and dignitaries, left from Berlin in their personal command trains, bound for Poland. Hitler was in his mobile *Führersonderzug Amerika* while Himmler rode in *Heinrich* his own fourteen-car luxury train. Each locomotive pulled an open salon car for its leader, a Mitropa dining car, another with quadruple 2cm anti-aircraft weapons, a luggage van and several office and sleeping coaches.

To address a chronic nervous condition, Himmler brought along his Finnish masseur, Felix Kersten.[23] The German foreign minister, Joachim von Ribbentrop, was also with Himmler's group, although provided with less luxurious digs than the Reichsführer's lavish antique car. Eicke, meanwhile, was onboard Hitler's train to coordinate the murder teams of the Einsatzgruppen; Karl Wolff and Peiper were also there as liaisons from Himmler. As an SS officer with weapons experience, Jochen drew the heady assignment of accompanying Hitler and his entourage.[24] The privileged in the trains were delighted to travel from Silesia to Poland to glimpse the war up close.[25] Yet Peiper knew his comrades in the Leibstandarte were elsewhere in the thick of the fighting.

Later he would learn that no formation had experienced more casualties than Dietrich's command. Although their combat record in Poland was mixed, the unorthodox fighting style of Dietrich's men's did not please the army: even in their first combat, the Leibstandarte seemed fond of the torch, setting fire pell mell to the villages of Żdżary, Piaski, Boleslawiec, and Mieleszyn. The most infamous incident involved the director of the Leibstandarte's regimental band, SS Hauptsturmführer Hermann Müller-John. On September 18 the army arrested him for shooting some fifty civilians just west of Warsaw whom the Obermusikmeister judged "Jewish criminals."[26] And that was not all: there were documented instances in which Leibstandarte troops brutally killed dozens of defenseless civilians in Boleslawiec, Mieleszyn, Wieruszów, Łęki Duże, and Zloczew.[27] Yet Himmler was not about to allow punishment of Waffen SS zeal, and he put a stop to prosecution of the SS band leader.[28]

But Peiper was not even with the troop during these reprehensible episodes. His only real presence in the Poland endgame was a momentary stop with Hitler and Himmler at Bzura on September 25 to give Dietrich a slap on the back for his battle performance. But if not able to participate in the fighting, Peiper did at least see the conquest up close. Himmler's train steamed through some of the most densely populated *Ostjuden* villages in Poland. The weather was hot, and the dark-roofed railcars broiled in the hot September sun. The train staff, including the clutch of secretaries, suffered the sweltering heat amid the nonstop din of the teletype machines. As adjutant, Jochen traveled away from the trains during the day with the escort column. Returning at night, with the batteries on Heinrich's cars often running down, the Reichsführer's staff had to pass out candles in the darkened cars.

By day, Hitler and his escort would take their convoy of glossy, beige, six-wheeled Mercedes cars out for surprise visits to the front of the newly conquered Polish countryside.[29] Peiper accompanied Hitler and Gen. Erwin Rommel in these voyages as part of Himmler's liaison team. His tanned young face sported goggles for travel across the dusty Polish roads while a comrade adjusted a light machine gun on their open-topped car.[30] In one of the forays on September 4 Peiper and Rommel moved with Hitler and his cortége from Bad Polzin to pay a visit to the old aristocratic general in charge of Armeegruppe Nord. Peiper recalled,

> In the Polish campaign, I was with Hitler and Genfldm. [Fedor] von Bock. He was a true Prussian. Hitler was very polite to him, but I remember one incident clearly where Hitler made a fool of Bock with his exact knowledge of the ammunition and gas situation. He enumerated all the details. I was a young officer who listened and became enamored with Hitler. . . . We were astounded by his memory.[31]

On September 6 Hitler, with Peiper and the others in the van, paid a surprise visit to Gen. Heinz Guderian in charge of the XIX Army Corps. Hitler marveled at the blown bridges across the Vistula River near Graudenz and the low losses sustained by Guderian's forces. "Tanks save blood," Guderian explained to Hitler.[32] The day before, the Polish Pomorska Cavalry Brigade had attacked the 3rd Panzer Division near Plenow—horse and lance against armor and cannon. The brave but foolhardy Polish mounted troops were nearly wiped out. It was the Blitzkrieg—lightning war—moving so fast that by the end of the fifth day of fighting, Gen. Franz Halder, Hitler's head of his general staff, concluded that "the enemy is all but beaten."

Meanwhile Rommel, Peiper, and the others were back on the road, galloping along at breakneck speed to meet the Führer at the next airstrip. On September 11 they escorted Hitler to meet Gen. Walther von Reichenau near the front at Tomaszów. Peiper knew the monocled general well enough—there were family connections. Here was a true Nazi general, unflaggingly loyal to Hitler, and the old Prussian who had aided Peiper's ascent in the SS through the Reitersturm.[33]

The days with the "gray column" were long but fit Peiper's audacity, driving like crazy all hours through the swirling dust. One day in the north, the next in the south. It was a long line of vehicles, the heavy gray Mercedes with a tanker car, a repair vehicle, radio car, and field kitchen that cooked while it drove. Ahead ran a fleet of motorcycles sporting machine guns and expert marksmen. The long days racing across Poland made a big impression on Peiper. These big cars bristling with weapons were like the fast gasoline-powered cavalry! They met Hitler at makeshift airfields all over Poland, traveling over seven thousand kilometers on primitive roads, with their keepers often sleeping under the stars in the "Hotel Mercedes."[34]

The reaction of the Führer's entourage to the Polish locals? On September 10, near Kielce, Otto Dietrich, Hitler's press secretary: "The appearance of these human beings is unimaginable," he reported. "Physical repulsion hindered us from carrying out journalistic research."[35] Peiper seems to have agreed; when pointing out some of the elderly Jewish Poles to comrades with a stick, he later referred to them as "parasites."[36]

Hitler did not intend to see the war from coach seats. Each morning "*Der Chef*" would venture away from his train for another trip to the front.[37] September 13 was no different. At 9 a.m. Hitler flew off from Nieder Ellguth for the short trip to the grassy airfield southwest of Łódź. There he was greeted by Gen. Blaskowitz leading the 8. Armee., Hptm. Erik Bertram, Peiper and the other SS men were waiting to provide escort to the front lines north of Łódź. Later that Wednesday Peiper was photographed during a roadside break with Rommel near Bratoszewice.[38]

On Friday morning, September 15, the escort column reached the airfield near Pawlosiów to meet Hitler at 8:30 a.m. Hours later Peiper, along with everyone else, enthusiastically cheered German troops as they stormed over the San River near Jaroslaw. When Hitler and the others scuttled across bridges erected by German engineers, bare-chested German troops on the other side stood in rows to give the raised-arm salute.[39]

By then the Polish armies were collapsing everywhere. Peiper and the others were exhausted. When they escorted Hitler back to the airfield that afternoon Peiper had been driving nonstop for twenty-two hours on adrenaline and coffee. By September 18 the long line of cars had rejoined Hitler's train, now idling at a rail station near Lauenberg.

Relishing his role as victorious warlord, Hitler journeyed on September 19 to the newly reclaimed old Hanseatic city of Danzig on the Baltic. With driver Erich Kempka at the wheel and Himmler and Peiper following in a vehicle just to the rear, Hitler rode in an open car through the streets of the city. Swastika-emblazoned flags fluttered out of every window. Flowers and banners streamed across the field of view; the streets lined with raised arms and the sonic atmosphere filled with shouts of "Heil!" A near-hysterical jubilation seized the population. Tears flowed; women fainted. To Peiper it seemed like Vienna the year before.

Hitler's headquarters triumphantly moved to the Casino Hotel in Zoppot on the shores of the Baltic Sea.[40] Where Europe's wealthy had once come to gamble, now an unusual spectacle unfolded. Over morning breakfast Hitler's entourage watched from the hotel terrace as two old German cruisers looking "like some old picture of a naval engagement" bombarded the Polish port of Hela some eighteen miles away. Later, with church bells ringing and flowers raining from enthusiastic onlookers, Hitler's motorcade passed through Oliva into Zoppot. At the end they finally pulled into the ancient Artushof Courtyard along the Langer Markt at the center of Danzig. There, in the late autumnal afternoon, Hitler joined a fleet of dignitaries, with Himmler and Peiper standing just to his rear.

A justified campaign was over, Hitler shrilly called out to the microphone, and it had only taken just eighteen days. Danzig was again German and German alone. Hitler pointed a finger. "Germany was grievously wronged by the injustice of Versailles."

> The land of Danzig also fell victim to the insanity of the time. . . . The last twenty years have proved beyond a doubt: the Poles who had not founded this culture were not even capable of sustaining it. . . . I must also mention, however, that this admitted valor of many Polish units stands in contrast to the dirtiest deeds perhaps committed during the past centuries . . . thousands of slaughtered German people, the brutishly butchered women, girls and children; the countless German soldiers and officers who fell wounded into the hands of the enemy and who were massacred, bestially murdered. . . . Under these circumstances, should one exercise restraint oneself? . . . I may lose my patience.[41]

Hitler referred to the four thousand German inhabitants of Bromberg that Nazi officials claimed were killed by angry Poles during the first week of the invasion.[42] However, in pondering his patience, the German leader must have been mindful of the far-reaching retaliation ordered by Himmler and the ongoing pogrom of the Einsatzgruppen.[43] Indeed, Reinhard Heydrich had just sent notice to SS commanders in Poland on September 21, ordering Jews to be concentrated in the Lublin area, grimly warning that the "*Endziel* [final goal], will take some time."[44]

News of the nonmilitary SS actions percolated down to the German army as well. On September 22 regiment Brandenburg of Eicke's Totenkopf, who had previously been concentration camp guards, began a wild four-day killing spree against Jews in the area of Wloclawek, northwest of Warsaw. The SS men from Buchenwald engaged in an orgy of plundering, dynamiting synagogues, and brutal executions.[45] When the general in charge of the Eighth Army, Gen. Johannes Blaskowitz, learned of these events, he composed a long memorandum cataloguing the savage crimes of the Totenkopfverbände.[46]

The insinuation did not go far. Instead, von Reichenau was praising the *performance* of the Einsatzgruppen, and the General of the Army, Walther von Brauchitsch, was unwilling to press the issue with Hitler. Instead of punishment, Himmler told Eicke to make sure to insulate army ears from such matters next time. This, Brauchitsch already knew, for Hitler had lectured the general in his private coach on September 7 on a vitally important mission for the SS with which the army must not interfere. What was that mission? "It is the Führer's and Göring's intention to destroy and exterminate the Polish nation," Eduard Wagner, the Quartermaster General on Hitler's train noted in his diary. "More than that cannot even be hinted at in writing."[47] Peiper's boss addressed the Leibstandarte:

> In some parts of Poland there have been sometimes real guerilla affairs which have been more painful than war itself. It is then that we need troops, formations and men who have received an ideological training for the occupation of these countries . . . we must begin to do with the Waffen SS what we have already done with the SS and the police.[48]

"More painful than war itself" was Himmler's unexpressed concern. What would be the effect of coldly executing Jews in the field?[49] Would his SS thoroughbreds be brutalized by their actions, go mad, or lose the sense of what it meant to be a

German? *Anständig*—decency! Prawdin's writings failed to provide a road map. What would Genghis Khan do?

Peiper not only heard the speeches but also had first-hand knowledge:

> Naturally, I have heard that Polish partisans have been shot. . . . I myself, at that time did not consider these actions contrary to law. I myself learned during the Polish campaign that Poles put out the eyes of German prisoners of war, cut off their tongues etc. . . . I had the impression that, in general, the Polish population was very cruel toward Germans and at that time considered the reprisal justified.[50]

In any case, the fighting in Poland was over. On the evening of September 26 Hitler's and Himmler's trains, with Peiper along, quietly returned to Berlin's Stettin station. The crowning moment came less than two weeks later when, on October 5, Peiper, with Himmler, Hitler, and a host of other dignitaries flew back to Warsaw to celebrate.[51]

At 11:30 a.m. the entourage landed at Kielce Airport, greeted by a jubilant delegation, including General Gerd von Rundstedt and Generals Blaskowitz and von Reichenau. An expansive victory parade flowed down Ujazdowski Avenue in the old Polish city, the procession filing by the diplomats' quarters for nearly two hours. Peiper stood at Himmler's side. The streets were partially destroyed from the furious artillery barrage that had pounded the city into submission. Although aides reported the macabre spectacle of destruction in the streets of Warsaw had shaken him, Hitler presided over the demonstration, dressed in a handsome full-length gray leather coat and holding his outstretched arm. As he did, legions of the German Eighth Army goose-stepped down the swastika-adorned streets.[52] Poland was now under German boot heels.

Later in the afternoon, after a tour of Belvedere Castle, Hitler and Himmler discussed the problems in Warsaw in the wake of conquest. Peiper followed behind his master. The Gauleiter of Greater West Danzig, Albert Forster—no friend to Himmler—complained about army interference with the "pacification" policy in his Gau. To solve the dilemma, two days later Hitler installed Himmler as the Reichskommissar for the Consolidation of German Nationhood. The head of the SS would spearhead the mission of a German settlement area in Poland. Most importantly he would make certain that the policy of eliminating Polish leadership and Jews continued full speed.[53]

When Peiper returned to his new bride in Berlin, he found the city as if in a prewar trance. Hitler himself had desired that the city show as little impact of the war on German life as possible. His underlings complied. The sports programs for the capital city were ambitious even by peacetime standards: track meets, a bicycle race between the homeland and Hungary, the national rowing regatta, and a schedule of a hundred all-popular football matches. The Berlin Grand Prix auto race at the Hoppegarten capped the sports fervor.

At the same time, Berlin cinemas sold out for early showings of *Sensationsprozess Casilla*, starring Heinrich George, a courtroom drama that mocked the American way of life. Meanwhile, Goethe's play *Götz von Berlichingen* drew big crowds at the Schiller Theatre as if to validate a veneer of Germanic normalcy.[54] "You would hardly believe there was a war on," an American war correspondent remembered.

Peiper had little time for the urban glitz that autumn of 1939. The decorative adjutant's braid that Peiper wore on his left shoulder continued to live up to a humorous German colloquialism—the *Affenschaukel*—or monkey swing. For, under Himmler, Peiper lived out of a suitcase and swung from one tree to the next, accompanying his superior on endless travel. Just about every week there was a two- or three-day trip, usually by airplane but sometimes by car. If it was a frequently visited place, there was a favorite hotel—the Vier Jahreszeiten in Munich, the Deutscher Hof in Nuremberg, or the Fürstenhof in Münster. In late 1939 many of the journeys toured newly seized Poland to monitor the progress of stripping Jews from the major cities there—hardly military.[55]

Amid all the travel, Himmler leaned ever more on Peiper. Himmler admired Peiper's measured thoroughness—his *Gründlichkeit*. For an SS man of low rank, his influence swelled disproportionately. SS Gruppenführer Oswald Pohl, Himmler's right hand man, often wrote to the adjutant with gushing salutations: "My dear Peiper!"[56] Within the strict hierarchy of the SS, with its terse and unemotive language, such an affectionate term would never be used unless the adjutant's status was something special beyond rank.

There was more. On November 8, 1939, Peiper accompanied Himmler to Hitler's annual address in Munich at the Bürgerbräukeller. Even before Hitler arrived, the gallery of the Löwenbräu was crowded with three thousand eager followers. A galaxy of prominent Nazis gathered: Goebbels, Ribbentrop, and Sepp Dietrich. The "Badenweiler Marsch," struck up and the "Blood Flag" was carried in as Hitler arrived. Seated close by Himmler and Peiper in the privileged front row was Hitler's adjutant, Max Wünsche. Hitler had asked Wünsche to reserve the early train back to Berlin, but his adjutant feared he would never make that. The packed beer hall crowd cheered so wildly that Hitler only began speaking at 10:10 p.m.

"What were the British aims in the last war?" Hitler raved. "Britain said she was fighting for justice!"[57] To onlookers Hitler appeared eager to pick a fight with the island nation, a fact only too apparent to his generals.[58] The bitter diatribe went on for half an hour and then suddenly Hitler stopped as if in midpassage. The usual drill was a painfully long speech, hobnobbing with the "Old Fighters" sipping weak beer followed by endless handshaking. Himmler was likely relieved since after the November 8 celebration, he usually headed off to a long vacation with his wife in Salzburg.[59] But unaccountably that Wednesday evening, Hitler ended his speech and made for the early train with his adventurous chauffeur, SS Col. Erich Kempka driving off. When Hitler and Himmler stepped onto the north bound train, adjutants Peiper and Wünsche followed in their wake.[60]

They arrived at the train stop in Augsburg to disconcerting news. Twelve minutes after Hitler left the Bürgerbräukeller, came a startling report. The podium exploded in a gigantic blast, ripping off part of the building's roof. Seven died instantly, with a further sixty-three wounded. Had Hitler been there, he almost certainly would have been killed. As soon as Himmler could get to a phone, he was speaking to his shrewd

SD agent, Walter Schellenberg, in Düsseldorf: "This evening, just after the Führer's speech in the beer cellar, an attempt was made to assassinate him . . . there's no doubt that the British secret service is behind it all."[61]

Himmler was obsessed with the British intelligence service, and his SD had known for some time that the supersecret MI-6 was considering ways to end Hitler's reign.[62] On orders, Schellenberg and his "gangster" sidekick, Alfred Naujocks, staged a daring raid near the Dutch border town of Venlo to trap British agents supposedly behind the assassination attempt. It was all Nazi James Bond, replete with a spy-versus-spy double-cross and a wild shoot-out at the border. When it was over, the two secret agents of Her Majesty's Secret Service were bound in shackles and heading in a speeding secure car back to Germany.

A few days later a thirty-six-year-old carpenter and watchmaker, Georg Elser was arrested attempting to cross the Swiss border. He was carrying a postcard from the Bürgerbräukeller and metal bomb-detonator keys. He was also found to have been a member of a militant Communist group and recently released from Dachau Concentration Camp. In the glare of the Gestapo's interrogation lamps at Prinz Albrecht Straße, the cabinetmaker readily admitted that he had constructed the bomb and covertly assembled it into the pillar behind the speaker's platform. Even under the pain of torture, the Swabian craftsman insisted he had operated alone. He had convincing details describing how the bomb was assembled. Moreover, Schellenberg, who had captured the two British agents, had time to interrogate them and found they were not responsible. Hitler would have none of it. "What idiot conducted the interrogation?" he scowled.[63] Hitler believed the Jews or the English had to be behind the attempt.[64] If a skillful craftsman, Elser seemed a half-wit.

So reprimanded, Himmler returned to Munich three days later to be present at Hitler's speech to swear in the new SS recruits at the Feldherrnhalle. After that, however, Himmler went directly to the Gestapo headquarters at Wittelsbach Palace to personally interrogate Elser. Peiper was present for the confrontation that would use *Verschärfte Vernehmung*—enhanced methods.[65] Dr. Albrecht Böhme, head of the *Kripo Leitstelle Muenchen*, claimed to observe Himmler assail the prisoner.[66]

Such treatment notwithstanding, Elser stuck to his story. Ostensibly Peiper was merely attending to adjutant duties and along for the ride. But practically, he had become a Nazi Everyman, a minor SS unknown, bumping along behind Himmler and witness to infamous events.

But if Peiper was attempting to insulate himself from the implications of the racial program to which his superior was committed, one incident in particular must have come as a shock. On December 12, 1939, Peiper was along when Himmler flew to Łódź, where a mass expulsion of Jews was underway. They watched as hordes were loaded onto cattle cars, supposedly for relocation. On the day-planner, Himmler traveled to inspect new housing being prepared for ethnic Germans being transferred from Russia.[67]

> Himmler believed after finishing the Poland campaign that the entire war was already won. He wanted to create new German Eastern provinces and he was totally obsessed with the thought to settle the new Eastern provinces with

> Germanic elements. I, by myself, had to visit together with Himmler these camps of re-settlement. But I never understood it to mean that in the context of the resettlement of the Poles, that they were to be annihilated to make new space for the new Volhynian Germans to settle there. As far as I know, at this time it was not planned to kill the re-settled Poles. They had been won for us with victory as new workers for the Reich.[68]

Afterward Himmler and Peiper journeyed to Posen for a special tour of inspection. Two months before, Hitler had signed a controversial authorization for euthanasia of institutionalized patients to purge weakness from the Germanic gene pool. Among other objectives, Himmler had come to Poland to witness a new "humane" method by which to rid the Reich of *lebensunwerten Lebens*—lives not worth living. The victims of the carbon monoxide gassing were insane Jewish inmates at nearby Tiegenhof Asylum. In any case, Peiper's account was startling in its detachment:

> One day during the winter of 1939/1940, I accompanied Himmler on a trip. During this trip, a euthanasia took place in Posen. There, the inmates of an insane asylum near Posen were killed by gas. The action was done before a circle of invited guests. At that time, I had the impression that people present were to be shown a painless mercy killing. The insane were led into a prepared casemate, the door of which had a Plexiglas window. The insane entered the casemate singing and laughing. After the door was closed, one could see how, in the beginning, the insane still laughed and talked to each other. But, soon they sat down on the straw, obviously under the influence of the gas, and soon thereafter laid down. Very soon, they no longer moved.[69]

How to ease one's conscience? The looming holiday season may have helped. On December 16, Peiper was at the Reich Chancellery in Berlin. While Hitler met with Philipp Bouhler, Martin Bormann, and Peiper's boss, two capped Jungvolk, young boys of the pre-Hitler Youth organization, knocked on the door to request donations. It was the Nazi winter fundraising drive. Peiper answered and showed them in. Hitler was soon there to smile as his personal photographer snapped photos. The Führer shook hands with the two delighted Pimpfe. Peiper stood smiling in the background, looking boyish himself.[70]

The following week, on December 23 Peiper was with Himmler and rejoined the Leibstandarte for the annual Christmas festival at the Bad Ems Casino. Eschewing the Christian calendar, the Reichsführer preferred to call it *Julfest*, but many traditions from *Das Weihnachtsfest* were retained. There was a bright green Christmas tree adorned in the Himmler-approved fashion: gold and silver painted nuts, marzipan cookies, red apples, and candles. Linen-covered tables shone with candles and pine garlands, and there was a big fire. For each SS man came a Christmas cake, tobacco, and a special bottle of cheer. The field kitchen doled out dinner, holiday punch, and steaming *Glühwein*.

Adolf Hitler arrived to a jubilant twilight celebration at 4 p.m. The sudden cheers drowned out Beethoven's inspiring chords. Frivolity and song followed. Sepp

Dietrich spoke first, imploring the Führer to give them battle. "As those who bear arms, we soldiers can only prove who we are and what we can do!" Later there was even a short address by Hitler himself. He took cheers as he announced his complete confidence in victory; things would be different from the previous war, he said. German weapons, after all, were insurmountable. "As long as I have the honor to stand at the lead of the battle," the German leader intoned, "it is for you, the men of my Leibstandarte, an honor to be the spearhead of the fight."[71]

In spite of the gloom, Hitler was satisfied when he left.[72] So was Peiper. "Christmas, what magic lies in that one word!" He took leave to return to his wife and family in Berlin, "to sip the delicious emotion of the Christmas eve when married."[73] With Sigurd now expecting, Jochen and his wife moved to a larger corner flat in Berlin-Wilmersdorf at Rüdesheimerplatz 7. That place seemed perfect for a new family; the building was right by the U-bahn station and was comfortably nestled on a street lined by stately chestnut trees.[74]

From their new front bay window Sigurd and Jochen could gaze out through the beech boughs to the Platz itself, decorated with frost-covered flowerbeds and watched over by aging stone statues of King Neptune. On Christmas Eve, in Berlin, Rudolf Hess spoke to the German nation over the radio from the naval base at Wilhelmshaven while Joseph Goebbels blustered at a celebration for the city's children at the Berlin Theatersaal. A special Bach recital and a performance of the Gross-Berlin guard regiment seemed designed to reassure as much as it was to inspire.

Back at the family Berlin homestead at Zähringerstrasse, the two SS Peiper brothers were united that holiday with mother and father. The family celebrated Horst's Iron Cross, 2nd class earned in Poland. Did the brothers confide in each other of the hard edge of war they had seen in the last year? Jochen himself had seen with Himmler a mass shooting organized by SS Oberführer Ludolf von Alvensleben near Bromberg at the close of the Polish campaign.[75]

Jochen's brother, Horst, had personally seen the outbreak of the first blast of the war when the *Battleship Schleswig-Holstein* fired on the fortifications on the Wester Platte. Horst had also participated in the combat operations of the SS Heimwehr Danzig—something of an illegal secret military formation—in the free city, an action in which members of the civilian Polish Post Office were later executed after surrender.[76] Moreover, Jochen's brother knew firsthand the cruel side of Eicke and the SS concentration camp scene. He had previously been with Oberbayern Totenkopf Standarte at Dachau for a year and a half and later was sent after the Anschluss of Austria to the newly created Totenkopf Standarte Ostmark, which was overseeing the creation of the brutal KZ camp of Mauthausen near Linz.

Beyond Danzig there had been other atrocities in Poland, and the *Selbstschutz*—organization for the protection of Germans outside of Germany—now included brother-in-law Kurt Hans Hinrichsen.[77] Horst was toiling under the misanthropic ideology of Eicke and the Totenkopf, while brother Joachim was now adjutant under the head of *all* of the SS, Himmler. Even their father was involved, if not directly for the SS, then eventually rejoining the army to extract work from impressed Polish workers appropriated by that conquest.[78]

But likely these were not the things to speak of over the holidays. Instead, it was to ponder if one could acquire a Christmas carp, the traditional holiday fare in Berlin, or otherwise secure enough eggs and butter to mount a holiday feast amid the increasingly difficult rationing.

On New Year's morning snow began to fall outside the Peiper family's new Berlin flat. By mid-January the German capital was in the clutches of the coldest winter in a century.[79] Even though Sigurd was now three months pregnant and heating fuel was dreadfully short, duty called for her husband to resume his travels with Himmler's couterie. Jochen's mother, Charlotte, saw to it that Sigurd was cared for and provisions obtained, even given the long queues in the streets to reach rows of empty shelves at Berlin's shops.

During that frigid time in Northern Europe, Himmler and Peiper departed Berlin's frozen streets to complete a inspection tour of Germany's concentration camps. The Reichsführer was particularly proud of these. Although approving of the "hard methods" of Rudolf Höss at Sachsenhausen in his surprise inspection, Himmler was infuriated that neither the prisoners nor the SS guards recognized him.[80] On their way back to Hamburg, Himmler and Peiper stopped at the SS KZ at Neuengamme, where a thousand famished inmates—many Jews from Kristallnacht—were slaving under brutally frigid conditions to produce clay bricks for the Reich. An accompanying photographer snapped a photo showing Peiper standing behind Himmler with local Gestapo operative Otto von Apenburg.[81] Undeniably, Peiper was familiar with the terrible reach of Himmler's ever-expanding empire.

Having given directions to the concentration camps to extract maximum work from the condemned, Himmler and his retinue, including Peiper, again took to the rails to return to Poland. This time the special Reichsführer train chugged eastward to the village of Przemyśl. Himmler's retinue was even larger than before. His traveling companions included his favorite poet, Hanns Johst, and his anthropological expert on Tibet, Ernst Schäfer. Schäfer was the most brilliant German explorer of his day—an expert marksman, scientist, and charismatic adventurer.

A year before Schäfer had returned from an ambitious quasi-scientific expedition to the lost city of Lhasa, where he and anthropologist Bruno Beger used calipers to measure the facial dimensions of Tibetan people, producing plaster face masks and thousands of photographs. Peiper and Himmler had enthusiastically greeted Schäfer immediately upon return from Tibet on August 4, 1939.[82]

A PRIMARY MISSION FOR THE ANTHROPOLOGISTS WAS TO FIND THE REMNANTS of an imagined Aryan race hidden somewhere in the mystical fog of Tibet. Himmler fervently believed that the legendary forefathers of the German race, the lost Aryan tribe, possessed supernatural powers that National Socialism could use to conquer the world.[83] Accordingly, everyone traveling with them seemed interested in speaking with the intrepid Schäfer. Had they found the Aryans and the Europids? In any case, a second rail car was required to carry all the travelers, although Peiper rode with the preferred Salonwagen.[84] But Himmler also had practical business in newly conquered Poland. The land was being cleared for resettlement by thousands of ethnic Volhynian Germans who had been living in a portion of Poland under Soviet rule. With land for expansion in the East, he would bring about Hitler's promised *Lebensraum* by providing Western Poland for German settlement.

Himmler's group left Berlin on January 25, heading for a meeting in Cracow, Poland. At Przemysl, the following day, Himmler welcomed one of the streaming trainloads of Volhynian settlers arriving to the new land. Things weren't going well, however. "You have to understand that you have to wait," he would later tell disgruntled German colonials. "Before you get your farm, a Polack must be thrown out."[85]

Himmler, Peiper, and his retinue then returned to Cracow for a morning review with Obergruppenführer Friedrich-Wilhelm Krüger of a police battalion and unit of the Totenkopfverbände. Krüger was the Higher SS and Police Leader for the Government (HSSPF). Later, on January 27, Peiper was with Himmler during an uneasy afternoon meeting with Minister Hans Frank and "Globus," the former Viennese Gauleiter and now police leader Odilio Globocnik. Krüger had control over "Globus," who would eventually be entrusted with Operation Reinhard and the plan to exterminate the Polish Jews. For now, however, Krüger and Himmler delivered the news that Globocnik would be responsible for rapidly resettling many thousands of Jews from the Polish territories that had been annexed by the Third Reich—the Wartheland, West Prussia, and East Upper Silesia. For the time being, Himmler would send them back to the strongly Jewish cities of Warsaw and Lublin. In particular, Lublin would become one vast concentration camp with grim prospects of survival for the thousands of Jews sent to its ghettos.

Back on the train, lighter topics were discussed. After dinner one evening aboard the train, Schäfer entered into a discussion with the Reichsführer himself. He learned that Himmler's strapping SS men could help to populate the cleansed landscape with illegitimate children. "It is important for us to consider that one man can have ten children a year by ten women," he posed, "while one woman can only have one child a year from ten men."[86] It was his conviction that through a genetic policy loosely modeled on "Mendel's law," the peoples of the East could be transformed to a race "authentically German in appearance."

With the borders of Hitler's Reich pushed out to the east, the existing towns in the conquered lands would be razed with a network of SS farming settlements to replace them. The indigenous peoples would be displaced or impressed under their German masters. And in Himmler's perverse utopian vision, his new peasant-soldier caste, the *Wehrbauern*, would reestablish ancient contact with the soil.[87] Polish territory would be annexed and resettled by the ethnic Germans from South Tyrol, the Baltic states, and the Soviet Union if all went well. Non-German owners would be expelled; Jews would be concentrated in ghettos and work camps or perhaps shipped off to the French colony of Madagascar.[88]

On March 20, 1941, Peiper attended an important planning meeting in Berlin with Himmler. Peiper calmly looked on while his boss, Rudolf Hess, and Martin Bormann examined scale-model housing developments for the Germanic transformation of Poland.[89] What did Peiper think of the resettlement program? "The assumption of making living room did not work out, because the number of settlers did not correspond to the capacity of the place. The population fled to the east. I drove through the area where one could not find any people around anywhere."[90]

As to other details of the program or any other executions, Peiper would beg ignorance, "I cannot tell you more about it, because individual co-workers had no need-to-know for secrecy reasons. I cannot deny that, as an escort of the Reichsführer that I was not ever everywhere present, but often I had no knowledge." See nothing, know nothing.

During the winter rain ride Ernst Schäfer mixed with Karl Wolff, Odilio Globocnik, and other high SS leaders, surprised to find them freely discussing their liquidation of Polish intellectuals over meals. Peiper was among the group. On January 27 in Cracow, an afternoon conversation between Himmler, Polish governor Hans Frank, and Globocnik shocked Schäfer when Globocnik proudly described how he himself had recently eliminated the inmates of a local mental institution. "Recently, we shot the inmates of a Polish insane asylum at a temperature of –20°," Globocnik loudly recounted to guests during the banquet. "The next day some were still alive." Schäfer watched several Wehrmacht generals exchange pained looks, but no one dared speak.[91] Down on his wanderlust, Schäfer longed to be elsewhere.

On January 30, as the train chugged back to frozen Berlin, the entourage paused briefly to celebrate Peiper's twenty-fifth birthday. Afterward Schäfer engaged Himmler's young adjutant in a friendly birthday conversation.[92] Peiper admired Schäfer, whom he considered "very well educated." As a scientist-adventurer, launching archaeological expeditions to Tibet, he was a Nazi version of Indiana Jones! The loud-voiced naturalist had colorful stories. In one he and Bruno Beger had thwarted British intrigue against their expedition in India to thread their way through the exotic heat of Calcutta and Sikkim before finally emerging into a lost horizon of verdant green hills covered with flowers.

Yet during lulls in the conversation Schäfer was surprised to learn that young Peiper seemed to have some weighty matters on his mind that had little to do with Tibet. The young adjutant told him that Hitler had personally charged Himmler with the elimination of the Polish intelligentsia. He and his superior had witnessed one execution in which twelve to fifteen people were shot outside Bromberg. Peiper professed to be shocked by the killing, "astonished by their composure as they died."[93] Afterward, Peiper alleged that Himmler would not speak for days.[94]

Schäfer later said that Peiper seemed to loathe these methods and "repeatedly remarked that he is just a soldier." Still, another conversation quoted by Schäfer revealed Peiper's darkening racial outlook. The SS officer glibly recounted how a former member of Himmler's staff, SS Brig. Gen. Ludolf von Alvensleben, claimed to have shot his own kin during the ongoing purge. He boasted to have coldly informed his half-Jewish relatives just before shooting them that he had no choice. He had to kill them now, he said. Otherwise, he would have to face them in the next war.[95]

"Now," Peiper sarcastically mused, "they'll all look at the potatoes from underneath."[96]

Part Two
ZENITH

"The Führer sometimes asks himself in a worried sort of way whether the white man is going to be able in the long run to maintain his supremacy over the tremendous reservoir of human beings in the East. . . . The Führer referred to the wars of the Turks and to the conquest of Genghis Khan, which led him far into the heart of Europe . . . the main burden of this fight must be borne by us. We don't know how later generations will stand up to dealing with it. . . . The Führer gave expression to his unshakeable conviction that the Reich will be the master of Europe. . . . From there the way to world domination is practically certain."

—PROPAGANDA MINISTER JOSEPH GOEBBELS
ON HITLER'S SPEECH OF MAY 8, 1943

Chapter 5

HUBRIS

In the spring of 1940 Peiper may have worried that war's glory might pass him by altogether. Having missed the fighting in Poland, what of his aspirations as a Waffen SS warrior? Although the prestigious stint with Himmler may have been gratifying, watching comrades glory from the Polish victory may have been a matter of growing dissatisfaction.

Meanwhile, nonstop travels with Himmler continued at a breakneck pace. Early March brought an inspection of the training SS Totenkopf (Death's Head) Division and a dinner meeting with the cold personality of Theodor Eicke at the Hart Hotel in Münsingen.[1] Eicke was obsessed with obtaining more camouflage uniforms for his troopers, as the preceding September Polish snipers had found it easy to pick out the nattily dressed SS officers. Peiper looked over Himmler's shoulder as his superior expressed satisfaction with Eicke's nonstop drills on everything from hand-to-hand combat to close assault tactics against fortifications using live ammunition.

Yet the unit had a seedy underside, reflecting its concentration camp guard origins. Totenkopf had developed a reputation for churlish behavior—drunken brawls in bars, alcohol-related auto accidents, and frequent fights with regular army soldiers. Himmler hastened to ensure that discipline improved. Eicke was happy to accommodate, forbidding his SS men to visit the bars around Korbach or to dance in public, which he considered a "degrading Jewish diversion."[2]

A week later, the itinerary took Peiper to Handorf near Münster, where Himmler met with SS Generals Dietrich and Hausser at the Hotel Fürstenhof: breakfast with the men of regiment SS Germania and a review of progress on armaments. But it seemed there was always something nonmilitary: a meeting on the resettlement question with the local Gauleiter and tea with SS Brigadeführer Ulrich Greifelt. Meanwhile, the rift of the newly formed Waffen SS with the army was growing.

On March 13 Peiper witnessed Himmler's apologetic evening speech in Koblenz to generals from Heeresgruppe A. Notes in Himmler's angular, spidery handwriting survive. His intention was to explain the controversial actions of his SS in Poland, already under assail from General Brauchitsch. And there was the uproar caused when Peiper's boss issued an "order" to all SS men to father as many children as possible, whether out of marriage or not. Himmler glossed over his moral faux pas, claiming misinterpretation of his intentions, yet reiterating the need for

German children: Without high-caliber descendants, who would replace the fallen Nordic blood?

What of the SS improprieties in Poland? The SS had protected the army, Himmler said, from any uprisings by partisans in the areas where they fought. Any inappropriate behavior had been punished. "Executions of all potential leaders of the resistance," he scribbled, "very hard, but necessary. Have seen to it personally. . . . No underhanded cruelties. . . . We must stay hard—our responsibility to God. . . . A million work slaves and how to deal with them."[3]

At the end of March 1940, Peiper accompanied Himmler to Wewelsburg, where he made notes for his boss about the continuing problems with providing the Totenkopf Division a heavy SS artillery battalion and engineer troops.[4] But then business moved to the dark side: in early April 1940 Peiper journeyed with the Reichsführer, Pohl, and Karl Wolff to the concentration camps at Buchenwald and Flossenbürg.[5] And on January 14, 1941, he walked in Himmler's shadow when they paid a visit to the all-female *Frauen-KZ* Concentration Camp at Ravensbrück, ninety kilometers north of Berlin. As the snowflakes fell, SS Stubf. Max Koegel greeted Himmler, Peiper, and the others at the camp gate. Koegel arranged to have the training SS female guards under SS Oberaufseherin Johanna Langefeld assembled in the frozen concentration camp courtyard for a Nazi salute to the visiting Reichsführer.[6]

Himmler was interested in the training of the SS female guards for use in other camps, but he also wanted to discuss the lack of progress in medical experiments he had ordered. What had happened to the work on mass sterilization from infecting female inmates with gonorrhea? SS Brigf. Dr. Ernst Grawitz responded that he and Dr. Karl Gebhardt at the Hohenlychen medical facility would now pursue these "experiments" energetically.[7] Satisfied, Himmler and the others drove south to Bavaria.

And so on January 20, 1941, both Peiper and Grothmann were with Himmler in a daylong visit to the KZ at Dachau. Starting out from the opulence of the Hotel Vier Jahreszeiten in Munich, the visit was arranged to show the Dutch NSDAP representative, Anton Mussert, and his entourage the "efficiency" of the SS concentration camp complex, with its Allach ceramics and textiles factories, greenhouse herb gardens, and production center. But one facet camp commandant SS Sturmbannführer Alexander Piorkowski did not reveal: on that winter day a total of eight prisoners died at the camp—a typical daily total.[8]

"When accompanying the Reichsführer SS," Peiper later described, "I saw concentration camps of Oranienburg, Dachau, Buchenwald, Mauthausen and Ravensbrück." What of the terrible reports? "I did not see any cruelty there," he observed, but then he contradicted himself. "Mauthausen made the worst impression on me with its granite quarries. The work there appeared to be excessively strenuous. The Reichsführer considered the concentration camps as work camps and an economic resource. . . . If somebody was shot dead trying to escape, it had to be reported to the Reichsführer via teletype. I remember from my time there that this happened twice to three times per week."[9]

Himmler had classified the concentration camps into three grades with progressively more severe treatment for prisoners.[10] Twelve miles outside Linz, Austria, Mauthausen was the only concentration camp classified as Grade III, and the mortality rate for Jews sent there—*Rückkehr unerwünscht*, or "return not desired"—realistically made it a death sentence. For it was there, on the camp's wooded slopes above the Danube, that Himmler had established his Stone Works. The inmates would carve out granite slabs from the quarry and then haul the sixty-pound rock up the 186 *Todessteige*—the "steps of death." And even though it was not an extermination camp, of the 200,000 condemned to Mauthausen from its opening in 1938 to its liberation on May 5, 1945, 150,000 perished.[11] Peiper had visited the camp twice in the spring of 1941 with Himmler, once on April 27, 1941, and then with Oswald Pohl toward the end of May 1941.[12] By the later date a retribution was in progress against Dutch Jews recently sent there from Amsterdam. The Mauthausen guards so abused the Jews that many chose suicide.[13] None survived.

The machinery of institutionalized genocide was also ramping up. Peiper was also in tow as Himmler courted industrialists in the Breslau area emphasizing that they must help him with the economic situation. Hitler had given him the assignment of resolving the Eastern situation, one that he maintained was more a racial than political dilemma. Construction of new concentration camps was part of his solution because those he considered undesirable had to be evacuated to make room for ethnic Germans.[14]

Peiper marked Hitler's birthday on April 20, 1940, with receipt of the Totenkopf "Death's Head" ring, a much-coveted prize for an SS man. Designed by SS choreographer Karl Diebitsch, most of the rings were made of smelted silver seized from Jewish synagogues.[15] Such moral questions seemed not to bother SS leaders one whit; Peiper proudly wore the runic band for the rest of the war.[16]

Seven days later there was a visit to Poland to iron out plans for the German transformation of that conquered land. After flying to the Polish town of Plock, the trip set out from the airfield as a seven-vehicle convoy. Peiper was in the Adler 28004, driving behind Himmler and Wolff in their armored Horch vehicle.[17] Officially the purpose of the visit was to meet the leaders who would make the resettlement program happen. In reality Himmler provided encouragement and guidance to men like Police Leader Wilhelm Rediess and Brigadeführer Otto Rasch, who had recently taken part in the shooting of 170 Poles near Soldau and were looking for further guidance on how more efficient "evacuations" might be accomplished.[18]

The Jews in the occupied areas, particularly Warsaw, were herded into ghettos, where they were deliberately denied sufficient food and medical care. On another occasion, on May 5, 1940, Peiper was present during a lunch at the casino in Lublin, where Himmler casually discussed the euthanasia program with the SS police leader of Lublin, Odilo Globocnik.[19] Himmler's driver, Franz Lucas, recalled Globocnik as a *Polterkopf*—a "head banger" of questionable character.[20] Hermann Fegelein, now the leader of an SS equestrian unit, was present as well. Peiper knew Fegelein well enough; they had seen each other all through his career. Just a few weeks before, he had seen him for a meeting on June 30 at Himmler's train at his *Hochwald* headquarters in East Prussia.[21] A way was to be found to do away with mentally retarded persons, Himmler explained offhandedly. The next morning Peiper jotted in Himmler's appointment calendar that this Monday was to feature "continuation of the program" for Lublin: "I heard then that Globonik was in charge of a huge great anti-tank ditch which would be made by Jewish workers. . . . They would build a huge East Wall."[22]

Peiper knew much more. "Globus" was now planning the construction of a massive concentration camp for Jews and Poles and three smaller ones that were to receive a continuous stream of prisoners with no word on how they would be accommodated. The vast reservation was to be a home for thirty thousand unskilled workers for construction of a massive *Ostwall Panzergraben* along the Bug River. The horrific conditions at the camp would condemn to death thousands of enslaved Jews who were sent there for a project with no military value.[23]

Military events were fast approaching. As Germany prepared for a decisive attack on France and the Low Countries, Sepp Dietrich concentrated his Leibstandarte for the surprise attack on Holland near Gronau.[24] Young Peiper was likely unhappy not to be involved. On the eve of the great offensive he was again ministering to Himmler on his superior's armored train, now standing on a railway east of Bonn at Altenkirchen.

On the morning of May 10 the Blitzkrieg exploded in the West. German bombers pounded Allied airfields, paratroopers seized fortified strong points, and tanks smashed quickly into France, Belgium, and Holland. The sudden advance of the motorized Leibstandarte completely surprised Dutch border guards. Within five hours, one of Peiper's SS officer contemporaries, Kurt Meyer, had taken the motorcycle company streaking on a forty-eight-mile ride through the Dutch countryside. By noon Dietrich's troops had reached the Ijssel River and, although finding the Dutch had blasted the bridges, quickly forced a crossing to the south.

Who was there? Max Wünsche! Now released by Hitler to fight with the Leibstandarte, the Führer bragged that his adjutants were not just "window dressing" but now combat soldiers.[25]

The quickness with which the Blitzkrieg slashed forward underscored that question. With the tanks of the 9th Panzer Division, the Leibstandarte helped secure Rotterdam after it had been pulverized by the Luftwaffe.[26] The SS troopers motored through the city on May 14 with little difficulty, as nearly thirty-five hundred Dutch prisoners passed to the division in a single day. The only great excitement came from the near-fatal wounding of General Kurt Student, the commander of the German airborne troops, by the eager advance guard of the Leibstandarte who, by some accounts, were inclined to shoot first and ask questions later. Any effective means to resist gone, the Dutch formally capitulated on Wednesday, May 15, 1940. On receiving the news on his train that night, Himmler was jubilant; now the Netherlands could be returned to Germany, the Reichsführer having considered it a rightful part of his nation since the Middle Ages.[27]

In the meantime Peiper pleaded with Himmler to allow him to return to the Leibstandarte. His boss gave his consent, but before this could be done both his combat unit and Himmler had a quick mission. With the Netherlands conquered, Hitler himself ordered Dietrich to take his troops on a grand tour of the countryside to impress the local populace of the power of the new German army. Dietrich's combat orders for the following day were ironic: everyone was to look their best for the propaganda march. On May 15, the shocked Dutch were subjected to an intimidating spectacle: the Leibstandarte in full uniform in their armored cars, parading arrogantly through Amsterdam, Utrecht, Nijmegen, Venlo, and Roermond.[28] Hitler, meanwhile, pondered his sudden victory from his *Felsennest* headquarters near Bad Münstereifel. Hitler desired a personal visit with von Rundstedt, who was guiding the great offensive from his Belgian headquarters not far from the fighting front at Bastogne. The commander of his command train examined the suitability of the road network through the Belgian Ardennes from St. Vith to a small crossroads village named Malmédy.[29] The roads, they concluded, had too many barriers to risk a Führer visit.

Yet on that same day Himmler, Peiper, and a few others took off to join the military parade through the newly conquered lands to the north. Also along for the journey was a sweet young thing: Hedwig "Häschen"—Bunny—Potthast. She was Himmler's *special* secretary.

Hedwig Potthast was only twenty-five years old when she met Himmler, having been recommended to the Reichsführer by Kurt von Schröder, a principal of the Bankhaus J. H. Stein and a central member of the *Freundeskreis*.[30] Himmler had asked the Cologne banker to find him "a hard working German girl," so Schröder suggested young Potthast, who had impressive secretarial talents—shorthand, obedience, and an ability with English. But the young Potthast also possessed *other* skills. Häschen came to work for Himmler in January 1936, and the SS leader did not fail to notice her charms. Himmler was uneasily married to Margarete Siegroth née Boden, an acerbic and corpulent *Hausfrau* seven years his senior.[31] Even Heinrich's older brother, Gebhard, found Marga "a cool, hard woman with extremely delicate nerves, who radiated no warmth at all and spent too much time moaning."[32]

The nagging may have played a part, as perhaps did his wife's inability to have further children after their first daughter.[33] Later Himmler would announce his intention that SS men surviving the war with sufficient battlefield accomplishments would take a second wife—a leniency he extended to himself in advance.[34] By 1940 Hedwig was Himmler's fawning mistress.

If not a real beauty, the new paramour of the Reichsführer was fit and lean: in 1936 the young woman had earned the standard sports certificate, the *Deutsches Sportabzeichen*, for her swimming, running, and jumping. But even though Häschen was cute, Himmler quietly had asked his ancestral specialists to investigate the girl's claim to Aryan roots. Meanwhile, to the younger set around him, he seemed relaxed as his SS slashed across Holland, sporting a more casual haircut. For Himmler, which was more sweet? The endorphins of European conquest or the gush of a young lover? The entire group drove about as if on a summer holiday.[35]

Peiper was along on the Friday drive on May 17, 1940 in Himmler's Horch staff car from Cologne to Aachen, and then Maastricht in Holland. To Himmler the Dutch made a positive impression: "The population was by no means hostile . . . a good race" he blithely concluded in a travel dossier. "They are an excellent gain for Germany."[36] Also along were good friends Dr. Karl Gebhardt, Dr. Ludwig Stumpfegger, and Himmler's driver, Franz Lucas. The day ended at the Hotel Warson in Hasselt, Belgium. At the nearby hotel restaurant, Zu den drei Pistolen, they were joined by two SS assault leaders who, over wine and dinner, regaled the Reichsführer with glorious tales of the fighting so far. Karl Wolff and Himmler could only lamely counter with anecdotes of their struggles in the early days of National Socialism. Wolff told a story he liked to repeat of how he was chosen early for the SS because "he had the height and the looks." Peiper had little to offer to the conversation, eager, instead, to reach the fighting. He was more than familiar with Karl Wolff's vanity.

The next day Himmler and his cronies drove off, leaving Peiper to be picked up by the Leibstandarte. Dietrich arrived later that morning. Now, fresh from Himmler's side, Peiper was installed as a platoon leader in the 11th Company of the 3rd Battalion of the Leibstandarte. At last he had a combat assignment.

On Monday, May 20, as the advance German tanks had reached the Channel coast at Abbeville, Peiper and the rest of the LAH marched in the sunshine into northeastern Belgium, crossing the Meuse River at Huy. They would be thrown against the French who, with English help, were still holding out against Hitler's onslaught. A desperate British counterattack near Arras against the German spearhead prompted the commitment of the Leibstandarte on May 22 to help fend off the attacks. This done, Dietrich's men were hurried off to help entrap the British Expeditionary Forces, now attempting to evacuate from France near Dunkirk.

On May 24 Dietrich's regiment moved in support of General Heinz Guderian's XIX Panzer Corps who were tightening the noose on the British forces in the pocket west of Ghent. With any luck, a concentric attack might drive the English into the sea. However, the objective for Dietrich would be to secure both sides of the Aa canal near St. Momelin, which had yet to be crossed.[37] Dietrich was none too pleased with his starting position, concentrating his troops in the open on the marshy tableland on the other side of the canal beneath French guns that commanded the Watten heights to the west. But before the order could be carried out, however, Hitler and some of his generals, suddenly losing their nerve, issued a controversial call for a halt to the German advance so the Luftwaffe could finish off the British attempting to embark from the beaches.

Showing his disfavor with Hitler, Dietrich ignored the Führer directive and told his men to secure the heights on the other side of the Aa canal without delay. At daybreak the next morning the 3rd Battalion paddled in rubber boats across the canal, with Peiper and the relatively untested 11th Company leading the assault. In the action that followed, Peiper distinguished himself in the short, sharp battle, personally leading the 150 grenadiers up the commanding heights to seize Mount Watten. Both speed and surprise were complete, and losses were light.

THE WATTENBERG HEIGHTS SECURE, DIETRICH MADE HIS NEW HEADQUARTERS IN the blasted-out castle there. Hearing of all the commotion in the distance, General Guderian motored up to find out why the halt order was being disobeyed. He had to advance, Dietrich told Guderian, motioning to the tableland to the east: the 235-foot cliffs of Mount Watten would have had left the defenders to fire on his otherwise hapless men below. Guderian was so impressed with Dietrich and Peiper's audacious advance to the West that he decided to phone up other panzer formations to get them moving.[38] Peiper was euphoric. On June 1, 1940, Peiper was awarded the Iron Cross, 2nd Class and promoted to SS Captain.

Even with the victory, however, the increasingly cavalier attitude of his troops troubled Dietrich. From now on, no dolls and trinkets and mementoes were to festoon Leibstandarte vehicles, and, worse, no dogs would ride in the front seat![39] In the meantime Hitler ordered the advance on Dunkirk to resume with the greatest possible speed. Dietrich's immediate objective on the way to pushing the British into the sea was the ignominious village of Wormhoudt. In their path were British territorial soldiers of the 48th Division.

The advance on June 27 was little like the experience two days earlier. The British fought bitterly for every kilometer and rained artillery on the heads of the Leibstandarte. Although over 250 English and French prisoners were taken, twelve SS men were killed, and twice as many wounded, including four officers.

But it was on the following day, May 28—Dietrich's birthday—that the Cinderella-like fortune of the Leibstandarte really began to unravel. SS adjutant Max Wünsche drove to Dietrich's headquarters at daybreak to convey regards and to receive the morning assignment for the 15th Motorcycle Company.[40] Soon came surprising news: the 1st and 2nd Battalions of the Leibstandarte were held up near the hamlet of Esquelbecq. Never before had they been stopped! Alarmed, Dietrich took SS wonder boy Wünsche with him to see for himself.

The rear zone of the battlefield was quiet as the pair approached Esquelbecq from the southeast. Rounding a curve, their command car was suddenly slammed by a hail of antitank and machine gun fire. It was an ambush—they were only fifty yards from enemy lines. Their driver was killed instantly as Dietrich and Wünsche leapt into the nearby ditch. As the two men flattened themselves in the depression, their Mercedes cross-country vehicle exploded in a ball of flames. The road itself seemed to be on fire. To avoid being burned, the typically fastidious SS men immersed themselves in dank ditch water and smeared mud over their uniforms. Bullets peppered the lip of the ditch. Wünsche crawled into a culvert to avoid the sharpshooters but passed out from the heat. Dietrich buried his head in the muck.[41]

Fortunately for the two, a radio operator behind the burning vehicles was able to signal the 2nd Panzer Division for help. However, against the British, the measures did not suddenly turn the tide as they had done in weeks before. Infantry rushes by both the Leibstandarte's 2nd and 15th Companies were checked by a storm of machine gun fire, and the first four tanks arriving on the scene were shot down like clay pigeons. The fighting grew in ferocity throughout the afternoon as Dietrich contemplated his birthday huddled in a ditch. Finally a company of German tanks breasted the English trap and blasted away the British antitank guns. That done, they clanked forward along the road strewn with pyres of flaming wreckage and drew sights on the building from where machine gun fire had pinned Dietrich and Wünsche. A single round blew the house apart. The rescue complete, tanks of the 2nd Panzer deposited the dripping Bavarian SS commander before a smiling Gen. Heinz Guderian.[42]

The SS men under Dietrich were not amused. Unaccustomed to a thrashing, the officers within the regiment were shaken by the near-loss of their revered leader and frustrated by their inability to waltz through the British as they had done so handily with the Dutch. Several infantry assault attempts were turned back with heavy casualties. Finally, as a last resort, a curtain of mortar fire was called down, after which the SS men rushed forward "in large numbers . . . and urged on by cries of 'Heil Hitler!'"[43] This sacrificial charge worked, and by 3 p.m. the 2nd Battalion wedged an embattled contingent in the village.[44]

House-to-house fighting raged throughout the afternoon. During these actions the commander of the 2nd Battalion, Sturmbannführer Ernst Schützeck, was severely wounded by an antitank grenade as his command car approached the town main square. Its leader gravely wounded, the brooding commander of the 5th Company, Wilhelm Mohnke, then assumed command of the 2nd Battalion. Tempers flared. French civilians in the village of Esquelbecq would later say of the SS in the village that "everyone talked of revenge."[45] Dietrich was still missing, Schützeck was near death, and many SS comrades had fallen trying to reach this northern French village. The heat of battle brewed up a mixture of adrenaline, tension, and rage. By late afternoon the Germans had gained control of the hotly contested place, taking many British captives. More than 750 prisoners were taken during the fighting, with most moved, as prescribed, to prisoner-of-war cages.[46] But not all.

A British antitank gunner, Arthur Baxter, was taken prisoner in the early fighting that morning and was beaten when he did not offer more than his name and rank. He considered this treatment bad form, but was horrified at what happened next. A British truck roared up to the German position—totally surprised to find themselves upon the enemy. The truck screeched to a stop, and its two occupants threw their hands up to surrender. They tried to edge out of their truck:

> Without any order given, the SS trooper with the light machine gun blasted the officer and the driver back into their seats. They must have had a full magazine blasted into their bodies . . . the SS men cheered and clapped their hands. Then one chap went to the back of the truck and pulled out a Jerri can of petrol. He splashed the petrol over the bodies of the officer and the driver and over the canvas roof of the cab and over the wheels, and then he put a match to it. They cremated them on the spot, and to this day I can still see those chap's faces disappearing behind the flames and the smoke.[47]

After filing past three British trucks with dead men sprawled out around each, some burnt to charcoal, another British POW, Bert Evans, saw the enemy line up a dozen of his comrades against the wall of the cannery and blast them with automatic fire. "They killed the whole lot," he remembered. "I shall never forget seeing them fall just like rag dolls."[48] At 4:30 p.m. the houses of the village burned furiously as a platoon commander from the 7th Company sought Hauptsturmführer Mohnke's advice regarding the deposition of the growing mass of prisoners. One POW, Richard Parry, had been brought by SS 2nd Lt. Heinrich for questioning to the Headquarters for the 2nd Battalion. Parry, who could understand German, was witness to a telling incident. A senior Leibstandarte officer, likely Wilhelm Mohnke, was seen to storm over to Heinrich and give him a thorough tongue lashing. "What do you mean bringing in prisoners contrary to orders?"[49]

Later that afternoon some ninety of the British prisoners were herded into a barn and hand grenades were tossed inside. When this did not kill all, separate groups of five were pulled out of the barn, lined up, and executed. Many attempted to flee the barn, only to be shot down as they emerged. Amazingly fourteen of the total managed to survive to tell of their horrific fate, many from feigning death.[50] All postwar SS accounts deny that anything sinister happened at Wormhoudt. One notable exception, however, was Korvettenkapitän Alfred Rodenbücher, with German Navy Station Kommando "Baltic," who had been posted to gain combat experiences with the Leibstandarte. Upon arriving at his temporary home at the 2nd Battalion on May 28, he noted that the talk of the battalion was that seventy British prisoners had been "all finished off."[51]

Peiper was not involved with the incident at Wormhoudt. In fact, the 3rd Battalion, to which he belonged, did not even see action in the battle. Yet the event was another in a controversial series of murderous episodes that would plague the Leibstandarte throughout its career. Moreover, some of those implicated within the unit, particularly Mohnke, would remain comrades as the war progressed.[52]

The fighting in France continued; the regiment watched agog as the Luftwaffe fiercely pounded the enemy attempting to escape from the beaches. That was over quickly. After the British exodus at Dunkirk, the whole affair became a mop-up. On June 2 the regiment took a break, relaxing on the Channel coast near Cap Griz Nez.[53] Some adventurous German youths took the opportunity of the radiant summer afternoon to swim in the Channel, while others peered through telescopes at England on the watery horizon. Would they go there?

Hitler wondered as well. Enraptured with the elation of a major military victory, the German leader visited a seemingly inconsequential place on the French-Belgian border near the village of Wervicq on Thursday, June 1, 1940. The small hill was called La Montagne. There, in October 1918, Corporal Adolf Hitler had been blinded by a British gas grenade in the final battles of the Great War. Now, twenty-two years later, Hitler returned to La Montagne as the vanquished-turned-victor. More than ever he saw himself as the self-vindicated Aryan messiah. Hitler was intoxicated! Extricated from his misadventure with Dietrich, Max Wünsche stood by Hitler's side, impressed by his leader's "powerful emotional experience" as he related every detail of 1918. But strangely the catharsis left Hitler not desiring a settlement with the British, who had blinded him, but with the Jews, who the German leader believed had undermined the Kaiser. A day after his epiphany he confided to a general that he hoped Great Britain would eventually come to their senses so that he could pursue the real task to eliminate "Bolshevik Russia."[54]

Yet the battle for France was not over altogether for those fighting for Hitler's namesake command. Soon assignments resumed for Peiper and the rest after their early June repose. On June 10, the 3rd Battalion was ordered to attack toward the Marne River. Despite disturbing artillery fire, Peiper's company quickly deployed and put in an assault that pushed the French back to Monthiers by nightfall. On June 12 the battalion reached Etrépilly, with no sign of the enemy. Even better, they had orders to rest in the small French village. Then, just after noon on June 14, word arrived by radio that German soldiers were marching through Paris! In celebration, Peiper's men rang the church bells in Etrépilly.[55]

On that same day Haupsturmführer Carl Marks was promoted, leaving a vacancy for the leadership of the 11th Company and Peiper drew the new command. On June 17 Himmler himself appeared at Dietrich's headquarters at Le Meriot to gawk over the shoulders of the fighting Leibstandarte. Extending greetings, he informed young Jochen he would shortly be back as his adjutant—this war was nearly over. Message delivered, Himmler hurried back to Brûly de Pesche along the Belgian border to be with Hitler at his headquarters when the French surrendered.[56]

Faced with that prospect, Peiper showed his penchant for the audacious, even in the twilight of the campaign. In the fighting on June 19 south of St. Pourçain in Central France, heavy French resistance rebuffed Kurt Meyer's 15th Motorcycle Company's plan to cross the Sioule River. However, at 2:20 p.m. that afternoon Peiper personally led the 11th Company in an end run to the south. In spite of wounds from shellfire, he struck suddenly in a brave straight-ahead assault that wrested the bridge from the stunned enemy. In the process Peiper's men managed to capture an entire French company with all of their equipment.[57] Later Peiper would receive the Iron Cross, 1st Class, for his overall performance as well as the *Infanterie Sturmabzeichen* for prowess in infantry assaults.

Even as Peiper captured the bridge, however, the demoralized French government sought surrender terms. The war in France was over and with it, Peiper's month of glory. A German war photographer clicked a picture of a smiling Jochen Peiper that would later dominate the cover of the *Stuttgarter Illustrierte* on January 8, 1941. "There is no happier soldier than a German soldier," pronounced the caption, "who knows clearly and confidently about the meaning and result of this war. An officer of the Waffen SS." Himmler must have agreed. Nine days later he ordered a copy of the magazine be placed in Peiper's personnel file.[58]

Meanwhile, on June 21, Peiper found himself reassigned as Himmler's First Military Adjutant. But more than that, Peiper exalted in his role as an SS warrior within the Leibstandarte—"the only unit in the army to bear the Führer's name."[59] Hitler himself added to the big-headedness, ordering the Leibstandarte immediately expanded to a brigade and awarding the Knight's Cross to Dietrich. The LAH moved to eastern France around Metz for the expansion. The Leibstandarte garnered one accolade after another, and Peiper was present with Himmler when Hitler proudly addressed the Leibstandarte in Metz the day after Christmas. A huge black banner with white SS runes stood on one side of the street across from the old caserne. Inside there was a big tinseled *Weihnachtsbaum* and privileged seating at Hitler's supper table. The Führer toasted his Black Guard with a raised glass of mineral water: "What your fate will be, oh my Men of the Leibstandarte, I do not know. But one thing I do know is that you will be at the forefront of every engagement. As long as I have the honor to stand at the fore of the Reich to lead this struggle, you who bear my name shall consider it an honor to lead every German attack."[60]

"Sieg Heil!" and a gulp of spirits. Both Hitler and his SS men seemed euphoric.

To the victors go the spoils. Like other soldiers, Peiper and Wünsche had brought back booty from France—only their souvenirs were SS officer-size. Both came away with exotic automobiles; Peiper had managed to snag a Ford sports car. The vehicle was officially added to the inventory of the Reichsführer SS at the decree of Himmler himself. However, their superior thoughtfully added that both men should be provided with proper German cars at the end of the war.[61] With the fighting done, Peiper was back with Himmler and Wünsche to Hitler.[62]

Then, on July 6, Hitler, Himmler, and the others arrived by train to Anhalter Bahnhof in Berlin to an astonishing reception—the German capital roiled in a wave of patriotic fervor. People waited for hours to see Hitler; women covered the sunlit streets with flowers leading up the Reich Chancellery, while radios from every street corner blared martial music. Church bells rang out, and swastika-adorned flags spilled from every balcony.[63] Streetside maidens and Hitler youth cried in shrill hysteria as their leader was called out to the balcony of his quarters. "Caesar in his glory," wrote a US newspaper correspondent, "was never more turbulently received."

The idyllic summer of 1940 continued for Peiper. In ten months of war, Germany had conquered seven countries: Poland, Denmark, Norway, Holland, Belgium, Luxembourg, and France. There had never been anything like it. For Peiper, the summer days boiled as if frothing champagne—victorious in France, medals, new cars, and heady celebration. There was an even more personal revelry, an auspicious event beyond all others. It could only be such fortune, for, in the world of an anointed SS man, there were no coincidences.

As if on signal, at the end of Hitler's triumphant parade, on July 7, 1940, Peiper's first child, daughter Elke, was born in Berlin. As with other SS men, Himmler sent the new parents in Wilmersdorf a ribbon and bib of blue silk.

For Woldemar Peiper, Joachim and Horst were the sons who had made it. Also with the Waffen SS, Horst was with the Totenkopf Infantry Regiment 2. By the summer of 1940 both sons had reached the rank of SS Hauptsturmführer (Captain)—their father's highest rank. Woldemar, now almost sixty, would soon leave his assignment with the Kraftfahr Ersatzabeilung 3 of the 153rd Reserve Division stationed in Berlin. In September he was assigned to Poland as a reserve officer in the Panzerwerkstatt in Litzmannstadt (Łódź). There the tank repair shop with which Woldemar held a desk job was converting captured Polish armored vehicles into serviceable vehicles for the Wehrmacht. Yet that job took place next to the massive Jewish ghetto under construction in Łódź—along with the unimaginable suffering for many of its inhabitants.[64]

Back in Berlin, that summer Peiper spent some time with Sigurd at their flat in Wilmersdorf to celebrate their first child. Yet given Peiper's schedule as adjutant to Himmler, his time there would be fleeting—he'd soon be off on another tour with his boss. On July 8, the day after Peiper's daughter's birth, his superior, Heinrich Himmler, had a long afternoon lunch with Hitler in Berlin. There is no record of their conversation, but the immediate result was that SS Gen. Wilhelm Krüger met Himmler later that afternoon to see whether the Reich's Jews could be sent to Krakau (Cracow). Peiper's boss instead informed Krüger they would be exiled to Madagascar by ship.[65] But the British air force would have to be dealt with first.

THE FOLLOWING DAY, JULY 10, HITLER HIMSELF HAD RETIRED TO THE OBERSALZBERG to contemplate his next move. Would he invade England, or could he entice Churchill to make peace? A truce seemed unlikely, for the English seemed stubbornly defiant. Then, on July 11, Himmler spoke to his head of SS recruitment, Gottlob Berger, telling him that there should be no demobilization of the SS Totenkopf Division—it would be needed for new assignments. How would England be subjugated if invaded? In the coming weeks Himmler would speak to Dr. Franz Six to take charge of London if occupied. Further, Reinhard Heydrich was to organize six *Einsatzgruppen*—the death squads that had killed so efficiently in Poland—for assignment in England. The job there would be similar. Meanwhile, Walter Schellenberg conjured up a bizarre scheme to kidnap the Duke of Windsor.[66]

There was also the possibility of dealing with Russia first. The German foreign minister, von Ribbentropp, along with Himmler puzzled with Hitler over Great Britain's latest rejection of peace, while Admiral Erich Raeder confronted the German leader with the immense difficulties involved in any invasion of the United Kingdom. But with no decision made, Himmler seemed intent on vacation. While his superior pondered war with England, on the afternoon of Saturday, July 13, Himmler and his little group flew off from Tempelhof in Berlin to Freiburg in the Black Forest.[67]

Then, from July 13 to 15 Peiper and Himmler took a grand sightseeing tour of conquered France, motoring along in a nine hundred–kilometer loop through Vesoul, Gray, Dijon, Chalon, Besançon, Montbeliard, and then back to Freiburg.[68] Himmler was obsessed with this land, where a Germanic tribe had once existed in Eastern France. Lothar, an heir of Charlemagne, had governed that kingdom from the Rhone to Antwerp. The long summer days in the Burgundy countryside, virtually untouched by war, passed warm, lush, and glorious.

The Reichsführer regaled his entourage with his grandiose plans to establish an SS racial paradise there. He would personally lead the new kingdom to form a racially pure enclave, something of gigantic Nordic boarding school. The Alsace-Lorraine of Eastern France would also play a large part in plans for expansionist SS settlements after the war.[69] These picturesque vineyard hills could be the long-awaited new home to the South Tyroleans and a fantastic new SS city with Himmler as first lord and master.

Heads spinning from such plans, the entire crew flew back to Berlin to participate in Hitler's triumphal proclamation at the Kroll Opera house. On July 18 the victorious German army staged a victory parade through the Brandenburg Gate for the first time since 1871. The entire city of Berlin turned out to cheer the tanned, hard-looking soldiers as they goose-stepped in robot-like precision down the asphalt streets. In the warm weather and heady atmosphere, dozens of swooning women fainted. The capital city had gone crazy.

And on the following day the *Grösster Feldherr aller Zeiten* addressed the Reichstag for "the most colossal honor in German history." As Peiper and Wünsche stood with the honored off to Hitler's left, the Führer dispensed a fountain of praise, punctuated by military promotions.[70] The entire opera balconies they faced were alight with gold-braided uniforms and chests spangled with crosses and decorations. A giant golden eagle with the Hakenkreuz grasped in its talons stood behind them as a bigger-than-life backdrop. But for the "brave divisions and regiments of the Waffen

SS," the shower of medals reached a downpour. To England Hitler continued to extend an olive branch. "I see no reason the war should go on," he declared. But the next day, when the British flatly rebuffed his offer, Hitler had altered the language for his audience: it was the English who chose war.[71]

That decision resurfaced the possibility of dealing with Russia first. Himmler himself had been studying this option when he was called to the Berghof to meet with Hitler soon upon his arrival. The meeting took place on July 29.[72] Peiper and Karl Wolff came along in the Mercedes; the afternoon vista from Hitler's alpine retreat was spectacular. Off to the north were the Untersberg Mountains, supposedly the former home of Charlemagne, and Hitler's beloved Austria. It was against this idyllic backdrop that Peiper posed with Hitler's dashing adjutant warrior, Max Wünsche, as Eva Braun tended Isolde, her black Scottish terrier. Everyone was smiling—the Polish and French were defeated—and somehow the war seemed already won. Peiper even had a laugh with Karl Wolff before table tennis with Eva Braun in the late afternoon.

Peiper must have sensed that Himmler's access to the Führer catapulted his own prospects. Soon Himmler and Peiper visited Hitler at the opulent Reich Chancellery in Berlin. Peiper remembered several occasions vividly. At the conclusion of the war in France, Hitler added twenty new recipients of the Knight's Cross to the Reich Chancellery in Berlin. It was a congratulatory occasion, with Himmler along to share in the good fortunes of adjutant Peiper, who had impressed in France. They arrived at Wilhelmstrasse in their limousine to climb up the marble stairs past Arno Breker sculptures to a five hundred–foot marble gallery, emerging into rooms that dwarfed human scale. Leibstandarte honor guards stood in their black and white uniforms beneath towering Corinthian columns adorned with Nazi eagles and gigantic bronze doors.

Eventually they came to Hitler's oversized study, where a crowd of guests were assembled, their uniformed chests emblazoned with medals. But the ceilings were so tall and the room so cavernous that everyone seemed lost in a pan-Teutonic acropolis. Yet Hitler soon emerged, the brown shaft of hair canted left across his forehead and his signature patch of moustache beneath his nose and a frowning brow. Peiper stood on the edge of the crowd of people as Hitler mechanically moved down the line in his plain gray army tunic to extend greetings. "He passed by me and then suddenly stopped, looked at me and then smiled and came back. . . . He took my hand in his two hands, but said nothing." To Peiper, Hitler's powder-blue eyes were earnest and mesmerizing. "For him, I would have put my head on the gallows."[73]

During another Berlin meeting there Himmler enthusiastically told Hitler about a bold new operation cooked up by SS spy-operative Alfred Naujocks. The idea was to flood the world market with counterfeit British pound notes to destabilize the English economy.[74] One audacious plan was to have the Luftwaffe drop millions of pound notes over England. Early in the process, Hitler and foreign minister von Ribbentrop were in the music salon when Himmler burst in excitedly with news from Operation Bernhard.

"Mein Führer, I have something to show you." The SS leader described how the early forgeries from counterfeiters at Sachsenhausen Concentration Camp looked so perfect that they would first be used by German foreign agents. He held out ten £10 British notes, not informing Hitler that only three of them were forgeries. Hitler examined the notes, pulled out three, and slapped them on the table. "I don't like these," he said, throwing them down. No one else in the room could see any difference, but the bank numbers told the story. They were the fakes. "He had a sixth sense." Peiper claimed. "We were stunned."[75]

In the middle of such wartime intrigue there were ominous developments in the skies of Germany. Since late summer the Luftwaffe had been bombing England in the Battle of Britain and, in the second half of August, began to hit London itself. On the night of August 25 air raid sirens wailed after midnight in Berlin, followed by searchlights, wildly firing flak guns, and loud explosions. Now, 4 million Berliners rushed to air raid shelters, lying awake in dank recesses until 4 a.m. as a group of British Wellington and Whitley bombers dropped explosives over the city. The following morning the bleary-eyed curious swarmed to find bomb craters in the Tiergarten not far from Peiper's office at Prinz Albrecht Straße. It was clear that the British had done what Göring decried as impossible.[76] Another raid, three days later, killed eight people, shattered a few buildings, and started numerous fires in the Kreuzberg district about seven kilometers east of Peiper's flat. Life in western Berlin grew edgy.[77]

Although he worried for Sigurd, Peiper had little time to obsess over a few stray bombs.[78] That month a new adjutant, Werner Grothmann, was brought into Himmler's fold to deal with his superior's rapidly expanding empire. Peiper knew Grothmann well; they had attended the officers cadet training course together in Jüterbog in 1935 and also the Junkerschule Braunschweig. As second adjutant, Grothmann would come under Peiper's wing. The two got along well—neither particularly liked Karl Wolff.[79]

At the end of August Himmler had visitors from Spain—the chief of the Spanish Police Forces, Conde de Mayalde. In Berlin, regardless of the gawkers around Görlitzer Station surveying bomb damage, Peiper was on call when the dignitaries came to visit Himmler at their offices. The Spanish police called on Gen. Kurt Daluege of the Order Police and Reinhard Heydrich with the Security Service on August 30. Himmler was anxious to show off his security services as role models for Fascist Franco.[80] Everyone was to make nice-nice. Hitler was, meanwhile, still deeply involved in diplomatic intrigue to convince the Spanish leader to allow German forces to seize Gibraltar and paralyze British shipping routes—a big potential coup.

Yet the German welcome must have seemed intensely self-focused, for the first order of business was to visit the Leibstandarte Adolf Hitler at the Lichterfelde Barracks, where they were treated to a demonstration of Peiper's alumni in precision marching. Next the Spanish Fascists were escorted to the Reichssportfeld next to Olympic Stadium in Berlin. There the female contingent of the RAD—the *Reichsarbeitdienst*—gave a demonstration of finely tuned Germanic womanly form.

To cap it off, the Spanish delegation, with Peiper in escort, was driven to Oranienburg to the KZ at Sachsenhausen. Many of the four hundred inmates were taken away so as to not affront the eyes of the guests. But would the rough edges of the concentration camp system shock the Spanish police chiefs? No, for even in late 1940 Franco's prisons still held hundreds of thousands of political prisoners who were being executed as fast as they could be tried.[81] Himmler held out the German model as the way to expunge these problem elements from society. To the Spanish contingent, he praised the potential of diet and natural cures in SS hospitals to promote optimum health.[82] Yet, by contrast, medical conditions at KZ Sachsenhausen were terrible: on the two last days of August ten inmates died from pneumonia or tuberculosis, and one was shot trying to escape.[83] Meanwhile, in Berlin, on July 28 newspapers reported that Himmler warned that a Polish farm worker had been hanged for sleeping with a German woman. "No race pollution is to be permitted."[84]

By now Himmler, the micromanager, was administering SS concentration camps, an SS agricultural center, and even medical, archaeological, and academic departments. These took on absurd guises, such as his ancestral wing, the *Ahnenerbe*, which sponsored pseudo-scientific archaeological expeditions to "explore the greatness of the German soul."

And then there was the *Lebensborn*—"Fountain of Life." The Lebensborn provided homes for children of unwed mothers of good racial stock—often SS men—and provided policies to encourage large German families.[85] Publicly the program was well-accepted and seen as a soft touch in an otherwise harsh series of National Socialist programs. Less in the public eye, however, were the factions harboring SS doctors and concentration camp guards.[86]

Meanwhile, with the German occupation, the Grand Duchess of Luxembourg and her government fled to Great Britain. The country was placed under a German civil administration headed by Gustav Simon, Gauleiter of the adjoining western German province of Koblenz-Trier. From August 16 to 18 Simon's operatives attempted unsuccessfully to incite the local population to riot against the Jews. Still, the pressure was on for Jews to leave the country so it could be *Judenrein*—Jew free. SS High Police Chief Theodor Berkelmann was assigned to accomplish that aim in the Alsace-Lorraine of France. Himmler and Peiper met with Berkelmann that same autumn.[87]

During those weeks of consolidation and conquest, Peiper was along on the "Day of Metz" on September 7, 1940, when Himmler addressed the motorcycle battalion and assembled officers of the Leibstandarte in the courtyard at Fort Alvensleben. This was an old citadel high above the city straddling the Mosel River.[88] The companies assembled in long, straight rows under a clear autumn sky. Himmler, with Peiper standing to the rear, slowly passed before each soldier.

Himmler moved to a podium, calling shrilly across the courtyard of "the SS and its tough obligations." He presented the regiment with its new standard—a swastika banner in red, gold, white, and black, mounted boldly onto a metallic SS shield—a personal gift from Hitler himself: "Everyone knows: now from this hour on, the Führer always stands among them—the highest obligation."[89] As Peiper looked on, Himmler reminded all that this territory along the German border had only been French since the Treaty of Versailles in 1919. "Lorraine spreads broadly at our feet," he began. Now it was back in German hands.[90]

Eastern France, he said, was rightfully part of the Reich. "Up here, the ancient German character of the land is visible. There is nothing to be seen of the whitewash that France painted rather cheaply across the Lorraine." Peiper listened. Himmler was no orator like Hitler, but he was animated. "We know and carry it in our hearts: this banner will always wave," Himmler paused and pounded his fist, "in war and peace, SS men!"

Everyone settled down in the lecture hall, where Himmler solemnly told of the great air battle raging over English skies—the Battle of Britain. The German Luftwaffe would prevail, he said. There was no mention of the bombing over Berlin. Then, Himmler spoke admiringly of Kurt Meyer. Because of men like him, he said, this place was now German once more. He praised Leibstandarte assistance in rounding up Alsatian Jews to be expelled from France:

> Very frequently the members of the Waffen SS think about the deportation of these people. These thoughts come to me today when watching the very difficult work out there performed by the security police, supported by your men who helped them a great deal. Exactly the same thing happened in Poland in weather 40 degrees below zero, we had to haul away thousands, ten thousands, hundred thousands; where we had to have the toughness—*you should hear this, but also forget it again immediately*—to shoot thousands of leading Poles, where we had to have the toughness, otherwise it would have been revenge on us later. . . . In many cases, it is much easier to go into combat with a company of men than to suppress an obstructive population of low cultural level in some area with a company, or to carry out executions, or to haul away people, or to evict crying and hysterical women.[91]

Himmler's speech was closed out by a ringing choral endorsement by the Leibstandarte men of "Wenn alle untreu werden" and collective shouts of allegiance to the Führer. What did Peiper think? We cannot know. Yet there he was, directly under Himmler.

"DINING WITH THE DEVIL," GOES THE OLD GERMAN SAYING, "IS BEST DONE with a long fork."[92]

Chapter 6

BARBAROSSA

DURING THE AUTUMN OF 1940 PEIPER CONTINUED WITH A DIZZYING TRAVEL schedule, accompanying his superior on one trip after another. Did the pace dull the moral judgment for Heinrich Himmler's adjutant?

There *were* fringe benefits. On October 17, 1940, Peiper and Himmler's immediate staff sauntered through conquered Paris and then flew to Bordeaux and picked up a Mercedes convertible. On the open road Himmler enjoyed driving himself, often at breakneck speed behind goggles and a leather driver's cap.[1] However, the Reichsführer was impulsive, frequently slowing his Mercedes to wave at any SS soldiers marching alongside or to stop altogether for a short conversation: How were they? Above all, how was the food? "If the troops are to solve the problems they are faced with," he wondered aloud, "one must under all circumstances see to it that the troops are not short of equipment or food."[2] A small package of chocolate or cigarettes from the food suitcase sealed the conversation.

On the first evening of the trip Himmler met with SS Standartenführer Eugen Dollmann over dinner at the Hotel Splendid to discuss the frustrating progress on acquiring weapons and equipment for the SS Totenkopf Division. The next morning the party drove to the French town of Dax so Himmler could drop in for belated well wishes for Theodor Eicke's forty-ninth birthday.[3] Given the SS leader's humorless nature, the occasion must have been less than festive.

With that obligation checked off the day's calendar, the group departed on a pleasant road trip to sunny Spain. And the Reichsführer traveled in style. Himmler, Peiper, and the others arrived at Irun and then proceeded to Burgos, where they made base in the posh digs of Madrid's Ritz Hotel.[4] The official reception the following day on October 20 took place at the Palace of the Prado before General Francisco Franco. Himmler had come to help convince that country to join Germany in the war effort. Had not Germany assisted the fascists with the German volunteer Condor Legion in their three-year civil war?[5] Yet, having achieved a ruthless victory in April of 1939, the prolonged conflict had cost Franco and his opponents over half a million lives. Spain was tired of bloodshed.

But beyond the official red carpet, the reception was lukewarm. Even the celebratory bullfight later that day was rained out, and a diplomatic effort disintegrated on the reefs of Spanish disinterest. So while their boss fawned over the new Spanish dictator, Franco, Gunther d'Alquen, Rudolf Brandt, Werner Grothmann, and Peiper took in the sights. The days that followed were a whirlwind of receptions, the Prado Picture Gallery, a visit to the Escorial Palace, and the laying of a wreath on the tomb of José Antonio Primo de Rivera. Nights were taken with official functions: pomp and circumstance.

Yet one very strange episode remained. While staying at Barcelona, Heinrich Himmler made an earnest pilgrimage to visit the famous Montserrat Abbey. It seems that Himmler believed that in the Abbey he might finally locate the Holy Grail![6] And in Himmler's legitimized lunacy, Nazi ownership of the chalice with which Christ had consecrated the Last Supper could help Germany win the war. In Himmler's tortured reasoning, far from being King of the Jews, Jesus was, in fact, descended from Aryan blood because Christ's father had been an Aryan as well. Himmler had studied all he could on the Grail and other religious artifacts: if he could lay his hands on the Ark of the Covenant or the Spear of Longinus, then his SS might bask in undreamt powers.

Himmler had been inspired by Richard Wagner's opera *Parsifal*, which mentions that the Holy Grail was kept in "the marvelous castle of Montsalvat in the Pyrenees." It was widely believed that this castle was, in fact, Montserrat, a belief bolstered by the first performance of the opera in 1913, held at the Liceu Opera House in Barcelona.[7] Himmler also had other foggy reasons: a folk song from the Catalonia region northeast of Montserrat told of a "mystical font of life" somewhere nearby. For Himmler that was close to proof. Yet, arriving at the castle with Peiper, Wolff, and the others, the SS Reichsführer was stymied. Andreu Ripol Noble, a monk, served as their interpreter and tour guide, being the only one who spoke German at the abbey. Although Himmler seemed eager to tell the simple monk about his outlandish reasoning, the curious group of SS men left empty-handed. They left empty-handed in other ways too: Franco did not agree to side with Germany in the war. Spain would remain neutral—at least officially.

After six strange days in Spain all returned to Berlin.[8] But even with no Holy Grail, on November 1 Himmler promoted Peiper to the heady status of First Adjutant with Grothmann assigned directly under him. For Peiper, back in Berlin, recent events tempered the joy of the approaching holidays; the British bombers had returned more than a dozen times, largely in response to the Luftwaffe effort now bombing London day and night. A particularly close call for the Peiper family came in a raid on Himmler's birthday on October 7, when the RAF arrived over Berlin at 10 p.m., catching many citizens out in the open, returning from work or leaving the cinema. Thirty-one died. Later in the month, after Himmler's adjutant returned home, Nazi propaganda minister Joseph Goebbels toured the damage in Peiper's Wilmersdorf neighborhood and nearby Steglitz. Clad in his characteristic off-white overcoat, Goebbels dismissed the significance of the raids. Yet in his diary he wrote otherwise. "Things are none too rosy," he confided. "Air raid alerts are making people nervous."[9]

Then, as the RAF bomber losses soared that November and the Luftwaffe raids of London faded as well, the nighttime raids over Berlin sputtered to a halt. The final strike on the night of December 20 damaged several Berlin museums, but did little more. For the rest of the holiday season a sense of normalcy returned to the German capital. The second Christmas of the war didn't seem particularly foreboding, although the idea of forcing England to capitulate from aerial bombardment had not panned out. For Hitler and Himmler, however, that failure would slowly draw attention to the East. The business of the war slowed only momentarily by the holidays; Jochen Peiper was soon back on the road.

In early January Peiper, with Himmler, ventured to see the glorifying vision of the Munich exhibit (*Kampfstätten der Waffen SS*) of the Reichsführer's favorite frontline SS artist, Josef Keller-Kühne.[10] And in late January 1941 Peiper, Grothmann, and Wolff were ordered to Norway as Himmler's attendants to help Totenkopf and police units address winter equipment needs.[11] Keeping this in mind was easy enough—the thermometer hovered at 30 degrees below zero. On Peiper's birthday, January 30, Himmler swore in 150 Norwegian SS volunteers in Oslo whom he would later organize as the new SS Kampfgruppe Nord. In typical style, the Reichsführer lectured the Scandinavians on the hallowed tradition of the SS and admonished them to marry and sire many children.

Afterward there was a meeting of the minds with the Gauleiter of Norway, Josef Terboven, who asked Himmler what should be done with ethnic German children. The Reichsführer responded that the children must be sent to the Lebensborn program in the Fatherland. Wouldn't taking children away from their mothers prove a hardship? Terboven wanted to know. Peiper, who witnessed the conversation, reasoned, "The women who had children by German soldiers were despised and persecuted, but it was valuable blood and it was desirable to bring them to Germany to educate them there." Valuable blood! The adjutant agreed completely with his superior's racial Weltanschauung. Himmler couldn't have said it better.[12] As always, there was a dignified ceremony in a great hall to welcome Norwegian volunteers.[13] But why were Scandinavian volunteers needed in the racially rarified strata of the Waffen SS?

The answer lay just to the east. But officially there were not even hints. On May 4, 1941, Peiper was along when Hitler and Himmler had strode through the rain-swept streets of Berlin on their way to the Kroll Opera. That place would serve as Hitler's platform to address the German people since the Reichstag had been burned.[14] Long swastiked flags hung ornately along the street as Hitler, in a long leather coat, held up his hand as he passed the ranks of the Leibstandarte showing fixed bayonets. Peiper, in jack boots, balloonish riding pants, and his decorative fourragère, strode confidently behind Himmler and Nicolaus von Below, Hitler's Luftwaffe adjutant.

Just like the previous summer, Peiper was also inside again for Hitler's long and ambling speech. "All my endeavors to come to an understanding with Great Britain were wrecked by a small clique," Hitler wrangled. "The man behind this fanatical and diabolical plan to draw us into war at any costs was Mr. Churchill. Behind these men were the great international Jewish financial interests." France had fallen, and the cream of the British army had narrowly escaped at Dunkirk. "And now he has got the war he wanted," the German leader blustered.

Less than week later, on May 10, after the Leibstandarte subjugated Greece in a short campaign, Peiper motored along through Larissa with the Reichsführer to get an accurate picture of the fighting there. It was over by the time they arrived. Later, on May 21, Peiper flew with Himmler to Oslo again and, the following day, reviewed the Norwegian volunteers of the newly formed SS Wiking Division. There were the usual speeches after dinner and mingled national anthems. Soon, Himmler hinted, the Norwegians would join the Germanic elite in a vast campaign of titanic proportions.[15]

Yet the frenetic travels were not over. At the end of May 1941, Himmler and Oswald Pohl, with Peiper in tow, made their annual tour of the cruel concentration camp at Mauthausen. In that single month eight thousand prisoners at Mauthausen perished.[16] Himmler's retinue showed little sign that the suffering made much of an impression."[17]

Soon thereafter, in early June, Peiper was with Himmler back in Poland in the Wartheland, where his boss was fawning over German school kids who would help resettle the annexed zone. And in that same trip Peiper was with Himmler for a celebration at Oppeln in Upper Silesia, where the position of Reichskommisar was handed over from Erich von dem Bach to SS Gruf. Fritz Bracht, the Gauleiter of the Upper Silesia. SS Brigadeführer Richard Glücks, the inspector of the concentration camps—and one of the most infamous war criminals of the Third Reich—was there with Himmler. Peiper held the requisite celebration flower bouquet.[18]

The group continued on to Łódź, Poland, on June 6, with Peiper driving Himmler in the shiny black BMW convertible bearing the license plate of "SS-1." Himmler's staff toured the tailoring factories in the industrialized ghetto where forty thousand slave workers, many of them young children, were producing uniforms for the Germany army in return for a starvation diet. Himmler impressed on Chaim Rumkowski, the head of the Jewish Council in Łódź, that production must be maintained at all costs.[19] There were promises of improved food supplies for the beleaguered workers, but the resources never materialized.[20] Peiper's memory of the event was a strange one: "We visited a working camp in which workshops for shoemakers, tailors and watchmakers were established. As during our presence several German police officers had been killed, orders had been given to demolish part of the ghetto. The demolition was carried out by the inhabitants themselves under the supervision of the police forces."[21]

With such disquieting preparations observed, Himmler and his headquarters hastily returned to Berlin to prepare for the biggest business of all: Operation Barbarossa. And Barbarossa would be *more* than military.

On the evening of June 11, 1941, Himmler secretly assembled a select group of senior SS officers and police officials at his sacrosanct ideological center at Wewelsburg overlooking the Alm Valley and the nearby Teutoburg Forest. In the remodeled castle, beneath a medieval coat of arms, the Reichsführer lectured them urgently on the approaching ideological war. Soviet Russia, he said, was the very root of the problem with Bolshevism. Also present was his expert on *Bandenkampf*—partisan warfare—in Poland, SS Obergruppenführer Erich von dem Bach-Zelewski. In actuality Bandenkampf had little to do with partisan warfare, which had not yet arisen in the East. Instead, it was a euphemistic expression used by the Nazis to give the killings of Polish intellectuals and Jews a military cover.

The population of Jews, Slavs, and *Untermenschen*—subhumans—Himmler informed his stunned audience, would have to be reduced by 30 million! "The war with Russia could become so costly, that German losses could nullify the victory," he warned. Yet now was the time to act. A leader like Hitler, he said, was born only every thousand years. According to Bach-Zelewski, others were present—Karl Wolff, Heydrich, Kurt Daluege, and the "young SS officer Jochen Peiper."[22]

Peiper now found himself part of the *Zauberkreis*—Himmler's magic circle! After interminable afternoon presentations at the castle came dinner with the high SS leaders. Later everyone climbed the ornate hand-carved wooden spiral staircase to Himmler's sacrosanct sanctuary. There, long talks took place around a round table by candlelight. The chat went on for hours; no one retired until midnight. What was discussed at the fireside talks is not revealed but can be largely divined from his speeches leading up to the big event.[23] Obsessed with the Germanic heritage, Himmler, like Hitler, reveled in the prospect of a momentous showdown with "the racial heathens" in Russia. "The Goths are riding again!" he would later exult.[24]

We do not know what Peiper thought of Himmler's announcements made on Friday, June 11. Yet we do know that by the time the meeting at Wewelsburg broke up on Sunday, June 15, Peiper had learned that his brother Horst had died on the very day the meeting convened. The Welwesburg conference concluded, he sped home to his mother and father in Wilmersdorf, seeking to learn what had happened. There was no news, only vague rumors and word that Horst had shot himself.

On Tuesday, June 17, Jochen was in Berlin for the funeral with Sigurd, his mother, and father. The 20th Wachbattalion of the Leibstandarte provided the honor guard. Now he was the only undamaged son—everyone was totally shocked. We know nothing of what Himmler himself might have told his adjutant, for the Reichsführer also had returned to Berlin to speak to Heydrich about Barbarossa. There were whispers alluding to Horst's homosexuality. If Horst Peiper was accused of being gay, there would likely have been little solace from Himmler. "We intend to get rid of homosexuals, root and branch," he once declared. And then perhaps thinking of himself and his adjutant too: "If a man has an affair with his pretty secretary, at most she will exert some influence on him, but she won't affect his ability to work."[25] That same tolerance was not extended to homosexuals, whom Himmler looked upon as worse than Jews.

That Tuesday was also special as Himmler celebrated the fifth anniversary of his appointment as the chief of the German military police. During the morning Heydrich had a closed-door briefing with the leaders of all his Einsatzgruppen at the RSHA headquarters at Prinz Albrecht Straße. There was something important to reveal, but only to the elite few.

"The Führer has ordered the liquidation of all Jews, gypsies and political functionaries in the entire area of the Soviet Union in order to secure the territory," one of those present would later report.[26] More than that, Heydrich seems to have fully bought into Himmler's illusory demarcation between killing and a justifiable racial war. The undesirables were to be wiped out efficiently and without vengeance, greed, bloodlust, or sexual motives, which he and Himmler considered to be un-German.[27] More than that, any SS men involved were to keep themselves impeccable with "smartness in appearance, both on duty and off."[28] Later Heydrich would solemnly explain that the information about the Führer's view was not to go further than the assembled Einsatzgruppen leaders.

Himmler now faced the greatest military operation in the history of mankind with likely knowledge that the brother of his adjutant had killed himself after being accused a homosexual. Not surprisingly, the head of the SS was again seeking healing massages from Felix Kersten for his nervous belly. Even more, Himmler indulged himself in carnal diversion with his pretty secretary, Hedwig Potthast, at her Grunewald apartment. In January 1940 her flat-mate, Käte Müller, met the Reichsführer. Since then, Himmler showed up at their four-story apartment building on Bismarckstrasse to drink wine in the evenings. By May 1941 Himmler was often spending the night.[29]

After their affair blossomed in 1939 Hedwig took the SS-compliant step of renouncing the church.[30] "Heinrich visited me regularly," she told her interrogators with a slight blush. "He said he wished to be the father of many children—not for himself, but the glory of greater Germany."[31]

For Himmler divorce was out of the question. Following his own recommended procedures for an SS man with a mistress, Himmler did not forget his wife, Marga, or his daughter in Tegernsee. What was an SS Reichsführer to do? Soak in *Gemütlichkeit*—a warm friendly atmopshere. Midweek Himmler returned home to wife and daughter for an idyllic weekend at their spread in Gmund am Tegernsee. Even though he had seldom been home over the preceding months, he endeavored that weekend to project a fatherly influence, particularly doting on his eleven-year-old daughter, Gudrun.

On the Sunday afternoon of June 19 the family journeyed to Himmler's Forsthaus hunting lodge at Valepp, some twenty winding kilometers in the hills south of Lake Tegernsee straddling the German-Austrian border.[32] Clad in traditional loden und lederhosen, Himmler, with his wife in a new dress and daughter in braids, picked wildflowers and munched on forest berries in the lush alpine meadows by the *Jägerhaus*.[33] Returning home there was gardening and smiling portraits before their big house at St. Quirin, although Himmler announced he would soon be gone for a big assignment. "Pappi is going away again," Gudrun wrote in tears, "this time into the field."[34] Her mother was more distraught. Marga Himmler was now fully aware of her husband's mistress—for Father Himmler it was the perfect Bavarian fest before Barbarossa.

Even so, the head of the SS was still anxious to take advantage of every available angle for the impending operation. Immediately after leaving his family at Gmund he consulted astrologers to gauge the cosmic prospects. One warned of zodiacal dangers on the horizon—Hitler had the same Saturn position in his natal chart as had Napoleon, and there were troubling parallels with their prospects in the East.[35] But Hitler had outlawed astrologers just that year, and there would certainly be no altering of the *Führerprinzip*—sacrosanct leadership principle—based on that curious source. Besides, Reinhard Heydrich, his security chief, derided Himmler's cautiousness. "He has been looking again too far into his horoscope," complained Heydrich.[36] Still, to steady their resolve, Himmler advised all SS men welcome the solstice with a blazing bonfire. "Yonder breaks already the dawn of a radiant time in history," he counseled. "The doors of the future are open to those whose hearts burn with love for the Fatherland."[37]

Whatever the presage of the stars that summer of 1941, Hitler was pleased with the historical coincidence to launch the huge offensive on the very same day—June 22—that Napoleon had invaded Russia in 1812. The German leader aimed to eliminate what he saw as the scourge of Bolshevism. Having paid a solemn visit to Napoleon's tomb after the conquest of France, Hitler saw himself taking over the task at which the French emperor had failed.[38] Himmler, for his part, met with Hitler on the day before the assault and urged him to consider the use of poison gas in the campaign if needed. Although Hitler looked warily at flouting the Geneva Convention, Himmler had no such scruples.[39] This was the ideological battle both men had sought all along—the Hitlerian holy war. "When Barbarossa begins," Hitler said of the codename for the operation, "the world will hold its breath."[40]

The Blitzkrieg unleashed on Soviet Russia on June 22 was a total surprise. Three million German soldiers and support troops flooded into the East. The panzer columns hurtled into Russia, with the enemy reeling so profoundly from the blows that total collapse appeared imminent. Indeed, Himmler was so confident from early reports that he paused the following Monday afternoon to play a set of tennis with Peiper outside his Berlin headquarters. His usually fastidious office manager and secretary, Rudolf Brandt and Erika Lorenz, did not record the score. Yet when the game ended at 8:20 p.m. in the long summer twilight, the Reichsführer, with his mind focused far to the east, must have considered the real match already won.[41] Certainly Hitler did. "You only have to kick in the door," the German leader scowled, "and the whole rotten structure will come crashing down."[42]

But even if Germany was on the verge of a fantastic victory, mid-June found SS officer Jochen Peiper disillusioned. The war had descended upon his family. At the end of the month Sigurd learned that her brother, Dr. Rolf Hinrichsen, a naval chief assistant surgeon, had died with all the others on the *Bismarck* when that battleship was hunted down and sunk by the British.

And now Jochen and his parents continued to anguish over the fate of his brother Horst, now dead and with no explanation. Horst had fought in Poland and was wounded in the campaign in France, rising to the rank of SS Hauptsturmführer, seemingly a rising SS leader. However, there were rumors in the regimental staff of the 2. SS Totenkopf Infanterie Regiment that Horst was homosexual. For Eicke, the odious head of that division, there was no infraction worse than that. Of course, Eicke was just following the lead expressed by the Reichsführer. Homosexuals "in every case will be publically demoted, expelled," Himmler told a group of SS leaders. "Upon my order, they will be transferred to a concentration camp and shot to death while escaping."[43]

One cohort, Alfred Roßdeutscher, told the story that the brutish Eicke had called Horst Peiper into his quarters and placed a loaded pistol on the table between them. Eicke told him he should shoot himself or let it go to the the firing squad. Horst was then relieved of command. Likely this event tipped the balance, for on the afternoon of June 11, 1941, while Eicke and the Totenkopf Division moved to East Prussia,

Horst Peiper shot himself in the head.[44] His official personnel file listed "death in an accident," but no one in his shocked family believed that tale.[45] Eicke and the Totenkopf had cost Jochen his closest brother.

PEIPER RESOLVED TO GET OUT FROM UNDER HIMMLER'S WING. "THE LONG ACTIVITY under the conditions well known to you," he later wrote to Himmler's mistress later that summer."[46]

The war offered no immediate distractions for Jochen's woes. With the expectation of another lightning campaign, on June 25 Himmler's train again pulled away from its Berlin moorings toward Hitler's bunker complex in East Prussia near Rastenburg. Rather than heading into battle with his comrades, Peiper again glided to the East with Himmler toward a field post some twenty-five kilometers northeast of Hitler on the edge of a large lake near Großgarten. If not spacious, the train was comfy—with a sleeper car, another for communications, and a well-equipped dining coach with thickly upholstered chairs set around round tables in front of big picture windows. When they finally halted, they found themselves at a rail siding between Lötzen and Angerburg. There they entered temporary quarters amid the East Prussian pines near Mauersee Lake.

The Reichführer's newly established headquarters eventually become known as Hochwald (High Woods), but for now the camp consisted of several temporary wooden barracks.[47] There Peiper and Grothmann attended to their superior not far from the front. All indications pointed to a short time there. Like the Blitzkrieg conquests of France and Poland, Barbarossa moved swiftly and looked to conclude with German legions fulfilling Hitler's dream of Eastern conquest.

On Sunday, June 29, 1941, Himmler and Peiper journeyed to Hitler's nearby *Wolfsschanze* to greet the German leader at his new field headquarters. The Wolf's Lair was a play on Hitler's own vision of himself—"Wolf" had been his cover name in the early days of the National Socialist movement. Beyond the name, Wolfsschanze was a gloomy collection of ten concrete bunkers with walls two meters thick hidden in a marshy Görlitz wood.[48] Hitler's retinue had been there only since the previous Tuesday. The place was hardly regal—the air was stifling and mosquito infested that summer—but the mood in the damp forest remained exuberant. When Himmler greeted Hitler on the ivy-covered west side of the Kasino I dining bunker, Peiper stood off to his side, hat under one arm with Himmler's leather notebook case under the other.[49] There in the sun-dappled woods, there were smiles. Keitel grinned uncharacteristically, while Hitler leafed through a report. Himmler was jaunty, and even Hitler appeared buoyant. His Luftwaffe adjutant, Nicolaus von Below, standing by Peiper, wrote to a friend,

> The ease of our early victories along the whole front came as a surprise to both the Army and the Luftwaffe. Enemy aircraft were parked in neat rows and could be destroyed without difficulty . . . the Russian is putting up a good fight everywhere, sometimes so tough and determined that our troops have fierce battle. The main reason is undoubtedly the Communist commissars who, pistol in hand, force their men to fight until shot dead. The Russian Communistic

> propaganda has succeeded in convincing their men that they are fighting a war against barbaric savages and that no prisoners are being taken. This explains why many soldiers . . . commit suicide when faced with surrender.[50]

Until now Hitler enforced a news blackout of the Russian campaign, but with things going the Führer's way, a series of twelve special announcements were aired over German radio. Introduced at half-hour intervals beginning at 11 a.m. by the "Russian Fanfare" based on Franz Liszt's "Hungarian Rhapsody," the breaking news told of a swift and crushing German advance—the destruction of 2,233 Soviet tanks and 4,107 aircraft. Two entire Russian armies were encircled at Bialystok while masses of prisoners streamed into German POW cages. Yet in many places the Russians fought to the death. Such encounters inflicted severe casualties on the German forces and reinforced Hitler's preconceptions about the enemy in the East. "Our enemies are not human beings anymore," the German leader told Japanese ambassador Hiroshi Oshima. "They are beasts."[51] Hitler's vision of his Russian enemy oozed with contempt:

> It is doubtful if anything at all can be done in Russia. . . . In the eyes of the Russian the principal support of civilization is vodka. His ideal consists of never doing anything that is not indispensable. The Russian will never make up his mind to work except under compulsion from the outside. . . . And if, despite everything, he is apt to have organization thrust upon him, that is thanks to a drop of Aryan blood in his veins. . . . What matters is that Bolshevism must be exterminated.[52]

The reality of such language became clear the following day. Peiper left with Himmler, Heydrich, and others from Hochwald for a tour of previously conquered Polish cities of Augustowo and Grodno. Before leaving on the bright summer day of June 29, Heydrich communicated to subordinates with Himmler's blessing: "self-cleansing measures" were to be instigated against Jews without leaving any trace—covert killing. His orders? "Ruthless and energetic execution of measures."[53]

Augustowo was not far away, just on the other side of the East Prussian border. Grodno was a bit further to the east. When Himmler, Heydrich, and the others in the entourage got to Augustowo, they encountered Einsatzkommando Tilsit, who informed them that they had just shot more than two hundred persons, "including one woman," in nearby Krottingen and Polangen for supposedly attacking Hans-Joachim Böhme's men. "The Reichsführer SS and the Gruppenführer who were by coincidence there [in Augustowo]," Böhme proudly reported the following week, "received information from me on the measures instituted by the Stapostelle Tilsit and sanctioned them completely."[54] Yet Heydrich and Himmler were not satisfied, for after next visiting Grodno, a city of fifty thousand with nearly half of the population Jews, they found none of the killing teams.[55] Making no attempt to hide his remarks, Heydrich, in the presence of Himmler and Peiper, roundly berated the head of Einsatzkommando 9 for having executed only ninety-six Jews on that day.[56] Cameras snapped photos as Peiper took notes and Himmler interviewed local peasant women. Beyond that, Himmler was briefed on the nature of "punitive measures" the Border Police were instituting.[57] The following morning Heydrich sent out an order, reminding those under him to keep pace with the military advance and *take the initiative*—a euphemism for outright murder.

On July 8 Peiper was along with Himmler when he and Order Police Chief Kurt Daluege showed up to the Polish city of Bialystok to follow the progress of the Order Police in fulfilling the intended mission. Eleven days earlier, on June 27, 1941, Order Police Battalion 309 and the regular army's 221st Security Division had brutally executed two thousand Jews in the town, in one case herding five hundred, including women and children, into a synagogue and burning them alive.[58] Others were systematically shot into trenches on the outskirts of town in a horrific scene.[59]

By July 8 the first wave of maniacal violence had faded, but Order Police Battalion 322 had just conducted a sweep through Polish and Jewish sections of the city and confiscated a great mass of material, supposedly having been looted by the Jews after the Russians had fled Poland two weeks before. On that basis Himmler asked for a briefing on the experiences of the battalion, as if it were a military operation, and inspected the seized booty. Later that Tuesday evening Gen. von dem Bach-Zelewski threw a princely banquet in honor of Himmler's visit. Yet the meddling Reichsführer SS took the opportunity to give Bach-Zelewski some command ginger. Himmler's specific order does not survive, but Bach-Zelewski would later indicate he was told to execute two thousand Jews as a punishment for looting.[60] Over the succeeding days a new wave of killings swept Bialystok. And on July 11 Bach-Zelewski broadcast an order for those under him to execute of all Jewish "plunderers" between seventeen and forty-five years of age.[61]

Himmler had other news for Bach-Zelewski. To help with this terrible job, he would have half of the strength of the twenty thousand men under the newly formed Kommandostab Reichsführer SS that was just arriving. Unlike the Einsatzgruppen or the Order Police, this was a special task force, not to be filled by police or ordinary conscripts but rather by members of the supposedly elite Waffen SS! Bach-Zelewski would have the services of the SS Cavalry Brigade, while the 1st SS Brigade under SS Gen. Friedrich Jeckeln would be assigned to the southern sector. What would be the combat assignment of these Waffen SS? They would go to the Pripet Marshes, a vast island-like expanse of nearly impassable swamps and roadless terrain. When Himmler visited SS Kavalerie Regiment 2 on July 21, he described their mission only in the broadest terms, but he sternly warned of a *schwere Aufgabe*—a grave task—that lay before them.[62]

If not a participant, Peiper was at the news center of the killing storm. In July 1941 Peiper was still at Himmler's side, fighting a war that was looking less like anything military and more like systematic murder. All the while, the young adjutant anguished of his mother's woes at now having lost one of her sons. Work was hardly more savory. Each morning Peiper and Grothmann would give Himmler a short briefing reflecting the most recent reports received, mindful of what each had been seeing during their travels with Himmler. Although a paper copy was handed over in a manila folder, the adjutants conveyed recent developments and the day's calendar while the Reichsführer shaved. Good coffee would be served each morning in the restaurant car.

The formal briefing came after that. A large hanging map-board in the train located the various *aktionen*—actions—during the briefing. One of the few surviving maps clearly shows the *Säuberungsaktion*—cleansing action—of the 1. SS Cavalry Brigade over the last few days of July.[63] Meanwhile the SS Reichsführer had developed a near-obsessional fixation on obtaining up-to-date reports from the field.

In Himmler's private war the "actions" transpiring behind the front featured detailed casualty figures describing a lop-sided slaughter. Thousands of Jews, partisans, and Bolshevists destroyed without friendly losses. At least once a day Himmler telephoned Karl Wolff to obtain an update, and then he called Berlin. Unlike the Berlin office, Peiper and Grothmann dealt with the phones and mail; they were aware of everything coming into Himmler's command train.

On July 13 Himmler journeyed from his headquarters to Stettin, the Polish city on the mouth of the Oder River, to produce some inspiring words for a group of Waffen SS replacements. Although counseling to be "merciless and moral," his words cast a shadow on the entire SS organization:

> This is an ideological battle and a struggle of races. Here in this struggle stands National Socialism: an ideology based on the value of our Germanic, Nordic blood. Here stands a world as we have conceived it: beautiful, decent, socially equal, that perhaps in a few circumstances is still burdened by shortcomings, but as a whole, a happy, beautiful world of culture; this is what our Germany is like. On the other side stands a population of 180 million, a mixture of races, whose very names are unpronounceable, and whose physique is such that one can shoot them down without pity and compassion.[64]

Himmler's appointment calendar frequently showed the young adjutant with his boss. On July 18 Peiper was on the phone postponing a trip by Himmler to Lublin to see Odilio Globocnik again. Himmler had charged "Globus" with "cleansing" Jews and Poles from the cleared territory, starting up an SS settlement program and building a massive new concentration camp. Two days later Peiper was pictured in Lublin with the Reichsführer, Globocnik, and Himmler's galaxy of assistants for discussions that scholars today posit concerned the decision of how the "evacuation" of the Jews would be accomplished.[65] While Peiper was present, Globocnik received orders to clear the Jews from Lublin so ethnic German settlers could be brought in—a genocide-based plan to completely redraw the ethnic map of Europe.

On another occasion, the records show Peiper present on July 24 for late-night conversations with Himmler, Rudolf Brandt, and others.[66] What the insiders discussed is unknown, but this was just before Himmler set off for a series of month-long tours to see how the Einsatzkommandos were disposing of undesirables in the conquered regions. All through July and into the early days of August, radio reports streamed into Himmler's East Prussian headquarters, telling of the human swath being cut through Russia by Heydrich's Einsatzgruppen, the order police battalions and the anti-partisan SS cavalry.[67] Himmler himself was out in the field, consulting his commanders and issuing oral instructions for something best not written down.

While Peiper took care of matters at the headquarters of the SS Reichsführer and accompanied him on trips, Himmler grappled with personal problems. Hedwig Potthast, who had left Himmler's office in early summer to serve as his full-time mistress, announced she was pregnant.[68] Although her brother, Walter, with the 2nd Panzer Division, supported the affair, her Catholic parents did not.[69] They went ballistic on hearing the news, cutting her off entirely from communication. That was a sticky situation, particularly as Himmler was still married himself. And now Hedwig was more than ten weeks pregnant. "In December 1941, I was able to inform him that he was soon to be a father," Hedwig later recalled. "I insisted he tell his wife, however, and after some deliberation he agreed. She didn't make any comment because I think she suspected it anyway."

"I would like to speak to your parents in Trier," Himmler wrote to her on July 28 from Hitler's field headquarters. For now he could not do so, Himmler said, as he was in the field"doing important work." "However, I can't tell you how happy I am to hear that you will be giving me a child." How would she face her family? "If there is an emergency need, Wölfchen [Karl Wolff] could make a house call to deliver something."[70] On July 29 Himmler wrote again to his mistress, who was seized with second thoughts about the pregnancy:

> Since 4 p.m., I am sitting in my office in my bunker at the FHQ and now my [* Hagall rune] will get a letter. Thank you for your nice and long one. . . . You must not think and write that you have the feeling that everything may be a deception. . . . I plan to go to Trier to speak to your parents, but I can only go there with extreme difficulty. . . . You should not worry about this issue; it only comes from love. . . . I cannot express to you how happy I am about the thought of the child that you carry. It will be for me a present and it will be a gift to you and me.[71]

On the same day Himmler wrote his paramour, he obsessed over the gritty mission of the Kommandostab Reichsführer SS in the Pripet Marshes. The day before, Hermann Fegelein,with the 1st SS Cavalry Regiment, revealed he had direct orders from Himmler that Jews were to be dealt with "for the most part as plunderers," another way of saying they should be shot. Now Himmler provided clarifications: there was more to do than to kill racially inferior men. That accomplished, the livestock and remaining women and children should be forced out of their villages with their peasant hovels then *burned to the ground*.[72] The war in the East was to be conducted just as Genghis Khan had done.

What was the impending "important work" Himmler had written his distressed pregnant mistress about? Over the next three days Himmler, Wolff, and Peiper would be in Kowno-Wilna-Riga, Dünaberg, and Minsk. The objective was to spread the message of genocide to the Baltic States. On July 29 Himmler and his coterie journeyed in the black Mercedes to Riga to meet with High SS Police Chief Hans-Adolf

Prützmann in the Latvian industrial city.[73] That Peiper was there during the driving across the delta lands of the Daugava River is firmly established by a photograph of the adjutant, Himmler, Prützmann, and others during a road-stop picnic during the trip on July 29.[74] The mission in Latvia and Riga went on for three days, during which Himmler issued instructions, preferring the privacy of face-to-face communication.

Just what had Himmler communicated to Prützmann before leaving? Understandably, no thread of their personal conversation survives. However, a clear indication of content came from Prützmann himself. After Himmler's departure on July 31, the High SS police chief announced to those under him that the Reichsführer SS had ordered "criminal elements" to soon be "resettled." One subordinate asked to where the Jews and others would be resettled. "Not what you think," Prutzmann clarified. Those "resettled," he made clear, would be "dispatched into the next world."[75] In the weeks following the visit of Himmler, Peiper, and the others, Jews killed in a nearby Lithuanian mass murder sharply rose to more than seventy-six thousand dead.[76]

Himmler, with Peiper and Wolff along, ended their three-day trip by flying from Dünaberg to Baranowicze and then one hundred kilometers onward to Minsk to meet Bach-Zelewski. There the horse-riding units under the Kommandostab Reichsführer SS were being assembled for further missions.[77] While Himmler personally communicated orders to Bach-Zelewski and Fegelein, Peiper was photographed with others looking inside a Russian war curiosity, one of the monster Soviet KV-2 tanks that had proven impenetrable to German tank guns. Knocked out in the reduction of the Bialystok-Minsk pocket in mid-July, the fifty-two-ton hulking steel form was hauled to the town square for Himmler and the others to ponder. As a result of the meeting, Hermann Fegelein advised his men that Himmler told him that "uncompromising severity" was necessary in dealing with their Jewish enemy. Moreover, he reminded them he would deal harshly with any commanders who showed weakness.[78]

The SS cavalry brigade was important to his mission, as were SS Standartenführer Hermann Fegelein and SS Obersturmbannführer Gustav Lombard, who were leading horse-mounted troops near the Pripet Marshes. And, Lombard, of course, had been Peiper's old cavalry instructor when he first joined the SS Reitersturm in 1933. Peiper and Himmler had inspected the SS cavalry brigade in Klausen on Saturday July 5 and topped off the event with a celebratory parade in which the SS Kriegsberichter snapped photos.[79] Fegelein, who had been quite the horseman before the war, had a scandalous reputation, castigated the month before for having impregnated a Polish girl and being well known for his sexual indiscretions.[80] At the end of July a coded radio message disclosed the nature of Fegelein's and Lombard's mission: "Express order of the *RFSS* [Reichsführer SS: Himmler]. All Jews must be shot. Drive Jewish females into the swamps."[81]

The radio transmission, received on Himmler's train, was simultaneously intercepted by Allied eavesdroppers and made intelligible by their cryptologists.[82] The visit Himmler had made with Peiper on July 31 seemed to inspire members of the Kommandostab beyond its exact wording. For, on the evening of August 1, while Peiper and Himmler attended to business back in Berlin, Gustav Lombard, in charge of the 1st SS Cavalry Regiment, issued a new interpretation of his orders: "Not one male Jew is to remain alive, not one remnant family [left] in the villages." In the following days Peiper's old head-strong cavalry instructor detailed a new *Entjudung* action in which *all* Jews, including women and children, were murdered with liberal use of automatic weapons. By August 11 Lombard proudly communicated that eleven thousand men, women, and children had been killed—over thousand done away with each day.[83]

Meanwhile, Peiper's old school instructor from Braunschweig, SS Obstuf. Franz Magill, was leading SS Cavalry Regiment 2 with the same assignment as the others to the north. Yet, unlike Lombard, Magill seems to have disappointed Himmler, for, on August 12, the former was explaining why he had not completely eradicated the "Jewish plunderers" in the Pripet marshes. "Driving women and children into the swamps did not have the success it was supposed to have as the swamps were not deep enough." That Himmler was dismayed by Magill's excuses was made clear in succeeding weeks. Lombard, who had taken it upon himself to enjoin the killing of women and children, found himself promoted. Franz Magill was not, soon banished to an unimportant post in Poland. The numbers told the story. By the end of August 13 the Kommandostab and the security police in the area of the marshes recorded 13,788 "plunderers" killed, with only 714 taken prisoner. At the same time, entire SS cavalry brigade of four thousand suffered only two dead and fifteen wounded. It was not battle, but murder.[84]

Similar communiqués funneled through Himmler's headquarters at all hours, grotesquely exacting reports of the number of "Jewish plunderers" liquidated.[85] Given Peiper's close association with many of those involved in the policies of extermination and their apparent openness with each other, it would be absurdly naive to believe that the young adjutant did not have intimate knowledge of the killing frenzy that summer. Peiper himself acknowledged as much: "A German soldier who doesn't want to know about these things going on now," he told one visitor to Himmler's orbit, "should go to the front."[86] Thus, the Berlin native was not along for the second interlude to Minsk in mid-August; Grothmann took his place, an unlucky choice for Peiper's stand-in, given the unsavory assignment, as Himmler wanted a personal demonstration of what an execution detail would look like.[87] Even for the Reichsführer SS it was an event so disturbing that he would later order that men forced to take part in such execution details should then be given time off to enjoy happy, carefree times with music, and good German food.[88]

Following his own advice, Peiper petitioned his superior to rejoin the fighting men.[89] Was it fear of further Himmler depravity or the desire for glory and medals? Likely it was neither. A clue comes from his communication with Hedwig Potthast five weeks later. "You know the intense pressure I have been under," he would write. That "demands a valve and some distance and time." The death of his brother, Horst, the previous month had been at least indirectly at the hand of Theodor Eicke. Himmler's refusal to do anything about that event must have cut deep. Certainly SS involvement in the murky intrigue associated with his brother's death in June must have created a powerful reaction from his mother, now with only a single son alive.

Charlotte had lost her son Horst under mysterious circumstances, and her other son Hans Hasso remained in vegetative state in a Berlin institution after attempting suicide. Jochen, of course, was still in service in the Waffen SS. He was still working for the homophobic leader of that entire organization that seemed at the root of the destructive fate of the other two sons.

Had Jochen and his brother communicated regarding his plight leading up to the fatal event? We will never know.[90] Sometime in July Peiper gave Himmler the negative word: he wanted out.In spite of an "angry reaction," the SS Reichsführer consented.[91] Further, even though Peiper knew Hedwig Potthast well—perhaps even much more closely than Himmler was aware—Himmler did not take the opportunity to inform his adjutant of Hedwig Potthast's pregnancy.[92] Or was Peiper's relationship with Hedwig the crux of the problem—two married men in love with "Little Bunny"? And now a dead brother? No matter. He was out of there—at least provisionally.

On August 1, before Peiper returned to the front, he and Himmler flew back to Berlin. There Peiper made another sudden appearance before Sigurd, who was now house-bound with Elke, their one-year-old daughter.[93] We know nothing of what Sigurd said to her husband about his change of assignment, but it seems to have been contentious. "Too bad, that Jochen went his own way and left K H.," Sigurd would later recall. K. H.—König Heinrich—was the in-crowd code for Himmler. "Jochen will forever regret it."[94]

So, at the end of the first week in August, Himmler sent his heretofore-faithful aide to go into the field, at first as his personal observer.

Peiper would go to Russia before that war was over.[95]

Chapter 7

LETTERS FROM THE WAR

In August 1941 the Second World War exploded in an Eastern European hell of guns, bombs, and shells. Beginning on June 22 Hitler's Stuka and tank-led legions plunged into the vastness of the Russia plains, intending to collapse the Soviet Union with their reach, speed, and firepower. Would it be a short, sharp campaign as with Poland and France?

Peiper may have been disillusioned. Not only shaken by his brother's death, but that summer Peiper knew enough from his time on Himmler's train in East Prussia that conventional battle was not what his superior's personal war was about. His mission was a terrible campaign of racial genocide.

Peiper aimed to get away, but first there was a brief interlude with the family. Life in Berlin was likely chaotic, as his wife was not in full agreement with his plans. Regardless, as he prepared to leave, he saw firsthand the effects of two years of war. Joining the family at Rüdesheimer Platz for a brief visit, the collective city-wide denial that had prevailed the previous year now gave way to forbidding developments.

By this time in Berlin many foodstuffs other than bread and potatoes—particularly real coffee beans, butter, sugar, and eggs—were in impossibly short supply. The meat ration in Berlin was cut to four hundred grams per week, although Peiper's first-rate connections insulated the family from most sacrifices.[1] Even though the cafes on the fashionable Kurfürstendamm promenade on the west side were still open, they served ersatz coffee with limited menus while patrons puffed on nontobacco cigarettes with the faint aroma of "burnt grass."[2]

With Berlin's nightly blackout, the city was plunged into complete darkness, and nocturnal sidewalk collisions became common. Other times in the dark, bleary-eyed Berliners, short on sleep, were forced to flee to cellars for air raids while blue-beamed searchlights, wailing sirens, and noisy anti-aircraft fire added to the fright. In the cellars the muffled explosions seemed terribly ironic as the head of the German Air Force, Hermann Göring, had assured before the war that Berlin would never see a bomb.

For a housewife like Sigurd Peiper, procuring groceries, even simple items like carrots and potatoes, meant standing in lines for hours. More grimly, the population of Berlin was now working fifty-six- to sixty-hour work weeks, with many silently depressed as the war continued.[3] Still, Sigurd and one-year-old daughter, Elke, were doing well enough during Jochen's short visit. All in all, Berlin still seemed reasonably safe when Peiper looked to head off for war at the beginning of August 1941. But not only would he be leaving Berlin, he would also be parting from Heinrich Himmler. But that Himmler still favored the Peiper family was clear: in mid-August, just after Jochen was gone, Sigurd received a special commemorative cake spatula emblazoned with RFSS on the sterling-silver blade and personally delivered by his faithful office secretary.[4]

Meanwhile, Peiper hastened to the front. In those warm August weeks the long-anticipated war in the East flared as if a massive fire. Daily the street side radio speakers blared out reports of fantastic tank advances deep into the heart of Russia. Would the Wehrmacht soon reach Moscow? Unlike the Blitzkrieg campaigns in Poland and France, however, rather than folding, the Russians seemed to be fighting back, even if composed of primitive forces. As the great conflict erupted, Peiper sought to return to his unit, the Leibstandarte Adolf Hitler, and join the fight with Himmler's other SS knights. On August 19, 1941, Peiper was photographed with SS Sturmbannführer Wilhelm Weidenhaupt, Max Hansen, and Albert Frey as they observed the shelling of an 88mm gun against the Russians clinging to the banks of the Dnieper River. With nearby Soviet resistance having collapsed on the southwestern front, the SS forces looked to secure the Black Sea port of Cherson.[5] Later that day Peiper seems to have taken temporary command of the 11th Company to reinforce the isolated reconnaissance battalion. Kurt Meyer had flung his armored cars against strong resistance at a fruit jam factory on Cherson's eastern edge. After breaking through he had boldly fought his way to the center of town, but he then advanced so recklessly that he left nobody behind him. One predictable delay came when the SS infantry and a journalist came across a huge cache of red wine and a platoon of drunken enemy Russians eager to surrender.[6]

The infantry advance toward Cherson was done in rushes across the open ground, completely exposed and devoid of cover save the occasional stands of sunflowers. The roar of artillery fire boomed, punctuated by louder explosions as the Russians detonated ammunition dumps. In the late afternoon the troops led by Peiper managed to reach the railway line to the northwest of the port city, supported by big 21cm army guns. The artillery fired as they moved forward, and "shorts" wounded several in his company.[7] By 6 p.m. Peiper and the rest of 3rd Battalion reported linking up with "Schneller" Meyer.[8] They were pitted against Russian sailors impressed as infantry, fighting from one house to the next, across gardens and public squares. Even after nightfall the streets were starkly lit, illuminated by furiously burning buildings.

In Cherson, now, were big, black, ugly clouds of smoke. The Russians were leaving, having put the torch to two fuel depots. The air was filled with the acrid odor of flaming wood and straw and the sulfurous stink of gunpowder. And where the stubbly plains met the late summer horizon there was an ever-present pall of flame and smoke. The thatched roofs of Russian homes blazed amid the rumble of guns and exploding shells. To Peiper, fire seemed to mark another victory—in a war that looked to be more brutal than any before it. How could one not think of Genghis Khan?[9]

Upon arrival to the division Peiper likely learned the news sweeping the ranks. Just days before, two companies of a neighboring division could not be located during the advance on Cherson. Erich Kernmayr, a Viennese SS war reporter with the Leibstandarte, followed along with the 4th Battalion. According to his account, on the morning of August 15 they found ninety-eight missing German soldiers, ghoulishly executed in a cherry orchard in the village of Nowo Danzig near Greigova. The victims were strung up in trees, their stocking feet having been doused with gasoline and set afire—"Stalin-socks." Retribution came swiftly:

> At noon the next day, an order was received by division to the effect that all prisoners captured during the next three days would be shot as a reprisal for the inhumane atrocities, which the Red Army had committed in our sector. It so happened that we had taken very many prisoners during those fatal days and so the lives of four thousand men fell forfeit. They scarcely looked up when our interpreter told them of their fate.[10]

According to Kernmayr, the executions were carried out by grim firing squads, felling one line of eight after another into antitank ditches. Although documentation of the Russian atrocity is complete, no direct evidence of reprisals can be found in German archival material—a hardly surprising fact.[11] "The other side carries it out with the meanest means," wrote one of Peiper's Leibstandarte contemporaries. "One gets very angry seeing again and again beastly massacred soldiers, who somewhere got lost or were taken prisoner."[12] Himmler threatened even larger horror:

> Soldiers of the Army and the Waffen SS! On 1 September, six SS officers were found in the Weniza forest in the following condition: They had been stripped of their clothing and hanged with their legs up. Their entrails had been taken out. Such an act demands revenge, and since it was the Jews who did it, we will utterly extirpate them. Even the brood in the cradle must be crushed like a swollen toad. We are living in an iron time and have to sweep with iron brooms. Everybody has therefore to do his duty without asking his conscience first.[13]

The war in the East seemed to spiral out of control. When Cherson fell into SS hands later that day, the enemy scuttled several Russian ships to the bottom of the Black Sea. Soviet hopes seemed similarly sunk, so much so that, on August 21, the Leibstandarte was temporarily pulled out of combat for rest and reorganization. The palace guard would be readied for the final coup d'grace.

With the pause in the fighting, Peiper took his leave to report on the war in the East to Himmler at his Hochwald headquarters near Grossgarten East Prussia. There, Peiper regaled his former boss with tales from the front of a war seemingly on the verge of final decision, the SS men of the Leibstandarte motored like tourists by the sand dunes of Chulakovka along the Black Sea coast. If Soviet soldiers seemed cruel, the Ukrainian locals welcomed the LAH release from Stalin's terrible rule. Civilians lined the roads, showering the SS men with autumn flowers and enthusiastic calls. The natives were decked out in colorful traditional Ukrainian costumes; some brought food—melons, eggs, and grapes. Others danced to balalaika music. They greeted the German invaders as liberators!

Away from the the Reichsführer SS for only a month, Peiper now earnestly wrote to Hedwig Potthast. Himmler's mistress was now four months pregnant and starting to show. It was now too awkward for her to remain with the Müller family at her flat at Bismarckstrasse 37C. Accordingly, she formally moved to the expansive villa at Caspar Theyss Str. 33.[14] That place in the well-to-do neighborhood of Grünewald had formerly been the home of Himmler's rune-mystic, Karl Maria Wiligut (he referred to himself as the incarnation of a Nordic god, Weisthor) before mental instability necessitated that he be forcibly retired from the SS in 1939. After Wiligut vacated, the location had been the discreet lovers' rendezvous point for their blossoming affair.[15] Now Caspar Theyss Strasse, the location of the love-nest, would be where Himmler's child would be born.

But what kind of relationship did Hedwig and Peiper have? Their relationship was *close*, but Peiper seems not to have known about the pregnancy yet. Was there a triangle? The normally reserved Prussian SS officer wrote longingly to "Little Bunny" on September 23, 1941. Peiper's prose was poetic, with the airy High German normally reserved for an intimate. "I always hoped you would send sometime short greetings into our desolate Steppe," he jotted from the Russian battlefield. "Unfortunately, you seem to have forgotten me totally. But, here, for me, it feels very different. Desire and the feeling of loyalty are growing in relation to the distance." *Desire?* Then the SS leader became serious in closing, almost as if to justify his departure: "I am happy to be permitted participation in this war that is so necessary for our people and for you to be taken care of at home. I am glad to have come out again to the fighting in the field which promises to be the last great campaign of our generation." If that sounded like a call to glory, Peiper also emoted a note of caution: "I am not a 'war junkie' looking for and desiring war." So why did he leave Himmler's services? Would he come back?[16] No, but he did have second thoughts.

Regardless of the the shadowy state of affairs, Peiper was officially transferred to the Leibstandarte Adolf Hitler by mid-October 1941. During the month an injury to the 11th Company commander gave Peiper the opportunity to resume leadership of his old unit. Under his command the infantry company fought at Mariupol and Rostov, with Peiper noted once more for an audacious fighting spirit. But there was a bloody cost: his company suffered terrible casualties in fighting along a rail line between Taganrog and Rostov. SS officers were shocked.[17]

Meanwhile the overall German advance along the front staggered and slowed. With the frustration, ugly noncombat actions erupted. Near the Black Sea the Leibstandarte killed a number of prisoners of war, as seen in the action at Greigova—a ruthless practice in which both sides increasingly engaged. And it was not only prisoners now but also the Jews. Jochen Peiper may not have directly observed what took place to the rear, but that he was aware of the killings is beyond question. Mobile killing team Einsatzkommando 10a made its headquarters in the port town of Taganrog on the Sea of Azov. And Taganrog, the birthplace of playwright Anton

Chekov, was where Peiper and the Leibstandarte wintered.[18] In fact, Peiper's division commander, Sepp Dietrich, ordered the Leibstandarte to assist Einsatzkommando 10a in the killings that would take place on the outskirts of the city. Einsatzkommando 10a was under Obersturmführer Heinz Otto Seetzen.[19] Peiper knew Seetzen as his old instructor when he was an SS officer candidate.

Indeed, the day after Peiper was formally installed to command, October 18, 1941, Himmler made his way to both the Leibstandarte and Einsatzkommando 10a headquarters in Taganrog near the Chekov High School. Stalin's forces had fled the city on October 22. Three days later, on October 25 and 26, 1941, SS Gen. Josef Dietrich, in charge of the Leibstandarte, offered to assist the SD by helping to seal off the town of Taganrog and deliver Jews. Almost two thousand Jews, gypsies, and Communists were collected on the Vladimirskaya Plaza. Afterward the victims were moved to the Petrushino Gully near the Beriev Aircraft Factory where, on October 29, the killing teams did the dirty work.[20] Seetzen informed laconically that "1,800 Jews were shot."[21] More killing actions took place on November 21, 1941, with Einsatzgruppe D reporting that the "commandos are proceeding via Taganrog, and Rostov. . . . The cities of Mariupol and Taganrog are free of Jews."[22] Peiper claimed he opposed such developments from the start:

> The Ukraine received us as liberators and waited to inherit their independence. The short-sighted setup of our civil administration created an enemy in our rear and also partisan fighting and in my opinion was a decisive error. It is my conception [*sic*: view] that the backbone of the Soviet Army was broken in the autumn of 1941. . . . Good treatment of the subjugated enemy would have started the mass desertion of the enemy. Instead, the contrary was done . . . and handed Stalin the slogan for a unifying national goal.[23]

With the advance stalled and the war now flung into uncertainty, the Russian weather changed from rain to snow on Peiper and his division as they dug dreary trench lines near the Black Sea at Taganrog. The Blitzkrieg stalled into a frozen remake of World War I. Living in a primitive frozen trench and without hot running water, Peiper sprouted a moustache.

Given that disappointing backdrop, it was clear that Peiper was elated at Himmler's decision to visit the Leibstandarte just before the Christmas holidays, so much so that he took the opportunity to send another letter to "Bunny" Potthast. Hedwig had sent Peiper some hundred-year-old Cognac and other very personal items. He was touched:

> 30 December 1941
>
> My Dear Little Sister:
>
> . . . If in the morning I shake the straw out of my head, I reach [into] the pocket and take out my comb with silver border. Do you still remember? It also will go this way in the future, when I shall reach into my breast pocket to feel the cognac still gurgling. . . .

All of us were naturally surprised on December 24 by the visit of the SS Reichsführer to the division. You can imagine my surprise, when I, unsuspecting, was called to the telephone and suddenly heard the familiar voice of K. H. Being together the next day not only was a change from my life in a hole, but beyond that a present that made me happy! (Please do not tell that to *anybody*!! [a euphemism for Himmler himself]) . . .

In other respects, time flies. The days are so short, that we spent most of our time in darkness. Things around me are full of activity: two men are sitting at the writing table, four are catching lice, and one is grinding coffee. The latter I must explain better. The preparation of this invigorating elixir is done in an old welding urn. Naturally, we do not have a coffee mill. So, the beans are wrapped into a relatively clean foot-wrapping rag, rolled and crushed with a hand grenade with a wooden handle.—After that, we serve it with a Stollen [Christmas fruit cake] sent by the Führer.

We have become wild mercenaries. We celebrate festivities as they occur, are rough and soft. Callous and sometimes a little sentimental. For you, my dear distant little sister, are all my heartfelt thoughts! Strength and health for the coming, fortune and fulfillment for the year 1942; those are my wishes! Don't forget me and write soon.

Always, your Jochen[24]

Mindful of his extended SS family, Himmler personally phoned Frau Sigurd Peiper the following morning in Berlin to extend secondhand wishes from her husband—likely leaving out the inglorious details of her husband's holidays in a frozen Russian trench. And on Friday, January 2, 1942, Himmler thoughtfully dispatched his personal secretary in Berlin, Erika Lorenz, to pay a special visit to "Mother Peiper."[25] Sigurd Peiper was pregnant again and due in late winter of the new year. All the while during those dark days at the end of 1941, Sigurd likely burned a bright yellow flame in the earthenware *Julleuchter* candle holder that had come specially delivered from the office of the Reichsführer SS on the occasion of the solstice.[26] In spite of hearts and Hagall runes under the candle, her husband still was not home. Sigurd was raising her baby daughter, Elke, alone in Berlin's increasingly uneasy west-side neighborhood.

1942

In Berlin the always anticipated New Year's celebration was muted. By that time the air raids on the capital city had become a weekly event, with everyone spending long fearful hours in air raid shelters. For Sigurd this was likely difficult due to her condition while taking care of daughter Elke, now a toddler. In the meantime Peiper's father had become ill in Panzerwerkstatt Litzmannstadt (Łódź), Poland. Soon he would be back in Berlin as a reserve officer in Wehrkreis III.

In the city, the wreckage of the bombs chipped away at Berlin's tidy reputation: the Reichstag was hit; not far from Sigurd, the Palace at Charlottenberg still showed damage. Even the Berlin Zoo and the American embassy were bombed. To be sure, spirited and efficient repair crews were ever active by day. And even though the Berlin street life seemed normal, there were troubling signs. Street signs themselves pointed out the nearest available air raid shelters. And Berlin's humiliated Jewish population, required to wear the Judenstern since the preceding September, were now disappearing. If the official ploy was to make these policies as inconspicuous as possible, almost no one in the city could fail to take notice as hundreds of Jews were marched down the city streets to the train stations at Grünewald or Anhalter Bahnhof. The trains were jammed with victims being shipped off to the Jewish ghetto in Łódź, Minsk, Warsaw, or Kaunas, Poland, or the concentration camp in Theresienstadt. Most would never return.[27]

In another bit of irony, German teenagers also vanished from Berlin's streets. In the fall of 1941 fifty-seven thousand adolescents were relocated from the train station to noncity locations. As Hitler had directed, the most important genetic stock of his future Reich would be removed to more rural areas so as to avoid the bombs: *Kinderlandverschickung*.[28] With those moves, Berlin was increasingly a city of elderly men and war-widowed women and children. Luckily, there was a long hiatus in the bombing of Berlin in 1942, when its citizens attempted to return to some form of normalcy.[29] Yet the war was always not far from word or thought.

On Berlin's west side, Sigurd Peiper and Hedwig Potthast watched over each other, checked on frequently by Erika Lorenz from Himmler's office. In the winter Jochen at last heard from Hedwig again. She had a surprising confession. Jochen knew that his wife was expecting his second child, but now he learned that "Bunny" was also carrying a baby from her extended affair with Heinrich Himmler.[30] Still, the inner ring remained intimate. As Himmler's former secretaries, she and Sigurd remained close as their SS men battled to the East. Both women were due to have children within weeks of each other, but the anticipation of the extended families were totally at odds.

Hedwig's family expressed profound disapproval for her decision to have the child out of wedlock. Since autumn, Hedwig's parents, Karl and Wilhemina, in Trier had totally broken off contact with their expecting daughter, shocked that she would carry on in a relationship "that is completely inappropriate to respectable norms."[31] Against all family advice, she would keep the child and continue as the devoted mistress to Heinrich Himmler. "I can't even describe to you the way things have been at home," her sister Thilde railed; indeed her father had a "nervous breakdown" and had been hospitalized in Trier.[32] Thilde held little back: "My wish is that during the birth of your child you'll feel some of the same hard pain your actions have caused our parents!" Even worse was news from her sister-in-law, Hilde Potthast, who had gotten a letter from brother Walter dated January 5, 1942. He had been badly wounded in bitter fighting in Russia on December 22. "Apparently, he was in an explosion with his small group. They had to retreat so quickly that he lost a great deal of his belongings. . . . He wrote that he has all sorts of things wrong; one certainly has to read between the lines there."[33]

Jochen Peiper was responding to a recent holiday missive he had received from Little Bunny. He took the news, still crouched in an icy Russian foxhole:

10 February 1942

Dear Häschen:

These days your detailed letter of 20 January arrived, with which you caused me a lot of pleasure! While we here stumble around in miserable stupidity, I often think about home and you too! . . . When you and Sigurd are together, there will be 300 pounds swaying along. And the Elke baby is growing from a baby into a small human child. And great events are about to happen and I cannot be there even once to make sure everything goes right. But knowing you and your vanity, I think you are quite pleased with that! Sigurd thinks that I shall receive leave at the earliest in fall. Should this happen, you will again have gone back to being 'girdle slim.' Then we shall push through the streets with our Kinderwagen caravan and let our three kids be admired!

But until then, a lot of water is going to flow under the bridge. During the last weeks we had a snow storm of until now unknown force! Now, it is raining since yesterday! On both sides of our ditches, snow is piled up 3 meters high! Now, all this will turn to water! . . . We all have a little bit of 'bunker tantrums.' We have been lying around here for already 2 ½ months! Now, three months of rain and mud weather are coming! But there is an end to everything! . . .

Always Your

Jochen[34]

Then, on February 15, 1942, Hedwig gave birth to Himmler's son, Helge. She had endured a difficult forceps delivery, traumatic for both baby and mother. And beyond that, Hedwig was deeply depressed. Amid family condemnation, her brother had at least maintained support for her decision to keep the child. But now due to his severe wounds, Walter's cascade of regular letters had suddenly stopped. Just days before she gave birth she had learned of Walter's fate: he had succumbed to his wounds.[35] Hedwig was nearly silent. After the birth of Helge, Himmler's long-anticipated son, Hedwig Potthast remained deeply hurt and withdrawn. Peiper, fighting in frozen Russia, knew nothing of it.

Finally, in March 1942 the Russian replay of World War I trench warfare was over, at least for Peiper and the Leibstandarte. Amid the icy boredom of Russia, there was both good and bad news from Berlin. On April 14, Peiper learned that his son Hinrich was born—a celebratory event. Yet less than one month later, a heavy letter arrived from Jochen's mother, Charlotte. His eldest brother, Hans-Hasso, had died in Berlin on May 11. Under treatment at a sanatorium, the official cause of death was tuberculosis. However, his father would later claim that his oldest son had been "a victim of war . . . sterilized by the Nazis according to a decision of the court and died a short time later. . . . " The sixty-two-year old father was relieved from his job at the tank repair facility in Poland and sent to a reserve hospital in Wilmersdorf. The reason: heart strain. Jochen Peiper was now the sole surviving son.[36] In spring the division moved from Russia to France, just west of Paris, for reorganization and as a hedge against an Allied invasion along the coast. Even so, France was almost casual—indeed, luxurious—as Peiper's battle command was expanded to a full battalion that would include armored halftracks, SPWs.

During the summer and autumn of 1942, amid the training and refitting with the new armored battle wagons, there was time for Jochen Peiper to get a dog and even to write to Häschen Potthast. He wanted to know: Why had he not heard back from writing the others in Himmler's close-knit office?

19 October 1942

Dear Häschen:

Heartfelt thanks for your letter of 15 September, which recently arrived here. I could not find an explanation for your silence and thought I had put my foot into my mouth somewhere. I have written to everyone (Erika [Lorenz], Kurt, Hermann Dörner, Grothmann, Sepp Kiermaier, Franz Lucas, Rudi Brandt) and none honored me with an answer. It does show that one has been away for over a year! Time flies! Imagine, in eight weeks it will be Christmas again. As you are never writing a word about yourself and Helge, I must obtain information about you via Sigurd. Apparently, you did not do so well during the recent days. I know absolutely nothing about your crown prince. Does he already have teeth, hair; can he already walk; does he have a sharp tongue?

All these things interest me, inasmuch as in our rough surrounding one needs some balance. For this reason, I bought a puppy. He is precious, a droll little guy of two months (Cocker Spaniel), who has conquered here the hearts of the girls in no time at all. . . .

Sometimes, I really cannot imagine that I am married and am supposed to have two children. Also, one cannot imagine that one day the war might be over! Fortunate are those who know their loved ones are cared for and under good protection in the homeland! Let us hope Tommie will spare Berlin. As you finally have servant girls, now everything in winter will be easier for you. I am always pleased to hear from Sigurd that you two have undertaken something together. Don't you want to go to the theater and to concerts together? It certainly should be possible to get the tickets! Don't forget me and you and your son are greeted heartily.

As always your,

Jochen[37]

1943

Peiper liked France, the entire thing: a restrained atmosphere, amid a flourishing cultural ambience and a clear national egotism. Good food, drink, art, and appreciation of it all. That may have struck his Prussian upbringing just right. Moreover, the French airs of unrestrained pride and aloofness were a good fit to his temperament, particularly since the German army had vanquished the Third Republic. Charlemagne's former kingdom was a place that was worthy of conquest.

There was free time in the autumn of 1942 as the Leibstandarte waited in case the Allies attempted an invasion. In France, not far from Paris, Peiper made himself friendly to the townspeople of Verneuil. Things got on well. In one gesture the SS officer invited a parish priest to his battalion officers' mess to share a meal.[38] The French reciprocated with goodies: fragrant baguettes and patisseries. And then there was Paris and its desirable trappings that Peiper and Rudi Lehmann sampled at length.

On December 12 the Musikkorps of the Leibstandarte put on a flamboyant musical event at the Trocadero in Paris, complete with a ninety-man chorus and orchestral music. Stodgy Germans? Sepp's Leibstandarte boys added a saxophone section—big band–style! To Peiper's clan, the crowd seemed to love it, even Strauss's Festival March. In the rousing close to the William Tell Overture, every piece of the orchestra played as loudly as they could—*Kultur* to the Parisians![39]

Yet the gaiety of France for Peiper did not extend to the war. With the cataclysmic capitulation of the Sixth Army at Stalingrad in Russia, Germany's war fortunes took a severe downward turn. After that calamity Peiper and the Leibstandarte moved back to the Eastern Front, where they were to help Hitler grasp the initiative for that great war once more. They loaded up on trains and chugged across Europe to the East.

Arriving back in Russia, campaigning conditions were abysmal. The weather showcased the frozen Russian winter: snow, ice, and blizzards.

Taking advantage of a winter interlude, Peiper took the opportunity to again write his "little sister," Hedwig Potthast. She now stayed at the SS estate at Brückenthin, Pomerania, with Oswald Pohl and his family near the SS main hospital at Hohenlychen. With the threat of bombs, Hedwig Potthast, like Sigurd Peiper, had moved out from Berlin. Hedwig's new refuge was eighty kilometers north of Berlin in the Brandenburg countryside not far from Hohenlynchen, an SS clinic that had been founded at the turn of the century as a tuberculosis sanatorium and converted to a main SS hospital compound. There Himmler's mistress and their son, Helge, stayed with Oswald and his second wife, Eleonore von Brüning, at their expansive Comthurey estate called Brückenthin.

A baron's estate, on the cold and bleak marshes and dunes in Mecklenburg, Brückenthin was financed "as if from a bottomless barrel."[40] At the time Potthast lived on the second floor of the Brückenthin Jägerhaus with her old friend and housekeeper, Frau Müller, and SA man Wilhelm Schmidt. More notorious, however, was her sponsor, Oswald Pohl, the slick and dogmatic inspector of the concentration camps. He lived there, as landlord of the SS manor.

As the business administrator of the concentration camp system, Pohl was indescribably rich, enjoying a cushy life at Comthurey. Meanwhile Pohl and his retinue, Potthast included, lived as if Prussian nobility. Not only was Hedwig a kept woman, but there were the other elements of the situation—secret rendezvous.

The Reichsführer SS came to visit on weekends when he was not in the East with Hitler. Typically Himmler arrived at Hedwig's quarters at the Brückenthiner Jägerhaus under cover and with careful subterfuge. Obsessed with propriety, Himmler always arrived in the train at Gut Comthurey in disguise, typically modestly attired as a Bavarian professor.[41] After he arrived, Himmler and his mistress would often take walks on the banks of the scenic Großer Gadowsees.[42]

If safe from the bombs, the lush place had a sinister lining. The women's concentration camp at Ravensbrück was not far away—the kept mistress had been installed at the epicenter of Himmler's expanding economic empire. The perfectly manicured yards, tree-lined lakes, and herb gardens were kept in perfect condition by more than 150 women prisoners who constantly toiled there from nearby Ravensbrück Concentration Camp. There, as Himmler's lover and mother of his son, Hedwig was a kept woman. An Estonian governess, Johanna Alber, helped take care of the house. They wanted for nothing.

From 1942 to 1943 Dr. Karl Gebhardt, Himmler's old school friend, was the head SS physician at Hohenlychen. There Gebhardt carried out fiendish medical experiments on Polish inmates from Ravensbrück to test antibiotics on gangrenous wounds.[43] Yet, at the nearby bucolic estate of Comthurey, none of these terrible secrets were evident.

Meanwhile, far away from Hedwig and Sigurd, in February and March of 1943, Jochen Peiper's command made a name for itself as the SS combat forces retook the Russian city of Kharkov. Peiper's command became famous for a daring, night-led attack on February 12 that rescued the 320th Infanterie Division, marooned deep behind enemy lines south of Smijew. Making contact, with sixty ambulances behind him, Peiper was shocked by the appearance of the frostbitten Germany infantry and was reminded of Napoleon's disastrous 1812 winter retreat from Berezina. Although getting little help from Genlt. Georg-Wilhelm Postel in charge of the 320th Division, Peiper escorted the frozen "parade of misery" back across the Udy River to safety on the 14th, culminating in a desperate, fiery battle with Soviet forces at Krasnaja Poljana. Upon entering the village, however, his troops made a terrible discovery. All the men in his small rearguard medical detachment, left in Krasnaja Poljana, had been killed and then brutally mutilated. An SS Sergeant in Peiper's ration supply company, Otto Sierk, claimed that Peiper responded in kind: "In the village, the two petrol trucks were burnt and twenty-five Germans killed by partisans and Russian soldiers. As a revenge, Peiper ordered the burning down of the whole village and the shooting of its inhabitants."[44]

The 1st SS Panzer Division was splashed all over German headlines and on optimistic radio broadcasts fervently followed by everyone in Berlin. Soon after the award, Hedwig sent Jochen Peiper congratulations on his latest battlefield commendation along a picture of her son, Helge, with herself and Himmler in the picture. Peiper responded,

> Command Post
> 24 March 1943
>
> Dear Little Sister:
>
> Thanks for the congratulation and above all for the charming little picture. Your demand to destroy it after having looked at it, is an imposition I must reject with indignation. Should unauthorized eyes look on the picture, I shall brag of Helge and proudly present him as my son, who as an exception, is permitted to sit on the arm of his godfather. You! The *kid* really is coming along well. I am a little envious and regret again and again that we have not yet

succeeded with a No. 3 child, inasmuch as out here in the combat environment one often pursues one's own thoughts.

Otherwise, everything is just fine. . . . We are aware that things could not get any worse and calmly look into the uncertain future. . . . We have become known beyond the borders of our division because of our successes and because of our persistence and enduring matter-of-factness. But even a bad reputation has its obligations—(I freely quote Zarah Leander) Our reputation precedes us as a wave of terror and is one of our best weapons. Even old Genghis Khan would gladly have hired us as assistants.

We are worrying about air raids where you are! The Tommie rather should drop more bombs around here and spare you. Thank god, nothing has yet happened. Continue to remain healthy and well and be assured that my thoughts are often at home. Bunny child don't forget me totally and accept greetings for all your loved ones.

Always,
Your Jochen[45]

Heinz von Westernhagen, fighting beside Peiper and leading the assault guns, also wrote home,

> What we left behind is appalling. A repetition of that is hardly possible. It could not get worse—you can't imagine. . . . If you were to come to Kharkov now, you would not recognize it. Hardly a house is left intact. Nobody is going to forget the street combat. . . . Nobody can describe what here happened during the winter fighting. Every single man deserves the Knights Cross. In Kharkov itself we drove to within 30 meters of fortified houses and fired directly into them with our panzer artillery. From above, the brothers bedeviled us with satchel charges on our heads. And after the dust from bricks and explosives had settled, these dogs continued to fire. From a distance of 100 meters we fired artillery into them and in places killed them with Cossack sabers.[46]

Even Peiper himself wrote, "I concede, that in those days the ideological war and propaganda brain washing had progressed so far, that neither a commissar nor an SS man counted on being captured."[47] Without question the veteran officers of the Leibstandarte knew of the killings going on behind the front lines.[48]

Amid the East Front heart of darkness the butchery escaped the confines of combat. After the war Obersturmführer Erich Rumpf described a horrifying incident in the village of Jefremowka during the fighting south of Kharkov in March 1943. Billeted in the snow-covered village, Rumpf heard a pistol shot at 10:30 a.m. in front of the house where he was staying.[49] He ran to the door and saw a scar-faced Hauptsturmführer, approximately thirty years old, standing there in a snow-camouflage outfit and a fur cap. The man angrily demanded that the company commander should be called there right away. Shortly Hauptsturmführer Nueske arrived on the scene to have the SS captain shout once more, "On the orders of [Kurt] Meyer, this town is to be leveled to the ground, because this morning armed civilians attacked this locality." At this he shot a "twenty-five-year-old woman who was busy cooking our lunch." Later Rumpf heard other shots and learned that the same man shot two other girls in the house nearby. Nueske stormed off, only to return thirty minutes later to confirm Meyer's orders. His soldiers, he railed, "had to act like wild men."[50]

According to Rumpf, the SS men killed all the village inhabitants, slaughtered all their cattle, and burned their homes to the ground.[51] Nothing was left. Not only were there Russian witnesses, but a separate testimony from captured SS Sturmbannführer Jakob Hanreich substantiates elements of the story:

> The reconnaissance battalion of the LSSAH made an advance at the end of February [1943] toward the East and reached the village of Jefremowka. There they were surrounded by Russian forces. Fuel and ammo ran out and they were supplied by air until they were ordered to try to breakthrough towards the West. Before trying to do so, the entire civilian population was shot and the village burnt to the ground. The reconnaissance battalion was at that time lead by Obersturmbannführer Kurt Meyer.[52]

If horrifying, any means of victory only reinforced SS resolve to pass out more medals. For his daring exploits in Russia, manifest in the reconquest of Kharkov, Jochen Peiper received the German Cross in Gold. News of the award arrived by radio from the Reichsführer himself. And unlike Himmler's typically emotionless homilies, this one gushed. Any hard feelings seemed forgotten:

> Heartfelt congratulations for the Knight's Cross my dear Jochen!
> I am proud of you! May your soldier's luck continue.
> Sigurd is doing well. Heartfelt congratulations from everybody.
> Heil Hitler![53]

After Peiper's recent award on May 6, 1943, the war's latest SS hero was given leave to go home. In any case, the advance in Russia slogged to a stop. The late winter sun warmed the Ukrainian countryside, and Peiper's detraining battalion of armored chariots, like everyone else in the German army, was stuck fast in mud. Every wheel, track, and boot that set onto an unpaved road marooned its owner in a gummy morass. Real movement was impossible. And that was the seasonal circumstance that played itself out each spring during the war in Russia. For the moment there was no fighting; indeed, there was barely any movement.

That June Peiper joined his expanding family, still in Berlin. For two weeks he was with Sigurd, two-year-old daughter, Elke, and baby son, Hinrich. Home life may have been awkward, if only because the kids hardly knew their wartime father. And to Sigurd, her husband presented an increasingly distant figure, gaunt and emaciated from a constant diet of cigarettes and coffee. Given her continued privileged status and access to Himmler's private stash of foods, Sigurd made an effort to feed her husband and build up his strength.[54]

Living conditions in Berlin remained civil enough—the bomber offensive had not resumed. Pushing baby Hinrich in a carriage, Sigurd could still see the fashions on display at the shops on the Kurfürstendamm or check the concert schedule at the Philharmonic, but outside the hall, Berlin's edges were fraying.[55] The final deportations of the city's remaining Jews was in full display in early summer, and the many carefully uniformed soldiers seen on the streets now included figures maimed on crutches or otherwise bandaged. In spite of the city's well-known *Ordnungsliebe*—passion for order without drama—a certain tension arose. Even the radio station Funk-Stunde Berlin, blaring from each street corner, restaurant, and café, now spoke of the war in increasingly hesitant tones. Bombastically prefaced by one of Liszt's Preludes, the exhaustive midday report of the Oberkommando der Wehrmacht now admitted "strategic withdrawals." And the scarcely concealed disaster of Stalingrad remained vivid. Secretly, many Berliners were listening to forbidden BBC broadcasts to get the story Deutschlandfunk didn't provide.

In spite of the brilliant victory at Kharkov that Peiper had helped lead, did Germany in 1943 already need a miracle to win the war? On the radio, rousing military tunes accompanied the many frontline reports, such as the lively Panzerlied or the equally popular *Panzer rollen in Afrika vor*—"Panzers roll in Africa." Yet the latter standard now disappeared from the airwaves since news came on May 13 that Rommel had been cast out of North Africa and the BBC was claiming that 150,000 Germans had been taken captive. Still, Jochen Peiper's favorite music featured the singing divas. He loved Zarah Leander, the throaty version of Greta Garbo. He knew most of the music by heart from her 1942 film, *Die große Liebe*. Indeed, many of the tall extras in the film were from the Leibstandarte and brought in from the Reich Chancellery![56] The number "*Ich weiss es wird einmal ein Wunder gescheh'n*"—"I know a miracle will happen"—was wildly popular throughout Berlin that summer:

> I know, one day a miracle will happen
> And a thousand fairy tales will come true
> No love can ever fade so soon
> When it is so great and wonderful.
> That's why a miracle will one day happen
> And one day we will meet again.

The veiled doubt of the lyrics seemed particularly poignant that spring, for Leander's own fashionable Grunewald flat in Berlin was demolished in air raids on March 1–3, 1943—big news in the papers. With that threat, the flame-haired diva of Hitler's cinema fled home to Sweden. Big bombs and incendiaries hit the famous city streets at the heart of Berlin—Unter den Linden, Wilhelmstrasse, and Friedrichstrasse. The elegant Prager Platz, scarcely four kilometers from the Jochen Peiper home in Wilmersdorf, was reduced to rubble. The largest tonnage of bombs yet dropped in the war—twice the weight of explosives unleashed in London during the height of the Blitz—had smashed Berlin. Five hundred civilians were killed, and even Göring's Air Ministry building was gutted. Smoky fires went on for days.

The air raid sirens in Berlin did not reassure. The British continued with nuisance aerial strikes, like the squadron of twin-engine Mosquito fast bombers that hit Berlin on April 20, 1943, Hitler's fifty-fourth birthday. They did little real damage outside of badly dinging any idea of German aerial infallibility. Worse, it seemed certain that the Allied bombing campaign would soon reach out to blast Hitler's power center. Indeed, on the night of May 29, 90 percent of Barmen-Wuppertal had been destroyed in an RAF raid. Weeks later the prescience of blazing Hamburg in July created a hushed fear in Berlin. Most believed the capital city would be next. There was a rumor that the real death toll in Hamburg was 150,000—it was actually only a quarter of that, but that was horrific enough. Every night air raid sirens wailed—mostly false alarms, but more and more evenings were spent in the cellar.[57] Then, at the end of July, Joseph Goebbels, the Reich propaganda minister and Gauleiter of Berlin, called for all women and children to leave town. Jochen and Sigurd agreed that she and the children should move right away to her sister-in-law's home in the Wartheland.

Far to the east, the war flared again with summer. By the time Peiper returned later to Russia at the end of June, the parched Ukrainian summer was in full heat. The Leibstandarte Adolf Hitler would fight in a titanic tank battle to regain the initiative in the East. Operation Zitadelle would become the largest tank battle of the war. Preceded by strong Luftwaffe close support, at 6 a.m. on July 8 the tank group, including Peiper's mounted grenadiers, attacked in the direction of the Panzer *Rollbahn*—assigned rolling road—toward the small rail town of Prochorowka. Supported by the tanks, Peiper's SPWs sped across the rolling grassy hills in a spread-out formation, sending plumes of dust skyward. His men seemed eager to challenge anything that would come forth. They didn't have to wait long.

Less than an hour passed before more than thirty Russian tanks assailed the panzer group, charging at them out of the north. T-34s were surging ahead everywhere, the dust was choking, and visibility went to zero. Peiper and the SS tankers swept into the tumult of jousting steel chariots at high noon. It was a tank battle fought at point-blank range in zero visibility, defying any plan.

There was no holding back Peiper. On they pushed into the yellow expanse. The further they punched along on the Teterewino to Prochorowka Road, the faster they rode. The tension was palpable. They were so far out ahead. "Faster, faster! Tempo! Tempo!" Peiper urged.

But in that short Russian moment, the tables turned. The enemy suddenly materialized out of the dust and shimmering heat. The lead armored vehicle was hit and spewed smoke. Within minutes it was clear that they were encircled—with more and more enemy flocking toward them to count coup. Would this be his Little Big Horn? Peiper, the press-celebrated magnificent SS warrior, was now encircled, with his men like Wild West cowboys fending off swarming Indians.

When this happened to George Armstrong Custer in another far-away hilltop grassland in another time, he had sent an immortal message to his subordinate, quickly scrawled on a tattered note and sent via galloping messenger: "Benteen, Come Quick!" For Joachim Peiper the modern messenger was the short-wave transmitter. When he told his old superior, Teddi Wisch, who was now in charge of the whole division, about his predicament, he laconically reeled off his position north of

Teterewino halfway to the golden prize of Prochorowka. What Peiper rattled off to the Leibstandarte headquarters is not recorded, but it may as well have been "Teddi, come quick!"

The Soviets were attacking with the entire 5th Guard Tanks Corps, immediately before Peiper came the 29th Tank Corps with 222 tanks.[58] Von Ribbentrop's panzer company had only seven battle-worthy Mk IVs, and the whole division had just sixty-seven tanks! The Russians, meanwhile, were firing with everything they had. Entire segments of the German line disappeared in an avalanche of explosions and smoke. SS Hauptsturmführer Siegfried Wandt, in charge of 13th Company, was badly wounded. Werner Wolff, Peiper's adjutant, quickly rallied the shaken men and organized a defensive front to engage the tanks and following Russian infantry.

A steel scythe of Russian tanks rushed forward so quickly that they ran right through Peiper's positions, suddenly coming upon an antitank ditch they themselves had created prior to the battle. They turned about, frenetically milling before the tank moat—shooting, firing, and clattering in the midst of Peiper's position. In a show of fool's courage, Wolff charged one of the T-34s with a half-track mounting only a puny 37mm gun. Wolff could not know that he had set upon the tank of the general leading the attack. He drew alongside, pumping rounds into the rear of the Russian T-34 until it halted. Wolff then boarded the tank, wrestled its emerging commander in hand-to-hand combat, and killed the Soviet general with his own dagger.[59]

Meanwhile the Russian tanks were headed right for Peiper's half-track. "Get ready!" he yelled to his men as he armed grenades. The Russian tanks were moving so fast that the usual tactic of slapping an antitank mine onto them was impossible. One armored beast slowed as it reached the Russian antitank ditch. Peiper sprang from the ditch, jumped atop the lumbering T-34, and threw open its turret hatch. He dropped two grenades inside and sprang from the tank to fall prone on the ground. There was a muffled explosion and a hollow metallic ring as the T-34 stopped. Another Russian tank clattered up behind the first. Peiper hurriedly shouldered a Karabiner 98k with rifle grenade. As he held the trigger, his blinking Knight's Cross shone out from his camouflage jacket, swinging a little as if moved slightly by nerves. The behemoth charged ahead as it reached the ditch across from him, only three meters away. Peiper loosed the grenade into the side of the lumbering tank near its weak point between the chassis and turret.

There was a loud explosion and fire, yet the tank was headed forward at such speed that it spun forward another twenty meters before shuddering, belching smoke, and stopping. The enemy attempting to charge outside the stricken beast were shot down, and in moments there was silence, broken only by crackling flames. Joachim Peiper grinned as he put down his weapons. Cheers erupted.

HIS TEETH WERE SHINING FROM HIS SUNBURNED AND POWDER-DARKENED face: "This should do for the close-combat badge, boys!"[60]

Chapter 8

FRONT AND FATHERLAND

PEIPER'S BRAGGADOCIO NOTWITHSTANDING, HE AND THE BATTERED LEIBSTANDARTE eventually escaped the inferno of the East Front in late summer 1943. Even with terrible Russian losses, there was no further German advance. The Soviets had stopped Hitler's final great attempt to win a decisive battle in that titanic struggle. Moreover, the Americans landed in Sicily, and the Italians teetered on the verge of capitulation. Hitler ordered the Leibstandarte to Italy to salvage the situation.

Meanwhile, Sigurd Peiper was now pregnant with her third child, having moved to Gut Staren in the Wartheland. On August 25, 1943, she wrote to her old friend in Himmler's office, Rudi Brandt, after having moved to the farmhouse of her sister-in-law, Vera Hinrichsen. In Gut Staren, word had already arrived about the bombing of Berlin two days before:

> I write to you to ask for a favor—I want to give my congratulations to our high chief, and his promotion to the head of the interior ministry. This big new promotion will bring a bright light too on you and your work. . . . Where did your wife and your boy evacuate to? . . . I am sitting here at the table writing you at night in the shine of the kerosene lamp. There is a phone, but is mostly dead. . . . I feel pretty good and the kids too. At the moment, I enjoy a lazy life with my children.[1]

Rudi Brandt wrote Sigurd back on August 28, 1943, with tardy birthday greetings to assure her that even with bombs and reverses, Himmler and the others were fine. "The tasks of our chief become even greater. The Reichsführer SS is very optimistic for this heavy work like he has done it every time before. . . . My wife and kids have had to leave Berlin to Schneidemühle. . . . During the last air attack on Berlin, I was here, but there was no damage to our bunker office."[2] On successive days the RAF struck Berlin in six to seven hundred aircraft bombing raids. Unlike the aerial assault preceding, the massive bombing attacks were immensely destructive.

Sigurd and the children needed to relocate for good. As before, being well connected had advantages. Peiper's former boss, Heinrich Himmler, had his highly publicized family idyll, Haus Lindenfycht, at Gemund on the shores of Lake Tegernsee in upper Bavaria. Why not locate there? Dotted by alpine lakes, it was safe and beautiful—a favorite haunt of kings and nobles. The place was nestled in the scenic valley surrounded by the towering Alps.[3]

Karl Wolff, Himmler's right-hand man in Italy, had also built a house on the Tegernsee and was raising his children there.[4] And in the same neighborhood lived Peiper's successor as adjutant to Himmler, Werner Grothmann. The mayor appropriately touted Tegernsee as "the first address in fine living," and devotion was certain: the town's main street had been renamed Adolf Hitlerstrasse. At the entrance to wartime Rottach-Egern was a telling proclamation: "This is a Jew-free village."[5] There Peiper's family would be far away from the bombs.[6]

So, with Himmler's assistance, Peiper moved his family to the two-story Gsotthaberhof Villa at 183 1/2 Wolfgrubstrasse in Rottach-Egern. By November 7, 1943, Sigurd and her children had completed the move, but the news was not all good.[7] From nearby Tegernsee, Himmler's own fourteen-year-old daughter, Gudrun, registered growing doubt in her diary. No longer did her idolized father bring brightly colored tulips and fruit from Holland:

> The fights are indescribably heavy. We were in the east before Stalingrad and now we are behind Kiev. . . . And the terrible terrorist raids from the air. Unfortunately, many Germans no longer believe in victory, but we must triumph. Pappi [father] is doing so much to contribute to our effort.[8]

What Gudrun Himmler did not know was that "Pappi's" contribution to the effort was methodically murdering Jews in Europe. In October 1943, in Posen, Poland, Himmler candidly addressed an assembled group of SS leaders:

> We can now talk very openly about this among ourselves, and yet we will never discuss this publically. . . . I am now referring to the evacuation of the Jews, to the extermination of the Jewish people. This is something that is easily said: "The Jewish people will be exterminated," says every Party member, "this is very obvious, it is in our program—elimination of the Jews, extermination, will do."

Several in the audience laughed nervously, and Himmler's voice was strangely nasal. But now the man peering from behind the round, rimmed glasses slowed his delivery to fish for words: "But of all those who talk this way, none had observed it, none had endured it." *What?*

> Most of you here know what it means when 100 corpses lie next to each other, when 500 lie there or when 1,000 are lined up. To have endured this and at the same time to have remained a decent person—with exceptions due to human weakness—had made us tough. This is an honor roll in our history, which has never been and will never be put in writing. . . . We have the moral right, we had the duty to our people to do it, to kill this people who would kill us.[9]

Himmler had long espoused a code of silence when it came to talk of dark matters. As if borrowing a page from the Sicilian mafia, he excluded stenographers from sensitive discussions. Yet this time, Himmler violated his own rule. A reel-to-reel recorder etched his words onto oversized red-oxide magnetic tape; he even arranged a sound check to make certain all was in order. For three long hours he spewed a litany of details of an officially sanctioned genocide.

He still believed the Germans would prevail in the conflict. That was nature's law, he said. Yet the real reason Himmler confessed all this was to cement devotion. The calamitous events of recent months suggested the need to improve the resolve within Himmler's SS. His generals needed to pursue this war without pity. In recounting terrible deeds, which the regime sanctioned, he, like Brutus, washed the hands of Caesar's lieutenants in a trail of blood.

Of this damning speech, Peiper may have known nothing right off. However, word of it spread like wildfire among high-ranking SS officers.[10] That night, Himmler's Posen audience indulged in a drunken revelry the likes of which was seldom seen in that staid organization. With such things disclosed, anesthetization seemed in order. The SS officers would be drawn into the *Blutkitt*—the blood cement—where all shared in the collective guilt if the war was not won. Peiper had long ago told those at Himmler's headquarters that SS men not wanting contact with such matters were best to move to the front. Still, Peiper maintained his relationship.

On each of his visits back, Himmler always seemed eager to keep Peiper in the loop of the deepening depths of SS depravity. In the summer of 1941 Peiper had summoned Rudolf Höss, who would become first commandant of the infamous concentration camp at Auschwitz, to the Reichsführer's office. Himmler gave him news: "The Führer has ordered that the Jewish question be solved once and for all and that we, the SS, are to implement that order."[11]

Returning to the front after one trip back to Germany, Peiper was remembered by SS Captain Otto Dinse as being unusually reserved and preoccupied. Finally, in one thoughtful moment, the SS leader confided to Dinse, "We had better win this war," Peiper warned, "or we will be in big trouble because of these things."[12] Otto Dinse knew the same. From 1940–1941 he had worked in Łódź, Poland, for the RuSHA at the *Umwandererzentrale*—the Central Migration Office—to arrange the "immigration" of Poles and Jews from the Warthegau.[13] Most would never return.

Yet now, with the failure of the Kursk offensive, Peiper and his battalion left to help disarm the collapse of their Italian ally—"just like the last war," as Peiper was fond of saying.[14] The division spent five days descending latitudes through southern Tyrol amid a spectacular mountain backdrop as they headed for Northern Italy. As Peiper's column geared through the mountainous countryside, they were greeted by enthusiastic Austrians.[15]

But the civilian response that September in their destination in the Piedmont region of Northern Italy near Torino was something else again. Arriving, Peiper's battalion disarmed Italians in the Cuneo region. Then, in a supposed "anti-partisan action" Peiper's half-track battalion was accused of an atrocity in the nearby small picturesque village of Boves. There, on September 19, 1943, his command set fire to numerous homes in the town, and thirty-three civilian inhabitants died from their actions, including the village priest.[16] Moreover, evidence suggested that Peiper's battalion was also involved in helping Himmler's security service to round up and deport Jewish refugees in the same area.[17] Peiper protested that Boves had been "not a massacre, but a battle."[18]

In any case, Peiper and his men did not remain long in Italy after the mess at the tiny town named for the bulls.[19] Just into October the battalion was sent from Cuneo to Alessandria, where training resumed. Unofficially the men of the division were still on an undeclared vacation: enjoying ice cream, pasta, the warm temperatures, and local spirits. Peiper himself drove Italian sports cars and even managed flying lessons!

If ever there had been worries about any combat in Italy, that had long since faded. On October 22 the Leibstandarte was officially designated a Panzer Division.[20] Could Peiper, the horseman-driving-halftracks, find a way to lead the tanks? He now had the close-combat badge in silver as well as the Tank Destruction Badge for his death-defying adventures at Kursk. He took the opportunity to catch up on correspondence with "Bunny" Potthast:

> 17 October 1943
>
> My dear Häschen:
>
> It is Sunday, once again! I sit in my robber-baron castle, look through the bull's-eye panes into the gray October sky, and think very dearly of you. Your last letter made me very happy, because I read in it that I had not been totally forgotten.
>
> Time flies! Your little Helge by now runs babbling behind his Mami. I cannot yet imagine it—just like Hinrich! Why don't you send me a more recent photo? I am immensely happy about the increase of our family being underway and grateful. Let us hope that everything will turn out well!
>
> While you at home are struggling with the present-day shortages, I am here leading the lazy life of a master. Thinking about the severely struggling comrades on the Eastern Front, one sometimes feels really bad. My most beautiful leisure-time activity is flying. I had a captured pilot instruct me for five days. Now I have already thirty glorious solo flights behind me. Besides, I am part-time owner of a wonderful horse and a racing car. Somehow, one must be able to keep your head for the long run.
>
> Despite that, I am wondering if one ever will get used to living in orderly circumstances? Occasionally, certain doubts arise! Above all, when one observes the moral conduct of comrades in high places. I am getting gray and old and am beginning to muse!
>
> I constantly think of the time, during which I was permitted to be with him! [Himmler] The longer the distance in time, the more one notices how much one absorbed knowledge that is giving direction for the entire life. Also in this respect, insight arrives, as one grows older! I am very happy about Sigurd's new alternative quarters. Too bad, that you have now rowed physically so far from each other. I always imagined it to be so beautiful for you to be together. What will become of us, nobody knows. Nothing is harder to endure than a series of good days. I think we are going to celebrate Christmas again in our second heaven.

Now, for today, deeply heartfelt greetings for you. This letter, please, is just for you! Wishing for you and for your two men all the best and beautiful, I am always

Your faithful Jochen[21]

Peiper's family had left just in time. The Berlin he had known as a youth was totally razed. That autumn, Arthur Harris, the commander in chief of Britain's RAF bomber fleet, vowed, "We can wreck Berlin from end to end. It will cost us 400 to 500 aircraft. It will cost Germany the war."[22] That month nearly four thousand Berliners were killed and half a million left homeless. Still, ideas of crushing Germans into submission under bombs failed and instead seemed to harden resolve.

With the approach of winter, the Leibstandarte left Italy. Rumors solidified with a delivery of winter clothing—a sure sign of an East Front destination. By November they were back to their "second heaven." But their arrival was a winter nightmare. Their halftracks and tanks unloaded off the trains into a blinding snowstorm near Zhitomir, made deadly by a Russian attack that threatened to envelop the railhead. Only with desperate fighting did Peiper and the others shake the trap. Later that month, when the long-term regimental commander of the panzer regiment was killed by a stray Russian shell, Peiper was designated to replace him. Yet Peiper had no experience leading tanks. Almost immediately he sought to transform the panzer regiment into an armored version of the heavy cavalry he loved. That winter, if Peiper could get fuel and ammunition, the panzer group was off on another slashing adventure, even if his new style of swashbuckling tank warfare was costly to man and machine.

For every mad tank–led dash there was another frozen hill or depression concealing another thicket of Russian antitank guns—a *Pakfront*. More and more tanks were shot up. In early battles Peiper had roared off on December 5 with sixty-six tanks, but four days later there were just four Tigers and only sixteen other Mk IVs or Panthers. "If we don't get new tanks up to the front in a hurry," Peiper worried over the radio, "the Russians are going to light a fire under our ass."[23]

Peiper's earlier superior, Albert Frey, in charge of 1st SS Panzer-Grenadier-Regiment, became critical of such foolhardy tank-led cavalry rides. The two faced off in a loud quarrel over who was in charge when tanks fought with the grenadiers. Everyone heard it. Peiper said he was in charge, but Frey said no, he outranked him. His grenadiers did not have steel protection, and Peiper's bold methods were too risky.[24] "Peiper burns up his men," Frey concluded with intended irony.[25] Yet Hans Siptrott, the hard-nosed NCO who had been on the sharp end of Peiper's hell-for-leather use of tanks, saw it differently. "I didn't realize he burned us down," he said years later. "Peiper was a *Draufgänger*—a go-getter—and led his regiment that way."[26]

By the dark days of the solstice, Peiper had few tanks left to command and indulged in a bit of nostalgia for his old life back in the comfort as Himmler's adjutant. How would he ever survive the fighting out here? He wrote again to Hedwig Potthast:

Regimental Command Post, 15 December 1943

Dear Little Sister!

Even though I am a little disappointed that I do not hear anything from you and that my last letter remained unanswered, I do not want to miss wishing you and your Helge everything good and beautiful from my heart for the coming Julfest.

During these very difficult times, it is a beautiful and calming feeling, to know that you all are safely in a warm nest. When on the 24th you will be standing happily and contentedly under the Christmas tree with your loved ones, and your crown prince cheerfully will put his little arms around your neck, and when you will be listening a little into yourself, you will notice good wishes and greetings drifting from afar. They should tell you that I am remaining the same old one in faithful friendship and affection, that is

Your Jochen[27]

In the dark days of December 1943, Peiper's regiment fought recklessly. Peiper led crazy night actions by attacking the rear of enemy lines; he captured four division headquarters. Still, his aggressiveness and lack of experience handling tanks caused some resentment.[28] By now hardly any quarter was granted in the East: on December 5 and 6, 1943, his tank regiment reported killing 2,280 Russian "enemies" and took only three prisoners.[29] During that heavy fighting the village of Pekartschina, north of Zhitomir, Peiper attacked "with all weapons and flame-throwers from his SPWs." The village was burned to the ground and "completely destroyed." The next day it continued.

At dawn on December 6 Peiper found himself before Andrejew, but he was faced with a bevy of antitank guns.[30] Undeterred, he bolted east with a clutch of Tiger tanks, his armored group smashing several artillery batteries, and by 10 a.m. he took the high ground on both sides of Styrty. Peiper's armored column moved so rapidly toward Kortschiwka that it took the 121st Rifle Division totally by surprise, destroying its headquarters and inheriting a "battlefield covered with many dead."[31] Tiger ace Michael Wittmann smashed three more T-34s that rose to challenge Peiper's approach, who then paused to take on supplies.

Divisional headquarters had other ideas. By radio the divisional adjutant, SS Maj. Rudolf Lehmann, encouraged Peiper to continue the advance. To Lehmann's dismay, however, he discovered that his radio-equipped tank didn't have Peiper's call signal. Knowing Peiper well, he broadcast clearly over the air without code. "Jochen, this is Rudi, come in please."[32] Peiper answered but was unresponsive.

"What are you doing?" Lehmann asked.

"We are frying potatoes!" Peiper sardonically responded.

Lehmann chaffed: "Are you stopping because you are tired?"

"Kiss my ass!" Peiper replied. "I am attacking, over and out."[33]

Within twenty minutes his tanks and halftracks were on the move again, firing madly at whatever came into view. The headquarters of the 322nd and 148th Rifle Divisions were run down and the Russians thrown into a panic. At 2:30 p.m. Peiper seized Tortschin and its nearby railway line. At nightfall Rudi Lehmann showed up to brief Peiper in the village. Peiper's forces were still clearing the enemy from houses now being put to the torch, and the crackle of gunfire and flames was the sonic backdrop for their winter discussion. Only at night in Kortschiwka, with the gas tanks dry, did Peiper finally stop—after a thrust of thirty kilometers behind enemy lines. The recorded additional destruction was tremendous: twenty-two artillery pieces, seventy-six antitank guns, forty vehicles, seventy-one horse-drawn wagons, and a total of 1,450 killed. There was no mention of prisoners.[34] "Where we were standing was Germany," he later wrote, "and as far as my tank gun reached was my kingdom!"[35]

Two weeks later Peiper still relished his success, even if homesick. "Far in the east, in my armored car," he wrote home, "I was allowed to keep watch for Germany on December 24,"[36] The *Schützenpanzerwagen*—armored halftracks—were now replaced by tanks. "Light a candle, roast a fir twig," he wrote his family, "and then shut the eyes to wander . . . to a Christmas tree, the inner light of which nobody can take from you!"

1944

Within a month of rejoining the desperate battle in Russia, Jochen Peiper was as spent as his tanks. On January 20, 1944, Peiper was ordered from the front to Hitler's Wolfsschanze headquarters in East Prussia. Four days later, Peiper paid a visit to Himmler's nearby Hochwald headquarters to catch up his former superior on events but was shocked by his diminished appearance. Even so, on January 27, with Peiper looking gaunt, pasty, and ailing, a smiling Hitler presented him with the Oak Leaves to the Knight's Cross at his headquarters.

Days later, on his twenty-ninth birthday, Peiper was promoted to *Obersturmbannführer*—SS Lt. Colonel. Regardless of accolades, Peiper was physically and mentally exhausted—a wreck—and after a medical examination at Dachau on February 11 and 12, he was sent home on medical leave.

Back in Tegernsee, Peiper visited his new address as the anointed SS war hero. He had earned the vaunted Oak Leaves. And his family had a new addition: his daughter Silke was born on March 7. Even if most of his tanks were lost, he was Himmler's favored warrior.

Later that spring the rest of his division followed, moving from near destruction in Russia to recover and refit in Belgium. His bodily condition was equally bad. At the end of March his doctor in Berlin declared him "unfit for duty," although releasing him days later.[37]

On April 2, 1944, the Leibstandarte Adolf Hitler, with Sepp Dietrich and Joachim Peiper in attendance, met Belgian SS leader Leon Degrelle and the Légion Wallonie at the Grand Place of Charleroi. There, military decorations were passed out and a borrowed Leibstandarte motorized column seventeen kilometers long traveled on toward Brussels in the bright afternoon sunshine. A large crowd of onlookers gathered to witness the parade of Hitler's Belgian propaganda pantheon.[38] Degrelle, the Ardennes native of Bouillon, was completely intoxicated by National Socialism, his arm outstretched in a Hitler salute while children rode atop his flower-draped half-track.

From Charleroi, Peiper moved on to meet his ragtag command. Slowly, from April to June 1944, they were built back up once more, although there was not a single surviving tank in the division! On April 17, 1944, Peiper met his wife in Hasselt with a bouquet of flowers charged to Himmler's office.[39] She and Jochen were together in Kiewit, Belgium, as the Leibstandarte trained once more, although Peiper worried about the quality of many of his replacements.

In early May some of the new troops got into serious trouble. Four young soldiers broke into a local farmhouse and stole chickens and a bicycle. Within the Waffen SS, theft was one of those egregious crimes, like treason, for which there was little tolerance. Indeed, there was record of a Hitlerjugend Waffen SS man who was sent to Dachau Concentration Camp for simply listening to a single Allied radio broadcast![40]

Formal court martial proceedings took place in a grassy meadow in front of the assembled panzer regiment on May 28, 1944. Peiper, Herbert Kuhlmann, and Werner Poetschke, with the tank regiment, presided before the divisional judge, SS Stubf. Markus Jochum. All four "looters" were found guilty and summarily shot before the assembled regiment. The real reason for the shooting likely had little to do with stealing chickens and everything to do with obedience in the rag-tag replacements.

Arndt Fischer, then in charge of a platoon in the 3rd Panzer Company, was mortified. He had been training these greenhorns. "We could barely stand it," he recalled. "Our operations were already suicide affairs. You could have at least given these young rascals a chance to redeem themselves in one of them!"[41] Who exactly gave the order for the execution is uncertain, but after the war the Chief Prosecutor's Office of Bavaria sought to question Jochen Peiper regarding the incident.[42] Peiper later admitted, "I was present during the shootings. There was a regular trial of the field court of the division. The men belonged to the SS Division Hitlerjugend as replacements for the SS. These people were fully trained, but sent away from their former unit. So, this was not the best *Menschenmaterial*."[43] *Human material?* Peiper approved:

> I can remember from the West, before the invasion, I had an incident in my regiment, where five young men were shot, who plundered and committed other things. Afterwards, nobody was more upset about them having been executed than Sepp Dietrich. I admit, we thought it to have been totally correct.[44]

Regardless of such controversy within the panzer regiment, it became clear that the re-forming Leibstandarte would fight the Americans and British, who threatened to smash Hitler's Atlantic Wall and liberate France.

That event happened on June 6, 1944—D-Day. As before, Hitler's battlefield micromanagement hurt any effective response. He had forbidden the panzer troops to be moved without his express permission. But given Hitler's odd hours—he did not go to bed until 3 a.m.—he was still sleeping the following morning, with no one willing to rouse him.[45] When Hitler was awakened he seemed strangely jubilant. "So this is it!" he proclaimed, pointing to the map. The German leader seemed pleased and even chuckled, careful to remind his audience that the invasion site was precisely where he thought it would come.

Hitler hastily drafted a fanciful order: "the enemy is to be annihilated at the bridgehead by evening of June 6."[46] Himmler, who was also present, seemed pleased too, even smiling. Martin Bormann had helped him obtain the funds to buy Hedwig a new and spacious abode at the foot of the Salzburg in Schönau am Königssee near Berchtesgaden.[47] Their two-story tiled-roof abode, *Haus Schneewinkellehen*, was something of a famous place. Nestled at the end of a private road at the edge of a luxuriant forest at the end of the Sportplatz in Schönau, it had been the home of composer Max Reger in 1912 and later the summer guest quarters for Sigmund Freud in 1929.[48] But in the summer of 1944 just after the Allied invasion of France, Himmler was happy. His mistress Hedwig Potthast, had just given birth to their second child, a girl named Nanette Dorothea, and his second family would be living in the new place.[49]

But, attempting to focus on things military, Himmler leaned forward to assure Hitler that his SS divisions were now headed to the danger zone. They would cut the Allies to ribbons.

Those plans came to nothing. By July 21 Peiper and his tanks were pulled into the fight to hold the Canadians near the beaches west of the town of Tilly. On that day, after a three-hour artillery pounding, the Canadian 3rd Division, supported by ten tanks, began to roll up German lines into the village. After breaking through the German infantry line, the Canadians surged into the village. Although the Panthers were up to their tracks in the rubble, when the enemy attempted to circle around to the southeast, one of Peiper's favored subordinates, Werner Wolff, pulled his tank out from cover and began to fire, exhorting his men to throw back the enemy. The Nova Scotia Highlanders reported heavy losses from an enemy who "shouted and threw grenades like wild men."[50] House-to-house fighting ended when the Canadians pulled back after losing nine tanks. Wolff and his men grimly held on.[51]

While the 7th Panzer Company dug in their tanks around Tilly, Jochen Peiper attempted to coordinate his armored counterattack from his first-floor headquarters in the castle at Garcelles. SS Untersturmführer Rolf Reiser, from the Panther battalion headquarters, was sent to the nearby command post of Obersturmbannführer Max Wünsche of the 12th SS Panzer Division to help coordinate operations. The artillery fire on the surrounding area was so dense that telephone lines were constantly being shot out. Radio communication was out of the question. Their clever enemy rapidly triangulated transmissions, with an avalanche of shells to follow. So old-fashioned messengers became the preferred method of communication. Reiser was returning to Peiper with news from the other tank leaders, Panzermeyer and Wünsche, when all hell broke loose. There was a droning sound overhead, and everyone craned their necks to look up the castle walls to the French sky. The air above suddenly glistened with what looked to be silver minnows in a blue stream. But the minnows were big Allied bombers high up. Pepper-like particles descended. Seconds later, orange flashes began to blast the road into dust.

Peiper and Reiser had their Panther tanks parked just outside the castle. The shell bursts thundered closer. "Under the tanks!" someone called. Without hesitation the men threw themselves out of a lower window in the castle and then crawled on hands and knees under the massive tanks. The bombs roared outside, and windows splintered and crashed. The ground shook horribly. Reiser instinctively pulled his hands over his ears and held his head close to Peiper. There was a momentary halt in the bomb bursts, and then they started again. Peiper looked at Reiser as both huddled under the tank, shouting above the noise. "I think they're trying to finish us off here," he said. After another burst faded, Peiper looked up once more. "Herr Reiser," he said, "I think we're going to win this war just like the last one!"[52] Not long after, Peiper was evacuated due to shell concussion. He was done in Normandy.

By mid-August the rest of the division, like Peiper, had been vanquished with the rest of the German army, in an attempt to turn back the invasion. Barely escaping the Falaise Pocket, the shattered rabble of the once-proud Leibstandarte Adolf Hitler was sent into headlong retreat to the border. Peiper himself was treated not only for concussion but also hepatitis and nervous exhaustion. He went back to a hospital near his home in Tegernsee to recuperate.

That autumn, as the supply-starved American forces stalled on the German border, Adolf Hitler schemed to reclaim the initiative.[53] He would attack one final time, hurling his best tank forces at the Americans in the sparsely defended Ardennes. For the huge offensive he would need to advance at lightning speed and mostly under cover of night or clouds. Even if still recuperating, Peiper was called back once more to lead the spearhead of the attack from the rebuilt 1st SS Panzer Division. He would be Hitler's favored warrior in the attack.

When SS Ustuf. Kurt Kramm arrived to take over responsibilities as an adjutant of the 1st Battalion of the panzer regiment that autumn near Rhaden, he came under the spell of its commander. Kramm found Joachim Peiper a charismatic panzer leader with "very blue eyes," starkly contrasting with his black panzer uniform. "He is just like Hitler," Kramm remembered, "for when he stands in front of you, he has so much fire and pep he gets you."[54]

Even if his men were pleased, Sigurd Peiper remained unhappy with her husband's return to a fighting command. She had been shaken at his appearance in September. Although her secretarial chum, Hedwig Potthast, had moved to the Obersalzberg that September, perhaps the SS Reichsführer's special *Geliebte*—lover—could pull some strings.[55] Could Jochen return to a desk job?

Rottach, 15 November 1944

Dear Häschen:

How I would like to telephone to you, to tell you that I had a high and dear visitor. But for eight days by now, the telephone has been out—electricity just has come back on yesterday. So I want to write to you quickly. I just had come back from a walk with my half-frozen children and still busy undressing them, when I heard a man's steps in the staircase. You can imagine my surprise, when I saw K. H. [König Heinrich—Himmler] in front of me. The children were immediately captivated by the chocolate bar he had brought, especially our always-hungry Hini. Elke examined the visitor very critically—in this respect, she is exactly like Jochen. I was really impressed by the visit and enjoyed it terribly. Too bad, that Jochen went his own way and left K. H.

Jochen will forever regret it. You know, how he loves K. H., appreciates him, and honors him. He has not seen him [K H] since January. I am again worrying about my Jochen, but that is what the failure carries with it. When Jochen took his leave from K H in July 1941, he must have said something like: "In three years I am going to get you back to me." Deep inside, Jochen seems to have counted on that. He indicated it variously at times, even though he is trying to dismiss it because of developments over time. . . . I only shall be relaxed and happy, when I shall have him healthily with me. . . .

Naturally, I did not tell that to K. H. and I beg you to understand that correctly, when I am writing it to you. It is so dumb that one does not have a soul around here with whom one can have a good conversation. If one sits here alone, day in day out, slowly the most horrible nightmares pop up. Just never let Jochen know that I have written you about that. . . .

With many loving greetings,
I am your Sigurd[56]

But the mood was hardly cheery for Hedwig, the letter's recipient. She was visiting once more her Brückenthin hideaway in Mecklenberg. There, soon after Sigurd wrote, Häschen met with Himmler. The atmosphere was grim. The occasion was a dinner with the boss of the SS economic head office, Oswald Pohl, and his wife, Eleonore, at the country estate. To Pohl's wife, Himmler seemed dejected, even maudlin. "The war," he announced wearily at the table, "must be counted as lost."[57] Oswald Pohl was shocked, but Hedwig Potthast nodded.

There was no talk of peace. What would happen at the all-female Ravensbrück Concentration Camp close by Gut Comthurey? None of the dreadful details were mentioned. Over the preceding five years 130,000 women and girls had passed through its gates and only one in three would survive.[58] And the annihilation of the Jews in Poland and their localized enslavement made any Allied concessions more than unlikely—Himmler's mistress boldly said so in her lover's presence. Himmler discussed how the upper-crust Nazi families might somehow escape.

He then waxed nostalgic about how *idyllisch* it might be to spend the December holidays at Achensee in the Tyrolean Alps. Nevertheless, such would not come to be—he had been promised a military command from Hitler. And the war ground on. Hedwig returned back to her new estate near Berchtesgaden.

Back at the alpine idyll of Rottach-Egern, Sigurd Peiper continued to worry about husband Jochen, again writing Hedwig, apologizing at the same time for attempting to intercede on Jochen's behalf.

Rottach, 11 December 1944

My Dear Häschen:

I did not have time until today to thank you heartily for your letter of November 25. . . .

Häschen, I already regret to have written at all. You must not think that I bared my heart to you, in order for you to talk with K. H. [Himmler] about that. It is not in me to want to do 'career adjustments' for my husband. . . . I must concur with the considerations of K. H. Jochen in a staff position would be intolerable in the end. There really is no work there, because his talents are really in the military leadership area. During my visits with Jochen, I observed repeatedly, how his men and officers love him, how he influences them, inspires, and electrifies them and how immensely Jochen enjoys them.

You know my Jochen's mission: guide young people and turn them into leaders. But only very few know, what it means to live through three years of such intensive front-line duty. When the comrades get together at night to relax, then Jochen sits and reads, books not of military matters in order not to become one-sided in his judgment and knowledge. I really admire his endurance and ambition, but I hope you will understand that I am worried about him. Because I know how worn out he is and it would really be high time to get an area of work where he could also consider his health, because his experience and skills will no longer be of use to anybody if he takes a bullet.

He is totally at the end of his nerves and no longer up to the demands of the front. The physician treating Jochen here has put a particular fear into me. He said, that people, who participate so intensively in everything and who store up within themselves all of it, are subject to an especially heavy load on their nervous system. One could compare it with a wire that can take a certain load under too much pressure will break. And that would have unimaginable consequences, which do not always manifest themselves in jaundice.

But things will happen as they should and we cannot change anything anyway. . . . Häschen, one is always egotistical and so am I in this respect: I worry about my happiness and I am afraid that one day there will be a terrible bang. But enough of that. Let us continue to have faith in our lucky star.

To you and your children many loving and heartfelt greetings.

I am Your Sigurd[59]

In the Great Ardennes Offensive Jochen Peiper had assumed a critical role to lead the assault for the 6th Panzer Army and had punched a dangerous hole in the Allied line and advanced ruthlessly, only to be surrounded, out of fuel, before the Meuse River. But during the advance, in the Ardennes, his command and that of Gustav Knittel had the dubious distinction of having shot dozens of civilians near Stavelot and executing captured American soldiers along the way.[60]

Most infamous of all was the action near the Belgian town of Malmédy, where eighty-four Americans were shot and killed after being taken prisoner. When Jochen Peiper learned of the disturbing complexion of the event on December 18, 1944, in La Gleize, it was described by Heinz von Westernhagen, in charge of the Tiger tanks, as a *Durcheinander*—a mix-up, a muddle, a confusion.[61] The incident was a blot within the expected brutality of modern war, a reversion to Russia.

Yet if the SS leader wasn't aware of the questionable nature of what transpired at the crossroads, how could one explain Wilhelm Mohnke's glowing official record of the incident? His division commander recorded the event on December 26 after Peiper had first come into his CP in Wanne, Belgium. Peiper had just escaped his furthest point of advance, at which he had been encircled and nearly captured. Even so, Peiper had lost every single tank that went with him. Still, his divisional commander enthusiastically recommended the SS Lt. Col. for commendation. Mohnke's composition at his division headquarters the day after Christmas spoke in admiring tones of Peiper's actions on December 17:

> Without regard for threats from the flanks, and only inspired by the thought of a deep breakthrough the Kampfgruppe proceeded via Möderscheid-Schoppen-Faymonville to Ligneuville and destroyed at Baugnez an enemy supply column and after annihilation of the units blocking their advance, succeeded in causing the staff of the 49th Anti-Aircraft Brigade to flee.[62]

As Baugnez was specifically named, there could be little doubt that the incident referred to in the report is what would become known as the Malmédy Massacre.[63] And by his own admission, Peiper had learned of the incident a day after it occurred and a week before Mohnke formulated his description. Why would such an incident—a smudge—be singled out for a decoration? Translation of the ambiguous German term used for annihilation—*Vernichtung*—provides one clue. Generally, within the National Socialist lexicon, vernichtung enjoined the killing of an enemy. After all, the concentration camps at which Jews were being liquidated were referred to as *Vernichtungslager*—elimination camps.

It seems likely that after years of savage ideological war on the Eastern Front, men under Peiper's command had come to admire such harshness. Certainly that is the way Himmler would have seen it. Rather than a stain on one's record, such an event was an accolade. As a convalescing Peiper witnessed the final winter battles around Bastogne, the recommendation for his promotion was speedily forwarded on to Hitler's headquarters.

Peiper's partner with the heavy tanks, Heinz von Westernhagen, was also exhausted. When he wrote home on Friday, December 29, he emoted pride and catharsis:

> Dear Mother!
>
> Christmas is over and we have some difficult days behind us. Right now we're resting for a few days, sleeping off the Christmas stress, while we care for our frostbitten limbs and gear up for new deeds.
>
> This time we were always in the thickest mess. We were at the point of the attack, and on the first day were already able to break through the American positions and push far behind their lines. It was a wild hunt with a great amount of shooting—but finally we were cut off and surrounded. For five days we sat without rations and with little ammunition while, like a mouse in a trap, we were smashed by American artillery.
>
> Early on 24 December we agreed to break out—it succeeded. For thirty hours we marched behind the American lines, breaking out on Christmas Eve around midnight from behind their positions. Then we swam a raging stream with a ripping current under MG fire, making it across only by summoning up

all our strength. Still, some brave soldiers died, either because their strength was no longer sufficient or their hearts failed. I dragged a wounded man along with me. And in the morning hours of the first day of Christmas we arrived back again in our lines, looking like walking icicles.

We thumbed our nose at the Americans and got the German Army 850 soldiers back. That is our pride. Now we prepare for new action. . . . I don't have any more time, and must go take care of my wild soldiers. To you I send heartfelt greetings and health in the New Year. I am convinced that this will be the last year of the war. I greet you.

—Your son, Heinz[64]

After walking for thirty hours behind American lines and swimming the Salm River, on Christmas Day, 1944, Jochen Peiper and the exhausted survivors of his command stumbled into the castle in Wanne looking "like walking icicles." Ralf Tiemann, the operations officer was there; it was 3 a.m. To Tiemann, the survivors of Peiper's battle group looked terrible—dirty and unshaven, totally whipped. At the aid station, Dr. Kurt Sickel bandaged Peiper's right hand, which had been wounded in the escape.

The SS Lt. Col. was visibly upset. "We left with 3,000 men from Germany and now we have 717," he said hoarsely, motioning with the back with his hand. "You can find the others the whole way along our path."[65]

Peiper threw back a cognac, complaining he had not slept in days. He fell into a deep slumber.

Part Three
FALL

"I have touched the highest point of all my greatness;
And from that full meridian of my glory,
I haste now to my setting; I shall fall
Like a bright exhalation in the evening,
And no man shall see me more."

—Shakespeare, *Henry VIII*, Act II

Chapter 9

OBLIVION

The new year of 1945 saw the racial war of mutual annihilation in the East reach a terrible climax. At Hitler's personal order, the Leibstandarte and Kampfgruppe Peiper shuttled to the East for a desperate attack to liberate the Hungarian oil fields.

As the Soviets gutted, raped, and pillaged their way across Prussia and pushed for Berlin, Hedwig Potthast pondered the future from Schönau and "Schneewinkellehen"—the moniker of her new abode. There the snows were thick and inviting for skiing with her sister, who had since reconciled with Hedwig and accepted her sister's children with Himmler. "I haven't seen much of Sigurd [Peiper] in the last month," she wrote, "while I've been together with Thilde these days. That crazy girl . . . seeing my new skis did this to her . . . and when I come up with a pair, we are going to run down the mountain together." Why, she asked, had her klutzy paramour never learned to ski?[1] Thilde, in fact, was pleased with Hedwig's children, "Helgi" and Nanette, and entranced by the postcard existence at Schneewinkellehen. The two Potthast sisters enjoyed lazy winter holidays together. For a few days the war seemed distant.

Heinrich Himmler thought nothing of skiing, struggling instead with the military leadership of Armeegruppe Vistula. In the meantime Jochen Peiper made his way out of the Ardennes. Peiper returned briefly to Tegernsee to visit his family. In the mail was a *weihnachtsgabe*—a special holiday gift for the exhausted SS officer from Himmler, including precious foodstuffs, now rare within the Reich: two pounds of coffee, special tea, bottles of red and white wine, cognac, and a hundred cigarettes.[2] Meanwhile, in Rottach, the flames atop the earthen *Julleuchter* burned while German defenses on the eastern border teetered and collapsed.

A massive daylight raid of a thousand US B-17s from the Eighth Air Force aimed to obliterate the Berlin rail system based on intelligence that the 6th Panzer Army was moving through Berlin on its way to the Eastern Front. The catastrophic blow not only wrecked the railways but also much of the unscarred portions of the city. The already damaged fashionable areas of Unter den Linden, Wilhelmstrasse, and Friedrichstrasse finally collapsed into a sea of ruin. Nearly three thousand Berliners died in the unsurpassed calamity.[3] Hitler, who was still characteristically sleeping at midday, hurriedly awakened to seek shelter. Two dozen bombs had rained on the Reich Chancellery and environs; the roof of its dining room crashed onto a hastily abandoned luncheon table. For Peiper the devastation must have been just as personal. Although his family had been gone from Berlin for more than a year, the bombing the previous autumn had destroyed his childhood Wilmersdorf neighborhood and home at Zähringerstrasse 17. Raging fires started and burned out of control for four days, leaving the entire city cloaked in smoke and ash.

In the meantime, surprised by bold Soviet advances, Himmler once more hastily moved his headquarters back to Birkenwald near Prenzlau, a wooded grove fifty miles north of Berlin and safely away from the bombing. It was the second move in five days. The surging Soviets had just crossed the Oder River and were now barely seventy kilometers away from the capital city. They had been close to Schneidemühle HQ when Himmler and his entourage fled with the refugees.

Simultaneously the 6th Panzer Army was in the process of transferring East. But where? Peiper left Rottach after only days and then motored to Berlin. From there, he drove to see Himmler, arriving at his final headquarters compound at the end of January.[4] Peiper had a new commander, Otto Kumm, who took over when the wounded SS General Wilhelm Mohnke was entrusted with the impending final defense of Berlin. All of the leaders of the Leibstandarte had been called back to Berlin with faked radio transmissions to lure the Soviets into thinking they would shortly be committed on the Eastern Front. We do know that Peiper was with Wilhelm Mohnke at that time. Mohnke supposedly had been injured in a Berlin air raid in January 1945 with damage to his hearing.[5]

The day after the devastation on February 3, Peiper arrived at Himmler's final headquarters. Birkenwald stood in a snowy birch forest between Haßleben and Prenzlau. Grothmann met Peiper, who quickly conducted his old protégé to Himmler's court. While his regular army staff lived in featureless wooden barracks nearby, Himmler led activities from his special train, the *Sonderzug Steiermark* surrounded by heavily armed SS sentries.

Peiper found Himmler's personal quarters at Birkenwald lavishly furnished in the curious manner to which he was accustomed. The decor reeked of SS austerity. The Reichsführer's barracks had a redwood-paneled bedroom and quilts, furniture covers, and light green rugs "more appropriate to the bedroom of an elegant woman than to a man directing an army." The accommodations were also ornately furnished—lounges, dining rooms with fine linen, and saunas and baths. The main entrance led into a vestibule arrayed with tacky handwoven SS carpets hung on the walls and expensive wooden furniture, all cluttered with porcelain knickknacks from the Allach SS-workshops.[6]

After the devastation to Berlin, was it possible to celebrate Peiper's recent birthday and the Machtergreifung of January 30? It was on that day, in fact, that Himmler issued a new draconian edict, *Tod und Stafe für Pflichtvergessenheit*—"Death and punishment of those who forget their obligations." The twelfth anniversary of National Socialism was now the second anniversary of Stalingrad, another Hitler-declared *Festung*. The Third Reichean penchant for irony was hardly lost on that day, for Himmler was celebrating the raising of a new 32nd SS Division, the "30. Januar."—a hodgepodge formation was formed around a core of convalescing wounded veterans.

Meanwhile, Sepp Dietrich also drove to see Himmler at Birkenwald, worried for his own family living on the Oder Front. What was on Himmler's mind?

It varied. Still playing field general, Himmler soberly told the Armeegruppe Vistula commanders that the Oder line could not be held after all. Just then, "It began to drip outside." A snow-eating winter wind left the Russian forces on the east side of the Oder, marooned in a sea of mud. "The thaw which has begun at this precise moment is a gift of fate. . . . God has not forgotten the worthy German people . . . we have been saved as through a miracle. Since then I have never doubted that we will win the war!"[7] Such bluster now fell flat, however. SS General Gottlob Berger informed Himmler that the civilian population now almost completely despised his organization, and even the army was "no longer on speaking terms with the SS."[8]

On February 4, Himmler did not rise until 8:30 a.m., for the attention of his obese Swedish masseur, Felix Kersten. More than usual, Himmler was overtaxed and stressed. After Kersten, Peiper was the first order of business on Himmler's calendar. At 1:30 p.m. the two met for a discussion.[9] Afterward SS Gen. Karl Wolff, Peiper's old superior, was also there for a sit-down lunch of simple Bavarian fare. Oberst Hans Eismann and SS Grupf. Heinz Lammerding were at the table. Released from leadership of the "Das Reich Panzer Division" in the Ardennes, Lammerding was now helping Eismann with staff work, unimpressed by Himmler as military leader.

At 3 p.m. Peiper met privately with Himmler once more. Perfunctory congratulations were in order for Peiper's new award from the Ardennes campaign, and there was certainly discussion of the crushing bombing raid in Berlin the day before. The long conversation with Peiper also surely touched on the certainty of the failed war. Perhaps Himmler told him of his evolving effort to seek a truce with the United States and Great Britain. He was about to send Karl Wolff off to Italy to enter negotiations with the Americans to seek an armistice there—a fact underscored by Wolff's presence that day. And there was Himmler's other favorite late-war topic: his unscrupulously efficient SS engineer Hans Kammler had brought the V-2 rocket into widespread use as a feared vengeance weapon and was manufacturing hundreds of jet fighters in deep caves in the Harz mountains. Now, the mercurial Kammler was secretly working on something even more diabolical. At the front new SS recruits talked of a massive counterattack with the new secret weapons on April 20, Hitler's birthday.[10] "*Die Vergeltung kommt!*" they said—"The Revenge is coming!"[11]

Nor had Himmler lost his love for crackpot science. During the last two weeks he had obsessed over an intelligence service report that said processing fir tree roots could produce high-octane gasoline! He had Oswald Pohl and Rudolf Brandt urging assigned SS engineers to produce rapid results. In the meantime he encouraged adopting Chinese rickshaws to ferry ammunition.[12]

There, too, was the Reichsführer mania for a miracle weapon based on a modern-day embodiment of Thor's Hammer. Himmler always kept Norse legend close; all the myths were simply ancestral keys to be unlocked to realize the full potential of the Aryan man and state. He waxed enthusiastic about a plan by an arcane company in Hildesheim, Elemag, to produce a gargantuan electric device that would use the atmosphere as a giant conductor.[13] With it, it might be possible to use the very air as a method to turn off all electrically operated machines. Imagine—no Allied tanks, planes, radar, or radio! *The Day the Earth Stood Still*, courtesy of Thor's Hammer!

Peiper stayed around Birkenwald until the morning of February 7, when he, Grothmann, and Himmler made a grim tour of the scarred and disfigured capital.[14] Hitler's Berlin nexus was smashed; grounds where Peiper and his youthful cohorts had once proudly paraded now stood wrecked from bombs and abatis. Deep craters pocked the previously stately gardens; tree stumps, rubble and debris covered everything. Nearby buildings burned and the ravaged streets were choked with smoke. What's more, Himmler's old SS headquarters at Prinz Albrecht Straße, where Peiper had spent so many days, had been thoroughly wrecked, with great holes punched in the roof and one floor sagging with bomb debris.

One night soon after the bombing, Himmler dined with Hitler, Hermann Fegelein, Martin Bormann, and Eva Braun.[15] Grothmann and Peiper sat at an adjoining table. The destruction of Berlin dominated the table conversation. With the wave of a hand, Hitler ordered that his mistress depart south the following day for Berchtesgaden. She didn't do so, but Peiper did leave—he had to be back to the Leibstandarte for *Operation Frühlingserwachen*—Spring Awakening—to take place in Hungary.

Then, in March 1945, Himmler, foundering in military ineptitude, came down with the flu and checked himself into Hohenlychen Clinic. He was despondent, having been relieved from a disastrous military command in the East and now laid low by influenza. Hedwig left her new home and the children in Schonäu with her nanny, Käte Mueller, and took the train to meet him at the SS hospital. Although Himmler and Potthast had seldom talked politics, a difficult discussion arose.

Before the Allied liberation of France, Hedwig remembered Himmler always being confident of winning the war. Now "he mentioned that he thought it was insane to continue fighting the Americans and that a separate peace ought to be made through a neutral country." He cautioned Häschen about the children now in Berchtesgaden. It would be okay "if the Americans enter it first," he told her, "but if the Russians were first I was to kill myself and my children," she recalled.[16] Oswald Pohl could provide Häschen with the requisite cyanide capsules. Courtesy of Pohl's wife, Eleonore, Hedwig also now had another address in Teisendorf near Salzburg where she and her children could take refuge if they needed to flee from Berchtesgaden.

Meanwhile the war went on for Peiper. The I SS and II SS Panzer Corps were essayed on either side of the Sarviv Canal to attack Hungary, about thirty miles to the west of the Danube River. Although the Leibstandarte was again brought up to nominal strength, the numbers were illusory. Tank, ammunition, and prime movers were in short supply, and the latest conscripts looked nothing like the strapping SS Zarathustrians of the early days. Even as the assault waves assembled in the muddy Hungarian beet fields, very young or very old replacement grenadiers arrived—young, homesick boys of seventeen just off the farm or old, unenthusiastic Schwabians of over thirty-five years. The last offensive failed with even Hitler losing faith in the Leibstandarte.

Peiper's battlegroup, had meanwhile pointlessly pierced deep behind Russian lines to Simontornya—to no avail. On March 22, the hydralike advance of the Soviet tank offensive split up the Leibstandarte in Hungary, prompting Otto Kumm, to send the tank battalion to open the Veszprém road. It was cloudless and warm at dawn the next day when Werner Poetschke assembled his tank commanders for a strike. Standing by a shed, he pointed out the enemy tank assembly on the horizon. Suddenly, there was a tremendous roar; a mortar bomb had exploded in the middle of the group. Poetschke staggered and fell. In great agony, he summoned his communications officer as they flopped his bleeding body onto a wooden door used as a stretcher. "Call Peiper on the radio," he urged, "and tell him what happened." Within three hours, the fierce panzer commander was dead. Under the heavy psychic blow, the entire division pulled back almost as in a rout. The few remaining tanks had to run a gauntlet, wildly shooting their way out of Veszprém. Peiper's tank was hit twice.

Kumm ordered a shaken Peiper to the rear. But that night, Peiper ignored orders and drove 30 kilometers to Mattersburg to be at the burial of Poetschke and Hans Malkomes. On March 27, a pale and sallow Peiper looked on as the coffins were nested in muddy, open graves draped with the SS runes and heaped with flowers. The band played the "Song of the Good Comrade," and the assembled honor guard fired a crestfallen salute. They were gone.

The morning after the depressing funeral, Peiper's orderly abruptly shook him awake. "Colonel," he said, pulling on his arm. "Get up! The Reichsführer wants to speak to you." Peiper angrily rolled out of bed and got dressed. After his relief of military command on March 20, Himmler's star had greatly dimmed. Everyone in the Leibstandarte knew that the SS Reichsführer was there to order everyone to remove their armbands on direct orders of Hitler. To Peiper, that was repulsive.

Himmler insisted he had nothing to do with the armband order and warmly offered dinner, treating Peiper "like a lost son." This time, though, Himmler was chagrined. "It's a terrible situation," he admitted, "but we can improvise. Remember Frederick the Great." Himmler rambled on as they took a short walk. "It's very important now to defend Vienna," he said blithely. "It shouldn't be difficult because it is a big city." Himmler was the perfect *Monokelfritz*! "I want you to come back with me. I need you urgently." Light rainfall added to the gray, and Himmler mumbled something about "going his own way." He had grandiose plans to raise a dozen SS divisions and Peiper could help with recruiting. It was farcical. "That's impossible," said the SS colonel, "I have no deputies. I can't leave my troops." That morning, his old cohort Jupp Diefenthal had been severely wounded by a machine gun burst. After dinner, Himmler smoked a cigar and offered red wine in an attempt to invoke the spirit of the old days. But Peiper's telling of the recent fighting put a damper on any rosy feeling—Diefenthal would lose his left leg. As Himmler said farewell, he seemed wistful. It was over.[17]

Returning, Peiper and his command were swept up in a losing battle with the Russians in the Vienna Woods, with one veteran after another dying in the hopeless sacrifice. Hedwig Potthast no longer received any letters from Jochen Peiper.

That same Easter, Thilde Potthast was writing to her sister, Hedwig, after having had to evacuate from Kolmar-Berg in Luxembourg with her Napola school girls to the old medieval abbey on Reichenau on Lake Constance.[18] Amid the calamity Thilde never received another letter from Hedwig, who was still at Berchtesgaden after returning from a frenzied visit to see a convalescing Himmler at Hohenlychen.[19] And Himmler himself?

On April 19 the head of the SS main office, SS Gen. Gottlob Berger, arrived on orders to Himmler's headquarters, now sixty kilometers northwest of Berlin. Peiper knew Berger well from his days with Himmler. Also there was SS Oberstgruppenführer Hans Prützmann, the man charged with the Operation Werwolf. Himmler ventured that his Werwolves would revive National Socialism after a guerrilla war thwarted the Allied occupation.[20] The logic was tortured at best, but Himmler cornered Berger: "Berger, I need you here," he implored. "I must have a sensible man at my side." History does not record how Berger responded to that irony.

In the evening Berger had dinner with Himmler and his head of the SS secret service, Walter Schellenberg. Swedish diplomat Count Folke Bernadotte listened incredulously as they discussed convincing Great Britain to consider peace negotiations through Sweden. Through Bernadotte, Himmler had just made secret arrangements to also meet Norbert Masur, a representative of the World Jewish Congress, whom he had covertly flown into Tempelhoff Airport that morning. It was clear to Berger that Himmler awkwardly sought surrender terms with the Allies—behind Hitler's back.

On that same Thursday morning, April 19, 1945, Hedwig Potthast received what would be her last telephone call from Himmler. In the conversation, they spoke only of personal matters, but Himmler warned, "The situation is getting more difficult each day." No matter, he said, promising to call the following day. And yet, strangely, that same afternoon SS Stubaf. Paul Baumert, who was serving as a courier, arrived with a personal message from Himmler. The message had the usual greetings but repeated there were "great difficulties." Then ominously, the communique closed with "the hope that God would protect her, the children and Germany."[21]

Peiper was still fighting on April 19, although increasingly disillusioned. The old trusted commanders and subordinates in his command had been killed off in the terrible fighting in Hungary in mid-March—Werner Poetschke, Werner Wolff, and Heinz von Westernhagen.[22] The very next day, Adolf Hitler's birthday, on April 20, 1945, saw Jochen Peiper's promotion to full colonel—SS Standartenführer. Indeed, Peiper would proudly claim that Hitler had personally called him in the field to bestow the honor.[23] But as if to underscore the desperate circumstances, on that day Peiper orchestrated the rescue of eight of his wounded out of hellish fighting in Rohrbach, Austria, when the Russians blocked evacuation by Red Cross ambulance with tank fire. Peiper retaliated with a counterattack against the Soviets probing Hainfeld. Hand-to-hand combat broke out amid a thick mortar barrage. Hardly a house was left standing in the Austrian village as the battle for its streets eddied back and forth. Peiper personally directed the assault, with all eight of the wounded brought out after being strapped on top of one of his tanks.[24]

Meanwhile Peiper's mother and father, Charlotte and Woldemar, fled bombed-out Berlin, not willing to be in the city to greet the Russians—a foregone conclusion. By April 15, 1945, Woldemar had reached Bad Gastein in Austria, some seventy kilometers south of Salzburg. That village and the sanatorium where he had recuperated from heart problems before being released from the army in 1942 was an ideal hiding place from the Russians. Woldemar listed his situation as "refugee without employment."[25] Yet his registry card there listed his most recent place of work as a businessman in Warsaw!

Now the Russians were at Berlin's doorstep. On Hitler's birthday, Friday, April 20, Himmler and Berger journeyed to Berlin, detouring via Nauen to avoid the closing Allied forces. They reached the city in the afternoon to find the streets wrecked and smoking. Whereas the capital often looked decorative for Hitler's birthday, only the most ardent fascist dipsomaniacs sought to display allegiance. Even so, those calling on Hitler saw red, white, and black Nazi flags limply draped on the walls of ruins while pathetic placards proclaimed, "*Die Kriegsstadt Berlin grüsst den Führer!*—"The War City of Berlin Greets Our Leader."[26] Meanwhile long-range Russian shells whistled overhead and exploded dangerously close. Debouching from their cars, the two men ran for their lives.

Passing the guards and reaching the inside of the Reich Chancellery, Himmler and Berger were greeted by a bleak sight. Göring, Ribbentrop, Karl Dönitz, Ernst Kaltenbrunner, and Albert Speer stood in the huge reception room of polished marble with thirty-foot high ceilings. It was now woefully ravaged. Once intended as the starting point for the reconstruction of Berlin and as a showcase of the Third Reich, the building was now in a splintered ruin, with fragments of concrete and stone strewn about. Almost all of the windows in the great building were shattered. Hitler's supremely ostentatious monument to his personal power looked meretricious and somehow deeply diabolic. Then the Führer appeared at the far entrance to the ruin, looking stooped and diminished.

With the others, Hitler made a solemn tour of the Chancellery. As he received the men, "his whole body shook violently."[27] The German leader blustered in mock confidence that the Russians were about to suffer their greatest defeat in Berlin. There were side glances as he spoke. No one said anything, but several, including OKW Chief Wilhelm Keitel, encouraged Hitler to leave while there was still time. "I know what I want," he said. "How can I call upon the troops to undertake my decisive battle for Berlin if at the same moment I withdraw myself to safety? I shall leave it to fate whether I die in the capital or fly to Obersalzberg at the last moment!" Their leader seemed bent on dragging all with him down to total destruction.[28] With that exchange concluded, the paladins of high Nazi power offered wishes for his fifty-sixth birthday. Each man stepped forward to clasp a feeble hand. Albert Speer was impressed by the maladroit silence: "No one knew quite what to say."

Outside, the booming artillery filled the air like a roaring thunderstorm. Soon the entourage moved back down into the musty confines of the bunker for Hitler's daily war conference. The usual situation map was present, with lots of ugly red lines outlining a penciled noose around the German capital. The Russians were encircling Berlin. Hitler told those assembled that he could see it would be a street battle—this would be the Soviet's reckoning as his had been at Stalingrad. Ignoring the vacuous historical parallels, several generals nervously pointed out that it would be necessary to move the headquarters to Obersalzberg before they were completely surrounded. Göring quickly agreed, pointing out there was now but one route through the Bavarian Forest to the south through which they might escape.

Later that afternoon Adolf Hitler emerged above ground for the final time. Hitler Youth leader Artur Axmann slowly escorted him out to the garden. Even the heavy jacket drawn around him could not hide his frail-looking figure. The grounds were scarred by shell craters and surrounded by great mounds of rubble. Gunfire crackled in the air. A small group of very young Hitler Youth had been assembled for the German leader to meet. Hermann Göring and Joseph Goebbels looked on as Hitler smiled tiredly and moved down the line, shaking young hands and doling out Iron Crosses. Although the youths wore duck-billed army caps, they were mere boys.

While Hitler pinched the ears of Hitler Youth in the garden, Heinrich Himmler engaged his tall former doctor, Dr. Ludwig Stumpfegger, in urgent conversation. Stumpfegger was now charged with caring for Hitler. Himmler announced that he had a very serious favor to ask of his old friend: if he cared for the fate of Germany, Himmler told him, he would covertly kill Hitler by lethal injection—he would not live for more than a few days longer any way. Yet that was not about to happen. Himmler described Stumpfegger as now completely under the Führer's spell, "so drunk with Hitler" that any sense of realism was gone.[29] Himmler turned to Hermann Göring, the head of the Luftwaffe, telling him that Count Bernadotte had come to see him. "You know, he must have been the man Eisenhower sent as a negotiator." "I can't believe that!" the rotund Göring said, turning away.[30] In a cold night rain Himmler got in his car and drove off to meet with the representative from the World Jewish Congress at Felix Kersten's estate—perversely ironic. He would never see Hitler again.

The following morning Hitler woke uncharacteristically early at 9:30 a.m. The deep underground bunker was shaking. He hurriedly shaved before confronting General Wilhelm Burgdorf, Otto Günsche, and Oberst Nicolaus von Below. "What's going on?" he demanded. "Where is this firing coming from?" Heavy artillery of the Red Army, Burgdorf replied. "Are the Russians already so near?" Hitler asked in disbelief.[31] Indeed they were. For, that same day, his SS adjutant had to inform him that the city was now as good as encircled with Soviet spearheads north at Oranienburg and south at Zossen. OKH and the armed forces high command fled hurriedly.

Nevertheless, it remained possible to get to Berlin through the narrow neck in the Russian tide. Unlike his SS master, Gottlob Berger remained loyal. On Sunday, April 22, he toiled his way back to Hitler's headquarters in another hazard-laden trek by automobile. The final approach was a dangerous gauntlet through a maze of streets blocked by rubble and carcasses of burned-out automobiles and tramcars. During a lull in the Soviet shelling he dashed inside the Chancellery headquarters to find another situation briefing in full swing. When Hitler came in at half past eight, he immediately obsessed over the progress of Army Detachment Steiner, a grandiose appraisal of a ten thousand–man SS force of limited means. He ordered Felix Steiner to counterattack the Russian right flank, threatening his officers with execution if they failed to heed his orders. "Whoever throws in the last battalion will be the winner," he bellowed, invoking Frederick the Great. Indeed, he was now taking to reclusive hours in his study, gazing at the huge portrait of Frederick the Great as if the historical figure might impart some mystical clarity to his dilemma.

The circle of officers was small, including Alfred Jodl and Hermann Fegelein, the arrogant liaison officer representing the SS. The ruinous military situation was explained while the bunker perceptively shook from shell impacts. At that, Hitler flew into an apoplectic rage. "Everyone has deceived me. No one has told me the truth. The Wehrmacht has lied to me and finally the SS has left me in the lurch." He continued in a loud voice as "his face went bluish purple." Berger thought he was having a stroke.[32]

Upon his return, Himmler announced plans: "You are my man of intrigue," he told Berger. Even though it was a Sunday, he ordered the SS general to drive to a bank, where he would be met by a representative who would give him eleven large bags of foreign currency, and then he would load them onto a waiting plane and fly south.[33] So, financially stoked, Berger would then take charge of the southern battle group that would fight on after Berlin capitulated. Berger flew off later that day, fully expecting that Himmler would soon join him, escaping on the wings of the supersecret Luftwaffe command, KG 200. Werner Baumbach still held the reins of a huge escape aircraft, fueled and waiting.[34]

On Monday, April 23, Peiper's former commander, Brigadeführer Wilhelm Mohnke, took over command of defending Berlin, now suggestively dubbed "The Citadel." Mohnke would fight by the Führer's side, as Hitler's own bodyguard, to serve as Hitler's last general. At the close of April 1945 a Wagnerian end seemed certain. There was little to work with. "Bring your own weapons, equipment and rations," Mohnke advised in the chaos of April 25. "Every German man is needed."[35] And German women too. The limping SS leader soon recruited "Mohnke Girls" to sacrifice themselves like the men.[36]

On April 25, at 5:30 a.m., the Soviet guns spouted great cascades of rockets and shells into Berlin. The thunderous salvo was to herald their final assault. Hundreds of Russian planes loosed more bombs to hit anything still standing. Buildings sank into grotesque piles of rubble and ash. Bitter street fighting raged. Russian tanks were shot down by flak batteries until they ran out of ammunition or were run over by fire-spitting T-34s. Desperate attack and counterattack eddied around the Olympic Stadium as Hitler Jugend battalions sacrificed themselves.

In the meantime Hitler called in his valet, Heinz Linge, to a private meeting. Hitler had surprising instructions: after the German leader ended his own life, Linge was entrusted with the task of carrying his body from the bunker and cremating it—thoroughly. "No one must see or recognize me after death," he said. "After seeing to the burning, go back to my room and collect everything I could be remembered by after death. Take everything—uniforms, papers, everything I've used—anything that people could say belonged to the Führer. Take it outside and burn it."[37] Only a single personal possession was to be saved: his portrait of Frederick the Great by Anton Graff. The portrait was to be somehow flown out of Berlin by Hitler's personal pilot, Hans Baur.

On April 26 the Soviet 79th Guards Division fought its way up the Landwehr Canal only four hundred meters from the Reich Chancellery. The approaches to that final bastion of the Third Reich were defended by a battalion of the Leibstandarte Adolf Hitler led by Valkyrie-like members determined to die rather than surrender.[38] Later that day the Soviets had reached the Alexanderplatz in the heart of Berlin. The Russians had the capital under a steel-jawed concentric attack. Hitler called for the defense to hold another twenty-four hours until Armeegruppe Wenck would arrive. But Wenck's forces were weak.

The German leader now lived in a fantasy. "I was more aware of the developments of the war than Hitler," said his longtime secretary, Johanna Wolf. "I realized much sooner that the war was approaching its end. He saw only the overall issues—unlike a woman, one of whose family had been lost due to the war . . . he had lost contact with the people. Up to the very last day, he still believed in victory."[39]

On Friday, April 27, Mohnke interrupted the morning military briefing to announce that Soviet tanks had smashed their way to the Wilhelmsplatz. Gen. Hans Krebs laconically estimated that the Russians would be crawling over the Führer's bunker in less than forty-eight hours. But it was the former commander of the SS Leibstandarte who capped off the flooding pessimism. "My Führer!" Mohnke blurted out, "We haven't quite brought about what we wanted in 1933!"

His sarcasm was barely noticed. Instead, Hitler and Goebbels floated off to recall the glory of the old days. When they were done, Hitler slunk down; he would stay in Berlin.[40] Mohnke, meanwhile, had cobbled together a desperate attack against the Soviet army bearing down on the Führerbunker and turned it back temporarily with volleys of point-blank gunfire and hand-to-hand combat. Few of the SS general's sacrificial warriors would survive.

Meanwhile Heinrich Himmler was not ready to end his life. In mid-April he recruited Werner Baumbach's KG 200 from its endgame sacrificial operations for a special assignment. Baumbach had recently been appointed *Chef der Regierungsstaffel*—a special detachment that could spirit away high-ranking Nazi leaders at the last moment. On April 28, 1945, Baumbach negotiated roads clogged with refugees after requested to urgently meet with Himmler in Güstrow in Mecklenburg.

When escorted up a spiral staircase to Himmler's study, Werner Baumbach found the head of the SS in a simple room, looking tired and unhealthy. A machine pistol, with its safety off, leaned against the nearby corner. There the Reichsführer SS, confident of his coming appointment to take Hitler's place, told the highly decorated bomber pilot of his grandiose plans to broker peace with the Allies,likely from a neutral country. "The war is entering its final stage and there are some very important decisions that I shall have to take. The Führer is isolated in Berlin. I shall be the only man to prevent chaos in Germany. . . . I think that foreigners will not negotiate with anyone other than me." Baumbach tried hard to not look away.

"The situation is far from hopeless," Himmler chirped. Then he pointedly asked about Baumbach's aircraft. He might need to be whisked to a neutral country to carry on the negotiations, Himmler said. "I've heard all aircraft available for that purpose are under your command. What possibilities are there?"

Baumbach gazed off through the windows of the estate. "I was examining a map of the world yesterday to see where we could fly to," he said. "I have planes and flying boats ready to fly to any point on the globe. The aircraft are manned by trustworthy crews." Himmler seemed to pause. "If I start negotiations, I shall need airplanes."

"I have enough aircraft ready to start any time." Himmler said if things went as expected, he could need those aircraft soon. Baumbach replied that big Blohm and Voss long-range flying boats would be at Travemünde, where he would be as well—the port on the sandy coast overlooking the Baltic northeast of Hamburg. Himmler told Baumbach he would be in contact soon.

But Himmler was not willing to face his death with Hitler in Berlin. On the evening of April 28 a radio operator in Hitler's bunker intercepted a BBC broadcast reporting Himmler's attempted surrender negotiations with the Western Allies. Hitler, who had long referred to Himmler as "*der treue Heinrich*"—the loyal Heinrich—flew into a rage.[41] He ordered Himmler's arrest and had Hermann Fegelein, his missing SS representative at Hitler's headquarters, located and shot.

Regardless of Hitler's rage at betrayal, within the *Führerbunker* it was endgame. On Thursday, April 29, Adolf Hitler married his mistress, Eva Braun, and composed a vitriolic last testament. Yet, in spite of his wrangle to vanquish Bolshevism, the collapse of Hitler's empire had instead brought it thundering into the very heart of Europe. After saying good-bye to his staff the next morning, he spoke to his SS adjutant, Otto Günsche, as the Soviet columns advanced within a single street of the bunker. He and his new bride would kill themselves the next day, he told him. Günsche quickly got on the phone to Hitler's driver, Erich Kempka. "I need 200 liters of gasoline immediately!"

"Impossible!" Kempka replied. "What do you need it for?" Günsche wouldn't say, but he ordered Kempka to produce the gasoline without fail.[42]

That next afternoon, at 3:30 p.m., Adolf and his new wife retired to their quarters. Sitting under the gigantic portrait of Frederick the Great, Hitler cradled a Walther PPK pistol, held it to his right temple and pulled the trigger. Startled by the sudden report, SS orderly Heinz Linge broke in to find Hitler sprawled out, face down on the table. On the couch next to him was Eva, pale and lifeless. The sickly sweet smell of almonds—cyanide—permeated the air. "The chief is dead!" Günsche called out. Erich Kempka came running.

Together with Hitler's manservant, Heinz Linge, the two men laboriously hauled the bodies up four flights of stairs. Reaching the entrance, the men dropped the corpses into a shallow depression not ten feet from the ruins of the bunker. Just then a Soviet artillery barrage detonated, sending everyone scurrying for cover. Only the two lifeless bodies of Hitler and his bride were unmoved, staring up in death from just outside the bunker. Between salvos, Kempa dosed one jerrican after another of gasoline onto the bodies—a revolting process. Finally, when the forms were almost floating in gasoline, Kempka found a rag and doused it with fuel.

During a pause in the shelling Günsche dashed from the bunker entrance to throw the incendiary. A pall of flame flared above the bunker. Against the backdrop of Berlin's rubble, the fireball twisted and roiled in ugly smoke and flame, hardly visible amid the larger pyrotechnic death agonies of National Socialist Berlin.[43] In a final act of obedience, all those in attendance "looked towards the fire and all saluted with raised hands." Yet the salute was only momentary, for presently, another salvo of Russian shells began landing on the Chancellery grounds. Over the next three hours the attendants poured gasoline on the gruesome pyre until there was little left.

There was more sacrifice at the bunker, but by the first day of May it was over. Joseph Goebbels and his wife poisoned their children and then had themselves shot by an SS orderly in the Reich Chancellery garden. Afterward they too were set ablaze; Wilhelm Mohnke ordered the same done to the Führerbunker. A few Jerricans sloshed about, a blazing rag, and much went up in flames. In the meantime Mohnke,

Artur Axmann, and Martin Bormann met in the cellar of the Chancellery. They would attempt to break out separately in ten small groups. Dressed in a plain field gray SS uniform covered by a leather coat, Bormann looked panicked, mumbling of his determination to escape. Donning a steel helmet, he darted off to the east with Dr. Ludwig Stumpfegger. Artillery shells exploded in the darkness, punctuating the crackling din of small arms fire. They headed toward the Invalidenstrasse, disappearing like ghosts into the night.

As Mohnke, Otto Günsche, and the others attempted to escape northwest on foot, the radio airwaves over Berlin were suffused with the dirge of *Bruckner's Seventh Symphony*.[44] Determined to flee, the two SS officers clattered downstairs into the underground U-bahn, but an impetulant station attendant rebuffed them. It was midnight, he complained; the subway was closed. Obediently, the SS officers turned back, moments later pronouncing themselves fools—they carried machine pistols![45] Just after midnight the music stopped. A drumroll faded to a sober-voiced announcer:

> Our Führer, Adolf Hitler, fighting to the last breath against Bolshevism, fell for Germany this afternoon in his operational headquarters in the Reichs Chancellery. On April 30, the Führer appointed Grand Admiral Karl Dönitz as his successor.

As Hitler and Berlin lay dying, Peiper and his men were still fighting in Austria. Word reached Peiper just as they received a new tank delivery. "On 1 May we heard on the radio of the catastrophe in Berlin and the death of the Führer. Dönitz spoke words of encouragement, but we knew our hour of defeat had arrived."[46] Peiper, for his part, agonized with regret: "In the end of the war, when the Führer was needing his Leibstandarte most," he later wrote, "fate separated us from him."[47]

An SS captain spoke candidly to Otto Wichmann, who, at twenty six, had been a tool weapons sergeant at the headquarters company of the 1st SS Panzer Regiment as the war fell in around them:

> I remember on the day that it was obvious to every SS man that the war was finally lost. It was the day which the death of the Führer became known, SS Captain Schulze said to me, "The Fuhrer is dead, but we will rally around our commander. In the future we must never lose touch with him. We will continue the work of the Führer with Standartenführer Peiper as our leader even after the war is lost."[48]

During those last weeks shocking radio dispatches came from the Western Allies describing scenes of horror as they liberated the German concentration camps. Peiper professed apathy. "When we heard about the things in the concentration camps in the last phase of the war," he would later recall, "I couldn't have cared less. Everything was crumbling—I thought, let this all go to hell. All my comrades were gone."[49]

Even delivery of six monster seventy-ton "invincible" Jagdtiger tanks waddling to 1st SS Panzer Regiment could no longer excite. Arriving straight from the Herman Göring factory works to St. Pölten, the SS colonel reckoned these behemoths would have to be blown up with the rest. On the night of May 7, 1945, Peiper met with his officers at an abandoned school in St. Anton. Ironically, he would announce capitulation next to the famous ski resort where he, Sigurd, and Häschen Potthast had once enjoyed carefree winter holidays. Now all was changed. He looked at each man. His voice was shrill: "The dream of the Reich is over!"

The rapidly increasing pressure by the Soviet 9th Guards tank army forced the Leibstandarte back in the direction of Mariazell and then the city of Steyr. A terse message arrived from the division—the war would end on May 9, 1945. The evening before, Gen. Dietrich urged all his units in contact with American troops to surrender to these forces along the Enns River; units facing the Russians were to hastily fall back to the Linz/Danube line.[50] Reinhold Kyriss of the 7th Panzer Company remembered the last day of the war with his commander, Werner Sternebeck:

> I was on the road, having been hurt by a falling fuel drum. Peiper showed up in a VW Kubelwagen and picked me up. "Where are our tanks?" I asked him. "The tanks can't get through," he told me. They tended to my minor injury. "You sit back," Peiper told me putting me in the car, "don't worry boy, you'll get home." Later the order of the day was passed down by Peiper. "The war is over. We shall meet in the city of Steyr and shall bring our tanks over to the American side." I had found Sternebeck in a nearby house. He sat at a table; he was totally drunk with riding breeches on, no shirt and suspenders wearing his saber on his waist. When he received the capitulation order from Peiper, he cried. He wept, but then regained his composure. I helped him on with his clothes. He then faced the men and told them the news with a straight face. Sternebeck struggled to reach an officer's composure. "We stand here . . . undefeated." Our mood was low.[51]

That morning Peiper met with the men of his command for the last time as the remaining tanks were scuttled and sent careening into the Enns River. Peiper stood tall on the bridge as his entire command filed past, looking immaculate in his tanker's uniform. "The war is over!" he shouted. That was all.

Throughout Berlin and on the Russian front SS officers were shooting themselves or crunching on cyanide capsules rather than surrendering. In a calm voice Peiper thanked his men for their sacrifice. The Leibstandarte prided itself as the *Garde Napolienne*: "The guard dies, but it never surrenders." With that in mind, Peiper warned his men against the wave of suicide sweeping SS ranks. "Look how to get home," he said. Germany needed each man alive for the new challenge.

LOYALTY FROM BEYOND THE GRAVE, PEIPER SAID, WAS BEST LEFT TO THE Nibelungs.[52]

Chapter 10

ENDGAME

In reality, at the end of the war Jochen Peiper, the man whom the U.S. Army intelligence services were desperately searching for, was not hiding.

Like many German soldiers at the end of the war, he merely looked to reach home. He hiked over the flower-sprayed alpine meadows, aiming for Sigurd, the kids, and the Tegernsee Valley. Peiper, the SS colonel, first started out with several others, but one by one they went their separate ways. In the end, Peiper marched only with SS Maj. Paul Guhl, who had been the last leader of his old SPW battalion. The fugitives threaded through the Austrian hills by day and slept in haylofts by night, surviving on food from accommodating farmers and quenching thirst with water from fecund mountain streams.

To evade road checkpoints they took a cross-country hike from Steyr to Reichsraming, Kirchdorf an der Krems and Gmunden, slogging wearily hundreds of kilometers across the hills. They threaded through the nearly impassable terrain south of Salzburg as they moved west. What would he do when he got to Rottach-Egern? Peiper was close on May 22, 1945, as he marched across a clay tennis court at Lake Schliersee. The Americans had occupied the region for three weeks, but Peiper walked carefully. Indeed, he was not ten miles from Sigurd and the kids.

"Hands up!"

The cry came from the other side of the tennis court. The voices were from members of the 222nd Infantry Regiment, US 42nd "Rainbow" Division, so named for the distinctive prismatic arch on their sleeve.[1] If these soldiers arrived after the end of the major fighting in Europe, their command lived up to a colorful reputation. After all, their commander was Maj. Gen. "Hollywood" Harry Collins, and everywhere the division went, rainbows were scrawled on walls—Kilroy with rainbows.

Peiper could see he was about to be captured, so he threw away the pistol he was carrying.[2] After all those years of war! And now all these days walking and this close to home! His world crashing down. "Thinking of the war," Peiper lamented. "I am not sure what we accomplished,"[3] He and Paul Guhl were held for two days by the 222nd Infantry Regiment as the dragline drew in a profusion of SS officer fish, of which Peiper remained a nameless minnow.[4]

Although the 42nd Infantry Division's 222nd Regiment was not long on experience, Peiper and Guhl may have been more worried had they known of an incident that had taken place three weeks earlier. On April 29, 1945, before the full extent of the horrors of Dachau were revealed, the 222nd engaged a company of Waffen SS men still fighting at the tiny farm hamlet of Webling, some ten kilometers northeast of Dachau. At a time when GIs in Europe were focused on simply surviving the last week of the war, one American of the group was gunned down as they approached the village. The incident so angered the U.S. infantry capturing the first SS contingent that seventeen of those surrendering were lined up against an earthen bank at the Furtmayer Farm and shot down in cold blood. Another group was dispatched nearby. In all, forty-one Waffen SS men were killed at Webling.[5]

Yet Peiper and Guhl were treated fairly by their captors from the 222nd Infantry Regiment that Tuesday. Neither made any attempt to hide their identity. Strangely, Peiper's name was not yet on the Big Fish radar screen, perhaps due to reports of his death. Unshaven, exhausted, and hungry, they were taken captive without ceremony. After a quick search, both were escorted into the back of a dusty two-and-a-half-ton truck and driven to the newly established collection point at Rottach-Egern.

There they were herded into an open outdoor POW enclosure set out before the majestic green of Waldberg Mountain and watched over by a GI squatting before a .50 caliber machine gun. There were nearly a thousand German soldiers there. Sigurd and the kids were just a few hundred meters away—with hundreds of other German army riffraff, Jochen Peiper was in the very town he had been plodding toward, but he might as well have been a hundred miles from Wolfgrubstrasse.

At least there was food and water. Sitting outside, beneath the green spire of the Waldberg, he squinted into the early summer sun and contemplated his new fate—prisoner of the US Army. The guards from the 431st AAA AW Battalion found their corralled prisoners listless and resigned to their fates. But not all Germans were so complacent. Word came from an upper-Bavarian woodsman that a group of fugitive SS men were hiding in the hills above Rottach and that they had weapons and explosives; indeed, the fugitive band appeared to be led by Peiper's old acquaintance and Himmler's hunting guide, Max Glasl. The proprietor of Hotel Maximilian in town was now holed up in the mountains near Valepp and threatening to shoot anyone with his hunting rifle who got close.[6]

The man for whom Glasl had served as a guide was on the run too. On May 21, traveling under a disguised identity and aiming to reach refuge in the Harz Mountains, Heinrich Himmler had been apprehended at a checkpoint near Neuhaus in Lower Saxony. While being interrogated in British custody in Lüneburg, he bit on a concealed cyanide capsule. Himmler died within minutes.[7] Peiper's old superior had killed himself a day after his own capture on the tennis court in Schliersee.

Peiper knew nothing of either episode. Instead, he waited with the others. There were more than seven thousand convalescing German veterans in Tegernsee to deal with, and on the day Peiper became captive, the 42nd Infantry Division reported taking on four thousand eagerly surrendering German prisoners. On May 24, forty-eight trucks came in the middle of the night to haul Peiper and 1,947 others to another collection point at Feuchtwangen, Germany, just southwest of Ansbach.[8] The four-by-four trucks stopped by the big granary silo near the railroad yard. Peiper and the other captives spilled outside to the big open field nearby. They sat on the ground by the railroad yard, guarded by guns, uncertainty, and apathy.

But as a full colonel, Peiper was the ranking German officer. On the afternoon of Sunday, May 27, a brown-haired, blue-eyed, twenty-six-year-old young infantry lieutenant from North Carolina arrived at Feuchtwangen. As officer with the 2nd Battalion, 22nd Infantry Regiment, Stephen J. Sanders Jr. had just received a new assignment. As battalion S-4, he would be responsible for the prisoners' food and supplies at the new POW camp. Sanders and his immediate superior, Maj. Clifford M. "Swede" Henley, were assigned to housing in the village of Dinkelsbühl some eight miles away, which served as their battalion headquarters. A tough football-type from Clemson, Sanders didn't see eye-to-eye with Henley.

Although Sanders, like many other American soldiers, had entered the conflict in Europe wet behind the ears—"a 90 day wonder," he called himself—he did not remain that way long. He fought in terrible infantry fighting in Luxembourg during the Bulge, reaching something of an epiphany when he faced a dying German soldier. Confronted by the universal human suffering, he saved his enemy whom he had professed to hate. It was as if he saved himself. "You will find two kinds of men in war," Sanders would later say, "those who actually like to kill and loot, and those who simply go about their business." Any glory he foresaw in war was long gone with the mayhem he had seen. Indeed, with the massive number of replacements from June 1944 through May 1945, some 1,547 members of the 22nd Infantry Regiment under Col. John F. Ruggles had died, and more than 7,200 were wounded, not to mention those, like him, whose spirit had been shaken. After his confrontation with death in the Ardennes, everything in Sander's life seemed to have deep meaning.

Sanders thought he would be in Feuchtwangen for a while; indeed, the others with him figured they would be there for a long time. Given the devastation he saw in Germany, it looked like the occupation would be needed for some time. He sought an interpreter. In Dinkelsbühl he was introduced to a poised, one-armed German interpreter, Eduard Dürr. Fighting for the German army in Russia, Dürr had lost his arm in the carnage near Kiev. Yet Sanders was amazed: the man seemed totally unfazed by his handicap. When Sanders mentioned it, Dürr shrugged; many of his comrades from the war were dead or had worse than a missing arm. "We are both alive!" Dürr laughed. His accented English was excellent; his mother had been from Virginia; indeed, her father had been a Union officer at Gettysburg. In any case, Sanders found his new sidekick completely beguiling—"a charming rascal."

When Sanders first arrived with Dürr in their jeep in the little German town, the prisoners were still unloading from the back of Ford trucks in an orderly fashion. Sanders was surprised at how well kept the German soldiers appeared. They were in uniform and looked like they had just come marching from their casern. It was a warm Sunday afternoon, and the prison yard was a large grassy meadow with a stout stone Lagerhaus by the railroad yard. By the time the day was done there were some five hundred, a mixed bag of army and SS men. Someone told Sanders that an SS colonel by the name of Peiper was the appointed senior officer in charge of the group. Sanders stepped up to the camp entrance to meet the man.

Peiper walked up as the trucks were still unloading. He stood straight and tall in a long coat. He had an adjutant at his side, a taller man with a glass eye.[9] Through Dürr, Sanders spoke with Peiper. "Colonel, I understand you are the commanding officer of the camp," he said. "I am Lt. Stephen Sanders, 22nd Infantry Regiment S-4. I will be taking care of food and supplies for your people." They saluted each other smartly. Peiper was older, and with much greater war experience, but Sanders did not feel fazed. Looking the German officer in the eye, Sanders thought the man had an unusual presence. "This will be your prison," Sanders told the men, motioning to the large Lagerhaus, "but it is not finished yet." Off in the distance they could see the village of Feuchtwangen.

The drab gray Lagerhaus was on a flat meadow, filled with sacks of grain. There was not even a fence around the camp. Sanders was worried—would the enemy try to take off? "Do not be concerned," Peiper told Sanders through Dürr. "Not one of these men will try to escape. You have my word."[10] Sanders told him the prisoners would have to begin working the next day to move the sacks of grain. Peiper agreed.

The following morning everyone was accounted for. The work began as planned, and the quarters took shape. Sanders said that his people would still need to build a fence for the camp, but he did not have the engineers to help with this task. "Don't worry, Lieutenant," Peiper told him. "Provide us with the materials and we will build the fence." Sanders was taken aback. "*Konzentrationslager*," Peiper winked—"We are experts at that, you know." Dürr's family owned a mill yard where they could get lumber. Sanders ordered barbed wire and post-hole diggers be made available to Peiper, and although surprised, the Provost Marshal approved.

Sanders drove back to Dinkelsbühl to check in. Later in the afternoon he and Dürr came back. When they arrived, the barbed wire enclosure was under assembly. The German prisoners were building their own jail from the inside!

As Sanders prepared to leave at dusk, Peiper suddenly appeared before him. He told the American officer that he had a special request: a radio and newspapers. Sanders told him he would have to check with his superior to see if this was possible. But quarters were being prepared for him as the senior officer of the prisoners in a small rail telegraphic hut, which was nearby the Lagerhaus and the railroad.

The next day Sanders drove back and met Peiper outside the Lagerhaus; it was a sunny June afternoon. Sanders told Peiper his superiors had denied his request for newspapers and a radio. "I've checked and it is not allowed." Peiper looked dejected after spending his first days at the camp. "Never mind," he said staring Sanders in the eye. "I would like to be shot."

Sanders was shocked and asked for him to repeat his words to make sure Dürr was translating accurately. Peiper repeated his request. "Yes, I would like to be shot."

"Listen, Peiper," Sanders told him earnestly, "there is nothing much happening in the paper or on the radio. The world is pretty much as it was just a few days ago."

Peiper shook his head. "Let me explain," he began. From where the two men stood, they could see from the camp meadow into the town of Feuchtwangen. The backdrop to their conversation was strange. As Sanders spoke to Peiper, he could see the prisoners behind him busy building their own enclosure fence from the inside. "Lieutenant," Peiper said to Sanders, "I have the Knight's Cross with swords—one of the highest decorations our country can bestow for fighting in its defense." Peiper motioned to the village of Feuchtwangen beyond the railyard. "Six months ago, if I had walked the streets of the village before us, the boys there would have recognized me and my medals and come out ask for my autograph. Today, if they recognized me there they would run to the Burgermeister and say, 'There is a dirty SSer in town!'"[11] Peiper looked deflated.

Sanders did not know what to say. "Goodnight, Colonel," Sanders said awkwardly. He left behind a few cigarettes.

Back at Dinkelsbühl, the lieutenant reported to Swede Henley. He had strange news: the ranking German officer in the camp wanted to be shot, but Sanders didn't understand why. Henley didn't understand it either; he just laughed and asked for another drink. "Can you believe it," he said slapping his thigh, "the German commander wants us to shoot him!"

Sanders came to visit Peiper on the third day with his interpreter again. Sanders did not speak of the request for execution. Nor did the SS colonel. It seemed forgotten, and somehow Peiper's mood brightened. Peiper glanced toward Eduard Dürr. "Lieutenant," he told Sanders in clear English, "you don't have to bring him along. I speak English." Sander's jaw dropped. Peiper told him he had helped host the Americans at the Olympic Games in Berlin in 1936 and had polished his English. Then Peiper struck a serious tone, confiding in Sanders that the German army had drafted a number of fifteen-year-olds in the closing months of the war. "They don't belong here," Peiper said quietly. "They should be back home with their families." Sanders passed the word on up to Henley, and soon the youngsters were released.

From then on, Sanders's visits featured an extended conversation. Each afternoon the two men met in the small, windowless telegraph hut, where Peiper made his quarters with a small desk at one end of the building. The SS colonel would sit behind the desk, and Sanders would post himself on the other side. Sanders first got the business out of the way. Were any of his men in need? Bread and other rations? Anyone needing medical attention?

"Everything is in order," Peiper said. Sanders was surprised that a beaten enemy remained in such form; he was always well groomed, even when the men at the camp were bathing from an outdoor trough. They smoked a couple of cigarettes over coffee. Why did the US Army, in all its material richness, Peiper wanted to know, still have such terrible coffee based on roasted barley? *Dark, tasteless brown water!* They should do something about that.

As not much was going on that June of 1945 at the camp, Sanders and Peiper would talk for hours. "I wanted to show him how impartial Americans could be—how fair we were," Sanders remembered. "And most of all I wanted to be an example to him of the goodness of U.S. democracy." It seemed to work. Peiper respected him, particularly after hearing Sanders's tales of the fighting in the snowy Ardennes. But how did Peiper feel as a captive?

> My thoughts were void of bitterness and resentment—though the end of the war and the way we lost it is another thing. We were still among front line soldiers—friend and foe—and the destructive force of press and propaganda had not yet made scape goats out of us.[12]

Sanders soon knew that Peiper had been in the Ardennes too—and with a key mission within the great German gamble. Sanders asked him about that famous operation, but Peiper dismissed it. "Maybe big for the Americans," he gestured. "The Ardennes operation was no extraordinary undertaking," Peiper said. "It was relatively harmless compared with the Russian theater of operations."[13]

Still, Sanders knew the American officer whom Peiper had captured and held for the fateful days in La Gleize, Belgium. Before coming to Feuchtwangen, Sanders had been with the 2nd Battalion S-2 (intelligence) with the 22nd Regiment. Earlier in the war Col. Hal McCown had been with the 22nd Regiment as a lieutenant. McCown volunteered to leave the 4th Division after learning that the 30th Infantry Division needed officers. When McCown's account of his captivity with the 1st SS Panzer Division was issued by the 12th Army Group in Luxembourg City in February, this tell-all quickly ended up at the 4th Infantry Division HQ near Junglinster.

Being an S-2, during a break in the fighting near Prüm, Lt. Sanders read this account with interest. Knowing about Peiper from McCown's intelligence report filed four months earlier, Sanders asked one question after another. Peiper recounted his time with McCown as a prisoner. He claimed he had told McCown to disappear as he, Peiper, and his men made a nighttime breakthrough to rejoin German forces.

In 1945 Lt. Col. John F. Ruggles was Sanders's regimental executive officer and had a nose for what was important. When he learned from Sanders that Joachim Peiper was being held at Feuchtwangen, he decided to drive down from Ansbach. He not only knew of the McCown piece, but also that Peiper's unit was possibly implicated in the incident at Malmédy. Why did Ruggles not immediately send Peiper off to the war crimes people? "No one was asking for him . . . they didn't know he was even alive," Ruggles said. With thousands of Germans and displaced persons processed every day, the confusion in those weeks was tremendous.

Yet Ruggles was curious about Peiper. Arriving at the camp, Ruggles came in with Sanders. Ruggles spoke quickly and asked about Malmédy. Had he shot those prisoners? Peiper's responded with dismay, "What would you have done?" It was a ridiculous question, he said; he had not ordered any prisoners shot. But he did tell them that the SS would have removed Julius Streicher, the Reich's leading anti-Semite and editor of the vicious journal, *Der Stürmer*. Corrupt, sadistic, and sexually perverse, Streicher was obnoxious, Peiper agreed—they should have gotten rid of him well before 1940. To Peiper's American audience, that edit sounded redeeming. But Sanders, who had seen the hideous photographs from the liberation of the concentration camps, wanted to know what he had to say about that. What about the terrible German abuse of the Poles and Jews? "All the Jews are bad and all Poles are worse," Peiper said without hesitation. "We have just cleansed our society and moved these people into camps and now you let them loose!" Sanders reeled. How could he believe that?

> I told him the Poles I had seen, seemed pretty decent to me. But Peiper was insistent regarding the Poles and the Jews, "They're dirty." I was surprised to hear such from a highly intelligent man. I did not know what to make of it. And of the concentration camps, he said that many of the prisoners held there

> were communists and if we released them, we would learn to regret it. He told me that we would have trouble with the Russians. He lamented the fact that we were not willing to take the SS into our army to prepare to fight the Russians. . . . I only wanted to set a good example as an American.[14]

Sanders looked to see if the SS colonel would change his mind. It didn't happen, but Sanders liked the talks—maybe he could begin Peiper's de-Nazification. Their conversations continued for nearly two weeks. Their hours together became something of a military epic, with Peiper speaking for hours about the fighting in the frigid tundra of Russia. How do you prevent the hands from frostbite in subzero and still handle weapons? What was the perfect time to attack? The legend of the German war in the East came flooding back to a little telegraph hut in Feutchwangen.

"The war there was absolutely barbaric and savage," Peiper said. "You wouldn't believe it. There is no Geneva convention in the fighting." He was amazed, he said, with "the Red Cross type of warfare" on the Western Front, where prisoners were accommodated. That was in stark contrast with the Eastern Front. There, no quarter was given or expected. Yet Sanders had his own experiences and couldn't agree. He told Peiper of his near-religious experience bandaging a German soldier near Osweiler, Luxembourg, after having so much contempt for his enemy. Peiper listened patiently but said nothing like that could take place in Russia.

But then, the daily "lessons from the war" suddenly came to an end. Sanders learned that the 4th Infantry Division would be called back to the United States. It was late July 1945. Sanders went into Peiper's little office at the railroad telegraph station. His unit was being reassigned, he told Peiper. The US 1st Infantry Division would take over the camp. This was good-bye. But as Sanders reached for the door, Peiper called out: "Lt. Sanders, may I ask you a favor?"

"Yes, Colonel?" Sanders paused in the doorway. The SS colonel reached out his arm. "I have been your prisoner and you have been completely fair." Somewhat surprised, the lieutenant shook his hand.

THE DOOR CLOSED BEHIND LT. STEPHEN SANDERS. HE WOULD NOT SEE JOCHEN Peiper again for twenty-seven years.

Chapter 11

MANHUNT

EVEN IF LOST AND ANONYMOUS IN THE MASS OF END-OF-THE-WAR GERMAN soldiery, there was good reason Jochen Peiper had implored Stephen Sanders to have himself executed. Shown pictures and newsreels of German atrocities that included the Malmédy crossroads incident under the same heading as the notorious concentration camps, the hearts of the American public hardened to clamor for vengeance. "The Germans who committed such crimes as shooting captured Yanks at Malmédy will be fairly easy to try—if they can be caught."[1]

Even as Peiper settled at Feuchtwangen on May 28, 1945, US Supreme Court Justice Robert H. Jackson arrived in Paris to tell reporters that an ambitious investigation into the Malmédy crossroads killings was under way.[2] President Truman had recently appointed Jackson as the chief American prosecutor in the coming international war crimes trials. However, as the travesty had occurred on the battlefield, it would be a military war crimes trial conducted by the army. Meanwhile Jackson and his civil team would investigate the top-ranking Nazis within an international tribunal, a process that would culminate in the famous trials at Nuremberg. All that would take time and coordination; there would be no similar delay in the Malmédy trial—or so Jackson said. The reality was quite different.

During the late months of 1944, as the war exploded on the Western Front, the US 12th Army installed a new judge advocate general to handle its legal affairs. The man was Colonel Claude B. Mickelwaite, an Iowan veteran of both the First and Second World Wars. His legal charge was this American army group that was assailed, battered, and nearly driven to the Meuse in the Battle of the Bulge. With war's end and the evolving war crimes programs, there was need for more legal staff. Brig. Gen. T. J. Betts with the SHAEF legal division called up Col. Clio E. Straight.

Other than his availability, Straight brought little experience to such a job. Before the war the redheaded lawyer had practiced in Waterloo, Iowa, but he had no experience in criminal cases or military law. Still, Betts needed someone legal of rank and in April 1945, ordered Straight to head for Paris to the Hotel Majestic to set up a war crimes section. At the end of June of 1945, while the War Crimes Branch was still in Paris, Lt. Col. Martin H. Otto of Red Straight's War Crimes Branch of the US Forces in Europe (USFET) handed a thin SHAEF file to Capt. Dwight Fanton, a Yale Law School graduate.[3] Fanton would be asked to help solve what was seen as the greatest war crime committed against US forces in Europe—the Malmédy Massacre.

Although the thirty-year-old Fanton had five years legal experience, most of it had been spent stateside with the Quartermaster Corps; the desperate US Army pleas for more staff soon took him to Europe.

When Fanton received his charge, the Malmédy case file was not much more than the forty-six-page report of the inspector general from January of 1945 along with the sobering testimony of some of the American survivors. Soon the operation in Paris swelled with a number of new faces, in particular a mustachioed Maj. Burton F. Ellis from Mariposa, California, who was to later head the investigation unit of the war crimes detachment. But with few leads and a cushy location in Paris, the summer proceedings of the war crimes unit featured an uneasy mix of booze, *Folies Begère*, sightseeing, and interrogation of what Nazi witnesses could be located. Like most others, Ellis longed to go home, particularly since duty in bombed-out Germany loomed.[4]

Although "wanted" notices for forty-two members of the Kampfgruppe Peiper were widely distributed, they dangled without result. Not surprisingly, Peiper's name headed that list. For weeks Fanton and his small staff were reduced to following numerous dead-end leads or taking in the beauties that Paris had to offer. Even so, Fanton and a translator bounced in a jeep all over Germany those first four weeks, journeying from one internment center to another, looking for members of the 1st SS Panzer Division. Each of the enclosures looked much the same—hundreds or even thousands of dirty German prisoners behind barbed wire and with rankled camp commanders. "Hell, we have no idea who we have here," one told Fanton. Few prisoners had been screened, any records were hopelessly out of date, and prisoners were continually being released.

Maddeningly, Fanton agonized that Peiper himself was rumored to be in captivity. But where? Some of the members of the battle group had been killed in the interim—an early rumor had even included Peiper. But such hearsay ebbed when Sepp Dietrich was captured with his wife at Kufstein on May 9 by unimpressed members of the 36th Infantry Division: when Sgt. Herbert Kraus of Cleveland, Ohio, recognized him in a POW cage, he described Dietrich as "not anything like an army commander—he is more like a village grocer!"[5] When Dietrich was debriefed at Wiesbaden days later by Lt. Col. Otto, he claimed that he and his wife were on their way to Linz in Austria, but more than likely they were looking to escape to Switzerland.[6] But Dietrich got himself into trouble with his interrogators when he was asked about his impressions of Hitler. "He was very clever," Dietrich stated. "He was human and could be superhuman!"[7] In any case, the "village grocer" told interrogators that Peiper was certainly alive and had already surrendered to the Americans. He had last seen him on April 25 near Lilienfeld in Austria. But where was Peiper?

He was still at Feuchtwangen. Stephen Sanders's replacement was a big Greek American, 1st Lt. Nicolas Katsiaficas with the Big Red One, the US 1st Infantry Division. Like Sanders, Katsiaficas found Jochen Peiper proud and steadfastly fixated with his integrity as a German officer.[8] Peiper later claimed that Katsiaficas allowed him to go home to Rottach-Egern for a single day, and he returned on time and was good to his word.[9] How that took place or whether it was even true was never clear. But in any case Peiper remained grateful, and Katsiaficas seemed to have taken a shine to him as well.[10] Even so, the budding relationship was short-lived. The New Hampshire native was soon closing the camp at Feuchtwangen at the end of July 1945 and sending all those to the much bigger enclosure at Langwasser, which would also be run by the 1st Infantry Division.

But now, in summer 1945, with the confusion of 4 million captured German prisoners and even more displaced persons, no one had managed to effectively get word to the US War Crimes Division that Joachim Peiper was already in American hands. So he was just another Waffen SS officer prisoner who would be sent to the expansive POW enclosure being prepared in the rural countryside near Nuremberg.[11]

The new camp was a step down. Unlike Feuchtwangen, there was nothing casual about it. Langwasser was a bleak sandy spit outside of Nuremberg used by the Wehrmacht during the war as its own POW camp for Allied prisoners. Now it teemed with thousands of SS men in grungy barracks or packed under two-man tents, crossed by stinking trench latrines. Strings of barbed wire and hat-roofed guard towers surrounded the place. The keepers in the late summer of 1945 were members of the US 1st Infantry Division's 26th Infantry Regiment. Special Agent Richard C. Lang with the 1st Counterintelligence Corps (CIC) Detachment of the US 1st Infantry Division was there with his Belgian interpreter and assistant, Jean Marie Centner. Together, they were in charge of day-to-day operations of the place. There were fifteen thousand prisoners—a mixed bag of everything from anonymous zeros to Nazi renegades on the wanted list. Many were SS men suspected of war crimes. Dick Lang was responsible for interrogating SS men, and Centner, who had grown up in German-speaking Belgium, worked as his assistant and interpreter. "In order to understand our state of mind," Centner recalled, "you must know that Dick and I were part of the groups who first entered the different German KZs. . . . Something that after only a few months was difficult to forget or forgive."[12]

The place was raw, something like a wild west for twilight Nazis.[13] Clouds of DDT hovered over the camp to control head lice, and after twilight, mayhem reigned. "Every night they were killing each other," Centner remembered. Many of these were concentration camp guards killing off those they knew could be witnesses against them. After sunrise Lang and Centner would find the bodies lying out in the street between the facilities or sprawled in the trench latrines, strangled with strands of barbed wire. "It was a dangerous place."

Each morning small groups of the inmates went to Nuremberg to pile up bricks and help clean up the city streets.[14] Still, Lang had no problem with prisoners trying to escape—there was nowhere for them to go. Inside the camp they got three square meals—2,200 calories; outside the camp nothing was assured. In one instance, a prisoner ran off from the work detail only to show up at the gate later that night: he had been off to see his girlfriend but wanted back inside!

Centner set up a motion picture machine in the back of a truck and arranged to show several films to two thousand prisoners at a time over a series of nights. The films depicted the gruesome liberation of some of the concentration camps. John Centner would then lecture. "We want these men to see what some of them were guilty of," he said. "The sooner you help us know who among you is responsible for this, the sooner we can all go."

In order to sort out whom they had at the camp, Lang had a list of sixty questions that were given to each prisoner, asking name, rank, military numbers, and many other things. This information was used to fill out a three-by-five information card on each inmate. Two dozen interrogators at the camp then systematically examined all the prisoners with the questions. Throughout the day they went through batches of prisoners, twenty at a time. After the Japanese capitulation in August, the tough SS men became easier to question. But the work was incongruous, Centner thought. Some of the accused "looked so nice and friendly—how could they have committed such crimes?"[15] As SS prisoners kept arriving every day, Lang and Centner slowly built up a big file of names they had at the camp.

One day Lang was absent mindedly thumbing through the card files in their ramshackle wooden barracks and saw a card: "Joachim Peiper." He quickly called his commander, Lt. Col. Henry "Red" Clisson, and told him they had Peiper. He could hardly believe it. "Joachim Peiper in our camp?" "That was the guy involved in the Malmédy Massacre. Send for this man at once."

Minutes later a guard brought Peiper into the barracks. Lang was surprised with Peiper's unremarkable height but "he looked like a pure soldier. He was thin and wiry, as if made out of spring steel."[16] The SS colonel was clean shaven and wearing a black duck-billed cap and a long feldgrau button-down greatcoat. Even his strange-looking Italian mountain boots looked well polished.

"Boy, I sure am glad we located that bastard,"[17] Red Clisson concluded.

John Centner was unimpressed. Rather than a tough SS officer, the Belgian thought he looked "as innocent as a new-born baby—a POW waiting politely to step into the rear of a U.S. command car." Clisson got on the phone to the War Crimes people in Munich. The message: Send Peiper immediately. "This prisoner is considered the most important single suspect involved in the Malmédy case."[18] The head of the war crimes division, Col. Claude B. Mickelwaite, further warned that "no one be permitted to interrogate Peiper relative to the Malmédy Massacre without written approval."

But Mickelwaite's proviso did not reach Jean Marie Centner. As Peiper stood outside waiting to be moved, the CIC man spoke to him briefly. In his native tongue, Centner told Peiper he was Belgian, born in Eupen. He had been in the region in the winter of 1944–1945, his mind flashing on Stavelot and the tiny hamlet around it where 128 civilians—many women and children—had been brutally murdered.[19] He had seen what his men had done, Centner told him. He couldn't resist a parting jab, wishing him "a peaceful conscience about what happened in the Ardennes."[20] Peiper was silent and stone-faced.

Within minutes Peiper was moved to the waiting car. Dick Lang rode with him in the backseat for the ninety-minute trip to Freising, a place about twenty miles north of Munich. "We didn't say much, but shared cigarettes along the way."[21] Lang turned him over to the Third Army Interrogation Center and drove off.

News of Peiper's discovery spread like wildfire. "GI's No. 1 War Criminal Seized" read the *Stars and Stripes* headline. Peiper's first interrogators claimed to find him "arrogant." He denied any knowledge of the Malmédy shootings, but CIC man Lt. Paul Haefner saw it differently. "He is a damned liar," he asserted. "We know that he knew about the slayings and knows exactly who did them." Once the story came out about Peiper, the army newspaper had former members of the 285th Field Artillery Observation Battalion writing,

> Concerning the capture of the Colonel of the 1st SS Hitler Division [sic] who massacred my buddies at Malmédy, I'd appreciate your help in getting those undersigned below and myself on the firing squad if he is convicted . . . we'd sure like to be in on it.[22]

Maj. Dwight Fanton had been frustrated that summer in his search for Peiper. Early on he and Lt. Col. Otto placed faith in CROWCASS, the Central Registry of War Criminals and Security Suspects that Eisenhower had established in November 1944. Yet although it was a well-meaning amalgam of the FBI and Scotland Yard, the sheer volume of the information and the ability to process it meant that Fanton's telex requesting suspects from the Leibstandarte Adolf Hitler produced only a handful of prisoners in two months.

Reasons for the failure of CROWCASS were obvious. The harried staffs of the POW cages around Germany were so overwrought with bulging prisoner populations that little cooperation was forthcoming. By late July no results had been obtained, and urgent appeals were sent to the US 3rd and 7th Armies requesting any information on the whereabouts of Peiper. But US Army communications were haphazard at best. Amazingly, the *Stars and Stripes* provided what US Intelligence could not. Galvanized by news that Peiper was being held in Freising, Lt. Col. Martin H. Otto, Maj. Fanton, and 2nd Lt. William E. Binder immediately left for Munich to see the long-sought quarry.

Peiper's first interrogation came from Maj. Edmund L. King, who submitted a terse preliminary interrogation report on Friday, August 25, 1945. King questioned Peiper extensively on his career but was hardly impressed. "Peiper appears to lie continuously," he wrote. "He is very arrogant and tries to give the appearance of a correct professional soldier." King went on to say that

> during the winter offensive, Peiper led the spearhead in the Ardennes . . . Peiper admits that his unit captured 150 U.S. soldiers near Malmédy who were shot, but denies having given such orders. . . . He is a typical SS officer and cannot be trusted.[23]

The following interrogations at Freising were exhaustive—Peiper afterward estimated he was interrogated six times.[24] Later he would claim that investigator Dwight Fanton had once held him in the interrogation chair for eight hours.

During those days Peiper would compose a long, rambling description of the military operation in the Ardennes. He went through one interrogation after another at Freising, spending most of August 25 and 26 composing his detailed opus. However, his interrogators' records left something to be desired. Columbia law student Paul C. Guth spoke to Peiper in the last days of August. The two participants' memories of the interrogation could agree only on topics but not on substance. According to Peiper, at Freising, Guth told him that he had a favorable picture of him as a panzer officer and fair soldier. Moreover, "as adjutant to Himmler I'm supposed to have been the only one who kept his personal integrity," and the report of American Maj. McCown would provide an advantageous light on his bearing during the Ardennes Offensive."[25] Yet Peiper said that Guth told him that although he admired the SS colonel, his days were numbered:

> By the means of newspapers and radio your name has become known as the No. 1 war criminal. You are the most hated man in America—GI enemy No. 1—and the public demands your head. . . . We assume that you are prepared to take full responsibility for your regiment. . . . I readily believe that you did not issue the order for the massacre. However, how much do you want to bet that I can find three, four or perhaps five soldiers who, due to certain promises, will testify that they themselves heard you give the order! You yourself know how the German people disintegrated after this total collapse.[26]

Guth's memory of their first meeting contrasted sharply, however. When Peiper was brought to his office for interrogation, Guth recalled, Peiper was less than cooperative, whereas he was correct and polite. Indeed, from Columbia Law School he had over a year's experience with this sort of situation. "I knew he was part of the Malmédy incident," Guth remembered, "but my charge was to get information from his position as Himmler's adjutant. I wanted information on the organization of the Waffen SS." On this topic Peiper was helpful, constantly maintaining that he was "purely a soldier." Yet Guth was unimpressed. "That was the line of all of them."

> Based on my experience, my immediate impression was that he was a fanatical Nazi. . . . His general atmosphere was one of full approval and admiration for Hitler and the regime. Yet, I tried to keep it on a certain level. He probably thought I was a goddamned fool for asking only about the SS organization."[27]

Guth spoke with him for half an hour, but, like King, he kept few notes. Peiper kept claiming himself responsible for any of Himmler's moral restraint. Guth said nothing about "GI enemy No. 1," although that moniker might have fit. Meanwhile, Maj. Dwight Fanton and Lt. Binder from the War Crimes Division showed up at the military intelligence interrogation center at Freising, anxious to see Peiper. Fanton interrogated him in lengthy sessions on August 25 and 26, 1945:

> He was a very difficult witness. He understood English perfectly, but insisted on being interrogated in German to allow himself more time for a response. I didn't speak German; but could understand it fairly well. He spoke English with an Oxford accent. He was a very personable individual. You could not help but admire him as a person. But on the other side, he was a dedicated Nazi. I interviewed him early on in August of 1945 and then saw him later during the trial. He never changed at all. . . . He admitted knowledge of the Malmédy massacre and stated that his division commander, Mohnke, had

ordered him to investigate this crime which the American government had reported to the German government through Geneva.[28]

Mohnke ordering the investigation of war crimes? How could that be taken seriously? Even so, Peiper claimed his "investigation proved negative." Meanwhile the US Army Historical Section also wanted a piece of the action. A detailed interview came on Friday, September 7, 1945, when Maj. Kenneth W. Hechler spoke with Peiper about the military aspects of the surprise attack in the Ardennes:

> Oberst Peiper is a very arrogant, typical SS man, thoroughly imbued with the Nazi philosophy. He is very proud of his regiment and division and is inclined to make derogatory remarks about other units.[29]

During the interview Hechler and his interpreter mentioned to each other regarding Peiper's possible complicity in the Malmédy Massacre while agreeing that they were not to ask about that—all the while totally unaware that Peiper understood every word.

> The first indication that we had that Colonel Peiper spoke English was on page 8 of the oral interview where, in perfect English, Colonel Peiper says "I am sorry" when informed that he came within 300 yards of a 3-million gallon gasoline dump at Spa. This so astounded both the interpreter and myself that we sat with our jaws hanging open for a full half minute. . . . On several occasions he turned heatedly to the interpreter and corrected his interpretation in perfect English.[30]

Later, on September 7, 1945, Edmund King spoke to Peiper a second time. "Peiper has lost his arrogance and has ceased lying," he said. King blithely claimed Peiper had covered German armored tactics in the Ardennes, the war crimes committed during that offensive, and "Himmler and the German master plan for the domination of Europe."[31] At best King was poor at documenting whatever he learned and agreed that the next step would be to move Peiper on to the USFET interrogation center just north of Frankfurt.

The story of Peiper's fateful encounter with Hal D. McCown, who was his captive for several days in Ardennes, was already being drawn into the melee. On September 19 the Office of the Director of Intelligence in Germany informed the Counter Intelligence Branch for USFET that the prisoner Peiper was identical with the one reported about by Maj. McCown in the Weekly Intelligence Notes of January 6, 1945. Not only had McCown survived, but he had testified that "concerning prisoners of the SS, I can state that at no time were the prisoners of this organization mistreated."[32]

As Peiper was getting ready to be moved, a major in the judge advocate general's office from California, Burton F. Ellis, was learning that he might soon "be top dog in the investigations of war crimes—quite a responsibility." Yet on August 29 Ellis was able to see enough of Wiesbaden, and a short trip to Heidelberg added to the gloom of the rain that seemed to come every day that late summer. He saw that the Germans were suffering:

> Humans lose their veneer of civilization very, very rapidly under certain conditions. It just beats the hell out of me...you know food and fuel is scarce in Germany . . . The women of Wiesbaden, come in from the surrounding countryside each evening, carry baskets of cabbage, potatoes, apples, or pushing carts, baby carriages, etc. loaded with wood. They are trying to prepare for winter the best way they can. It is really pitiful. I cannot hate these people because I know what happened to them could happen to any people who followed false leaders . . . On Sunday I went through Darmstadt . . . It was leveled. Block after block with nothing, but burned-out skeletons of apartment houses. It is a dead city. If your family, your home, your possessions were buried there—what would your reaction be? These people that lived there beat some airmen to death. I can see why they did what they did. I would have done likewise.[33]

Ellis seemed depressed to learn he would be assigned the Malmédy case and would not be going home for Christmas. "There are hundreds of thousands of prisoners of war that are held and no one even knows their names and as far as I know, few give a damn. . . . This is the most discouraging mess I've ever had the misfortune to be thrown into."[34] Then on September 19, as Ellis looked to find a way out of the army, his promotion came through to Lieutenant Colonel. There was a Mercedes sedan now to drive, an assigned staff, and chance for a little golf. "Of course we got drunk a bit, but then all promotions mean a big drunk."

While Burton Ellis recovered from his post promotion hangover, Jochen Peiper was moved again. Nestled in the Taunus Hills near Frankfurt, Oberursel, the leading interrogation center in Europe, the Military Intelligence Service operation required very little physical change when the Americans took it over. The Germans had used Dulag Luft as a transit center during the war to interrogate luckless Allied airmen. Now, under American ownership, it again harbored POWs. There at the same time the SS colonel arrived, was Karl Dönitz, the last head of the Third Reich, Hanna Reitsch, Hitler's favorite female pilot, and both of Hitler's doctors.[35]

With such infamous deposed dignitaries, Oberursel was less friendly than Freising or Feuchtwangen. When Peiper arrived, he was issued a shirt, trousers, and shoes. Although a toothbrush, bar of soap, and towel were provided, the razor blade was loaned by an emotionless guard in the morning with a washbasin and then taken away after shaving. Peiper was an ordinary prisoner on suicide watch. More than that, Peiper's ID card was marked with a big red "S"—solitary confinement. He was not allowed any contact with fellow prisoners—physical or even visual—and no exercise, bathing, or smoking.[36]

Almost as soon as Peiper arrived he was brought in for an interrogation. On September 15, 1945, Capt. Leroy Vogel spoke with him regarding the statements made by Maj. Hal McCown in SHAEF Intelligence Note No. 43 from the preceding January. They alleged Peiper had treated him well.[37] If true, Peiper's recollections of his conversation with McCown in December 1944 contained high blasphemy. For one, he indicated that the American major was not under guard and had given his word of honor that he would not attempt escape. Worse, McCown supposedly had advised Peiper when they should attempt to escape encirclement at La Gleize by providing information on American artillery practices. If true, both statements could all lead to court-martial, but uglier still were Peiper's claims that McCown had "expressed his regrets at the Russian-American alliance" and, not expecting to soon return to American lines, "offered his services to help fight the Russians." And then the bombshell: "He told Peiper that he could reciprocate by coming to America after the war and help him to hang the Jews."[38] Could any of that be true?[39]

Meanwhile Peiper's other compatriots were being sought out. At the end of the war over ten thousand SS men arrived by rail in a mass assembly at the formerly brutal concentration camp at Ebensee, Austria. There, in the highlands near the Traunsee, tunnels for future underground development of a Nazi intercontinental missile, the "*Amerika-Rakete*," had been built into the mountainside during the last two years of the war. Workers were concentration camp slave laborers toiling under horrific SS leadership. A subcamp of Mauthausen, Ebensee had been in operation since November 1943. During the first days of May 1945, SS Hstuf. Georg Bachmayer and SS Ostuf. Otto Riemer, the heartless and sadistic killers who led the camp, fled as the Americans approached. Peiper had met Bachmayer when touring nearby Buchenwald with Himmler exactly four years before. Now, on May 6, Ebensee shocked infantrymen of the 80th Infantry Division who liberated the wooded valley, finding it filled with starved skeletal corpses and sixteen thousand hideously gaunt "survivors"—emaciated beings still somehow alive. On May 19 Bachmayer first shot his wife and two children in Hintermühle and then killed himself.[40] Otto Riemer escaped and disappeared to an unknown fate.

The first trainload of two thousand SS men had arrived by train in June 1945 to the site of untold suffering only weeks before. Understandably, Poles and Jews in the streets of Ebensee took revenge with whips and sticks on the weaponless SS men as they marched to camp, their path being littered with decorations, armbands, and torn documents. Dr. Franz Loidl, a Viennese priest, volunteered to minister to the SS troops collected there—eighteen thousand by July 1945. Some of the younger SS men found the availability of a *schwarzer kuttenhengst*—a priest—an ironic twist. Yet Loidl hardly felt welcome; many of the incarcerated were "repellant and cold."[41]

Now, a huge collection of imprisoned SS men were interned there in the shabby wooden barracks and mass tent compound, but there was no control at all of what went on. Indeed, Loidl found the American officers amazingly casual, but hardly concerned for the SS connivances developing. The most important thing was to suppress the Hitler salute. Conditions at the camp were wild; SS men were also killing each other at Ebensee.[42] Even though he was an experienced priest, Loidl was shaken by the stories and rumors he heard. "Some SS men are surrounded by a spirit that is secretive and demonic."

In the late summer interrogations began, but ranks quickly closed. On August 29, 1945, Ostuf. Werner Sternebeck, Ustuf. Arndt Fischer, and Hans Hennecke, who had been right under Peiper, were ushered way from the sprawling camp for further interrogation by American CIC men. Hennecke went to the room where

Fischer was being held and there found Rolf Reiser, another of Peiper's officers. He and Sternebeck were steeped in conversation. "What luck the Americans haven't captured August Tonk," Sternebeck said. Hennecke asked why. "He was present when the shooting took place. . . . If the Americans will capture men from the 9th Panzer Engineer Company, they will fare badly too. . . . They were also present." Sternebeck then turned to Fischer and Hennecke with a stern look. "When interrogated," he began, "don't say a word about Peiper's personal order."[43]

WHAT EXACTLY WAS THAT PERSONAL ORDER? ALLIED INVESTIGATORS NEVER found out.

MEANWHILE, BACK IN GERMANY, ON SEPTEMBER 28, BURTON ELLIS, THE NEW Malmédy investigator, stopped by Oberursel to meet Joachim Peiper for the first time. Alerted by *Stars and Stripes*, he learned that fifteen of the survivors of the Malmédy Massacre were located at nearby Bensheim/Bergstrasse. Could they place Joachim Peiper at the scene?

> Friday, I tried to get Col. Peiper identified as having been present at the Malmédy massacre. A number of the survivors were close by so I took him over to see if he could be identified by any of them. He couldn't be. Several said that as much as they would like to see him hang, they had never seen him before.[44]

Ellis was surprised by his own reaction:

> He is the youngest full colonel in the German army—30 years old. Speaks quite good English. Definitely not the sadist type, but a bold courageous soldier. There has been a lot of bad newspaper publicity about him such as being in disguise in a PW camp as a common soldier and not using his correct rank. On the contrary, he was the German commanding officer of the POWs where he was held, always went by his right name and has conducted himself as thoroughly honorable as far as I can determine.[45]

So impressed was Ellis after his first contact with Peiper, that in his first remarks to his superior, Col. Claude Mickelwaite, he suggested the newspapers were off their nut.

"WHILE THE HELD PRISONER WAS DEFINITELY PEIPER," SAID ELLIS, "AT THIS time it is very doubtful that he is guilty of any war crimes."[46]

Chapter 12

ON TRIAL

In the autumn of 1945 the U.S. Army war crimes team was still looking to break the Malmédy case. After being interrogated extensively at Oberursel, Jochen Peiper was moved, with about a thousand Leibstandarte men, to an old army barracks at Zuffenhausen, Germany. But that proved to be ineffective too. Quite naturally, the prisoners aligned themselves into their old units with their former officers. That is, except for Joachim Peiper. The principal suspect was isolated and kept under continual guard."[1] Regardless, Fanton claimed to learn that even from solitary confinement, Peiper had sent out word to the members of his command to say that SS Maj. Werner Poetschke had given the orders for the shootings at the Malmédy crossroads.[2] Although Fanton's suspicion couldn't be proved, it was an effective ploy.[3] Poetschke was not only conveniently deceased but was already a major suspect in the crossroads incident. "Some of the men who were not involved . . . told us that Peiper had instructed the entire group to keep quiet about the crime," said Morris Ellowitz, a short, bespectacled New Yorker who was now part of the investigation.[4]

At first there was practically no lead as to who was responsible. Every man that admitted to being there at the crossroads, recalled seeing the bodies, but when it came to the actual question of who did the shooting, they knew nothing about it. But Ellowitz did interrogate SS man Otto Wichmann, who confessed that even though he knew he'd likely be hanged for his admission. He advised the Americans that "Peiper and his men of his type must be executed, because some day, if German rearmament occurs again, and there is a new government of Nazis, Peiper will be one of their leaders."

Later, at the beginning of December, the SS men were moved once more to the big prison Schwäbisch Hall, where extensive interrogations took place in the winter and spring of 1946, some under circumstances later to be widely questioned. Prisoners of the highest importance to the investigation were salted away in solitary confinement. First and foremost was Peiper. Ellis, meanwhile, stayed at his office in Wiesbaden. But even if remote from his Malmédy investigators, Ellis had not forgotten about Jochen Peiper. He wrote on Sunday, December 9, 1945, that "I must turn the heat on Col. Peiper and see what I can get out of him. He wants to '*tell me all*.'"[5]

Curiously, there is no evidence that Peiper told Ellis anything of substance. Indeed, Peiper continued his vehement complaint that one of Ellis's investigators had seized his chestful of combat decorations, which he considered the "greatest degradation of my life." He claimed that Ellis had promised to return the valuables to his wife.

Later he would bitterly recall an encounter at Schwäbisch Hall with Harry Thon, who brazenly wore Peiper's medals during one of the interrogations. It was "extremely depressing," claimed the ex-SS colonel, "and made me lose faith in humanity."[6]

To the extent possible, all the suspects were kept alone in individual cells, particularly after interrogation. Those not yet probed were unable to learn what those already processed might have said. Although Peiper was in Cell E-73 in solitary confinement, he did have some special privileges befitting the most infamous of those incarcerated: Dwight Fanton personally brought him reading material and he had a desk and access to a typewriter.[7] Passing by Peiper's cell, Fanton often saw him sitting with his back to the door peephole, reading or writing.

> Peiper was kept by himself in a very fancy setup, compared with everyone else. Our theory was that we are not after the *kleiner Mann*; we are after the upper ones and we would show the little guys Peiper reading and looking very comfortable in his accommodations at Schwäbisch Hall. Naturally, there was some resentment over the way he was treated and we made the most of that. We had one fellow, Gustav Sprenger who turned over to our side and gave us a lot of detail and information. He was really helpful.[8]

The controversial interrogations went on for over three months. However, in May 1946, Peiper and about two hundred others were then moved to Dachau, Germany, for the big trial of the defendants accused of the Malmédy Massacre. The ironic setting for the trial—Dachau and its infamous concentration camp was not lost on the public or the SS defendants. Most, like Peiper, knew it well.

The trial took place from May 16 to July 16, 1946, before a military tribunal of senior American officers operating under rules the Nuremberg International Military Tribunal had established. Lt. Col. Burton F. Ellis led the prosecution in the trial, the US Army deciding to try the defendants en masse rather than individually. The seventy-four defendants included SS-Oberstgruppenführer Sepp Dietrich, 6th SS Panzer Army commanding general, as well as Joachim Peiper, commander of the 1st SS Panzer Regiment, which was identified as the main SS unit associated with the crimes at the Malmédy crossroads.

At the trial the accusations were mainly based on the sworn confessions provided by the defendants in Schwäbish Hall. The lead defense attorney, Lt. Col. Willis M. Everett, tried to show that these statements had been obtained by inappropriate methods. However, even the witnesses presented by the defense made admissions that established the guilt of many of the SS men.

Before Peiper, Everett had called Lt. Col. Hal McCown to testify about Peiper's troops' treatment of American prisoners at La Gleize. McCown, who, along with his command, had been captured by Peiper and held at La Gleize, testified that at no time had he seen American prisoners shot or otherwise mistreated.

When Peiper took the stand on Monday, June 17, 1946, he carefully rose from the seats of the accused, and as he approached the bench, he held his head high, giving the court a dose of superiority. Even in the drab, featureless uniform, stripped of all medals and accoutrements, Jochen Peiper still looked the part of the proud SS officer.

Sensing a critical moment in the trial, when Jochen Peiper would testify, the wives of the accused now entered the Dachau courtroom in solidarity. And well behind Jochen, in the last row of the courtroom witness area, was Sigurd Peiper, sitting quietly beside Frau Ursula Dietrich.[9]

At that point the trial had already been in progress for several weeks and was going poorly for the defense attorneys who sought to save Peiper and the others from the gallows. Unlike some of the other defendants, who looked disheveled in physique as well as psyche, Peiper remained well groomed, with his carefully parted hair and neatly arrayed lapel. He still wore his oversized Italian Alpini mountain boots, held his knees close together, and looked straight ahead into the cameras with his hands folded in his lap. Everett's assistant defense attorney, Lt. Col. John Dwinell asked the questions. Name, age, status? A brunette female interpreter in a light-colored sweater translated his statements into English. Peiper canted his head up and gave his name, "31 years, married with three children."

"Would you briefly describe your military career?"

"In 1934, I joined the Waffen SS. After I graduated from the war school, I became an officer. . . . I came to the Leibstandarte Adolf Hitler and I belonged to the Leibstandarte until the end of the war. I held all the positions, beginning with platoon leader and regimental commander. My last position was commander of SS Panzer Regiment Number 1."[10]

Had he participated in combat in World War II?

"Yes, I participated in all the campaigns."

"Were you a member of the Nazi party?"

"No," he said. Strictly speaking, that wasn't true, but he claimed ignorance.[11]

Then Peiper recounted his time with Himmler.

> I was detailed as an adjutant of the Waffen SS in 1938 to the Reichsführer. In this capacity I was in his company for three years without interruption and I was responsible for all matters which concerned the Waffen SS which at that time was still known as the "Verfügungstruppe." During the campaigns that happened in the meantime, I was again with my troops. . . . I was responsible for all matters concerning the available troops and Waffen SS and that means mainly personal political problems, training problems and organizational problems.

Peiper told the court he had been interrogated six times at Freising in September 1945, and at the beginning of November, again at Zuffenhausen and then Schwäbisch Hall.

> In Zuffenhausen I was held for five weeks in a cell which was nearly completely dark and there were no facilities through which light could enter the room and in the course of four weeks I could wash myself only once. . . . There was no physical exercise.

He had been grilled at Zuffenhausen by a 1st Lieutenant whom he would later learn was Lt. William R. Perl.

Peiper said that he was moved to Schwäbisch Hall on December 3, 1945, and then was interrogated there during the winter of 1946. After making a statement on March 21, 1946, Peiper said he had been confronted by members of his own command—Capt. Hans Gruhle, Capt. Oskar Klingelhöfer, Lt. Rumpf, and Lt. Kurt Kramm. While Peiper faced the men, Perl addressed them, asking whether they believed he himself knew everything about the case. All agreed in chorus. Rumpf even said the prosecution knew more than the German officers present! As Peiper told it, Perl then turned directly to him. "At first we believed that you didn't have anything to do with that and suddenly you became a very harmless case for us. The man whom we want now is General Dietrich."

> Thereupon I was told that at the beginning of the offensive in the Ardennes that a fundamental order was issued by the army wherein it was ordered that prisoners of war were not to be taken, that they were to be shot in cases of military necessity; and that, furthermore, the order was issued that our offensive had to be preceded by a wave of terror and fright and that in recollection of the bombing terror at home, we should forget all humane inhibitions. . . . Subsequently, my adjutant [Gruhle] confirmed this in all the points and told many details. . . . Thereupon I signed it, but I was stupid enough to sign it without having read through it.

In any case, Peiper said he was soon confronted still again by others of his command a day or two later—Gruhle, Hennecke, 2nd Lt. Reiser, and Sgt. Hillig.

> Hennecke gave me the impression to be completely down on his nerves . . . and he told me that he was before a court for 14 days and that because I gave him orders in La Gleize to shoot prisoners. I was lightly astonished by what Hennecke told me . . . and had the impression to be in an insane asylum. . . . I was told by 1st Lt. Perl that he [I] had given orders in La Gleize to have 180 prisoners of war shot, but since I was positive that there were only 150 prisoners in La Gleize and those 150 prisoners had been turned over to the Americans. . . . Thereupon I was told, "We know that you personally did the shooting in many places, and that in other places you have the order." Thereupon I was not able to say anything. When Sgt. Hillig was introduced to me, then he was asked, "Did you shoot American prisoners of war on the 19th of December in Stoumont?" His answer was, "Yes." The next question was: "Who gave the order?" And he replied, "Col. Peiper." And he was taken out again. Then my adjutant [Gruhle] was called in. He was asked the same questions and he gave the same answers.

Peiper told the court that he was dismayed by what he was hearing, particularly from Gruhle who was an SS officer.

> When my own adjutant made these statements against me I was disgusted and I told Lt. Perl that I would dictate whatever he wants me to. I will sign everything. Worst of all, Peiper claimed, "Comradeship had broken down too."[12]

How had he been treated, defense attorney Dwinell asked? For six days at Schwäbisch Hall, Peiper claimed he had been locked in a "punishment cell—a death cell." Although sensory deprivation sounded to be the drill for him at Zuffenhausen, he was assaulted only once he said, and that was just as he was leaving Schwäbisch Hall. "I was struck several times in my sexual parts with a stick."[13] He could not see who did it, and so surmised it was the Polish guards who were conveying him away before the black hood was placed over his head. "I was only beaten on this occasion," he said.

Had the statement about the order to shoot prisoners in the 6th Panzer Army been untrue? "In every respect," Peiper replied. Could there have been an order to not take prisoners that Dietrich had received in his conference with Hitler? "I am not certain that such an order existed," Peiper said, "but if it did, the creator of the Order of the Day would have been the Führer." But then the defense pressed Peiper. Had not Wilhelm Mohnke, the divisional commander, relayed a zealous intent at the beginning of the attack? The defense counsel read his statement of March 21 in which he quoted Mohnke as saying that the "offensive had to be fought with special brutality." "My divisional commander was very enthusiastic about the speech of the Führer," Peiper admitted. "It was the demand of the hour to pursue the coming offensive with ruthless harshness."

The court recessed for a short morning break, but Everett worried over coffee and a cigarette. Peiper's recall of Mohnke's words seemed not so different from what Dietrich had written after all. And in another statement, just before they adjourned, Peiper had indicated before the court of his willingness to give Diefenthal permission to shoot troublesome prisoners if circumstances warranted. That seemed hardly reassuring for prospects of an effective defense for Everett's clients.

When the court reconvened at 10:30 a.m. the attention shifted to the accusation that Peiper had been involved in the shooting of a frozen American prisoner at Petit Thier in early January 1945. The SS colonel's damaging statement of March 26, 1946, was again read to the court. But in a surprise move, Peiper did not deny that the American was shot, but said that his recollection was that the decision to shoot the man had been totally that of his subordinate, Dr. Kurt Sickel. Peiper claimed that his admission for having given the order to Sickel to shoot had come from his desire to take the heat for all of his men. Had he ordered Hans Hillig to shoot the American prisoner in Stoumont? He had accepted responsibility, he said, after being confronted by both Hillig and Gruhle, who alleged he had ordered such.

Next Peiper gave extensive testimony describing how the orders had been issued to himself and his men during the days leading up to the attack. Although any organized Belgian resistance was "to be put down ruthlessly," Peiper repeatedly insisted that there had been no special mention of prisoners in the orders of the day, either from the higher or lower echelon. If anyone came across as a fanatic from Peiper's lecture on the days leading up to the big attack, it was the division commander, Wilhelm Mohnke, who "expressed the special confidence which the Führer put in the Leibstandarte." Peiper began a long description of the opening of the Ardennes offensive—a half-mocking treatise on how not to launch tanks in a desperate winter battle. "The traffic on the road turned out to be totally chaotic." he began. The horse drawn artillery of the 12th Volksgrenadier Division was on the road with "a terrible heap of King Tiger tanks and four-legged mules." Soon Peiper was on the jammed road, directing traffic himself. The implications were clear; the local infantry combat leaders were idiots.

The court took a break for lunch. On their return at 1:30 p.m. Dwinell took pains to establish that more than one German officer was wearing a yellow jacket. "Do you remember the names of any officers in particular who wore yellow jackets?"

"I only remember 1st Lt. Thiele for certain from the 3rd battalion and Capt. Gerhard Nüske from the Division headquarters." But Peiper was very conveniently forgetting that his old Waffen SS buddy, Jupp Diefenthal, and the Leader of the 3rd Battalion was wearing a tan jacket as they rode around in his halftrack during the offensive. The prosecution was asking because, before the mass shooting at Baugnez, several of the American survivors had observed an SS officer in a tan jacket dismount from his armored halftrack.[14]

After establishing that fact, Peiper resumed his discourse on the attack. Peiper took the court to Honsfeld in Belgium, on the morning of December 17, 1944, the scene at which a number of Americans claimed his troops had shot down captured American soldiers. "Did you see any prisoners in Honsfeld at that time?" Dwinell asked.

Peiper seemed annoyed to have his tactical treatise interrupted. "I saw some individual American soldiers jump around from house to house," he said. The enemy was looking to get away.

"Do you know whether any prisoners of war were shot in Honsfeld at that time?" Peiper was quick. "I didn't hear anything about that."

"Have you heard the witnesses' statements in this case—Wilson, Morris and White, who testified that prisoners of war were killed in Honsfeld?"

"Yes," Peiper said. "I can't state anything about this, because I wasn't present."

> It was later reported to me that resistance started up again several hours after my passing through Honsfeld and that the troops who were following us up and who at the time considered Honsfeld to be safely in our hands, considered themselves to be secretly ambushed. . . . The American troops had realized their surprise only rather late and proceeded to fire again on the units of my troops, which were further behind, and that therefore serious combat again resulted.

Later Peiper took his audience to the dashing assault on Büllingen, where he took matters into his own hands and overtook the route assigned to the 12th SS Panzer Division and how, at 9 a.m. just south of Büllingen, they came upon a small airfield dotted by a dozen American Piper Cub observation planes. Peiper's tanks and half-tracks soon shot up the flimsy aircraft, with the Americans who owned them coming forward with hands held high. "Did you see any American prisoners of war at that time?" Dwinell asked. "Yes, seven, eight or possibly twelve prisoners of war came towards me along the road. They dropped their arms and were sent to the rear by us. No guard was sent along since a continuous convoy was right behind us along the road."

At about 9:30 a.m. on the 17th they reached Büllingen. In the village, Peiper said they collected about sixty prisoners of war. And here he was careful: "I ordered Captain Diefenthal to see to it that these prisoners were sent to the rear in American trucks which were standing around there, so that the prisoners and the trucks could be put in a safe place at the same time." Peiper's tactical lecture took the court by panzer all the way beyond Schoppen on muddy narrow roads, where Diefenthal's half-track came upon a jeep with an American officer in it. "I left Diefenthal's vehicle for a short time between Ondenval and Thirimont because a jeep was standing along the road there with a driver next to it and, since I had nothing to do at the moment and was very much interested in a the tactical situation around Malmédy. I questioned the driver about this briefly." Peiper said he was still questioning the jeep's occupant when he heard sounds of firing and then quickly drove the jeep on toward the Baugnez crossroads. There he briefly joined the tank of Poetschke, where he ordered the shooting stopped. "I then mounted Diefenthal's vehicle and followed the other vehicles which had already proceeded to move towards the crossroads."[15] Peiper was pointing to the big map on the wall in the courtroom. "The road here between the crossroads and the beginning of the forest was pretty well blocked by American vehicles." He tapped the map south of the crossroads to a stand of trees.

> And a Panther was right in front of me and it was pushing the shot American vehicles into the ditches by moving to the left and to the right alternately. I, myself, with the vehicles followed at a speed no faster than walking. At that time I saw a large number of Americans.

"Did you stop?" Dwinell asked. "Not at the crossroads—no." But Peiper said he did halt soon thereafter about five hundred meters further along, "where the road disappears in the forest."[16]

"Did you know what was taking place at the Malmédy crossroad at the time you passed and the time you stopped?"

> I saw a large number of American soldiers at the time, 40 to 60 at my estimate, some of them were standing in the road already, some of them were lying in the ditch and the great majority of them were lying on the west side of the road in the open area. . . . Some of the American soldiers played dead; some of them slowly crept towards the woods; some of them suddenly jumped up and ran toward the forest and some of them came towards the road. Grenadiers which were in the halftracks fired on those who carried rifles and were running towards the forest. . . . I do remember that about 50 meters from the place we were off the road, there were several American soldiers who played dead and that either [Hans] Assenmacher or some other soldier told these soldiers to get up. I also remember that one or two of them were dead.[17]

"Were these American soldiers that you're referring to prisoners of war?" "At that moment, no," Peiper said.

"Did you give any orders to any American soldiers who were standing or walking in that vicinity?"

"I motioned to those soldiers with my thumb for them to go back and it's possible I told them in English too."[18]

"Did you see Diefenthal there at that time?"

"Yes," Peiper replied, "we were in the same vehicle."

"What did he do?"

"According to my recollection, Diefenthal motioned with his hands to the half-track behind him in order to make them speed up, because the many trucks which were standing around there represented quite an attraction to our men."

"Did you see Poetschke there?"

"No, I saw Poetschke a short time before the road crossing where I gave him the order to send the radio message." Dwinell then wanted to know how long Peiper stayed in the location south of the crossroads.

> In my estimate, about two or three minutes. . . . The reason that I had stopped in the first place was as I didn't see any vehicle in front of me any more and that I had the impression that I was the first vehicle and since I knew with certainty that we would meet resistance in Ligneuville, I had no desire to be the first one. . . . I motioned to my rear and three half tracks and the tank of 1st Lt. Fischer, the Adjutant of the 1st Battalion, passed by me. They continued towards Ligneuville at great speed and I attached myself to their heels.

"In the vicinity of the Malmédy crossroads, did you see any prisoners of war shot?"

Peiper's arms were folded. "No," he stated flatly.

"Did you secure the corner at the Malmédy crossroads?"

Peiper paid careful attention to each question. "I myself, did not do this," he related, "but I am convinced that this was done by Poetschke because tactically this went without saying."

Dwinell wanted to know about Diefenthal's behavior at the crossroads. Peiper recalled the previous testimony of Diefenthal's radio operator, Hans Assenmacher, for the prosecution. "Did you hear him say that Diefenthal got out of his SPW at the crossroads?" Peiper nodded. "Did you see Diefenthal do that?"

"No," Peiper said, Diefenthal had been in the SPW with him the whole time. Yet he did admit allowing Assenmacher to loot the American jeep as he had claimed. That much was true. But the bit about Jupp Diefenthal leaving briefly at the crossroads, that was potentially incriminating—and carefully not mentioned. Peiper did describe his dress: "a yellow fur jacket."

Peiper then described his harrowing entrance into Ligneuville behind the exploding Panther of Arndt Fischer. After stalking the American tank responsible with a Panzerfaust, he had bandaged the badly burned Arndt Fischer. One of the tank crew was killed and the others wounded. "Did you see Poetschke there at that time?"

"No. . . . After about 45 minutes, Poetschke arrived at that place on foot."

Jochen Peiper (right) and brother, Horst, shown circa 1924.

Nuremberg Party Rally 1936. Heinrich Himmler presents Jochen Peiper with the *SS Ehrendegen*, or dress sword. (BA-MA)

Taken at the wedding of SS Lt. Col. Richard Prutchnow with Himmler's immediate staff, January 29, 1937. From left to right in the front row: Lina Heydrich, Reichsführer SS Heinrich Himmler, bride Martha Dickert, Prutchnow, and SS Maj. Gen. Reinhard Heydrich. In the second row from the left are SS leader Karl Wolff and Sigurd Hinrichsen (future wife of Jochen Peiper), leaning over Himmler's shoulder. (BA-Lichterfelde)

In 1936, Hedwig "Häschen" ("Little Bunny") Potthast joined Himmler's secretarial staff. Eventually, the young, athletic woman became Himmler's secret mistress. Potthast was also very close to Peiper before and after the war, and they maintained an intimate correspondence. (BA-K)

On May 20, 1939, Himmler and Peiper joined Adolf Hitler at the Munsterlager training grounds where a group of assembled generals observed a demonstration of the newly trained SS combat forces using live ammunition. (BA-K)

On December 16, 1939, Peiper was at the Reich Chancellery in Berlin when Hitler met with Philipp Bouhler, Martin Bormann, and Himmler. After the meeting, two capped *Jungvolk*—young boys of the pre-Hitler youth organization—knocked on the door to request donations for the Nazi winter fund-raising drive. (Völkischer Beobachter: Monasensia Verlag)

During the December 1939 Christmas holidays at the Peiper household, Peiper (on the left) wears the adjutant's aiguillette. Horst Peiper, on Woldemar's left was with the Totenkopf (Death's Head) Verbände. Woldemar wears a regular army captain's uniform.

Peiper and Karl Wolff at Hitler's Berghof on July 29, 1940. Both accompanied Himmler to Hitler's mountain retreat where the SS Reichsführer met to discuss the possibility of a campaign against Russia. (Frentz)

Peiper is shown with SS Obersturmführer Fritz Darges during a break from escorting Hitler's armored column in the campaign in Poland, September 1939. (Frentz)

Peiper and SS officer Max Wünsche pose for Hitler's photographer, Walter Frentz, on July 29, 1940. Both were SS officers with the Leibstandarte Adolf Hitler. While Peiper was Himmler's adjutant, Wünsche was Hitler's SS aide-de-camp, even sharing Hitler's birthday. (Frentz)

Inspection of the Dachau concentration camp in January 1941. SS Maj. Alexander Piorkowski, the camp commandant, salutes Himmler, while Peiper stands just behind. Wolff is just getting out of *SS-1*, Himmler's Mercedes. On the right is SS Maj. Gen. Richard Glücks, Himmler's inspector of the concentration camps. At the end of the war, Glücks committed suicide and Piorkowski was hanged at Landsberg prison on October 22, 1948. (KZ Gedenkstätte Dachau)

On March 20, 1941, Peiper, along with Himmler, attended the Berlin exhibition "Structure and Planning in the East." Also in the photo are Gottlob Berger, Rudolf Hess, and Martin Bormann. After destroying or deporting Poles, Wehrbauer or SS soldier-peasants, were to be settled in model farms, similar to the one pictured, along a fortified line in conquered Poland. SS leader Reinhard Heydrich alleged German settlers would act as a bulwark against the "raging tides of Asia." (BA-K)

On June 29, 1941, Himmler visited Hitler at his Rastenburg headquarters, just after the opening of the massive German attack on Russia. Peiper is seen at the right edge of the photograph. Himmler is speaking to SS Gruppenführer Karl Wolf. Behind Peiper is another of Hitler's adjutants, SS-Obersturmführer Hans Pfeiffer. Out of view: Hitler, Wilhelm Keitel, and Dr. Theodor Morrell. (Frentz)

On July 29, 1941, Himmler and his inner circle journeyed by car to Riga, Latvia, to meet with Higher SS police chief Hans-Adolf Prützmann to discuss a matter so sensitive it could not be trusted to telephone or telegraph. From left to right: Franz Lucas, the driver; Josef Kiermaier, Himmler's bodyguard; Himmler, seated, with Peiper behind him; Karl Wolff, Himmler's chief of staff; Prützmann; and SS Gen. Karl Gebhardt, Himmler's physician. (Heidemann)

Peiper and Himmler arrived in Grodno, a city of 50,000 with nearly half of the population Jewish, on June 30, 1941, with Himmler complaining that none of the killing teams—the *Einsatzgruppen*—had yet arrived. Photographers recorded the scene as Peiper took notes and Himmler interviewed local peasant women.

From the right, Peiper (wearing a steel helmet) watches as an 88mm gun shells Russian ships on the Dnjepr River in the August 19, 1941, assault on Cherson. SS Capt. Albert Frey is next to him, then SS Maj. Wilhelm Weidenhaupt and SS Capt. Max Hansen. (BA-K)

Peiper, having grown a mustache in the frigid Russian winter, is seen peering through a periscope during the static, snowbound trench warfare that took place in Taganrog along the Black Sea in December 1941.

Peiper addresses the audience at a competitive SS sporting event in November 1942 in Verneuil-sur-Avre, France, west of Paris, where the Leibstandarte was being retrained and equipped. On his right is Peiper's adjutant, Otto Dinse.

Peiper and SS Brig. Gen. Theodor Wisch plan the coming attack to free the 320th Infanterie Division surrounded near Liman, south of Kharkov, by the Soviet winter advance. Photo likely taken on February 11, 1943. (NARA)

Peiper shares a friendly moment with SS Maj. Heinz von Westernhagen during the winter warfare in Russia in February 1943. At the time, von Westernhagen was in charge of the assault guns that supported Peiper's III Battalion, 2nd Panzergrenadier Regiment. (Westemeier)

Peiper seen in his command SPW prior to the attack, which was photographed by SS Kriegsberichter Paul Augustin. (NARA)

As one of the Sturmgeschütz assault guns accompanying Peiper's troop dashes across the frozen Russian steppe, a Soviet soldier throws up his hands in surrender . . . (NARA)

. . . only to be shot down as the assault gun continues the advance. February 20, 1943.

During a typical action in March 1943, Peiper's *Lötlampen Battalion* (Blowtorch Battalion), in concert with the 5th Panzer Company, conduct a search-and-destroy mission through a small Ukrainian village, setting fire to buildings. In one image, an SS leader with an uncanny resemblance to Peiper lights his cigarette from the burning thatched roof while SS Kriegberichter Paul King records the action. King operated with Peiper's battalion during this time. (BA-K)

Peiper seen during the desperate fighting of Operation Zitadelle, near Kursk, July 1943. (Westemeier)

On September 19, 1943, Peiper's command with self-propelled artillery, shelled the town of Boves in Northern Italy. Peiper is observing with binoculars while his adjutant, SS Capt. Otto Dinse, looks on. In the ensuing "anti-partisan" action, thirty-three civilians in the town were killed and many houses burned. (Insituto Storico della Resistenza)

Blowtorch Battalion: After a relentless tank advance on December 7, 1943, Peiper attacked the tiny Ukrainian village of Tortschin north of the Teterew River, which was burned to the ground after being captured. Shown in the photograph are tanks of the 5th Panzer Company. (BA-K)

On January 27, 1944, Peiper was received by Adolf Hitler at his Wolfsschanze headquarters in East Prussia to confer the award of the Oak Leaves to the Knight's Cross.

In November 1944 Peiper's refurbished tank regiment was training in the Westphalian town of Rahden. He conferred awards to those who had fought through the destruction in Normandy the previous summer. With a new offensive coming, Peiper sought to inspire his command on the *Schicksalstag* on November 9, 1944—the celebratory National Socialist occasion when Hitler had staged his famous *Bierkellerputsch* twenty-one years earlier. (Lippl)

Even with the failed attack in the Ardennes, Peiper was awarded the Swords to the Oak Leaves of the Knight's Cross by Hitler's personal order on January 11, 1945. "During the German winter offensive in the West, SS Obersturmbannführer Peiper commanded the panzer group engaged at the fulcrum of the attack through the Eifel in the Ardennes. . . . " Upon receiving the award, Peiper journeyed to Berlin where he was photographed by Heinrich Hoffmann. (Bayerisches Staatsarchiv)

Lt. Col. Burton F. Ellis questions Jochen Peiper in the Dachau courtroom in on June 22, 1946. The interpreter was Lt. Herbert Rosenstock. (NARA)

Durings the final Malmédy trial proceedings, Sigurd Peiper (hat) and Ursula Dietrich leave the courtroom after final arguments are heard. (NARA)

On July 16, 1946, Peiper receives the sentence of "death by hanging" from the Dachau court while defense attorney Col. Willis M. Everett solemnly looks on. (NARA)

In February 1959, at Glemstal near Stuttgart, Peiper meets with other Leibstandarte SS veterans. On his left is Kurt "Panzer" Meyer, with Josef "Sepp" Dietrich on his right. The location of the HIAG treffen is housed today in the *Hotel Kulinarium*. (BA-MA)

Peiper's former command tank radio operator, Fritz Kosmehl, meets with Peiper and Sigurd in the summer 1960 at their home in Stuttgart. Kosmehl was blinded when his Panther tank was blasted by enemy fire in Normandy. (Kosmehl)

Portrait of Peiper taken by his friend Benno Müller in 1960 while Peiper was with U.S. sales at Porsche AG Automotive.

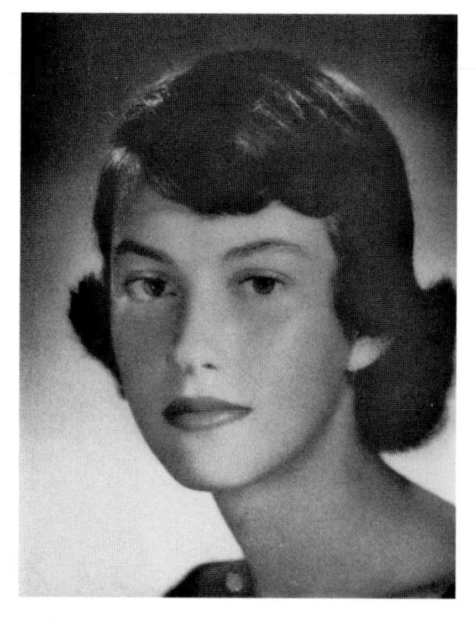

Judith Mutke, who with her Porsche-enthusiast husband, Dr. Peter Mutke, befriended Peiper and Uli Wieselmann in Stuttgart in 1964.

Peiper in Traves, France, in 1967, takes his small boat out on the Saône River for afternoon fishing.

During the summer of 1972, Fritz Kosmehl stopped by Peiper's home in Traves. From left to right: Mayor Ernest Rigoulot, Jochen Peiper, Erwin Ketelhut, and Fritz Kosmehl. (Kosmehl)

During Peiper's last year in Traves, his friend Dr. Benno Müller and Müller's wife would frequently stop by, bringing wine from Germany. Here is Peiper seen with Timm, one of his two Drahthaar wirehaired pointers. (Müller)

On June 21, 1976, graffiti appeared on the roads in Traves, some said written by Paul Cacheux himself. (Paygnard)

Peiper's house, "Le Renfort," at Traves as it appeared on June 22, 1976, when Marc Paygnard took photos during Peiper's only interview. (Paygnard)

"I am tranquil here . . . listen to the birds." André Moissé interviewed Peiper at his home in Traves on June 22, 1976, as photographed by Marc Paygnard. (Paygnard)

Curious onlookers gathered on the morning of July 14, after a fire consumed Peiper's home. Captain Pierre Marchal points out the place where his alleged assassins had cut the barbed wire fence. (Paygnard)

Lt. Stephen Sanders met Peiper after the war and later in Traves.

Police Inspector Roger Lavaux, of Dijon, investigated Peiper's death.

A Traves fireman sprays water on the still-smoldering ruins of Peiper's home on the morning of July 14, 1976. (Paygnard)

For a long time after Peiper's end, the tiny village of Traves was troubled by the memory of what took place during the pre-dawn hours of Bastille Day 1976. (Paygnard)

Reclaimed by nature: the ruins of the balcony of Peiper's house, where he met his fate, as it appeared in 2000. (Paygnard)

"Did he say where he had been?" "No, he merely reprimanded his adjutant [Fischer] because he was wounded."

"Did you see any prisoners of war in Ligneuville?"

"Yes," Peiper said, "I saw several and I think that they remained behind with our wounded." And although Dwinell asked point-blank, Peiper too denied having seen any Americans shot in the town. Instead, the SS colonel seemed to swell with arrogant pleasure, describing how they interrupted the lunch of an American general who escaped just before they arrived. What now seemed like Peiper's Ardennes tactical debriefing now moved on to the problems of reaching Stavelot in the late night and morning of December 18. Feeling their way along in the dark, they had reached that place in spite of terrible terrain and increasing resistance from the enemy. Fighting their way across the bridge into town, he complained the natives were unfriendly. "When we penetrated Stavelot, many civilians shot at us from the windows." But Peiper seemed to shrug that off. "My only goal was for the bridge near Trois Ponts."

"Were there any prisoners of war shot at Stavelot that you know of?" Dwinell asked.

"No," Peiper insisted, pulling the conversation back to their rapid advance to seize a bridge at Trois Ponts, an effort soon thwarted by American engineers who blew the span before them.

"Did you see [Heinz] von Westernhagen at that time?" Dwinell knew that von Westernhagen was the commander of Peiper's improvised Tiger Battalion, SS Heavy Panzer Battalion 501.

"Yes, I asked him about the situation in his battalion and about his casualties." Peiper paused, as if considering his words. "Among other things he told me in this conference that a mix-up had happened at Ligneuville and that a rather large number of prisoners had been shot there. He did not know any details, nor who had given the order to do that."[19]

"Was this the first time that you heard of the incident he spoke about?"

"Yes," Peiper said, and he had seen it himself. "He had passed by there," he recalled, but there were more pressing problems. "My road of advance from Trois Ponts on west could not be maintained and I had to find another crossing somewhere. . . . I decided to take the route by way of La Gleize to cross the Ambleve southwest of there in order to get back to the main road."

This was done speedily, Peiper told the court. Without resistance, his serpentine column was soon racing through the little hamlet of La Gleize and crossed the Ambleve before heading off to the southwest to the little bridge across a small creek, the Lienne, where he planned to regain the main road to Werbomont. "We saw some persons rushing around the bridge, and since we had to expect that this bridge would be blown right in front of our noses, the point stopped and opened fire." Just then there was a heavy air attack on his column. Scurrying for cover, his vehicles stopped firing as the American planes strafed and bombed them.

> The street on the other side [of the creek] takes a sharp curve and goes up to Cheneux and the tank at the point was blown to pieces by a direct hit from

> a bomb right there. It was therefore not possible to pass by this tank for a while. . . . I then ordered Diefenthal to proceed at once in the same direction at great speed and reach the main road and to prevent by all means, the blowing of the next bridge which was near Veucy.

Peiper described the Panzer march to Cheneux, passing through that town at about 4 p.m. on December 18. Peiper told how his column now passed through Cheneux just south of La Gleize: but the bridge across the Lienne Creek to Werbomont was blown in their face, just as he had feared. He had to turn his column around and backtrack—an arduous and fuel consuming maneuver.

> I arrived in La Gleize for the second time about midnight, December 18–19. I immediately proceeded to reconnoiter Stoumont. . . . Upon that I planned and prepared an attack on the town on Stoumont for the early hours of the 19th. . . . The attack itself was studded with severe crises and in one of these crises, the tanks of the Battalion Poetschke attacking on the right flank proceeded to pull back, so I gave Poetschke the order to take a hand there at once. Poetschke himself left his tank, took hold of a rocket launcher, went over to every tank and threatened every commander to shoot him down at once if he would go back even one meter. In that manner, the backward movement on this flank was stopped, . . . I myself organized everyone that was lying in the ditch, including the Company Rumpf, for an attack on the town, which made the decision. About 30 prisoners of war were brought back from the main line of resistance, which continued around the edge of town. I gave the order to send them to La Gleize at once.

Dwinell read the prosecution statement of SS Maj. Tony Motzheim. Motzheim's statement had him seeing the capture of the main group of prisoners on the morning of December 19. According to Motzheim's statement, just then Werner Poetschke, standing by Gustav Knittel, said to Peiper, "Here are two more prisoners of war." And then Peiper supposedly answered in an indifferent and disdainful manner: "As usual."

What did Peiper have to say about that? Before the court Peiper turned on the sarcasm. "It is rather unusual for a high-ranking officer to personally bother with prisoners of war and it is even more unusual for a major to come up with two prisoners of war and ask me what is to be done with them."

Dwinell wanted to know whether Peiper remembered the trial testimony of SS men Walter Landfried and Georg Ebeling, who saw him near a house in Stoumont around noon on December 19? Yes, Peiper said. Both German enlisted men had testified at the trial of seeing Hillig speaking with Peiper on December 19, and soon thereafter Hillig took a prisoner in a field and shot him. And then there was the statement of Hillig himself, who claimed the same.

Peiper denied the whole thing, changing the subject again and launching off into a personal drama regarding his bold strike beyond Stoumont. On the morning of the 19th he ran headlong into an American antitank ambush west of Stoumont just as his Panthers were running out of fuel. Near the railway station west of Stoumont, Peiper held a frenzied meeting with Poetschke and Diefenthal in a ditch as they crouched for cover amid the heavy enemy fire and decided they would pull back to La Gleize. Dwinell sought to bring Peiper, the military hound, back to the issues causing all of the trouble: had he heard the statement of Sievers read by the prosecution where he said he had shot several American prisoners in Stoumont? Yes, he had heard it, Peiper admitted, but "I don't know anything about that." Instead, Peiper described the action where he had captured McCown and safely conveyed him back to La Gleize. "Did you have any conversations with him at La Gleize concerning prisoners of war?" Dwinell asked.

"McCown was very much interested in the questions as to how we would treat POWs," Peiper said. "I could reassure him on that. I told him that I was no '*Genghis Khan*' and that went without saying with us." Peiper's retort struck a strange chord—even the mention of Genghis Khan seemed a telling gaff.

In harrowing detail Peiper recounted the fighting in La Gleize over the following days, but at one point he admitted that on the evening on December 22nd he came upon about half a dozen American soldiers on the outskirts of town who looked to have been shot. "I wasn't able to make any investigation since it was dark and very lively firing was going on. I continued on my way to the C.P. of Maj. Poetschke and I asked him whether he knew anything about those American soldiers I had seen out there. And he said, 'Yes, they had been shot in the course of an enemy attempt to escape during the afternoon of the 21st.'"[20] Peiper said he had a heart-to-heart with McCown, warning that anyone attempting to escape would be shot.

But the following day of December 25, 1944, in La Gleize it was Peiper who would be seeking to escape the American noose being prepared for his battle group advancing deeply into the Allied lines. Peiper carefully described leaving the American prisoners behind in La Gleize, even though he took Hal McCown with him—why? At least nominally he hoped to have some bargaining power to eventually get some of his wounded officers back in exchange for the American major, a crazy scheme that McCown roundly denounced.

Abandoning all his tanks, Peiper's column trudged through the forested hills for over a day, crossing the icy Salm River, where his troops were recognized. He was wounded in the hand—a minor thing, but Peiper told the court he was totally exhausted, having not slept for nine days! He collapsed upon reaching the divisional outpost at Wanne. "I had a violent heart attack," he said, "and was taken down there unconscious."[21] After sleeping for twenty-four hours, Peiper was summoned to the divisional C.P., where he had a debriefing with Wilhelm Mohnke in which Mohnke wrote up a commendation for Peiper that would tout his unit's eradication of an enemy column at Baugnez—the 285th FAOB. After that, Peiper said he drove onto Blanche Fontaine to set up his own command post at Petit Thier.

But Dwinell wanted to know about the Petit Thier event that took place days later in which an American prisoner was brought to him. "The man was half dead," Peiper said. He was frozen severely—third degree and completely exhausted and starved." Peiper interrogated the American soldier who was brought in supported by two of his men. The SS officer had a chair placed under the man while he asked a few questions. Peiper's story of the frozen prisoner's fate was virtually identical to what he had told at Schwäbisch Hall, with the unlikely addition that he and Dr. Sickel discussed whether to put him in an aid station where his frozen limbs could be amputated.[22] After the man was removed, "The atmosphere pervading the room was one of pity."

Dwinell kept on going. Did Peiper hear about Werner Kühn, who was accused of shooting civilians at Lutrebois? Yes, Peiper said, he knew this man. Indeed, on December 21 he recalled having demoted him from an Obersturmführer to an enlisted man for leaving his platoon during a critical moment in the fighting in Stoumont. As for the rest of Kühn's story, Peiper could not say—he was not there. But Dwinell pressed on. Had he heard Heinz Hennecke accuse Peiper of having ordered an execution detail on December 22? Yes, Peiper said, this was true, but the execution detail was not to shoot Americans but rather to put an SS deserter to death. "The shooting was to occur at noon on the 22nd," Peiper said, "but it was delayed by the American attack and the man was shot in the evening in La Gleize by a summary court."

But if Peiper saw his behavior as honorable, to the court it must have seemed damning, for if a Waffen SS commander was readily willing to shoot one of their own for desertion, how much more eager might they be to eradicate true enemies who might have surrendered? It was on that note that the court and Jochen Peiper adjourned at 3 p.m. that Friday.

When the German newspapers came out the next day, there was Joachim Peiper sharing the bold type with Albert Speer at Nuremberg, the latter now informing the world that reputed Nazi progress on atomic weapons was a bluff. Yet Peiper's share of the newsprint was more personal, telling English readers how at Zuffenhausen he had been informed of his doom:

AN ARMY INVESTIGATOR—WILLIAM PERL—RECOMMENDED HE SETTLE HIS affairs: "Not even the President can save you now."[23]

Chapter 13

ELLIS

THE COURT IN THE MALMÉDY TRIAL RECONVENED THE FOLLOWING SATURDAY morning, June 22, 1946, at 8:30 a.m. It was a steamy day in Dachau, unnoticed as the fifth anniversary since the cataclysmic German invasion of Russia in 1941.

Again Jochen Peiper took the stand, but the complexion of his testimony changed. Pointed questions now came from Burton Ellis and the prosecution. "Peiper, you speak and understand English, don't you?" Peiper said yes, but did so in German. "Isn't it a fact that you didn't surrender to the Americans on the capitulation, and that you tried to go home and were apprehended within 20 km of your home? And you were carrying a weapon when you were apprehended?" Yes on all counts.

Peiper's answers were emoted carefully. And then at other times, when his footing seemed certain, his answers came quickly. His knowledge of English and the time it took his bespectacled interpreter, Lt. Herbert Rosenstock, to compose the questions into German provided an unmistakable advantage as the ex-SS colonel's body language clearly suggested he knew the meaning of the questions before they were translated into his native tongue. "You went into the Headquarters of the Reichsführer in August 1938, didn't you?" Peiper nodded. "And in 1940, you became adjutant to the headquarters of the Reichsführer . . . and in that capacity you became quite well acquainted with Himmler?" Yes, Peiper admitted; all was true.

But now Ellis began to turn the screws. "Now, in direct testimony, you stated that you were a military adjutant; as a matter of fact, you were more than just a military adjutant weren't you? Isn't it a fact that you accompanied Himmler on inspections that were of a character other than military?"

Peiper looked straight ahead. "Yes."

"And as a matter of fact, didn't you accompany Himmler on an inspection of one of the first gassing experiments on living subjects?" Yes, again, Peiper agreed. Hadn't he made a long report on these gassing experiments while he was confined at Oberursel?

"Not a long report," Peiper countered, "only a very short one." Standing on the sidelines, Everett winced—how did that admission help his star witness?

"Have you listened to the testimony here in the court about the famous Genghis Khan?" Peiper said he had listened to it. "And isn't it a fact that you have told Lt. Perl that it was sort of a hobby of Himmler's to inculcate to the SS the idea of fighting like Genghis Khan?"

"No." Peiper denied, but in his heart he knew differently. In fact, he had been required to write an essay during SS officers' training school about Genghis Khan.[1] And he asked the man under him to do the same! Peiper further asked the men under him to do the same! And he knew that Gottlob Berger had a personalized copy of Michael Prawdin's book about Khan given to each SS officer at Christmastime. Earlier in the trial Hermann Priess had testified of Himmler's interest in Genghis Khan—it was an established fact. And unknown to the court, Peiper had written of his admiration for the Mongol lord from the Eastern Front in 1943.[2]

"Didn't you also tell Lt. Perl that Himmler said in substance: 'Pyramids of skulls have to impress the enemy and create panic amongst them?"

Peiper held his body firmly. "No."

"Do you deny that Himmler advocated such measures of fighting?"

"Yes, absolutely." He was defending SS Reichsfüher Heinrich Himmler, the head of the SS and the architect of the Final Solution. In fact, Peiper knew the contrary: Himmler was obsessed with Genghis Khan.[3]

Ellis changed the subject. Now he was talking about the "death cell" that Peiper told the court he had been confined to at Schwäbisch Hall. How long had he been there? Peiper had to admit that he was there for only six days. On December 10, 1945, he was moved to a hospital cell, where he remained for three months prior to the trial, eventually being moved to a standard jail cell where he bunked with Arndt Fischer. The hospital cell had a bed, night table, chair, and a toilet as well as a typewriter.

Peiper complained that he had composed more than half a dozen statements since his captivity.[4] Ellis asked Peiper whether his statements had been under oath. He agreed that they had. So were the statements the truth? Peiper complained the Schwäbisch Hall statements were not the complete truth as he was accepting the blame for his men.

Ellis ran circles around Peiper. Had he written statements while at Dachau? Peiper said no, he was sure of it, only to have the chief prosecutor produce a piece of paper with his handwriting and signature. "Is that statement true?" Ellis asked.

"May I read through it?" Peiper asked, seemingly caught off guard.

"It is sworn to, is it not?" It was. "You believe in the sanctity of an oath do you not?"

"Yes."

"Was it signed under pressure?"

Peiper protested.

Ellis sniffed. "If the contents are not damaging, then it is true and if the contents are damaging then it is not true, is that correct?"

"I was never afraid of any damage," Peiper declared. "Do you usually read statements before you sign them?" Peiper said he did.

"I will read this paragraph in the statement of yours is dated April 25, wherein you were referring to the conversation with Hardieck. 'To my question of what he would do with prisoners, he answered, "We do not give pardon. If we get caught, we will also be bumped off. . . . "' Is that paragraph true?"

"This paragraph is true." Peiper then reminded the court that Willi Hardieck with Skorzeny's troops had died on the first day of the offensive.

"If you saw Hardieck kill an American prisoner of war, you could have stopped him, could you not?"

"I could not have prevented it after he was already dead," Peiper said, loosing a bolt of sarcasm. After Ellis recast his question, Peiper admitted that, as senior commander, he did have authority to prevent the execution of prisoners.

Ellis pressed. "Do you think that a statement that was sixty-seven pages long and taken over a period of two days would be untrue?"[5] Peiper knew what they were asking about: his long first interrogation at Freising by Dwight Fanton and others in September 1945.

"That was a very long interrogation report and furthermore, the first one which got me into connection with the Malmédy incident. I would have to read it very exactly in order to find contradictions."

Ellis looked as if he had bitten a sour apple. He said Peiper's judgment was predictable: damaging statements would be untrue and innocuous ones would be fine. Peiper shook his head. "I personally do not care what could do me any harm."

Where had the notes gone that he had at the opening of his testimony? Since Zuffenhausen, he told the court, he had kept notes on scraps of paper, often hidden in his sleeves.[6] "The guards wanted to take them away from me, but I directed their attention to the fact that they were very important for the prosecution." After that fib, they left him with his notes that he had then copied down onto the sheaf of papers he carried into the courtroom.

Ellis asked Peiper whether he remembered the statement he attributed to Perl of having been told that "the sons of two influential persons, one a senator and the other an economist's son were killed at Malmédy" had not actually come from the statement he made to Paul Guth at Freising. Ellis insinuated that Peiper had made that up.

Peiper said no and had more: "I might remind you, Lieutenant Colonel, of the fact that on December 7 or 8, 1945, when you visited me in Schwäbisch Hall, I told you the contents of the conversation I had with 1st Lt. Perl and that you told me at the time that you were very sorry and that Lt. Perl did not have the authority to make such utterances and that I should not pay any attention to them."

Ellis was chagrined. "Do you have anything else that you want to remind me of?"

"At the moment, no," Peiper said smugly.

Ellis launched off in a different direction. Hadn't Peiper signed those statements he made in Schwäbisch Hall in March 1946? And weren't the drafts in his handwriting? All true, Peiper agreed, but some of what he wrote in the statement of March 26 was not true, as "it was made under the circumstances under which I had to believe that my comrades betrayed me, and I was very disgusted and it did not matter . . . and I told Lt. Perl he could dictate anything."

"How does it make a difference to you now?"

"Today, I was able to find out that the comradeship, which at the time I believed to have disappeared is not an empty illusion. . . . *It is my duty to testify clear and distinctly so that the German people would learn who we were in reality and that we fought for their Fatherland for six years desperately and fanatically.*" Peiper seemed fired up—again he was the proud SS man.

To throw water on Peiper's gloating testimony, Ellis changed the subject to Schwäbisch Hall. "You remember don't you, that when confronted by Knittel in the presence of Mr. Thon [that] you told Knittel that he should confess as you had told everything?"

"That did not occur in this manner. . . . One day Mr. Thon said to me, 'Don't you want to say hello to your old comrade, Knittel?' And I said, 'Of course, with pleasure.' The door to Knittel's cell was opened, I greeted Knittel and he asked me what is going on around here. Thereupon Mr. Thon said to Knittel, 'Go ahead, ask Peiper. We know everything.' Thereupon Knittel asked me, 'Did you testify?' and I said 'Yes.' And he asked me 'What do they know?' and I said, 'Well, they know more than we.' Thereupon the door was closed."

Ellis asked whether Peiper hadn't requested that he be allowed to visit Georg Preuss. Peiper agreed he had requested that, but the "only reason was about the Knight's Cross." Peiper was troubled in endorsing the commendation for a subordinate who was lying. That was terrible form for a Waffen SS officer.

"Isn't it also true that after Lt. Perl came back to you and told you what I said, that you then confronted Preuss in the presence of Lt. Perl and you told Preuss that: 'They know all about the killing of the flyer' and that Preuss then confessed the killing and also taking the flier's ring—isn't that true?"

"Yes," Peiper agreed, "that is correct." Georg Preuss looked shaken in the defendants' dock. Peiper's testimony had seemingly sealed his fate. Ellis pressed—hadn't Peiper said that if they looked to be making a last stand in La Gleize that he would liquidate prisoners?

"I decided to keep La Gleize until the last man, up to the 23rd at noon, and I told my commanders, if all of us should perish here, our prisoners are not going to survive us, since I thought it impossible [would not allow it to happen] that all of us would die here and the next day a hundred and fifty Americans would get new weapons and fight against the German Army."

The defense was staggered—one admission from Peiper after another. Poetschke had killed eight prisoners trying to escape in La Gleize, the frozen American prisoner at Petit Thier was shot even without his orders, Preuss had shot the flyer, and now Peiper was admitting that if he went down defending La Gleize, he would have the American prisoners shot before the final battle. Disaster.

"How do you account for the fact that all of your company commanders and many of your platoon leaders held meetings before the offensive began and told their troops to kill prisoners of war and allied civilians if it hadn't been ordered by someone?"

"I heard the testimony of the company commanders here and I also heard the testimony of the enlisted men. . . . It was clear to me that everyone was looking for some protection and for some straw, and since the men were constantly told, 'You couldn't have done it on your own, you must have had an order,' it is very understandable that drowning young men seize this—grasp this straw and allow that such an order was suggested."

Ellis looked to have him cornered again. "Now, were all your men so undisciplined that they killed prisoners of war without orders?"

"During combat," Peiper huffed in a superior air, "there are situations about which one cannot talk [about] on the green table."[7]

"Can you answer the question without talking about green tables? I'll ask the question again. Were your men so undisciplined that they would kill prisoners of war without orders? Answer yes or no." It was a cheap trick. To answer was quagmire.

"No, this question doesn't have anything to do with discipline. . . . I cannot answer it yes or no." Ellis dropped the word disciplined in his question and Peiper finally gave in. "During combat, there are desperate situations, the answer to which is given out very fast to main reactions and which do not have anything to do with education or training."

"Well, is there anything desperate about a situation where you line a hundred and fifty men, prisoners, up in the pasture without arms, and there is no enemy in the vicinity and you are still advancing without opposition, and there prisoners are shot?"

Dwinell jumped up to object. "Counsel is assuming a state of facts in asking that question . . . I object." Ellis argued loudly that the question was legitimate. But even the law member was confused on proper procedure. The court took a midmorning recess while Abraham Rosenfeld gauged the law and spoke with Josiah T. Dalbey, the president of the court.

When the court reconvened the question was allowed and then repeated. Was there anything desperate in the posed situation? "No," Peiper said. Moments later Ellis was determining the colors of the uniforms of the SS panzer men clad in black leather and the panzer grenadiers in gray. "You rode with Diefenthal quite a lot during the offensive, didn't you? Did he wear a yellow-colored jacket at the crossroads on the 17th of December 1944?"

Peiper said yes to both questions. "What time did you testify that it was when you entered Honsfeld on the 17th of December 1944?"

Peiper said it was about seven o'clock. He had learned about the fighting there secondhand from Gerhard Nüske, his adjutant Hans Gruhle, and Heinz von Westernhagen. "Did they tell you about prisoners of war being killed in Honsfeld?" Peiper said no. "When you left Honsfeld, do you remember the graveyard on the right side of the road?" Peiper said he couldn't remember. "Did you kill the prisoners of war that were lying opposite the graveyard in the pasture, where the statements have placed [Max] Hammerer and [Ernst] Goldschmidt?"

"I know nothing of that."

"Were you present when they were killed?" And then a second question: "Do you know who killed them?" No, two times.

"I believe you said yesterday that you saw civilians firing from the windows in Büllingen. Is that true?" Yes, Peiper said. "How did you know they were civilians and not American soldiers?"

"I have had some rich experience in this field and a sharpened eyesight."

"How close were you to these people that were firing in the windows?"

"I was driving right past these houses underneath the window. I had to get my head down several times and I saw these people shoot. Also [I] saw and heard the bullets hit my vehicle."

"Did you see any eighty-year-old women firing at you from the windows in Büllingen?" Ellis asked sarcastically. He was trying to draw the court's attention to the more than a hundred civilian men and women killed by Peiper and Knittel's command in the Ardennes.

"In those short moments, I had no occasion to determine the age of the persons firing." Ellis already looked like a fool.

"Did you see any one-year-old baby firing at you from the windows in Büllingen?" Ellis asked.

"No, not even in Russia did I see any one-year-old babies firing." Peiper's replied acidly. There was a quiet chortle in the court. Ellis straightened his posture in surprised embarrassment. The SS colonel's satiric response would make headlines the next day.[8]

Peiper testified about having seen a line of prisoners as he approached the town. "Could they be the same ones that Jaeckel in his statement says he fired on?" Peiper said he could only vaguely remember Jaeckel's testimony. "What time was it that you got to the crossroads south of Malmédy?"

"According to my estimate today, approximately 1330. It might have been somewhat earlier."

"Now, do you remember who had the lead vehicle there at the crossroads in Malmédy?"

"1st Lt. Sternebeck conducted the column point all the time. And I also saw him in Engelsdorf [Ligneuville]; he was among those tanks who arrived at Engelsdorf before me. I did not see him at first because he was standing in cover behind some houses. . . . I also think that he had some combat with an American Sherman that I mentioned yesterday."

"Recall the testimony of former Lt. Lary where he said that the leading tanks sprayed his men as they were trying to surrender. Would that change your answer about who had the third tank?"

"No," Peiper said, he had no idea who had the third tank. "What time did you get to Ligneuville?" Peiper said he thought it was shortly before 2 p.m. Ellis gave up. "What position in the column was the vehicle you were riding in?"

"My impression was that I was in the second or third vehicle. I testified yesterday that I stopped south of the crossroads. I was under the impression that there was no vehicle in front of me and I then motioned three half-tracks and one panzer in front of me—to pass by me. So that they were for sure in front of me when I arrived in Engelsdorf. Also at that time the following were in Engelsdorf for sure: Sternebeck and perhaps one or two more tanks under his command."

When Peiper got to Ligneuville there was the fighting with the American Sherman tank, but Peiper said there were at least one or two more in the town. Who had knocked the Sherman out, Ellis wanted to know. "It must have been one of my tanks," Peiper said. "All I know is that I looked out of the window and ordered it knocked out with a rocket launcher: it blew up in the air about that time."

"I thought you told me in Blankenheim, last fall, that you personally knocked it out?" That was when Ellis had brought Peiper close by the Ardennes.

"No," Peiper said, "I said that I attempted to knock it out."

"When did you leave Ligneuville?" Ellis asked.

"It is hard to estimate time," Peiper replied. "I spent about forty-five minutes among the burning ammunition there in the house and this was a situation that was so extremely unpleasant that one could easily make mistakes in time. My whole stay in Engelsdorf might have amounted to an hour and a half."

"What time did you reach Stavelot?"

"In my opinion, at about 2000 or 2100 hours."

Peiper said they thought a small infantry column on their left attacked them and that ended any attempt to take Stavelot that night. Instead, he moved from his post in Jupp Diefenthal's half-track to a house about a kilometer southeast of Stavelot to dispense orders to his commanders to attack after dawn the following morning. "Did you order the killing of eleven American PWs and three civilians that were found dead by that house on the 18th?" Ellis was referring to the US soldiers and Belgian civilians killed near La Vaulx Richard.[9]

"I neither ordered that, nor did I hear about it."

Then Ellis said, "If the court please, I would like to request that Hans Hillig . . . stand up." General Dalbey gave the order, and Hillig rose from his seat curtly and then sat back down. "Do you deny that you ordered the accused Hans Hillig to kill an American PW on the 19th of December 1944 in Stoumont?" Ellis posed.

"Yes," Peiper said.

"You stated yesterday that Sprenger told an untruth." Yes again.

"Do you deny that Sievers shot any PWs in Stoumont?"

"Completely." Ellis took Peiper to task for his memory of time and dates, but that got nowhere; indeed, it smacked of repetitive whining. Suddenly, Ellis addressed Gen. Dalbey and the court, as the Saturday court was to end at noon.

"At 0900 hours this morning, some undisclosed information was brought to my attention, which makes it necessary to recall Lt. Col. McCown for further cross-examination. We request permission to recall Col. McCown when he arrives . . . and also to recall this witness."

The news seemed to animate Rosenfeld. "When is Col. McCown going to return?"

"We have wired for him," Ellis offered. He knew McCown was already supposed to be on a plane to return to the United States. "They are trying to stop him." Dalbey seemed satisfied. The court was adjourned until 8:30 a.m. on Monday, June 24, 1946. Willis Everett was disgusted.

> I am pretty well whipped down after the first week of the trial. At noon, Lt. Col. Ellis announced to the court that due to certain development, which had just been discovered, that it was necessary to have Lt. Col. McCown recalled as a witness. None of us defense know what he expects to pull unless it is to impeach or discredit his testimony. We have had a meeting with our staff this afternoon and every one of the lawyers are clamoring to stop our case and give

> up trying to defend these people as the court appears so one-sided and the prosecution appears to be trying to slur all our efforts.[10]

But Ellis failed in his attempt. McCown was already in the air and had returned stateside. That was one small victory for the Everett; another was Peiper's testimony:

> This morning Lt. Col. Ellis cross-examined Col. Peiper and it was a pity to see a German officer run rings around an American officer. Not one time, did Ellis trip up Peiper, but I know the questions, which Ellis asked in a sneering manner, could not help prejudicing the court. The pity of the whole thing is that Ellis is not representative of the high principles of American justice and all the people in the audience must have some opinion of Americans.[11]

When Monday morning, June 24 came around, Peiper was back once more on the witness stand. After a day to mull things over, Ellis lit into Peiper, intent on tarnishing the German star witness with what was learned from him when interrogated at Oberursel the preceding summer. "Do you recall what dates you were there?" Ellis began.

"I remained there from the middle of September 1945 until the first part of November," Peiper replied.

"You were interrogated there weren't you?"

"I was questioned about several points once or twice in an oral conversation. . . . I talked to the man conducting the interrogation about experiences I had with American prisoners, including McCown. I told the gentleman, in the course of the conversation, that I did not have any intention of saying anything which would do any harm to Maj. McCown since my meeting with Maj. McCown at the time had occurred on a very human basis and our conversations too."

"Then you would not have made any statement about Col. McCown that would have hurt him, would you?" Peiper agreed that he would not.

"As I recall, you testified, I believe it was at La Gleize, a Belgian civilian clubbed one of your wounded to death."

"I said in La Gleize a Belgian civilian hit one of my men over the head with an axe crying 'Vive la France.' Actually, it was in Cheneux. Whether the man died or not, I don't know."

"What happened to the civilian?" Ellis asked laconically.

"He was shot on the spot," Peiper said without hesitation.

"Didn't you give him a trial?"

"No," he said, "that happened in combat, while the Americans were attacking."

Ellis seemed satisfied. He turned the questioning back over to the defense. First Dr. Eugen Leer spoke up, asking the court to strike Peiper's courtroom testimony about his witness of an early gassing experiment with Himmler. It was irrelevant to the case, he insisted. But Ellis was not about to let that happen and pointed out that it was the defense itself that had brought up the issue. Round and round it went, but soon Rosenfeld ruled that Peiper had taken the stand of his own volition and had testified accordingly. The evidence would remain.

So chastised, Leer still got around to his questions, but these promptly backfired.

"This book about Genghis Khan was mentioned repeatedly. In what manner did you come into contact with the book?"

"All SS officers who had to go to military academies were, during 1937, forced to write a thesis of a tactical nature concerning military history. And in that connection, we also received an order in 1937 to write a theme on the subject—the significance of the Yassah for the Mongolian empire, and sources for this in a number of books were given, including two books by Prawdin."

"You mentioned the name Genghis Khan in your cross examination," Leer asked.

"When I first talked to Maj. McCown I said, laughingly, 'You are really suffering a stroke of bad luck by falling into the hands of us bloodhounds here.' Upon that, he himself laughed and said, 'That is propaganda. I know very well that these are the best troops in the world, for any other troops in your position would have surrendered a long time ago.'" The US Army officer in the room flinched: the *SS—the best troops in the world!?* Had McCown said that? But Peiper seemed suddenly unrestrained; Dr. Leer was his lawyer, and he plowed on, with an altogether unhelpful confession.

> The only thing that happened during the Ardennes Offensive which I know was not proper was the complex or incidents at the cross roads near Malmédy. . . . That incident at the crossroads, I therefore never denied in any manner. However, I was only able to maintain that at the time in which I was at the crossroads, nothing extraordinary had yet happened.[12]

If Peiper didn't believe his Kampfgruppe had been involved at Malmédy, who could he reasonably suppose had been involved?

> Upon returning to the Division C.P. on the 25th of December I received an order to determine whether any men of my regiments were involved in this incident at the crossroads; at that time I promptly ordered the commanders of my two battalions, that is, Maj. Poetschke and Lt. Col. von Westernhagen, to institute such an investigation. And I also gave similar instructions to Capt. Diefenthal. . . . [But] the commencing American counter-offensive did not leave us any time to concern ourselves with the matter. I considered the negative reports of my commanders as sufficient.

Poetschke investigating the incident? The fox finding out about the disappearance of the chickens! Peiper went on: "I remained convinced, until my interrogation at Schwäbisch Hall that nobody in the regiment was involved."

For even the most dispassionate bystander, it was an amazing display. How could Peiper say that when, on the previous Friday, he had described his conversation with von Westernhagen on December 18, 1944? "Among other things," Peiper said, "he told me in this conference that a mix-up had happened at Ligneuville and that a rather large number of prisoners had been shot there. He did not know any details, nor who had given the order to do that."

But Peiper obviously felt safe in speaking before his own attorney, reflecting a loosely prepared agenda. "I was told by 1st Lt. Perl on March 21 . . . [that] I really wasn't such a bad man as they had assumed. I was at the beginning and that they intended to go much higher now to incriminate my superior, General Dietrich." Peiper said he was confronted with a statement of Dietrich in which his superior had said the fighting was to be "done with brutality and terror without humane inhibitions."

Peiper claimed that the testimony he was shown was erroneous because Dietrich did not even arrive at Schwäbisch Hall until the day after the event. Yet that wasn't true. Dietrich had been brought in the same day that Peiper confessed, Thursday, March 21.[13]

After that, Dr. Leer sought to show that there was anti-Waffen SS bias. "Did you have the experience that prisoners of war were expecting to be killed by the Waffen SS?" posed Leer.

"I found that most of the prisoners of war that I talked to believed that they would be shot, which is probably based mainly on radio propaganda."

"Did the appearance of the American prisoners of war agree with the picture that your men had of them?"

"No, in war, it is usually like this," mused Peiper. "One attacks one another with great fury and when one meets face to face, one generally find that after all, you are not as bad as I thought you were and that fundamentally, it really would be very stupid to bash in each other's heads."

As if on cue, Peiper began a long animated lecture on his "severe responsibilities in the Ardennes" and the "very larger burden" of prisoners of war:

> During the whole mission prisoners did not interest me at any time. In the meeting of many commanders and officers in Blankenheim, I expressly told them that I was not a bit interested in prisoners of war and that the only important matter as far as we were concerned was to break through fanatically at maximum speed and that anything which in the course of our breakthrough would remain lying in the ditches, be it prisoners of war or material or tools of war, that they would later be picked up by the infantry following us. . . . In the course of many other breakthroughs we really had nothing to do with prisoners of war. . . . We were driving at great speed and firing from all barrels. We penetrated the soft spots of the enemy like an arrow.

Peiper's eyes glimmered as if he felt himself once more in the saddle of a Panther tank. Dr. Leer ended his questions and handed the baton to the prosecution.

"Poetschke reached you in Ligneuville about 45 minutes after you arrived there, is that not true?"

"Yes," Peiper said, "that is a rough estimate." "Is it true that Poetschke is dead now?" Ellis posed.

Now Peiper seemed bold—even arrogant: "Yes, unfortunately."

"Now, the fact that you had been given an important mission to perform, does that relieve you from all other command responsibilities?" Ellis asked incredulously.

"I have always been known to be exceptionally eager to take responsibility and if I am not mistaken, the question as to how far I am responsible in this matter will be cleared up by the court." Peiper was sardonic now, even mocking.

"Well," Ellis charged, "are you responsible for the name that was given to your battalion on the Eastern Front as the 'Blowtorch Battalion'?"

Dr. Leer jumped up to defend his client. He was here to defend his actions in the Ardennes and not in Russia. Dalbey sustained the objection. Ellis asked Peiper if he had known about American prisoners being used to carry ammunition in La Gleize. "Given our supply situation," he responded sarcastically, "there was hardly any to carry."

"Now, you have denied that you have given any orders to shoot prisoners of war at La Gleize, isn't that true?" Peiper agreed. "Now, if you know that Rumpf, in his own handwriting, in a statement not introduced in evidence before this court stated:

> During the conversation in the C.P. of the Regimental Commander, Peiper mentioned that he had ordered a part of the Americans to be shot right away because the American soldiers had refused to work. This would be the best means to make them obey, as the others would notice right away what's happening to those who do not return. . . . Contrary to this, Peiper treated an American major in a very friendly way and talked with him for many hours. . . . He took the major's name and his home address."

"Do you deny the truth of the statement of Rumpf?" Ellis asked.

"Completely," said Peiper. Ellis read one statement after another by Rumpf. Peiper denied them all. Ellis came back to Peiper's own statements of March 21 and 26, both of which he had denied at the trial. "You knew that I was present in Schwäbisch Hall and that I visited your cell several times after both these statements were taken. . . . Never on one occasion did you ever tell me that there was anything in your statements that were untrue, that you wanted to change, did you?"

Peiper said that after speaking with Paul Guth and then Lt. Perl earlier in the investigation that he got "the impression that the truth was not one of the material points in this investigation." "Upon that, I permitted everything to be dictated to me lethargically, and from that attitude, I therefore did not have any reason to talk to you about this."

After a few more jousts Ellis threw in the towel. "No further cross examination."

Peiper suddenly piped up. "I ask the court to be permitted to make one further statement in connection with the cross examination by Col. Ellis."

Dalbey seemed surprised, but Ellis was thunderstruck. "Go ahead," said the president of the court. "Early in May," Peiper began, "I had a personal conversation with Lt. Col. Ellis. This conversation occurred on a personal human plane—fundamental—and in that connection I asked Col. Ellis whether he personally really believed all the things I was accused of here."

Ellis ran over to the bench. "I object to that. It is irrelevant whether I believe what is going on here or whether I don't," he said.

Dalbey stared back at him. "Objection overruled." Peiper charged on:

> I had told him that Col. Ellis surely would know that all my testimony resulted only from my attitude that I wanted to save my men and wanted to cover them. Upon that, Lt. Col. Ellis said, "I admire you and I hardly know another soldier who I estimate as highly as I estimate you, but you are sacrificing yourself on an ideal which no longer exists. The men whom you today think you have to cover up for are bums and criminals. I'll prove that to you in the course of the trial. We are now parting as friends and when we see each other in court, as enemies, and I'll have to paint you in the most bloody colors, but you'll understand that I'm only doing my duty."

As Peiper fell silent, Burton Ellis flushed beet red. He insisted that Peiper's testimony about him be stricken from the record, stating, "I don't believe I am on trial." But the law member did not agree, and Peiper's last laugh remained.

When court resumed after a brief recess, Ellis was still hopping mad about Peiper's last statement and asked that Paul Zwigart's statement that had previously not been admitted to the court case now be allowed. The portion of Zwigart's disallowed statement had described Peiper's typical modus operandi on the Eastern Front, a terrible commentary. "In Russia, generally we did not take any prisoners at all," Zwigart's statement began:

> When the fighting became heavier and the German advance slowed down, prisoners of war were only taken in special instances. On various occasions we burned down whole villages with our blow torches. I remember two cases; one in the spring of 1943 when we expressly received the order near Kharkov to set a village afire and "bump off" all inhabitants "including women and children." When I say we, I mean the third battalion which at that time was led by Hauptsturmführer Peiper. As far as I know he originated the order personally. . . . I myself did not see Haupsturmführer Peiper, who was with us at the time, shooting at civilians. However, it was generally known that he actively participated in this action. . . . I saw in this village which was of medium size (approximately 500–600 inhabitants) how our battalion set the houses afire with the blowtorches. I was a tank [*sic* SPW] driver and on that occasion I did not leave my tank. I stood with my SPW at the entrance of the village and watched the infantrymen of our battalion running around in their vehicles with blowtorches and saw at least one who set a house on fire . . . [they] ran around between the burning houses with machine guns and rifles shooting into the houses.[14]

Dr. Leer again rose to object that Peiper was not on trial for the Eastern Front nor for his character. Ellis was incensed. "If the court pleases," he blustered, "over my objection this accused testified about what a wonderful person he was and if that is admissible, he certainly has placed his character on issue by the court."

But Rosenfeld was emphatic. "The motion of the prosecution is denied." The mud-slinging was over. Then, in a parting gesture, the law member himself had a question for Peiper: "Will you give the court the details of the beating you alleged you received at Schwäbisch Hall?"

Peiper obliged:

> On the last day of my stay in Schwäbisch Hall I was called for interrogation and received, as usual, a black hood over my head. And I had to wait down there in the hall of the prison for about five minutes, since the American sergeant who came for me went to get some other comrades of mine from their cell. During this occasion when I was standing there quietly waiting, I was struck in the face by a person unknown to me, and several times in my sexual parts with a stick. I was of the opinion that they were Poles.[15]

In the end Abraham Rosenfeld, the law member, was impressed with the former SS colonel. "One of the finest witnesses I ever heard in my life was Joachim Peiper," he later said.[16]

Yet when court was adjourned and Peiper and his men shuffled back to their bunker, their defense attorney, Willis Everett, was seized by despair. "We got a few breaks in court today," he said, referring to Peiper's bravado, "but they were too small to be of any material consequence."

> All my staff wanted to quit again today, but I have been able to hold them together. . . . They feel it is so hopeless that we should rest our case and not try to prove anything further.

"PERSONALLY I DO NOT KNOW," EVERETT WORRIED, "BUT I AM STRONGLY OF the opinion that if we stop now, we will have 74 death penalties."[17]

Chapter 14

VERDICT

IF PEIPER'S TESTIMONY HAD BEEN AT TIMES BRILLIANT, IT ALSO FREQUENTLY IMPLODED on his arching ego. For he was clearly too proud to argue ugly questions that might hurt his reputation as a modern-day Siegfried. Instead, he embraced the role of the irascible SS Panzer officer. Rather than exoneration, he seemed resigned to proud martyrdom on the steps of Valhalla.

Tuesday, June 25, Everett and the defense wallowed in despair. The wayward course of the trial now jerked about, led by Peiper's subordinates, who demanded their time on the witness stand. Against his better judgment, Everett allowed their testimony.

German SS officers, in particular, wanted to be heard: Friedrich Christ, Franz Sievers, Heinz Tomhardt, Hans Hennecke, and enlisted SS man Marcel Boltz, who was accused as being one of the crossroads shooters. However, the entire affair proved a major legal miscalculation, for when the prosecution cross-examined the defendants, they behaved as Everett had predicted—like "a bunch of drowning rats . . . turning on each other." During the withering cross-examination of Boltz, Willis Everett suddenly rose from his seat and announced to the tribunal that he was cutting short his case by discontinuing the appearance of defendants on the witness stand "because of the fear of the prosecution still lingers in their minds after months of solitary confinement."[1]

"They put four of their defendants on the stand," Ellis would later gloat, "and we really cut them up."[2]

That night Willis Everett and John Dwinell went to the Munich home of Dr. Eugen Leer, who sought to defend Peiper even amid his sacrificial stance. "These Germans don't know American psychology and laws and procedures," he complained.

> This morning with the approval of four of our American counsel, I requested a 30 minute recess during which time we suggested to the accused to stop the trial as all they were doing was to hang each other. They decided to take the stand and we went on with the trial. The next witness [Boltz] . . . well, when he finished, he not only hung himself, but seven other defendants.[3]

When court resumed on Monday, July 1, prospects appeared exceedingly grim for Everett. "Toward the end of the trial I threw in the sponge . . . the continual overruling of what were obviously proper objections particularly when we were limited in impeaching witnesses of the prosecution."[4]

Jochen Peiper used July 4, the American holiday of declared independence, to write a personal appeal in English to Willis Everett:

> Although my mens' attitude during the Battle of the Bulge was better than during the Battle of Dachau, nevertheless I'm glad to share the fate of my comrades. From the point of view of the old commander, I have to feel ashamed of my outfit, especially of some officers. But attitude without support is rare! Today we are going to be cradled for the last time. Then hearing of investigation circumstances, the old front line soldiers can only be silent scornfully and smile ironically. From a psychologist's standpoint, the development is naturally quite easy to understand. I also try to see it with these eyes. Besides, I'm on the point to become a philosopher owing to the splendid isolation in American custody.
>
> My boys may charge me with all they want. The main thing is, it helps them. They are not evil and no criminals. They are the products of total war, grown up on the streets of scattered towns without any education! The only thing [they] knew was to handle weapons for the Dream of [the] Reich. They were young people with a hot heart and the desire to win or to die, according to the word: right or wrong—my country!
>
> Therefore Colonel, I beg you to tell the court that these ones who have to die, may die as soldiers. After having served six bloody years in all theatres and burning points, I think we have merited a firing squad! . . .
>
> I'm your,
> Jochen Peiper[5]

Here was Peiper staying true to Hitler and the Third Reich.

It was still and hot that Thursday night while the prosecution and others of the defense attended a big dance and noisy drinking adventure on the terrace by the officers club. But Everett stayed in his quarters, stripped down to boxer shorts for comfort in the hot, still night. He composed his closing argument for the case, working until midnight, smoking and writing until he felt worn out.

When court resumed on Friday, July 5, all seemed anticlimatic; now the courtroom chemistry focused on somehow finding a way to end the proceedings. Still, the defense had their prearranged witnesses who were paraded forth one after the other. Dr. Leer, attempting to come to Jochen Peiper's aid, called up former SS Rottenführer Georg Freitag. In the Ardennes Freitag had been with the driver of an SPW in the headquarters company of the 1st Panzer Battalion.[6] He too had arrived in the late morning of December 19 just outside Stoumont to collect the German wounded from the fight there. He claimed that he not only had orders to pick up German wounded but also to take along any American medical personnel he ran across.

Freitag told how he had picked up the first wounded by the Robinson house. "On the right side of the house there was a knocked out Panther." Inside the home in an upstairs room toward the garden Freitag found a dead American medic and looked around for blankets to help protect the other wounded from the cold weather. "Did you see any officers outside the house?" Leer asked.

"Yes, Colonel Peiper," Freitag said.

"Did you see any American soldiers next to the house?" Leer asked.

"At the time we stopped next to that house, about thirty armed Americans were taken out of the cellar by paratroopers." Freitag said there was another American medic among the prisoners taken. He received orders from Peiper to move the prisoners back to the aid station at the castle between La Gleize and Stoumont. Freitag claimed the thirty prisoners were treated well. By the time they got back to the castle the number of American prisoners there swelled to more than a hundred, tended by German medics.

Next on the stand was Albert Braun, an SS corporal who would be questioned by Dr. Leer to elicit some positive things about Jochen Peiper. In quick fashion he described the happenings in Büllingen on the morning of December 17, when his tank rushed through the village, only to be knocked out 150 meters beyond. Although emerging wounded from the stricken tank, he took fifty prisoners himself on the western outskirts of the town.[7] They were soon disarmed, after which Braun ran into his regimental commander:

> My driver went back and picked up the tank which was standing out front, and after we had taken these prisoners to Büllingen, I left the group in order to look for a truck so that the prisoners would be transported. . . . At the time, I met Col. Peiper who was coming my way in a car. . . . Col. Peiper went to the prisoners and in his presence, they were loaded into the truck and moved back.[8]

Well and good for Peiper, but when Ralph Shumacker came up to parry, he questioned Braun about his statement from Schwäbisch Hall, in which he was told before the offensive that "whatever stands in our way will be mowed down" and "no prisoners of war would be taken."[9]

Mowed down? "Now, you claim that your statement 'No prisoners will be taken,' means that the infantry behind will take care of them," Shumacker asked.

Braun gestured affirmation. "The last sentence, yes. That's how I explained it to you at Schwäbisch Hall too."

Whatever stands in our way will be mowed down. How did that fit with the infantry behind taking care of things?

That Friday afternoon former SS Hstuf. Rolf Möbius, leader of the 2nd Company of the elite heavy panzer battalion, strode up to the motley, elevated chair serving as the witness stand. Like Peiper, the SS officer held his chin up in a defiant air. Möbius testified that he had entered La Gleize with his lumbering King Tiger tank on December 19.[10] There Peiper and his CO, SS Ostuf. von Westernhagen, informed him to appoint an American to be responsible for the expanding number of prisoners. Möbius said he was aware of one man shot in La Gleize during his stay there, but that was a German deserter and not an American. Yet when questioned by Dr. Leer, Möbius soon showed his colors, painting Peiper and the Leibstandarte in glowing terms. Had he heard anything before the offensive about the treatment of prisoners? "We oriented our men to the effect that we were in a different theatre from the East, that we were getting into combat with an enemy whose fair methods of combat were known to us." Although intended as balm for American ears, the clear indication was that the combat in the East to which the Leibstandarte was accustomed was a savage, no quarters game. Then Dr. Leer asked Möbius what he knew about Malmédy.

> Col. Peiper asked me in La Gleize, very excitedly, whether I knew that American prisoners were supposed to have been shot. I told him, "No, I don't know anything about it" and asked him whether they were supposed to have been members of the regiment. Col. Peiper answered no, but that he would follow this matter up.

That all seemed self-serving to Ralph Shumacker. When he cross-examined the company commander of the King Tigers, the young officer could not recall when the conversation had occurred with Peiper in La Gleize. Shumacker was sarcastic: "Are you sure it did not take place here at Dachau?"

Möbius now pumped up his chest. "I saw Colonel Peiper for the first time since the surrender today." Shumacker asked when his King Tiger had passed by the Baugnez crossroads. Had they not seen the executed Americans lying in the field? No, Möbius claimed they had come by the Baugnez crossroads in the middle of the night. Shumacker sneered, and Dr. Leer objected, stating that Shumacker was taking Möbius on a path not covered in the direct examination. What might his witness say?

Still, there was no defensive disasters for the moment, and Möbius was soon telling about how Peiper had gallantly treated three American prisoners in his presence, one being Maj. McCown. "You say you are a firm believer in the fair methods of fighting, do you not?" Shumacker asked. Möbius agreed. "Is that the reason that you joined the Allgemeine SS in 1931 when you were a national of Austria?" Shumacker reminded the court that from 1933 to 1938 the SS had been outlawed in Austria. The implication: Möbius was a true believer; he had joined the Waffen SS in 1938, becoming an officer on Hitler's birthday in 1940. Dr. Leer was seething in contempt for this line of questioning, but the law member allowed it. His witness was now revealed as a Waffen SS devotee with crumbling credibility.

Then Gerhard Walla, from the headquarters company of Poetschke's 1st Panzer Battalion, was back up to the stand to testify about seeing Peiper in La Gleize on December 22, with defense attormey Herbert Strong looking for some positives.[11] Walla had been in the cellar of the schoolhouse in La Gleize—Werner Poetschke's command post—on that morning as the Americans were pulverizing the place with a terrific artillery barrage. Besides Poetschke, Peiper himself was there as well as SS. Ustuf. Rolf Ritzer, Ustuf. Herbert Steininger, and SS Ostuf. Ernst Rumpf in the small cellar. They talked over the situation, Walla remembered; things weren't looking good, and some of their men were looking to bug out. Indeed, Rumpf told Poetschke and Peiper that one man had left his position and removed his SS insignia. What was the response? "Peiper said this man had to be shot."

Rumpf was soon out of the CP on other business when SS Ustuf. Hans Hennecke entered. "After Hennecke entered, Lt. Col. Peiper told him to tell Rumpf to form an execution detail for this man." The detail was to report to Hennecke, who promptly left. According to Walla, Hennecke suddenly showed back up at Poetschke's CP five minutes later "and reported the execution of the order."

At 5:18 p.m. that Friday the court adjourned. When proceedings resumed the following Monday, the prosecution called up William Perl to contradict the testimony given by several defendants on the stand.[12] "Were you present in court when the accused Peiper testified?" Perl said he recalled it. "Did Peiper ever complain to you about a beating he received from Poles the day before he left Schwäbisch Hall?"

"No, sir," Perl said.

"Did you ever say to Peiper in Zuffenhausen, the following?"

> It is a personal misfortune that, amongst the prisoners who had been shot, there are the sons of two very important Americans. . . . It enraged them and the people demand your head since they know your name. . . . You are an extraordinary soldier. . . . That is over now. Your life is completely ruined today and there is no sense in it anymore. . . . As long as men like you are alive, there can never be any talk about peace treaties.[13]

Perl did not deny the gist.

The short Austrian American, guided by the prosecution examiner, quickly offered a litany of denials to testimony recently heard, including accusations of beatings and threats and claims that Perl saw the blood on the insides of prisoners' hoods.

Strangely, the defense knew something about Perl that they never shared with the court. Early in the work to prepare the case, Lt. Col. Dwinell came to notice that papers in their offices seemed to go missing. As it seemed to happen more frequently, Everett took pains to have the outside gate to their offices locked during lunch and at night, and sensitive papers were then stowed in the clothes locker. But one day, while in the courtroom, Everett saw Perl climb over the fence and duck into the bunkhouse. Ten to fifteen minutes later, he emerged with an armful of papers and climbed back over the fence. Soon he entered the courtroom and spoke with Ellis briefly. Dwinell then reported this to the lieutenant provost marshal, and, thereafter, Perl was found in Ellis's office, translating the stolen documents. Perl gave the papers back, and the issue became a hidden embarrassment for the prosecution, but for better or worse, Everett never brought up that gaff during the trial.

At 8:30 a.m. on Tuesday, July 9, the trial resumed when investigator Harry W. Thon took the stand.[14] "While you were at Schwäbisch Hall, did you see or interrogate the accused Peiper the day before he was transferred to Dachau?" asked Shumacker.

"I did not interrogate him," Thon said, choosing his words, "but I am quite sure that I talked to him."

"At that time," Shumacker asked, "did the accused, Peiper complain to you that he was beaten by Poles in his sexual parts, just before you saw him?"

"Peiper never said a word like that to me," Thon told the court. He had often stopped by his cell and shared a cigarette and conversation with Peiper. But like Perl before him, Thon then denied one defendant witness claim after another. He remembered the testimony of Heinz Tomhardt, who alleged Thon had struck him in the face and stomach. Neither was true, he said, nor was he aware of anyone else abusing Tomhardt. "I never touched him." The same was true for Sievers, Motzheim, and Boltz. All had alleged abuse in their courtroom appearances, but Thon denied each. Thon was excused as the parade of witnesses came to a close.

Now the trial's closing began, and as it unfolded, Peiper was clearly singled out in Shumacker's parade. Within the sixty-eight-page statement Peiper's name appeared on nearly half of the pages. "The case against Peiper must not be overlooked," the Tennessee attorney admonished. He urged weight be given to the mass of confessions obtained at Schwäbisch Hall, knowing that the defense would decry the mock trials, hoods, and other artifices needed to extract confessions from hardened SS men. Yes, they had seen the witnesses now charging that statements were dictated. "If the accused were willing to write down anything suggested by the interrogator," Shumacker illustrated, "why, for example was Peiper unwilling to confess the details of the Hillig shooting in Stoumont, when he freely admitted the shooting by Wichmann of the starved and frozen prisoner in Petit Thier?"

In one case, according to the closing statement, the prosecution seemed to overextend themselves, claiming that Peiper had decided to have American prisoners shot in La Gleize on December 22. "Peiper testified that he had decided to fight to the last man in La Gleize, until he received a garbled radio message from higher headquarters advising him to evacuate La Gleize and return."[15] Yet even the summary of evidence for this charge looked deficient, with no evidence of any shooting. Peiper's Schwäbisch Hall confession of March 26, 1946, was brought up again. There he had admitted giving Diefenthal and other subordinates the authority to shoot prisoners of war if they refused to obey orders. Still more damaging in that statement, Peiper acknowledged the shooting of a prisoner by Hillig in Stoumont. Moreover, two German witnesses, Georg Ebeling and Walter Landfried, had described the killing in detail to the court.[16] Then there was the even more personal death of the frozen American soldier in Petit Thier, with a multitude of corroborating statements from Sickel, Gruhle, Wichmann, and Peiper himself.[17]

Ironically, Shumacker quoted Peiper's witness stand affirmation that there had been orders to take no prisoners. "Peiper admitted that he was stupid to have signed this statement," the prosecutor told the court, "but never did he deny the truth" before the court. Unless such behavior had been sanctioned, he reasoned, then the observed killings would have been isolated and helter-skelter. For such a long trail of blood, Shumacker insisted, it must have been sanctioned from the top.

Shumacker's final legal assault anticipated the defensive strategies and sought to dismiss them. Everett would probably contend that the executed Belgian civilians were partisans and could be shot. But the prosecution said even partisans were entitled to a trial. Instead, the SS had summarily executed them.

There was one other obvious defensive stratagem. "The youth of these accused," he said, "cannot help but have impressed the court." But Shumacker reminded everyone that some seemed to relish their bloody work and, because of these acts, were "no longer the beardless, unsophisticated, naive youths they appear to be." Besides, he pointed out, many of the civilian victims were women or even infants. For sure, the defense would contend Germany was in a desperate situation and in its most desperate offensive and "that the method of warfare they employed . . . stemmed from their loyalty and devotion to country." But some of the crimes reflected a moral depravity that demanded punishment.

It was a bloody record, Shumacker said; his team estimated 150 civilians killed and 750 American soldiers shot. Those figures were clearly hyperinflated, but the reality of the crossroads shooting and the mass atrocities of Belgians at Stavelot and the surrounding villages made the fundamental contention undeniable.

And then there was the case of Hans Hillig, where the defense did not argue that he had shot an American soldier in Stoumont—he had done so on direct orders from Peiper, his regimental commander.[18]

In the closing statements, German attorney Dr. Pfister attempted to defend Dr. Kurt Sickel, whose fate was inextricably entwined with Peiper's in the Petit Thier incident. Sickel had clearly incriminated himself in his own statement. And even though testimony of Peiper, Gruhle, and Otto Wichmann had corroborated his story in convincing detail, the attorney said his client's statement was untrue. There would be no question of mentioning the particulars of Sickel's unsavory career in the SS, where he had been responsible for "the health of Jews" brought to Lublin and Madjanek.[19]

Then Dr. Eugen Leer rose to defend the star of the case, Jochen Peiper himself.[20] Unlike the other German counsel, Leer read his statement in English. Peiper could follow along.

> The charges against Jochen Peiper has—just as the charges raised against all the other defendants—been based by the prosecution upon a number of statements given by the defendants themselves. . . . What distinguishes Col. Peiper's statements from those of most of the other defendants is the fact that Peiper intentionally and contrary to the truth, assumed the responsibility for a number of cases which were completely unknown to him in order to protect his subordinates.

Leer's statement was hardly a thing of beauty, but its composition was far ahead of the other German attorneys before him. "It is therefore my duty to clarify Peiper's real participation in the alleged events," he said motioning to the SS colonel on the sidelines.

Leer took up the allegation that earlier in December Peiper, with Poetschke and others, had told everyone at a joint sand-table exercise that the humane methods of warfare in the West would soon be suspended. That was according to SS officer Kurt Kramm, who had nervously testified with such great damage before the court on May 17, 1946, his face still bandaged from wounds.[21]

More trouble for Dr. Leer were the murderous episodes themselves. First there was the incident near Cheneux on December 18 in which Paul Zwigart, in Diefenthal's half-track, had crashed into a jeep carrying two Americans. One had been shot right away after the collision, but it seemed pointless to argue that Zwigart had not executed the second American as he emerged from his vehicle. But there was a problem: not only was Jupp Diefenthal in the SPW, but Jochen Peiper was there as well. Yet Leer conveniently ignored the more numerous testimonies of Hans Rineck, Hans Assenmacher, and Paul Zwigart himself that Peiper had not only been in Diefenthal's half-track at the time but was also preoccupied with reading a map and did nothing to stop the shooting.[22]

Even more damaging to the SS colonel's legal prospects was the incident in Stoumont on December 19 in which Peiper had supposedly angrily ordered Hans Hillig to shoot an uncooperative American prisoner. Predictably, Leer dismissed Hillig's statement, but problematic were the testimonies of Walter Landfried, whose credibility he needed, to keep Peiper out the SPW with Paul Zwigart, and Georg Ebeling, who verified the key aspects of the incident. Less threatening was Peiper's supposed guilt in mass shootings in La Gleize. This allegation by the prosecution had only produced embarrassment for Ellis. It seemed all too clear that the fabled incident had not taken place, the 30th Infantry Division not finding more than ten bodies in the entire village that had been the scene of intense shelling during the battle. Moreover, US Maj. Hal McCown had testified of Peiper's proper behavior relative to prisoners in the town, with a group of more than 120 being released unharmed when American forces entered the village on Christmas Eve.

Yet it was with the charge of Peiper's involvement in the shooting of the frozen GI at Petit Thier that Dr. Leer could offer the least help for his client. At Schwäbisch Hall Peiper had done what he did for his other men: he aimed to take the rap for Dr. Sickel. But it was Peiper himself, in his courtroom testimony, who really set Leer back, for his client had acknowledged that the frozen American was killed but in a "pronounced atmosphere of compassion"—it was a mercy killing.

Finally there was the charge that Peiper was personally responsible for all the war crimes wrongdoing under his command. On that treacherous ground, Dr. Leer reminded the court that Rolf Möbius testified that Peiper was very disturbed when he learned of the crossroads shooting and that "it is known that he suffered a nervous breakdown after the campaign. All this, together with Col. McCown's testimony, shape the picture of a man who is above all, conscious of his duties."

When the court reconvened on Thursday, July 11, for its close, Willis Everett made a long, impassioned plea, at the end turning again to Gen. Dalbey, appealing to the fairness of the court to kindle democratic nationalism to rebuild Germany. He closed with a quote from the American patriot Thomas Paine. "He that would make his own liberty secure," Everett said, looking up from his statement, "must guard even his enemy from oppression, for if he violates this duty, he establishes a precedent that will reach himself." He paused briefly and dropped his papers. It was a dramatic movement. "I leave in God's and your hands the fair judgment of these seventy-four accused."

The Atlanta attorney returned to his seat. If Everett's delivery was awkward at times and the language tortured, his closing remarks were impassioned—particularly for the men whose lives were held in the balance. In the defendant's dock Peiper looked on without a hint of emotion. Nearby, tears flowed freely from defendant Fritz Kraemer, the former 6th Panzer Army chief of staff.

By 4:20 p.m., some two hours after Everett's closing appeal, an attendant rang a bell to announce that the court had reached a verdict. The spectators, defendants, prosecution, and defense teams streamed back into the courtroom. The camera and news people set up expectantly. On July 11 the American military court, in a mass verdict, found guilty all seventy-three of the Malmédy accused.

Then, a parade of the accused stood up from the dock to make short statements, asking for mitigation of their sentences.[23] Most were enlisted men or NCOs. Some begged for mercy, while others claimed they would have been shot if they had not obeyed—even if orders involved shooting prisoners. "I have never denied what I have done," announced Kurt Briesemeister. "I appeal for a mild sentence," mentioning he had been wounded five times in battle.

Roman Clotten revealed he had joined the SS at the beginning of the war, but spent a stint as a driver for Hitler! But the statement garnering most attention came from young Georg Fleps, accused of firing the first shot at the crossroads. Fleps revealed that in January 1943, he was drafted into the Rumanian Army. In May 1943, he was discharged again and drafted into the "*Volksdeutsche*" for the German Army and into the Waffen SS. "We have never been considered as real Germans," he told the court. Later, he received very tough basic training in 1st SS Panzer Grenadier Training and Replacement Battalion 12 in Arnhem. "I was instructed that all orders had to be carried out without asking questions, even if the orders are connected with death."

For Peiper it all must have been galling—Waffen SS men reduced to begging for their lives. At 5 p.m., after eight pleas were entered, the court recessed. But the continuing pleas the following day were even more damaging—several statements read before the court were not pleas for mercy at all. Former SS Oberscharführer Hans Siptrott, who was accused of commanding the tank from which Georg Fleps had fired the first shots at Malmédy, read aloud a statement that oozed with pride. And Siptrott had been a favorite tank commander of Peiper's. Unlike the enlisted men who claimed they had been drafted against their will into the Waffen SS, Siptrott emphasized he had *volunteered* for the Leibstandarte, emphasizing it was Adolf Hitler's Bodyguard Division. Two of his brothers died during the war, he said. He had been trained both as an infantryman and later as a panzer man. "During a total of 680 combat days on all fronts," he read, "I was knocked out with my tank eleven times and wounded three times." He participated in all campaigns from Poland in 1939 up to the capitulation in May 1945. "I always took pains to fulfill my duties and serve my Fatherland."[24]

Yet it was the speech of Hans Hillig before the court that really vilified Peiper. In his plea he said that he had volunteered for the Waffen SS at the beginning of the Polish campaign when he was only seventeen years old. Unlike many others, Hillig had been with the Leibstandarte for a long time. Even during his early military training, "we were told that we had to carry out every order of our superiors . . . refusing an order on the front would be punished by death." Then something seemed to shock Ellis:

> When Hillig finished reading his plea in German, Mr. Harry Thon, US civilian employee, who was acting as my check interpreter, whispered to me and said that "Hillig admitted he shot the Sergeant on Peiper's orders." When defense counsel read the English translation of Hillig's plea, I immediately noticed that he failed to read the admission of guilt. I immediately objected to the translation whereupon Defense Counsel Lt. Wahler stated that he had requested Hillig to delete that paragraph. The German statement read by Hillig was then obtained and the paragraph which defense counsel had admittedly omitted, was then read to the court.[25]

When translated, it was a real zinger. "I state that my testimony is correct as the prosecution witness testified before the court," Hillig said. He verified that he had shot an American soldier in Stoumont. "I felt very sorry about the shooting of the American soldier, but I was in an unfortunate position. How could I have refused the order of my regimental commander? I request the court be considerate."[26]

And before the tirade of pleas was done, there was another that dimmed prospects for Jochen Peiper. Twenty-four-year-old Paul Zwigart stood up to recite his appeal, which read more like a confession. Zwigart repeated his story of the jeep incident near Cheneux, Belgium, where he had confessed to having shot a hapless American driver after he surrendered to the SPW containing Jochen Peiper and Josef Diefenthal. There were extenuating circumstances, he claimed. Zwigart was exhausted on December 18, having been awake for three days and constantly urged on by his superiors.

Before the court, Zwigart again affirmed that he had shot the American soldier in the jeep that day while Peiper himself had looked on. "In the presence of my superiors, and on instigation of my comrades standing around me, I interpreted it as an order, which was my highest military duty. . . . In the heat of battle, I lost my head. . . . Soon thereafter I considered the wrong that I committed." Then Paul Zwigart, Peiper's half-track driver at the crossroads and beyond, choked with emotion and tears. "I beg this high court to place themselves in my position," he implored, "and bring out a merciful sentence."

One could have heard a pin drop after Zwigart's final words. There was an uneasy silence. The court judges looked to Everett, who nodded faintly—there was nothing more.

"The court will be closed," announced Dalbey, with seeming relief. It was 12:05 p.m. on Friday, July 12, 1946. The court recessed to determine the individual sentences; it would not reconvene until the following week. All the spectators rose, including the German accused in the dock, waiting to be escorted back to their barracks. Amid a hubbub of activity, a reporter approached Joachim Peiper.

WAS HE SURPRISED BY THE VERDICT? PEIPER SMILED IN AN AMICABLE BUT condescending manner: "Of course not, I am not in the least surprised," he replied in English. "I knew all the time what the findings would be."[27] The court took over four days to sort through the evidence and mete out appropriate punishment. At 1:30 p.m. on Tuesday, July 16, the court reconvened. Everyone took their seats again;

this time the sweltering courtroom was filled and overflowing with spectators, wives, families, and reporters. The cameras and bright lights were back and seemed only to add to the perspiration and discomfort.

Gen. Dalbey squinted into the lamps, looking stern and determined. He had an announcement, he told the court: those sentenced to death would not be shot, as requested by the accused. "The court has been directed to conform to current regulations, which prescribe death by hanging." With that there was a short gasp in the court. Each of the accused was called up individually. Walking forward, they stood before the judges while their sentences were read aloud.

One by one they came and stood before Dalbey, who read the sentences aloud. Many got death; some got life, and a few received shorter sentences. The oldest and highest ranked, Dietrich, along with twenty-one others, was sentenced to life imprisonment.[28] Finally it was time for Jochen Peiper.

All of the men took their sentences calmly, the only signs of emotion were slight smiles of relief on those who did not receive the death penalty. Peiper's body language was smoothly martial—the obedient Prussian soldier. He stood rigidly at attention before the court, with fixed unblinking eyes on Brig. Gen. Josiah T. Dalbey while his sentence was read. "Joachim Peiper, the court in closed session sentences you to death by hanging." An interpreter echoed the words into the German tongue: "*Tod durch Erhängen*." Even though standing, Everett's shoulder drooped. He swallowed and wavered.

Peiper smartly turned on his heel and proceeded to the rear of the court. As he strode back, one reporter saw Peiper smile sardonically when a photographer's flash bulb exploded in his face after the death sentence was pronounced.[29] To Burton Ellis looking on, "They showed no more emotion than if they had been eating a meal. They marched in, snapped to attention, listened to their sentence and did an about face and marched off."[30] The same could not be said for their families who made up over half of the spectators. To the rear of the crowded courtroom women openly wept as the sentences were read. One was Sigurd Peiper.

Back in his Dachau cell Jochen Peiper took to pen and paper:

> Lt. Colonel Ellis,
>
> The theatrical performance is over! You have won a credible victory! May I congratulate!
>
> I'm convinced that your admirable work, borne of deep ethics, will contribute to over-bridge strained relations between our countries and will represent an important stone for the mighty building of the United Nations! . . . During your amusing cross-examination I sometimes forgot that you are no opponent for me and therefore, now and then, became a little acute and ironical. You have committed a fault when you attack my character. In interest of my other comrades I was forced to reveal the tenor of our last conversation, in order to attack your credibility! . . . After you already took care of my medals, I should only like to get back the photos of my family because I believe that Lt. Perl does not need them any longer for interrogation purposes!

Now, when you . . . catch your next victim, don't forget my last word: You can warp justice, but you never can bend the neck and pride of an old Prussian front-line officer!

For the future, good luck and good health,

Jochen Peiper[31]

He then wrote to his defense attorney, Willis Everett:

Dear Colonel Everett!

When overlooking my life today I may say, that it has been a rich one! Should I begin it once more I would march once more the same straight way, the milestones of which were: idealism-faithfulness and sense of duty!

During six bloody years I fought and bled in all European Theatres and became a preferred favorite of the God of Hosts! In spite of it all—it was a proud and heroic time. Where we were standing was Germany and as far as my tank gun reached was my kingdom! We had no personal aspirations! Our vision always has been the "Dream of the Reich."

In the end of the war, when the Führer was needing his Leibstandarte the most, fate had separated us from him and we were to fight a desperate way through Hungary and Austria! I was even grudged on the last merited shot, in this war!

When seeing today the defendants on the dock, don't believe them to be the old Combat Group Peiper. All my old friends and comrades have gone before! These people who plead for mitigating circumstances are only the negative selection! The real outfit is waiting for me in Valhalla!

Life of an old Prussian officer is no more worth living today! Better dead [than] a slave! Besides my charming children I leave my wife, the last and bravest comrade I ever met. Unfortunately I'm not able to do anything for her protection. On the contrary, I know that only my presence would do harm to her—The thankful population wishes me to be a "criminal" and my family has to suffer from this fame. That's the worst, Colonel. The own countrymen, for whom you always were prepared to sacrifice your life are enemies of today and deprive your wife's last property, in order to please the new potentiates!

In my position it's difficult today to believe still in Germany. I'm fearing that my wife has to undergo further reprisals when court is over. . . . My greatest sorrow is the fact that I don't know how she is going to get a living now! We have become the pariahs of the nation and may say with Shakespeare: "the evil that men do lives after them, the good is oft interred with their bodies."

Before our steps separate, I want to thank you especially for all help you gave us as a human being, as a soldier and chief counsel of the defense during the past eight weeks. In a time of deepest human disappointment, you and McCown have returned to me much faith I already had lost. This will remain one of the best remembrances and was worth the whole procedure of the Malmédy case.

> I'm very glad to know that you are going to continue the work in my Germany. Time heals all wounds! Only men with your character and chivalrous attitude are able to build peace and to over-bridge the strained relations between our countries. Perhaps our end will contribute a little to this goal. . . .
>
> Joyfully to live, smilingly to fight, laughing to die! That's my watch word. It arms me also today. I'm going to die as one of the last soldiers of this terrible war, but not as a criminal! I have a good conscience and the conscience of performing my duty. Stronger than the fate is the will that bears it unshaken! May God give you a long and successful life and protect your family.
>
> In sincere friendship I remain your devoted,
>
> Jochen Peiper[32]

Everett, for his part, was devastated: "Well I couldn't write much yesterday after that verdict," he wrote home. "43 deaths."

After the death sentence for her husband, Sigurd joined Dr. Leer in Everett's office briefly. It was a difficult conversation. "She was very brave and he [Peiper] was worried about treatment for her and her children. I told her if anything of this type should occur, it should be reported to Dr. Leer or myself." Everett felt lost and unanchored.

> My heart is crushed, not for the 43 especially, but over the principle of condemning 18 or 19 year old boys who has never known anything else and would have been instantly shot if he refused to obey the order of his superior officer.[33]

Nonetheless, even among the disappointed members of the defense, there was awareness that the trial, while crossed by shortcomings, had essentially been fair:

"Undoubtedly there were some who were guilty," Everett wrote home, "There were others who were innocent or at least guilty by association. We pursued the defense with vigor hoping to separate the wheat from the chaff." Another on the army defense team, Ben Narvid, poignantly observed, "If the situation had been reversed," National Socialist justice would have been different.

"Most of the American accused would have faced a firing squad," he opined, "after a very, very brief and cursory trial."[34]

Part Four
IN EXTREMIS

"Society, as we have constituted it, will have no place for me, has none to offer; but Nature, whose sweet rains fall on unjust and just alike, will have clefts in the rocks where I may hide, and secret valleys in whose silence I may weep undisturbed. She will hang the night with stars so that I may walk abroad in the darkness without stumbling, and send the wind over my footprints so that none may track me to my hurt: she will cleanse me in the great waters, and with bitter herbs make me whole."

—OSCAR WILDE, *DE PROFUNDIS*

Chapter 15

LANDSBERG

Together, with forty-two other defendants, Joachim Peiper was sentenced to death by hanging on July 16, 1946. Yet after the Dachau trial in 1946, doubts remained.

The sentences generated large controversy in German circles, including the church, leading the commander of the US Army in Germany to commute some of the death sentences to life imprisonment, particularly for the younger defendants. In addition, the SS men's defense attorney, US military attorney Lt. Col. Willis M. Everett, awkwardly appealed to the US Supreme Court, claiming that the defendants had been found guilty by means of "illegal and fraudulently procured confessions." Based on the accusations, Kenneth Royall, the Secretary of the Army, created a commission, chaired by Judge Gordon A. Simpson of Texas, to reexamine the evidence.

The commission arrived in Europe on July 30, 1948, and issued its report two months later. Its finding recommended that the twelve remaining death sentences be commuted to life imprisonment. The commission affirmed Everett's misgivings regarding the mock trials and neither disputed nor denied his charges of torture of the defendants. But the commission expressed the opinion that the pretrial investigation had not been properly conducted and believed that no death sentence should be executed until a more detailed review was completed.

In response, General Lucius Clay altered six more death sentences to life imprisonment. However, he refused to commute the six remaining sentences, including Peiper's, though the executions were postponed. The turmoil roused by the commission report along with an inflammatory article by Judge Edward L. Van Roden caused the US Senate, led by sensational US Senator Joseph McCarthy, to investigate the trial.[1]

Later, in an investigation of the trial, the Senate Committee on Armed Services determined that improper pretrial procedures, such as mock trials—but not torture, as often later claimed by the defendants—had adversely influenced the trial process, if not the outcome. Even so, there was no doubt that some of the accused were indeed guilty of the Malmédy massacre. However, there was also little question that some innocents were unfairly sentenced—a miscarriage of justice.

In the end, the sentences of the condemned were first commuted to life imprisonment and then to time served. Throughout the early 1950s one after another of the Landsberg men were released. After a long campaign by the German church and German citizens, on Peiper's birthday, January 30, 1951, his death sentence was commuted to life in prison.

If Peiper was no longer condemned to the gallows, he didn't look to get out anytime soon. Peiper knew in his heart that he was in the debt of Willis Everett. A memento of thanks came in June 1951, when the fifty-eight remaining Malmédy boys sent a handcrafted brass lamp to Willis Everett. Sepp Dietrich signed the keepsake, with the base of the lamp embossed in gold and with the emblem of the Leibstandarte Adolf Hitler. The hand-stitched lampshade emoted placid scenes from Landsberg. "Not even one member of the Malmédy case will ever forget your successful assistance."[2]

Locating the lamp in his study, Everett wrote in catharsis to sympathetic North Dakota senator William Langer: "It was on the last day of the last month that the Army announced that the last six of the death penalties meted out to those defendants would be reduced to life imprisonment. This took me almost five years, a heart attack and the expenditure of about $35,000. It was all worth it, because I am able to live with myself."[3]

At Landsberg, slowly, every single confession of wrongdoing by the Malmédy men, either from Schwäbisch Hall or the trial, was recanted in formal affidavits. Yet from his vantage, Peiper was inclined to still judge his cup half-empty.

The former SS colonel denounced most of the rest of his old comrades. In particular, he was dismayed by his old rival, Max Wünsche, who was out scot-free. "There are quite a number of former friends, who lightly drive about the landscape in the Mercedes and do not know they are permitted to write me," he wrote bitterly. "There is a whole world between a Mercedes and a writing hand!"[4] Meanwhile, back in Rottach-Egern, to make ends meet, Sigurd Peiper had taken to working in Tübingen, only able to come home on weekends. Still, that summer of 1951 she and the kids returned for summer holidays to her hometown of Kiel, spending three weeks at Schönberger Beach.

Sigurd's brother Kurt Hans Hinrichsen lived there with his family, having fled the Warthe District during the war. He had been with Heydrich's SD in those days and married his brother's widow after Dr. Rolf Hinrichsen had died on the Bismarck on May 27, 1941. Jochen Peiper himself had interceded on the part of brother-in-law Kurt Hans with Himmler himself on July 11, 1942, to gain permission for the marriage.[5] In any case, there were plenty of playmates in the summer of 1951: the Hinrichsens had nine kids between them. Peiper's girls and the Nathan kids loved the sea. Did she discuss bigger plans that summer vacation?

Meanwhile Jochen lingered in the prison hospital with thrombosis. He was writing to her to encourage her to learn whether his old friend Benoni Junker was soon to be released. A week later, on September 23, 1951, Sigurd requested permission to visit Jochen. She was staying close by Rolf Reiser at the Hotel Windenhof in Augsburg. But their "little mafia" was looking to spring her husband out of prison:[6]

> Peiper was guarded by Polish guards who liked to drink. We planned to add a little something to their drinks. To make sure this would work, we tried it out on one of our own and he slept for six hours! I worked at a hospital in

> Landsberg after being discharged. Peiper was on the first floor of the hospital and had only one sentry. Once we got through an open window, it was only 3 meters up a fence and then the street to a waiting car.[7]

As envisioned, Otto Skorzeny, Hitler's favorite commando, who had rescued Mussolini in the fall of 1943, would meet Peiper on the Swiss border before he was spirited off to Spain. Jochen was unaware of the plan until two days before the scheduled escape. But when Sigurd Peiper visited him in the hospital to whisper the news, he objected right away. "I won't leave as long a single man in my command is still in prison." That was that. Back in Landsberg, Werner Roesch was dismayed. "We were always talking about a breakout," he recalled, but Peiper's wife put an end to that.[8]

The mental outlook of the others in his family remained cynical, if defiant. Contrary to his letters of supplication to American authorities, Peiper's father, Woldemar, remained unreconstructed. "Even though there are certain circles in the government which more or less support the enemy during our difficult struggle for existence and as a result, commit treason," he wrote to another SS veteran in 1951, "we will continue our firm stride in the future." One day in the future, he imagined, "the youth will one day whisper to another, '*That one, he was in the LAH*' and remove their caps in respect.'"[9]

Had Woldemar's son's ideology changed? Hardly. On July 21, 1952, Peiper's old battlefield surgeon friend, Dr. Robert Brüstle, paid him a visit in prison, ostensibly to discuss his wife's condition. She was ailing recently; he judged her condition to be hepatitis. The old circle of friends circled on: Brüstle now was treating Sigurd Peiper and her three children in Rottach-Egern.[10] At the visit in Landsberg Jochen Peiper professed unending loyalty of the old troop to Brüstle. He still looked for recognition for the old Blowtorch Battalion while condemning those on the outside as ape-like heirs to the Bolshevists:

> It doesn't matter where they stick you—be it a bordello on the Champs Elysées or a U.S. Military court in Dachau—it matters less *where* one is, than *what* one is. . . . All is just a question of attitude and requires that one not take things too seriously. Nevertheless, the isolation from these people—this half emancipated breed of monkeys—really is a blessing. It is pleasing to hear occasionally that there are still survivors who deserve the designation "comrade." The old Don Roberto [Dr. Robert Brüstle] is a diamond in the coal mine and helped me to remember the forced slaughters in our ranks. In case they should have references from the war about the earthly wanderings of our blessed Blowtorch Battalion, I would be grateful if they would pass a copy of it onto my boys . . . Never mind that—*nitschewo!* Take it easy good buddy and be happy. . . . good wood and fair winds.[11]

In nearby Miesbach, Frau Peiper ran into Lina Heydrich, the widow of Reinhard Heydrich. Looking to travel to Kiel, Sigurd, Lina's old school-day chum, located two former German soldiers to escort her on the trip. Later Lina would move to a place of her own in Rottach-Egern according to her "standing" where she would be among friends.[12] The *Lago di Bonzo*—"Lake of the Bosses," that included Rottach Egern—was a secret postwar Nazi convivial, that much was clear. After the war sixty-eight people in the local government of nearby Landkreis Miesbach were dismissed for overt participation in NSDAP activities, and the American occupational government struggled against engrained anti-Semitism.[13] The week before Christmas old SS veterans with HIAG in Miesbach near Tegernsee would turn out with presents for the kids and assemble a big gathering at the Hotel Waitzingerbräu.[14] And the local populous was frequently agitated over trials at Dachau; for instance, they expressed sympathy for Dr. Klaus Schilling, who had conducted diabolical malaria experiments on Polish priests.

West Germany's postwar chancellor, Konrad Adenauer, soon broke an uneasy silence on the war criminal controversy by concluding that "it is too late to kill." However, neither he nor the tireless Nazi guardian angel, Princess Isenburg, could save cunning Otto Ohlendorf.[15] Here was a man who had openly admitted at Nuremberg of killing thousands while leading Einsatzgruppen D and still endeavored to justify his actions.[16] In spite of constant petitions and interventions—and even the offer by the Catholic priest of Landsberg to take the place of the accused on the gallows—Ohlendorf and the other six Red Jackets were hanged on June 7, 1951. The condemned included Oswald Pohl, Himmler's head of the concentration camp system, his doctor, Dr. Karl Gebhardt, and Wolfram Sievers, the SS Reichsführer's director of the Ahnenerbe.

In a case of bad company, Peiper knew all of them well. Yet, as if to balance that act, John J. McCloy, the US High Commissioner in Germany, substantially reduced the sentence of seventy-nine other major war criminals—Einsatzgruppen members, concentration camp administration, and convicted criminals in the Krupp corporate slave labor case. Upon release, a convicted I. G. Farben executive put it simply: "Now that they have Korea on their hands," he mused, "the Americans are a lot more friendly."[17] None of the Malmédy men had been executed.

By the winter of 1951, the prosecution of Nazi criminals effectively stalled. Publicly Truman and top officials thoroughly condemned Hitler, the killing of the Jews, and the SS involvement. Privately, however, senior US government operatives prepared to drop the prosecution of the horrid acts of the German *Endlösung*—The Final Solution—all to preserve West German support for the Cold War. Beyond that the US intelligence services were even employing their former enemy! Hundreds of SS men were covertly working for the US Counterintelligence Corps (CIC), gathering information on Soviet Russia along with German scientists dredged off for rocket knowledge.[18]

The most senior member of the German intelligence community, Reinhard Gehlen, was recruited by OSS Chief Allen Dulles to resurrect his espionage teams who had infiltrated wartime Soviet Russia. His network held obvious importance to the American Cold War warriors. So with US intelligence blessings, Gehlen wielded a free hand to hire whoever was needed. And many times the chosen included former SS men with shady pasts.

All such intrigue evidenced the sharp right snap of European political winds. On October 26, 1952, five thousand former members of the Waffen SS held their first mass reunion since the end of the war, convening in Verden in Lower Saxony. The crowd widely cheered its spokesman, Herbert O. Gille, when he declared that "the frightful words 'war criminal' did not apply to the Waffen SS." The quarter of a million of that troop who had died in the war had not fallen for National Socialism, he claimed, but for Germany! Then Gen. Bernhard Ramcke, who led wartime *Fallschirmjäger* troops—German paratroopers—rose to the podium. Although not Waffen SS, he was clearly of the old Nazi coterie. The blacklist of SS members, he said, would eventually become "a list of honor!" "Who really are the war criminals?" he chided. "They are those who made the tragic peace, who destroyed whole cities without any tactical justification and dropped the bomb on Hiroshima!"[19]

Amid the strong political current, public demands for a general amnesty increased loudly; almost everyone in German society knew someone living under a false name to evade being handed over to foreign states. And although the Waffen SS had been branded a criminal organization at Nuremberg, Adenauer stood up before the Bundestag on December 3, 1952, and *apologized* to soldiers of the German armed forces who had fought in World War II. They should be respected, he said, not scorned and outcast from society. Two weeks later the Adenauer wrote to Genobst. Paul Hausser in Ludwigsburg. "[The] apology to the soldiers of the German Wehrmacht also includes the members of the Waffen SS."[20]

Much of the change had to do with Adenauer's move to bring Germany into the North Atlantic Treaty Organization (NATO). That strategem might have come right from Peiper's wartime warning to Col. Hal McCown of the coming "Bolshevist" threat.

At Landsberg, too, the progression swerved in Peiper's favor. Each year the cardinal of Cologne, Josef Frings, appealed for a generous Christmas amnesty. The Vatican did not attack the legitimacy of the Malmédy trial but rather called for mercy even for the worst of criminals.[21] In 1952 eight more Malmédy defendants were set free, including Peiper's adjutant, Hans Gruhle.[22] At the end of the year Peiper again appealed to the parole board.

> The crime for which I have been imprisoned and that is supposedly to have taken place during the "Battle of the Bulge" was, as General Handy attests himself, "associated with a confused fluid and desperate combat action, a last attempt to turn the tide of Allied successes." . . . It was certainly no deliberate killing by Nazi hordes running amuck, but an ill-fated occurrence in the heat and turmoil of battle. . . . I was a professional soldier and served my country in a long and hateful war. . . . Should I have really failed then [it was] only in the unselfish endeavor to save Germany in the hour of greatest need. I was in solitary confinement for 5 1/2 years and for 55 months under the sentence of death. This alone should be punishment enough for an unprovoked incident which, however deplorable, repeats itself time and again in today's merciless warfare.[23]

Peiper implored the review board to consider the plight of his family. Sigurd, he said, "suffers most and is on the verge of physical and psychical collapse . . . [consider] the future of our three minor children." Each month Sigurd Peiper would journey from Rottach-Egern to Landsberg prison to spend two hours talking with her husband. The visits were hardly intimate: the meeting room was a cold concrete chamber, a wire screen separated husband and wife, and two guards looked on while the two talked—often for two hours. Peiper's own son judged the circumstance "very hard on my parents." The prisoner and their wife were allowed to one precious embrace at the beginning of the session and again when saying good-bye. They were perfunctorily searched at the end of the visit.

Some days at Landsberg Peiper rationalized his incarceration: What good would it be to be out in Germany where "the free have no understanding of their serfdom. . . . Where ever you look, you find egocentric wailing, materialism and thrashing around in shallow waters."[24] Christmas amnesty? On December 25, 1952, Jochen Peiper only benefitted from an afternoon holiday concert for the inmates. The music came from the orchestra of the Town of Landsberg accompanied by the local glee club reciting Christmas carols and ironically entitled "Cheerfulness."[25] There remained four hundred inmates still in Landsberg for the concert, more than nine hundred having been released so far. Even so, Peiper was no longer under threat of execution—a total of 286 had met the gallows he had narrowly avoided.[26] That same winter Peiper wrote a rambling essay that would later be included in an apologist SS work composed by SS General Paul Hausser, who claimed the Waffen SS "were soldiers like any others."[27]

> In his monkish seclusion a war criminal sits on his fold-down bed and daydreams. The sign on the door reads "Life Sentence" and the calendar is at October 1952. The stove sings, the spider reconnoiters new winter positions, and fall rattles the steel bars with a rough hand. Thirteen years of marriage apart, five times birthday as a man condemned to death, and now the eighth Christmas in prison. Really, a sunny youth. One should not treat any animal that badly. People: to what sacrifices and to what meanness are they capable?

Other SS veterans saw it differently. "The Waffen SS was a phenomenon," remembered one, "being a mixture of regular soldiers, old brutes from the days of the struggle and genuine nuts."[28] Indeed, the Waffen SS did not even exist before 1940, so anyone joining before then was part of the regular SS anyway.

Regardless of their classification, however, the number held at Landsberg fell each month, but Peiper remained. A number of those now on the outside made pilgrimages to visit Peiper. In October 1952 his old panzer officer friend, Benoni Junker, came by, himself just recently released. Over the coming months Peiper would see him along with Dr. Joseph Goebbel's SS war reporter, Schwartz van Berk, and even Dr. Eugen Dollmann, a former SS colonel and Himmler's courtly Italian interpreter.[29] In August 1954 Arndt Fischer and Anton Motzheim, also previously imprisoned there, stopped by for personal greetings.

But strangest of all was a visit later that year from Luftwaffe tank-busting ace Hans Ulrich Rudel, who had come all the way from South America.[30] Rudel was arguably the most legendary Stuka pilot with the Luftwaffe during the war. Flying more than 2,500 missions in spite of being shot down thirty times and losing a leg, Rudel's exploits were so extraordinary that Hitler created a special medal just for him: the Golden Oak Leaves with Diamonds and Swords to the Knight's Cross, a military pomposity that was Germany's highest decoration.

After the war Rudel moved to Argentina, where Juan and Evita Perón gladly received him. Officially Rudel served as an aviation adviser to Argentina, joining a fleet of former members of the Focke Wulf aircraft corporation under Dr. Willi Tank. Unofficially he became Perón's glamour boy at lavish state dinners and gala receptions. Scandalous rumor even had Rudel carousing with the luscious beauty Evita Perón. And some said it was no rumor.

Upon Rudel's return to Germany in 1951, he became spokesperson for the ultranationalist *Freikorps Deutschland.* So inflammatory were Rudel's speeches, by 1953 he was banned from speaking engagements in Bavaria, where he scurrilously referred to the leader of West Germany as "Rabbi Adenauer." "What good would it do Germany if the Americans won the last battle?" he asked in one. "No one would be left to see a '*nigger* division' marching in Germany over the atom-bombed graves of German people." True to his National Socialist allegiance, Rudel founded the *Kameradenwerk,* an organization to aid imprisoned comrades and assist them in relocating, along with tens of thousands of others, to a South American haven. During the summer of 1953, before visiting Peiper, British intelligence exposed Rudel as the mastermind, with Otto Skorzeny, of a fantastic plot featuring a daring helicopter commando raid that was to free more than a hundred Nazi war criminals still held in captivity at Spandau Prison![31]

What was the true extent of the Nazi underground movement? The last few months of the war had seen speculation reach a new height. No one knew what had become of Martin Bormann and there was great uncertainty of the death of Hitler himself. Disquieting rumors said the German leader was living on a huge Patagonian estate in Argentina![32] That was at least partly due to far-fetched rumors of a network of supersecret resistance cells established deep in the Bavarian Alps, each lavishly stocked with food, arms, communications, and, above all, money. There Werwolf was to carry on a years-long campaign to preserve the old ideas.[33] Fueled by massive gold shipments covertly moved to Swiss banks in the closing days of the war, ODESSA (Organisation der Ehemagligen SS-Angehörigen—Organization of Former SS Members) was to lay the foundations for the establishment of the *Fourth Reich.* For the remaining underground leadership of the Reich, there were specially equipped submarines that would spirit the Nazi brain trust out to distant havens.

The rumors and wild tales of ODESSA ended up as a best-selling novel and later a movie.[34] There was much, too, beyond fiction. The real ODESSA was a small clandestine organization set up in 1947 by Otto Skorzeny and Alfred Naujocks as an underground SS network.[35] Many important Nazis now managed to gain political asylum in Argentina, with Skorzeny and Rudel operating from Spain and South America. Would Peiper join them there?

Aided by the shadowy network, Eichmann had left Germany in 1950, finally resigned to the fact that he would be hunted for all time. Not only did Eichmann leave on board the Italian steamship *Giovanna C,* but his escort to the port of Buenos Aires was none other than Peiper's old SS panzer leader replacement in Normandy, SS Col. Herbert Kuhlmann. He was the same blonde-haired panzer man who had saved Peiper's radioman, Fritz Kosmehl, from death in a flaming tank in Normandy in August 1944.[36] And Kuhlmann was also the old fighter who had testified in Peiper's behalf at the Malmédy trial on June 21, 1946!

Now, four years later in July 1950, Kuhlmann arrived in Argentina with forged papers. Eichmann became Riccardo Klement while his escort, Kuhlmann, assumed the identity of Pedro Geller—a tenebrous German businessman who was shortly living the Viva Loca in the fashionable Palmermo Chico neighborhood. If Kampfgruppe Kuhlmann had gotten nowhere in the Ardennes, Peiper's old running mate with the "Hitler Jugend Panzer Division" was now doing pretty well for himself. Buenos Aires had not earned the honorific "Paris of South America" for nothing. Kuhlmann ended up living in fashionable digs on embassy row, only a short walk from the presidential palace of Evita and Juan Perón.[37]

Fascist dictator Juan Perón was an egomaniac and also pro-Hitler; he provided thousands of blank Argentinian passports to Nazi fugitives during the closing days of the war. Meanwhile anti-Semitism was so institutionalized in Argentinian life that some people like Rudel felt more welcome in Buenos Aires than in Germany. Indeed, Rudel had befriended Josef Mengele, the heinous Nazi concentration camp doctor and war criminal, after his arrival in Argentina in late 1948.[38] Adolf Eichmann too.

And here was Rudel planning a visit to Joachim Peiper. Peiper had received packages with food and goodies from Leibstandarte veteran Robert Sell, then living in Argentina. *Kameradenwerk*, another group of clandestine SS veterans, even left their return address on Christmas packages sent to Peiper at Landsberg! For Peiper, it was as if Sell had parachuted from South America to rescue his battle group in La Gleize, Belgium:

> When you had to cower behind prison walls in this way for five years, as the pariah under arrogant victors and with a Diaspora going on in the middle of your own people, it was a very odd feeling when a flare shows up from the other side of the ocean. It is like an air drop to a surrounded Kampfgruppe, you know. Here, as there, the important thing isn't the number of calories brought in, but just the amount of moral support, the spiritual ammunition. . . . .[39]

Did Rudel hope to jail break Peiper from Landsberg? He visited Peiper on March 23, 1954. There was the fact that the single postwar escapee during transfer to Landsberg Prison had been assisted by none other than Otto Skorzeny, and the only German to escape the prison proper had been one of Skorzeny's wartime commandos![40]

MEANWHILE, COURTESY OF THE ANNUAL REVIEW BOARD, LANDSBERG PRISON rapidly thinned. In December 1953, nine more Malmédy men were released, including Hans Hennecke and Gustav Knittel.[41] For sure, sentiment for old SS warriors was changing.

But Joachim Peiper remained as one of the four hundred prisoners the Americans still held. Peiper was now taking commercial law courses and adding to his proficiency with English and its literature. Although his superiors rated his performance as excellent in the gardening, school, motor pool, and carpentry section, he did little to hide his bitterness.[42] He wrote directly to the members of the parole board in English on December 28, 1953:

> The rough fingers of violent experience have harped upon the souls of Germany's war generation, and many a young man's hair has become gray behind bars. Let bygones be bygones, and give a chance to a man who is sincerely willing to contribute his share to a common cause. Decency, good will and reconciliation thrive only in the tolerant and unprejudiced climate of free human relations whereas, as Oscar Wilde puts it,
>
> "The vilest deeds like poison weeds
> Bloom well in the prison air
> It is only what is good in Man
> That wastes and withers there."[43]

Despite Peiper's English literary debut, he was denied parole again.[44] In 1953, Sigurd Peiper and her children moved from the Gsotthaberhof Villa in Rottach-Egern to Sinzheim in Baden.[45] She first moved to Hauptstrasse 65, moving in with her old Himmler secretary friend, Hedwig Potthast![46] A few months later Sigurd took a modest one story flat at 32 Bergstrasse. The place was small but cozy; a framed picture of Jochen Peiper, with the Oak Leaves to the Knight Cross, occupied a prominent place over the living room mantle.

It was no coincidence that Sigurd first moved in with Hedwig, the former mistress of Heinrich Himmler, when coming to that town from Rottach. And then after Sigurd settled in Bergstrasse, Häschen became her next door neighbor.[47] When Sigurd moved to Sinzheim, she helped locate a job for Hedwig there, both women working as clerical help for Dr. Wolman GmbH, a wood treatment company—they were secretaries working together again.[48] Hans Joachim Freiherr von Kruedener had helped both to find flats in town within walking distance of the factory, and the two worked as a team—clerical ghosts of Himmler's former empire.[49]

In fact, the job was not far removed from the old SS. In wartime, their boss, Baron von Kruedener, was in charge of a failed industrial plan by Oswald Pohl's late-war SS economy to extract fuel oil from shale. Operation Wüste had been run by the SS, using slave labor in seven concentration camps in the Schwäbian Alps. Mining shale by hand with pick axes, thirty-five hundred of the laborers died. And so, von Kruedener knew Himmler's former secretaries from the old days of the circle of friends. Yet, those who met them in town saw them as unremarkable: working single mothers, like so many others in man-short postwar Germany.[50]

HIMMLER'S SON FROM HIS BIGAMOUS LIAISON, HELGE, WAS IN THE SAME class in high school with Hinrich Peiper in Baden-Baden.[51] Nanette Dorothea, Himmler's daughter, attended school with Peiper's youngest, Silke. And Sigurd Peiper remained good friends with Häschen. Even though Frau Potthast had a Berlin notary in 1949 (a former SS colonel) nullify Himmler's paternity over her children, she decided to have Jochen Peiper inform her kids of their father's identity. That was to happen when he was released from prison.[52] The *Sippengemeinschaft*—Himmler's clannish SS community—was still alive. And just what kind of person was Sigurd's neighbor and the close friend, Frau Potthast?[53]

At the end of the war, as the Allied advance threatened to engulf Berchtesgaden, Potthast had fled. Even before news was broadcast of Himmler's death on May 23, 1945, both women had arranged to meet in the Tyrolean countryside near Rosenheim. Not only were they keen on avoiding the Soviets, but the area was also where Himmler had designated for the Alpine Redoubt, the envisioned final bastion of National Socialism.

In those chaotic weeks at war's end, Hedwig joined Eleonore Pohl on her family estate, Brünings Au, in Halfing.[54] It was in the same spectacular alpine region where others of Himmler's inner circle made their homes, but the US Army investigators found her. There, in Upper Bavaria, an interrogator from the US 7th Army—likely Walter M. Baum—pronounced her "a prototypical Deutsche Frau" and a "loyal and devoted mistress to Himmler" who could not bear to destroy letters from her former lover.

Later they returned her briefly to Augsburg for an interview with Maj. Paul Kubala and interpreter, T/4 Sgt. G. K. "Joe" Guennel.[55] Hedwig Potthast gave the impression of being the dedicated simple-minded Nazi mistress who only discussed personal matters with her prominent paramour and naively believed that "everything he did was for the sake of Germany." Of the excesses of the SS and the concentration camps, Miss Potthast claimed to know nothing. "I don't understand all these nasty things they say about him. He was really the nicest man!"[56]

In fact, however, Hedwig Potthast had pulled the wool over American intelligence eyes. She had been Himmler's lover and the mother of two of his children, but she was hardly a simple-minded concubine. And Frau Potthast's knowledge of the odious goings on in Himmler's world had not come late in the war.

In the spring of 1938, conditions in Buchenwald had become so desperate that inmates with nothing to lose killed an SS guard and escaped. Later one of the men was captured. Determined to make an example, Himmler ordered that the man be hanged in a grim spectacle before the assembled three thousand camp inmates. As Himmler was spending the weekend at Tegernsee, Hedwig, his devoted secretary, went along and wired his office in Berlin from *SS Kommandostelle Gmünd* with macabre instructions to Theodor Eicke that "the Reichsführer SS wishes for a precise report over the attitude of the prisoners at the hanging of Bargatzky."[57] So much for secretarial innocence.

When she gave her only interview at the age of seventy-five to a Hamburg journalist, Hedwig recalled how she was Himmler's "sole confidant" who could talk to him at any time about *any* subject. *Nothing* was off the table. Indeed, it was she, Häschen later claimed, who had suggested that the Reichsführer SS enter into negotiations with the Allies in late 1945.[58] Further, there is strong evidence she was well aware of the murder going on at the elimination and concentration camps, one of which she lived close by. Although secretive and so horrifying as to engender doubt, one troubling story was repeated by young Martin Bormann Jr. of having visited

Potthast's home in late 1944 with his mother and sister and seeing items gifted to her from Himmler: a table and stool supported by legs of human thigh bones![59]

AND THEN THERE WAS THE SEEDY CONNECTION OF POTTHAST WITH ALFRED Kurzmeyer, the Swiss wartime director of the Deutsche Bank and the private financier of Oswald Pohl—a job that would later earn him the dubious title as "Banker of the Holocaust." It seems that in February 1945, just before the collapse of the Third Reich, 239,000 Swiss francs were transferred from a Swiss bank account that had been seized from a Hungarian Jew to the SS in Berlin to help Hedwig Potthast get along after the war.[60] On April 25, 1945, as the Reich crumbled, Potthast, her children, and the other Pohl neighbors fled back to Upper Bavaria with Eleonore Pohl to Brünings Au.[61] The following month, Oswald Pohl went into hiding, posing as a simple farmhand disguised behind a gigantic Bismarkian mustache. For a year it worked, but Pohl was one of the most wanted persons of Hitler's legacy. His arrest made headlines in early May 1946.Taken into custody, Pohl readily admitted the existence of the *Vernichttungslager*—the elimination camps—saying, "everyone down to the lowliest clerk knows what went on in the concentration camps."[62]

With three kids and a husband in prison, Sigurd Peiper was scraping by, supplementing her meager income by selling Persil laundry detergent on weekends. Unlike the financial situation of Sigurd Peiper, after the war Himmler's mistress and her children seemed better off. The difference may have been special knowledge of SS riches, as was suggested by Frau Margarete Himmler when she was apprehended in 1945.[63] First, Potthast lived with the Eleonore Pohl near Halfing until Oswald Pohl was captured and then hanged on June 7, 1951.[64] Then Hedwig and her children moved to Tiesendorf near Traunstein until April 1952, when *Newsweek* reporters discovered her. It was then, after she was uncovered, that she moved to Sinzheim to stay with Sigurd Peiper.[65] At that time she wrote to Eleonore Pohl, saying, in the interest of her two children she was "burning all bridges and breaking all contact."[66]

When interviewed after the war by a Pohl biographer, Potthast insisted on leaving the past behind. Remarried, she had changed the surnames of her children.[67] In public she never spoke of the past. The Peiper kids likely knew nothing about the dark side of Hedwig Potthast, but the same claim for Sigurd strains credibility. Even so, there was no denying that it was a hard time for Sigurd Peiper; after all, she was raising three children alone, with all the exhaustion that entailed. Her local internist, Dr. Günther Zimmermann, worried of her blood condition, given that her father had died of leukemia.[68] He argued that Jochen Peiper should be released to rescue the family.

In 1954, seeing others leaving Landsberg, Peiper and his attorney, Dr. Eugen Leer, doubled down in seeking parole. To that end, he enlisted the help of his old SS friends, Rudi Lehmann and Willi Bittrich, who had led the 2nd SS Panzerkorps in the Ardennes Offensive.[69] On May 14, Peiper wrote to Lehmann, thanking them for helping to "find me a way into a civilian existence."At the time they were proposing that he work for Schnellpressen A. G. in Heidelberg with Lehmann. Although Peiper said his French was sufficient for his wartime adventures with Lehmann to Paris, his command of the language was not up to translation. And Heidelberg did not seem attractive, as parole did not allow travel outside geographic limits. Sigurd would not be moving from Sinzheim, where she had built up a career and landed an apartment. "Understandably, she refuses to give this up for more or less blue sky," Peiper wrote. The kids were in school, and that was a big factor.[70]

On May 21, 1954, the US Army reduced Peiper's sentence to a prison term of thirty-five years—hardly different from life, in a practical sense, but still a reduction. Energized by the news, Peiper requested clemency right away, calling himself "a fatalistic optimist." The answer was no again.

Later, on December 20, 1955, Sigurd Peiper wrote from Sinzheim to his potential parole officer, Dr. Theodor Knapp: "So it is the 14th time that I will have to light the Christmas candles for my children without my husband. The disappointment is very great, indeed." But it didn't work—Jochen was still in prison.[71]

Then, in late summer 1956 came signs that Peiper's clemency application might finally be approved.[72] Because the parole board objected to Peiper's initial plan to work at Porsche due to suspicion of Albert Prinzing and the Porsche family, Dr. Knapp crafted an alternative for employment at the chemical firm of Paul Lechler. Peiper objected, however, holding out for Porsche. Unsaid was that Lechler was an evangelical Christian, anti-Nazi zealot—a *Weltanschauung* totally at odds with the unreformed Jochen Peiper. "In view of his training, a technical occupation would suit him best," Knapp argued.[73] Then Porsche's personnel director, Alfred de Maight, replaced Prinzing as Peiper's potential sponsor.

But a big bump threatened to derail everything. An incendiary article in *Neue Illustrierte* revealed that Peiper and other Leibstandarte officers had presided over the execution of several German SS enlisted men near Beverloo, Belgium, in May 1944. Again the muddy water was stirred, but former Leibstandarte pharmacist Helmut Seidenglanz contacted the parties involved—SS judge Dr. Christian Jochum, Dr. Gerhard Franz, Hans Gruhle, Gerhard Nüske, and Teddi Wisch—to coordinate a common thread. Seidenglanz even visited Peiper in Landsberg on several occasions to make sure everyone would be on the same page with their story.[74]

When the legal authorities spoke to Peiper about the incident on July 30, 1956, he was primed. "The article of the news magazine '*Neue Illustrierte*' is known to me," he began, "but is totally wrong. There was a regular trial of the field court of the division. The men belonged to the SS Division Hitlerjugend as replacements for the SS. . . . These people were fully trained, but released from their former unit," Peiper said. "So, they were not the best *Menschenmaterial*."[75]

But Peiper's choice of words—*not the best human material*—struck an ugly chord. Even still staying with Nazi-speak, however, Peiper and the others managed to blame the SS regime for the orders to have the men shot, and not themselves. Yet, as summer faded to fall 1956, Peiper was still in his concrete abode. On November 7, 1956, a Flensburg attorney general wrote that Peiper would not likely be singled out for charges in the affair.[76] On November 30 even Georg Preuss, disdained by his own Leibstandarte comrades, was released.[77] What would it take to get Peiper out?

The approaching yuletide did the trick. On December 6 his waiting parole officer appealed to the federal judge in Bad Godesberg. None of the alleged allegations of wrongdoing from the article in *Neue Illustrierte* were going to be taken to court. It had been very heavy for Peiper's family over the last year, his attorney told the mixed board, and Peiper's wife was now suffering ill health. Would she have to light the Christmas candles a fifteenth time without Jochen at home?[78]

On December 21, at 3:53 p.m., a teletype machine inside Landsberg rattled off a classified message to prison director Maj. Daniel W. Stubbs:

> Pursuant to unanimous recommendation of the Mixed Board, order signed 21 December 1956 release war crimes prisoner Joachim Peiper on parole. His release will be effected 22 Dec 1956 at 1400 hours.

THE SECRET US ARMY ORDER EMPHASIZED THAT THE CONTENTS OF THE message were to be classified until the day after Christmas.[79] Peiper's release would be a bombshell—a Cold War seismic event.[80]

Chapter 16

STEEPLECHASE

On December 22, 1956, two American soldiers at the sprawling prison at Landsberg-Lech came to see prisoner number 99, Joachim Peiper. Their footsteps echoed down the brightly lit hall as they approached cell number 216, resonating with a lonely schuffle among the gray walls of prison.[1] The heavy wooden door swung open. The two Americans, clad in olive drab, poked their heads in to see its occupant, seated in a chair. He looked up rather surprised. "Peiper, you are going free," one told him. The other guard wrinkled his brow. "Doesn't he understand?" They were both staring at the well-groomed inmate incongruously clothed in a prison smock for whom orders had just come for a Christmastime pardon. The second man turned to the first: "I think I saw an eyelid blink."[2]

His family knew nothing when Joachim Peiper walked to freedom that Saturday afternoon. At the prison entrance, Helmuth Meng, the German point of contact for the parolee, and the US parole officer, Deforest A. Barton, were waiting. Barton, a native of Austin, Texas, shook Peiper's hand. At 2:05 p.m. Peiper signed the papers and checked out beyond the snow-encrusted prison gate.[3] He had been incarcerated at Landsberg for over ten years. Soon he was outside. It was cold and cloudy, but he instinctively looked up—a winter sky without walls. Walking ahead with Meng, Peiper shuffled across the road before the spired prison and its iron gate. To reach the Bahnhof, they simply crossed the street over Hindenburgring. Soon the former SS colonel and Meng boarded a train, outlined in red, that would take them to Augsburg and, from there, to Stuttgart. Through the slab-like plate-glass windows of their train car, the view gave way from the streets of Landsberg and then the quickly passing countryside. To anyone else the panorama was bleak, but to Peiper, the gliding scenery was euphoric. At last he was leaving that cursed point of bondage that had been Hitler's own place of incarceration thirty years before.

Peiper was free, but with qualifications: as a charged war criminal, he was on parole. In Feuerbach in Stuttgart he checked in with his new landlord, Dr. August Hartmann, and Dr. Theodor Knapp, his sponsor. After registering with the police, several hours were spent discussing his parole plan with Dr. Knapp. During the day Peiper would work his new job at the Porsche automotive company, returning at night to sleep in his one-room apartment at Klagenfurtstrasse 4. He was to make an effort to move his family to Stuttgart, but given the housing shortage, that could take some time. Until then he was encouraged to visit his family in Sinzheim on weekends and holidays.[4] With official business done, that afternoon Jochen again took the train to be with his family near Baden. It was just days before Christmas.

A telephone call from friends listening to the radio first told Sigurd that her husband was released from prison. The long-missing family father arrived on Christmas Eve. The circumstances for his homecoming were cathartic and emotional even for Prussian sensibilities. Peiper was thrilled to have his freedom, but expectations were great, and the family welcome was likely awkward. Fourteen-year-old Hinrich was more concerned with planning a ski date with friends than with seeing his estranged father over the holidays. Elke was now sixteen years old and a *Backfisch*—a young teenager. "We were glad to have him home, but as a family we had been just with my mother for years,"[5] Hinrich said later. There was the traditional goose and *Rotkraut*, but Christmas Eve dinner fell strangely flat.

Even between husband and wife the relationship seemed strained. Sigurd had seen painfully little of her husband during the war—there were only short visits—too little to give her three children, all born during the war years, any clear recollection of Daddy. After the war she had lived in the shadow of his impending death, raising a family as a single parent for eleven years. As he had been cloistered in Landsberg, the kids barely knew their father. He was the war-time hero whose uniformed photo lived on the mantle.

> When my father was released, he came back to a family in which mother and half-grown children already formed a firm community. Papa was known to us solely through letters and the occasional visit to Landsberg. It wasn't easy to become accustomed to him and it took some time before he was finally accepted really into the family community.[6]

Not surprisingly "Papa" seemed ill at ease—indeed, shocked—by mundane things, such as the liberal use of butter on bread. Peiper had saved everything he could at Landsberg, hoarding pats of butter and exchanging them for candy for his kids. Such frugality now seemed misplaced. The new Germany was bustling with business and Western capitalism.

Whereas Sigurd remained steadfastly centered on rearing her children, Jochen was still obsessed with the war and his time in prison. "At first," his son remembered, "it was very difficult for him. He was focused on his past and I was not interested in his past. We didn't want to hear about that." In any case, their newly arrived father was not around often. With parole limitations, he spent most of his time working in Stuttgart or in his little apartment. On weekends he traveled three hours by train to Sinzheim to see them.[7]

Officially, the tension didn't show. When Dr. Knapp visited his client on January 15, 1957, he found him adjusting. Alfred de Maight, the chief of personnel at Porsche, made a favorable report on Peiper's work for the sales department. He "was on good terms with his work colleagues," but Maight complained the "public attacks in the press must cease as soon as possible." The negative notoriety of their new employee did little for Porsche. And Knapp noted his client was nervous, but that was understandable—his release had created an uproar.[8]

The US Army had done their best to cushion the blow. Certainly the holiday slowed the awareness of Peiper's release. Yet a day after he was set free, *Stars and Stripes* quoted US senator Estes Kefauver of Tennessee in a scathing indictment. "Peiper and his group were the worst kind of sadistic murderers," he said.[9] Similarly, former chief justice William Clark of the Allied High Commission courts in Germany sharply criticized Peiper's release: "I think it is a disgrace for our State Department to set up a board with three West German members to release these criminals."[10] Most poignant, however, was the bitter complaint of Lt. Virgil Lary Jr., the only US Army officer to survive the shooting at the Malmédy crossroads. "The screams of my men who were massacred still ring in my ears," he wept. "For those of us who survive, our hearts are sick after each release."[11]

Ex-Waffen SS veterans rejoiced. In the January issue of *Der Freiwillige*, Peiper was epitomized as their long-suffering "comrade and colonel of the Waffen SS with the Oak Leaves and Swords to the Knight's Cross" who had been held unjustly at Landsberg. For him there was "heartfelt greetings and best wishes for the start of a new life." That groundswell was ever so apparent when Peiper was released. Although it was important to keep it quiet, given his touchy parole status, there was an understated celebration. From the old comrades, Frau Peiper was deluged at their home with congratulatory telegrams, Christmas packages, flowers, and even money. In the same issue of the SS publication of the Hilfsgemeinschaft auf Gegenseitigkeit (HIAG), Jochen asked ex-SS Unterstürmführer Helmut Seidenglanz to relay his appreciation to the many veterans, both named and anonymous, who sent him good wishes and more.[12]

Regardless of adoration from his old comrades, Peiper emerged into a changed world. The National Socialist culture he had embraced during the war had vanished—at least publicly. Nobody talked of the days just twelve years before when Germany was master of the continent! Everyone seemed to have a profound collective amnesia, a constant undercurrent of angst and sulking guilt. As much as possible the war was not discussed, particularly not the supposedly "criminal" Waffen SS. And the name Hitler—or, even worse, Himmler—was part of the forbidden lexicon. Unless being roundly denounced, these names did not appear, not even in whispers.

Meanwhile Peiper's employer, Porsche K. G., was teeming with SS men. Its head, Ferry Porsche, was the gold-handed son of Dr. Ferdinand Porsche who himself had worked with Hitler to produce fine fighting machines during the war. Ferry's personal memoirs claimed that Himmler capriciously bestowed on him SS membership for his part in designing the highly successful amphibious jeep, the Schwimmwagen. Yet, in actuality, he had *volunteered* for the SS on December 17, 1938, including the requisite paperwork for the Race and Settlement Main Office—the Rasse und Siedlungs Hauptamt.[13] Later Himmler awarded Porsche the Totenkopf, or "Death's Head," ring.[14] Company employee rolls bulged with former SS men. These included Huschke von Hanstein, who was one of Himmler's chief racing men and Hans Klink, son of Gertrud Scholtz-Klink and who would later be made chief of Porsche sales to

France. Porsche had even hired Erich Kempka, Hitler's coarse-talking, womanizing driver, who gave the cars the final touch before handing them over to customers. At least in part, Porsche K. G. in the *Wirtschaftswunder*—the German economic miracle of the 1950s—was a modern-morphed SS company!

Even with the country split in half from the Soviet occupation, the average West German seemed to be doing well. But matters were touch and go for Peiper's family in Upper Bavaria. Peiper received a prisoner of war indemnity on his release, but that would hardly make ends meet.[15] Peiper's morning newspaper opened to bitter headlines. In 1957, the Cold War accelerated as if under rocket power. The Fatherland was split in half at its heart, right through his hometown of Berlin. The very danger of the Bolshevists of which he had warned the American colonel McCown back in those December days in the Ardennes in 1944 seemed more real than ever. Soviet Russia—Peiper's despised enemy of those years—threatened Europe as never before. Now the Russians had nuclear weapons! Within months of his release they launched Sputnik, revealing a rocketry program of shocking technological dimension and the prospect of global atomic Armageddon. To Peiper's mind, the German failure on the Russia steppes loomed more painful than ever.[16]

Even though Germany had become an important ally of America and Great Britain, there were many thousands of SS veterans living in Adenauer's Germany who also cast ballots and wrote vitriolic diatribes to the newspapers. Adenauer himself came right out with it: "I think it is about time to end the witch hunt for Nazis."[17] Were German comrades-in-arms more important in Cold War Europe than the memories of murdered civilians and Allied soldiers? Was it possible for those who won the war to judge fairly whether war crimes had been committed?[18] And so in the spring of 1957 none other than old Kurt "Panzer" Meyer rose to a podium in Karlberg, Bavaria, to address eight thousand members of the former Waffen SS. "SS troops," he railed, "committed no crimes except the massacre at Oradour, and that was the action of a single man."[19] Even the mention of Oradour created a firestorm of protest from veterans from Das Reich, and Meyer never repeated that mistake again! At the close of Meyer's speech the SS veterans spontaneously broke out into song—the emotionally charged first stanza of the forbidden Nazi anthem, *Deutschland, Deutschland über alles*.[20]

Since the final curtain in 1945, veterans of the Waffen SS sought to distance themselves from the atrocities committed in the name of National Socialism. Yet could a military force created in the ideological mold as the elite standard bearer of Nazism ever succeed in such a venture? In some ways it hardly mattered, Meyer was wildly popular with the old SS men. When he showed up for the meeting in 1958, fifteen thousand admirers looked on:

> Things happened during the war that were a disgrace to the German nation. The former soldiers of the Waffen SS are man enough to know that there were war crimes and to detest them as such. It would be silly to reject all the events with which we were charged by our former enemies as propaganda inventions. . . . They obviously made propaganda out of them. . . . They were the

victors, after all, and we had no rights as the losers. But crimes did happen. . . . Those in prison cannot defend themselves. Those who lie in countless graves no longer have a voice.[21]

But Meyer's appeal for sympathy for the Waffen SS did little for Peiper. Judged by the victors, Peiper, the loser, had fallen from the lofty height of fabled SS war hero to *Vorbestrafter*—with a criminal record. And Porsche was his employer—Prof. Porsche, who had built some of the Tiger tanks with which Hitler's forces had endeavored to conquer Europe! As he always told it—Peiper's favorite tale—his first job at Porsche the first day of January 1957 was to wash cars for the company.[22] But the truth, as evidenced by reports of his parole officer, was less colorful. Because of his affliction with phlebitis, Peiper was almost immediately confined to office work. Pay was 477 marks per month—equivalent to US$120 at the time.[23] Putting his best foot forward, he presented himself as Jochen Peiper, "the pure soldier."

Even though his parole conditions warned Peiper to avoid any contact with old SS comrades during his parole, being a hero to that organization made compliance unlikely, particularly given the avalanche of letters just after his release.

On February 15, 1957, his family joined him in Stuttgart. Peiper moved from Dr. Hartmann's tiny apartment to a flat at Waldstrasse 32, spacious enough to provide room for Sigurd and the girls.[24] Meanwhile Hinrich stayed behind in Sinzheim to finish the high school year at Baden-Baden. But somehow word of his father's identity had made it through the community grapevine. In April 1957 the principal of his school in Stuttgart refused admission for "the son of a war criminal." But that ended when Jochen threatened legal action.[25]

Things got better. When Peiper's parole officer visited on August 5, 1957, he reported "the parolee is respected by the firm and he is satisfied with the work." Assigned to the sales bureau, he even made trips to attend auto expositions in Garmisch-Partenkirchen and, later, Frankfurt/Main. By May 1958 his monthly pay at Porsche had doubled to 900 marks, and the American Embassy recommended to the parole board that Peiper's need for supervision cease. Officially, at least, the shackles were gone.

Peiper stayed with his sales job for a year and a half until Ferry Porsche recognized his unique credentials. Peiper had a certificate in the English language from Landsberg; he was fluent, and that was useful. He thrived with the export sales department under Erich Hirsch.[26] Reborn by the economic miracle of Konrad Adenauer's *West* Germany—the *Wirtschaftswunder*—Peiper threw himself headlong with the others into the "the steeple chase for money."[27] Porsche now had a hit with the 100-horsepower 1956 Porsche 356a that designer Dr. Ernst Fuhmann called "my youthful sin."[28] Porsche was making it, and Peiper too.

Although focused on his family matters, Peiper's adjustment to home life remained challenging. The relationship with his children was stormy—he was from a different era.[29] His daughter Elke was preparing for college, and Hinrich was in his final year of high school, although, according to Jochen on his birthday in 1960, his son was "far better on skis than in school."[30] Peiper's father was ailing as well.[31]

Peiper, meanwhile, sought to resume a halfway normal life.

But even as he came to grips with the modern age, Peiper's past was never distant. In November 1957, the successful US writer John Toland approached him for his help with a book he was assembling about the Battle of the Bulge. Toland was keenly familiar with Peiper's controversial role, but the former SS colonel was unwilling to be drawn into the fray:

> Regrettably, I must disappoint you. The U.S. Army, whose prisoner I still am as a "parolee," is not interested in a truthful description to the same extent you are. To the contrary, I specifically had to assure in writing to remain silent about these things. . . . Well, I bear this with composure and a whispered smile. Truth is a daughter of time and history is nothing but a fable, the interpretation governed by expediency.

Peiper invited the author to meet when he was in Germany next.[32] But otherwise, generally Peiper closed the door. Meanwhile Toland pursued other connections. Working on several books, including one detailing Hitler's life, the author was in nearly continual contact with infamous SS commando Otto Skorzeny. Having escaped from the Americans at Darmstadt on July 27, 1948, Skorzeny went underground, moving from a Bavarian farm, Paris, South America, and then to Spain, using the pseudonym Rolf O. S. Steinbauer, living well on loot hauled from the collapse of the Reich.[33] In Spain he engaged in military consulting and engineering as well as sponsoring Nazis in hiding.[34] Frequently he and his "Circle of Friends"—fascists and ex-Nazis—would hang out at Horchers, a sympathetic Austrian watering hole in the Calle Alfonso XII, where they would plot their next move or consider those like Peiper, who might still need help.

For most old Nazis, such dealings would have been a full life of intrigue. Yet, Skorzeny, who was never shy of reiterating his dedication to Hitler, also looked to redress the condemned historical lot of National Socialism.[35] To help that, he did little to deny unsubstantiated reports of his wartime largess. He befriended John Toland, who was in awe of the towering Austrian.

On September 28, 1957, John Toland interviewed Skorzeny at length in Spain. Had he really been assigned to assassinate Eisenhower during the Bulge? "Only a rumor," Skorzeny chortled, "but you can be sure if it had been attempted it would have succeeded."[36] Skorzeny managed to slowly put the American author in touch with any of those in the "inner circle."[37] Toland really wanted to speak with Peiper. Skorzeny contacted HIAG:

> Some days again I had the visit of the American writer John Toland. He has the intention to write a book about the Ardennes Offensive in our sense in a correct way. He showed me some already written pages that prove he has good intentions and his intent to bring justice to both sides. I now urgently need the addresses of Dietrich Ziemssen and Jochen Peiper—and perhaps even Panzermeyer.[38]

HIAG quickly put Skorzeny in touch with Peiper. "I am wondering what you finally wrote about the Peiper case," Skorzeny soon wrote to Toland, "As you know, I talked during many hours this summer with Colonel Peiper. I am only sorry that you were not able to talk to him personally."[39]

In any case, through Skorzeny's strident advocacy, Peiper agreed to help, if not in a meeting, at least by correspondence. Provided with Toland's prepublication draft, Peiper gave a caustic critique:

> I have gained the impression from both your letter and the conversation with Mr. Skorzeny that you sincerely endeavor to serve the truth rather than sensationalism—although your story contains much fiction. . . . Having read the whole excerpt of yours, I regret that you do not write history, but prefer to still cling to the old and primitive pattern of the Nazi brutes slaughtering civilians and violating the laws of war and peace. Admitted, it was a very successful weapon of psychological warfare and is still a safe means to sell a book or movie. . . . However, for a man with intelligence and reason, such a one sided and biased story should be under his dignity. And above all, what good is it?
>
> Don't you think I could write an analysis myself on how the U.S. courts of vengeance violated the Geneva convention and all existing law on 3rd degree interrogation methods and fabrication of evidence and confessions. Or give an account on how the U.S. Army, retreated terror stricken without need during the Battle of the Bulge, and what a poor show three U.S. divisions put up when they failed to crush a small German task force without fuel and ammo, and how the latter blew up all material before it walked out right through the sleeping foe, stubborn and unbroken. But what would be the good of it? Is it not much more important for all of us to settle the old feuds and shake hands, to let bygones be bygones instead of scraping off the crust from never healing wounds. . . . I am firmly convinced that the heroes and scoundrels were equally distributed on both sides.[40]

Unknown to Peiper, Toland would also approach Peiper's former defense attorney, Willis Everett, for help. "I want to tell what happened at Malmédy . . . without prejudice."[41] Everett wrote back that he had received requests to write a book on the trial, but that such a book, no matter how factual, would be poorly received so soon after the war.[42] "It is probably true that I am the only one who can give you the facts pertaining to this ten and a half years of strategy and battle that I have single handedly waged." He offered Toland access to his records in Atlanta.[43] Toland responded, "Your opinion has great weight. . . . And even though it will undoubtedly bring the wrath of the American Legion on my neck, I will print the truth as I see it."[44]

Later Toland sent Peiper a copy of his book. "I have been careful to exonerate you from all blame." The author claimed to have provided balance by describing the Bulge shooting of German soldiers near Chenogne, Belgium, by the green US 11th Armored Division. Peiper wrote back,

> Well, I cannot help smiling. Don't you understand that this is of no concern to me at all? I am used to being a scapegoat. . . . It has no bearing on the course of events, nor has your unbiased attempt to report on the murder of 60 German soldiers—much as I acknowledge your courage. But what is the good of washing dirty linen? He who is a soldier knows that war is not fought in kid gloves. . . . I was not upset with the material you sent me, but simply disgusted. Not because of myself or the way others describe me—I couldn't care less—but because of the stupidity of man and the immortality of propaganda stories that keep producing poison. If you attack me, I won't move a finger. If you attack my men—unfair and unjustified—you'll find me on the barricade.[45]

Meanwhile Peiper's old SS buddies rose within the Waffen SS organization, the HIAG. By July 1958 Dr. Ernst Klink was the press chief for the Tübingen section of the organization, and Hans Siptrott, of Malmédy fame, was the secretary contact in the Esslingen area. In Stuttgart, the old SS Kameraden normally met at the Tübinger Hof the first Friday of each month where a now-free Peiper was venerated, if seldom in attendance.[46]

While John Toland sought to resuscitate the past, Peiper looked to lose it—at least officially. Now he devoted his energies to his job. Most days he returned home from Porsche exhausted, but his star rose quickly. By 1959 he was still in the sales department and paid well in spite of a relatively minor post. But Peiper's English skills were increasingly important. Nearly half of Porsche sales were to the United States, and the SS colonel slowly became famous with the American Porsche-nut crowd. "He was a handsome man," remembered Evi Butz, the young female assistant to Baron Huschke von Hanstein, the racing director the company. Of Peiper she recalled, "He looked like a gentleman of the old school, good looking and charismatic. . . . In those years we were trying to forget the war and everything connected with it."[47] Indeed, Butz toed the line, careful not to inquire of the past of Peiper or her boss either.

In the meantime Peiper had been befriended by Dr. Benno Müller, a physician-turned-photographer from the Black Forest Kirchhofen who had himself been with the 5th SS Panzer Division Wiking.[48] Likeminded—both professing an interest in music, culture, and literature—they shared essential political sympathies, even though at odds with the politics of the Bonn government. In Müller's photography he specialized in black-and-white portraits, particularly of the glamourous women at the horse races in Baden-Baden or the rich and famous at the auto races.[49] Müller added Peiper to his list of the beautiful people and clicked away raptly.

And when Peiper spoke appreciatively of Willis Everett who had legally defended him, Müller impulsively wrote to the Atlanta attorney, enclosing a carefully crafted image of Peiper. There he was smiling above a white shirt and carefully groomed hair. "Peiper spoke about you with great admiration," Müller wrote.[50] When Everett received the envelope he quickly wrote Müller, thanking him for photos of the "gallant soldier." Within days another letter arrived, addressed to Peiper himself. For Willis Everett, contact with Peiper was an epiphany. "During October I received one of the most gratifying letters that I have had in many years," Everett began. The photos were on his mind:

> The one in which you were smiling brought great joy to my heart. I had never seen that smile and I can not say that I ever expected to see it after the ten-and-a-half year ordeal you went through. Frankly, I never smiled inwardly during that time and it was not until December 22, 1956 that I could feel that I had done my duty and complied with my assurance to the 74 defendants in our case that I would continue this fight until everyone of them had received a fair trial or been released.[51]

In his next letter Müller attempted to bring Everett up to date on Peiper's circumstances. He claimed Peiper's family was "without any signs of stress, which could be assumed regarding the long separation." Although Müller deemed Peiper's wife a "lovely personality," Jochen confided to him of "how difficult it was to adjust himself to the manner of his grown children, who regarded him as a foreigner, and for all decisions to be taken, turned to their mother and not to him." And the job at Porsche? "As such his clients are mostly Americans, who are all very satisfied by the way he handles their affairs, all of this seeming to be a slight parody of fate."[52]

As Müller responded, the "slight parody of fate" closed in once more at Porsche automotive. The problems began in 1959 when Peiper made a proposal to reorganize the sales department within Porsche by removing the public relations department from von Hanstein's racing department to a new overall PR department that he would lead—and with a lucrative salary. At first Porsche agreed to the idea, but all the affected department heads vehemently objected as well as the union, the Deutscher Gewerkschaftsbund (DGB).[53] In particular, Baron Huschke von Hanstein was incensed, even though he himself had been designated Himmler's official SS racing driver in 1940![54] All the while von Hanstein was attempting to curry favor with Europe's upper crust so counts, barons, and old money would be buying Porsche automobiles. How could having Peiper as the PR department head help with that? *The man had been accused of war crimes!* After all, the United States was Porsche's largest car sales market. Could that be good for public relations?

It didn't seem to matter. Peiper's reputation with German sports car afficionados in America blossomed. In 1960 the executive secretary of the Porsche Club of America, William J. Sholar, a commercial artist-turned-Porsche buff, approached Willis Everett with a strange request. "I have come to know and be very fond of Jochen Peiper and his charming family," he wrote. As Sholar was now planning a gala "Porsche Parade" for July 1960, in Aspen, Colorado, he wanted to bring along Peiper. "He and his wife have made so many friends among our membership. Jochen has done such an outstanding job of organization of our tours to Germany . . . we hope that they will be able to come with the group to be with us next summer."[55]

Ferry Porsche would be there. Sholar saw it only appropriate that Ferry's power US sales rep should come over for the big event. They could really experience America and its beautiful roads. Yet there was one big rub. As an accused war criminal, how would Bill Sholar secure a visa for Jochen Peiper? Responding by letter, Everett lamely suggested that Sholar simply submit the request along with other German personnel at the last minute. Perhaps Peiper's name wouldn't raise any red flags.[56] "The most important thing that must be safeguarded against is any publicity of any kind regarding Colonel and Mrs. Peiper coming to America. A great issue was made by the Jewish War Veterans . . . following Colonel Peiper's release."

When Everett wrote to Peiper, he was more pointed: "I would like to add that in view of the very hostile attitude of the American Legion as well as certain other segments of the American public, absolutely no publicity should be released about your coming." Still, Everett planned a reception at his home. "I am sure you will enjoy the hospitality of the South and will not regret this extra time involved in your visit to Atlanta."[57] An SS colonel in the Deep South! But if Everett's suggestion was naive, Peiper's first communication to Everett in three years was not:

> It was with deep joy and sincere appreciation that I recently received your long and friendly letter, the first sign of life since we saw each other last. Although many years have gone by and the whole ordeal today seems to have been nothing more than a bad dream, scarcely a moment elapsed without our knowing that you were doing your best for us, fighting against overwhelming odds and battling against a biased and revengeful world. . . .
>
> Though we did not hear from you, you were always present in our discussions and not for a moment we gave up our belief in you. I wrote you my last letter upon my release back in 1956. It was not necessary for me to get an answer, as I never lost inner touch with you.

But Peiper had doubts about the plans to come to the United States:

> I am very busy today and strangely enough, am primarily engaged with American tourists. There is not the slightest vestige of resentment or revengefulness in my heart toward the nation that robbed me of the best 12 years of my life and put my family to endless hardship and trouble, this solely is up to you, to your upright and unfailing example and the unsurpassed way in which you represented your country. You have been America's best ambassador to Germany. . . . I am really looking forward to seeing you in the coming spring and all my family is joining me in this wish. . . . Unfortunately, however, it will be impossible for me to accompany you, both for business reasons and because my wife and I already have a skiing engagement in March. . . . My trip to the States, on the other hand, is more improbable. Though your counsel is sound and wise as always, I am not yet convinced that Bill Sholar's anticipated scheme will materialize.[58]

Having received the letter, Everett responded promptly. "I wish I could share your patient understanding since 1946." he said, "but very frankly, I can only condemn the Army for putting these boys in the position they occupied."[59]

Everett did enclose a copy of John Toland's new best-selling book, *Battle: The Story of the Bulge*. It was the book over which Everett had made an attempt to balance the coverage. "You are mentioned many times," he said. Everett saw Peiper in a trusting light. You are "an outstanding soldier and true commanding officer," the Atlanta attorney concluded. In any case, he told Peiper, "I certainly believe that we all have much to thank God for."[60] Everett was convinced of the fundamental moral rectitude of the universe.

Not Peiper. He already saw storm clouds gathering at Porsche and likely took little comfort in Everett's Christmas-tide homily. He had been a proud SS soldier in Hitler's praetorian guard as well as Himmler's one-time adjutant. Could the world forget that?[61]

Willis Everett had not shared with Peiper the gravity of his failing medical condition. Ten years earlier, in March 1949, Everett had sustained a major heart attack. His physician, Carter Smith, had managed to pull him through, blaming too much stress from the Malmédy affair, made worse by chain-smoking. "He put me back on my feet so we could continue our fight." Now, there was more trouble. On February 5, 1960, he confided at last,

> I am still hoping to come to Stuttgart in April, but due to medical treatment for the last 60 days with Dr. Smith and others for the uncommon malady of lymphoma, I may have to delay my trip a little.[62]

That was an understatement. Everett was gravely ill, even though he still planned to come to Europe. He told Peiper he wanted to purchase one of the new Porsche four-passenger sedans "for a tour of Europe." "You and your wife might be able to take a little vacation with us, which would give us a glorious opportunity of going over the last 14 years."[63] He would pay whatever the cost. As befitted Everett's situation, money didn't matter. But time did.

In March, the Atlanta lawyer weakened and was confined to bed. His medical condition faltered, and on April 4, 1960, Willis Everett died. How Peiper reacted is unknown, but he knew he owed his life to the man. "Henceforth, in Germany," Peiper had written years before, "your name will stand for honesty, justice and democracy."[64] Later, when he decided he would write his own book about Malmédy, Peiper planned to dedicate it to Everett. That would have been fitting.[65] For, without Everett, Peiper would have likely have died on the gallows at Landsberg long before.

On the surface, Peiper's life during the summer of 1960 seemed reasonable enough. Even if he kept his visibility out of the public eye, he could still be found at unofficial events harkening back to the Third Reich. In July 1960, he attended the funeral of Genflm. Albert Kesselring in Bad Wiessee. Although only a colonel at the end of the war, there was Peiper, along with other former NSDAP illuminati on the invite list to the Bergfriedhof: Ferdinand Schörner, Karl Dönitz, Sepp Dietrich, and Otto Remer.

He also still had time for the younger LAH veterans with whom he had fought. When his old blind panzer radio operator, Fritz Kosmehl, visited him in Stuttgart during those warm days, Peiper was still working unperturbed at Porsche.[66] Returning from vacation, Peiper had picked Kosmehl and his wife up in a new red Porsche and greeted the blind man with a hug. It was the first time Kosmehl had encountered Peiper in fifteen years. Kosmehl's wife saw Peiper as a "noble general," a wiry man with gray temples. Peiper's wife seemed more aged—"the hard years of separation and anxiety had left their traces," Kosmehl recalled. Peiper greatly respected Kosmehl—a man who had lost his eyesight in tank battle in Normandy. But then, after the war, Kosmehl had maintained a steady communication with his former commander still held in prison at Landsberg. More than that, Kosmehl was an avid reader, an intellectual, and also a man who did not let his disability still him. Even blind, he trained at winter sports.[67]

Fritz and his wife enjoyed a little summer party on the balcony of Peiper's Stuttgart flat with Peiper's children. "Everything radiated relaxation and security," Kosmehl said. He was pleasantly surprised to hear his old commander laugh—he seemed at ease. Peiper pulled out a three-liter bottle and popped the cork and explained that it was *Asbach Uralt*—special brandy. To be sure, there were serious conversations about Landsberg and Porsche. But that seemed to fade with the alcohol. There were even jokes and laughter that summer afternoon.[68] Perhaps, Kosmehl thought, "he still believed that he would be able to make a normal life for himself."

Yet Peiper's ascent at Porsche ended abruptly in the spring of 1961. With little explanation, management advised that he would not receive the requested new position and must stay in the sales branch. However, he would receive more money—2000 marks a month.[69] Not enough! Peiper refused, informing management that he would contest their decision.[70] His daughter, Elke, had just ventured off to the university, but when home on weekends, she listened as her father complained of collusion developing against him at Porsche.

Peiper threatened Porsche with a lawsuit for breach of contract. He appeared before the Stuttgart court a "tall, well-groomed gentleman head to toe, superficially the Dieter Borsche type." The man who looked like a thirties movie idol was not a criminal, he maintained, but his speech that followed brought the past surging back to life. In his language the injustices of the Americans at Schwäbisch Hall and the disreputable Dachau trial were all to blame. Unable to prevail in the court battle, Peiper was done with Porsche and able to win only six months' severance pay. The German trade union gloated over their victory in the association newspaper: "Porsche Put the Brakes on Leibstandarte Officer: SS Colonel Aimed Too High."[71] There were awkward social ramifications. At the Uli Wieselmann gatherings in Stuttgart the social mix had to be adjusted if Peiper would be there: no Ferry Porsche, no Huschke von Hanstein. There was mutual disdain.

Meanwhile the daily news told of continuing danger for accused war criminals of the former Third Reich. Those hunting the suspects were busy—everyone was looking for Josef Mengele and Martin Bormann. And in May 1960 the word came that Adolf Eichmann, a primary manager for the Holocaust, had been captured in exile in Buenos Aires and returned to Israel to stand trial. In spring and summer of 1961 the court proceedings captivated the world. Peiper and other old members of the Waffen SS watched warily. Before Christmas 1961 Eichmann was sentenced to death for crimes against humanity. He was executed in May 1962.

The Eichmann case presaged a dramatic swing in German politics away from Hitler's Waffen SS. During the Adenauer period, from 1949 until 1961, the unspoken credo was that if SS men stayed out of politics and overt trouble, the government would shelter them—say nothing, hear nothing, know nothing.[72] Yet with Eichmann's arrest, the unspoken safety net for the old SS veterans vaporized. In cultural circles there was the highly acclaimed left-wing literary icon, Günter Grass, chastising Germans for energetically embracing a collective historical amnesia. "Perhaps if I rubbed my typewriter superficially with onion juice," the main character wrote in *Katz und Maus*, "it might communicate an imitation of onion smell which in those years contaminated all Germany . . . preventing the smell of corpses from taking over completely."[73] Suddenly that sentiment was everywhere. Within a year, the courts were prosecuting one German war crimes case after another.

And the renewed deliberations over SS guilt in the war brought new problems into the Peiper home. Now, vaguely aware of the closeness of his father to Himmler, Hinrich frequently had arguments with his senior. "How many Jews have you sent up the Schornstein?" one visitor to the family overheard the junior Peiper snidely question.[74]

AN SS HERO—QUESTIONED EVEN IN HIS OWN HOME.

Chapter 17

"WE ALL HAVE OUR CROSSROADS"

Postwar Germany was a discreet place. "The defeated must keep their mouths shut," ran the old German proverb. Like an ethereal mist, a general amnesia had settled over the country in 1945, and for more than a decade almost no one could be found who remembered anything about the war.[1]

Not surprisingly, Peiper was careful not to associate too closely with his old SS comrades and their aid organization, the HIAG. At least publicly. In mixed company he claimed he was consumed by his work and that his Prussian sensibilities did not lend themselves to the "old slap on the back" comradery that pervaded the meetings.[2] Peiper, seeing himself an intellectual and honorable soldier, said he could not identify with many of the old vets in the Waffen SS—the street brawlers, beer guzzlers, and old fighters.

But in fact, Peiper was *much* more involved with the SS crowd than he let on. In 1959 Peiper attended the national Ordengemeinschaft der Ritterkreuzträge (OdR, Association of the Order of the Knight's Cross) meeting in Regensburg, although he himself was not a member. Indeed, when he agreed to drive from Stuttgart with the former commander of the 10th SS Panzer Division, SS Obf. Walter Harzer, he had hoped to see Kurt Meyer.[3] Although that event had a certain legitimacy, given the attendees, the meeting was now held behind closed doors. Sepp Dietrich was there along with Archduke Franz Joseph, the last commander of the Imperial Austro-Hungarian army.

SS officers from the 2nd SS "Das Reich" Division sat with Peiper at his table at the formal dinner. There was Ernst-August Krag—his daring double from the reconnaissance battalion, Ernst Barkmann—of panzer fame and Heinz Lammerding, the division commander who was still hounded by the French over the terrible killings at Tulle and Oradour-sur-Glane.[4] It was the first time the old veterans and Bundeswehr alike were allowed to wear the Ritterkreuz in the old style around the neck. Of course, there was no Hakenkreuz—the Swastika was the ultimate taboo. Looking pensive, Peiper, wore only a simple white shirt with a dinner jacket.[5]

And he attended other events as well. On February 15, 1959, Peiper met the old comrades at a big gathering the Waldgasthof Glemstal, nestled in a secluded resort in the Rotwildpark just west of Stuttgart. There was Kurt Meyer, now too out of Canadian captivity, heading HIAG, and recently having penned his memoirs.[6] Also sitting by Peiper was Otto Günsche, Hitler's last SS adjutant who had torched Hitler's lifeless body at the Führerbunker.[7] Attired in ties and arrayed around a table, the former SS men—formerly condemned war criminals—basked in a genteel atmosphere. Comrades came by the table to shake hands, bowing curtly in deference. Meanwhile a hotel band squeezed out the old wartime tunes as the beer flowed. There was even singing.

But in the early 1960s, when Jochen Peiper's name kept bubbling up in one war crimes trial after another—even with Malmédy all but forgotten—he had to be careful about appearing too chummy with some of his old comrades. The investigation against Himmler's senior adjutant, Karl Wolff, began soon after West German authorities arrested him at his villa at Kempfenhausen on Starnberg Lake on January 18, 1962. The charges against him were damning, but the man whom Himmler called Wölffchen was cunning and slick.[8] He adroitly denied the most horrific charges, accepting those that were merely damaging, all the while playing a befuddling game of interpretation with the German language. Still, the circle was close, and Wolff remained in close contact with Hedwig Potthast and others of Himmler's inner sanctum.[9] Although Peiper laid low, he was nevertheless mentioned several times in the proceedings.[10]

Wolff steadfastly denied knowledge of the death camps and proved an exceedingly difficult witness.[11] However, in the course of the trial, letters emerged from the summer of 1942, in which he professed to be "particularly gratified with the news each day that a trainload of 5,000 of the Chosen People has been sent off to Treblinka."[12] And SS Ogruf. Erich von dem Bach-Zelewski, already under a sentence of life imprisonment for complicity in mass murder, damned Wolff, with whom he had a *Dutzen* relationship. "It is simply unbelievable," he told the court regarding the shooting of Jews, "that someone with such a high position can say he knew nothing."[13] On September 30, 1964, Karl Wolff, standing tall and pumped with vanity, though shackled with handcuffs, was brought into a Munich courtroom and sentenced to fifteen years imprisonment.

Within the proceedings, Peiper's name was sullied along with the likes of Heinrich Himmler; his driver, Franz Lucas; mistress, Hedwig Potthast; and others. Lombard himself was now under grave suspicion and strangely unable to remember anything about the Einsatzkommandos or the infamous *Kommissar Order*. Rather than mention his cavalry's Jew killing spree near Minsk in the July 1941, on the record Lombard referred to the action as a siege battle "*Kesselschlacht*." Indeed, he lied continuously in Karl Wolff's trial, but no one called him on it. "*Nichts!*" was his constant rejoinder.[14]

In fact, Peiper's successor as Himmler's adjutant, Werner Grothmann, also sat on a sizzling seat. While prosecutors pondered his amazing inability to remember the Russian partisan war, the Final Solution, or the extermination of the Jews, he professed dunce-like confusion. "My brain is so muddled by reading newspapers," he claimed, "that I can no longer remember whether things happened in the war or on the printed page."[15] But others could remember. Himmler's bodyguard, Josef Kiermaier, described in detail Himmler and Grothmann's presence at the shooting of Russian "partisans" at Minsk in August 1941. And on July 24, 1964, Gen. Bach-Zelewski testified that even before the war in Russia at the meeting at Wewelsburg, Himmler had spoken of the need to rid that country of 30 million Slavish people, and after his presence at the Minsk killings, "Himmler made it crystal clear to all his subordinates that he determined to eliminate the Jews."[16] Peiper had been with Himmler during that time but had escaped to a field assignment after his brother's death.

During the war Werner Grothmann had lived in Tegernsee for a time, much like Sigurd Peiper—close by the Lake of the Bosses and the National Socialist upper crust. Grothmann had many "old friends" among community neighbors in the splendorous Tegernsee Valley. That idyllic place was, after all, Himmler's power center of the SS Sippengemeinschaft in upper Bavaria. Nestled in the mountain dwellings about the alpine lakes was Karl Wolff, the head of the adjutants Reichsführer SS; Sepp Kiermeier, Himmler's personal bodyguard; and even Paul Baumert, also from Himmler's office.[17] Sepp "Tüpferl" Tiefenbacher, Himmler's ultra-efficient office security director, was there too. He had gone for a stint to Egypt as a security adviser to Abdul Nasser along with other old SS commando types.[18] Returning in 1954, he ended up with a security job for the local BMW factory and unknowingly was tracked by the US CIA!

But amid the unending controversy in which he found himself, the politics of the old SS veterans could not be helpful. Although Peiper avoided the more visible displays, in private he nurtured contact with veterans. There were a lot of them. During the 1960s HIAG's roster had swelled to over 70,000 of the 250,000 Waffen SS veterans who had survived the war. In 1963, Peiper was working with Walter Harzer of the 10th SS Panzer Division, the ranking SS general, and now in charge with HIAG of coordinating the writing of the divisional histories of the Waffen SS Divisions.[19] Over a period of years, Peiper had the old veterans over to Harzer's Stuttgart flat: Sepp Dietrich, Harzer, and Ernst Klink, their "in" at the Federal Archive in Freiburg.[20] Surreptitiously Ernst Klink was helping the old veterans, serving as an inside man to expunge their personal papers of any damaging personal admissions.[21]

There were also personal visits to Johannes Göhler and even Gustav Lombard, his old instructor at the 7th Reitersturm in Berlin. Göhler had been Hitler's dedicated SS adjutant at his headquarters when Peiper had his reckoning in the Ardennes. Both he and Lombard (who had been Peiper's old riding instructor in Berlin) had been associated with the 1st SS Cavalry Regiment implicated in the savage killing of Jewish "partisans" near Minsk.[22]

In 1973 Peiper met with the last division commander of Leibstandarte, Otto Kumm, in Offenburg. Kumm remained the ever-unreformed Nazi enthusiast. And on other occasions he and others visited SS General Paul "Papa" Hausser, who so staunchly defended the troops at Nuremberg.[23] Understandably such meetings would be held in private gardens in Stuttgart, where Peiper, Müller, and the other SS comrades would gather to renew the revelry.[24]

Further, Jochen was now actively helping HIAG and the old SS men, and this was clearly in evidence in the publishing world. In 1973 he worked with Paul Hausser jointly to edit and translate a massive five hundred–page SS picture tome, nostalgically titled, *Wenn alle Brüder schweigen*—When All Our Brothers Are Silent.[25]

Yet for Peiper and his wife, these connections were of lesser importance than Sigrid and Friedrich Wilhelm Mayr in Miesbach, another family of well-heeled Nazis who said little about their past before 1945—or at least kept it all quiet.[26] Mayr was an old fighter from Hitler's street-brawling days before 1933 and the truest of true believers. During the National Socialist heyday, Mayr was the part-owner of the regional *Miesbacher Anzeiger*.[27] Hitler considered that newspaper to be the real Bavarian voice of National Socialism—nationalistic, extremist, and anti-Semitic. Well connected, SS Obersturmführer Friedrich Wilhelm Mayr exerted enormous influence, but for his wife he chose a striking Danish beauty. But Mayr's marriage choice got him in trouble with Himmler's obsession for unflagging racial SS purity, when the head of the SS learned she was one-quarter Jewish. It was only because Mayr was a prominent SS officer, old fighter, and ran a favorite Hitler publishing house that Himmler allowed the marriage to continue. In any case, he forbade her to have any more children. Although Sigrid Mayr complained of having been racially persecuted by the SS, the fact that both were intimately connected to the SS organization throughout the war. She and Jochen's wife had become close while Sigurd Peiper was Himmler's secretary. After the war, if the Mayrs suffered, it was in luxurious style. Indeed, Mayr had become so rich as the publishing magnate for the National Socialists out of Miesbach that his financial empire became like the Rockefellers of Tegernsee.[28]

While Jochen was in Landsberg, the lines of communication with the Mayrs was never long interrupted. And while Sigurd had lived in Tegernsee after the war Sigrid Mayr had been her best friend.[29] Once Peiper was released from prison the first holiday he and Sigurd took from Stuttgart was to visit the Mayrs in Upper Bavaria for coffee, cakes, and a sympathetic ear.[30] Amazingly, Mayr was allowed to resume the lucrative journalistic business in Miesbach, albeit with a new name for the newspaper.

"He was very bitter and unhappy from his days in prison," remembered one of the Mayr children. The little kids, carefully shielded from their parents' National Socialist days, dreaded Peiper's visit—they just wanted to have fun. "When Mr. Peiper arrived, all laughter ended," remembered one. "When he came, he brought with him a gray shadow."[31] And Frau Peiper was a strict disciplinarian. She didn't like children speaking in the presence of adults and worried that her son and daughters would pick up the bumpkin Bavarian dialect. The family was standoffish too when they visited—friends had to go. Peiper wanted no contact.

Still, Peiper benefited from some other old connections. Shortly after leaving Porsche he moved forty kilometers away to work for Volkswagen in Reutlingen, where he took advantage of his association with its burly owner, Max Moritz. Moritz had joined the Nazi party early on and owned his own service station in Reutlingen before the war. During the conflict Moritz joined the regular army and had been stationed at Sochaux, France, continuing to ply his mechanical knowledge.[32] As another old comrade, he was sympathetic to Peiper's difficulties. Peiper was placed in charge of sales promotion of Moritz Autohaus, which sold everything from puttering Beetles to high-performance Porsche racing machines.[33]

But with passage of time itself, more and more of the old hares vanished. In April 1966 Peiper attended the memorial service of Sepp Dietrich in Ludwigsburg along with six thousand other SS faithful.[34] Yet Peiper, whom Dietrich had once derided to Albert Frey as "an arrogant swine," was faithful to his old superior. At the funeral Peiper looked uncomfortable, his "narrow face was still marked by ten years of prison."[35] "He despised intellectuals like me," Peiper recalled of Dietrich. "He was a primitive type of warrior." But of the many things Peiper had to admire about Dietrich was that, unlike other opportunists, "He never pretended to have forgotten Hitler."[36] On February 10, 1968, there was a supersized wingding of the I Panzer Corps—they always left off the SS modifier for obvious reasons—at the Hotel Heim in Ludwigsburg. Not only was Peiper on the invite to the "*Grosser Kameradschaftsabend* im Fasching" but the bygone cavalcade as well: Wisch, Kraas, Dinse, Trabandt—even Max Wünsche.[37] Later that summer there was another big celebration, this one including Albert Frey, who had returned from precautionary exile in Argentina. Each year the celebrations seemed to get larger.[38]

The 1968 Fasching meeting had also discussed a more pointed objective—to begin the project to rewrite the history of the Leibstandarte, the way the old comrades wanted it remembered. Peiper's old friend Rudi Lehmann worked tirelessly to compose an exculpating multiple-volume chronicle of the Leibstandarte and even the Malmédy Massacre.[39] During this time he enlisted the help of a legal consultant to check that the history being composed of the Leibstandarte did not affront the strict German laws on *Jugendgefährdung*—not glorifying the Nazi war.[40] This work had originally been the domain of Dietrich Ziemssen, Rolf Reiser, and Arndt Fischer, who now became Peiper's dentist. Both Reiser and Fischer had been Poetschke's adjutants and now became the keepers of the secret. It was these three, along with Rudi Woch and Gerd Walter, who maintained a steady correspondence with the Landsberg men. And while they had been in prison Ziemssen and Reiser had orchestrated the exculpatory manifesto authored by Ziemssen.[41]

The literary subversion worked. Now the SS veterans moved themselves from the persecutors to the persecuted! Five years later old comrades were still spilling out of West German closets. Peiper's unit once again proudly called its members by its infamous moniker, the Lötlampen (Blowtorch) Battalion.[42] But despite invitations in the spring of 1973, Peiper stayed home:

> When your announcement "*Achtung*, Blow Torch Battalion," came to my attention by chance, I won't lie that my heart beat faster for a moment. I have always considered the III. Gep [*gepanzert*—armored] with its creation, victories and its particular elan—which was alone the high point of my military career. I felt closer to it than any other unit. That developments after the war forced me into prison and then alienation and finally to emigration, doesn't change things at all. Please tell this to the comrades when they get together on 19/20 May and convey my greetings and very best wishes to the meeting of the Blowtorch Battalion.[43]

In the generation after the war many Waffen SS veterans turned inward, finding solace in veterans' organization such as HIAG and their house organs such as *Wiking Ruf* and *Der Freiwillige*. These journals swelled with accounts of heroic Waffen SS deeds, biographical sketches and the ever-popular stories of persecuted old fighters. Meantime, nefarious SS notables such as Bach-Zelewski, Pohl, Eicke, Fegelein and

Himmler himself were silent—dead or in prison—unable to communicate the dark side of the story. Only a few SS men complained that the story being told was not the complete one. In print, the Waffen SS repeated Hausser's mantra: they were an honorable combat fraternity of noble "soldiers just like any others." There was even an underground movement in the early 1960s. Felix Steiner and the old vets were again celebrating the SS-pagan holidays of Julfest and Sonnenwende in Munich.

Peiper's old rival, Max Wünsche, was out too. He was the lucky one. Released from England in 1948, he was one of those few who had worked closely with Hitler and yet was around to tell about it. Close enough but not close enough for the dirt to rub off, he had avoided close contact with the war crimes that had so tarnished the reputations of Peiper and Meyer. "Whoever loses the war," he insisted, "must live with the results." He was interviewed by writers and reporters, publicly expressing one view while still privately insisting that Hitler knew nothing of Kristallnacht, much less the extermination of the Jews.[44]

But even as Peiper was looking to avoid unwanted attention, he nonetheless dallied with a few libidinous distractions. In the summer of 1964 he met Judith, the alluring wife of Dr. Peter Mutke, a German veteran who had served in the Wehrmacht in 1944 and was made captive by the Russians. After traveling to the United States and making his fortune as a doctor, Mutke had met Uli Wieselmann in Stuttgart in the 1950s when stationed there as a drafted US soldier. He soon became an avid Porsche owner with a penchant for amateur racing. When Mutke returned to Stuttgart with his young American wife, Judith, in the summer of 1964, Wieselmann invited them to stay with him. When they pulled up to Wieselmann's hilltop abode, Uli warned them that they would soon meet his close friend, a famous SS colonel who had been one of Germany's "brightest and most highly decorated heroes."[45]

The twenty-eight-year-old woman expected to meet an stodgy, monocled Prussian. Instead, she was introduced to a soft-spoken, unpretentious man who barely said hello. And for an impressionable Stanford graduate, rather than coming off as a cold aristocrat, Joachim Peiper seemed more than handsome. Although at first Judy found him standoffish, that soon melted. And Judy herself was striking—brunette, tall, and curvaceous, she had lovely gams that sprang from an *I Magnin* miniskirt.

Peiper grew more friendly, and the young woman found him strangely charming. They soon learned of a mutual interest in horses. Her husband, Peter, had fought with a German horse cavalry unit on the Russian front. Horses against tanks! She told how they recently bought a stable of Arabians and taught dressage in Carmel Valley, California. That was the proper way to ride, Peiper agreed. Even if just mentally, Peiper began intently probing.

What was life really like in America? Each thing Peiper learned sparked a new question. Soon it was clear to her that this man was very intelligent and seemed to know a lot about everything. He suddenly began speaking English, and she was amazed at his command of the language; here was a man who knew most English literature as well as she did—and she was the Stanford English major. He continued with questions: Where was she from? California. "Why did you incarcerate the Japanese during the war in concentration camps?" he asked. Judy tried to explain, saying she knew Japanese who had been interred in those camps, but it was no big deal.

Peiper couldn't agree: "A blot on America," he pronounced, but said nothing about the KZ in Germany nor any mention of the murder camps in Poland.

Yet now the SS war hero showed a bitter side. He pointed out that her country could not be so free as it claimed. "As a former SS man, I can't visit," he said, thinking of his recent inability to come over on the Porsche junket. Peiper told Judy about Willis Everett, the brave Atlanta lawyer who had saved him. Obviously, there are some good men in the United States! Yet she could see that, for all his reading and knowledge of geography, Peiper really didn't understand Americans.

Peiper didn't bother to tell her of the wellspring of his latest resentment. His world had begun to fracture once more when, on July 1, 1964, the *Stuttgarter Nachrichten* had reported that the former partisan Dr. Ettore Gerbino from Cuneo, Italy, had submitted to the Central Office for National Socialist Crimes in Ludwigsburg—charges of his responsibility in the deaths of scores of civilians in Boves, Italy, in 1943. And within week a headline in *Die Tat* besmirched his name: "Joachim Peiper—the SS Incendiary of Boves."[46] No, the attractive young American woman knew nothing of that.

On her second day with the Wieselmanns, Judy and Peiper were often off talking while the boys' club in the next room loudly crowed over racing tales and politics. Peiper seemed to enjoy talking with her. Here was a German really interested in what she had to say. She had a strong intellect, and he was a keen listener. Classics, Cold War, and horses.

Then, at some point, it happened. Within a conversation his eyes locked onto hers, sky blue and penetrating, and Judy felt herself go warm and blushing. It was like a forbidden secretive household romance. She didn't know anything about his family—he didn't even mention he had a spouse! She was happy hers was along. Hours went by in conversation.

Later in the afternoon the others played Skat, the characteristically German card game. And Uli Wieselmann started to drink, endlessly chain smoke, and emote the pratfall yarns. That broke up their conversation. Peiper played too, with the conversation invariably moving to the Cold War and the Russians. As the booze started flowing, Uli grew loud, bubbling out the old propaganda. "Too bad Hitler didn't win the war. . . . He did so much for the country." Peiper looked on silently, sipping less. He was too canny for pro-Nazi remarks; instead, he smiled weakly, pointing out that he used to play Skat daily when he was in prison at Landsberg. One fellow player had been the now-rich and released industrialist Alfried Krupp! Guffaws. The boys' club buzzed.

At one point during the weekend, Peter Mutke told how he was experimenting now with hypnosis, even considering it for surgery. There were special powers in this, he opined. That seemed to animate Peiper. The former SS colonel proudly launched into tales of how charismatic Hitler had been during the war. Once, he said, he had been in a room with others awaiting Hitler's arrival at the Reich Chancellery. When the Führer entered, he said things to people before they could tell him. Joachim's eyes gleamed. "Hitler was a clairvoyant!"[47] Judy's heart beat a little faster: Peiper was saying things contrary to everything she believed. She looked over to her husband, who was strongly anti-Nazi. He stared on blankly. The former SS colonel seemed to really admire Hitler. But Peiper said nothing of what he surely thought. When the day was done, Peter and Judy Mutke pulled out from Wieselmann's house in their fire-red Porsche. She seemed oddly relieved. Such a handsome Hitler lover!

What did Peiper really believe about Hitler?

> I would have put my head on a scaffold for him. This only changed in Hungary [in 1945]. . . . So remember that everyone who lived near Hitler saw that he was a genius while we were only puppets. Hitler had a sixth sense. . . . [About him,] my heart has two chambers—in one harbors the memory of a young and unimportant man who met a great man. I could give my all idealism for that . . . my personal experience always remains thankful for this particularly historic moment in which I lived. . . . On the other side, as the father of the German children, as creator of what happened, I would say "Never again." Such a dictatorship caused the complete destruction of our nation.[48]

And there were other women, even another American Judith, this one more at ease with Peiper's past. At around the same time he met the first Judy, the suave General Walter Warlimont introduced Peiper to Judith Ann Weller.[49] The cultured Warlimont had been a Peiper family neighbor in Tegernsee prior to the war and afterward had covertly continued his allegiance to National Socialism. His wife was American, an heiress to the Anheuser Busch brewery empire in St. Louis. Weller was a local German-speaking equestrian, and a darling to that circle. What's more, she was a young, headstrong American woman with strong right-wing leanings and an interest in German military history.

What kind of other company was Judith Weller keeping? The young woman stayed with the family of Dr. Hanns Dietrich Ahrens, a right-wing industrial public relations figure with a expressed interest in Jochen Peiper, though he was considering writing a book about Reinhard Heydrich.[50] On July 14, 1967, Weller was also visiting Dr. Werner Best in the company of SS wartime *Schwarze Korps* propagandist, Günther d'Alquen. Now under investigation for his responsibility in the murder of the Polish intelligensia in September 1939, Dr. Best met with Weller and d'Alquen to discuss collecting documents that would help to exonerate the embattled figure. As an American, Weller could lend legitimacy for the search for documents or at least provide cover for the SS inner circle behind the effort. Yet the secret plan did not remain so. Suspicious German authorities raided Dr. Best's home in March 1969, uncovering letters documenting not only Weller's involvement but also Peiper's coordination with Best to obtain favorable testimony![51] Dr. Best, meanwhile, sought damage control within a network of SS Kameraden that reeked of collusion.

During the time when she was helping Dr. Best, Weller occasionally visited the Peipers at their flat in Stuttgart. Weller, who taught horse-riding skills at William Woods College in Missouri, and Peiper, the old cavalryman, hit it off too. Weller was interested in warhorses stretching back to Roman times. Staying at his home, she saw the SS colonel as a "very refined man—a very proper Prussian." Peiper spoke candidly to Weller about Malmédy. The problem, he told her, was the youngsters fighting in 1944. "He told me the men under his command in the fighting were very young and inexperienced—not the veterans he had with him before." He wasn't able to control what they did.[52] Peiper's men claimed the US soldiers were worse, however. "The American prisoners were undisciplined. They were moving around and talking while being held prisoner."[53]

Weller even began her own research on Malmédy, the result of which would later be published as the central thesis in a German language book *Der Malmédy Prozess*.[54] It was part of a continuing campaign by Waffen SS veterans to counter the traditional wisdom. Weller was elevated to professor of history.[55] In fact, Weller twisted evidence within the records at the US National Archives to match the objective: all incriminating German evidence came from "false confessions extorted by the prosecution," whereas the mass of damning testimony from the Malmédy survivors reflected American perjury. "The fact that somebody wore the uniform of the U.S. Army," Weller recalled acidly, "is not a guarantee of truthful testimony; liars wear all kinds of clothing."[56] If reeking of historical revisionism, Peiper still recommended the treatise to British author Charles Whiting.[57]

Peiper also told Weller of receiving a letter from Burton Ellis from out of the blue in April 1966. The note clumsily proposed to patch old wounds: "Nearly 20 years have passed since the beginning of the trial," Ellis began, "of which you no doubt have nothing but bitter memories." Toward the end of the note, Ellis casually asked whether Peiper would like his wartime medals returned. "If so," he announced glibly, "I will be more than happy to send them to you."[58]

Peiper promptly replied, more than a little shocked to hear from his old tormentor. "Your letter has been received—with a surprised frown and a pensive smile," he wrote. With regards to the medals? "Go ahead and rid yourself of the items in question," he offered. And then Peiper added a zinger: "We all have our crossroads."[59]

A short time later Ellis wrote again, informing Peiper that he could no longer find his decorations! But returning to the United States, Weller was incredulous and somehow learned Ellis had the decorations up for sale to the highest bidder! She contacted the attorney in Merced, California, reminding him he had sworn under oath in 1949 to the senate that he had no knowledge of the whereabouts of Peiper's medals. Obviously that was not true. Weller managed to get the medals from Ellis and then returned them.

"You won't believe it," Peiper later told his old comrades. "Last summer [1968] I received a small package from America—contents: my decorations." Weller had included a note, Peiper said, indicating that she "was returning these things for the sake of the honor of America."

And then there was Peiper's old nemesis, William R. Perl, the Jewish US Army interrogator who had allegedly tormented prisoners at Schwäbisch Hall in early 1946 to obtain confessions. "He knew how to get at my softest spot," Peiper said, "and put me under psychic pressure by appealing to the ethics of an officer and Prussian tradition . . . this was my personal bad luck—the press and public opinion had already hanged me."[60] After Perl and Ellis's rebuke during the Senate hearings in 1949, Perl had returned to what Peiper had imagined was his devotion: Jewish affairs.[61] By the 1970s, when Peiper was taking refuge from the world in Traves, Perl was a highly vocal street activist in the Washington branch of the Jewish Defense League.

Perl had become obsessed with the Soviet persecution of Jews in Russia and even advocated violence. In a strange twist of fate, by 1976 that mania found Perl under FBI investigation for a bold plan to shoot out the windows of Soviet diplomats in Maryland. Even more worrisome, the FBI uncovered that Perl allegedly wounded a German prisoner in an interrogation long before Schwäbisch Hall in June 1945, at the 15th Army Interrogation Center in Rheinbach. It was a fact the US Army had covered up since 1951.[62] Perl was arrested in late summer 1976 and convicted by a federal jury, but he worried that anti-Semitic Palestinians would try to assassinate him at his Baltimore trial.[63] Peiper's old adversary, William Perl, was paranoid to the end.

Peiper, for his part, claimed to have left the past behind. But his associations after release from prison boldly contradicted any such view.

"Show me your friends," went the old German saying, "and I'll tell you who you are."[64]

Chapter 18

UNDER FOUR EYES

ALL THROUGH THE 1960S IN GERMANY, WITH ITS CHANGING AND LESS friendly political climate, Peiper remained vigilant in his affairs. Not so different from the Sicilian mafia, the SS in those days preferred to coordinate their response to the various investigations using the most secure methods: preferably face-to-face meetings or a private, unlikely-to-be-tapped telephone. Letters and correspondence that might be seized or reappear (as with the Dr. Best trial), were particularly dangerous. When the investigations began of the SS cavalry in the 1960s, the SS men involved began intensively traveling around (*Reisetägtigkeit*) to meet personally *unter vier Augen*—under four eyes.[1] The frequent veterans' meetings served other purposes than just reestablishing wartime camaraderie; it was a chance to coordinate stories and alibis among members under investigation. Peiper's Italian misadventure at Boves seemed a likely source for new trouble.

By 1964 Peiper had learned from the magazine *La Stampa* that a memorial had been installed in Boves, naming his command as the source for the civilian killings in the town.[2] Peiper got in contact with Otto Dinse at once. Now Peiper, Dinse, Gührs, and an old friend, Dr. Robert Brüstle, met in Traves at Peiper's newly purchased vacation home.[3] In all likelihood they crafted a basic defense strategy for Italy: all those blaming the SS for the killings in Boves were doing so based on political motives, and all accusations were pure lies coming from Italian Communist propaganda. In the conjured SS scenario, the killing and burning of Boves came from a fierce battle with the partisans. Given the fact that the Cold War was at its height, any accusations against the Communists would probably stick.

As the investigation drug on, all had to file statements. Dr. Friedrich Breme, Peiper's battalion surgeon in Boves, met with Dinse in July of 1964 to speak about Boves.[4] Breme and Dinse's explanations were exactly the same in their prepared statements—a necessary agreement, as the "ferocious battle" never happened. Although, no explicit evidence can be found of collusion among the three men, even a cursory review of the statements of Dr. Friedrich Breme and Otto Dinse filed at Ludwigsburg reveals almost exact matches on numbers, facts, and even language!

Within Peiper's group, Otto Dinse functioned as a go-between, the veterans using the meetings of the Stuttgart HIAG as a means of preparing for further investigations. What to do if the police showed up? "We were given instruction last evening by comrade Johannes Göhler who has already been interrogated several times," revealed one SS man. "Now we know how we should react."[5] And Göhler would know—he had been under Gustav Lombard with the SS cavalry, a unit under increasing scrutiny for a murder campaign in the East.[6]

For Peiper and Dinse, Boves would not go away; it was like a haunting. Even living quietly and working at Max Moritz Autohaus in Reutlingen, Peiper did not escape unwanted attention. The source came from two former Italian partisans, Giuseppe Biancani and Giuseppe Pruneto, who had managed to trace Peiper to Stuttgart. Biancani had recognized Peiper in John Toland's book about the Bulge.[7] The investigation into the incident at Boves aimed to bring Peiper to stand trial. Charges were filed on June 24, 1964, which included statements as well as several photographs of Peiper cooly watching with binoculars as the Northern Italian town of Boves burned below their position.[8] Later Robert Kempner, one of the principals at the Nuremberg Trials, took up the case on behalf of nine Italian plaintiffs. Kempner was now the famous anti-Nazi Goliath. This is the man who helped send Eichmann to the gallows.[9] Now he was after Jochen Peiper.

The original charges showed Peiper responsible for the deaths of 146 civilians in the Cuneo region. On September 17, 1964, Peiper went before the office of the state prosecutor in Stuttgart to deny the charges. "It is not true that I selected the two men [Vasallo and Bernardi] as emissaries, shot them afterward and torched their bodies. . . . The civilians who died in Boves were victims of combat events and not because of my intentional acts or those of my unit."[10]

At a meeting with a journalist on October 6, 1965, Kempner condemned the SS colonel. If he would atone, that would be one thing, said Kempner. Yet "Peiper is just like the other criminal Nazis; he is silent or unloads the responsibility onto others." He then discussed the trial to come. "It will be a difficult battle," he said from his journey to Cuneo to collect evidence. "The judge has interrogated the former major and he first claimed he had not been in Boves due to stomach trouble. Then he claimed the fire and bloodshed were the results of higher orders. Yet finally he claimed the result was simply a combat event." Kempner was dubious. "False testimony," he concluded.[11]

Maybe Peiper would have to flee. The SS colonel was still in contact with Otto Skorzeny, who was wheeling and dealing in the world scrap metals business from Spain when not jet setting with his wife, Ilse, to South America, Paris, or the Alps.[12] Even if unspoken, Skorzeny always made it known to Peiper that should things get too bad in Germany, there was always a haven for him with others under Franco's protection in Madrid. For his part, Skorzeny was living openly, completely unafraid, and a publicity hound. Amazingly, Skorzeny was working with a literary agent in Los Angeles, attempting to bring his life story to the big screen in Hollywood: *Commando Extraordinary!* Warner Brothers and United Artists nearly bit on the script. But such cinematic planning halted suddenly when focus groups revealed a shortcoming in brilliant contrast to the box office smash of George C. Scott as Patton; the new story would glorify a Nazi hero![13] In the end Skorzeny's efforts to portray himself as an apolitical commando hero disintegrated with only a little investigation from the studio.[14]

But the bombastic commando was not willing to be shut out of Hollywood wartime exploits for which he felt himself uniquely qualified. Skorzeny wrote Peiper in 1964 that he now weighed the wisdom as to whether to be a technical adviser for a new American war film being produced by British director Ken Annakin on the Battle of the Bulge. A good part of the film would be shot in Spain. But soon Skorzeny had negative reports—the developing movie looked to really be terrible. Originally the bloated cinematic epic on the Battle of the Bulge was to focus on the exploits of charismatic panzer leader Peiper and the Americans who opposed him. One of the buffoonish Americans was Henry Fonda as Lt. Col. Daniel Kiley, a loose caricature of controversial US First Army Intelligence Officer Benjamin A. "Monk" Dickson. But for Peiper, being cast in a movie could only be trouble—big trouble.

When the writers learned that Peiper was, in fact, still living in Stuttgart and under investigation for war crimes in Italy, the Warner Brothers legal team sounded the alarm. The script was hurriedly altered to redline him out of the story. Colonel Martin Hessler became a fictionalized Peiper, albeit a snarling regular army officer portrayed by Robert Shaw. Skorzeny then wrote to John Toland in the summer of 1965: "At the moment, [Charles] Bronson is making here a big film about the Battle of the Bulge in Spain. First, I was asked to be an advisor, but then they finally engaged a young German general retired [Gen. Meinrad von Lauchert of 2nd Panzer Division] who told me that they are making such nonsense of the film that he furiously left a few days ago in Madrid."[15]

Back in Stuttgart Peiper was depressed.[16] With Boves and now the Battle of the Bulge movie, it had started again. He confided to Otto Dinse that he could not face another trial; he was doomed. To Dinse, Peiper presented a terrible appearance, all indications of a mental breakdown. Somehow his old comrade changed his mind, but the Italian investigation dragged on for three years.[17] At first both Dinse and Peiper were involved, but when Ehrhard Gührs presented himself as a witness for the defense, he was then charged too. Worst of all, the Italians demanded Peiper's extradition. If that happened, all bets were off. One of Peiper's old friends tried to convince him that now it was finally time to join Skorzeny and the others in exile in Spain or, perhaps, beyond. After all, old Ludolf von Alvensleben, another of Himmler's adjutants, had fled to safe haven in Argentina! The inner circle prepared passports and made appropriate travel arrangements, but in the end Peiper demurred. He would stay to battle the charges.[18]

Peiper maintained that he had simply fought uniformed partisans at Boves. But who was guilty for the deaths of the civilians there? Eventually over a hundred members of Peiper's battalion gave testimony along with 14 Italian witnesses and 114 Italian depositions. The statements of the former SS men alone filled 1,800 pages.

In spite of the mass of testimony, some facts could not be verified. Still, there was no changing the fact that Italian people were killed. Some were clearly victims of the artillery. This is not only confirmed by the German witnesses but also by Italian accounts.[19] But others had died under much more sinister circumstances.

Several Italian witnesses testified that Peiper's battalion set houses on fire and then shot those attempting to escape. Members of Peiper's command even confirmed that homes were burned. One has to only recall this was the Blowtorch Battalion, just back from the Russian front. However, none of the German witnesses claimed to know anything about shooting civilians. It was unclear as to whether the twenty-three citizens of Boves were killed by SS excesses or as a result of fighting. Each side disagreed on that issue completely.

Predictably, all the 127 Germans interrogated denied intentionally torching houses and killing civilians. And it was not true that Peiper sent out two negotiators to bring back the prisoners. Otto Dinse said he tried to negotiate with the Catholic priest of Boves, but the priest refused to take over such a task as intermediary. In this however, Otto Dinse was in the hottest water. After all, the priest he admitted speaking with had ended up shot through the head and then burned to a crisp in a flaming house.

Yet Dinse flatly denied culpability: "As I had spoken to the priest," Dinse later testified, "one could impute that I was the one who shot the priest and the business man. . . . If these two men lost their lives at that time, in my mind, it could have only happened during the fighting over Boves."[20] In flat contradiction, Boves attorney Faustino Dalmazzo provided a damning contradiction:[21]

> Two SS were made prisoners by some Italian patriots. The SS men came in vehicles at around 11 o'clock. At 11:45, two trucks came to Boves commanded by Captain Dinse, the direct subordinate of Peiper. There was an altercation with shooting and the Germans retired from the scene. Later they returned to Boves and were joined at about one o'clock by the armored battalion of the SS who had occupied Cuneo. At the order of Peiper, two ambassadors, the priest and Mr. Vassallo, were asked to help with the return of the German prisoners and if that was done, there would be no reprisals. Around 3 PM, Don Bernardi and Mr. Vassallo brought back the two prisoners safe and sound, and their vehicle with all their stuff. From this moment, the action foreseen by Peiper develops. He had sealed off all the roads from the town. He then began to burn down the houses in the locality of Rivoira. A further 22 men were shot at the time when they were attempting to escape. . . . Most of the inhabitants of Boves, when seeing the Germans arrive had run away earlier. The priest, Don Bernardi and Mr. Vassallo were placed under an armed guard who forced them to watch the village being burned and then were themselves shot, dumped into the cellar of a home which was then burned to a cinder.[22]

And then, in December 1964, Simon Wiesenthal, the Viennese Nazi hunter, filed new criminal charges against Peiper.[23] Peiper was said to have demanded in September 1943 a list of Jews residing in the town of Borgo San Dalmazzo. The Jews had eventually been rounded up and shipped off to Auschwitz in Poland, where nearly all perished. Most suspicious was Dinse's testimony about the disposition of Peiper's various units during those days. Even though Peiper and Dinse claimed not to know an SS Capitano Müller who had posted a command to collect "all foreigners"—a euphemism for Jews—in Borgo San Dalmazzo, the commander of the 12th Panzer Grenadier Company in that hamlet was an infamous name from the Malmédy trial:

SS Obersturmführer Georg Preuss.[24] Although suspicious, Peiper's direct involvement in that episode remained unproven.[25]

Then, in the summer of 1968, Peiper's domestic scene grew unsettled. One morning the former colonel noticed a large van with the Italian television network RAI, with men setting up cameras and floodlights in front of his house. Their purpose: a live report from the home of a supposed war criminal. Peiper and his wife stayed inside rather than be thrust before the lights and cameras. Eventually tiring of the unproductive stakeout, the camera van went on its way.[26] German newspapers also got wind of the affair and called attention to possible legal subversion in the Stuttgart court through use of the statute of limitations.[27] And the peculiarities of German law did not make superiors responsible for the military actions of their subordinates.

Publicity notwithstanding, by September of 1968, Kempner realized the Boves investigation was coming unglued; indeed, the efforts to make the charges stick was poorly orchestrated.[28] Simon Wiesenthal was brought in to help. Together, with the ten Italian families represented, they petitioned for an extension of the case to bring in more witnesses, a request that was denied. And more and more, Kempner found himself leaning on the damning facts of Peiper's past with Himmler rather than on the merits of the case of Boves itself.[29] That got him nowhere. The defense attorney Dr. Egon Schneider, challenged 113 testimonies by citizens of Boves on the grounds that they did not understand German!

Even though there was no denying that questionable things had happened under his watch, there was no proof that Peiper had intentionally ordered the town burned. In any case, within the vagaries of German law, charges against the three SS men were dismissed—there would be no trial. For Peiper the storm had again blown over, even if Wiesenthal looked to renew the accusations.[30]

> Dr. Kempner . . . let himself be employed to represent the interest of the Italian village of Boves near Cuneo which considers itself to be the "Cradle of Italian Resistance." . . . They kidnaped one of my men and wanted to pressure us to withdraw. Instead, we rescued the man and fell into an ambush. The sad end was a burning guerilla village. . . . Kempner got in touch with his soul-mate Simon Wiesenthal. . . . A press conference was called and, alternately, I was made into a second Eichmann and the executor of the Final Solution of the Jewish question in Upper Italy. The result: dismissal of the case after four years of preliminary investigations because of proved innocence and the ruination of my civil existence.[31]

On December 23, 1968, Dr. Schneider closed the case, stating that there was not enough evidence to open a trial.[32] They could not determine whether the accused had killed the emissaries or burned the houses or just watched as subordinates killed or burned (*billigend in Kauf genommen*—"you did not order it, but you did not interfere"). Schneider believed that there was a battle in Boves, as the SS officers maintained, but he was equally certain that Peiper's men had intentionally burned down the houses and killed most, if not all, of the Italian victims. But why open a trial if not one of the 127 former battalion members could be singled out for a criminal action?

There was also evidence in the statements, based on exact duplications of language, that Leibstandarte witnesses coordinated testimony; indeed, some of those that were central to the investigation may have been pressured. As a key witness and a man who had been captive by the Italians, Kurt Butenhoff was caught off guard by investigators when asked whether the Italian emissaries rescued him. In answering, he contradicted the official SS story.

After that, Otto Dinse counseled Butenhoff and suggested he only show up at the police station with his lawyers and then follow his written statement *exactly*. The text was, in fact, an affidavit prepared with the lawyers of Dinse and Gührs. There was a second interrogation of Butenhoff by Pfister on April 12, 1967. This time, Butenhoff dictated a detailed description in which he said he had freed himself. However, the court also did not look at any earlier investigations. If they had, they would have realized that Butenhoff gave statements about the killings in Kharkov in 1943 and said he had taken part in SS reunions since 1953 and was well connected with all the old comrades. Collusion!

Nevertheless, in the end Peiper came away unaccused, but not without tarnish. The investigation continued listlessly on from 1964 to 1969; the SS colonel was interrogated three times and once handed in a written statement from his lawyer. If the investigation didn't alter Peiper's *Alltag*—history, ordinary life—there was plenty of anxiety.When Peiper had met Gührs and Dinse at his new vacation refuge in Traves, France, the three cleared underbrush and around the campfire agreed that if a formal investigation began, they would move to Spain.[33]

Italian victims and their families, however, were incensed. The German state attorney appeared to have dropped the case on a technicality that served to protect the guilty. The investigation never disputed that twenty-three Italians were killed in Boves and that the houses in town had been intentionally burned. And yet, because they could not identify who did the killing or who had ordered the action, the entire investigation varporized. Regardless, the colonel could stick to his attractive story: regarding the Boves affair, SS warrior Jochen Peiper was innocent.

BUT OTHERS OF THE LEIBSTANDARTE IN ITALY IN SEPTEMBER 1943 WERE not as fortunate. The atrocity case against members of the 2nd SS Panzergrendier Regiment emerged from an incident that had taken place just after Peiper's reckoning in Boves. In that sordid affair Leibstandarte troopers had arrested several dozen Italian Jews in several towns around Lago Maggiore on September 24 and murdered them the following night.

The accused perpetrators were from a sister 1st battalion in the same 2nd SS Panzer Grenadier Regiment under former Obersturmbannführer Hugo Kraas, to which Peiper had belonged in Italy. Named in the investigations were Hans Röhwer, Teddi Wisch, Hugo Kraas, Sepp Dietrich, Christian Jochum, and Josef Diefenthal. Peiper's old friend Jupp Diefenthal in particular was good friends with Röhwer and advised him that he should simply say that he knew nothing about the affair—a strategy that quickly fell flat.[34]

Not surprisingly, after the war's end the suspect members of the Leibstandarte uniformly claimed no knowledge of the misdeeds. Still, there were three separate investigations into the Lago Maggiore affair: an Austrian inquiry in 1954, one in 1955 in Italy and then another in Germany in Osnabrück in 1965. The trial in Italy reached a clear judgment: guilty. But each time the case was attempted in Germany it was dropped due to lack of evidence.

Indeed, in 1950 Peiper's old friend Rudi Lehmann, who was the divisional chief of staff, insisted that the killings were the work of a commando of the SD and had nothing to do with the Leibstandarte.[35]

The case may never have broken open had it not been for an SS man troubled by terrible guilt. Herbert Gerretz, who had been at Lago Maggiore, could no longer live with his conscience.[36] He had nightmares. Gerretz's cathartic confession in 1964 was the key development in the case that led to the imprisonment of the SS men accused in the Lago Maggiore case.

In 1968 the court in Osnabrück found the five accused guilty of murder, but all were later released due to changes in German law. Although Peiper had nothing directly to do with this incident—he knew well the accused battalion leader, Hans Röhwer—it was again Leibstandarte men with murderous behavior in Italy.[37] Again, postwar Leibstandarte claims of war crimes innocence took a big hit. In the divisional history Lehmann was forced to admit that the killings at Lago Maggiore did, in fact, take place.[38]

But even with Boves dismissed, there were still other war crimes trials swirling about Peiper's orbit. On January 19, 1967, Peiper appeared in a Stuttgart court, summoned to testify in the war crimes trial of Dr. Werner Best—a free-floating SS attorney with a shifting sense of morality. In spite of Dr. Best's selective memory in his trial, all the investigational winds pointed toward Best being central to the murder of Polish Jews and intellectuals in September 1939.[39] Regrettably for Peiper, Dr. Best knew Himmler's adjutant well from his time with the SS head office. Regardless of a late-found sense of morality, in 1948 a Danish court sentenced the SS lawyer to death, although his sentence was later commuted, with release in 1951. Now, in 1969, Dr. Best was detained for a new round of investigations—complicity in mass murder in Poland.

Once again Peiper found himself trying to distance himself from intimate dealings with Himmler, Globocnik, and the rest. His presence at the execution of Polish partisans near Bromberg in 1939? He knew nothing about them, he said. And on the orders for the elimination of the Polish intelligensia that Ernst Schäfer overheard him mention? Schäfer must have him confused with Ludolf von Alvensleben, whom Himmler had sent to Poland to attend to such things. All this in spite of having given earlier testimony to the contrary.

> Naturally, I have [had] heard that Polish partisans have been shot. . . . I had the impression that in general the Polish population was very cruel toward Germans and at that time considered the reprisals justified.[40]

Had he given reports to the SS Reichsführer on the operations of the Einsatzgruppen? No, he knew nothing of it. The Final Solution, the *Endlösung*? Peiper was now taking pages out of the Karl Wolff legal playbook—he was lying like hell and hoping no one had the information that might ensnare him in his tangled web:

> Even though it might sound incredible, I can only emphasize again that at that time nothing became known to me about the Endlösung to the Jewish question. I was in Russia with combat troops and did not move around the rear echelons . . . I once visited the Warsaw Ghetto at the end of the Polish campaign. There, we were offered a macabre picture. The Jewish Ghetto Police, wearing rimless caps and armed with wooden clubs ruthlessly made room for us. The senior Jew even offered Himmler a bouquet of flowers. But only after the war did I learn about the destruction of the Eastern Jews during a conversation with Ohlendorf.[41]

How was that possible? "Naturally, Himmler often spoke during meals about the general situation and problems," Peiper admitted, "but any orders or instructions, he issued only in a narrow circle. The sensitive discussions on such subjects took place in small intimate meetings and behind closed doors." Rudolf Brandt knew more, Peiper said, as he "was Himmler's memory." Peiper, according to his own view, was just Himmler's flunky, answering the phone.[42]

The investigators did not know of the testimony of one of Peiper's contemporaries to British intelligence before war's end, one Jakob Hanreich. Although haughty and arrogant, Hanreich off-handedly indicated that Peiper and his comrades knew of the actions of the Einsatzgruppen in the fall of 1941.[43] That could not have seemed controversial in 1944, when Hanreich said it, for at that time, within the SS, it was common knowledge. The court also could not know of the conversation with Otto Dinse in 1943 in which Peiper disclosed the nature of the elimination camps: "We had better win this war, or we will be in big trouble because of these things." Now he claimed to have known nothing of them until after the war![44] Yet, for the court, Peiper's claim of ignorance seemed to suffice.

Still, in 1970 he was summoned once more to the continuing investigation of Dr. Best. This time the web grew more twisted. Three years after his previous testimony he told them, "I cannot say with certainty whether I heard at the time of the actions of the Einsatzgruppen or the security police" and their actions in Poland. "My recollections are blurred," he claimed.[45] But this time the court had brought forward August 1945 testimony of Dr. Ernst Schäfer that was damaging to Peiper's professed ignorance of the elimination of the Polish intelligentsia. For one, it was brought out that he had witnessed an early gassing experiment. That was bad enough. But then a highly inflammatory statement was brought to the attention of the court. Supposedly upon that hearing of the shooting of Poles, Peiper had remarked to Dr. Schäfer, "Now they will look at the potatoes from below!"[46]

With that accusation, Peiper went on the offensive. In sworn testimony he emphatically denied just about everything that Dr. Ernst Schäfer heard him say in 1940. "Objectively untrue," he said. He had not seen the executions of Polish partisans, in spite of having testified earlier to the contrary. He never made those incriminating remarks to Dr. Ernst Schäfer. The anthropologist was misleading his interrogators, Peiper ventured. Schäfer had not even been along with him during that train trip in January 1940!

But it was all untrue. Himmler's meticulous daily appointment calendar from 1940 survives and shows Peiper and Dr. Schäfer both present in a detailed itinerary that showed who got on and off at each train stop![47] And Peiper changed his story on his presence at the Bromberg executions, in spite of testimony corroborating his previous version from the likes of Karl Wolff.[48]

MEANWHILE, AMID ALL THE LEGAL INTRIGUE, PEIPER CONTINUED TO WORK at Max Moritz Autohaus. Some at the car dealership feigned ignorance of Peiper's past or were careful not to ask. In a typically postwar German fashion, none of them talked about 1939–1945. The workers at Moritz knew about Peiper's experience at Porsche. And there was old Harald von Saucken, who had come out of the SS officers school at Bad Tölz the same year as Peiper emerged from Braunschweig SS. In recent years von Saucken, who was now quite wealthy, was racing Porsche automobiles as a private driver.[49] The SS good-old-boy network was alive and well.[50]

Moritz liked Peiper. More than liked him—even though Peiper was forty-nine years old, he still had his fire, and those there knew that he was the best motivating instructor in the sales force.[51] Even though he was at Volkswagen, all the Americans came to Moritz wanting to buy their cherry Porsche from the famous Mr. Peiper. He made money hand over fist while working with Moritz.

Well groomed and good looking, women too were crazy about Jochen (*zu Füßen gelegen*—at his feet). Some of the women gossiped in admiration, and a few claimed more. Still, one coworker was negatively impressed. "He was very handsome," she said, "but there was something about him. He seemed unapproachable. And when he looked me in the eyes, it gave me goose bumps. His eyes were ice cold—I didn't want to be around him."[52] Yet everyone agreed that Peiper conducted himself at Moritz Autohaus as if he was still an officer—and the officer in charge.

"He was a friend to those he liked, but he was cold to everyone else. I first met him in 1963, when Moritz told me to report to Mr. Peiper. I didn't know anything about him. But when he looked at me with his blue eyes, I was somehow afraid. I felt intimidated and nervous. You could tell he felt superior. The whole sales staff felt it. But he was the 'shining example' for Mr. Moritz."[53]

The "shining example" was always careful to stay out of pictures—no photos, not even grouped with the other staff. When he entered the service area where mechanics were working he always entered with rigid attention, chin held high. "It was like an inspection," remembered one, "but we admired him. Everyone stood at attention if they saw him."[54] Similarly the head of the cafeteria found Peiper "arrogant" and sought to avoid him, while another coworker at Autohaus Moritz raised troubling questions, claiming that Peiper made fun of people who lacked proper Aryan features.[55]

Every other Monday Peiper showed up in his dark green Upper Bavarian Loden hunting jacket and conducted his sales training meetings in casual enthusiasm. He sat on the table, encouraging everyone to move Volkswagens. "If you eat the bread," he was fond of telling everyone, "you had better sing the song!"[56] The sales meetings were animated. On one occasion the little group became very noisy. Suddenly big Max Moritz himself burst in. "What is this? It sounds like a *Judenschule* [school of Jews]!" Peiper quickly reprimanded his coarse-spoken boss. "Out! There'll be no anti-Semitic commentary in here!"

Yet, when interviewed in 1967 by a Belgian writer, Peiper projected a defiant image. After the trouble with the Italians and then the Dr. Werner Best trial, he was clearly disgusted:

> I was a Nazi and remain one. We were betrayed by unscrupulous people. This includes the cowards of 20 July 1944, orchestrated by the little general of the opera, Rommel. . . . Today's Germany is no longer a great nation; it has become a province of Europe. That is why, at the first opportunity, I shall move elsewhere, to France no doubt. I don't particularly care for Frenchmen, but I love France! In any case, the materialism of my compatriots causes me pain.[57]

In closed company, Peiper showed much the same color. In March 1969 Peiper gave a rousing talk to the Stuttgart section of the OdR. "His tales were almost incredible." He spoke to the old comrades of his current life and of times gone by. "The vanquished and particularly the members of the Waffen SS had to be punished before the entire world so their alleged misdeeds could be atoned for." With the retelling, the past was magnified and embellished. The events at Schwäbisch Hall, thirty-three years before, had become diabolical. Whereas before, suspects were threatened and beaten, now they had been tortured—strangled by a makeshift gallows with a hood over their heads until a confession came forth. "My men were ill-treated and tortured with refinements that would have created envy even from Nazi interrogation specialists."[58]

But what *really* happened at Malmédy? Everyone wanted to know that. He had not been there when the prisoners were shot, he told his audience. The guards "were just a few men against a multitude of prisoners. They took advantage of the weakness and started a mass escape that caused the otherwise helpless guards to open fire. Naturally, that can rapidly kill a few dozen. . . . I was up front and had other problems than 'letting prisoners be shot.'"[59] There were several Malmédy stories in the queue, each one slightly different.[60]

In the 1967 interview, the Belgian reporter candidly asked Peiper whether he claimed that no war crimes had happened at Malmédy. No, he would not say that:

> I admit willingly that after the Normandy battles, my unit was composed of young fanatic soldiers. Many of them had lost their parents, or brothers and sisters in the bombardments. Some had seen for themselves at Cologne where thousands of bodies were crushed after the terrorist raids. Their hatred of the enemy was such that I admit that I could not always control them. At Malmédy, there were, no doubt, some excesses.[61]

"So, for you was this normal?"

"It was normal to the extent that such happens in a merciless war. The day will come where we realize that those excesses were committed by both sides. They are blameworthy of course, but they are the usual fate of those battles where each person fights for his life. I have never given the order for an execution and I did not take part personally in this operation."[62]

Given the wilting impact of SS association, did Peiper now finally eschew his old comrades? Hardly, even while the Boves process was going on, he was enlisting the help of his old buddy Ernst Klink and Walter Harzer, the rough-talking, scar-faced Ritterkreuz hero of the battle of Arnhem. They would continue the task to write a history of the glory of Kharkov's recapture. In 1964 they got together with Paul Hausser, Rudolf Lehmann, Sepp Dietrich, and Otto Weidinger. It was a closed affair. "Let's discuss things at a war history party," Peiper suggested to Klink. "I would be particularly glad if we could get together one evening as otherwise we just see each other at funerals."[63] Peiper personally picked up "the old warriors" from the Hotel Schatten. "*Gospodin*—Sir," Peiper announced, "Kharkov will be conquered again on 6 March 1970."[64]

Meanwhile, quietly Peiper began to assist Karl-Heinz Schulz, who was helping Rudolf Lehmann write a "chronicle" of the Leibstandarte.[65] Given the subject, that had to be careful work, tiptoeing around the war crimes issues. Thus, whatever Peiper contributed for the research would be not cited but rather attributed to Schulz. Eventually some of the research showed up in *Der Freiwillige on the* Ardennes Offensive, but nowhere was Peiper's invisible hand to be seen.[66]

Meanwhile, other authors continued to make contact. By now John Toland had become something of a friend. In late 1964 Toland asked Peiper whether he would participate in a television documentary on the twentieth anniversary of Malmédy. Peiper declined, citing his past and ongoing trials, investigations, and persecutions, noting that any media attention, including Toland's book, only served to reinvigorate his enemies.

WITH DRAMATIC FLAIR, TOLAND'S BULGE BOOK HAD CLEARLY MADE PEIPER something of a dark-side celebrity. Only three years later, his old troop was again trying to get him to go back to the Ardennes. "If I go to Belgium," he responded, "it is my own fault if I am arrested by the Belgians."[67] He was having none of that.

In 1970 Toland was writing again. He enclosed a copy of his Pulitzer prize–winning book on the war in Japan, *But Not in Shame*. Now he was working on a biography of Adolf Hitler. "I did not know Hitler intimately," Peiper told him, "but if my modest support can contribute, I am at your disposal."[68]

But later that autumn Peiper was writing Richard Schulze-Kossens, nicknamed Rix, about the need to have Hitler's adjutants write something more balanced: "Toland is writing to me these days. As an American author, for sure he is known to you, that he wants to make a book about Adolf Hitler in a certain way to answer Shirer's book, *The Rise and Fall of the Third Reich*. He wants to take five years for this project and to speak to as many people as possible and to see the archives and protocols of the trials." [69]

To write a proper and balanced history of Adolf Hitler, Peiper had in mind Hans Schwarz van Berk rather than Toland. According to Peiper, Schwarz van Berk, having been trained under Goebbels, possessed a "good writing style," was "unbelievably mentally fit," and had a view of Hitler that matched his own:

> Hitler was lonely, joyless, but he had a good nose for things—nearly clairvoyant. He possessed a strong will, with a good knowledge of history and—for a long time—he was master of the time and situation. But he was without limits, rampant, greedy and wildly ambitious. Then he became ill and was doped [by drugs]. From that moment on, a change began in his nature which could only be recognized by the people who were around him. And this is the moment where the testimonies of his adjutants are becoming important. They should show the climax—the great coming, the rise and then, the tragic fall.[70]

Meanwhile others were writing too—and on subjects that could be more personally damning for him than biographies of Hitler. In 1969 Peiper learned that an English author, Charles Whiting, was writing a book about Malmédy. He spoke with Whiting later that summer at his Stuttgart office:

> I am a fatalist today. The world has branded me and my men as the scum of the earth. No one will ever be able to clear it up now. They see us as German gangsters—Al Capones, the lot of us—with a revolver under each armpit and a tommy gun in our hands. . . . Me, I've emigrated within myself. Let the so-called government do whatever it likes. Germany—don't make me laugh! Malmédy? Who knows and cares anymore? No one will ever sort out this mess now. Too many lies have been told after many years.[71]

Max Moritz and Peiper remained good friends, but it had become clear that there could be little continued peace for a former SS colonel in Germany. In 1962 Moritz invited Peiper along on a trip to France. Later they stopped by the St. Tropez villa of SS reporter Hans Schwarz van Berk. His old SS war correspondent buddy had written him often while he was in Landsberg—he had even visited at prison. In fact, Schwarz van Berk had been incarcerated himself after the war—the price for being one of Goebbel's star war correspondents. After testifying for the Nuremberg trials he had escaped from CIC detention at the US detention camp at Ludgwigsburg.[72] Now he and Peiper were sunning themselves on the beaches and enjoying his palatial digs. Attractive young women strolled along the tidal edge, and one could often practice English. Here was a loyal comrade.[73]

The trip rekindled Peiper's love affair with France and particularly with the area near east of Dijon, known as the Langres plateau. For years Peiper had told those around him that he would like to find a wooded lot in a quiet place. He looked for something harkening back to a simple time—a retirement home in the country. Moritz told Peiper this might be the place: the Haute Saône region was tranquil, reasonably priced, and close to Germany.

Along the way Max Moritz re-introduced Peiper to Albert Gauthier, a man from Chauncey who had a modest property to show him. Peiper knew Gauthier from 1940. After the conquest of France Hitler's Reich had negotiated an agreement with the installed Vichy government such that for every voluntary French worker going to Germany to work, two French POWs would be permitted to return home. Thus, due to Peiper's influence with Himmler, Gauthier was chosen in an exchange to return home. Gauthier, a pro-German French nationalist, never forgot the favor. At least that was the way Peiper later described it.

When the retired SS colonel saw "Le Ranfort," it was love at first sight. Or was it second sight? Indeed, Peiper had motored right by Traves with Himmler on July 13, 1940, in search of the Reichsführer's future SS Burgundian-Eastern France fantasy estate.[74] "I know France because during the war, we were sometimes here. I like the size of the country . . . I believe the French are freedom loving and have buried hostility which existed between France and Germany."[75]

So, under his wife's maiden name, Sigurd Anna Hinrichsen, Peiper purchased one hectare in Traves along the Saône River. In May 1964, he applied for a building permit, listing his employment as a "commercial editor living in Stuttgart." He spent part of that summer of 1964 on the property with his son, Hinrich, in an old Bundeswehr tent. They grew reacquainted, steeped in contact with the earth, far away from automobile magnates, courts, newspapers, and the noise of the city.

When autumn came, it was hard to go back to Stuttgart. Jochen Peiper had fallen in love—in love with a wooded refuge in the remote French countryside of Eastern France.

Chapter 19

OLD HARES

Over the years in Stuttgart Jochen Peiper and his family had become close friends with Heinz-Ulrich Wieselmann. In early 1957 Wieselmann sought out the vanquished SS war hero after being introduced by Benno Müller. Wieselmann himself had spent the war in the regular German army with the antitank troops, much of the time in Paris.[1] After the war he had written a book on the reconstruction of bombed-out Berlin where Peiper had grown up.[2] The two became fast friends, and along with Peiper soon became part of the boys' club. He, Wieselmann, and Dr. Müller were often over to the Moritz household to talk about fast cars, politics, and the national scene.[3] The joke-like status of the Bundeswehr and the corruption of the new German generation were common themes.[4] Peiper's Stuttgart pals shared a love of "man's best friend," both Müller and Wieselmann touting their choice of the boxer purebreds. Wieselmann was the irascible author, penning everything from books on all-out racing to a touching missive on the thoughts of dogs![5]

Even though Peiper drove a modest dark blue Volkswagen fastback, he cultivated a love for cars and racing. Courtesy of sympathetic auto dealers, he was often driving a Porsche "loaner" about town. This passion was natural; during the war he had spent many hours behind the wheel of quality autos as he drove Himmler all over Europe. And within the SS there was a daredevil mystique associated with racing.[6]

Contrary to the others in the boys' club, Max Moritz was the chubby, common mechanic who had ascended fortune through hard work but felt somehow uncomfortable within the group. To him, Wieselmann and Müller seemed like rich playboys, hauling along the famous SS colonel for their escapades. There always seemed to be buxom, juicy femme-rockets following the well-heeled racing crowd. It was more than tempting.

Peiper's and Wieselmann's children knew each other well from school, and Wieselmann's young intelligent daughter, Bettina, became close to the family. Knowing that Jochen was financially strapped, Uli convinced Peiper to approach his boss, Paul Pietsch. Before the war, Paul Pietsch was a famous race car driver, and after the conflict he drove in several races and began publishing a highly acclaimed newspaper review, *Das Auto.* Later this became *Auto, Motor und Sport*, a publication of incalculable importance to the German automotive renaissance in the West German Republic. If Paul Pietsch was the towering tycoon behind *Auto, Motor und Sport*, Uli

Wieselmann was its motive force and mercurial chief editor. What did it mean for Pieper? Uli "pulled some strings" for the former SS colonel.[7]

Soon Wieselmann had Peiper working for the magazine at the big downtown office complex. There Peiper met the man who would be his editor in later years, Wolfgang Schilling. Peiper was working only three days a week, and then he would go to France for the rest. Even if Schilling thought his hours odd, that gave him and Peiper something in common, for Schilling went to France with his wife often on holidays as well. During one meeting he asked Peiper why he worked only part time. "You have to know that a man who has been under the gallows several times like me," Peiper said, "has a different perspective on life and money is not so important."[8]

True enough. It was like the title of one of Wieselmann's books: *Als gäbe es kein Morgen*—"As if there was no tomorrow." Peiper was making up for lost time. With many free days, Peiper and Wieselmann took auto-touring trips, testing out the latest hot cars while whooping it up across Europe, even attending the Grand Prix in Monaco in May 1964![9] There was also always "*Swatt*," their rich friend Hans Schwarz van Berk in the South of France. And when back in Stuttgart at Römerstrasse, Schwarz van Berk would join the boys' club with Benno Müller.

Wieselmann had a penchant for fast cars, and the two men zipped about for a time in one Porsche 356 after another. Each was faster and more powerful. "With such an engine," pronounced Wieselmann, "one is king." There were touring trips to France and Italy that Wieselmann ostensibly wrote about in the magazine. Uli and Bettina would sometimes travel to Traves to Peiper's holiday home in France. One could get there quickly, Wieselmann joked, which was good with these cars—there was no room for luggage! Even with Peiper owning the place in France, both men contemplated investing in another property together. Would it be Italy or France?

Young Bettina Wieselmann loved visiting Peiper at his place in Traves—her first big adventure with nature. They hiked about, hunting for mushrooms until they got lost. Together they even planted a walnut tree by the entrance. "Everyone should spend one night of their lives in a tent!" Peiper announced on one trip. For Bettina, that one night was miserable with dripping rain. But beyond roughing it, there was the ever-popular barbeque at Le Renfort. Or it was another day paring the underbrush or chopping firewood? But Peiper was very close to Uli's daughter; they had long conversations each day—politics, hippies, pollution. Was Hinrich's hair too long? Had she read Hemingway? Peiper passed on a copy of *For Whom the Bell Tolls* to her.[10] Nothing was off the table. She knew he had been considered a war criminal, but Bettina had grown up with Jochen; as her father's best friend and the cherished stand-in uncle.[11]

The good-old-boy circuit in Stuttgart was tenuous, though. In 1968, at a big auto show in Geneva, where Peiper was in attendance, Wieselmann had a heart attack. Yet Wieselmann was the proud editor of *Auto, Motor und Sport*, and he continued to smoke and drink the same way he drove hot sports cars—hard.[12] Even so, it was a big shock in May 1970 when Uli Wieselmann died suddenly. Peiper was so close to the family that he offered to help Bettina as a legal guardian. Peiper even drove Frau

Wieselmann and the kids to the funeral at Kirchhofen. There, Jochen made an impassioned eulogy for Wieselmann, evoking the image of Nils Holgersson, the Swedish tale of a boy bewitched by a troll, enabling him to ride the back of a swan named Martin. Just like the boys and the swan, Peiper lamented, he and Uli had enjoyed the most magical adventures together.[13]

Those days were gone. At the family boundary, the old allegiances withered. Peiper was promptly let go from *Auto, Motor und Sport.* No one claimed to know why, but Pietsch was calling the shots. In any case, there was now little to hold Peiper in Stuttgart. His children were grown and away from home, and he saw himself a "persecuted man of the Third Reich for whom there is no longer any room in Germany."[14] Without a steady income he could no longer afford his flat in the city. Rather than start a new career at fifty-seven, he would go to France.

The decision stunned Sigurd, even if faced by the stark economics. Jochen could continue to work for Wolfgang Schilling at Motorbuch Verlag, translating English titles into German under the pen name of Rainer Buschmann.[15] So it was on February 18, 1972, that Peiper received a certificate of employment from *Presse Verlag* allowing him to apply for residency in Traves, France. Still in Stuttgart in May, he was exhausted but encouraged that Hans Schwarz van Berk would visit.

> If we did not have wealthy friends in Gassin which we could visit once a year, the future working in the coal mine would be indeed depressing. . . . At night I sit shot, and worn out in my chair like Robert Blum and I think of the time when everything around me was well groomed and undisturbed. . . . My wife is a little worried about our transfer to Traves and she worries that her nice furniture will end up on green grass. . . . We want to move by mid June.[16]

Peiper and his wife boxed up things in Stuttgart on Thursday, June 13, 1972, and drove off the following morning.

On June 24—Johannistag—Schwarz van Berk came for a housewarming visit, pleased to get away from it all and to see his old comrade's new home, even as he suffered from cancer.

> The trip to Traves on the Saone on Johannistag was once again a discovery. Every contemplative trip should be like this. I hadn't seen the village for a long time, and hadn't seen the house in its completed state. One passes all the way through the village, then through meadows on the left and right. Right before the valley with its springs feeding his half-clogged lake is the old mill, whose walls crumble like a decayed tooth when trying to force new windows into it. That's how my friend pointedly described it. So, still before reaching the mill, to the right behind the meadow, we passed through a nearly impenetrable forest of which Jochen had cleverly bought: 2 hectares plus another 20,000 square meters. One must open one or two fence barricades, which are detached from the fence posts with rusty loops of barbed wire. You must make your way through or around innumerable cow patties through an entry gate made of sticks, and then hike up in the cool forest near the meadow toward the house.

The silver river already glitters through the cleared areas of the forest, but underneath the branches almost hang in the river. A fisherman sits in his shallow four-cornered boat without moving. The fish aren't biting, either, although in Jochen's purchase contract the water is described as being rich with fish. The white house has a red saddle roof, with two windows facing south looking out on the meadow. The house presents itself with a natural-stone outside chimney and offers a view stretching over the ridge. But without a new "surgical intervention" this chimney is never going to draw properly. As I came home to Stuttgart and unpacked my pajamas in the evening, I still smelled the smoke residue from the wood fireplace, which had settled everywhere within the walls.[17]

On July 20, 1972, daughter Silke was married at Tegernsee, which provided a good opportunity to visit Sigrid Mayr in Miesbach. "It is good timing," Peiper wrote to Schwarz van Berk on August 13. "Silke is the last of ours to be married." Upon returning to Traves, Peiper then relished a late summer visit from Manfred Schönfelder, a close classmate from SS officers school at Braunschweig and the chief of staff of Herbert Gille with the 5th SS Panzer Division "*Wiking*." He was another of Benno Müller's buddies.

Soon Peiper's daughter, Elke, her husband, Toni, and their baby were visiting. "It is not only nice, but the dealing with a little human being is really new for me and also to my surprise, I discover real grand-fatherly feelings in my breast."

The autumn went by quietly. Now, long after the war, Peiper would recall November 9 while in retirement in faraway France. That was the day in 1935 he had vocally dedicated his life to Adolf Hitler at the lavish ceremony at Munich's Feldherrnhalle some thirty-seven years before. "At least a quiet 9th of November," Peiper sighed that Thursday in 1972, "without parade marching and fiery pylons."[18] For sure, Traves was quiet—too quiet for his wife.

The mayor of the village, Ernest Rigoulot, was friendly enough and cheerfully approved Peiper's application for residency, "He owns a house here for the last eight years and wants to make his retirement and establish himself in our village." Peiper had spent a good amount of time at Traves by himself, as his wife preferred Germany.[19] Some even rumored that Peiper took up with a French woman, yet this remained the thing of idle gossip.[20] Although occasionally he returned to Germany to see the old fellows, mainly the old SS colonel kept to himself.[21]

IF NOT A FULL FRANCOPHILE, PEIPER WAS STILL FASCINATED BY THE REGION. "He liked France," his son recalled. "The atmosphere, its way of life. It was the time of de Gaulle and Adenauer and he was persuaded that the two countries would be good neighbors from now on."[22]

Peiper was careful to say nothing of the war in encounters with French neighbors. Privately was another matter. Given what his father had told him, Peiper's son saw the Malmédy trial as revenge: "The Americans had a need after the war for a symbolic condemnation of the Waffen SS," he would later recall. Or so his father had spoon-fed him.

Although self exiled to Eastern France, Peiper's appetite for reading in isolation only grew. Knowing the SS colonel's fondness for literature and his fondness for the outdoors, Dr. Benno Müller's attractive second wife, Uta, had given him a copy of Ernst Wiechert's *The Simple Life*. Peiper at once identified with Wiechert's vision of a quiet life in East Prussia and the author's troubled life after the war.[23] For Peiper, Traves would be his best hope for "Wiechert's island," the life of anonymous solitude.

Even by 1970, Peiper saw the Americans getting a taste of their own medicine in the failed Vietnam War. There was the well-publicized case of Lt. William Calley and the US 23rd "Americal" Division who, in a fit of battlefield frustration and violence, on March 16, 1968, had slaughtered hundreds of innocent Vietnamese women and children in the village of My Lai. Lt. Calley, the leader of the troop, served no more than a few weeks of house arrest.[24] "They have lost some of their naive sense of mission and penetrating self-righteousness after Vietnam, My Lai and Watergate."[25] Peiper said of the Americans, "Would you see a moral difference between setting a house on fire with a flame thrower from a distance of 50 meters . . . or massacring civilians with submachine guns from a distance of 50 meters or from a height of 50 meters from a helicopter? It is really nothing but hypocrisy to bless war and condemn its methods. Fresh wars of aggression have been waged and war crimes committed without ever again invoking the international law so solemnly postulated at Nuremberg. The Americans are no longer the infallible interpreters of the conscience of the world."[26]

Nonetheless, Peiper saw that he and many of his old SS comrades needed to give up their fixations with the war, particularly now, as he was taking his leave from Germany. "History is always written by the victor and histories of the vanquished belong to a shrinking circle of those who were there."

> After thirty years we are no longer so sure in the saddle of our own recollections and naturally, never objective. I made myself available for such things entirely too often. . . . As I am growing older, I am dropping more and more.[27]

In spite of Peiper's warnings, twenty-one Kameraden of the Leibstandarte informed their former commander they would venture back to the Ardennes. The nostalgic trek was organized by panzer men Karl Wortmann and Rolf Ehrhardt, assisted by Gerard Gregoire, the curator of the Expo 44 museum in La Gleize, where the big Tiger tank had been restored.[28] There was no way Peiper would attend. Outwardly the famous SS colonel gave the impression of trying to leave the war behind. The inner man, however, was another matter.[29]

Nowadays, Peiper, the Ernst Wiechert-sage, voiced gentle criticism of his old superior, Heinrich Himmler, referring to him as King Heinrich, a moniker he had used many years before:

> I spend my time at the typewriter and outdoors. . . . There are hundreds of trees to be felled for making living conditions better for other ones, thin out branches, planting and transplanting, and above all to remove *toutes les petites cochonneries* [brushwood], which is well known to be more fit for life than

all cultivated plants. "King Heinrich," who studied agriculture, should have known that before he descended as a race fanatic on the Untermenschen.[30]

Had Peiper really been reformed? One letter to Ernst Klink strongly questioned that notion. "A book by a Frenchman (!) fell into my hands, which I would like to recommend to you warmly," he wrote. By Dominique Venner, it was an ode to the nihilistic pre-Hitler Freikorps, a right-wing anti-Semitic and pro-Nazi polemic.[31] "It provided me with more clarity about the history of the Third Reich, than any other literature on that subject," Peiper concluded.[32]

And when Charles Whiting interviewed Peiper in the summer 1969 at the Stuttgart editorial offices of *Auto, Motor und Sport*, he found the SS Colonel bitter and fatalistic.[33] Age was catching up. True, unlike most of the flaccid workers at the complex, Peiper was still trim and fit, but he wore his graying hair sharply parted and slicked down in the style from German days gone by. There was a tie over a white nylon shirt, but he was no fashion plate; his collar was too large, and his neck showed wrinkled wattles of age. He needed reading glasses to refer to written material. Whiting told Peiper of the book he was writing. He seemed unimpressed. The British author asked about the Malmédy crossroads. Peiper described hearing of the incident from Gustav Knittel and Heinz von Westernhagen and ventured his own theory. He shrugged.

Peiper was a war icon passed by history. His sarcastic tongue was laced with the dated jargon of SS troopers as he complained to Whiting of the stodgy modern-day German middle class. They had sold out, he said. "You know that Tiger of mine in La Gleize [Belgium]," he grinned, "Well, I'd like to drag the damned thing here to Stuttgart and put it outside the entrance overnight and see the looks on their faces next morning. That would show them!" It would be a shock, his interviewer agreed. "I'm sitting on a powder keg, you know," he said with dramatic effect. "Ellis, Kempner and Wiesenthal—they all have tried to get me in the past."

"One day someone will come along with another 'story,'" Peiper nodded, "and the powder keg will explode under me. Then it will all be over at last."[34]

Part Five
REQUIEM

> "After his work was done, he swam once more far out into the lake, smoked his pipe on the shore, and slowly changed his uniform. It hung a little loosely on him, and he looked down at his medals thoughtfully. It was a long time ago that he had won these ribbons and crosses. . . . The world appeared to him to be especially beautiful. The light on the pine trees was beautiful and so was the reflection of the heron in the motionless water. This was a festival of youth, and he was no longer indispensable. He did not care anymore for festivals. He did not have much time left, and he could be happy without them."
>
> —Ernst Wiechert, *The Simple Life*

Chapter 20

THE OLD GERMAN HERO

JOCHEN PEIPER'S WIFE, SIGURD, WORRIED FOR HER HUSBAND'S SAFETY IN France. Yet the old SS colonel loved the place. His friends would later claim he was a Francophile, even if the cloistered way he lived there contradicted that view.[1] Peiper was far too sheltered and private to embrace the *joi de vivre*—the open casual enjoyment of life—exalted by the French. Even more cool and aloof by demeanor, Frau Peiper was even more out of place. Yet, with the permanent move, both Sigurd and Jochen were alone there. Jochen Peiper wasn't hiding in Traves, but neither was he broadcasting his presence. He seldom went out; Sigurd usually drove their BMW from the rented garage in town to the grocery in the nearby town of Vesoul.[2] But mostly they stayed to themselves—expatriated Germans living in remote Eastern France.

But strangely, Peiper's closest neighbor was also German. Erwin Ketelhut had an expansive estate on the old mill property less than three hundred yards away to the west. From the perspective of the past, the two men were similar. Both were veterans of the same combat unit. Indeed, the two had gotten to know of each other on the Russian front in the same outfit.[3] After the war, Ketelhut rekindled relations with his comrade while he was working as chief of advertising for Max Moritz in 1963. Peiper told the businessman about the place he had in Traves. Interested, Ketelhut came to the village and in 1971 decided to purchase the adjoining mill property. The price was a bargain, the Moulin de Velet was in ruins. But soon, Ketelhut built an expansive estate at the mill.[4]

When Ketelhut moved to Traves in 1971, the two met frequently. Peiper had all kinds of enterprising ideas to make money—they would raise ducks or trout; he would grow Christmas trees. Ketelhut had the money; he had the ideas. Yet his new neighbor was unreliable. The former artillery captain fancied himself "a Bohemian" and frequented *Chez Néné* to drink and cavort with the locals. Each evening he would invite the willing customers at the cafe to share a liter of Côtes du Rhône. Although he invited his German neighbor, the proper old soldier declined. Even more, Peiper's wife found Ketelhut abrasive and improper; the man sometimes showed up at the door in undershirts!

Given the silent-treatment with his neighbor, visitors were special. Every so often Peiper's old veteran friend Dr. Benno Müller brought goodies from Germany, including his fetchingly attractive young wife. Not only was there the war in common, but also a love of intellectual distractions. Sometimes at his country table they would tackle the philosophers, both famous and arcane: Schopenhauer, Nietzsche, Jacob Burkhardt, Tucholsky, Ringelnatz, Knut Hamsun, or Gottfried Benn.[5] With music, it was Bach versus Telemann. Evening required sampling and discussion of the quality of the latest red wine delivery. And there was always racing and the good old days with the jet setters in Stuttgart: bon vivant Kaj Keser or racing mogul Uli Wieselmann. Nor must one forget the dogs: the pure bloods had advantages but weaknesses too. *Mendel's law!* More red wine.

Even if such discussions and an existence in the country seemed to satisfy Peiper, the visitors could tell his wife was unhappy. When his editor, Wolfgang Schilling, stopped by with his wife to visit one summer, Sigurd had sandwiches, inviting them to spend the night. They parked their mobile home in the neighbor's nearby grassy meadow, marveling at the remoteness of the location. At night the sky was sprayed with stars and only crickets and the bellowing French cows broke an uncommon peace:

> It was a very simple home and they lived in a simple way. Outside the house, there was a flower bed with roses and the dogs were running over them and Mrs. Peiper didn't approve. . . . But while we talked, his wife seemed a little distant. [She] was a nice lady, but it was lonely there and she seemed a little sad.[6]

Sigurd often had long phone conversations with her children and made frequent trips back to Germany to see her grandchildren or her sister in Stuttgart. During these trips her husband stayed alone in Traves—there was a hint of marital discontent.[7] Still, the cavalcade of friends stopping by for visits found his retreat almost bucolic. Schwarz van Berk, Jochen's outspoken friend from the South of France, approved:

> A forest house. One sits wonderfully in the sun on the terrace and hears an unending chorus of bird songs. In the oaks and ashes and birches, the bright yellow Pirol birds are now feeling especially well. One or two pairs gave a fantastic concert, morning and evening. . . . I have never been so conscious of their beauty . . . It is almost impossible to enumerate all the trees, bushes, and plants in the forest. Also, the ground is covered with ivy, blackberries, ferns, and other creeping plants with blue blossoms. . . . There are walnuts and ashes, alders, and beeches, oaks and firs and larches, pines and spruce. The forest has been growing at least fifty years undisturbed. . . . Twice I've been swimming in the river. You can scarcely feel any current in the warm clear water, though it's a little murky now from the rain. On both banks, fishermen sit in green boats or stand in the water along the edge in high boots. Like hunting, fishing has been a privilege since the French Revolution, which has plundered the waters, forests, and fields. But no politician, including De Gaulle, would dare to take away this wild freedom from the citizens.[8]

Although Peiper mostly kept to himself, Mayor Rigoulot of Traves was at least *French friendly*, particularly with a few glasses of wine. When Peiper was by himself during one of his wife's frequent trips to Germany, he was sometimes the dinner guest of the mayor, or at least he would eat at Chez Néné for lunch.[9] To Schwarz van Berk the villagers were boorish likeable hicks. "Someone recommended that Jochen plant mountain ash trees by the house, which he did," he recalled. Then one of them said, "See, isn't it good that you can sit here and shoot birds out of those trees through your window?"

> The village is no idyll, but it is also not without heart and friendliness. When we go to the tavern on the long street, we have trouble not getting drunk, because a cup of wine and an aperitif are presented to us as we greet people in the village.[10]

To be sure, most German visitors stopping by had been connected with Peiper during the war. These included his old combat leader, Otto Dinse, or tank commander, Dr. Arndt Fischer, now his dentist. And there was his devoted tank radio operator Fritz Kosmehl, now blind from his last desperate day fighting in Normandy:

> On the return trip from our vacation in Spain in 1972 we drove our trailer to Traves. The surrounding landscape was wavy with juicy meadows and laced with forests. Soon we were 400 meters on a narrow path along a meadow, arriving at a barbed wire fence. We stopped at the gate, no house to be seen. Fifty meters away there was a downward sloping strip of forest. There was just a mailbox at the path along the fence, but they must have been noticed as two people stepped out from between the trees. They approached and waved and were obviously happy. As always, we were received heartily, especially by his wife Sigurd. She always hoped our presence would loosen up the occasional melancholic mood of her husband. . . . In the evening we sat in front of his fireplace and talked. . . . He works a lot in the forest, clearing trees and planting new ones. He called his domain in the forest, "Le Renfort," his paradise.[11]

But then, at the end of the evening, the feeling changed. "Despite the heartiness, a depressed mood hovered over the meeting. . . ." The next day, there was a trip with the old colonel in his rowboat on the Saône and a visit to see Ketelhut at his mill with the trout farm, but Kosmehl could not avoid the heavy atmosphere once more. There was a reason for Peiper's dark side. His wife's health was failing: she had cancer. "When we moved here in 1972, I imagined I would have some ten years of time left," he wrote to a friend, "but the calculation does not work out. The illness of my wife was not planned into it."[12]

Peiper also wrote his son:

> Ma seems to be safe in Munich. That is a stone off my chest. What a great friend she is. How she kept you all above water during difficult times. And how she gets along nowadays, in this not always beautiful present, and above all with this devilish disease. All that, only a later retrospective look will make clear.[13]

For a time he thought they would have to leave, yet radiation and chemotherapy brought the cancer into remission. Looking at the Saône, he dreamed that their spirits might dwell "sometime in the future on the bank of the river in the shape of twin oaks."[14] Sigurd also eventually grew to accept the place:

> In many respects, these years in Traves were not easy for me in moving there. This existence, so strange from my normal life style, was an enormous change. But as the months passed, I became more adjusted. Inner ballast dropped off and I rediscovered nature in her origin and in her beauty. With Pa together, I again became cheerful and easygoing. We made plans and we enjoyed every day. I again had found my Jochen. Our innermost wish was to let our lives end there like Philemon and Baucis. The years in Traves will remain the most beautiful ones in our lives together, because, there, Pa had times when he was really happy and I with him.[15]

For Peiper the eleven years he had spent in prison after the war imparted a strange appetite for solitude. When Sigurd was away in the winter he could follow his nose in complete freedom and even let the dogs into the house.

> At this time of year, it is cozy and very comfortable in the forest under the warm roof. If the swollen Saône did not gurgle menacingly by and the dogs bark occasionally, one could feel like being on a distant star. . . . We three can pursue the inclination to grow wild without being disturbed. In the mornings, I work on a book about Napoleon's army and in the afternoon I look after felling wood for the next winter. At present, it is "tea time and blue hour." I listen to Telemann and Correlli, listen to the peaceful snoring of my four-legged Trabants and let my thoughts wonder.[16]

"On good days this unadulterated piece of nature can become a link," he wrote to his wife, "and on bad days—a refuge!"[17] He was happy to be out of Germany. The war having been lost, he considered it morally bankrupt.[18] Nature, however, could not be subverted. Here were the trees and the animals of the forest—the world in a pure state. He carefully built wooden bird houses that he set about his property and planted trees and nurtured a garden.

> Much water has flowed down the Saône since the bushes in front of my last retreat closed behind me. . . . Now that the children are all taken care of and married, the baggage had become lighter. Now I only have to worry about my wife, dog and whatever is nearest to the land. For me, there is little point in thinking about tomorrow. I hope that no donkey comes up and eats our clover, and that we stay healthy, and that I may be granted peace and quiet after all the worrisome years, without persecution, slander and constant discrimination. And if not, then just that time which we have spent here and which no one can take away from us will have to be enough. In brief, my wife and I live entirely

in the present, with our friends the trees and plants, music and books, and comfortable conversation before a glowing fire.[19]

Perhaps the times were affecting Peiper. The hippie movement of the early seventies espoused visions with which he was already familiar: the flower children of his German childhood were like *Wandervögel*—wandering birds—colorfully dressed youths who traipsed about the German countryside in search of a natural way of life, distrustful of society and impelled by idealism.

> Civilization does not release its children unharmed. Despite all that, here it is incredibly beautiful—ignoring the invisible chains one still drags along. Where I stand, the perspectives change and everything falls into place. . . . There are many positive things on the island. May it tolerate us for a while longer and later be available for other shipwrecked people.[20]

As for the dark memories he carried with him into his sanctuary, he admitted that "everyone has regrets." Yes, he had fought in the war and with the palace guard institution of Hitler's National Socialist Germany.

Those muddy waters did not easily settle. In his dreams Peiper was sometimes back in Landsberg Prison. There was now a dream within a dream. He recalled his dreams years before within the cold, gray walls of Landsberg on the Lech River near Munich. In those distant visions in prison, his heart often left the shabby confines to find a free place where the past no longer needled him and all the ugliness of life evaporated. He craved freedom in the outdoors under a blue sky.[21]

That dream had come true. Living as an expatriot in France, he was doing whatever he could to make ends meet, but he was outdoors and breathing fresh air. During the day he was at his typewriter, translating books.

Still, the books reminded him of unpleasant things of his life. Under the pen name of Rainer Buschmann, he translated volumes about "Old Fritz"—King Frederick II of Prussia—and the memoirs of French SS Division Commander Gilbert Gilles. The translation was "enough for restful sitting," he said, alluding to ten years at Landsberg, "and I know something about that."[22]

> The material is depressing for me—it already was during the war—certainly not because of the destructive madness of these days, rather from the realization that such relapses into barbarity are not just attributed to Hitler or my contemporaries. Pure and simple, it is people who do not change and have lived by murdering their neighbors to assure their survival since the olden days. *Survival of the fittest!* Formerly the one who was fittest did the deed with a stone mallet. Today the job is done with a preemptive strike or an atomic club. The result of this realization is resignation. Lucky is the man who closes himself off the world without resentment and without leaving altogether. Submerging oneself in paradise is not enough. Above all, it is important what luggage and ballast one drags along.[23]

The SS organization to which he belonged had been demonized; the country for which he had fought had disowned him, and the ideals in which he had believed were now judged as criminal. And now, after losing the war, the Soviets had threatened for twenty years to gobble up Europe as a plum for Communism. The H-bomb was the only deterrent. "Even if we had been the victors," he sarcastically wrote to his old tanker friend in 1974, "we couldn't have created a bigger chaos than this."[24]

"This is not a dark pessimism," he said of his fatalistic outlook, "but rather it is my experience since 1945 that I have never been left alone." The world he sought now was the simple natural life, like that popularized by Wiechert. "It is quiet and peaceful here," he told one friend, "like on another star."[25]

Was all fleeting? "Aware of a likely fateful future, I try to live very much in the present,"[26] Peiper wrote. For him the years in the woods had worked magic. Here he had found, he told a friend, "the way of tranquility."[27] The aging, sympathetic anonymous SS officer.

A SINGLE DAY IN 1974 SHATTERED HIS SANCTUARY FOREVER.

Chapter 21

BLOW-UP

On Tuesday, June 11, 1974, Paul Cacheux sat behind his shop counter. For the last two years the fifty-two-year-old clerk had been working at the Mégnin-Bernard hardware store on the bustling Rue Paul Morel in Vesoul. He had lived better days. During the war he had been part of the Nazi resistance as part of an Alsatian Group in Eastern France. Cacheux was tall and stern, with graying wavy hair and horn-rimmed glasses riding on an upturned nose. Wearing an ill-fitting gray hardware smock, he looked like a guileless clerk. As with many of the former partisans, those glory days thirty-five years before were the most important of his life. After the Germans had invaded France in 1940, he had been incarcerated for two years. When the invaders released him, he joined the French resistance.

Now, in 1974, he was a dedicated French Communist and obsessed with apprehending the Nazi war criminals. He would speak frequently to those who would listen of the *Boche*—Germans—and the need to bring to justice those who are hiding in France. With his simple job, counting flower pots and tools, his hobby created interest in an otherwise routine life.

It was a quiet day at the shop. Sometime in the afternoon a tall, older man entered. In good French he asked about fence wire. Cacheux immediately noticed a German accent. "*Sind sie Deutscher?*" Cacheux asked.

The man hesitated. "*Ja*," he answered. "Where did you learn to speak German so well?"

"I am Alsatian," Cacheux explained, peering into the man's blue eyes. "Where did you learn to speak French so well?" The man did not answer, but slowly repeated his question about fence wire in French.

"I was sent to Germany in the war," Cacheux continued, explaining that he was cast out of Alsace after the invasion of 1940 as an *Unerwünschter*—an undesirable. "So you were in Vesoul during the war?" Cacheux finally asked.

The customer hesitated. "*Nein!*"

"I feel like I know you," Cacheux squinted. He thought he saw the man's face whiten, almost to the pallor of his hair. There was an uneasy silence as he filled out the order slip. "So where should I deliver the fence?" Cacheux continued.

"Peiper . . . at Traves," he said.

"Peiper . . . Joachim?" Cacheux asked, searching his eyes.

"Yes," the man said. He did not blink. The customer gave directions to his house for delivery of the wire, paid, and left the shop.[1]

At his home that night Paul Cacheux eagerly pulled out the *Livre Brun*—the Brown Book. Its pages identified all German war criminals still at large. He thumbed through his worn copy, as he had done so often before. On page 103 he found the man he had seen in his shop—Joachim Peiper! His heart beat faster. Peiper had been in high places in the Waffen SS and had been accused of war crimes both in Belgium and Italy. Now he had a big fish!

It was true. Cacheux learned his given name was Joachim Peiper, but he preferred a shortened version of the first; his close friends knew him as "Jochen." The man had been with the 1st SS Panzer Division, the Leibstandarte Adolf Hitler—Adolf Hitler's bodyguard: the name of that formation was enough to bring back memories of the war. And, more, Cacheux learned that Peiper was something of an SS idol, one of Germany's great war heros. At age twenty-five his battlefield exploits had become legend. Flashing and bright, he had a reputation as a *Schneidiger*—a total daredevil. His combat citations were one audacious operation after another. Without fear, bold and dashing, the SS man was holder of the Knight's Cross with the Oak Leaves and Swords, one of the very highest German military honors. And from a military standpoint, his big error had been to find himself in the camp of the defeated.

Woe to the vanquished. Cacheux was excited to learn that Peiper was charged with war crimes. One incident had taken place in Italy near the tiny village of Boves in 1943 and another a year later near Malmédy in Belgium. For the latter incident he had received a death sentence from the Americans, but this was commuted, and he was released in 1956. Now he was here in France!

Proud of his discovery, Paul Cacheux got the word out to others in the local French Communist Party. At first those in Vesoul did not believe him—another false alarm from the doddering old resistance fighter. "Cacheux, you see SS everywhere!" A year went by as the simple ironmonger sought to learn more about Peiper. Villagers in Traves were little help with his obsession. "He is just an ordinary German," one complained.[2] Then Cacheux learned that there was yet another German neighbor—now he had visions of a Nazi stronghold in Eastern France! And through a sympathetic informant he was able to learn a few intriguing facts about his quarry: the German had been a colonel (that fit!) and an advertising chief at Volkswagen and had received a lot of mail. Locals said he could be heard typing all day. Did that make him a dangerous criminal? Spying on Peiper seemed unlikely—the man had two big dogs. Try as he might, Cacheux found nothing evil. Peiper, meanwhile, carried on with a quiet life.

> My wife is in Hamburg for the last three weeks to help a new grandchild with the first deep sighs in this questionable earthly existence. We three dogs live all by ourselves in the forest and give in to the inclination to become feral. In the morning I sit at the money machine, at the present working on a book about Napoleon's Army. In the afternoon, wood is being cut down for the coming winter. In between, are improvised meals and the evening music and reading.[3]

Yet there were signs of malaise. When his old comrade Fritz Kosmehl visited Traves, again returning from a sun-drenched vacation in Spain, Sigurd Peiper seemed edgy. "It's nice that you are visiting us again, Mr. Kosmehl," she said. "It will be good for him to talk to you. Unfortunately, he will not be back until late tonight." To Kosmehl's wife, she no longer seemed carefree as during their previous visit. There were new lines of worry in her face. Later that night the three sat around the fireplace with wine, and the mood loosened. "Oh, if my man could laugh like you!" Sigurd Peiper sighed. But when Jochen returned from a business trip at 10 p.m. he seemed preoccupied. Outwardly there were greetings; he seemed happy to see Kosmehl again, but Peiper said nothing about his own personal affairs. The next day Kosmehl thought his former tank commander looked tired. They took a tour of Erwin Ketelhut's thriving trout hatchery next door.

Later that night the Kosmehls retired to their house trailer just in front of Le Renfort, only to have someone softly knock on the metal door. It was Erwin Ketelhut. He was eager to talk to Kosmehl and his wife; a long conversation began. He described his relationship with Peiper, which seemed to have gone wrong. In the beginning they had started a duck farm, but Peiper seemed determined to remain a soldier and knew nothing of animal husbandry. That venture failed. Finally Ketelhut got around to the subject on his mind. "Could you not get him to stop this new wave of visitors?" he asked earnestly. "A certain unrest has been created in the village." Kosmehl was surprised. Peiper had enjoined Kosmehl not to tell others about his whereabouts, and as far as he was aware, only a few veterans knew. Yet Ketelhut insisted there were many others.[4] Ketelhut seemed deeply troubled about something he couldn't bring himself to say. After he left, Kosmehl had trouble going to sleep.[5]

Jochen Peiper's neighbor, Erwin Ketelhut, may have seen trouble coming, for in May 1976, the whole thing exploded. The obvious trigger was a long exposé on Peiper that Cacheux sent to Pierre Durand on May 13. Durand was the editor of the French Communist newspaper *L'Humanité* who had lived in Lure, near Vesoul. One thing was certain: Durand, a former concentration camp survivor, went on a month-long trip to the archives in Stuttgart and then the Stasi in East Berlin. Ostensibly, at the Stasi he was looking for information on other survivors from the Dora-Mittelbau Concentration Camp in Nordhausen, Germany. But Durand did take time out to request Stasi files on Jochen Peiper. From that, he must have verified that Paul Cacheux was not imagining Nazis hiding in the Haute Saône—it was true! As evidence of intrigue, he took a trip to Milan and nearby Boves in Italy.[6] The latter was particularly telling, for tiny Boves, was one of the places that had accused the old man of war crimes. Whatever the circumstances, by the spring of 1976 even Peiper knew something was afoot.

Tied to the fence post by the road, his yellow metal mailbox was frequently pilfered; letters disappeared. Although his telephone number was unlisted, he suspected his line had been tapped; sometimes there were strange sounds. Behind the scenes Paul Cacheux worked diligently to accumulate as much dirt as possible on the old

German. But it was not easy. A quiet life did little to brand a sixty-one-year-old retiree as a dangerous Nazi.[7]

Since the end of the Great War, France has always had a leftist streak, an admission within its popular politics that left open the door for parties of alternative persuasion. After World War II the French Communists were well established yet not receiving the recognition they felt due. Things were no different in the summer of 1976, except perhaps the existence of a ruling republic under President Valéry Giscard d'Estaing, who was a readily identifiable antagonist to their aims—he was working to *improve* relations with Germany. Exposing the existence of a former German war criminal on French soil could embarrass Giscard and his conservative politics.[8]

Then, on April 18, came a disturbing development in Paris. Eight men in white hoods held a press conference in the Grand Hôtel in the Place de l'Opéra in the city. "If the escaped Nazis continue to avoid justice, they will be led before God's judgment sooner than they think."[9] Two months later, on June 21, a group of seven young French Communists distributed crudely mimeographed yellow flyers from door to door on the streets of Traves.[10]

On June 21, 1976, twenty-eight-year-old André Moissé was at the offices of the *L'Est Républicain* at the big quarry-stone building at Place du 11ème Chasseurs in Vesoul. Moissé had been a journalist for three years at the tiny newspaper—there were only four others in the Vesoul office. But Moissé thought of himself as the cool correspondent. He looked the part: neat, but longer hair and beard—seventies French neo-hip.

It was a normal Monday, but it was also the longest day of the year and very warm. That afternoon, while Moissé considered the mundane stories being followed, the fifty-two-year-old leader of the local Communist party in Vesoul, André Vuillien, walked inside their offices. "Here," he motioned to Moissé, "this might interest you!" Vuillien flipped over a flyer. It had two pictures of an SS officer, one grinning derisively from the upper left and another with the lightning bolts on his collar at the bottom of the page.

> Inhabitants of Traves! A War Criminal Lives Among You, an SS Man!
> Out with Peiper!

Monsieur Vuillien departed, and Moissé was left staring at the oversized leaflet. Was there really a big-time German war criminal living in tiny Traves? Vesoul was sometimes referred to as the "Nice of the East." But altogether it was an unremarkable French town, with fourteen thousand Vésuliens made slightly infamous in 1968 by the accordion-laced waltz of Jacques Brel. The Belgian songwriter was right—it was no Paris! But if Vesoul could hardly be compared to the City of Lights, Traves was so much less! This hamlet never saw any news, nothing really of note, even for a small regional edition on the newspaper. But Moissé was always eager for a story, particularly one like this—an SS colonel here in the Haute Saône?

Looking to see for himself, Moissé jumped in his small car and drove the twenty-kilometer winding roads to Traves. Reaching the village, he motored slowly down its one street, looking from one side to the next, but there was nothing to really see. This was the usual place, no sign of new construction and no door that said *Peiper*. Then he spied a farmer. Was a German man named Peiper living here? Moissé wanted to know. Yes, the farmer nodded, but he didn't know where he was exactly. Moissé spent a few more minutes before returning to Vesoul, where he had a deadline. He quickly wrote up a short story with information from the flyer about a German SS war criminal supposedly living in Traves. But his editor from Nancy, Roland Mével, took one quick look and nixed any plan to go to print. Moissé had not found the German, and who knew whether the flyer was even true.[11]

But the very next morning young André Moissé picked up the latest copy of the French Communist party newspaper, *L'Humanité*, which was out on the street. There was the story on the front cover. What a headline! "Un membre de état-major de Himmler en Haute Saône—A Member of Himmler's Staff Living in the Haute Saône."[12] Moissé studied it over coffee. The piece detailed Peiper's past in lurid detail, alleging horrific murders in Italy, Belgium, and elsewhere. According to the Communist publication, the persona of "Eichmann Number 2" was living in luxury in Traves. "Who Protects War Criminals in France?" *Humanité* editor Pierre Durand asked rhetorically.[13]

At 8 a.m. Moissé knocked on the door of Gérard Sebille, the local editor in Vesoul. Seeing the *L'Humanité* headline, his boss finally agreed it was time to get on this story. Moissé proposed an interview to get the scoop, but the initial challenge was to find Peiper's house. A phone number should do the trick, but it wasn't in the phone book. But Moissé had a friend in the newspaper with access to "red-listed numbers." They looked up Peiper's name in that clandestine source, and there it was: 74.10.67. Moissé called Peiper right away. It was just after 9 a.m.

Moissé didn't know it, but at that very moment Lt. Col. Pierre Chappaz and Capt. Pierre Marchal, out of the Gendarmerie headquarters in Vesoul, were at Peiper's house. They told the German man they were investigating the accusations in the flyer that had appeared in Traves.

Peiper immediately identified himself on the phone, as did Moissé. But Peiper put him off. "Look, I can't talk now," he explained, "because I have to talk to the police who are here."[14]

But Moissé was not dissuaded. He repeated his intention to meet. "If you want any information," Peiper insisted, "then please speak to the Gendarmarie."

"In France the journalists write the newspapers," Moissé told him, "not the police."

Peiper listened, but said he had to go. "I'll give you a call after the police leave," Moissé said finally.

"You can always try," Peiper said before he hung up.

At about 5 p.m. Moissé called again. "Well, the gendarmes are now gone and you can come," Peiper said. "I'll wait for you at the letter box by the road."

There was no time to waste. At the news desk in the Vesoul office Moissé grabbed newspaper photographer Marc Paygnard. They had an important interview, Moissé told him. After grabbing pads and camera, the two men jumped in their car. Although late afternoon, it was still bright and sunny as Paygnard drove across the rolling, alternately wooded and green-fielded hills that separated Vesoul and Traves.

It was very hot that day, and the hot air fluttered through the rolled-down windows of the little Renault sedan.

Just twenty minutes later Moissé and Paygnard geared down to arrive in the tiny village. Just beyond the west side of Traves, on the narrow road that led to Cubry, they spotted the yellow mailbox to which Peiper had alerted them. As they drove up, a tall, wiry, white-haired man approached in khaki pants, unbuttoned plaid shirt, and sockless sneakers. They parked the car off the shoulder of the road by the mailbox. He looked more like casual country gentry than a dangerous SS man. After a quick introduction Moissé was surprised when Peiper unhitched the barbed-wire fence and motioned them to cross into the green pasture beyond. There were cows and all that went with that! But where was the house? They walked behind Peiper steadily as he muttered to them, "I still can't understand why you are here." There was still another gate across another barbed-wire fence in the middle of the pasture. That was odd, Moissé thought to himself.

Arriving at the edge of the pasture another fifty yards to the north, there was then a third gate at the barbed-wire fence. Reaching the edge of the "*le bois de Ranfort*," they found a worn path with steps leading beyond. Reaching the tree line and descending down some steps suddenly revealed a big two-story rectangular house with a red-tile roof in the middle of the woods. Peiper took the two men past the dogs in the kennel on the east side. The police had been there to talk to him about the dogs that morning, he explained. "See," he said, "I keep them under a double lock." But the dogs commenced barking loudly and charging the pen. Moissé was happy to move on. To him, the wired-haired German pointers seemed ferocious. Still, Peiper appeared confident as he led them to the south side of his property. There was even a narrow, green, manicured lawn on the south side with flower pots, planters, and even a rose bed.

Peiper motioned the two Frenchmen to a table by the terrace covered by a parasol. Moissé sat by the south wall on a wooden bench and leaned over the table with his pad. Peiper's wife briefly appeared, bearing a bottle of Perrier mineral water and some juice on a lacquered tray. Much younger than Peiper, Moissé waited for his host to drink. The sun was still bright and the afternoon exceedingly warm as they sat down. The house looked like a carefully groomed oasis in the middle of the thick forest. Peiper's plaid shirt was rolled up at the sleeves and, in the afternoon heat, was casually unbuttoned at the neck. In contrast, Moissé had a Beatles-like haircut, round John Lennon glasses, and a stylish goatee. The casual old SS colonel met the hip young French journalist. Meanwhile, Paygnard, the photographer, waited by the terrace, snapping images on his 35mm camera.

"I can see you live peacefully here," Moissé ventured to break the ice, "and we'll give that impression in the article."

Peiper gesticulated with his arms, saying he only wished to live here quietly with nature. "I am tranquil here," he said. "Listen to the birds." His bushy eyebrows revealed lines of concern on his face, even with his relaxed manner. Moissé thought he looked tired from the long questioning by the police, but his French seemed quite good, if obviously accented.

Like any good journalist, Moissé had a pad and took notes, but he made up most of his questions as he went along. Could Mr. Peiper describe his path in the war? Peiper told him he had spent a long time on the Eastern Front, but then after the Kursk offensive, he came to Italy in September 1943. Why so? Moissé wanted to know. "What!" Peiper exclaimed. "You ask me about my time in the war as a journalist and you don't remember Mussolini's fall in Italy!" Moissé was mortified. It was true, he didn't know the war well at all—he was only twenty-eight! He blushed but continued; he still had some hard questions to ask. "The massacre at Boves—was it you?"

"With regard to this affair, Simon Wiesenthal, the hunter of Mr. Eichmann, has said of me, that I am Eichmann Number 2 because he needed to find guilty culprits. . . . At Boves one of my artillery sergeants had been taken prisoner by the Maquisards of the Italian Army. We gave an artillery barrage on the village as a preparation for a rescue operation. It was very hot, like today. The houses caught on fire."

What about the shooting of American prisoners near the Malmédy crossroads during the Battle of the Bulge in December 1944?

Peiper didn't flinch. "Here is a probable version of the events: An armored half-track lost a track. Some US prisoners tried to escape in the woods. We did not have infantry to guard them. The driver shot his pistol. Confusion. The machine guns opened fire."

"You, then, were guilty?" Moissé asked.

"Concerning Malmédy," he began, "I was in charge, and therefore I was responsible. But even if I was personally guilty, I spent ten long years in Landsberg prison in Bavaria. I've paid." Moissé copied his response down, a bit surprised.

"With the passage of time, what do you think about the war?"

"I fought for my country. I did my duty as the young Frenchmen did their part. But with the history of today forgets the complex situations of the past."

"So you have regrets?"

"Yes," Peiper replied, "everyone does."

To Moissé, Peiper seemed confident. But then the French journalist felt it was time to play all his journalistic cards. He had a zinger he had composed at the Vesoul office.

"What do you think of the Nazi ideology?" Moissé posed expectantly.

"It's a ridiculous question," Peiper said. "Should I say something about this?" He seemed agitated. "I was young, idealistic, and idealistic against Bolshevism." With his blustering retort, Moissé was convinced Peiper kept his old convictions. He seemed proud. "Besides, I don't understand why people want to revisit these stories."

What did Peiper mean by that?

"As one says in Italian, 'The coffee is cold.' I think we need reconciliation in Europe."

"And the SS organization?"

"I was never political," Peiper retorted. "I was never a member of the Nazi party. I was a soldier. I've never been a member of any of the old SS veterans clubs. I'm not against them. I just don't have the time."

Moissé wanted to know what kind of work Peiper now did. "I translate military books and histories. . . . But this afternoon I am cutting wood because of my good fortune to find this marvelous place. One can enjoy nature, the fish, and the birds."

Moissé could tell the conversation was over. "Why did you accept this interview?" he asked.

"When I arrived with a camping tent, I thought the France I loved was a democratic country, respectful of the individual." Peiper paused thoughtfully, then concluded, "Maybe there are people deserving of trust."

Moissé thanked Peiper, who escorted them past the dogs that snarled loudly once more. "*Au-revoir*," Peiper called out in French. The two men crossed the pasture and opened each of the wire fence gates to reach their waiting car. Moissé made a mental note: the access to Peiper's house seemed like that for a secret German military headquarters. It was a very strange situation.

The interview had lasted about one hour. But in the end Moissé had the feeling that Peiper hoped giving a good impression would cause things to quiet down. Reaching the road, the two Frenchmen jumped in their car. Soon they were speeding back to Vesoul. In the car on the return trip Moissé spoke eagerly about the last hour, but Paygnard shrugged. Being an artist, he wasn't interested in history.

Soon they were back in the office. Paygnard headed for the dark room while Moissé sat down with his notes and recomposed the interview. By early evening he was speaking with the stenographers in Besançon who moved the story to Teletype. The short exposé, "'Ten Years in Prison: I've Paid,'" would appear the following day.[15]

In any case, Peiper's idea of defusing the whole thing backfired spectacularly. After Moissé's interview everyone was calling. Peiper consented to a radio interview on June 23, but then after that he drew the line. No more! Even German journalists started contacting him. There was a telephone call from the editors of *Der Stern* who wanted to publish a series of articles about the SS colonel and asked for assistance. When Peiper declined, the reporter was agitated. "If you do not go along, we shall finish you!"[16] In another case a Belgian author showed up at the doorstep of one of Peiper's old comrades, demanding Peiper's address. But Peiper wouldn't make the same mistake twice; Moissé's visit would be the only newspaper interview Peiper ever granted.

Was the whole thing orchestrated? The East German Communist secret police, the dreaded Stasi, maintained a simple dossier on Peiper. When *L'Humanité* sounded the attack on June 22, East Berlin had already provided basic assistance to Pierre Durand.[17] Armed with a letter from Cacheux, Durand had visited the East German archives in early 1976, where they produced a file.[18] Cacheux felt vindicated, satisfied that he had gotten word to the right people.

The French Communists called for Peiper's immediate expulsion and chided the local police commissioner for harboring someone "who had been on the staff of Himmler." Henri Bernard Pélagey, the commissioner, issued a simple statement: "His past was not known to us when he asked to establish himself in France."[19] But the Communists claimed to have more. André Vuillien, the party secretary in Vesoul, unintentionally gave away one secret when interviewed: "He was and remains leader of the HIAG (Cooperative of Former Members of the Waffen SS) for Baden Württemberg," he told the press. "This organization owns a large publishing house in Hannover, for which Peiper translates military texts. He often has German visitors and every evening he telephones the headquarters of the former SS in Hannover."

That Vuillien had the former fact wrong was one issue; another was how did he know who Peiper called on the telephone? Perhaps the answer lay with Emile Michel, then twenty-eight years old and the letter carrier for Traves. Three weeks before the events he told a reporter, "Soon it will bang at Peiper's."[20] Did Michel have access to unlisted phone numbers?

The question of whoever was eavesdropping on Peiper's phone, whether Emile Michel or someone else, was up for speculation.[21] They reported to the French Communist party of hearing about "military instructions" via his telephone number. Actually, instead of communicating with old SS members, he was speaking with his Stuttgart editor about translation problems with his latest project, *The Army of Frederick the Great*, to be published in 1977 by Motorbuch Verlag.[22] "Military instructions to the leadership of the SS" were actually mundane conversations concerning the translations. As to leadership within the HIAG, Peiper was emphatic. It wasn't true."[23]

The mayor of Traves, Ernest Rigoulot, was in a difficult position. He had been about as close to being a friend to the German colonel as anyone in the village. He had even had Peiper and some of his old veteran friends over to his restaurant! Yet now, under scathing public scrutiny, things were different. Even Rigoulot himself began to receive threatening telephone calls: "Send Peiper away or we will kill him!" one said. There were other letters too:

> Mr. Mayor,
>
> How can you tolerate in your town the presence of Joachim Peiper, ex-SS Colonel, member of Hitler's personal guard and war criminal?
>
> I cannot understand the Traves inhabitants and yourself for not reacting to this scandal. It is unacceptable that an odious individual like this now lives peaceful days on French soil. . . . I talk to you this way since I have lived the war of 1939–1940 and the sad years of the German occupation. . . . Justice be done, this man has much blood on his hands; his victims ask to be avenged.[24]

On June 26 the Federation of Resistance of the Haute Saône angrily called for Peiper's prompt ejection from France. Under pressure, the besieged administration agreed to rescind Peiper's occupancy permit, which was set to expire the following February. Rigoulot informed the members of the snarling Communist Federation that Peiper would be gone soon: his *permis de séjour* would not be renewed. Perhaps now the whole thing would gracefully settle. However, Vuillien couldn't be placated: "The Peiper affair should make the public know of the pro-German politics of Giscard."[25] Where would it end?

Threatening graffiti, scrawled in enormous white-washed letters, suddenly appeared, smeared on the pavement across the Route départementale 3 on the way out of Traves:

> PEIPER SS

No one seemed to have seen the source of the handiwork. Or so they said.[26]

Peiper's daughter Silke and her daughter Kajta were staying at Traves when it all happened. Family friend Bettina Wieselmann was there too. The whole thing was scary; the phone in Peiper's study kept on ringing. There were so many threats that Peiper did not know which to believe. Reporters flocked to his once-private haven and stalked him with microphones and telephoto lenses. The press in France, never well paid or overly considerate, staked out Le Renfort and pursued the old German each time he left his home.[27] The reporters tried to find someone in the village with ill to say of the quiet man they called *Monsieur Pépère*, but the only complaint faintly newsworthy, came from a woman who said Peiper's dogs scared her sheep. Another local was more direct with his rebuff: "He's paid his debt to society," he scowled. "Anyway, he's committed no crime in France." At Chez Néné a French pensioner sensed growing hypocrisy and threw up his hands before one reporter. "Do you think we only did good in Algeria?" he asked.[28]

Still, the press was relentless. When would Peiper leave? "I will stay in Traves," he told one reporter in exasperation. "I will not leave. I have been happy here for four years. That means a lot." Le Renfort was the only long-run peace he had known in his adult life.

> I live in an area where law and order exists. France is peace loving and they have buried the hostility which existed between France and Germany and I think also that it is very important that Germans and French people should meet and talk to understand that the future is only possible if we become friends and the political grudges are now forgotten. . . . I would like to stay here because I like France and I like this little village of Traves. Until now the contact and the situation with the neighbors in this little village was very good. We've never had any problems and that's why the leaflets distributed yesterday was such a big surprise for me.[29]

"Aren't you worried that the people in the village may look at you differently?" the reporter asked.

"Yes, I'm sure they will. But what should I do? I've nothing to hide and I don't need to defend myself. If someone attacks me, there is the French police who will protect me. And I'm under the impression that I live in an area where there is law and order."

But law and order meant little to rabid reporters—a story was everything. We are "in the craziness," one said of the siege.[30] Peiper agreed when he wrote a friend:

> The atmosphere and reporting is now as if I had been found hiding after a long hunt. There are demonstrations in Vesoul in front of the police headquarters by the "anciens combattants" and the "résistance." An intimidation campaign is underway. Threatening letters, "Red commandos" announce kidnapping me to Italy. Shouting and telephone calls announce the burning of my house, which has to be put under police protection. My dogs—in the meantime, are promoted by the press to wolves. So is the fact that I make my rounds with

binoculars and a hunting rifle. In other words, overnight the peaceful paradise has become a position under siege. I shall move in the fall, in case the Communists give me that much time.[31]

At one point Peiper momentarily lost his patience. "If I am here now," he said in exasperation, "it is because the French lacked courage in 1940." Each who spoke with him asked about his presence in Italy where the northern village near Cuneo was burned. "Boves was not a massacre, but a battle," Peiper insisted. "War is war."[32] Always they asked him about Malmédy, where the American prisoners were shot. For the pesky reporters he produced at least two versions. "So, the ultimate responsibility was mine," he said. "I have paid my debt to society. Even if I had been guilty, I have spent more than ten years in prison. I have paid dearly. I deplore the publicity that has surrounded my past life and would like to just live in peace."[33]

It was useless. Journalists knew nothing of the terrible ferocity of modern combat. "He who is a soldier," Peiper sneered, "knows that war is not fought in kid gloves. What is the good of washing dirty linen?"[34] Blame for the loss of his peaceful idyll? "Scab scratchers," Peiper concluded.

For the gray-haired Mayor Rigoulot, the threats, the crazy press, and an increasingly scornful public brought the matter to a head. That he had nearly been a friend to the German seemed carefully forgotten. On one hand he feigned defiance. "We know Peiper here," he told reporters. "If we wanted him to leave, we would tell him ourselves. We don't take orders from others."[35]

In spite of his professed independence, Rigoulot's worries grew. He went to see Peiper at his home on Tuesday, July 6, 1976.[36] When Peiper invited him inside, he was shocked by the man's diminished appearance. Three weeks of siege had taken their toll. Rigoulot laid the whole thing out. Peiper admitted the police in Vesoul had told him that they could not assure protection; they could patrol only during the day. Between taking statements from Peiper and reporting on his dogs' worsening habit of chasing local sheep at Scey sur Saône, the gendarmes were becoming familiar guests. Peiper reassured the mayor. "He said he would never shoot French people if they attacked him," Rigoulot said.[37] But that was hardly of comfort. He begged Peiper to leave.

"I can't," he insisted. "They'll burn down my house."

The mayor agreed. "I know they will," he implored, "but they'll burn it down whether you go or stay. Save yourself, man!"

"They won't try anything if I'm in the house," Peiper opined. Traves was all he had. "Besides," Peiper flatly stated, "no one can hate that much after thirty years."[38]

As Rigoulot left, he shook his head. Did Peiper really believe that? "Le passé n'est pas mort, il n'est même pas passé." In France Albert Camus had made William Faulkner famous with a single line.

"THE PAST IS NOT DEAD," CAMUS CHOSE FOR HIS THEATRICAL ADAPTATION of *Requiem pour une nonne*, "it is not even past."[39]

Chapter 22

LA FÊTE NATIONALE

BY THE END OF JUNE 1976, JOCHEN PEIPER HAD REACHED A POINT AT WHICH he knew he would eventually need to leave. On Friday, June 25, and again on July 1, heckling French youths appeared close to his house, throwing stones and dirt clods. Shouts drove them off, but Peiper saw that as a portent of things to come. "The porcelain is broken," he wrote one friend.[1] Maybe he could lease the place. "Such a rental income and my lecturing and translation work would enable me financially to stay in the city—what a terrible thought."[2] For now, however, he would have to protect the place from those who wanted to torch it. On July 9 he wrote to his old tank-leader friend Arndt Fischer, who had been asking to visit:

> Dear Arndt,
>
> I regret very much that at present the visit did not work out, because of the situation here, the more it so appears that it cannot be either in the future. The expulsion from paradise started on June 21 with a malicious article in *L'Humanité*, the official newspaper of the Communist Party of France. . . . The other day a leaflet campaign followed nearby then a road painting action in Traves and finally, the press, radio and television upon me.
>
> The next step of the organized campaign was murder threats by telephone, announcements that my house would be set on fire and my dogs poisoned if I did not leave the country immediately. . . . Briefly my peaceful haven and retreat turned overnight into a fortress under siege. . . .
>
> My wife and I must count on another change of position. We may have little more than half a year for its preparation. If possible, we want to go to Bavaria—in case it is possible, within reach of the suburban traffic of Munich. We would consider a small apartment, if we can, surrounded by greenery. . . . I would very much like to come over for a personal discussion, but it can't be done for the reasons mentioned above. I must hold the position in the literal meaning of the word.[3]

The week before, he drove his car to Stuttgart to visit with his longtime editor, Wolfgang Schilling, at Motorbuch Verlag.[4] He had one manuscript to deliver and another he needed to discuss. When he arrived, he handed over the completed package. On the new one, he told Schilling, his progress was delayed. He described the chaos of recent days—they were writing "SS Peiper" on the streets of Traves in big white letters. He would have to drive back that same day, he informed his editor, because his tormentors might try setting fire to his home.

"At least in the war, when you were stuck in an untenable position," he lamented, "you could at least retreat from those shooting at you from the front. I cannot leave." Usually calm, Schilling thought his old associate looked surprisingly old and frail since their last meeting. As Peiper left his office, the former SS officer sighed as they shook hands. His thoughts returned to the 1940s. "You know, it is a little bit like during the war, there is the feeling in the gut," he said, looking Herr Schilling in the eyes. "It feels like that." He knew that back then Schilling was a veteran too—if just with the regular army. "It was better during the war," Peiper said. "Then you always had comrades on your left and the right."[5] Schilling nodded. Peiper returned to his car and drove off.

At Peiper's home, the phone was a constant irritation. It was either reporters wanting to talk or anonymous threats: "We shall burn your house down!" Later there was another: "You will be killed on the 14th."[6] He shrugged it off, or at least pretended to.

The old SS colonel was still feeling defiant as he watched the summer thunderstorms roll through Eastern France. If his past would not let him be, then he would seize the offensive and return to his neglected book on Malmédy. On Monday, July 12, he wrote to his friend Rudi Lehmann, the chronologist for the Leibstandarte Adolf Hitler. He would write a book, he said, about the long persecution of their troop and the ruinous campaigns of the Nazi hunters Simon Wiesenthal and Robert Kempner:

> I have come to the conclusion that now more than ever, I must write the book of the road from Malmédy to Landsberg. It does not matter where to we shall be driven. I shall find a place for setting up my typewriter; I shall not have a lack of words in order to tear off the masks of people who put the rope around our neck in 1946 and who today continue with their execution helpers, Wiesenthal and Kempner, to make capital from their revenge. . . . I just received another ultimatum from the "Brigade Rouge" that they would put the red rooster [fire] on my roof. . . . May they come. I have loaded and armed my gun. I would prefer that these heroes would not come until fall, when my wife will again be in Munich and we have calmly made the anticipated move to Bavaria. Thank God, eternal wandering makes the luggage lighter.[7]

As if pressed by time and events, he was typing away each day on the book about Malmédy. He had consciously decided against an appeal for material from his old comrades in Der Freiwillige—he wanted facts rather than saccharine remembrance.[8]

In a letter written on Malmédy's thirty-first anniversary, December 17, 1975, Peiper joked with his comrades about the possibility of revisiting the Ardennes and writing a best-seller. The tremendous monetary success of Albert Speer's *Inside the Third Reich* was on his mind. He had also recently read the memoirs of Gerhard Engel, *Army Adjutant with Hitler* and derisively suggested *A Spy in Hitler's Court* as a more descriptive title. Like the Speer book, Peiper saw Engel's as an abomination:

"opportunistic contemporary history and not the historical truth."[9] For his story, he would do better.

Just a week later, he was writing to his old buddy Ernst Klink in the Federal Archives on the same subject. He would write a book about Malmédy, he emphasized, but "I would like to add something that is extraordinarily important."

> During our trial the prosecution always started out about a "criminal Order of the Day of the Army," in which the troops allegedly were called upon to do away with prisoners of war. Despite this obvious nonsense, we did not succeed to find anywhere the Army Order of the Day issued before the Ardennes Offensive. It certainly existed, but the prosecution sat on it. And that had a good reason. I am hoping that this document is no longer out of circulation, but in the meantime has emerged. Can that be determined? It would be great, if I could bring it into my book, and thus, after the fact, show the entire trial *ad absurdum*.[10]

In one collection, Klink was able to locate the 6th Panzer Army address before the attack, but, as Peiper suspected, there was no mention of "taking no prisoners." But was that *the* order?[11] He began writing with the new year, appealing to the widow of his former defense attorney for help.

> Dear Mrs. Everett,
>
> . . . Many years have elapsed since you heard from me last, years in which history has been repeating itself and the human nature has not much changed—despite all the bombastic statements and solemn vows of the post war era.
>
> Today, my wife and I are very retired in our romantic little refuge, surrounded by virginal forests, water and animals and are having peace and independence at long last. Nevertheless, man cannot escape the past and discard his memories like an old suit—particularly if one is confronted with it, time and time again in a distorted version.
>
> In the coming summer, thirty years have gone by since the Malmédy trial made headlines, time enough to look back at it in a dispassionate and—if possible—unbiased way. I am therefore planning a book on the fate of my then combat group "From the Battle of the Bulge to Landsberg." The motives that guide me to tackle such a venture are not of a materialistic nature, but rather I feel obliged to the great number of my former comrades—soldiers who did nothing but their duty—who have collectively been discriminated against by the wicked political move of an insolent victor.[12]

Peiper asked for help with documents and photographs for his book. Only in the postscript to the letter did Peiper indicate there was any concern. And there, he carefully asked Everett's widow to leave off his former military rank in addressing a response. Otherwise, he feigned indifference and informed his old comrades that he would forge ahead.

Each morning he was typing. It was quiet then and the best time for him to work. First tea, a look at the paper, and then reading and typing. And more typing. Tapping away amid the pines and the birds, toiling on his long-considered book."I feel obligated to our old bunch to finally open my mouth," he said. "They have a right to that."[13] But not all the veterans wanted him to stir the pot. Most critical of all was Dietrich Ziemssen, who had dealt with the Malmédy issue for years—and had tired of its poisonous effect. Peiper had written the former divisional operations officer for documents on the Malmédy case, but now received a salvo of dismay.

Ziemssen addressed Peiper as *Gaeta*—as if he, like Mussolini—was exiled. "After this, I don't want to know anything anymore about the Malmédy case," he said flatly. He was sick of it. "And I promise you already now that I will not read your upcoming 'standard' work."[14]

Why *was* he writing it now? Undeterred, Peiper fired back. It was something he *had* to do:

> Much evil was done by Germans or in the name of Germany under Hitler—there are no excuses—but not everything blamed on us is true—particularly what professional scab-scratchers want to perpetuate as reasons for restitution.
>
> Yet as certain as death, there cannot be a trusting and unprejudiced common future as long as the victors do not concede that they too have not always been angels and should grant us good faith and the same ideals for which they have purported to have crusaded. The Second World War dug a deep ditch between the winners and the losers, between good and evil. If we do not succeed to bridge this ditch by an honest and trusting handshake, we shall all fall into it together.[15]

Peiper appropriately closed his freshly typed book forward with a stanza from the first Greek master of tragedy, Aeschylus:

> If the victors
> Respect the temples and gods
> Of the vanquished,
> Then, perhaps,
> They will not be defeated by
> By their own victory.

Having written a forceful opening and collected archival materials, Peiper seemed poised to move ahead. But *From Malmédy to Landsberg* was not to be. Despite professed enthusiasm for the project, the disquiet of the New Year derailed the book's progress.

In Traves at Le Renfort, Peiper circled the wagons once again. Although he referred to his tormentors derisively as "the heroes," even to his old war buddy Lehmann, there was a certain desperation in his language over the weeks. By July 12, he wrote the German ambassador in Paris for help. Above all, Peiper feared the Communists. He was convinced they were at the bottom of the poisonous proceedings.

> As a German residing in France for four years, I am turning to you with the request for legal protection. . . . On 21 June, 1976, a local leaflet and graffiti action against me took place, which was used by the Communist Party of France to call attention of the population that a former SS Colonel and war criminal lives in the middle. . . . It was the start signal for a well-organized press campaign in which old resentments were stirred up, horror fairy tales from the war were warmed over, and a general hunt for the Fascists began. . . . M. Henri Bernard de Pelagey, the Prefect of Vesoul, is under continued political pressure from the left. . . . So far, he has suggested that I leave the country until the grass has grown over the story. I do not consider such a retreat to be a solution, inasmuch as the local gendarmes are convinced that immediately after my departure our house will go up in flames as a sign of victory for the Résistance.[16]

That same day, on July 12, 1976, Peiper's old Waffen SS veteran friend Dr. Ernst Klink was writing to him, reporting on his efforts to help with the new book. A long-fighting machine gunner from his outfit, Klink now worked at the Institute for Military History of the German Army, the Militärgeschichtliches Forschungsamt, (MGFA) in Freiburg im Breisgau as a historian.[17] He had spoken to attorneys about Peiper's dilemma. "There is no basis for immediate expulsion based on the facts, but the Prefect might deny any extension based on the reasoning that your presence alone is a constant threat to peace and order. . . . ." No dice.

Klink candidly suggested Peiper request for a stay of his expulsion until February of 1977 and to use the time to arrange for a favorable sale of Le Renfort. "I can imagine that you now think of me as cowardly or stupid," Klink emphasized in his letter, "but I would not condone any persuasion for 'perseverance' or 'holding the position' to be anything but absurd and destructive."

"We know each other from desperate situations too well. You know I do not advise against my convictions. It is understandable that you have given up writing the Malmédy story, among other reasons for the lack of enthusiasm from the old bunch. . . . After solving your current problem of existence, we can talk about all that calmly. Until then, I am offering you, and especially your wife, our protective harbor to weather the storm."[18]

Klink's offer for refuge was still in the mail on July 13 as the eve approached of the most honored holiday in France. Calling back to the storming of the Bastille in 1789, it is most famous as a day of unbridled French passion, celebration, and bacchanalia: exploding firecrackers and dancing in the streets until dawn with wine and more wine.

The 187th celebration, on Wednesday, July 14, 1976, was little different. The bright vertical panels of blue, white, and red fluttered patriotically under the Arc de Triomphe, although it was beastly hot in Paris on the holiday's eve. But as the colorful annual military parade strode down the Champs-Élysées, the marching khaki clad soldiers were drenched in a sudden downpour. Onlookers took to umbrellas, but the drought-stricken farmers around the city were delighted. Yet there was no rain 360 kilometers away in tiny Traves. Temperatures there soared as if to mirror everyone's enthusiasm for the glory of France.[19] It was *la fête nationale*—the great French national holiday.

On the eve of the holiday on Tuesday, July 13, Peiper was up early. At 7:30 a.m. he was on the road to Traves. When Madame Louette saw him striding toward her farm, she thought the old German was coming for milk, but he passed without stopping. A little bit later he came by again. Sigurd drove off in the powerful BMW coupe to see her friend, the sister of Mercedes legendary press chief Artur "Kaj" Keser in Bâle, Switzerland.[20]

Jochen had told her of the threats and intimidation of the local youths. They were nothing to worry about, he said. But his tone wasn't reassuring. She had been planning the trip for some time, and he thought it good reason for her to stay away a few days until the ruckus died down.[21] He expected his old buddy Ernst Klink, but he hadn't shown. And the letter Klink had sent the day before was still in the mail. He sat down to the typewriter to bang off another quick note:

> Traves, 13 July 1976
>
> Towaritsch:
>
> Obviously, I misunderstood, waited vainly for you, and telephoned around without result. As one does not yet know how the experiment here with the German-French friendship will end, I have packed together all my records for my book for you. It is not advisable to keep it here and I will have to do the writing elsewhere. If Miss Wieselmann should approach you (our deputy daughter)—trained journalist and interested in my press documents—please be of assistance to her. In the meantime, good vacation, heartfelt greetings. See you soon.
>
> Jochen Peiper[22]

Now he was alone.

On the way to Switzerland, Sigurd Peiper stopped by the Black Forest abode of their family friend Dr. Benno Müller at his home near the church in Kirchhofen. She visited with them for a few hours by the big church there before heading on. Over lunch she described the mounting harassment and threats. Traves was becoming unbearable, she told them. While she was there, to reassure her, Benno telephoned Jochen in Traves. "I am here," he told his old friend, "and standing guard duty." Although Müller assured Sigurd that her husband was okay, he saw good reason to worry.

Benno did not tell her of the conversation he had the previous day. As he had been speaking with Jochen nearly each afternoon, he had noticed his friend seemed depressed. As if to reinforce his impression, Sigurd told them the episode was taking its toll. Her husband was "profoundly disturbed by the telephone threats" she said.[23] The Müllers listened with concern but could do little more than bid Frau Peiper well as she motored off to Bâle.[24] Benno Müller had advised against Peiper moving to France in the first place. His young wife patiently listened.

Late that morning, at 11 a.m., Peiper met his moody German neighbor, Erwin Ketelhut, by his yellow mailbox at the road. He slipped the letter to Klink inside. Ketelhut was off to do errands in the village. Although the men seldom spoke, each was quietly aware of the renewed threat. Ketelhut saw that there was a letter with the newspaper in the bright yellow metal box. Without opening it, Peiper held up the envelope. "You see," he said, "here are the threats again." He told his German neighbor that his agitators had just called on the phone. "They warned me that tonight I and my dogs will be dead!" Peiper laughed. "They say the day will be hot!"[25] He waved his hand in dismissal. Yet his neighbor sensed a palpable tension.

Ketelhut offered to help and suggested that he come to stay at his big house by the mill. Even the request was awkward. Peiper thanked him, but politely refused. "He was absolutely calm and quiet," Ketelhut recalled. "When I offered him my help, he declined it. Peiper looked a bit frail, but defiant, 'I could be shot dead, but I won't let myself be beaten into a cripple. When they come, I shall defend my house!'"[26]

"Besides," Peiper concluded, "these people are not very courageous." He did accept Ketelhut's loan of a shotgun and the offer to stand guard over the approach to his property. Would he reconsider the offer to stay? "Bah!" he waved his hand again before heading back to his house across the pasture. "I will wait for my aggressors. They lack the nerve."[27]

Later that day, at 3 p.m., three policemen came to Le Renfort to confront Peiper-about a new complaint regarding the dogs. It seemed that a farmer had lodged a legal action in Vesoul; Peiper's "lions" had killed some more of his sheep. The police, escorted by Monsieur Caillet, the bailiff, served a summons. Peiper would have to pay to appear at the Vesoul court on September 29. It was more bad news, but the old SS colonel seemed unfazed. He politely invited the men into his house and calmly acknowledged the problem with his dogs. He showed them the new kennel. He had said nothing to them about the threats he had received that morning.[28]

At about the same time in Vesoul, Jacques Delaval, the owner of the café Champ de Foire and a former partisan himself, tacked up an announcement for the enjoyment of his patrons. Everyone in town called him by his nickname, *Riquette*. Known for practical jokes, he had been following "*L'Affaire Peiper*" closely. "Tonight," the crude poster announced, "big fireworks in Traves."[29]

JUST BEFORE DARK, PEIPER PREPARED HIS WEAPONS—SHOTGUN SHELLS, RIFLE rounds, and a loaded revolver. He prepared a vigil on the balcony of the upstairs east part of the home and another position facing west from the terrace on the west. Not far away, Erwin Ketelhut did the same, arming himself with two loaded rifles at his side on the balcony, facing Le Renfort from the west. He could not see Peiper's house for the trees, particularly in the night. Ketelhut's aches and pains were bothering him again. He pilfered the medicine cabinet.

Meanwhile, Peiper also posted himself on the eastern balcony, spread out the revolver and placed the shotgun with ammunition on the table. By the west terrace he left his loaded rifle, where he faced the access road that led from Traves to Cubry. There, he kept a pair of powerful binoculars within easy reach.[30] Twilight came.

Nothing happened. The night was hot and dry—an airless heat. At sunset, he opened the wooden shutters on the windows downstairs to let things cool off. The dogs were in the kennel; anyone approaching from the road would have to pass their attentive guard. To his front were the trees he had planted as saplings—oaks to remind him of his native Prussia and the linden trees that held a special place. All was quiet.

Hours earlier, at 7 p.m., he had briefly phoned Ernst Klink to see why he hadn't shown. The two men spoke briefly. Peiper told him he was sending material he intended for use on the autobiography that would be published by Motorbuch Verlag.[31] But that was not the focus of their conversation. Peiper had invited Klink to come down to stay with him through the craziness of Bastille Day. But aside from their conversation, both men really thought back to another desperate summer day, long before 1976.

On July 12, Ernst Klink always thought of Jochen Peiper with great poignancy. It was that day, long ago in faraway Russia during a cataclysmic fight near Kursk in 1943, that Peiper had saved his life. Klink was severely wounded on a tank-strewn battlefield and collapsed near death. In desperate combat Peiper repulsed a desperate Russian tank counterattack on the knobby grassland of Hill 252.2 with a shouldered Panzerfaust. One of his men had mounted a Russian T-34 and killed its commander with his knife. The enemy assault turned back, Peiper had packed the wounded SS sergeant onto one of his halftracks. The SPW transport took him to a waiting Fieseler Storch. Then, flying through explosion-torn skies, the plane took Klink to a field hospital, where toiling doctors stopped the loss of blood.

Ernst Klink knew he owed his life to Peiper. Now, he would come to Traves if Peiper needed him. Yet, in July 1976, Klink was ailing; the same war wound was acting up; his leg had never been the same after his last fight at Operation Zitadelle. And the broiling summer heat only made things worse. For relief, he spent most days in the cooler forested hills near his home around Baden.

"Stay home," Peiper said. That was an order. Over the phone the two briefly discussed his plight. They had just called, Peiper told Klink. Their words were short:

"We are going to get you tonight," they said.

"Fine. I will wait for you."

Klink noted no sign of worry in his friend's voice as he recounted the threat. On the contrary, he seemed "merry and in good spirits."[32]

A Waffen SS hero never shrank from confrontation.

Chapter 23

RECKONING

It was just before 9 p.m. on the night of Tuesday, July 13, 1976, that the pale yellow moon inched out from behind the fir trees and oak boughs lining the Saône River. It was near Traves, France, that the frogs croaked and the crickets sang in the dry evening air. Along the road that led out of the tiny village, on the balcony of the house he called "Le Renfort," sat Joachim Peiper.

The sky was clear, and other than the ordinary noises of the night, there was scarcely a sound. The old SS man sat patiently on the balcony, paying more attention to the full moon and the washed-out stars than anything else. Although he had bolted the other doors, the one leading out to the terrace on the west was open, and he left the window shutters open downstairs in his library on the west side to the terrace as well as one leading into the kitchen. Likely he sought to bring some fresh air into his home and to provide a vantage toward the road and Ketelhut's house.[1] When posted on the terrace, he kept his E. Leitz-Wetzlar binoculars handy to survey the road to Cubry. Then, as if on patrol, he slowly made his way back to the balcony on the east, which had the most commanding view.[2] It was hot—unusually hot for Eastern France. The evening air was sultry and warm, punctuated by a light summer breeze rustling the birch leaves to waft from his flower boxes.[3] The moon cast an eerie glow over the scene as he gazed across the wooden balcony rails with his back to the gurgling river. His thoughts wandered. His wife was away. Although his friends in Germany called regularly, he was alone.

And not all telephone calls were friendly. Anonymous threats over the preceding week warned of intentions to set his house on fire that night. These were local Communist "heroes" with whom he had become all too familiar. He had driven off several harassing youths over the last two weeks, once on the evening of June 25 and again on July 1. Peiper tended to discount their hazing—the worst the delinquent kids had done was to pelt his house with dirt clods. Still, he stood guard. A shotgun he had borrowed from his German neighbor was close at hand, leaning against the edge of the door leading out to the balcony from his bedroom upstairs. He sat by it on the east side of the house.

He trained his ears on the night for unusual sounds—only faraway laughter from the village and an occasional forbidden firecracker. It was, after all, Bastille Day. As hours passed, the glowing moon loomed high overhead, casting an amber light on the pine boughs and the parched fields beyond. He peered out into the blue shadows in the forest.

Scarcely two hundred meters away to the west his German neighbor, Erwin Ketelhut, walked out onto the terrace of his expansive Bavarian-style home. He looked through the balmy night toward the woods that concealed Peiper's abode. It was 11:30 p.m. All was calm. His harassed neighbor must have been right—the threats were a bluff. He returned inside to go to bed. With age and arthritis, his left shoulder was bothering him and insomnia had recently made nights restless. He took a sleeping pill and retired to his bed to read.

At about the same time, Madame Maria Thérèse Guyot was chatting with another farmer's wife as the two sat on the steps of their home in the center of the village of Traves. They took in the beautiful summer evening. The sky was clear with stars. So modest was their village that there was hardly ever any traffic in the middle of the day, much less late at night. Yet as they spoke, the women were surprised to see several cars drive past. First came a metallic-colored Volkswagen, then fifteen minutes later three cars in a caravan. The middle vehicle was an ambulance. "That's funny," Madame Guyot remarked to her friend. "It's driving with its headlights off." The two women shrugged and said good-night.[4]

Even in the middle of summer, many French sleep with their windows and shutters closed. In little Traves a closed shutter helped avoid being awakened at 4 a.m. by boisterous fishermen making their way down to the Saône for the daily contest with the *truite*—trout. Madame Guyot, however, liked the sounds of the street and the fresh air, particularly on a night as warm as this. She left her casement window swung wide open. She was lying on her bed at the edge of sleep when she heard five loud explosions. She rose from her pillow, a little startled. "Oh, yes," she smiled to herself, reclining back to her pillow. "Bastille Day!" Soon she was dreaming again.

Not far away, explosions also woke Madame Madeleine Rollin. "Oh," she thought to herself, "the youths of the village who have not gone to the dance are now setting off firecrackers." Seeing the luminous hands together at the top of her alarm clock, she too settled back to sleep.[5] Two other local farmers, Messieurs Jean-Michel Farque and Robert Bournon, also heard a series of loud bangs just before midnight. But they too were not alarmed.[6]

Across the great nation, Frenchmen danced through the night. Storming of the Bastille! Rockets shrieked into the dark sky, and firecrackers popped and banged. In Traves the local firemen roasted a whole pig behind the church as they always did. There was laughter and drinking—a French redneck holiday. Everyone ate their fill of pork washed down with red wine, and then stumbled home. That was the extent of the big celebration; the fireworks, normally on tap at 10:30, were canceled due to the drought. Even so, no one paid attention to the dull thud of explosions from around the mill just after midnight. Ketelhut would later vaguely admit hearing what sounded like a hunter's rifle.[7] Yet soon he was snoring from the sleeping pill. Just revelry—it was the great national holiday!

While France celebrated, events closed in on Jochen Peiper. How it all began, no one knows. Yet, somewhere before the woods, cars driving quickly without headlights pulled off the road. Peiper sat waiting on his balcony. Fence cutters clipped the barbed wire to the west, and dark shapes moved toward Le Renfort. Steps at the edge of the woods. Barking dogs and shots near his dog kennel off to the southeast. Perhaps they taunted the SS man; perhaps there was only shooting and shouts. One assailant pumped bullets into the dog kennel, the hounds tearing off the wire mesh door in panic.

In the darkness the assailants surrounded the house, at least one on the east and at least two on the west—but likely a number more.[8] Did he see torches being lit or his assailants moving around the house in the moonlight? The phantom on the east firing at his dogs kept Peiper to that side of the house while the others worked their way to the west side. Several 6.35mm (.25 caliber) rounds were fired from a small-caliber weapon at the dogs and toward the house. It was no more than a percussive pellet pistol, but the reports were loud enough in the night. Peiper let loose first with the Remington shotgun from the balcony on the east, blasting off a deafening warning shot upward into the dark trees. Shredded leaves floated down.[9] At first he stood, but with his assailants still firing, he dropped momentarily to a prone firing position. He fired two more shots to the right; the last one fired from the doorway to the balcony.[10] The three expended shell cases spilled onto the balcony or to the ground, and the shotgun was out of ammunition. Peiper abandoned the gun on the concrete balcony floor near the bedroom entrance, its breech still smoking. He tucked the short-barreled .38 caliber Colt revolver into his belt.[11] There was smoke. His house was on fire! He ran inside.

On the west side he had left open a shuttered window to the library from the veranda, likely for a field of view to the west, as he left his binoculars on the terrace outside. But his assailants seem to have found that weak point. At least one Molotov cocktail splattered against the walls inside the library downstairs, the ugly orange gasoline flames instantly setting ablaze everything they touched.

After the short encounter with his attackers on the east side of the house, and even though hobbled by the phlebitis in his right leg, Peiper moved swiftly through his upstairs bedroom to the study on the west side, where there was already dense smoke. Holding his breath, he trotted quickly down the stairs right into the blaze, the pistol in hand. Could Peiper have summoned help? The telephone downstairs was working. Yet who could he call?[12] And besides, the fire blazed there and he was still under attack.[13] Instead, reaching the bottom of the stairs on the west side, he emerged on the glassed terrace, banging away in the darkness with his pistol toward the woodshed to the west.[14] He fired with the rifle as well. The fire bombers seemed to have come from there. Scare them off!

His assailants likely ran, but the house was really burning now.[15] His study blazed—his books! His favorite chair! Parched from the hot July sun, Le Renfort was surrounded by dense shrubs and undergrowth. He had planted oaks and ash saplings less than a meter from the house walls. Flames quickly spread across the hardwood floors and wooden furniture. Within minutes the entire house burned like a torch. Flames raced up the varnished wood-panel walls. The roof trusses caught fire above.[16] Amid the leaping flames his mind raced: save all that was precious—his nascent manuscript on Malmédy![17]

Peiper had crammed valuable papers into two wooden drawers and an attaché case. The contents were a hodge-podge of legal and insurance forms and even the recollections of an old French SS veteran. The manuscript was tied up with string, addressed and ready to go to the publisher. Yet more important were personal items from his life: letters from his children, written during the long years while he awaited execution in Landsberg as well as an old copy of *Mein Kampf*. The latter had sentimental value—it had been given on his wedding day. He likely fired a couple of times with the pistol to make sure his attackers had not returned. With the leather attaché and drawers in his arms, the old man ran down the stairs and out through the glassed-veranda to place them safely out of harm's way near the garden. Dashing out beyond the smoke, he stacked the valuables by a pile of his carefully cut firewood in the wood shed.[18] Yet in his haste some papers were strewn about the yard.[19]

Where would he go? To Ketelhut's house? No. Instead, he ran back to his burning house to the stairs just inside the west veranda where the fire was spreading. If he had wanted to call, there was no way now; the library just inside the veranda downstairs with the telephone was a sheet of fire. There were more important things upstairs! With the revolver in his belt, the old Waffen SS commander ascended the stairs into a hell of fire and heat. In the bedroom on the east side by the balcony he scooped up armfuls of clothes and flung them out of the bedroom window off the balcony. He headed back to the library on the west side, where there was more pistol and shotgun ammunition as well as his Anschutz .22 caliber carbine.[20] He had only a single round left in the pistol.

Flames towered from the lower floor, sucking all oxygen from the hot air. The fire roiled with noxious smoke from the burning lacquer paneling. He choked on carbon monoxide, unable to see or breathe in the acrid atmosphere.[21] The entire floor below him was alit from the kerosene and the wood paneling. And now the roof above was a sea of flames. Suddenly it ended. The heavy tile roof and upstairs floor, a curtain of fire, crashed onto him. Jochen Peiper disappeared.

From the road that led west to Cubry-lès-Soing, two youths, returning from the dance, spotted the fire at 1:10 a.m.[22] At first, they took the orange glimmer for fireworks. Yet this seemed strange, as the prefect's police office had strictly forbidden them due to the extraordinary dryness. Drawing closer, the youths saw the Bastille-eve apparition was a blazing house. At first, they screeched to a stop in Traves and sent out an alarm. Soon the village siren wailed. It was 1:15 a.m. The warbling siren woke Madame Rollin again, and she hastily left her home in her nightgown to join others sleepily taking to the streets. In the sky to the west, there were rising flames. "It is the house of Peiper burning!" someone yelled.[23]

It was true. Yet by the time Traves's volunteer firemen arrived and were able to cross the pasture-like field and reach the house, Le Renfort was burning furiously. And when the eleven frustrated firemen under Lieutenant Raymond Obriot got their aging equipment in place, they found the hydrant pump not working.[24] All they could do was hook up to a puny garden house faucet at the house, which made little difference with a blaze like this. By 1:40 a.m. the inferno had consumed most of the villa. And still it burned.

Thirty-five minutes later another group of firefighters from Vesoul arrived. With the great heat of the fire and the dry heat of the evening, they could not get close. When they at last could bring cascading sheets of water onto the conflagration it was too late—save the eastern balcony, the house was completely burned. When the hydrants shut off, only blackened block walls remained.

Raymond Louette was one of the first on the scene when the firefighters arrived. The farmer had a cold from spending long days on his tractor and had slept upstairs on the eve of the Bastille. He had the shutters open for fresh air. "We heard people talking excitedly outside the house," he said. "It was the local priest who woke us up. We hurried down the road. When we got there the firemen were already on the scene." The fire crew pulled out the fence posts in the field so they could turn the tank truck around, but they seemed to be having a lot of trouble with their equipment.[25]

Other villagers trampled across the pasture toward the fire, some wearing raincoats over their pajamas, with the flames turning their sullen faces a dull red. Police Inspector Roger Lavaux was awakened at his home in Dijon at 3 a.m. by a surprising call: there was a fire at the Peiper place in Traves. He hastily left for the little French village, reaching the scene just after 6 a.m. He arrived at the crossing from the road, where he saw "flames leaping into the night." When he arrived at the house it was still burning furiously. There was, he recalled, "a great, great heat." There were papers and clothes strewn about the base of the burning home. Captain Pierre Marchal, in charge of the Gendarmerie in Vesoul, and seven other gendarmes from Scey-sur-Saône were already there. Dozens of cars were now parked on the edges of the field, and a crowd of shocked onlookers gathered.

But to Roger Lavaux on the scene, it quickly became apparent that the fire was no accident. About ten meters from the house Raymond Louette called police attention to an empty beer bottle filled with kerosene and stuffed with a Dacron rag—a dud. One thing was interesting about that: it was tied onto the bottle with twine in a style reflecting a local farmer's knot. Somewhat further back from the house, the metal top to a Jerri can was found, not far from where the barbed-wire fence had been clipped. A pair of abandoned wire cutters was found nearby. Not far away was an oddly pressed and folded half-empty cellophane package—the powder blue Gauloises cover, with six unsmoked cigarettes still inside.

Peiper's two hunting dogs, Timm and Tamm, were nowhere to be found. When located later the next day near Cubry, one of the two hounds, Timm, was wounded with a 6.35mm bullet in its jaw and had also been grazed across the head by another bullet.[26] The small slug removed from Timm, the dogs were otherwise okay. By morning the ruins were still smoldering. The Remington Sportsmaster Ketelhut had loaned to Peiper was found on the southeast balcony. The binoculars were discovered where Peiper had left them on the west end of the house. Several shots had been fired from the semi-automatic shotgun; three empty shell casings were strewn about the ground below the balcony at the foot of an oak tree.

On further examination, the barbed-wire fence on the southern boundary of the property had been cut in not one, but two places. Near the woodshed on the west side of the property Lavaux discovered two wooden drawers full of documents, a briefcase, and what would turn out to be Peiper's uncompleted manuscript on Malmédy. Some women's clothes had been thrown out on the yard.[27] The documents included identification documents, insurance papers, medical records, an unfinished manuscript, a copy *Mein Kampf*, and a last will and testament to his wife. Tantalizingly, on the end pages of *Mein Kampf* was a handwritten dedication from Adolf Hitler.[28]

LAVAUX FRETTED OVER THE EVIDENCE; WITH THE HUNDRED-ODD ONLOOKERS, he had no idea whether things had been moved around. It was obvious things had been taken. In the days that followed, he and his assistants pieced together the evidence. They found evidence of bullet traces that had ripped through the crowns of the overhanging trees: several of the shots had been fired upward. Unable to make out his assailants in the night, but warned by his dogs, it appeared that the former SS colonel had fired warning shots into the air. The first shot had been fired to the southeast toward the village, the second shot from a prone position and upward into the trees. The third and final shotgun blast was evidently fired from the doorway from their bedroom to the balcony, almost straight to the east. He had expended all the shotgun ammunition he possessed and had not attempted to reload in the darkness. Instead, he grabbed the .38 caliber pistol and perhaps the hunting rifle and headed inside, for the house was already on fire.

Reaching the burning west side of the house, Peiper had rushed to that side of the house, found it on fire, and sought to repel his attackers. He fired the revolver several times into the darkness toward the woodshed, from where his assailants had likely emerged to throw firebombs. One slug was recovered from the ground nine meters from the southwest terrace.[29] Five of the six chambers of the revolver were fired, and the rifle, found in that corner of the house, had also been fired once.

Outside, lodged in one of the wooden planks of the dog kennel, the inspectors found a small 6.35mm slug. Two expended cartridges of the same type were scattered nearby with traces of blood spattered on the ground below.[30] The obvious conclusion was that the small weapon had been fired at the dogs. But where was Peiper?

With first light and cooling water over the smoldering ashes, the investigation was able to gather more clues. As the earliest evidence would suggest, it appeared that several homemade fire bombs had started the fire, two of which had been thrown through the ground-floor window, likely from the terrace on the west side. Combing through the ashes, Police Inspector Lavaux and Captain Marchal came across guns, spent cartridges, and a pitifully charred form.

The dark shape was still immersed in blue flames when Lavaux found it on the lower floor of the building on the left corner of his burned-out library. At first he and the firefighters mistook it for the remains of a dog, nearly buried in ashes and blackened roofing tiles. The figure was a body—incinerated, shrunk, and carbonized. It was burned totally beyond recognition.[31]

By this time Erwin Ketelhut had appeared at the scene with everyone else.[32] As Lavaux poked about the charred form, the Bavarian spoke up from the crowd. The head of the carcass was only the size of grapefruit but remained grimly expressive. "That's Peiper," Ketelhut ventured, "only he is miniaturized." Lavaux said nothing and continued to examine the smoking form. There were no arms, only a torso. The priest thought the blackened shape looked unreal, not like a body at all. However, also in the crowd was Raymond Louette, the dairy farmer, who had grown to know Peiper as well as anyone in Traves had over the years:

> The priest was at the fire just before I got there. I saw Peiper's body in the burning house. He was like a shrunken black coal. He was lying on a bed. The bed had burned away, leaving him lying on the bed springs. There was a blue flame next to the body, and they kept trying to rake over it to put it out, and it kept coming back. They hauled it away in a wheelbarrow. I saw the shape of the skull and it was Peiper's. I saw him every day, and he had a distinctive profile.[33]

Not far from the charred form still burning on the exposed springs of a couch or chair Lavaux spied a spread of unexpended ammunition. The cache had been found downstairs in what had been Peiper's library on the west side of the living room. On the remains of a bookshelf his investigators discovered thirteen boxes of unused .38 caliber rounds. Nearby a box of shotgun shells were discovered, spread out on a charred table facing the window. Oddly, the ammunition was not far from the remains of one of the Molotov cocktails.

The difficulty identifying Peiper's body promised big trouble in the entire affair. The shocked adjunct of the attorney general from Vesoul, Robert Finielz, was out of his league. He sent for assistance from police in Paris.[34] In time, the French fire expert, René Pouillaude, was able to examine the remains of where the kerosene fuel had burned just inside the window from the terrace in the library and near the foot of the stairs. The fire bomb appeared to have bounced before exploding and bursting into flame.

Under the carbonized human remains the Anschutz rifle was found. In the same vicinity was the burned pistol and his scorched stainless-steel Heuer watch.[35] The blackened body was in the southwest corner of the charred home, just inside from the terrace. Peiper's timepiece had stopped at exactly 1:00 a.m.; the scorched ceramic clock in Peiper's study had stopped seven minutes later.[36] Lavaux was puzzled by one vexing question: Peiper was still a reasonably fit man. Why had he not fled the home? Or had he?

The Gendarmerie Vesoul brought "Edo," their favorite tracking dog, to the ruins, suspicious that the German owner might have left the scene. If Peiper was still about, the police were confident Edo would find him. Early in the morning, after the fire, René Bourgeois gave the scent of the missing man to the dog from some clothes found on the premises. The "best tracking dog in France" promptly left the ruins of the house and headed diagonally across the meadow toward Ketelhut's home. There, the dog took them to the place where the barbed wire was cut. Edo circled and sniffed hesitantly by the road. The trail faded not far from the balcony by Ketelhut's home. That was strange enough.

They brought the dog back and he repeated the trail, stopping again at the road. After several hours they tried again with the same path. What did all this mean? Had a car spirited Peiper away?[37] Or had he taken refuge with his German neighbor? To the outspoken village priest, Ducros, it all added up to a clever escape. "Peiper was too malicious and too hard for anyone to get him in such a stupid fashion." But no one, he said, was willing to listen to him.[38]

But to Inspector Lavaux, the early evidence pointed to Peiper being surprised by the rapidity of the fire's spread, as the staircase worked like a chimney to funnel the flames quickly from the first to the second floor. Peiper appeared to have been overcome by toxic smoke in the library of his home where the fire had burned most furiously.[39] Had he died when he returned to that burning room to obtain more pistol ammunition? That was at the west end of the house. Had he still been firing? Or had the burning roof crashed down on him? But the larger question for the police was: Who had tossed the Molotov cocktails that had set Peiper's house alight?

When questioned by Captain Marchal and Inspector Lavaux the day after on July 15, Ketelhut was evasive. "Young fire-bombers," he speculated, had come to set fire to Peiper's house, arriving by boat on the River Saône. Though possible, the police could find nothing to confirm this hypothesis.[40] But Lavaux found Ketelhut tight-lipped and cagey. At first he claimed not to understand French well enough to communicate. Then, when a German interpreter was brought in, he seemed even more elusive. "He seemed to be hiding something from us," Lavaux concluded.[41] As for Ketelhut's "assassins arriving by boat" scenario, that only had the attraction of being an explanation from a man who had been in place to perhaps see something. But why did Ketelhut not believe the more mundane explanation, that the arsonists had arrived from the road? Was it because he would have had to see them? To add to the suspicion, the following day Ketelhut departed for Germany and was gone for two weeks.

By 7 a.m. on July 14, 1976, the story blared over the radio and the press took their cue. All through the day, reporters flocked to the otherwise anonymous village. First they came from Vesoul, then Paris, and finally from Germany. Each was manic to get the big story. The dismayed mayor of Traves, Ernest Rigoulot, attempted to deflect the negative suspicion threatening to engulf his village. "No one in the community ever had trouble with Peiper," he stated flatly.[42] But it didn't matter. "SS Man Executed" blared the front-page headline of *France Soir*.

Journalist André Moissé, who had interviewed Peiper at his home in Traves on June 22, had been sleeping that night when he received the startling call at 2 a.m. from his boss, Gérard Sebille. "The Peiper house has been burning for an hour!"[43] The news sent him driving, bleary-eyed to Traves before daybreak. He arrived at the chaotic scene with everyone else on the morning of July 14 while the house still smoked and fumed. Marc Paygnard came too, taking photographs as Captain Marchal examined the cut barbed-wire fence and firefighters sprayed the steaming ruins with water. Yet by the end of the holiday, *L'Affaire Peiper* had taken a life of its own. More press kept arriving all afternoon. The gendarmes had trouble holding back the curious crowds. It took only a day more for the whole thing to reach a public uproar. The wounds of the war were open again!

Many outsiders first hearing of the story doubted whether an "old hare" of the SS like Peiper could be so easily killed off. After all, they could not identify the body, with the "whole drama becoming a complete mystery."[44] Still, those who knew Peiper saw signs of a last battle. The revolver found under Peiper's body had five of its chambers empty—they had been fired—and a single .22 caliber round had been fired off from the rifle.[45] Peiper had been carrying two guns when he fell. Mayor Rigoulot was seized by the drama. "He fired until he was overwhelmed by flames," he somberly told reporters. "That's how he was."[46]

A German veteran was more bitter: "If one studies the tragic, unfortunate and botched life of this man," said one friend of Peiper who preferred to go unnamed, "one can only make a cold-hearted reproach. He should have put a bullet through his head in 1945!"[47] No one noted the irony of July 14, 1976: it was just two days shy of thirty years from when Peiper had been condemned to death in a Dachau courtroom. Meanwhile, as HIAG and the SS apologist machinery in Germany looked to begin their effort to martyr Peiper, Rudolf Lehmann, one of his oldest comrades at the SS Junkerschule from the class of 1936, was responding to the wishes of the family to keep things quiet. But even that suggestion kicked up the mud.

Erich Kernmayr, with the right-wing *Deutsche Wochen Zeitung*, was critical of Lehmann's muzzling. Lehmann had told Kernmayr that no one wanted to hear anything more about "SS heros and such shit." Kernmayr was not about to let that pass, even if Lehmann had fought for a long time with the staff of the Leibstandarte. "I have seen you as a sympathetic SS man in the LAH, and during that time I admired you," the Austrian wrote.

> I now hear these words from you, and wonder are you now not still believing in "heroism and shit like this"? Dear Mr. Lehmann, under your leadership, many thousands were killed, trusting in the oaths of soldiers and not in "such shit."[48]

The events in Traves had once again showcased the war, even within the world of old SS men.

In the days following the fire, speculation continued as to whether the body found smoldering in the coals was indeed that of Peiper. The favored journalistic rumor was that the carbonized form was some poor sot, which the crafty SS colonel had pulled into the burning house before making his escape. The blood found near the dog kennel, the theory went, was one of the attackers who Peiper had wounded, dragged inside the house, and set alight. After putting aside insurance papers that would allow his family to claim the restitution, he hastily departed by car or boat for an unfettered life elsewhere. Why else had Ketelhut disappeared after police questioning? He had likely spirited Peiper away!

"Hitler's bodyguard, SS Colonel Peiper is Alive and on the Run," offered one sensationalistic newspaper headline two days after the event.[49] Another hypothesis played on the wound to the chest of the discovered body. Tired of life as an undeclared fugitive, Peiper had shot himself in the heart.[50] Until the body could be identified, there was no stopping such rumors.

Staying with the sister of Artur "Kaj" Keser, in Switzerland, Peiper's wife learned of the tragic events when Dr. Benno Müller called from his office in Bad Krozingen.[51]

Müller had been in surgery that morning when his receptionist called him out urgently. The doctor's friend, Jochen Peiper, the receptionist interrupted, had been killed the previous evening. A friend had just phoned from Munich; the news was all over the radio.[52] "White as a sheet," Benno Müller took the phone and dialed Basel. Soon Sigurd Peiper was on the line; Benno broke the news.

Deeply shocked, Sigurd quickly made her way to the Black Forest home of the Müllers where her son, Hinrich Peiper, met her on the evening of July 14. Just before dawn the next day, Hinrich's father-in-law picked them up for the drive to France. The three arrived in a spotless gray metallic Mercedes 380 SE at the police headquarters in Vesoul that Thursday morning.

Sigurd was the embodiment of composure. She arrived at 10 a.m., conservatively dressed, with carefully coiffured hair and a guided poise behind sunglasses. She walked hand-in-hand with her son. Both showed little emotion as they were escorted into a waiting police vehicle that took them to Vesoul, where she met the examining magistrate, Daniel Clerget. Not long afterward they stood stone-faced in the coroner's office to view the charred remains of the body that had been found in Le Renfort. There was scarcely anything to see; the blackened cadaver was only two feet long. She spoke quietly in good French: "It is absolutely impossible for me to say if this is my husband," she began. "It is out of the question to identify what has been shown to me. It is gruesome."[53]

Under close police escort, Sigurd and Hinrich Peiper appeared at the house at 3 p.m., with the gendarmes resolutely herding back eager journalists. At the house, grieving as they fished through the ashes, Sigurd and her son collected several unburned items but stayed for only half an hour. She listened intently to an explanation from the investigators. "My husband was expecting an attack," she told the police. "We had received so many threats! The last phone call really frightened him. He wanted my daughter and me to leave."[54] Yet, if unsaid, Sigurd Peiper resented speculation that she had abandoned her husband.[55] The Peipers said nothing more, leaving stoically for the police station in Vesoul and refusing to speak with reporters whom the police cordon barely contained. The gendarmes had something more.

Peiper seemed to have had a premonition of his fate. Among the documents stacked in a drawer on the wood pile was a final letter that he had written to his wife, the woman he called "the last and bravest comrade I ever met."[56]

> Traves, 22 June 1976
>
> My Sigi,
>
> As the ghosts of the past again are after me and all signs indicate that I shall take the great journey before you—we know that no cure has been found against the idiocy of the aroused masses—I would like to thank you once again for everything: You have been a magnificent companion and I only regret, that I was not able to provide you with a life with fewer worries.
>
> Therefore, my last thoughts will be for your security and safety. The former should be attained from insurance and pension; the latter, hopefully, you will find in the Munich area.

I would find it wrong to sell Traves; leasing it would be better. The children should handle the low maintenance costs and from time to time look after things. In good days, this unadulterated piece of nature can become a link and in bad days a refuge—despite the current persecution! I have it at heart, if, later on, in the course of succession you would bequeath Traves not only to our three children but also to Bettina Wieselmann. She understood me better than our epigones and is more attached to it than they are.

And then my dogs—they only had a few good years and I wish for them an equally good and totally unexpected jump into the Eternal Hunting Grounds, where I hope to find them.

My funeral, cremation or whatever, I ask to be done without announcement, family participation or comrades' performances in the place that causes the lowest costs.

Let me put my arms around you, enjoy a few more carefree and healthy years in beautiful Bavaria and, please, count only the beautiful hours together of our marriage.

—Jo[57]

The letter had been written at the very beginning of the trouble in Traves. Local French Communists were unmoved. "There is a burned out house and a cadaver, that is all," shrugged André Vuillien. "Isn't this all an elaborate ruse to allow the ex-colonel to go elsewhere and continue the mysterious business in which he was engaged?" He accused Peiper of being the mainspring of a secret organization of former SS officers, not yet given up on the hope of a Nazi comeback.[58] Several anonymous callers boasted to have the inside story on the intrigue. Some said it was a commando squad from Italy intent on revenge, while others identified the killers as French resistance fighters, the Baader Meinhoff gang, or possibly an Israeli combat team! One even claimed to know Peiper was now headed to South America, courtesy of a shadowy group of retired SS officers with ODESSA. There he would join Martin Bormann![59] Perhaps it was all imagination or a public so conditioned by *Escape from Colditz* or the novels of Leon Uris that inspired readers to pretend there was still a war going on. Some had obviously neither forgiven nor forgotten.

Police investigators accorded attention to one telephone message apart from the many crank calls. It came from a French caller to the Paris newspaper *L'Aurore*, insisting the carbonized form *was* Peiper. A Communist group called the Avengers claimed credit:

The Peiper incident, that is us. It is more than just a warning. Our revenge will hit not only the Nazis who are hiding in France.[60]

Strangely, during that crazy week, Peiper found defenders in Serge and Beate Klarsfeld, the husband-and-wife team who made a career of hunting ex-Nazis. The attackers in Traves, they objected, were "trying to collect a debt from someone who had already paid it to society."[61] An elderly woman from the village of Traves echoed the sentiment. "We had Germans here in the war," she told investigators, "and they were just like him—scrupulously correct at the same time they were shooting people and deporting others—including my brother. But we thought it was all over. There is no sense in carrying on a war forever."[62]

In criminal cases such as that with Peiper, French law is strict. Prosecutors, police, and magistrates can disclose no information until the case is closed or after a century has elapsed. The autopsy report for the case was never made public, and the immediate lack of hard evidence intensified rumor, greatly aided by an eager press. Months after "L'Affaire Peiper" nine out of ten people in France still believed the SS colonel had managed a sleight of hand. By placing a body in the house from an unfortunate victim to burn rather than his own, he had gotten away. An SS Houdini!

Paul Cacheux, the hardware store clerk who had first found out Peiper two years earlier, was unapologetic. "It was unthinkable that such a man should try to live in France—we were five years under German boots here. I'd do the same thing again."[63] Peiper was alive, he assured a reporter, "with another murder on his conscience." Meanwhile German newspapers were less sanguine. The dead man was Peiper, ventured the *Frankfurter Allgemeine*, and the local authorities had known about the murder threats against the man. Although French speakers had been on the other end of the phone when Peiper received threats, the German newspapers looked warily at East Berlin as the source of the mayhem. Reporters from Frankfurt even claimed divination of the crime scene scenario: "The murderers arrived during the night of the national holiday with four cars and one ambulance. Village inhabitants claimed to have seen and counted them . . . but his body has not yet been identified, so authorities continue to respond haltingly."[64] Editorials a few days later were even more accusing: "They burned him alive." Had the French authorities intentionally neglected their protection duty? "Rarely was the public opinion so perfectly, so systematically prepared for political murder," concluded the German journalists.[65]

Could the charred remains be conclusively identified? The police closely examined the blackened vestige of a human body. There were only withered stumps of arms or legs; the majority of it was the burned-out crucible of a shrunken torso barely sixty centimeters long. Within twenty-four hours the chief examiner in Vesoul, Daniel Clerget, moved to bring in experts to help with identification. The prestigious French criminal forensic, Professor Pierre-Fernand Ceccaldi, flew from Paris to Vesoul on July 16 and brought with him Messieurs Henri Teisseire from Lyon and Pouillaude from Marseille. They were experts in dealing with the grisly business of fire victim identification. At 4 p.m. that Friday the autopsy began.

The head of the team, Professor Ceccaldi, was already a great name in French forensic criminology—the prestigious director of the Parisian Laboratory of Judicial Identity. The collective credentials were a clear indication of the concern for L'Affaire Peiper in higher echelons of the French Republic. Expectations were great when the gifted team began a thorough examination at the mortuary at the Vesoul hospital. The investigators took many photographs, X-ray sections, and performed a lengthy dissection. Yet, even after a "long and meticulous analysis," the three experts found it impossible to identify the charred form. About all they could say was that no bullets had been discovered.[66] The fire, they estimated, had reached foundry temperatures: over 1,400 degrees Centigrade.

To be sure, there were other problems in the evidence before the police. Why had Peiper's dogs, which were so attached to their master, run away from Le Renfort and not stopped until they reached Cubry? Even if escaping from a burning building, dogs typically try to stay in the vicinity of their master. If, however, Jochen had escaped by car, the dogs would be inclined to chase after him.

There was also the issue of time. Other than Ketelhut, the closest neighbor, Jean-Michel Farque, who lived about 500 meters away, estimated that he heard half a dozen shots at fifteen minutes after midnight on July 14. Three others soon followed, but all the gunfire ended within a few minutes. Yet Peiper's watch and the clock in the kitchen showed that the fire consumed the house at approximately 1:00 a.m., when both timepieces stopped. The question was this: What transpired in the forty-five minutes between the initial shots at 12:15 a.m. and the fire consuming everything at 1:00 a.m.? That seemed a long time if Peiper's shots scared the assassins away just after the fire bombs were thrown. There was at least half an hour for him to take action.

The papers and documents had been placed rather neatly on the wood pile, but others were scattered on the ground as if Peiper had moved them with great haste.[67] It would seem more reasonable to have either fought the fire first, or to have carried the papers hurriedly out while battling the flames. At least that part of the theory seemed feasible, as some of the papers had been scattered on the ground between the veranda and the wood shed. After all, he could not have been unaware of the operable garden watering hose just outside the glassed veranda, which the frustrated local firemen eventually used. Perhaps he was unable to fight the fire, instead shooting with the pistol from the west side of the burning house as he made multiple trips to move documents to safety. Had he been preoccupied with keeping his assailants at bay? What exactly had happened?

The only certain finding was that he had not been shot; there were no bullets or traces of their path found in the autopsy. The discovered hole in the middle of the chest, examiners concluded, was not from a projectile but rather from something falling onto the body. And although the corpse had a broken shoulder blade, the examiners could not tell how this happened. The press, of course, fancied a fierce scuffle in which his assailants overcame Peiper, placed him inside, and then doused him with ignited fuel.[68] The police offered a more prosaic explanation: the shoulder was fractured when his body fell or when the roof collapsed onto him. And although the fury of the fire had left precious little evidence for establishing the identity of the carbonized cadaver, the most important evidence was the left segment of the charred upper jaw that had survived with a single intact second molar. The autopsy report was only able to establish that had come from a man older than fifty-five years.[69] Doubters made much of the fact that Peiper's gold tooth, so obvious when he grinned widely, had mysteriously disappeared.

A more positive identification would require dental records. Peiper's old friend and comrade in the Ardennes, Dr. Arndt Fischer, was contacted to help. He had been Peiper's dentist in Munich after he moved to France. In fact, Fischer had offered several

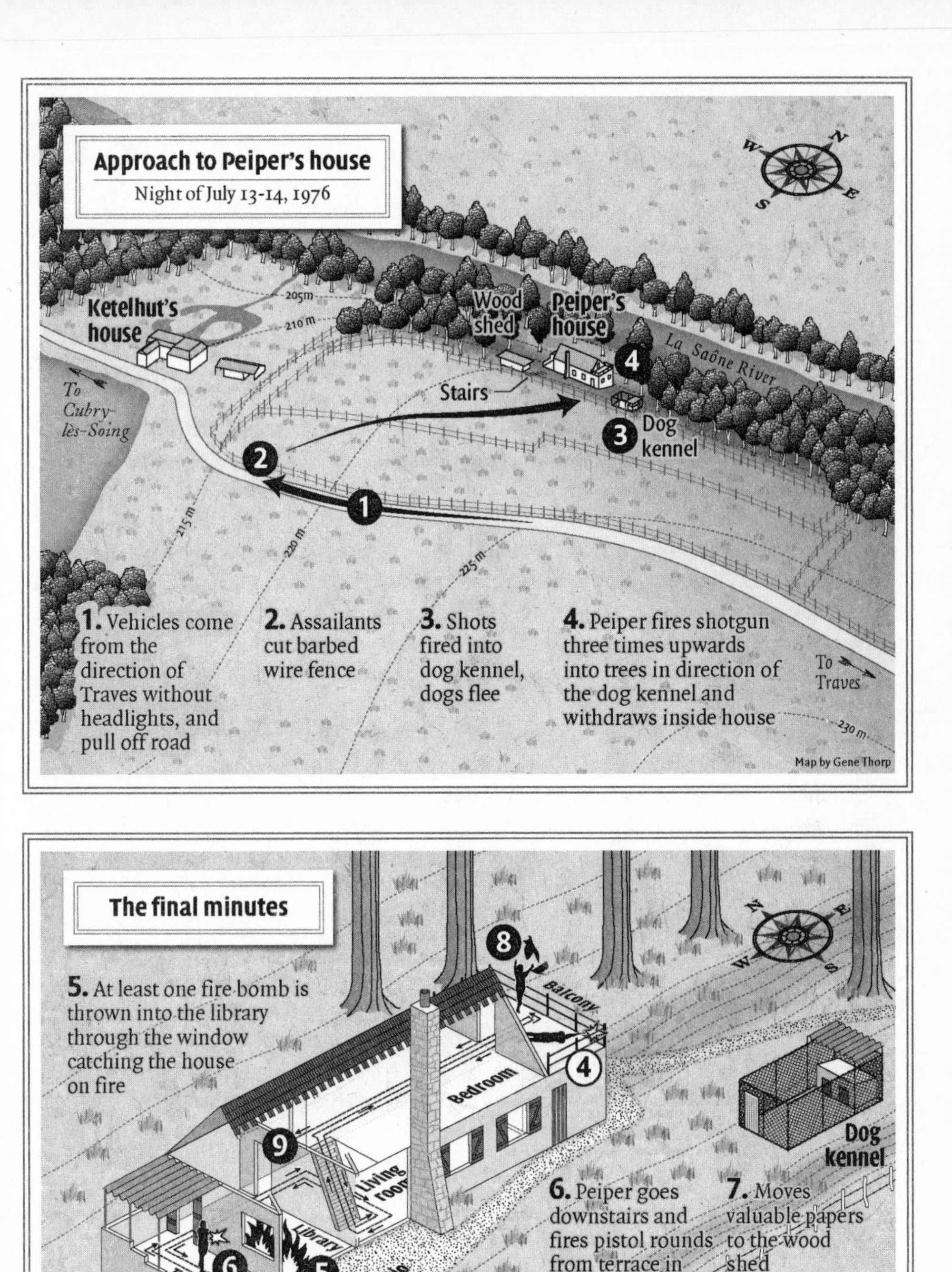

Approach to Peiper's house
Night of July 13-14, 1976
N
E
S
W
205m
210 m
215 m
220 m
225 m
230 m
Ketelhut's house
Wood shed
Peiper's house
La Saône River
Stairs
To Cubry-lès-Soing
Dog kennel
1. Vehicles come from the direction of Traves without headlights, and pull off road
2. Assailants cut barbed wire fence
3. Shots fired into dog kennel, dogs flee
4. Peiper fires shotgun three times upwards into trees in direction of the dog kennel and withdraws inside house
To Traves
Map by Gene Thorp
The final minutes
5. At least one fire-bomb is thrown into the library through the window catching the house on fire
Balcony
Bedroom
Living room
Library
Terrace
Patio
Steps
Wood shed
Dog kennel
6. Peiper goes downstairs and fires pistol rounds from terrace in direction of the wood shed.
7. Moves valuable papers to the wood shed
8. Returns to the bedroom and throws clothes off balcony
9. Heads back to the upstairs study to reach stairs, but is overcome by fire
Map by Gene Thorp

times to help with the early attempts at identification, but the French authorities seemed uninterested.

Peiper's dentist had last seen Jochen in March of 1976 and had taken X-rays of his patient a year before in February of 1975. "His [Peiper's] wife called me up and asked if I could help with the identification of the body. I told her, 'I can identify him because I have X-rays of the teeth and mouth.'"

> Two days later, a French investigator and a German police official came by my office and picked up the X-rays and records I had on his mouth. I had X-rays of Peiper's jaw and one day men suddenly came to my office and took the X-rays. I made another copy. I told them I was willing to go and testify to help with the investigation, but they never came.

Fischer remained incredulous: "It has never been proved that the body was that of Peiper. . . . Why had the jaw been destroyed? Why was the body cut up?"[70] His friend Benno Müller also doubted the official version of the events. Peiper, he believed, killed himself when he saw that his house would burn.[71] After all, the .38 caliber revolver was found underneath his body and rumor had it that the head was never returned to Germany before the burial. The latter was untrue, of course. Police Inspector Lavaux told the author that the head was retained for some time as a key piece of evidence, but there was no sign of a headshot wound that would have been obvious through personal examination as well as within the autopsy report. Peiper's son was quite cognizant of the potential for lingering scandal. "For the sake of clarification," he told the newspaper *Die Welt*, "we did not urge the French authorities to hurry, because there has to be absolute certainty, so that the heretic charges will not continue after my father's death."[72]

Yet doubts remained. The evening before Bastille Day Benno Müller had remarked to his wife, after speaking with Peiper on the phone, that his friend seemed depressed. And Peiper's son, Hinrich, believed his father's spirit was faltering in summer 1976. "Physically he was strong," he remembered of his sixty-one-year-old father, "but mentally he was broken. He realized it was all starting up again." Jochen Peiper would not leave his beloved Traves home. Nor could he shake his past. Until his own death, Dr. Müller was unable to accept his friend's passing. Today Peiper's son believes his father was killed rather than murdered. It is a time-worn view reflecting personal acceptance of the events.[73] Years later he explained the situation to a family friend:

> The investigations of the French authorities against unknown ones still appear to be underway. However, someday they will be discontinued silently. And for what? It would not bring back my father. By the capture of the culprits and in the case of a trial, his name would not be enhanced. Sympathy and public opinion would be for the culprits and not with the victim.[74]

Life in Traves was also unsettled. During the first days at Chez Néné, the local fishermen had difficulty finding a seat for their afternoon Pernod. The place was now taken over by a craving press looking for any comment from the public. "I knew that one day we would all be sorry that he had chosen to live here," Mayor Rigoulot offhandedly told the buzzing media.[75] Anything he said would become a headline. As he spoke, Rigoulot's ruddy cheeks grew more red, his previous casual friendship with the German conveniently forgotten:

> What happened last Tuesday evening was not a surprise for us. It was certain that something would happen to Joachim Peiper. He had received too many threats of death and intention to burn his house. Personally, I had to try to make him understand to leave the country. Not because that he was doing wrong, but for peace for us. One thing is for sure: it is not the inhabitants of the parish that made the hit. It was certainly a well-organized group. It was likely a revenge of war perpetrated by old members of the *Maquisards* [Resistance Movement]. I think it is normal that people who suffered very much in the past can keep a tenacious hatred.[76]

Regardless of what the mayor said, Traves would never be the same.

Chapter 24

GHOSTS OF THE PAST

IN THE YEAR AFTER THE SUPPOSED DEATH OF JOCHEN PEIPER HUNDREDS OF people came to the tiny village of Traves. What was all the commotion about? Clattering Volkswagen minivans teeming with tourists sputtered down the small streets, and curiosity seekers from the city converged on the weekends. They sported cameras and paraded past the burned-out home as young boys lurked about, looking for souvenirs while vendors hawked ice cream and pommes frites. Traffic jams crowded farm tractors off the narrow village byways.[1] It was like a morbid carnival.

Mayor Rigoulot received letters congratulating him for seeing the SS colonel to Valhalla while others enclosed razor blades so he could cut his own throat. "I urged him to leave," Rigoulot maintained. "He did not want to. Tough break for him."[2]

> August 1976
> Mr. Mayor,
>
> Bravo for the hospitality that you reserve in your town for honorable strangers. They assassinate a hero of the Wehrmacht, the renowned Colonel Joachim Peiper. That crime is due to some scum resistance fighters such as the famous Cacheux.
>
> But don't fear, all is not yet done. This is only the beginning. Colonel Peiper will be avenged! Your bastard communists and Resistance fighters will get their turn. . . . Your town will soon know some hot days.
>
> Glory to the memory of Adolf Hitler and Peiper,
> The Society of the Swords and Oaks[3]

There were more letters full of poisonous accusations about the Jews. The worst of the war bubbled up. "Joachim Peiper's friends are always there," said one note. "And they are going to complete their mission!"[4] The local *curé* of Traves, Father Louis Ducros, made a statement to French television that only a priest could make: "I deplore the murder of Peiper and blame the communists not the Catholics." Although he would not say mass for such a man, "I will pray for him, and his murderers," Ducros intoned, "but the peace of the village is destroyed for good."[5]

In Boves, Italy, where twenty-seven had died on the hot days of September 1943, there was no remorse. "Peiper did not pay but for a part of the crimes he was guilty of," the Boves mayor Anselmo Cavallera insisted. "We would have preferred a sentence from justice rather than a private execution." They called the incident near Cuneo the "Oradour di Piemonte." Old fighters from the French resistance chimed in, "As a former exile, I say it is a job well done!"[6]

In Germany the tragedy aroused the opposite. "In going to France to live, Peiper put himself in the mouth of the wolf," surmised the *General Anzeiger*, a Bonn newspaper specializing in foreign affairs. "The constant attempt to revive past passions more than thirty years after the war emanates from a very precise intention of certain forces."

Certain forces were the French Communist Party. For its part, however, the local Communist chapter of the Haute Saône labored to shift the blame. "The main responsibility," they declared, "lies with the public officials who refused to expel him."[7] The police remained skeptical: here was the organization that started the whole thing with inflammatory flyers in Traves, and there was Paul Cacheux. Soon police inspectors drove about Eastern France to interview the organization all the way down from André Vuillien, the outspoken secretary of the Communist Federation in the Haute Saône. Neither Vuillien nor his nine lower lieutenants and underlings ventured anything.[8] Vuillien said they wanted Peiper expelled, not dead, but his protests didn't sound convincing. And even though the police requested help from the public, no one came forward.

Old French resistance fighters were also on the suspicion list. The chief of the ancient Resistance Haute Saône, Colonel Reuchet, was emphatic: "God has willed that we do not find the culpable," he said, "but if that should happen, we will be behind them even if they are louts."[9]

Why had there been no police protection during the critical night of July 13? The furor did little for the amity of French-German relations. "This is less a French matter, than a political one of people who want to split our two countries," said *L'Aurore*. "One has to invoke the old devil of Nazism for disturbing the relations between Germany and France."[10] The German press charged the Peiper murder as "the result of a communist campaign" but laid the direct responsibility on locals in Eastern France.[11] Sarcastic reporting followed:

> The French Interior Minister, responsible for political terrorism keeps steadfast silence. Nothing serious was undertaken to prevent the announced murder. Despite the unmistakable threat, the murderers could come, murder and get away completely undisturbed. . . . The head of state of France has not seen fit to send a condolence letter to the Peiper family. One has not even heard in France that the murderers were wanted.[12]

Less than a week after the fire, Monsieur Paul Cacheux, the French Communist hardware clerk who had exposed Peiper, received a rash of death threats. "You are going to pay for the death of our friend, wherever you go."[13] With the warning was a hideous photograph of a human body strung up, marked with a swastika and bearing Cacheux's name.

Outside of the Haute-Saône there were other developments in the emotionally charged atmosphere that summer. On July 18, a pro-Nazi clutch, calling themselves

Groupe Joachim Peiper, claimed responsibility for a grenade attack on the Jewish community center in Marseille. No one was hurt, but the center was badly damaged. Later a time bomb at a synagogue in the same city was defused. And within days of the incident Nazi hunter Beate Klarsfeld received a letter accusing her and her representatives of having killed Peiper. The threatening missive warned Klarsfeld never to return to Germany, to stop "persecuting" former comrades, and to donate 300,000 Deutschmarks to the Peiper family or suffer revenge. Ominously, the note warned that Groupe Joachim Peiper knew Klarsfeld's daily movements in Paris.[14] All the while police hunted the chimera of the Avengers in Paris who had claimed the work of revenge as their own. Arrests were made, but no one could be connected to the Peiper killing. And that was just the beginning.

On August 19 plastic explosives blew apart the entrance of Paul Cacheux's house, and only early intervention by Vesoul firefighters saved his place from burning to the ground. And two weeks later a powerful bomb splintered the storefront of the Mégnin-Bernard hardware shop in Vesoul after it had been marked with Neo-Nazi graffiti.[15] The Federation of the Communist Party in Haute Saône claimed that the conspiracy against Cacheux and his organization was wider than just Peiper revenge; the conservative Giscard d'Estaing government was behind it, they said.[16] The French Communist *L'Humanité* emerged with a twisted headline: "In Traves, Freedom for Neo-Nazis, but Police Harassment for Patriots and Militant Workers."

Yet the news pointed out that the French government, both in Vesoul and Paris, wasn't acting to needle the French Communists to find out who had done the deed. An investigation designed to impress rather than succeed?

All this seemed more insidious when the German press learned that Peiper had appealed directly to the French ministry of the interior to "protect me against further persecution." The request went nowhere and was revealed only after his home burned to the ground. Within both countries the incident touched off a torrent of extremist threats. Bombs went off in Paris at the building sheltering the Miroir-Sprint, a press agency linked to the French Communists. Another exploded at the door of Joe Nordman, the attorney for Paul Cacheux.[17] And in little Traves, which had no police force, gendarmes had to be brought in to protect the peace. On July 25, an anonymous caller to the village priest threatened to execute ten "hostages" unless those responsible for the act were identified by the end of the month.[18] Another gruff phone voice warned that ten homes would be burned on the night of July 31.

Officials hurriedly canceled the scheduled parish fair—the *Kermesse*. Not that anyone would want to come to go bowling or play cards with the volley of threats to the village; it was a good time to be gone. Peiper's mysterious and tight-lipped neighbor, Erwin Ketelhut, had driven off to Germany and couldn't be found. And Captain Marchal and Inspector Lavaux both took a vacation. But when the time came, the last night of the month passed quietly. Thirty heavily armed gendarmes posted a round-the-clock vigil at the village. A house-to-house search found no explosives. While others left town, others were unafraid. The church bells pealed to echo the wedding of a local girl who was married that night as if all was normal.[19]

Yet the lack of revenge that final July night was no indication of a cleansed atmosphere. In the little military cemetery in Vesoul white swaths of spray-painted swastikas intermingled with "Traves-Red" scrawled on a wall were discovered after the entrance was set on fire with bottled gasoline. Soon after that, a rash of threatening anonymous letters arrived in the mailboxes of the mayor and the priest: "If in three months the police have not unveiled the murderers of Peiper, we will settle the account with those who are at the source."[20] The threats were postmarked from Belgium. Cancellation of the town annual fair promised a fiscal disaster.[21]

Later that fall, those behind the threats seemed ready to act. In late November "We will revenge Peiper!" was amateurishly painted in green on the Traves post office. Strangely, villagers discovered the message just after the funeral of M. Michel Obriot, the mason who had crafted the walls of Peiper's burned-out home. The scrawl was signed "Rex"—evoking the past of the Belgian fascists. There were more threats by mail to the people of Traves. And another discovered bomb in Vesoul had to be defused. Just a few days before Christmas the Curé Ducros had organized a holiday card game to substitute for the canceled Kermesse that had so damaged the parish annual fund raising. But when two hundred squeezed into the parish hall that holiday someone yelled "Fire!" Everyone dropped the cards; there was panic as all rushed for the door. Someone had set the adjoining room ablaze. That was quickly put out, but the perpetrator was never discovered and the Kermesse was canceled for good.[22] That same month graffiti-brandishing youths—"*Groupe J. Peiper Vengeance!*"—were defacing cars and walls in Vesoul with fire bombs, crude threats, and spray-painted swastikas.[23]

"*Hitler revient*," they scrawled—"Hitler will come again."

The final police investigation was thorough but did not lead to much. "No detail escaped Captain Marchal or myself," Lavaux recalled. "Everyone involved made a large effort to uncover everything."[24] At its peak, the investigation had nearly sixty people working to track down leads. Lavaux constantly reminded those under him of the need for speed: "Either you solve the case in the first 48 hours or it goes on and on."[25]

Yet the local inhabitants of Traves were inclined to close ranks, and no reliable witnesses could be located. Few clues were discernible in the burned-out wreckage. "One thing is certain," ventured Raymond Louette, "there were tire tracks in the dew-soaked grass when I went down there."[26] The police, too, looked closely at the tracks, which crossed the field and had crossed near the lane. Nothing, however, could be learned about the vehicle or the tracks. Police dogs found the same, but all the trails ended at the road.

Always the investigation seemed to come back to the village, the police privately professing that if the "fire commando" did not originate in Traves, then the threads of evidence pointed that way.[27] At first the police thought they had something on Saturday, July 17, when they questioned two youths from the village.

The boys, Raphaël M. and Jean Marc-H., were workers at the Peugeot plant in Noidans-lès Vesoul. They had been bragging for days that they aimed "to get the Boche." So suspicious were the circumstances that the police questioned the two again the following Wednesday, holding them at police headquarters in Scey-sur-Saône. Yet, like other leads, this one dissipated when "reputable" individuals could place the two boys elsewhere on Bastille eve. They had been drinking, the youths confessed. After too many afternoon Pernods, they had boasted of an act they hadn't done.[28] The police also brought in the son of the baker, Jacky Gauthier, to whom Peiper had given his private telephone number that the assailant seemed to have possessed. That was reason enough for suspicion.[29]

All three called in the village priest to testify on their behalf. The burly Curé gave them an earful. "The cops think them to be bad, but they won't find anything. The people of Traves are stronger than they!"[30] A challenge? The priest declared that the boys had been at the church rectory that famous night, playing cards. He was witness to it. The word of a priest against the accusations of the police! Although six hours of interrogation scared the youths witless, it became obvious to the gendarmes that they had no proof these two kids were Peiper's killers.[31] Back to square one.

With each new effort, the investigation still seemed to keep looping back to the village. On July 23 the *L'Est Républicain* reported that the police had already interviewed some three hundred locals, and everyone had to account for their whereabouts on Bastille Day eve. Cars were searched, and the police confiscated the wire shears and bolt-cutters found on the scene, looking for the instruments that cut Peiper's barbed-wire fence. "For the time being," wrote one, "it seems that Traves and its immediate surroundings are the key to this drama."[32]

In response to Erwin Ketelhut's apparition of a water-borne team of assassins, the police had frogmen comb the silty bottom of the Saône. They found nothing. A helicopter photographic survey was equally unproductive. The growing frustration was large enough that officials offered a reward of ₣20,000 for decisive information to solve the case. No one came forward.[33] The inaction frustrated one farmer in Traves. He saw Lavaux on his way back from work one morning. Was it another government cover-up like Algeria? Certainly, Giscard d'Estaing couldn't afford a scandal now. "You've had three hundred policemen working for the last three weeks," the farmer complained., "Why can't you find out who did it?" He looked the capped gendarme in the eyes: "Who is paying you off?"

Lavaux was taken aback. "No one is paying us off," he insisted. "We know who did it and we're not going to let go!"[34] His admission surprised the farmer. Perhaps justice would be done. Yet weeks became months and then years, and no one was convicted. What happened?

The official theory, as expressed by the Vesoul prosecutor, Marc Dreyfus, was logical and straightforward.[35] A group of punk kids—the exact number was unknown—had attacked Peiper's house. Why else would they have small 6.35mm pistols and crudely made gasoline bombs? Their intention was to own up to their recent threats to convince the aging SS colonel to leave France. Peiper had driven them off with guns, fired not at his assailants but into the air. Yet the aging German had not vanquished his adversaries before they set his house on fire. Peiper was then overcome by smoke while trying to rescue his possessions.[36] The idealistic hoodlums' harassment went further than intended, with a fatal result.

A popular hypothesis—that professional killers were involved—was much less credible, though hack journalists enthusiastically embraced it.[37] According to such "theories," Peiper's killers were commandos, either from the Avengers hailing from Paris or from Italy, and had struck that night to see that Peiper's perceived crimes were avenged.[38] So fantastic were each day's headlines that September found the newspaper

France Soir giving credence to the outlandish rumor that Joachim Peiper had been an agent for the KGB![39] And a Parisian television documentary, airing on September 28, wondered aloud whether Peiper was still at large. Such twaddle persisted, fueling acrimonious reaction from the German right wing, but nothing from French officials had Peiper as a Soviet James Bond nor escaping to an SS haven in Paraguay.

Colonel Reuchet and the old members of the wartime resistance were insulted by the insinuation that they were responsible for Peiper's execution. Too sloppy! He rightly pointed out that any operations from their quarter would be more professional. First off, the telephone line would have been cut, when, in fact, it was still intact when the fires consumed the house. Certainly larger weapons than a feeble 6.35mm pistol would have been used in confronting a Waffen SS colonel! And rather than primitive fire bombs made out of beer bottles, any self-respecting commando descendant from the Armée blanche would have thrown incendiary grenades!

What of the opinion of both Peiper and his neighbor Ketelhut that the fountainhead of his tormentors involved militant Communists? Were they acting, as Peiper said, on orders from East Germany and orchestrated by the local Communists looking to unsettle French-German relations? In their official investigation report, the police seemed to look at it that way.[40]

AT THE END OF THE MONTH THE POLICE FINALLY GOT THE BREAK THEY HAD been waiting for. If it was true, the truth of Peiper's demise was much more mundane than spies and international intrigue. A young man, Didier B., came to the police to tell them of overhearing a conversation between some friends who said they had "killed the SS man." The youth who had overheard Daniel D., was brought into the Gendarmerie headquarters in Vesoul on July 31. There, he confessed to participating in the crime and gave a lengthy statement.[41] Having made attempts to harass Peiper before, the youths decided to make good the threats. They made up about ten crude Molotov cocktails, and one of the youths provided a 6.35mm revolver to subdue the dogs.

Daniel said he had driven three other lads to the scene that night, parking the car a dozen or so meters from Ketelhut's mill, and although not participating himself, he knew the others had done the deed. They went off to cut the barbed wire. Then everything happened quickly. Daniel became anxious as a series of gunshots erupted. From behind the wheel he saw the first flames spout up from the house. He was relieved to see the other three hurriedly run up to the car and jump inside. "*Ça y est, ça grille!*" one exclaimed, closing the car door—"It's done. It's torched!"[42] The four roared off quickly for home.

Daniel's story was compelling in another sense for French police: it neatly fit the facts. There were other small but perhaps important pieces of physical evidence. Several scattered articles were found along the trail located by the police dogs that led from the house to the cut barbed-wire fence by the road. One was a crumpled light blue half-empty cellophane pack of Gauloises cigarettes. This was not particularly important except for the peculiar way it was folded—vertically in half. It seems that one of the four accused youths was in the habit of folding his cigarettes in exactly that fashion. Nearby, at the base of a tree only four yards from the doghouse, was another unused Molotov cocktail crudely fashioned out of a bottle, filled with kerosene, and fitted with a nylon rag. A fuel-can stopper was also discovered close by where the barbed wire had been cut. And the youths often traveled with a fuel can. Still, although compelling, these tidbits did not add up to a case.

Yet within French law suspicion alone is grounds for arrest. The police subpoenaed the other three young men and brought them in. They had no jobs, drank excessively, and had been involved in petty theft. The police characterized them as "young crooks." The suspects lived in Gray, another small French town about forty kilometers from Traves on the way to Dijon. The big break seemed to be when the police found a letter addressed to Peiper when searching the home of one of the youths. They apparently were the same group who had broken into his mailbox on June 25 at 9 p.m. That evening they had gone to challenge the SS man but had turned tail when the lady of the house challenged them. According to the statement of twenty-one-year-old Daniel D., they had also made an expedition to Traves in his Ford Escort to harass Peiper on the night of July 1. The youth shouted insults and hurled dirt clods and rocks. They were scared off only by the sight of the approaching owner brandishing a hunting rifle.[43] As the French police saw it, the group that threw stones later lobbed amateurish Molotov cocktails. It was a logical synthesis of detective work and confession. Case closed?

There was a critical shortcoming. Given the lack of witnesses and incriminating physical evidence, all hinged on the youth's confession. And the boy was psychologically unstable. After a single night at police headquarters under observation, Daniel clumsily recanted his statement the following morning.[44] Some said the police had encouraged him to change his story. The other three youths were held with him for a few hours until Monsieur Clerget ordered the police to let them go.[45] In spite of strong circumstantial evidence, without Daniel D.'s confession there was nothing on which to hold them. "We were at the ball with some girls," the others said.[46] The police interviewed the girlfriends, who seemed very nervous, but they stuck to the boys' story. The rowdies were released. On September 30, the police again heard from Didier B., who claimed that D. "had lied to us about their whereabouts on the evening of July 13, 1976."[47] Yet there was no one who could corroborate him.

Ultimately sympathetic Frenchmen argued that Daniel sought only to draw attention to himself given the emotional atmosphere in Traves that summer. Certainly his young life showed little to admire: he later confessed that rather than burning Peiper's house, he had often set fire to the local dump to drive out rats, a morbid pastime for the troubled youth. The sorry tale did not end there. Two months later, on September 26, he was arrested for involvement with his friends in a local theft. Somehow he managed to escape from the police only to take refuge at his grandmother's house. There he would unsuccessfully attempt suicide with sleeping pills. He left a short note. "I am fed up to always be accused of everything," he said, "particularly this Peiper affair. I prefer to die."[48] He survived, but said nothing further about L'Affaire Peiper.[49]

Although the youths were implicated as having broken into Peiper letter box, there was no other physical evidence to tie them to the events of Bastille Day. The youth's retraction of his confession did the rest. "After that," the chief inspector ventured, "everyone in the village clammed up. Nobody was going to talk."[50] Lavaux's office dutifully followed dozens of other leads to their ultimate end. They had nothing more.

Had it been the kids from Gray? Not according to the recalcitrant priest:

> It's not true; it's crap. I am sure of this. The police tried to turn people here against each other. During the war, there had been people here who were with the resistance and those who were for the Germans. They tried to bring all this to the surface again and set fire to the countryside with it. They tried to get people to accuse each other. It was the strategy of the police.[51]

Lavaux was convinced that the enigmatic Ketelhut knew much more than he was telling. Even with a sleeping pill, how can someone snooze through a half-dozen gunshot blasts fired scarcely two hundred meters away? And with open windows! Soon after the fire and before being interviewed by police, Ketelhut took off to Germany and spent two weeks there before returning to speak with impatient authorities. Interrogators found him less than frank: even though the police knew otherwise, the German neighbor denied knowing anything of Peiper's military past.[52] He seemed intent to confirm Peiper's demise:

> I have given the entire matter much thought. Now, I think the attackers came in a small boat going down the Saône. That explains Peiper's surprise and the fact that I didn't hear anything. He is dead. For me, it is a certainty. I immediately recognized him as soon as I saw the body.[53]

And soon after the uncomfortable police session Ketelhut made plans to sell his Moulin de Velet estate and move out of town. Was he afraid for himself, or did he have something to hide?[54] Could he be telling the truth? "Unthinkable," Lavaux concluded in his report.[55]

That Ketelhut claimed not to have heard the shots seemed particularly ludicrous after a midnight test Lavaux and Marchal concocted in Traves a week after the incident. The French police fired Peiper's hunting rifle from the remains of his burned-out balcony. By the time the last shot was fired, a breathless and anxious Ketelhut came rushing up to Peiper's abandoned house to find out what was going on. The police told him of their ballistics tests but made the mental note that Erwin Ketelhut had heard these shots clearly enough to come running.[56]

Two years later the judge magistrate left in charge of the case, Christian Nannini (successor to Daniel Clerget of Vesoul), would unsuccessfully attempt to reopen the case to subpoena the four youths and Erwin Ketelhut as well.[57] "It will be interesting to hear Mr. Ketelhut before the Chief Examiner," Marc Dreyfus posed. "It is evident that he was not directly mixed with the affair, but he is likely to have seen something that night that he did not talk about until now for fear."[58] Although unable to prove it, Lavaux believed that as well.

On January 26, 1977, the commission heard Ketelhut once more. There was more background on their relationship in 1967 when Ketelhut worked with Volkswagen:

> We all knew Peiper as an ordinary person among us, but we knew that he was an old colonel of the SS. . . . Peiper did not hide from it. I knew that he had been tried and that he had paid and that he has been freed. . . . Peiper was above all a soldier. In any case, the war was not pretty.[59]

As before, Ketelhut described how their friendship slowly fell apart amid their differing sympathies. The only real difference with his original account was his acknowledgment of "hearing some gunshots." Yet he did not admit to not hearing barking dogs. He said he walked out onto the terrace after hearing the gunshots but decided it must be hunters. Hunters blasting away on a July night? If not very convincing, Ketelhut stuck to the new story and continued to lamely suggest that the assassins had come by boat. There was an obvious advantage with this theory for Ketelhut: no assassins parked by his home to have escaped notice. "*Ich hatt' einen Kameraden*—I Had a Comrade" went the old German soldier's song. If Ketelhut got on poorly with his neighbor, he still maintained loyalty. Or did he?

If he had heard the shots, why had he not helped Peiper as he had promised earlier that Tuesday evening? Ketelhut flushed and stammered:

> I was not targeted by anyone, because [Paul] Cacheux had assured me, when he distributed the leaflets in Traves, that I had nothing to fear from them. . . . So I did not want to spill French blood [that night] in an armed intervention.[60]

With that, Ketelhut admitted not only to hearing the shots but also to deciding not to come to Peiper's defense. But if Cacheux had told him that he was not a target, what else had they told him? And more than that, what else had he seen? Ketelhut hurried off once more, the headless horseman of L'Affaire Peiper, disappearing into Germany and the hinterlands of Eastern France. Even his lawyer seemed to know little of his whereabouts. All of this was "deeply disturbing" to Lavaux. Had Ketelhut seen what had happened to Peiper? Without more evidence, why did he insist that the assailants came by boat? Had he recognized the aggressors, but was threatened with his own life? Or did he know something even more mysterious? Why else would he endeavor to leave as if Peiper's ghost chased him?

In August 1979 a frustrated Nannini announced a plan to rehear the four suspects originally interrogated on July 30, 1976. The public buzzed in anticipation, and headlines announced "the threads tighten around the four suspects." Yet when the four youths were heard they steadfastly held to the previous alibis of three years before. And in spite of additional details, nothing really came of that part of the investigation either. In an attempt to bring some closure, the Court of Vesoul had earlier made out a death certificate on May 24, 1977. Even that was lacking: "While there does not exist absolute evidence of the death of Joachim Peiper, that the evidence is sufficiently compelling as to consider it as certain."[61]

Years after Inspector Lavaux had retired in 1990, Daniel D., the primary witness in the abortive investigation, called the police in Dijon. He wanted to speak to Lavaux, he said—he had something important to relate about L'Affaire Peiper. He would not speak to anyone other than Lavaux. His voice, the operator recalled, had sounded tortured, even desperate.

At the time the troubled youth was a shepherd in the nearby town of Savoie. The former police inspector found the youth's address and sent him a letter. Daniel never responded.[62]

It remains a mystery.

SIGURD PEIPER'S HEALTH HAD BEEN POOR FOR SEVERAL YEARS BEFORE JOCHEN Peiper's Bastille Day reckoning. She carried on a long fight with cancer, but increasingly after the terrible July day she was worn down, even though careful of her privacy. In public she was careful not to speak to her family of her own past. It was an old burden she and Jochen had both hauled around for years. If Jochen had been Heinrich Himmler's adjutant, she had been his secretary.

A month after the tragic events of July 1976, Sigurd wrote a letter to her son, now an attorney:[63]

> Whatever happened that gruesome night no longer matters. Pa could not and would not have left Traves. If he had not been able to see Traves, his present dream of happiness and peace, would have made life seem not worth living; his heart would have been broken. Finally now, Pa has his peace. No one anymore can hurt or torture his soul.[64]

Still, it was difficult for the family to put the passing to rest. On September 17 Sigurd Peiper came back to Traves with her son. Hinrich had already come unannounced to inspect the ruin, speaking to locals of an intention to rebuild it, "as if attachment to the green country on the banks of the Saône was stronger than all else." Publicly the mayor of Traves said that their return would be welcomed, but privately he expressed unease. Ketelhut was back and exhibiting his wood sculptures, but looking to sell his place. The police were still posted to the town, although fewer in number, and the atmosphere seemed to be calming. But rebuilding Le Renfort could surely stir things up.[65]

On October 22, 1976, Sigurd Peiper showed up in Vesoul to assure Captain Marchal that although they had doubt before, "that they had, indeed, very firmly identified the carbonized body as that of Joachim Peiper."[66] In his report to police headquarters Roger Lavaux concluded the same thing. Yet that didn't settle the matter for cautious French authorities, and the burnt corpse remained in Vesoul. Without the body it wasn't possible to conduct a proper funeral. On People's Mourning Day of November 14, 1976, Sigurd and son Hinrich attended a memorial service held by the veteran's organization of I SS Panzer Corps in Marienfels. Hubert Meyer, the federal spokesman of HIAG, the Waffen SS veterans' organization, gave a short speech. "We have not been able to carry the earthly remains of our comrade Jochen Peiper to the last resting place," Meyer began ruefully.

> Twice after the war, he had to stand up for us: In the Malmédy Trial at Dachau and during the cowardly assault in Traves. For a broad public in Germany and

> even more throughout the rest of the world, he has become the embodiment of that which all of us were clearly, intentionally and wrongly burdened in Nuremberg.... We have not forgotten what Jochen Peiper wrote to us from Landsberg Prison in 1952: "Don't forget that the first Europeans killed in action were in units from the Waffen SS, that the ones beaten to death during the post war period mostly were men from our ranks. They had become fair game because of their belief in the indivisibility of Western Europe. Remember these martyrs."[67]

In some ways Hinrich Peiper agreed. Six months after Traves he wrote a letter to the newspaper *Die Welt.* "Our history was taken over officially without reflection, just as the victors have written it," he lamented on January 10, 1977. "Not even the obvious attempt was made to let truth and justice be heard. If the one-sided reporting of our past continues, our heritage cannot be corrected. Indeed, we are in danger of becoming a country without history, a country without a future."[68]

Even so, Hinrich Peiper was thoroughly displeased with efforts to martyr his father. "Radical circles on the right abused the tragic fate of Jochen Peiper," he complained, "as a vehicle for spreading their ideas." Dr. Gerhard Frey of the *National Zeitung* made clear his intention to erect a memorial to Jochen Peiper. When his son indicated his father's will had specifically requested no memorials, Frey brashly asked to see the will. Hinrich Peiper denied the request. Dietrich Ziemssen wrote another letter after hearing that protests were planned. "Please, no demonstrations," he wrote. "It is not in Frau Peiper's interest now to politically game the person of her husband."[69] But that caution was for naught.

Organized by Dr. Frey on September 12, 1976, three hundred militants converged in Cologne to demonstrate in favor of the memorial. And later, on November 7, a thousand demonstrated in Mannheim to protest the execution of the ex-SS colonel.[70] Although most claimed to be "brothers in arms," this was hardly the case; many were Neo-Nazis barely twenty years old. Hinrich fought against a campaign to erect a memorial to his father (in Dachau of all places!) and disdained the firebrand of the right wing. "My father was apolitical," he protested. "He wasn't focused on the past any longer, he lived in the present."[71] Just to make sure, Hinrich Peiper orchestrated a legal restraining order against the moves of the extreme right to canonize his father.[72]

Amazingly, Gerhard Frey filed a reactive criminal lawsuit against Hinrich Peiper alleging perjury. How could Peiper's son make such an assertion, when his father had been a wartime hero to the Waffen SS? "Originally, I did not find fault with my statement," son Peiper maintained, "but certainly today I would not express myself in this manner having read some things about the SS." In writing to Dr. Klink at the Militärgeschichtliches Forschungsamt, he seemed initially ignorant of the particulars of his father's historical persona:

> Now, in what organizations was my father involved? He entered the horse-riding squadron, the SS Readiness Troops (LAH), Waffen SS, and apparently a member of the SS (automatically?) upon entering the SS and Readiness Troops. He attested them to be of non-political origin and emphasizing that they were

> military units like the rest of the troops. But Readiness Troops and Waffen SS. Can one call these two non-political organizations? Or did they have at the time my father joined them (as such actually only the Readiness Troops, which later were transformed into the Waffen SS) only a political past, but were not actually a political organization. For me, joining the SS was not equivalent with expressing a political will.

It was all a matter of legal semantics. If joining the SS was not political within Hitler's Germany, then what did constitute a political will? Klink, the adroit historian, carefully sidestepped the treacherous territory: "Under no circumstances will I let myself be drawn into arguments about the political orientation of the Waffen SS."[73] Soon Hinrich and his wife both found themselves learning many details that Jochen had never made them aware of.

"My husband did not repeat anything that we had not heard over and over again from my father-in-law." Jochen had been careful to shield the family, a tactic made more successful by generational disinterest. "You see my father-in-law as the soldier in history," Dorothee Peiper-Riegraf wrote to Peiper's wartime underling Klink. "We never really found our way to that part of him—there was always an impenetrable wall about him, but he was and is an example for us in his human bearing."

> He [Jochen Peiper] said that he who had always been non-political had been pulled into the political mill in connection with Nazi politics. I remember his testimony so well because I never accepted it, because I am of the opinion that one cannot separate soldiering from the desired political aims for which the soldierly effort is done. . . . I can't read about Boves or Malmedy, because it makes me ill. War does not legitimize killing. I see in every form of force and aggression—and war is the most perverted form—only the expression of political inability and human erring. . . . But to accuse my father in law of anything would mean to ignore the Zeitgeist and would deny that one must be educated into democracy and to deny the modern understanding of a soldier.[74]

In December 1976 Harvey T. Rowe, a prominent journalist working for *Quick*, approached Hinrich. The magazine was looking to feature a nine-page exposé on the Peiper affair in February 1977 timed to coincide with a television documentary being done by Chronos Film GmbH in Berlin.[75] Peiper's old editor at Motorbuch Verlag, Wolfgang Schilling, had suggested Rowe write a book. In contacting Peiper's son, Rowe termed the Malmédy trial a "screaming injustice." However, Hinrich Peiper was cynical, considering helping only "out of the fundamental consideration that I have promised to support everything that can be of benefit to my father's reputation."[76] Then, only weeks later, Peiper's son expressed doubt about Rowe's newly conceived plan to write a biography of his father. Although Schilling vouched for Rowe's qualifications, there was a more basic problem: "My mother does not care much for this idea." In exchanges with Ernst Klink and Chronos producing the film on his father, Hinrich waxed fatalistic. "They want to make a movie that fits into the political landscape as they do not want to cause any damage. One must remain skeptical."[77]

Meanwhile the SS veteran's organization, HIAG, was working on its own attempt to get a favorable Peiper biography written for Motorbuch Verlag. In one letter old SS officer comrade and HIAG coordinator Walter Harzer opined that they enlist the help of Herbert Reinecker, creator of *Derrick*, an enormously popular German television detective series; otherwise, Erich Kern, that crazy SS loose-cannon author, might do something![78] Even though Reinecker himself was an ex-Waffen SS man who had fought in Normandy, none of the HIAG plans came to fruition. It was more lucrative—and a lot less controversial—to compose scripts for *Derrick*.

Back with the family, by February 1977 Hinrich Peiper, the attorney, was asking for more information on the Boves affair as a method of clearing his father's name—a radical move that Ernst Klink questioned. Why stir the pot again? "Inevitably during a discussion of the affair, names of comrades will be used who would not want to be again in the center of public interest." There were other reasons. "Dr. Kempner has not forgotten the old defeat and would be ready this time . . . and the investigation looks to find comrades willing to make statements and commit perjury. . . . I would ask you to not undertake anything without approval of your mother, because for years, she has kept the bad luck of this episode from you."[79]

Things did not get easier. Sigurd Peiper moved in with her daughter in Munich and for a time lived in Miesbach close to her good friend Sigrid Mayr, who helped her by furnishing an inexpensive flat. At the foot of the Bavarian Alps, surrounded by mountains and highlands, Sigurd felt at home, even if ill. To the Mayr family, Sigurd Peiper looked "drawn and terrible," with little money.[80] The Landkreis of Miesbach was typical of those alpine rural communities that the Nazis favored; even after the war it had that reputation.[81] Indeed, the old SS officers school at Bad Tölz had been only a few kilometers away during the war. Sigrid had also been the wife of an SS officer, Sturmbannführer Friedrich Wilhelm Mayr, and Sigurd knew her during the war. "Jochen always appreciated her," Mayr wrote of Peiper; the bonds were strong. Indeed, with some Jewish blood and married to an SS officer, Himmler himself had forbidden her from bearing children. "She is one of those types who always stands up for justice; as she was 'racially persecuted' her word carries some weight."[82] When Sigurd visited, the two women talked:

> It is difficult to adequately express one's feelings about the events in Traves. Still today, I simply cannot get over the incident. Jochen and I so much hoped and wished that after all that had happened, we at least could look forward to a peaceful and tranquil old age. But things happened differently and I feel left behind and alone. . . . Unfortunately my health is not doing well. . . . The heavy burden on my soul has eaten away my physical resistance and I am not longer up to much.[83]

Regardless of failing health, detectives shadowed Sigurd at her apartment. Family mail was checked, and friends endured the embarrassment of interview and interrogation. And although Sigurd had legally declared her certainty that the charred corpse in the ruins of Le Renfort was that of her husband, the pitiful remains were not returned to the family. The Foreign Office, to which the family had appealed for help, remained silent for weeks.[84] Without an official act in the matter, the French claimed it was impossible to return the remains still held at the mortuary in Vesoul. And in absence of positive identity, the crazy French laws indicated that Joachim Peiper would instead be considered "legally missing," a delay that could suspend resolution of the issue for thirty years.

That the French still held onto Peiper's body would eventually raise such a stink that the fifteenth session of the German Bundestag forced the consulate general in Lyon to expedite the matter.[85] All the while the Nazi hunter Simon Wiesenthal brooded. The blackened corpse was not that of Peiper, he grumbled to the press. "They are experts at arranging convenient disappearances." Why the amputated limbs, the body burned so badly that reasonable identification was impossible? The reason: Peiper was still living. The yellow press, quoting Wiesenthal in Vienna, had Peiper wintering in the modest suburbs between Ipanema and Copacabana along with Brazil's other curiously welcomed immigrants.[86] The whole thing developed into a huge scandal.[87] The hastily produced Chronos Film Peiper television special aired on February 17, 1977. And in a television documentary entitled *Das Gericht der Sieger*—The Justice of the Victors—the Peiper affair featured prominently.[88] Even then, the Boves story came off as a bad mark on Jochen Peiper.[89]

Under mounting political pressure the French government moved to bring a close to the episode. The straightforward way to do that was to produce certain proof that the carbonized mass being held in France was that of Peiper. On March 6, 1977, Attorney General Marc Dreyfus in the Vesoul police office made an official statement to the press. Even with proof not available, Dreyfus was inclined to see the cup half full. "Nothing was opposed to this being the body of Joachim Peiper," Dreyfus read from the official autopsy report, "but the condition of the carbonized body does not permit the identification to be more 'affirmative.'" Dreyfus put on the best spin possible: there was "a very strong probability that Joachim Peiper perished in the fire on the night of July 14."[90] But for fain journalists, Dreyfus might as well have said Peiper was on a jet bound for Rio de Janiero.[91]

In reality the former SS colonel was returning home to Germany. Amid chaos and calumny, Peiper's incomplete and fragmented body was at last returned to the family.[92] At 6 p.m. on April 1, 1977, a French hearse from Vesoul, bearing a closed casket, arrived at the Munich Forest Cemetery. Inside, supposedly, were Peiper's earthly remains. Yet without a proper death certificate, the final burial could not take place. A rather fantastic piece of paperwork accompanied the body:

> On 14 July 1976 at Traves at the place called le Renfort,
> a person of male sex died, whose identity could not be determined
> and whose personal description is: None.[93]

With that confusion, Hinrich Peiper involved himself in elaborate legal maneuvering. Accepting the corpse as Jochen Peiper would close the case in France, but without a death certificate of certain identification, no insurance or other compensation could be recovered. The son persuaded the Munich district attorney's office to confiscate the body and to conduct their own attempt at identification. Yet when the autopsy was conducted on April 5, no one at the Munich Forensic Institute had counted on a corpse with a missing head. Two steps back.

This disturbing event delayed final arrangements for over a year until the French could produce the missing head. The fantastic claim: they had misplaced them!

In the meantime, Georges Arnaud and Roger Kahane began a seven-month investigation with the aim to air a special on the Peiper story. During trips stretching from Belgium to Italy, the French journalists conducted dozens of interviews of many people associated with the affair at Traves. On December 6, 1977, their story was ready for Parisian television but would not be aired—it was too controversial. For over a year Antenne 2's producers struggled with a thorny problem. Although most of what Arnaud and Kahane found was completely mundane and in keeping with the official story, one facet was deeply disturbing. Arnaud was something of a maverick journalist (some say that designation was a stretch), thriving on controversy, and a known Communist sympathizer. Arnaud claimed to have spoken with a "very reliable witness" who told the writer on the strict condition of anonymity that Peiper was still alive. The corpse at Le Renfort was not that of the SS colonel! Try as they might, the producers could not get Arnaud to reveal the identity of the secret informant, and without proof, they steadfastly refused to televise the documentary.

Undaunted by the move, Arnaud and Kahane quickly composed a contentious book to air the theory that Peiper might still be living. The book, *L'Affaire Peiper*, came out in May 1978, an ode to yellow journalism. Splashy headlines quoted Arnaud, "I Have Proof That Peiper Is Alive!" There seemed no end to it.[94]

Reaction to the book reseeded the storms of controversy. Amid all the rukus, Mr. Christian Nannini, the new magistrate of Vesoul, decided to reopen the case that summer. Arnaud would be called as a witness. Nannini was exceedingly dubious of his claims yet inclined to weigh them along with everything else.[95] Letters in the press, both in Germany and France, took Arnaud to task: "Rejoice Mr. Arnaud that you live in a Country where justice does not condemn such unsupported arguments." Others called for him to reveal his secret source, even on betrayal of his confidence.

Nannini reacted rapidly: on June 23 he heard the chain-smoking Arnaud in his private office for three hours. They released no transcript, but when the bushy-haired Frenchman descended the steps, he professed triumph. "My hearing means the case is not closed and one day the investigation will open on the truth," he boomed. "Peiper's affair is not buried, it has just begun!"[96] But his enthusiasm seemed unfounded. Nannini brought in other witnesses and the police records were reexamined. Nothing came of it. The four young men from Gray again all stuck to their stories. Even so, Arnaud was right about one thing: the controversy would not die.[97]

Legal moves assailed Antenne 2 to release the film. The petitions came from the International Anti-Semitic League and a left-wing organization, Fédération nationale des déportés internés, résistants et patriotes. The controversial television piece finally aired, on Sunday, January 21, 1979, but not before the rather extraordinary step of allowing the Vesoul attorney general, Marc Dreyfus, the opportunity to rebuke the documentary in *Le Monde*. He complained that the story in *L'Affaire Peiper* outlined "a false scenario at the expense of the facts." All this made little difference; the Peiper affair in France had become something akin to the assassination of President John F. Kennedy in the United States. Phantom SS men staging a death in Traves and Jochen Peiper escaping to a Nazi haven had replaced the ghostly shooters on the grassy knoll, with chain-smoking, French Communist, Georges Arnaud as Oliver Stone.

Nor did Peiper's supposed death do anything to quell conjecture about what had happened at the Malmédy crossroads on December 17, 1944. There were now some misguided German souls who posited that Americans killed in an errant air attack on Honsfeld in Belgium had been later moved to the massacre field. But Ernst Klink, Peiper's old wartime confidant and historian at the MGFA, rejected that outlandish theory. He had seen the autopsies. How could one explain the powder burns on faces twisted in fear and others frozen in death with upheld hands?

> The air attack thesis is known and untenable, based on the examination of the corpses. Also, neither Peiper nor any of the other participants denied the shooting of the Americans. Only the question of orders remains. In this respect, final clarity about the participating persons cannot yet be established. Even the inner circle does not know more.[98]

Nor did efforts to revise the Peiper story end there. In 1986, as Belgian researcher Gerd Cuppens, sought to get to the truth of Malmédy, he encountered resistance from the Waffen SS *Kameraden*. "German veterans don't want to be reminded of Malmedy," he wrote to an American historian. "They want me to omit the massacre at Baugnez which I most stubbornly refuse to do."[99] The same effort at expurgation continues today.

And was Peiper himself really dead? To be sure, many in Traves and the surrounding farmland still fancied him alive. The priest of Traves, Louis Ducros was emphatic. "People in Traves believe different things. Ernest Rigoulot believed Peiper was murdered. I was always against that. I thought the whole thing was a set up. I never believed it." Like the eerie escape of Adolf Hitler in the novel by René Fallets, *Ezarts*, Ducros believed Peiper had shrewdly escaped. The priest remained bitter at the refusal of the press to print his stories, blaming the police and corrupt journalists. The police, however, dismissed him—a disgruntled parish crank.[100]

There are a garden variety of opinions. The farmer who delivered milk to Peiper, Raymond Louette, and Mme. Guyot, who cooked for Ketelhut, both believe Peiper was murdered.[101] The mayor's son and others unwilling to be identified, told the author the same. Typical of the other side is the story of Jacky Gauthier, the baker's son in Traves, who was a one-time suspect, but said he was managing the oven late the night when Peiper was killed: "What do I think happened that night? . . . I doubt it was Peiper who was killed. He was too smart and cagey to be killed on his balcony. . . . I think his friend the doctor brought a body to the house which was placed inside and Ketelhut took him to the train station. Authorities here don't agree with my story. But I'm skeptical that he died here."[102]

Perhaps most disturbing was the author's final interview with the village priest, Louis Ducros. We met inside the church of Traves, standing by the pews amid the dilapidated interior. Upon informing him that I looked to understand what had happened that July night, he flatly impugned my motive. "You will never be successful in what you want to know," he said, pointing a finger at me. "Peiper had too much blood on his hands."

The curé's voice was loud and echoed in the chamber of the church while statuesque saints looked down on us from the front as if to chastise the questioner. Our conversation went on for half an hour, covering recollections of the summer of 1976, including his continuing conviction that it was not Peiper's corpse that was hauled out in a wheelbarrow. At that point the priest looked sullen. "Now," he said with drama, "I am going to tell you something really important."

The priest began to explain a perplexing encounter with Erwin Ketelhut. In 1996 or 1997 Ketelhut came to Traves and looked up the priest. They met at the café and shared a couple of glasses of red wine. Ketelhut had something on his mind. "It was the only time he ever spoke with me about Peiper," the priest said. "It wasn't a long conversation, but it was serious." Ketelhut was well aware of the Curé Ducros's doubt regarding Peiper's death.

The priest whispered to me inside the church, almost as if this was a deep secret. "Here were his exact words to me," he said, to quote Ketelhut from five years before:

"You were perfectly right in saying to me that Peiper wasn't dead. He died a long way away from here from lung cancer."[103]

Even with his conviction, the priest said he was surprised. "Well, then," he stuttered, "he got away." Ducros asked Ketelhut to elaborate. "He didn't want to tell me where he died, but added that proof his story was true could be verified. Said Ketelhut: "The proof is that before the house burned, he had increased his insurance so he would get more money."

Seeking verification, the author asked the priest about Ketelhut's whereabouts. "He is dead," the priest told me. "He lived with a much younger woman in Cussey-sur-l'Ognon, but she doesn't know anything." That seemed final. For everyone the author had spoken with over several years, from Inspector Lavaux, to the priest, to reporters and even friends of Peiper, all confessed to believe that Ketelhut was the key to solving the enigma. "He knew much more than he said," Lavaux told the author.[104] Now final resolution seems impossible. We only have the word of the Curé Ducros and his fantastic tale up against much contrary evidence that Peiper did, indeed, perish in his home that warm summer night.

The truth? With Ketelhut dead, we will likely never know. The mystery of Traves lies enshrouded in a secret web buried in a dark well of the collective unconscious of Eastern France. It is the place in the old territory of Burgundy and the Franche Compté where Heinrich Himmler had planned a secret postwar SS state—the Zone Interdite—the French forbidden zone. Did Peiper unconsciously carry on that legacy?[105] "Ten years ago, Peiper was a nuisance," the local newspaper declared in 1987. Now the little village of Traves seemed cursed, holding some deep secret. "Today this phantom still haunts us."[106]

The fiery end of Jochen Peiper hung like a wartime albatross over Traves. The absurd contradiction of an SS war hero living in a backwash provincial French village had settled into the inky shadows along the Saône River and refused to depart. Was it simply the chimera of the dead SS hero? Or was it something more complex and unforgivable—the trace of collective suffering of millions slaughtered in Hitler's immensely destructive war?

RESTLESS GHOSTS HAUNTED TRAVES, THE VILLAGERS, AND THE MEMORY OF Jochen Peiper himself.

EPILOGUE

JOCHEN PEIPER'S FAMILY REMAINED PRIVATE AMID THE YEARS OF GRIM speculation. In accordance with her husband's wishes, Sigurd Peiper told her children she would never sell the property in Traves.[1] She remained gravely ill and resigned to unfolding events:

> Life is the best, but the hardest teacher. Afterward one smiles with amusement about so many things about which one formerly got all worked up and exasperated. Despite all the not always beautiful experiences and events, I must and can say that I am far from bitter and resigned. Naturally, it is not always easy to find sense in all the things that happen. One cannot dismiss everything as fate. One must endeavor to realize how unimportant and small we are as individuals and despite that, to make the best of one's life. I would like to live some more years with my interests and with my children, but the decision unfortunately is not mine. I am now quite content and must take things as they come.[2]

On April 10, 1979, Sigurd died in Munich, only a few weeks after German authorities finally released her husband's body for burial. Even a private bereavement was difficult—the family had to deny a request from suspicious French police to attend the funeral! A joint memorial service was held in the Waldfriedhof in Munich, where son Hinrich gazed from present to past:

> Even though my parents did not have their wish fulfilled to grow old together on their own soil and die together like Philemon and Baucis and subsequently be transformed into trees, they planted and pampered many of them as living proof of their activities and existence on earth. Similarly we, their children and grandchildren, obtained from our parents a piece of immortality, be it only via Mendel and his inheritance principles. The trees planted by them will survive us all and certainly will see times during which we or our children may peacefully gather together in their shadow.[3]

Sigurd and Jochen were together; the son and daughters placed the two urns containing ashes at the cemetery on May 30, 1979, marking the formal end to three difficult years. The resting place at Schondorf-Ammersee near Munich is a secluded spot by the local church.[4]

Soon after his father's death Hinrich revealed deep feeling:

> Sometime during summer or fall, I want to drive to Traves on a weekend, at least to show the flag and take inventory. Certainly there will be moments there where we can get together with our children peacefully and undisturbed in the shadow of so many trees planted and nurtured by my parents. That is a comforting thought, that what our parents had built there would be kept for their children and grandchildren.[5]

Hinrich Peiper's view evolved over time. Leaving a difficult past behind, he moved away from his homeland to live in New York City. There he worked as a senior German officer for the Dresdner Bank until retirement. Had his father been murdered or was it manslaughter instead?[6] And in the end, did it matter? The wounds of 1976 healed only slowly.

> Their generation was different in their frequent confrontation with death. My father had that experience. Whoever has seen so many dead in war, who has lived in that time, being aware of millions of people losing their lives, to whom death and transitoriness has become daily experience, to them, death has lost all shock and sorrow.[7]

Over time, Hinrich's appreciation of his father changed substantially, to the recognition that his father had been a war criminal. Coming to terms with that reality in recent years, Hinrich Peiper's family has devoted themselves to the Freya von Moltke Stiftung, which seeks to heal the relationship of Germans to Poland after the great tragedy of World War II. The new generation of Peipers has broken with the sensibilities held by Jochen Peiper during the war, even if his older sister, Elke, retains a different opinion. Yet even then, Jochen was Hinrich's father—at once and always a complex relationship:

> To properly deal with a father like mine has never been easy; knowledge, approach and responsibility we are taking has changed over the years and it continues to be a difficult path and I am not always sure how to judge. One will come to the conclusion that not only Himmler, but also his assistants were criminals, murderers since we tend to look at the Third Reich from its results and not at the circumstances of the individuals and the society how it all developed into a system with little resistance or opposition. Observing such a murderous system by how it all ended up, makes it rather easy for many people today to claim that they would have fought it all along and that they would never have followed a Hitler. I do not claim to have at all times succeeded—not even within my own small family—in making the distinction between my father as a father and as compared to the public person [where] he was an assistant to Himmler and a Waffen SS-man.
>
> So my inability and difficulty to justly and adequately deal with my father will continue.[8]

Father and son were of different generations, a chasm that is still being spanned by generations in Germany.[9] Hinrich Peiper has accepted his father's past, even if the constant prodding has become a source of irritation. "My father was a man of his time," he says. Hinrich Peiper is of another epoch, and one with different aspirations.[10]

Even at the turn of the century Traves seems ageless. Farmers in overalls work the fields and tend the *bêtes*—beasts. Old men, holding canes and topped by felt berets, sit under shade trees by the old World War I monument and ponder the French sky. Not far away, patrons no longer argue the afternoon over wine at Chez Néné. With a fallen economy, the place is now closed. But at times of weakness, hungry bygone ghosts haunt the village. "It's not the same," the priest says. "A lot of the young people have moved away. There isn't a lot of money here and things are getting bad." Another local complains that since the Peiper affair "this place seems like Sicily."[11]

Along the narrow road leading west of the town there is nothing obvious to suggest the former domain of a retired Waffen SS officer who sought haven by the Saône River. The only sign is a power line draped on concrete poles. The black cable stretches from the road across the bright green pasture populated by affable French cows. From there, it simply disappears into a dense thicket of trees before the riverbank.

Traipsing across the muddy pasture and peering into the wood, one finds the moss-covered concrete steps that lead down to Le Renfort. The dog kennels, with their wire enclosure that started it all, still stand just off to the right. Below the steps is the crumbling ruin of the former house, being fast reclaimed by the verdant forest growth. Ivy covers the standing walls, and snails creep up the sides of the moss-covered hearth that Peiper once held dear. New birch and conifers are now thick over the lot where the old SS man spent so many days to hold their growth at bay. The way down to the Saône, where he enjoyed a swim or paddle, is nearly impassible with dense stands of sprouting firs. The muddy river can't even be seen.

Peiper's labor is still evident in the neatly stacked firewood in the shed that he built by hand. Strewn about the grounds one finds shards of clay roof tiles mixed with bits of the burned-out house. Outside the basement, encrusted in the ivy and mud, are empty Weck glass jar lids that once held blackberry jam canned by Frau Peiper. In front of the ruins the walnut tree set out by Bettina Wieselmann is huge. The oaks Peiper planted himself now tower over the property, disappearing slowly in the vines below. Standing in the midst of the vestige of Le Renfort, the huge trees whisper in the wind, unable to communicate their witness. And time consumes all.

What remains of the ruins is still owned by the family. Hinrich Peiper reflects sadly on the disheveled state of the property and sometimes ponders the difficult questions he would now ask of his father. It was ten years before Bettina Wieselmann could hazard the emotional reckoning of going back. Silke Peiper could only return after twenty; Elke Peiper has never traveled again to Traves.

At police headquarters in Dijon, France, the case remains unsolved.[12] Nearly forty years later, no one really knows what happened to Jochen Peiper.

NOTES

Prologue: The Simple Life

1. *Les Mystères de L'Est,* Collection "Reflets et Racines," ed. *L'Est Républicain,* 1988.

2. André Moissé, "L'affaire des chiens de Peiper renvoyée sine die," *L'Est Républicain,* September 1976. The sheep's owner, Joseph Noël, contacted the police. "He loved his two dogs, . . . Timm and Timm might have killed a sheep at night, but he doubted his dogs had really done that. But he wanted to avoid anything that could bring a conflict so he constructed a kennel." Frau Dr. Uta Müller, interview by author, May 19, 1999.

3. Details of the man's daily life and routine in Traves are taken primarily from Hinrich Peiper, interviews by author, May 5 and May 21, 1999, as well as a detailed discussion with a close family friend: Bettina Wieselmann, interview by author, May 13, 1999.

4. Letter to Fritz Kosmehl, August 6, 1973. Courtesy Fritz Kosmehl.

5. Letter to Rudolf Lehmann, December 6, 1975.

6. Letter to Elke Maierl, December 2001, anonymous source.

7. H. Peiper, interview, March 2009.

8. Müller, interview.

9. Ernst Wiechert was an East Prussian poet and novelist whose stories were set in the prewar Weimar Republic. A veteran of the First World War, Wiechert's rich poetic imagery was populated by lush East Prussian landscapes and sympathetic rural characters living through the upheavals between wars. At first the Nazis claimed Wiechert as a "blood and soil" author embracing their vision, yet in 1937 Wiechert warned an audience at Munich University that Germany "stands already on the edge of an abyss." Declared "a corrupter of youth," Wiechert was sent to Buchenwald Concentration Camp in 1938. He wrote *The Simple Life* (trans. Marie Heynemann [London: Quartet Books, 1994]), immediately after his inhumane experiences at Buchenwald. The story describes a disillusioned Prussian naval officer despairing of the lack of national repentance after the end of the First World War. Living in a wooden hut on an island, he finds that hard physical labor amid nature liberates him from his unpleasant memories of the war.

10. Stephen Sanders, interview by author, January 21, 1999. Sanders visited Traves on June 2, 1973, and found the old soldier jovial and in good spirits. Regarding SS heroes: "All people need heroes, even if they end up on the junk pile of history." Letter to Fritz Kosmehl, August 6, 1973.

11. Details of the home provided by Inspector Roger Lavaux as well as author's visit to the property in May of 1999, and deed to property, held in Vesoul. The home was six-by-twenty-two meters with two floors. "L'Inspecteur Divisionnaire Roger Lavaux à Monsieur le Directeur du Service Régional de Police Judiciaire à Dijon: Service Régional de Police Judicaire à Dijon: No. 2 400/SC," no date. This official report, prepared for M. Daniel Clerget, the examining magistrate in Vesoul, was provided to the author, hereafter: Lavaux Police Report, 2–3.

12. Numerous descriptions refer to the property as "Le Renfort"—"the fortress," and some say this was an invention from an eager press looking to turn Peiper's Traves abode into an armed bunker. In actuality the property was known as Le Ranfort from the local name for the woods where the home was built. However, that the old man himself called his property Le Renfort is established in a scene of the home's entrance and its mailbox in a French television documentary: Georges Arnaud and Roger Kahane, *L'Affaire Peiper*, January 21, 1979. Within the narrative I use the old soldier's own preference for the place. For the official designation of Le Ranfort, papers showing the deed designation from Vesoul.

13. Jacques Gauthier, interview by author, August 16, 2001. Gauthier was the baker's son.

14. Martial Rigoulot, interview by author, Traves, August 15, 2001. "You won't find anyone to say anything bad about him here," said Rigoulot, the son of the deceased mayor. "The man was someone refined with an imposing presence. He was someone the people respected. He had an air about him."

15. Craig Unger, interview by author, April 2, 1999. Unger visited Traves in 1978 and spoke with many villagers.

16. Background from author's visit to Traves in May 1999 and summer 2001.

17. "He was reserved and cold. Very cold." Curé Louis Ducros, interview by author, August 16, 2001.

18. Sanders, interview.

19. Raymond Louette, interview by author, August 16, 2001.

20. Ibid. "During the war, there was occupied France and unoccupied France, but our whole region was sealed off and no one could come in or go out. We were a special zone, and in 1942, there were SS men here on R&R."

21. All but one of the names were from the Great War. One, Charles Rigoulout, who died in 1918, was undoubtedly a relative of the town mayor.

22. André Moissé, "Dix ans de prison j'ai payé," *L'Est Républicain*, June 23, 1976.

23. WASt file for Max Moritz, was born February 11, 1912, in Reutlingen, he later became a party member and joined the regular army as a Schirrmeister (Feldwebel). In 1942 he was assigned to Heereskraftfahrpark 513, later serving in 1944 on Panzer Ersatz Abteilung 7 in Böblingen. He became a French war prisoner May 10, 1945, and was released the following January.

24. *Les Mystères de L'Est*. The trip to St. Tropez with Moritz was to visit SS war reporter Hans Schwarz van Berk as well as Nachlass Schwarz van Berk, BA-K N-1373, Band 6. For the trip with Wieselmann and "too many uniforms": Wieselmann, interview.

25. Peiper statement to the police in Vesoul, France, June 22, 1976. The police visited his home for a three-hour interview. The purchase price of Le Renfort was ₣110,000.

26. Raymond Louette, interview. Louette brought milk to the German colonel. "He felt he was a burden to society," he said, "but he had a good opinion of France." Louette knew Gauthier. "Albert Gauthier had been a supporter of Petain and Vichy France during the German occupation."

27. Jean Michel Bezzina, RTL Radio interview, June 23, 1976, recording in author's possession.

28. H. Peiper, interview by author, May 21, 1999.

29. H. Peiper, "Letters to the Editor," *Quick*, No. 36, August 26, 1976. Also, H. Peiper, interview, May 5, 1999.

30. Ehrhard Gührs, interview by author, December 17, 2004. His bushwhacking helpers, seen in photos, were Otto Dinse, Dr. Robert Brüstle, and Walter Kern, all former officers with his wartime battalion.

31. *Les Mystères de L'Est.*

32. J. Peiper, statement, June 22, 1976.

33. Jochen Peiper to Karl Wortmann, November 28, 1974.

34. Jochen Peiper to Fritz Kosmehl, February 8, 1971.

35. *Les Mystères de L'Est.* The inscription on the mailbox read simply "J. Peiper."

36. Peiper to Fritz Kosmehl, November 29, 1974. "For us, however, it was strenuous, because such a back woods couple has their rhythm. We are no longer used to all that talking."

37. J. Peiper to H. Peiper, undated, Traves. Source: Nachlaß Ernst Klink, BA-MA, Zur Trauerfeier am 17.4.1979.

Chapter One

1. The Feldherrnhalle (Hall of Generals) had originally been built by King Ludwig I of Bavaria in 1846. Bronze plates on the rear of its limestone walls commemorated both the German fallen in the war of 1870 as well as the First World War. For the service to the Third Reich, Hitler consecrated it on November 9, 1933, as the Platz der Helden (Heroes Square) for the martyrs of the failed 1923 Putsch in Munich just outside the Feldherrnhalle, in which the seemingly vanquished National Socialists had attempted the overthrow of the Weimar Republic. All official consecrations of the heroes of National Socialism and the swearing in of members of the SS would be held on the same spot. November 9, according to German pagan tradition, was the Feast Day of Quatuor Coronati, the four crowned martyrs, an ancient and obscure celebration dating back to the fourth century. In 1933 Hitler declared November 9 as the Day of National Solidarity, harkening back both to his failed Putsch in 1923 as well as the same date in 1918 when Kaiser Wilhelm II was forced to acknowledge the end of the First World War and the Kaiserreich. Description of the November 9, 1935, swearing-in ceremony is taken from detailed records of the Leibstandarte SS Adolf Hitler at the National Archives, "SS-eigene Veranstaltungen und Veranstaltungen der Bewegung in der Zeit 7.-9. November 1935," NA RG 242, "Captured German Records," T-354, R226, F3894617–4831. Period press coverage was obtained from the *Münchner Neueste Nachrichten*, "Vereidigung der SS: In Anwesenheit des Führers vor der Feldherrnhalle," November 11, 1935, 10; "Die Weihenacht am Odeonsplatz"; and a series of articles appearing in the Munich newspaper from November 8–11, 1935, *Monasensia Literaturarchiv* und *Bibliothek*, Munich.

2. Nominally the SS was formed to safeguard Hitler, the National Socialist party, and its leaders.

3. Himmler considered the S-rune to be an emblem of an Aryan semireligious order. It was not by chance that the SS uniform colors were black and white, as these were those formerly worn by the Deutscher Ritterorden or the Order of Teutonic Knights. The Order had been founded in 1198 by Hermann von Salza as an organization to assist German knights who had been wounded or taken ill during the Medieval Crusades. The original order was exclusively German and expanded to lead great conquests eastward into the Baltic. The Teutonic Knights reached its apex in the second half of the fourteenth century but were suddenly halted on July 15, 1410, at Tannenberg by a coalition of Poles, Lithuanians, and Mongols. Although the ancient order was destroyed, Himmler adopted the vision of Teutonic Knights for his own modern SS.

4. Long after the war Peiper would recall this evening from retirement in faraway France. Peiper to Hans Schwarz van Berk, November 9, 1970. "At least a quiet 9th of November without parade marching and fiery pylons." BA-K, N 1373, Band 6.

5. Like Hitler, Himmler had unremarkable origins. He was born into the family of a university-trained schoolteacher in 1900. His parents administered a strong education and a fairly strict Catholic upbringing. Intellectually, Himmler held his own, but was physically unimpressive. In school he did poorly at sports and, at thirty-five, was prematurely balding and badly nearsighted. One Nazi party Gauleiter (regional party boss) ribbed, "If I looked like him, I would not speak of race at all." Louis P. Lochner, *The Goebbels Diary* (New York: Doubleday, 1982), 507.

6. The Thanksgiving prayer for Dutch freedom fighters from 1586. Music by Adriannus Valerius (1625) and words translated and adapted by Eduard Krumm (1877).

7. "Vereidigung der SS," Völkischer Beobachter VB, November 11, 1935, microfilm at Library of Congress. The oath administered on November 9, 1935, comes from NA R-242, T-354, R-226, "SS-eigene Veranstaltungen und Veranstaltungen der Bewegung in der Zeit 7.-9. November 1935," F3894831.

8. The Nazis claimed their regime was the natural historical successor to other major periods of German history. The Third Reich was the German empire proclaimed by the Nazis and was to last a thousand years. They referred to the first as the Holy Roman Empire, which came to an end in 1806. Their second empire encompassed Bismarck's Deutsches Kaiserreich, which stretched from 1871 to 1918.

9. "Vereidigung der SS," VB, *op. cit.*, November 11, 1935.

10. "Wenn alle untreu werden" was an old German spiritual adopted by the SS for their ceremonies. Music by Friedrich Ludwig Jahn (1724), words by Max von Schenkendorf (1814).

11. *Münchner Neueste Nachrichten, op. cit.*

12. Historically the Germanic ruler of the eighteenth and nineteenth centuries had *leib* (life) bodyguard units assigned. The Prussian Army of Frederick the Great included the Leibregiment zu Pferde and the Leib-Karabiners. During the campaign of 1809 the Leib-Regiment marched with the Bavarian contingent under Napoleon's La Grande Armee. The Leibstandarte Adolf Hitler was formed on March 17, 1933, by Sepp Dietrich two months after Hitler came to power. Originally there were 117 picked SS men installed as the *Stabswasche*—headquarters guard. On November 9, 1933, the annual personal oath began when the unit, now expanded to 835 men, swore allegiance to Hitler at the Feldherrnhalle. Afterward it was officially known as the Leibstandarte Adolf Hitler. For the early history of the Leibstandarte, see James J. Weingartner, *Hitler's Guard: The Story of the Leibstandarte SS Adolf Hitler* (Edwardsville: Southern Illinois University Press, 1974).

13. The Horst Wessel song was not an original composition but rather an old German folk tune common in Northern Europe. Horst Wessel himself was a party tough who died in February 1930 at the hands of political enemies, likely Berlin Communists. His life was martyred by the National Socialists with the song that would become the official party anthem. See Daniel Siemens, *Horst Wessel: Tod und Verklärung eines Nationalsozialisten* (Munich: Siedler Verlag, 2009).

14. This infamous verse of "Und Morgen die ganze Welt" is usually mistranslated: "Today Germany belongs to us," *Unser Liederbuch* [*Our Songbook*] (Munich: Reichsjugendführung, Zentralverlag der NSDAP, 1939).

15. For "we had no personal aspirations": Peiper to Willis Everett, July 14, 1946. Willis Everett Papers, courtesy Willis Everett and James Weingartner. Peiper's recollection of his first meeting with Hitler recounted by John Toland in letter to author, December 11, 1994. For "I was ready to die for him": Peiper quoted by John Toland in interview with Max Wünsche, November 19, 1971, Library of Congress, Tape A, Pt. 1.

16. With a disability after World War I, Woldemar Peiper had become a lottery official and made at least a few enemies. "After World War I, he became lazy and dissolute and lived on credit." Unidentified optician residing at Westfälische Str. 12 in Wilmersdorf, letter to military court in Dachau, July 28, 1946, NA, RG-153, Box 83.

17. Peiper was fond of telling this story of his almost-substitute name. Wieselmann, interview, June 17, 2004. During the First World War German troops occupied all of Belgium except for the part southwest of the Ijzer. The little river became part of the northern line of defense, which ran from the English Channel eastward to Germany. Allied Supreme Command assigned the defense of the sector of Dixmude to the Belgian army. As a result, the area was completely destroyed during four years of bloody fighting, which never changed the front line. For historical background on Dixmude: Robert De Cort.

18. "The Nazi movement was born in the dragon seeds planted at Versailles and brought to monstrous growth the world depression." Freda Utley, *The High Cost of Vengeance* (Chicago: Henry Regnery, 1949), 1–2. Thanks to Neill Thomson for Peiper's birth certificate.

19. That Woldemar Peiper was convinced in Hitler's leadership and at the same time was a convinced anti-Semite is evident in two revealing letters written in 1948 to Bishop Theophil Wurm in Stuttgart. While praising his son's unit, the Leibstandarte Adolf Hitler, in one letter, he refers to "Jewish troublemakers such as Mr. Kempner and the other members of the Jewish forces in America and Israel are now so strong," he claimed, that justice from the United States was increasingly impossible. Letter to Wurm, June 19, 1948, Landeskirchliches Archiv, Stuttgart, Bischof Wurm Files.

20. Herbert Peiper, as overheard by his son, in 1938. Interview with Hans Jürgen Peiper, March 7, 2012. For background on the family: Dr. Matthias Peiper, interview by author, March 10, 2010.

21. The Wandervögel movement began in the suburbs of Berlin in 1896 as a youthful response to the oppressive social conditions of the Wilhelmine period. It became a formal association in 1901 and adopted a special style of dress, mannerisms, and speech, idealistically focused on German folk tales and a natural life.

22. For background on Peiper's school days, see his Berlin Document Center (BDC) file, NA RG-242, A 3343-SSO-368A.

23. From Peiper's curriculum vitae within his application to SS Senior District East in Berlin, December 21, 1934. At the time he was a *Rottenführer* (squad leader) in the 1. Sturm of the 7. SS Reiter Standarte. He closed the letter with an indication of his sincerity for the National Socialist movement: "[I] declare myself to be ready to make the profession of SS officer my career. Heil Hitler!"

24. "Circumstances are unclear." H. Peiper interview by author, May 21, 1999. *Schöngeist* is a euphemistic term for a homosexual man. It should be noted that in 1930, when Hans Hasso Peiper was twenty years old, the gay Berlin cabaret scene was near its apex and one of its centers, Nollendorfplatz, was not far from the Peiper home in Wilmersdorf. For an inside perspective on how the Nazis shut down the gay scene beginning in 1933, see Christopher Isherwood's famous novel, *Goodbye to Berlin* (London: Hogarth Press, 1939).

25. The hospital where Hans Hasso was institutionalized was on the other side of Berlin from where the Peipers lived. The institution still exists today, seemingly possessing the same tragic gloom likely present in the 1930s. For the relationship of the Peiper sons with their mother and father and the mother's care of Hans Hasso; H. Peiper, interview by author, May 21, 1999.

26. In everyday life in Hitler's Reich dates and their significance both in German history as well as that of the movement was accorded special import. Thus, January 30, the date Hitler took power in 1933—and Peiper's birthday—was widely revered, and Hitler used it each year to present "a state of the Reich" address.

27. Song of the "Jungvolk" from Gregor Ziemer, *Education for Death* (New York: Oxford University Press, 1941), 120. On June 20, the longest day of the year the song was sung around a blazing campfire of pine logs. The song was adapted to the melody of "Fredericus Rex," the old military march of Frederick the Great.

28. Bernd Wegner, *The Waffen-SS: Organization, Idology, and Function* (Oxford: Basil Blackwell, 1990), 11; The SS tribute "Your honor is loyalty" reflects differing sentiments from the motto of the German army, "God with us."

29. Himmler speaks to men of the Leibstandarte in Metz on September 7, 1940, NA RG 238, US Evidence 304, Box 18, Also IMT, *op. cit.*, Vol. 29, 1918-PS, 101. See also Josef Ackermann, *Heinrich Himmler als Ideologe* (Göttingen: Musterschmidt Verlag, 1970), 206–207. "All the good blood in the world, the Germanic blood, which is not on our side, one day can be our ruin." Himmler to the SS Gruppenführer, November 8, 1938, BA, NS 19/422.

30. See James J. Weingartner, "The SS Race and Settlement Main Office: Toward an Orden of Blood and Soil," *Historian* No. 34 (November 1971), 62–77.

31. See larger discussion of the Reichsführer's racial plans in Ackermann, *Heinrich Himmler als Ideologe.*

32. See "Weltanschauliche Schulung in der Leibstandarte SS Adolf Hitler," NA, RG-242, T-354, Roll 218, F3884560–61. For numerous examples within daily instruction to the Leibstandarte: "Standartenbefehl," 1936–1937, NA RG 242, T-354, R212.

33. For background on SS ideological indoctrination: Jürgen Matthäus, Konrad Kwiet, Jürgen Förster, and Richard Breitman, *Ausbildungsziel Judenmord? 'Weltanschuliche Erziehung von SS, Polizei und Waffen-SS im Rahmen der Endlösung'* (Frankfurt: Fischer Verlag, 2003). For the SS leadership magazine serving as an ideological resource for the SS officer corps: *SS Leithefte, M. Müller und Sohn* in Berlin from 1934–1945: NA, T-611, Rolls 43–45.

34. Peiper BDC file, "Lebenslauf," December 21, 1934.

35. For background on this period, see "Triumph and Consolidation," in William L. Shirer's, *Rise and Fall of the Third Reich* (New York: Simon and Schuster, 1959). Also, "An Unguarded Hour" in John Toland's *Adolf Hitler* (Garden City, NY: Doubleday, 1976).

36. Moissé, "Dix Ans de Prison J'ai Payé."

37. Capt. Horace R. Hansen, letter, War Crimes Branch, quoting a Herr Rohrbach in Gotha, 1946. Evidence of Hitler's impressive but fragmented public approval within Germany is seen in the last popular vote within the republic on March 3, 1933. Hitler won a decisive victory, the National Socialists taking 44 percent of the popular vote, but this exceeded that of any other party. However, it must be noted that by this time the election was no longer democratic, as the Communist party was outlawed as well as other irregularities. "Statistical Yearbook of the German Reich," Office of US Chief of Counsel for Prosecution of Axis Criminality, *Nazi Conspiracy and Aggression* (hereafter NCA), 2514-PS, US Vol. 5 (Washington, DC: Government Printing Office, 1946), 254.

38. Jochen took weekly riding lessons with Mr. Beerman at the Tattersall Beerman at Hardenbergstr. 25, in Charlottenburg. Being Jewish, Beerman later had his operation taken over by the SS. According to Woldemar's own self-serving testimony, he claimed to have sent in Jochen's name as a potential candidate to the Cavalry Regiment in Potsdam. Woldemar Peiper, "Petition for Pardon of my son, Joachim Peiper," letter, August 30, 1946, Salmünster, National Archives, RG 549, "Records of US Army Europe, Entry 143, "War Crimes ("Cases Tried") 1945–49," "United States vs. Valentin Bersin et al.: Case 6-24: Review and Recommendations of the Deputy Theatre Judge Advocate for War Crimes" (hereafter NA: Case 6-24), Box 83.

39. The episode regarding Gen. Walther von Reichenau is related in Charles Whiting, *Massacre at Malmedy: The Story of Jochen Peiper's Battle Group, Ardennes, December, 1944* (New York: Stein and Day, 1971), 16–17. The story likely comes from tales that Peiper told Whiting during their meeting in 1969. Although this may be exaggerated relative to Peiper's political motivations, it seems clear that the cold and calculating Nazi General von Reichenau was a social friend of the Peiper family. Significantly, von Reichenau showed himself a confirmed anti-Semite during the war: he issued the infamous "Severity Order" to his troops on October 10, 1941, emphasizing "the necessity of a severe, but just revenge on the sub-human species of Jewry." Johannes Hürter, *Die deutschen Oberbefehlshaber im Krieg gegen die Sowjetunion 1941/42*, (Munich: R. Oldenbourf Verlag, 2007) 579–588.

40. The Reiter SS, to which young Peiper belonged in 1933, was made part of Himmler's Allgemeine SS to boost the membership and power of his fledgling SS organization. Himmler established the equestrian SS with an eye toward creating a branch of his Black Corps, which was more "socially respectable."

41. "Lombard, Gustav: Lebenslauf, June 26, 1935," NA BDC file, A 3343 SSO-275A. Lombard had come to the United States with his father in 1913 and remained there until 1919. For admiration of horsemanship in the SS: "Aus eigener Kraft" and "SS Reiter in guter Form," *Das Schwarze Korps*, 1936.

42. Later, in the war, Reiter-Standarte 4 was made part of the SS Totenkopf Reiter Standarten as part of Himmler's infamous mounted killing squadrons on the Eastern Front. For details of the wanton killing spree of Lombard and the SS Cavalry: Martin Cüppers, "Gustav Lombard—ein engagierter Judenmörder aus der Waffen-SS," in *Karrieren der Gewalt. Nationalsozialistische Täterbiographien*, eds. Klaus-Michael Mallmann and Gerhard Paul (Darmstadt: Wissenschaftliche Buchgesellschaft, 2004), 145–155.

43. Hitler's praise of the SS within the Night of the Long Knives quoted in the VB, July 26, 1934. NSDAP: Nationalsuzialistche Deutsche Arbeiterpartei.

44. For details on the 1934 "Party Day of Unity," see, Hamilton T. Burden, *The Nuremberg Party Rallies 1923–39* (New York: Praeger, 1967), 76–99.

45. Ancestry was scrupulously checked, and recruits had to have a "Jew-free" pedigree stretching back to the year 1750 in the case of officers or 1800 for enlisted men ("Merkblatt für den Eintritt als Freiwilliger in die SS-Verfügungstruppe," BA-B, Sammlung Schuhmacher/V 432/ I). Ideally Himmler wanted the ancestral search eventually carried back to 1650, a goal that proved ludicrous. Bradley F. Smith and Agnes F. Peterson, *Heinrich Himmler: Geheimreden 1933 bis 1945* (Frankfurt: Propyläen Verlag, 1974), 61. Later the height requirement was relaxed, since at five feet six inches, even the burly head of the Leibstandarte, Josef Dietrich, did not meet that requirement. See BDC files for Dietrich: NARA (A3343-SSO-152).

46. The first squadron of SS Reiter Standarte 7, to which Peiper belonged, was chosen as the "diplomat platoon" for the Party Day in 1934.

47. Hitler's speech from the Nuremberg rally in Leni Riefenstahl's motion picture, *Triumph des Willens*, 1934.

Chapter Two

1. Both the teachers at Jüterbog and Braunschweig did not encourage a view of the SS Verfügungstruppe as "soldiers like any others." In July 1941 Emil Sator ordered the 10. Infanterie Regiment of the Totenkopf to round up and kill the Jews in the town of Ostrog near Rowno. An estimated 2,600 were shot that day. For details, see Martin Cüppers, *Wegbereiter der Shoah. Die Waffen-SS, der Kommandostab Reichsführer-SS und die Judenvernichtung 1939–1945* (Darmstadt, 2005), 167f. Moreover, the class included individuals like Paul Werner Hoppe, who would play a large role in the concentration camp system where thousands died. Peiper knew Hoppe well; he too had been born in Wilmersdorf, where both took paramilitary training with the Reichskuratorium and then later the pre-officer course at Jüterbog. Karin Orth, *Die Konzentrationslager-SS. Sozialstrukturelle Analysen und biographische Studien* (München, 2004), 118–124.

2. See NA, BDC files for Karl Künstler (A3343-SSO-226A). Künstler would later command the concentration camp at Flossenberg, where many Soviet prisoners were killed during the war. Later he was removed from the office—by Himmler himself—due to problems with alcoholism. Amazingly he was then posted to a command within the 7. SS Gebirgs Division Prinz Eugen, where he served to the end of the war. See Tom Segev, *Soldiers of Evil: The Commandants of Nazi Concentration Camps* (New York: McGraw-Hill, 1987), 70.

3. BDC File for Rudi Lehmann, A3342-SSO-250A, Certificate of service, October 24, 1934.

4. See Rudolf Lehmann, *The Leibstandarte*, Vol. 1 (Winnipeg: J. J. Fedorowicz, 1987), Appendix 3: "Recruit Training in Jüterbog."

5. For detailed research on this episode, see Jens Westemeier, "Bedingt geeignet"—Die Psychologische Prüfstelle der Reichswehr," in *Himmlers Krieger: Joachim Peiper und die Waffen-SS in Krieg und Nachkriegszeit* (Paderborn: Schöningh-Verlag, 2014), 50–52.

6. BDC files on Peiper, "Psychological Testing Station X Opinion of the Testing Committee, April 4, 1935." "The subject is intelligent and energetic, but still immature and

opaque. . . . Tends to criticism and sarcasm." The team of examiners, led by a Dr. Kleemeister, deemed Peiper "conditionally suitable" as officer material.

7. Given that German people are by culture allowed to be more critical than in the United States, the evaluator's report of Peiper would indicate a strongly arrogant streak.

8. It must be noted that Hausser was not in any way a revolutionary military figure but wished the future Waffen SS to follow the regulations of the ordinary army, a perspective that was in stark contrast to those of other more radicalized SS generals, such as Sepp Dietrich, Theodor Eicke, or Felix Steiner. Heinz Höhne, *Der Orden unter dem Totenkopf. Die Geschichte der SS* (Gütersloh: Sigbert Mohn Verlag, 1967), 442.

9. For the emphasis on proper appearance, dress and behavior, see Richard Schulze-Kossens, *Militärischer Führernachwuchs der Waffen-SS: Die Junkerschulen* (Coburg: Nation Europa Verlag, 1999), 266–271.

10. BDC file for Karl Heinz Brohl, NA, BDC, A3343-SSO-108.

11. Börchers, diary, *op. cit.*

12. Waffen SS leaders such as Peiper endeavored to diminish any ideological influence within their history. As example, see Peiper to Weingartner, April 9, 1976: "Just imagining [ideological training] would cause everyone to laugh. . . . Sepp Dietrich didn't have the slightest appreciation for that and the troops rejected any kind of ideological training—to the constant annoyance of Himmler." Peiper's claims that the prewar ideological training was poorly received is substantiated by a speech given in January 1939 by Dr. Joachim Cäsar, the head of the SS Training office, who complained that emphasis of important racial and eugenics questions and the "choice of mate (*Gattenwahl*)" were met by growing apathy among SS men. See Wegner, *The Waffen SS*, 198–199. Even the head of ideological training, Fritz Weibgen, worried that plans to interest young men in the vagaries of *Mein Kampf* had gone awry. Weibgen, who Peiper derogatorily referred to as the "Priest of Wotan," complained that when asked for his reason for joining the troop, one SS man responded, "For the nice uniform." BA-K, NS 17, LSSAH, "Rasse und Schulung" and "Erfahrungsbericht 1937." However, as described by Wegner, many of these denunciations came from postwar attempts by Waffen SS men such as Richard Schulze-Kossens to distance themselves from National Socialist ideology. See Wegner, *The Waffen-SS*, xv, 151. Similar conclusions relative to the real importance attached to ideological instruction at the Junkerschule have also been reached by Martin Cüppers and other contemporary historians.

13. BDC file for Otto Eysell (A3343-SSO-193). Contrary to Peiper's later protest, Eysell was "popular and well liked" with the SS officer candidates asking for more ideological instruction, rather than less, at Braunschweig.

14. Hitler's instruction calling for the Leibstandarte as an armed force exclusively at his disposal: "Tagesbefehl No. 265," January 3, 1939, R199, 3860161. Some went so far as to naively claim that the Leibstandarte had "nothing to do with the SS and National Socialism." See statement of Unterscharführer Hans Prack, 1938, NA, RG-242, R88, F2611499. However, realistically one could agree with Dr. Bernd Wegner that if Dietrich and the Leibstandarte were not Nazis, then there could be none in Germany at all! Wegner, *The Waffen-SS*, xvi.

15. BDC file for Matthias Kleinheisterkamp (A3343-SSO-178A), who became a commander of Das Reich in 1942. Letter of Himmler to Kleinheisterkamp, October 9, 1942: "You really deserve to be relieved as division commander. . . . I only don't remove you because we would have to explain this to the Army. . . . As you are not able to deal with alcohol at age 49, I order you not to drink any alcohol for the next two years."

16. Westemeier, *Himmler's Krieger*, 52–63. For background on all of the instructors at Braunschweig—tactical, military affairs, engineer, sports, riding, Weltanschauung—see his section "SS Führerschule Braunschweig," 3.3.

17. Many fanciful stories of SS training are of specious origin. Perhaps the most famous of these mythic tales found its way into the Nuremberg proceedings (Nuremberg Document,

PS-2825). A famous apocryphal legend claimed that a live grenade was placed on the helmet of a prospective SS officer who had to calmly stand at attention while it exploded! (Even with a helmet on, he would have been instantly killed.) Another fabled test of courage had cadets frantically digging foxholes while tanks approached to prevent being crushed on the proving ground.

18. The riding lessons at Braunschweig were particularly easy for Peiper. James J. Weingartner, "Sepp Dietrich, Heinrich Himmler and the Leibstandarte SS Adolf Hitler, 1933–1938," *Central European History* 1, no. 3 (1968), 282. For the original source: Ernst-Günther Krätschmer, *Die Ritterkreuzträger der Waffen-SS* (Göttingen: Plesse Verlag, 1955), 11.

19. Albert Frey, *Ich wollte die Freiheit: Erinnerungen des Kommandeurs des 1. Panzergrenadierregiments der ehemaligen Waffen-SS* (Osnabrück: Munin Verlag, 1990), 115.

20. Lochmüller, January 31, 1936, BDC file for Peiper, *op. cit.*

21. Paul Hausser, *Soldaten wie andere auch. Der Weg der Waffen-SS* (Osnabrück: Munin Verlag, 1966), 46.

22. After the instructional course at Dachau, Heinz von Westernhagen, unlike Peiper, would be transferred to the SS security service, the SD, in Berlin. This was likely due to his travel experience as a sailor in the Far East. Unlike as has been claimed, however, von Westernhagen was pleased to be working with Heydrich's SD. In May 1938, when Hitler met Mussolini in Rome, von Westernhagen functioned as an undercover agent in Rome to coordinate the use of other V-men—Nazi secret agents. On March 17, 1939—the invasion of Czechoslovakia—he wrote to his brother Harald: "Unfortunately I could not participate in the invasion. . . . However, my work at the moment is of huge interest, so I'm not angry to be here." Von Westernhagen would only later transfer to the Leibstandarte in May 1940, seeking at last to fight the war with "more than a pen." Thanks to Dörte von Westernhagen for clarifying on this matter.

23. Dr. Barbara Distel, interview by author, KZ Dachau Memorial Site, March 7, 2006. Not surprisingly, nowhere in the selective memories of Waffen SS men can they recollect the days at Dachau in 1936.

24. Peiper's grades at the SS Officer School in Braunschweig were "rather good" in the SS rating system in most categories; he finished sixteenth in the class. The assessments of his performance are in the BDC files, January 31, 1936. Graduating the same year as Peiper in April 1936 was another handsome SS officer who would figure prominently in the Leibstandarte: Max Wünsche. Unlike Peiper, Wünsche came from the other SS officer school at Bad Tölz. BDC file for Wünsche, RG 242, A3343-SSO-014C and 015c.

25. For the Leibstandarte as "an honor every German dreamed of," Peiper to Modification Board, Landsberg/Lech, October 5, 1950, NA, RG 549, Case 6-24, Box 61.

26. Horst Peiper, curriculum vitae, circa 1937. See BDC file, NA RG 242 (A3343-SSO-368A). Horst graduated from SS officer candidate school at Bad Tölz on April 20, 1937, exactly a year after his brother. He then took over a platoon of the SS Totenkopf Standarte "Oberbayern," which was charged with guarding the Dachau Concentration Camp.

27. Hitler was a devoted apostle of the venerated German philosopher Friedrich Wilhelm Nietzsche (1844–1900). Within Hitler's Munich apartment he maintained the philosopher's silver-knobbed walking cane which Nietzsche used for strolls along Lake Geneva with the equally venerated composer Richard Wagner. See David Irving, *The War Path* (New York: Viking, 1978), 54–55.

28. By 1934 Hitler saw that he could no longer maintain the cooperation of the army with the unruly SA waiting in the wings and let it be known that Ernst Röhm had to go. Himmler and Heydrich were only too happy to "uncover" a conspiracy by Röhm to overthrow Hitler. Their artifice translated into the Night of the Long Knives.

29. For a good early account of the Röhm purge, see Höhne, *Der Orden unter dem Totenkopf,* 109–112. And more recently, Richard J. Evans, *The Third Reich in Power 1933–1939*

(New York: Penguin, 2005), 31–41, and Ian Kershaw, *Hitler: 1889–1936* (New York: Hubris, W. W. Norton, 1999), 510–517.

30. For the actions during the purge in Berlin at Lichterfelde: Ian Sayer and Douglas Botting, *Hitler's Last General* (London: Transworld Publishers, 1989), 14–16.

31. From the SS ideological training manual *SS Leitheft*. Thanks to James Weingartner for recommending this unique source. "Unsere Härte," SS Leithefte 9, 1943, 1–3, NA, RG 242, T-611, Nonbiographic material microfilmed at the Berlin Document Center by the University of Nebraska, Roll 44.

32. "Rede des Reichsführers SS auf der Ordensburg Sonthofen," May 5, 1944, T-175, R92, F2613496.

33. James J. Weingartner, *Crossroads of Death* (Berkeley: University of California Press, 1979), 10. Original citation: Oskar Winter, "Gott," SS-Leitheft, Heft 4, 1942, 3–7, National Archives, T-611, R45.

34. For particulars of Himmler's SS pseudo-scientific brand of mysticism, see Walter Schellenberg, *The Labyrinth* (New York: Harper and Brothers, 1956), and Felix Kersten, *The Kersten Memoirs* (New York: H. Fertig, 1994). In particular, the skull-adorned Totenkopf ring was coveted by Waffen SS officers. Peiper always wore his band and at one point interceded on behalf of Hauptsturmführer Josef Diefenthal to obtain one for his adjutant. See Peiper to Himmler, handwritten note, no date, NA RG 242, T-175, "Records of the Reich Leader of the SS and Chief of the German Police," R112, 2636740–41.

35. Höhne, *Der Orden unter dem Totenkopf*, 170–175. It was named Wewelsburg after the Knight Wewel von Büren. For details on Wewelsburg: Dr. Jan Erik Schulte.

36. Conversation of SS Gruppenführer Siegfried Taubert with Himmler regarding Wewelsburg on Peiper's birthday, January 30, 1939. The place was to be kept as secret with no tourists allowed. NA, RG-242, T-175, Roll 88, F2611425–26.

37. Karl Hueser, *Wewelsburg 1933 bis 1945. Kult und Terrorstätte der SS* (Paderborn: Verlag Bonifatius-Druckerei, 1982), 274.

38. For photographs of the Lichterfelde barracks, see BA Bildarchiv Koblenz. Also, Paul Hausser and Jochen Peiper, *Wenn alle Brüder schweigen* (Osnabrück: Munin Verlag, 1973).

39. Hermann Stahr, as cited in Patrick Agte, *Jochen Peiper: Commander Panzerregiment Leibstandarte* (Winnipeg: J. J. Fedorowicz, 1999), 13.

40. Reinhard Rürup, *Topographie des Terrors: Gestapo, SS und Reichssicherheitshauptamt auf dem 'Prinz Albrecht-Gelände'* (Berlin: W. Arenhövel, 2002), 232.

41. Information on the day-to-day activities at the Lichterfelde barracks is covered in the daily "Standartenbefehl," 1936–1937, NA RG 242, T-354, R212.

42. For the Nazi poet's European travelogue: Hanns Johst, *Maske und Gesicht* (Munich: Albert Langen and Georg Mueller Publishing, 1935). For a contemporary biography, Rolf Düsterberg, *Hanns Johst: Der Barde der SS. Karrieren eines deutschen Dichters* (Paderborn: Schoening Ferdinand GmbH, 2004).

43. "Ein Besuch bei Obergruppenführer Dietrich," December 1936, NA, RG 242, T-354, R 210, F3874673–78.

44. "I improved my English speaking with Americans at the 1936 Olympics.": Peiper statement to Stephen Sanders, June 1945, in Feuchtwangen, Germany. Sanders, interview, January 21–22, 1999.

45. There is doubt about this episode, as it likely stems from postwar attempts at political correctness for an incarcerated SS man. Hellmut Meng to Parole Application, letter, files for Peiper, on testimony of Frau Constanze Kröger-Kment, November 14, 1955. The BDM, or Bund Deutscher Mädel (League of German Girls) was established in 1930 and eventually became mandatory for all girls between fourteen and twenty-one. It was Himmler's desire to set up a Women's Academy for Wisdom and Culture to educate females selected for their intellect, grace, political reliability, and Germanic racial purity. The tacit expectation was that

these Aryan beauties would bear many children for National Socialism. Frau Kröger-Kment remembered Peiper as "an exceptionally gifted young man . . . whom the girls at that time especially admired." Kröger was later killed in Russia in 1943. Later Constanze married SS man Kment, also from the same Junker class Bad Tölz 1936. Thus, Kröger-Kment married two SS men in succession.

46. For Peiper's participation in events during the summer Olympic games: "Standartenbefehl," August 1936, and "Empfang der deutschen Frauen Olympiamannschaft," NA RG 242, T-354, R213, 3877317–35. A specific requirement for the escorts: "fresh haircuts; dress and grooming must be immaculate."

47. Himmler's handshake with young Peiper at the Reichsparteitag was recorded on film. BA-MA, Sammlung Vorpersal, NS 756/105. Unless otherwise noted, the primary source of fundamental information on Peiper in his early years is taken from his BDC file and the reproduction of these files at the NA. Particularly CV dated December 21, 1934 and January 14, 1935.

48. Abteilung Schulung, February 4, 1935, NA, RG 242, T-354, Roll 218, F3884526.

49. Der Freiwillige, no date, "Aus dem Tagebuch eines gefallen Kameraden: 18.4.1937–1.8.1937," Sammlung Vorpersal, BA-MA, 756/105.

50. For story of Karl Hollander, Agte, *op.cit.*, 15. Description of Hitler's motorcade being cheered into Austria: Max Wünsche, interview by John Toland, November 3 and 19, 1971, LOC "The Austrian people were wildly enthusiastic after the *Anschluss*. . . . Later people would deny it, but that is not true. It was incredible. . . . There was nothing else like it in my life."

51. Marga Himmler, diary, USHMM, 1999, A.0092, entries for March 13–27, 1938.

52. Peiper's story of his recollections after the Anschluss as related to Heinz Stutterecker. Stutterecker, interview by author, in Vienna, February 28, 2009.

Chapter Three

1. BA-MA, RS 4 /15760: May 22, 1938, Peiper received free tickets to the International Avus Rennen 1938, along with twelve other officers, including Fritz Witt in Berlin.

2. BDC file for Wünsche, *op. cit.* From his assignment to the Leibstandarte in April 1936, he was assigned to the Führer Begleit Kommando, which served as ceremonial honor guards for Hitler. In that capacity, at the Reichschancellery and the Berghof in Bavaria, Wünsche's military bearing resulted in Hitler's request for him to serve as his personal adjutant, which he officially assumed in November 1938. Wünsche, taped interviews with Toland, November 1971, LOC Sound Division, C-36–C-39.

3. "My impression of him [Hitler] was favorable. . . . He had a strong personality with fascinating eyes. Women seemed drawn to him. . . . He didn't anger easily, but he hated smoking. . . . He was thoughtful—in nightly loneliness he made his big decisions often pacing his balcony for hours. . . . Hitler had no fear. He rode to Austria in an open car, but he was determined not to be killed by idiots in meetings. . . . You had excitement before meeting him, but afterwards he made you feel comfortable. . . . Today, people make him a devil, but for me, he was a very human and very sympathetic person." Wünsche, interview by Toland, November 3 and 19, 1971.

4. For Wünsche perspective on Peiper's superior: "From my point of view, Himmler was an unsympathetic man. I was glad I didn't have to deal with him much. He was responsible for the security of Germany and because of that he was associated with negative things. And people who have to deal always with negative things—they rub off a little color [*abfährben*] on you." Wünsche, interview.

5. Peiper's story as related to Heinz Stutterecker. Stutterecker, interview, February 28, 2009.

6. Marga Himmler, diary, USHMM: 1999, A.0092, February 14, 1941.

7. Although nominally part of the SS and the Verfügungstruppe, the Leibstandarte took its orders directly from Hitler, and this unavoidably reduced Himmler's control over the unit.

See James J. Weingartner, "Sepp Dietrich, Heinrich Himmler and the Leibstandarte SS Adolf Hitler, 1933–1938," *Central European History*, Vol. 1, No. 3, 264–268, 1968.

8. For the "Reichsführer SS befohlene Ausgabe," see John Michael Steiner, *Power Politics and Social Change in National Socialism: A Process of Escalation into Mass Destruction* (Atlantic Highlands, NJ: Humanities Press, 1976), 274–275.

9. For Himmler's obsession with astrology, staffing, and day-to-day decisions, see Schellenberg, *The Labyrinth*, 185. Also, Wilhelm Wulff, *Zodiac and Swastika* (New York: Coward, McCann and McGeoghegan, 1973), 163–164.

10. The pilgrimage to Braunschweig and the following ceremony is described in Himmler's adjutant's records: "Zeitfolge der Heinrichsfeier am 1. Juli.1938 in Quedlinburg," NA, RG-242, T-175, Roll 112, Frame 6851. Peiper was simultaneously assigned to the staff of the SS Reichsführer, as shown in his "Dienstlaufbahn" in his BDC personnel file. Arising as a clever prince from the French Capetian dynasty, King Heinrich I (876–936), was crowned leader of Germany in 919. The former Duke of Saxony unified the German Grand Duchies of Swabia and Bavaria after conquering Lorraine, forbidding the church to interfere in his expansionist plans. Heinrich saw the Slavic tribes to the east as the natural enemies of his dynasty and successfully repulsed the Hungarian invasions of Germany at the Battle of Riade. In a speech on the millenary of King Heinrich's death on July 2, 1936, Himmler referred to the Russian Slavs to the East as the Hungarians of the present day. Whereas the Hungarians had hordes of horsemen, the Russians now had tanks. See Frank Helzel, "Himmlers und Hitlers Symbolpolitik mit Mittelalterlichen Herrschern," Bad Wildungen, November 1, 2006, www.himmlers.heinrich.de.

11. Günther d'Alquen, *Reichsführer Rede zu Quedlinburg* (Magdeburg: Im Nordland Verlag, 1936). The head of SS propaganda, d'Alquen, added to the Himmler's self-proclaimed myth: "A thousand years ago one of the greatest Germans ever died, but today he is so much alive, so close, that we believe to be seeing him physically in our midst."

12. Peiper himself used K. H. to refer to Himmler.

13. Himmler envisioned that after the war, SS peasant-soldier farms ("a return to the soil"—a return to nature and a simple nonindustrial life) would transform the conquered east into an idyllic land teeming with SS feudal lordships.

14. The senior adjutant was Dr. Hajo von Hadeln, who had most recently been a platoon leader (SS-Untersturmführer) in the SS Totenkopf Standarte "Oberbayern." Hadeln held the post for two years.

15. For example, see letters of SS Strm. Hermann Hellman, who wrote to Peiper on November 1, 1938, seeking help with his endangered post with 7th Company of the Leibstandarte. NA, T-175, Roll 28. Description of the office layout and activities are taken from Peiper testimony at the investigation against Dr. Walter Best, Strafsache gegen Dr. Werner Best u. a. wegen Mordes: Joachim Peiper, January 19, 1967, 1 JS 12/65 (RSHA). For Himmler's daily office routine, see Peter Witte, Michael Wildt, Martina Voigt, Dieter Pohl, Peter Klein, Christian Gerlach, Christoph Dieckmann, and Andre Angrick, *Der Dienstkalender Heinrich Himmlers 1941/42* (Hamburg: Christians Verlag, 1999), 29–30.

16. Testimony of Joachim Peiper to State Prosecutor Filipiak, *Strafsache gegen Dr. Werner Best u. a. wegen Mordes*, January 19, 1967, 1 Js 12/65 (RSHA), E16, Stuttgart.

17. A small collection of Peiper correspondence on these everyday matters within Himmler's office can be found at the Institut für Zeitgeschichte: IFZ: MA 778/6731, 778/6765–6768 and 778/6820. In one, Peiper was asked to intercede on the part of SS Untersturmführer Paul Erdmann, who had been excommunicated from the troop in March 1939 for marrying a racially suspect bride. NA, BDC File A3343-SSO-189.

18. Testimony of Edith Franke in investigation of Karl Wolff, November 9, 1962, BA-L Wolff, Z-Prot. II, 10 Js 39/60, Bayerisches Landeskriminalamt.

19. "Kiermaier statement," *op. cit.*, PRO: WO/208/4474. For other details of Himmler's daily routine: Felix Kersten, *The Kersten Memoirs: 1940–1945* (London: Hutchinson, 1956), 303.

20. "Programm des Führers," NA, RG-242, T-175, Roll112, F2637010.

21. USHMM, Himmler Collection, Photo No. 60392, showing Himmler with children, picking flowers, July 30, 1938, near Graublau, as described in the rear photo caption.

22. See Himmler's obsession with Karelian witches and sorcery: Heather Pringle, *The Master Plan: Himmler's Scholars and the Holocaust* (New York: Hyperion, 2006), 81–90.

23. On December 8, 1938, Himmler had made public a circular on the need to address "the gypsy problem" and its threat to the German race. Guenther Levy, "Himmler and the Racially Pure Gypsies," *Journal of Contemporary History* 34 (1999): 201–214.

24. "Der Reichsführer SS Persönlicher Stab an SS Obstuf. Karl Diebitsch: Betr. Besuch des Reichsführer SS im Sachsenhain am 18.6.1938" NA, RG-242, T-175, Roll 112, F 2636754.

25. "Communication SS Personal Office to LAH," October 19, 1938, BDC file for Peiper, *op. cit.*

26. BAB, NS 19/ 3951, Himmlers Dienstkalender, October 18–25, 1938.

27. Kristallnacht came to be known for the broken storefront windows across Germany brought about by the rampage. That Hitler approved of the violence is abundantly clear in the Joseph Goebbels diaries for November 9, 1938, which were reproduced in *Der Spiegel* soon after being discovered in a Moscow archives. "Big demonstration against the Jews in Kassel and Dessau, synagogues set on fire and businesses demolished. . . . Now that's done it, I go to the Party reception at the Old Town Hall. Lots going on. I brief the Führer on the matter. He orders: let the demonstrations continue. Withdraw the police. The Jews should for once feel the people's anger." And the following day: "The Führer has ordered that 20,000–30,000 Jews are to be immediately arrested. . . . The Führer wants to take very sharp measures against the Jews." Excerpt from the Joseph Goebbels diaries for November 9 and 10, 1938, Die Tagebücher von Joseph Goebbels, Teil I, Aufzeichnungen 1923–1941, in Auftrag des Instituts für Zeitgeschichte, edited by Elke Fröhlich, Vol. 6 (August 1938–June 1939), Munich 1998, 180. For the scripted midnight ceremony at the Feldherrnhalle on November 9 for Hitler, Himmler and Sepp Dietrich: "Der Chef des SS-Hauptamtes:Verteiler V," October 20, 1938, NA, RG-242, T-175, Roll 32, F254964–66.

28. For several converging sources on Himmler's involvement and motivations in Kristallnacht, see Kurt Patzold and Irene Runge, *Kristallnacht, Zum Pogrom 1938* (Cologne: Pahl-Ruggenstein, 1988).

29. For the Wolff myth, see "Testimony of SS Gruppenführer Karl Wolff," IfZ, ZS-317, Band II, Folder 28. For the involvement of the SS, even of the militarized VT troops, see Peter Longerich, *Heinrich Himmler. Biographie* (Munich: Siedler Verlag, 2008), 423f.

30. For Himmler's clearly anti-Semitic speech to the assembled SS Gruppenführer the evening before: "We must be clear that in the next ten years we face unprecedented conflicts of a critical nature. It is not only the battle of the nations, which has pushed forward only in the case of the opposition, but it is the ideological *(weltanschauliche)* battle of the entire Jewry, freemasonry, Marxism and churches of the world. These forces—of which I assume the Jews to be the driving spirit, the origin of all negatives—must understand that if Germany and Italy are not eradicated, *they will be eradicated* (*vernichtet werden*)." Referring to the "coming wars," he indicated that an SS man should never be taken prisoner; he would be expected to make an honorable end of himself beforehand. And while his Black Knights should remain "kind and decent to people of German mothers," when it came to the undesirable races no pity would be expected, "then it should be a matter of indifference if, in a town, a thousand [people] must be put down. I would do it myself, and I would expect you to carry it out." Speech of Himmler at the Conference of the Gruppenführer on November 8, 1938 at Officers's quarters of the SS

Standarte 'Deutschland,'" NA RG-242, T-175/R 90, F261258–62. Also, Smith and Peterson, *Heinrich Himmler*, 21–47.

31. Peiper claimed to Charles Whiting in a 1969 interview never to have received a party number, a fact clearly disputed by the historical record (see following note). See Charles Whiting, *Jochen Peiper: Battle Commander, SS Liebstandarte Adolf Hitler* (London: Leo Cooper, 1986), 12. Whiting, interview by author, August 19, 2001.

32. The National Socialist Party was the Nationalsozialistische Deutsche Arbeiterpartei (NSDAP). In spite of claiming to never have been a formal member, Peiper was actually given a party number, 5,508,134, on March 1, 1938 with a *signed* application. Claiming to be unaware of this fact, Peiper later attempted to emphasize his career as the unpolitical professional soldier. See BDC files and Moissé, "Dix Ans de Prison J'ai Payé." The letter from Himmler's office requesting a party number for Peiper is dated April 27, 1939 with an acknowledgment letter on May 6. "Joachim Peiper is now the adjutant of the Reichsführer SS and naturally the RFSS desires that this SS-Captain Peiper be given a party number." However, the issue was cleared up by the Berlin NSDAP office in an award letter on August 1, 1939, from Otto de Mars, in which he indicated that Peiper already had a membership number and sent along a second membership card. That Peiper received this card is beyond question in that the final letter requested acknowledgment of receipt. Peiper had applied for party membership on December 10, 1937, in a signed application, with receipt nine weeks later. It is possible that Peiper did not receive his first membership card or otherwise lost it. However, the missing party ID card clearly became an issue after February 2, 1939, when Peiper applied for marriage and Himmler noted the deficiency within his assigned adjutant. NA, RG-242, NSDAP Partei Korrespondenz, A3340-PK-J019, correspondence for Peiper, Joachim.

33. "I was no member of the Nazi party," Peiper maintained, "[And] Not out of opposition! Being a professional soldier with all my heart, I was simply not interested in politics." Letter Peiper to Modification Board" October 5, 1950, NA, RG 549, Case 6-24, Box 61. In recent years, casting doubt that Peiper was a member of the party has become a rallying call for those attempting to maintain the "pure soldier" image of Peiper. When viewed from the perspective of archival sources, this matter is beyond doubt.

34. Special thanks to Dr. Michael Heim and Benno Eisenburg, local historians in Tegernsee, for helping the author with background in a visit in October 2002. The Benedictine monastery was founded in 746 AD, and the shield of Tegernsee shows two crossed leaves alongside the three crowns of Burgundy. Information on Himmler and Lindenfycht is from the Himmler Dossier: PRO: WO 208/4474, in which associates of Himmler were interviewed, including his drivers, bodyguard, household maids, and servants. Himmler's next-door neighbor in Tegernsee was Max Amann, Hitler's military superior in World War I and publishing magnate for the NSDAP. "Amann's Control of German Press," Seventh Army Interrogation Center, SAIC/24, May 26, 1945, NA, Records of the Central Intelligence Agency, RG 263, File: CIA-RDP83-0041R006200020002-7, Declassified February 19, 2004.

35. Sigurd Peiper: BDC RSHA file, A-3342-RS-E0552, "Fragebogen: Sigurd Hinrichsen": "I was born on 16 August 1912 in Kiel as the fourth child of the dentist, Kurt Hans Hinrichsen. . . . From Easter 1929 until fall 1930 I attended the home economics school in Kiel. Sigurd learned typewriting and shorthand and worked in her father's dental office, later working as an apprentice nurse. Since October 1936, I am working on the personal staff of the Reichsführer SS as a secretary." For the political perspective of the Hinrichsen family, see Sigurd's testimony: "My father, Kurt-Hans Hinrichsen, has been a glowing proponent of the National Socialist movement." Her brother, also Kurt-Hans, was an SS Obersturmführer in the head office of Heydrich's SD office in Berlin and her brother Rolf, was a doctor in the Allgemeine SS. Also, Spruchkammer 19/1106/46, Miesbach, April 30, 1947, Denazification file for Sigurd Peiper, Staatsarchiv München, SpKa Karton 3499: Peiper, Sigurd.

36. Lina Heydrich on Marga Himmler: "That narrow-minded humorless blonde female . . . size 50 knickers, that's all there was to her." Sigurd Hinrichsen had met Lina von Osten at a dance for naval officers in Kiel. They became close in the early 1930s, attending school together at the Kiel School of Home Economics. Sigurd was also "a friend of my husband [Reinhard Heydrich]." See Lina Heydrich, *Leben mit einem Kriegsverbrecher* (Pfaffenhofen: Verlag W. Ludwig, 1976), 140–141.

37. Felix Kersten, *Totenkopf und Treue, Heinrich Himmler ohne Uniform* (Hamburg: Robert Mölich Verlag, 1952). This summary "Der Dogmatiker und Romantiker" with Himmler's intention to surround himself with blue-eyed, blonde-haired secretaries appears only in the German edition on page 392.

38. Peiper's office romance with Sigurd Hinrichsen: Charles Whiting, December 23, 1998, describing his interviews with Lina Heydrich. "The men closest to Himmler, his secretaries, aides and adjutants . . . were all youngsters under thirty. None of them had any technical or economic training; some of them could not even speak or spell properly. But they were tall, they were good-looking and they lived in the Spartan fashion of their master." Third Army Interrogation Center, IPW Report #20, May 17, 1945. "Character Sketch of a War Criminal," NA RG 319, Investigative Repository Records (IRR), Himmler files, XE-000632. Author of the report is unnamed, but is Felix Kersten, Himmler's personal masseur.

39. Handwritten statement of Sigurd Hinrichsen in marriage application to Jochen Peiper, April 1939, BDC RuSHA (Rasse und Siedlungshauptamt) File A-3343-RS-E-0552.

40. Born on February 5, 1912 in Cologne, Hedwig Potthast had finished school in Trier before spending some time in England in 1933. There she learned English before studying economics, typing, and shorthand at Handels Hochschule in Mannheim. In 1935, at twenty-three years old, she ventured to Berlin, seemingly looking for the excitement of the big city. In January 1936 she was hired on as a personal secretary for Himmler, at first assisting Erika Lorenz to manage the ongoing distribution of presents and gifts. With a student roommate, Käte Müller, she rented an apartment at Bismarkstr. 47C in Steglitz, where she remained until fall 1941. "Urkunden und Abstammungsunterlagen Hedwig Potthast," BA, Nachlass Heinrich Himmler, N 1126, Folder 38.

41. The wedding took place on January 29, 1937. Also present were Lina Heydrich, Karl Wolff, Reinhard Heydrich, and the Pruchtnow couple. Smith and Peterson, *Heinrich Himmler*, 123.

42. Sigurd Hinrichsen was once leafing through files in Himmler's office, to be disturbed by the contents. "If you are interested in sleeping at night," she later told someone, "you had best not read through such papers." Apocryphal story told by Sigurd Peiper in the 1960s and related by anonymous source.

43. See extensive correspondence from H. P. to various members of the secretive SS school in Wewelsburg from 1937–1939, BA-K, Himmler Files, N 1126/21.

44. For instance, Hedwig Potthast writes to Hstuf. Dörner in Berlin *from SS Kommandostelle Gmünd* on July 27, 1938, NA, T-175, Roll 40, F2550705-06. For Peiper's assignment to plan traveling routes and to accompany Himmler to Gmund, Lindenfycht, and Dohnensteig in Berlin, see "Dienstalterslisten 1938 haben erhalten," and same for 1939, T-175, Roll 37, Folder 116.

45. "SS Oscha. Ernst Glasl to SS Ostuf. Schwarzhuber," Gmund am Tegernsee, June 16, 1938, BDC file for Ernst Glasl, NA, RG-242, A3343-SSO-015A. Glasl joined the NSDAP in 1931. He would eventually serve with the artillery regiment of the LAH from 1940–1942 and then as an artillery instructor as SS schools at Bad Tölz and Braunschweig. Today the Hotel Maximilian is still surviving in Tegernsee as something of a historical ruin. At the time of writing neither side, wrangling over its fate (preservation or demolition and transformation into a grocery plaza), is aware of its unusual place in the history of the Third Reich. The author unsuccessfully sought to contact the Family Glasl in the area who still operate a resort. After

the war Glasl continued with a high profile in Gmund am Tegernsee, operating his hotel and serving as the annual master of ceremonies for Fasching.

46. At least two native German speakers reviewing the wartime correspondence of Jochen Peiper and Hedwig Potthast (revealed to its full extent for the first time in this volume) are of the opinion that Peiper's choice of language is too intimate and personal to reflect only a platonic relationship. The author's very professional translator and German-English linguist, Helmut Thiess, was insistent in his opinion: "Peiper was Prussian and terms of endearment like that are unlikely from a man of his persuasion unless there was a serious relationship." However, Katrin Himmler, the great-niece of Himmler himself, reviewed the same letters and rendered the opinion that although the two had a very close relationship, it was not necessarily romantic. Even so, Peiper's letters are salted with suggestive innuendo and unusual word choices that appear to times to be a code for terms that will only be clearly interpreted by the intended recipient. Clearly, however, Hedwig Potthast, Sigurd Peiper (née Hinrichsen), and Jochen Peiper were very close before, during, and after the war. Peiper met both Sigurd and Hedwig by the summer of 1938, and by the end of that year Himmler was in a serious relationship with Potthast. Whether Jochen had an earlier involvement remains a question and one that will not likely be revealed, as Hedwig Potthast died in 1994.

47. "Aktenvermerk für Frl. Potthast," December 18, 1938, NA, RG-242, T-175, Roll 88, F2611412. The conversations were recorded by Himmler's office manager, Rudolf Brandt. For the comment on Pope Pius XI, Himmler's dinner table conversation with Frl. Potthast on January 30, 1939 (F2611420–21). Pope Pius died under mysterious circumstances on February 10, 1939, the day before he was scheduled to give a speech vehemently denouncing fascism and anti-Semitism. The text of the planned speech has been lost to history, even within Vatican archives. His replacement, Pope Pius XII, was a controversial religious figure during World War II for his lack of action during the Holocaust. John Cornwell, *Hitler's Pope* (New York: Viking, 1999).

48. Hedgwig Potthast to Thilde Potthast on November 10, 1941, and response on November 15, 1941. In the communication, Hedwig described to her sister how the romance began in December 1938. BA, Nachlass Heinrich Himmler, Bestand N 1126, Folder 37. Hedwig's decision to take up with Himmler outside of marriage and to give him children caused her parents to cut communications with her unmarried sister serving as an uneasy intermediary. In reviewing the diary kept by Himmler's wife during this time it seems she sensed something was up, being seized with bouts of hypochondria. "The year is over," she wrote on the last day of 1938. "I spent Christmas in bed with stomach trouble. . . . Tonight we went to play with the children and light the tree." Marga Himmler, diary, *op. cit.*, entry for December 31, 1938. Two years later Frau Himmler's diary described even greater angst, for her husband had clearly informed her that he was taking a mistress: "I am alone today, like every day. I wonder if H. is coming home for dinner?" she wrote. "It is midnight and I cannot sleep. Thinking, thinking. One has to believe everything and be ready for everything. Life is hard. I have a daughter. . . . And every young woman craves a man. If only they knew how bitter life is. If only I could protect my daughter from the worst!" Diary entries for December 7, 1940, and February 14, 1941.

49. "Ausgestaltung der Winter Sonnenwend Feier," 1938, NA, RG-242, T-175, Roll 38. The music: Beethoven, March from the "Die Ruinen von Athen"; Grieg, "Solveigs Lied aus Peer Gynt"; and Wagner, "Freiheitsmarsch der Römer a. Rienzi" and "König Heinrichs Aufzug und Gebet aus Lohengrin."

50. This letter is part of the group of letters from Himmler to Hedwig Potthast that were illicitly seized at the end of the war and are now sold all over the Internet. A copy of this particular letter, dated February 4, 1939, was provided to the author from an auction house. In the letter Himmler indicated that he had just written Hedwig regarding her worries from Tegernsee but was now back in Berlin.

51. For information on Sigurd Peiper, née Hinrichsen, the couple's marriage application and genealogy, see NA BDC A-3343-RS-E0552. Within the application Hinrichsen mentions that her entire family, in particular her father, was "very enthusiastic about the National Socialist world view" (Frame 67).

52. "Marriage in its current form is the Catholic church's satanic achievement. . . . The fact that a man has to spend his entire existence with one wife drives him first of all to deceive her, then makes him a hypocrite as he tries to cover it up. They avoid each other's embraces. . . . This is the reason why millions of children are never born, children that the state urgently requires." Himmler in Salzburg on May 4, 1943: Kersten, *The Kersten Memoirs: 1940–1945*, 176–177.

53. On Himmler's personal approval of prospective brides for SS men, see discussion by the nonconformist editor of *Das Schwarze Korps*, Günther d'Alquen, *Unterredung* (Munich: IfZ, March 1951). Himmler made an attempt to replace the Christian marriage rites with a Germanic ritual. For Himmler's comments on the need for "houses in which to raise large families with lots of children," see his address to one company and 120 officers of the Leibstandarte SS on the Day of Metz, NA, RG 238, US Exhibits 304, NM-66, Entry 2A, Box 18. Also, NA, RG-242, T-175, Roll 112.

54. Max Domarus, *Hitler, Speeches and Proclamations, 1932–1945*, Vol. 3 (Wouconda, IL: Bolchazy-Carducci, 1997), 1437–1449.

55. A photo of the fierce-looking Hinrichsen, replete with a dueling scar, appears in Burkard Baron von Mullenheim-Rechberg's *Battleship Bismarck* (Annapolis, VA: Naval Institute Press, 2002).

56. "Hitler's Himmler," *Time*, April 24, 1939. The Reichsführer's likeness was on the cover of the popular news magazine.

57. "Heldengedenktag: Goebbels, Keitel, Hitler, Brauchitsch, Stumpf und Bock beim Festakt in der Staatsoper Unter den Linden in Berlin, 12.03.1939," Ullstein Bild, No. 00041118. Also, Himmler's schedule for March 12, 1939, NA, RG-242, T-581, Roll 38A. Built in the Prussian classical style in the middle of Berlin, the impressive building was constructed as the Royal Opera from 1741 to 1743 by Georg Wenzeslaus. By Hitler's time Richard Strauss was the chief conductor.

58. For the Czech episode, see Dr. Paul Schmidt, *Hitler's Interpreter* (New York: Macmillan, 1951), 122–126. Also, Ian Kershaw, *Hitler: Nemesis* (New York: Norton, 2000), 169–171.

59. For witness to the climatic scene at Hradcany Palace, see Jochen von Lang, *Top Nazi: SS General Karl Wolff: The Man Between Hitler and Himmler* (New York: Enigma Books, 2005), 116–117. Later, on March 22, 1939, Peiper received a commemorative medal for the occasion.

60. Archive Gedenkstätte KZ Dachau, program for Himmler visit on April 24–25, 1939. Within the folder on the SS visit to Dachau the high officers for the long program at the concentration camp, ended with an inspection of the SS Standarten Oberbayern that would later be part of the Totenkopf Division. Thanks to Albert Knoll for assistance in locating the photographic album of SS Führer von Grävenitz, which contains the image of Peiper. Documentary records of the visit to Dachau and the wide-ranging SS activities during these data are found with Peiper's handwritten notes in the margins on RG-242, T-175, Roll 112, F2637871–7880.

61. "Zeitfolge beim Besuch des Reichsführers SS in Anhalt am 5. Mai 1939," T-175, R112, 2637859.

62. See photographs of Peiper with Hitler and Himmler inspecting the Westwall on May 14–19, 1939. Bildarchiv Preussicher Kulturbesitz, BPK No. 50048936 and 50048905.

63. "First Detailed Interrogation Report on SS Oberführer Eugen Dollmann," PRO: WO 208/4474. Himmler made frequent enquiries as to the progress of Italian authorities in looking for treasure—so much so that, Bocchini, in despair, seriously considered "faking" a

discovery by removing some antiques from a Roman museum and burying them in the area of interest to be later dug up in triumph by the Nazi archeologists.

64. The show was orchestrated by Felix Steiner, although the degree to which it influenced his audience likely grew in his own mind in postwar conversations with Höhne and others. (See citations in Höhne, *Der Orden unter dem Totenkopf*, 442–445, and George H. Stein, *The Waffen SS: Hitler's Elite Guard at War* [Ithaca, NY: Cornell University Press, 1956], 25–26). It must also be pointed out that the original description of this military exercise comes, as cited in Stein, from a sympathetic summary given by Kurt Kanis and other Waffen SS veterans (Angehörige der ehemaligen Waffen SS) in the picture book *Waffen SS im Bild* (Göttingen: Plesse Verlag, 1957), 12.

65. Peter Padfield, *Himmler: Reichsfuehrer SS* (New York: Henry Holt and Company, 1991), 252.

66. Photo of Peiper at the celebration at Kassel is from the BA Bildarchiv in Koblenz.

67. Program of the meeting of the Ober and Regierungspräsidenten from June 26–28, 1939, BA-L, NS 19/1792, 178–185. The program bears Peiper's signature.

68. For a detailed discussion of Daluege and his career, see Richard Breitman, *Official Secrets: What the Nazis Planned, What the British and Americans Knew* (New York: Hill and Wang, 1998), 27–34.

69. Himmler denounced Christianity, which he considered to have polluted the Germanic race when Charlemagne introduced it. "What is Christian, is not Teutonic; what is Teutonic is not Christian!" he emphasized. "Male pride, heroism and loyalty are Teutonic—not gentleness, contrition, misery of sins and a hereafter with prayers and Psalms." *SS Leitheft* 3 (August 1937). Himmler desired that all of the SS members would renounce Christianity for Gottgläubigkeit. More than half of the enlisted men in the SS Verfügungstruppe made the desired conversion and fully 70 percent of Eicke's Death Head units. See Höhne, *Der Orden unter dem Totenkopf*, 417. However, in the realm of the SS leadership, the conversion was over 90 percent. Peer pressure within the officer corps was particularly intense. "We believe in God, but not in his son," Eicke wrote in a 1940 circular, "for that would be idolatrous and paganistic. We believe in our Führer and the greatness of our Fatherland. For these and nothing else we will fight. If we must therefore die, then not with 'Mary, pray for us.' We will depart as freely as we have lived. Our last breath: Adolf Hitler!" Ackermann, *Heinrich Himmler als Ideologe*, 93.

70. Memo of LSSAH to SS Gruppenführer Heydrich, March 19, 1936, BA NS 17/44. Also, Dietrich to O. Sauer," May 8, 1936, BA, NS 17/33. See also, "Vorträge über Glaubensangelegenheiten in Ackermann, *Heinrich Himmler als Ideologe*, 256. That Hitler himself agreed with the thrust of Himmler's approach to religion is illustrated by his stated intention to do away with Christian influences. "I have six SS divisions," he boasted on December 13, 1941, "composed of men absolutely indifferent to matters of religion. It doesn't prevent them from going to their deaths with serenity in their souls," *Hitler's Table Talk* (New York: Enigma Books, 2000), 143.

71. "Rede des Reichsführers SS auf der Ordensburg Sonthofen," May 5, 1944, T-175, R92, F2613495.

72. RuSHA file for Sigurd Peiper, BDC-A-3343-RS-E-0552. "Totally suitable for marriage to an SS officer," was SS Oberführer Karl Diebitsch's effusive endorsement on April 3, 1939. "I have known her for four years and find her to be absolutely reliable, loves children very much, an exemplary comrade, a strong housewife and an absolutely reliable defender of the National Socialist *Weltanschauung*. . . . Both applicants are well known to the Reichsführer. The issuance of permission for marriage is recommended because the Reichsführer SS agrees." Diebitsch was an old *Freikorps* fighter and an early convert to the NDSAP, joining the SS on October 20, 1933. Beyond being a long-term head of the adjutants with the staff of SS Reichsführer Himmler, Diebitsch was something of the Ralph Lauren of the National Socialists—the designer of the SS uniform and many of the legion's medals and badges and even *Julleuchter*.

And more important for the Peiper wedding, it was Diebitsch himself who had designed the SS wedding ceremony! A personal friend of Himmler, Diebitsch remained with his office through 1943 and then was sent to Italy with Karl Wolff. Although without military qualifications, Diebitsch was given the command of the 11. SS Totenkopf Standarte who were involved in the killing of Jews in Radom, Poland in January–June of 1940. There was an investigation into the killings in the early 1970s, but the proceedings ended without conclusion in 1973. See BAL, B 162/15131. Diebitsch survived the war, living in the Tegernsee area, similar to Karl Wolff. He passed away in August 1985.

73. The couple had applied to the racial office for approval of their marriage the previous March, and Himmler had personally approved their joining. Marriage of Jochen Peiper, see RuSHA file for Peiper at NA BDC A-3343-RS-E0552. For the date of the Peiper wedding: Standesamt Berlin-Wilmersdorf Marriage Act No. 887/1939.

74. Eschewing anything dealing with the Christian church, Catholic or otherwise, the Peiper ceremony was nominally a civilian wedding at the town hall in Wilmersdorf, with the SS ceremony and reception following at the mansion and gardens of Viktoria von Dirksen at Margareten Str. 11 near the Lichterfelde Barracks. For a description of the SS marriage ceremony: Jeremy Noakes and Geoffrey Pridham, *Nazism: 1919–1945*, Vol. 2 (Atlantic Highlands, NJ: University of Exeter Press, 1984), 497–498. For the June 29, 1939, telegram to Peiper's wedding reception at 11 Margaretenstr from SS Gruf. Wolfgang Schmitt: BDC file for Peiper NA, RG-242, A3343-SSO-348A.

75. The silver badge on the right breast of the Gesellschaftsanzug featured a death's head on a scroll with the SS motto "Meine Ehre heisst Treue."

76. Himmler himself was at Peiper's marriage ceremony. His pocket diary entry for June 29, 1939, simply has a handwritten note: "9.30 Hochzeit Peiper." NA, RG-242, T-581, Roll 38A. Ludolf von Alvensleben (Himmler's head of the adjutants), Karl Wolff and Reinhard Heydrich and his wife Lina were also present. Lina Heydrich nee von Osten, was Sigurd's old chum from Kiel who had become an early Hitler devotee when he spoke in her hometown. All had just come from the big meeting at the *Haus der Flieger* the day before (NA, T-175, Roll 112, entries for June 28, 1939).

77. For personal dedication from Hitler in wedding copy of *Mein Kampf*, letter Hinrich Peiper to author, May 7, 2000. For a "manual of conduct" for SS families over the year, see SS Oberabschnitt West, *Die Gestaltung der Feste im Jahres und Lebenslauf in der SS Familie* (Wuppertal: Völkischer Verlag, 1940). After their marriage the couple lived in a flat at Rudolstädter Str.123.

Chapter Four

1. "[Peiper] was among the small number of officers of the Waffen SS who appreciated the Reichsführer SS as a person." Jens Westemeier, interview by Otto Dinse, May 28, 1994. Himmler's outlandish ideas of mysticism, religion, and pseudo-scientific racial policies left him open to ridicule, even from Hitler, himself. However, much of the overt criticism of Himmler within the Waffen SS was a postwar invention (see, for example, Toland, interview by Richard Schulze-Kossens, May 8 and October 30, 1971, FDR Papers, Box 56). That Peiper continued to speak of Himmler in his later life: Walter Harzer to Peter Strassner, July 31, 1976, BA-MA, HIAG Archives, B-438 V/320. "Peiper told me many anecdotes about the Reichsführer SS which won't soon be forgotten."

2. For background on Himmler: Padfield, *Heinrich Himmler*, and Longerich, *Heinrich Himmler*. The swastika was an ancient Indian symbol of good luck and also the traditional symbol of Thor, the Norse god of thunder. The Swastika was derived from the Norse Hakenkreuz rune, as adopted within the murky occultism of the Thule society. In 1920 Friederick Krohn suggested the symbol to Hitler as the bold logo for his new National Socialist movement.

3. Himmler had an SS Captain, Wilhelm Fuehrer, from Kiel Observatory, who instructed him on astronomy. Fuehrer was eventually with the Ahnenerbe, where he helped Himmler toy with ideas of constructing an astronomical observatory for Wewelsburg Castle. "To further his aims, Himmler wanted to make it possible for everyone to observe the cosmos—especially the stars. He hoped to establish small observatories in SS schools and camps." "Notes on Himmler and his Staff by Wilhelm Fuehrer, Adj. to Himmler," NARA, RG-407, 7th Army G-2 Records, 7th Army Interrogation Center, SAIC/FIR/15, July 27, 1945.

4. "Notes on Himmler and his Staff by Wilhelm Führer, ADJ to Himmler," Seventh Army Interrogation Center, July 27, 1945, NA, RG-407, US First Army G-2, PWI 101-2.13, Box 1510.

5. For Himmler's belief in the Welteislehre: "The Activities of Dr. Ernst Schäfer, Tibet Explorer and Scientist with SS Sponsored Scientific Institutes," NA RG 338, US Third Army Interrogation Center, OI-FIR/32. See Brigitte Nagel, *Die Welteislehre: Ihre Geschichte und ihre Rolle im Dritten Reich* (Diepholz: GNT Verlag, 1999). For Himmler's fascination with astronomy: *SS Leitheft*, Heft 10, 1943, NA, RG 242, T-611, Roll 44.

6. Himmler believed the descendants of the Atlanteans from the legendary polar island of Thule near Greenland eventually settled in Tibet and South America. Himmler hypothesized some of the island's giant superintelligent Übermenschen had survived and that the "truly initiated" could establish contact with them through mystical practices followed by a spiritual pilgrimage to contact the ancient ones. As a result, Himmler began to sponsor pseudoscientific expeditions to explore and nurture the cradle of the Aryan race. "SS Esoterik," *NS Gedenkstätten und Dokumentationszentren in NRW* (Büren: Wewelsberg Museum, 2001).

7. Rudolf Brandt to Walter Schellenberg, February 23, 1945, NA, T-175, Folder N443, Roll 20.

8. The belief in racial superiority as a new world religion also emanated from Hitler. While incarcerated at Landsberg in 1924 Hitler became fascinated by the writings of Munich Professor Karl Haushofer. Later Rudolf Hess introduced Hitler to Haushofer, who was an eager advocate of *Lebensraum* (living space), a theory popular with German ultranationalists. Proponents felt it was evolutionary fate that superior Germans would reconquer and recolonized the Slavic lands formerly conquered by the Teutonic knights in the Middle Ages. Lebensraum would then reunite the German populations of Eastern Europe as a precursor for a great modern Holy German Empire that would exceed that of Rome. Haushofer's theories were supported by the famous Swedish explorer Sven Hedin, who had suggested that the "'Aryan cradle" would be discovered in Tibet. In accordance with his stature with Hitler, Sven Hedin was chosen to make the opening remarks at the 1936 Berlin summer Olympics. Christopher Hale, *Himmler's Crusade* (Hoboken, NJ: John Wiley and Sons, 2003).

9. "First Detailed Interrogation Report on SS Oberführer Eugen Dollmann," PRO: WO 208/4474. Eugenics, the belief that human beings could be selectively bred for intelligence and strength, was widely accepted in the early twentieth century, leading to widespread sterilization of thousands of people in the United States and around the world. Embraced by the Nazi hierarchy to promote German racial superiority, eugenics had been conceived at the turn of the century by an English scientist, Sir Francis Galton, a pioneer of modern heredity.

10. "Plan zur Erforschung des Gregorianischen Gesanges im Hinblick auf seine Bestandteile germanischer Musik," NA, T-175, Roll 20. Himmler ordered that his ancestral organization, the Ahnenerbe, would study the supposed German origins of the music.

11. "Himmler Dossier: Statement No. 521 of Josef Kiermaier," August 5, 1945, Westertimke, PRO: WO208/4474.

12. Evidence of Himmler's cruelty: he called for executions as punishment for officers involved in stealing or corruption, but SS Hstuf. Walter Hennings (BDC file: A3343-SSO-87A), the highest legal officer in the SS High Office, refused to enforce that policy. Enraged, Himmler requested that Hennings should be removed and condemned to a front-line command in

Russia. Rudolf Brandt to Gottlob Berger, October 4, 1943, letter, BDC file of Walter Hennings. Rudolf Brandt ultimately persuaded Himmler to not follow through, and in an ironic twist, Hennings became Gottlob Berger's lawyer, successfully defending him after the war.

13. Heinz Guderian, *Panzer Leader* (New York: Ballantine Books, 1957), 374. Carl J. Burkhardt, *Meine Danziger Mission 1937–1938* (Munich: Verlag George D. W. Callwey, 1960), 123.

14. "Amann's Control of German Press," Seventh Army Interrogation Center, May 26, 1945, CIA Release RDP83-00415R006, NARA, February 19, 2004, College Park.

15. For "never sloppy": Arndt Fischer, interview by author, May 15, 1997.

16. For this section: Richard Breitman, *Architect of Genocide: Himmler and the Final Solution* (New York: Knopf, 1991), 39–41; Michael Prawdin, *Tschingis-Chan, der Sturm aus Asien*, Deutsche Verlags Anstalt, Stuttgart, 1934 (a second volume appeared in 1935). For Prawdin's book in Himmler's recommended reading lists: "Bücher für Reichsführer SS," NA RG 242, T-175, Roll 112, 2636687. For the creation of the SS edition: "Interrogation of Gottlob Berger, 30 October 1947," NA, RG 238, M-1019, Roll 7, and further interrogation on March 4, 1947 (Roll 6, F491–492). See also, RG 242 T-175, R128, 2654350. Modern scholars agree with Prawdin's fundamental assertion: Khan's empire, stretching from Afghanistan across China, resulted in nearly complete genocide in many of the conquered lands. Himmler did see Khan as having made one egregious error: by "mixing blood" with the women of the conquered territories, he diluted the racial purity of his Mongol warriors. This was a mistake Himmler did not intend to repeat. For Germany he planned to maintain a pure Nordic race in any future conquests. See Otto Heider to Himmler, letter, June 3, 1943, NA RG-242, T-175, Roll 29, 2536756. Even today about one in twelve men in Asia carry a form of the Y-chromosome that originated in Mongolia nearly one thousand years ago, the unusual prevalence of this genetic variant likely being tied to Khan's brutal military success: John Travis, "Genghis Khan's Legacy?" *Science* 163, no. 6 (February 8, 2003).

17. SS Gruppenführer Hermann Priess recalled receiving his copy of Prawdin's book at Christmas in 1937, NA, Case-24, RG 549, Box 61. Himmler saw to it that young SS officers who were detailed for military positions were given a written assignment that helped them to think about the Mongol lord: "By what means did Genghis Khan win his battles?" For "The first attack . . . " Presentation by SS Oberführer Cummerow at the Haus der Flieger in Berlin: "Militärische und wissenschaftliche Weiterbildung der jungen SS-Führer, Vorträge anläßlich der SS-Gruppenführerbesprechung vom 25.1.1939," Persönlicher Stab Reichsführer SS, Bundesarchiv NS 19/29.

18. Karl Hollander, as cited in Agte, *Jochen Peiper*, 14.

19. See open letter written from Landsberg by Jochen Peiper, October 15, 1952 as published in one of the first SS apologist works, Paul Hausser, *Waffen SS im Einsatz* (Gottingen: Plesse Verlag, 1953), 257. Peiper saw vindication in the immediate troubles of Western Europe with the Soviet Union: "Where would ripped apart Western Europe be today, without the dikes of German bodies that history can no longer deny? . . . One must thank this avant-garde of the European idea, that the heirs of Genghis Khan aren't stopped only by the waters of the Atlantic ocean." After the war Hausser argued that the Waffen SS was the "first European army" and the predecessor to NATO.

20. Presentation by SS Oberführer Cummerow at the *Haus der Flieger* in Berlin: *Militärische und wissenschaftliche Weiterbildung der jungen SS-Führer, Vorträge anläßlich der SS-Gruppenführerbesprechung vom 25.1.1939*, Persönlicher Stab Reichsführer SS, Bundesarchiv NS 19/29.

21. Breitman, *Architect of Genocide*, 43, Louis P. Lochner, *What About Germany* (New York: Dodd, Mead and Company, 1942), 2. The secret address of Hitler to his army officials in Berchtesgaden on August 22, 1939, was noted by an informant within the audience (many believe this was the chief of the *Abwehr*, Canaris) who turned over notes to Lochner, then the Berlin correspondent to the Associated Press. For the German original: *Akten zur Deutschen*

Auswärtigen Politik 1918–1945 (Baden-Baden: Serie D, Band VII, 1956), 171–172. Corroboration of the explosive speech are also given from a separate source in the Nuremberg trial: International Military War Crimes Tribunal (IMT), Vol. 36 (1946): 338–344, which is less vitriolic but conveys the same ideas: "What matters in beginning and waging war is not righteousness, but victory. Close heart to pity. Proceed brutally. . . . Supreme hardness."

22. See Charles W. Sydnor's seminal treatment of Eicke and the Totenkopf, *Soldiers of Destruction* (Princeton, NJ: Princeton University Press, 1977). The pogroms of the Polish campaign is described on pages 37–45. Immediately after the actions in Poland, Eicke's killing squads were organized into a Waffen SS infantry division—Totenkopf—that would quickly develop a reputation for sacrificial fighting and pitiless brutality. Also Niels Weise: *Eicke Eine Karriere zwischen Nervenlink, KZ-System und Waffen-SS*, (Paderborn: Schöningh Verlag, 2013).

23. A source account survives of the history of Himmler's mobile headquarters: "Erfahrungsbericht über die bisherigen Einsätze im Hauptquartier," Sturmbannführer Tiefenbacher, NA RG242, T-175, R129, F2655585–95. Also, "Special Führer Trains: Report on information obtained from PW Kan. Bock," CSDIC(UK) SIR 547, Combined Services Detailed Interrogation Service, RG 338, 290/56/1/1–2, Box 3.

24. For Peiper's presence with Hitler's and Himmler's trains during the invasion of Poland: Jochen Peiper, "Kommentar zum Buch *Massacre at Malmedy* von Charles Whiting," September 1971. This important document courtesy of James J. Weingartner, Southern Illinois University. Also, "Kurierverbindungen von Sonderzug nach Berlin: 4.9.1939," NA T-78, R351, F6310682–683. Details of the composition of the two trains: Richard Raiber, "The Führersonderzug," *After the Battle*, No. 19, 1977. Also on Hitler's train was Generalmajor Erwin Rommel who acted as the Kommandant Führerhauptquartiere.

25. Himmler's train trip to Poland is well documented, both by microfilm records as well as by the accompanying Reich Press Chief who would later write a short book on the journey: Otto Dietrich, *Auf den Strassen des Sieges: Erlebnisse mit dem Führer im Polen* (Munich: Franz Eher Nachf, 1939). The foreign minister's perspectives are described by John Weitz: *Hitler's Diplomat: Joachim von Ribbentrop* (London: Weidenfeld and Nichols, 1992), 228.

26. "Handwritten message of Hauptsturmführer Hermann Müller-John to Sepp Dietrich," NA, T-354, Roll 609. Frames 937–938. No date, but late September 1939. For acknowledgment of war crimes by Müller-John from a Leibstandarte man taken captive in August 1944, see "Interrogation of Sturmbannführer Jakob Hanreich," August 19, 1944, PWIS(H)/LDC/299, NA RG-332, Loc: 290/56/1/5, Box 30. According to the division chronicle (Rudolf Lehmann, *The Leibstandarte*, Vol. 2 (Winnipeg: J. J. Fedorowicz, 1988], 233–234), Müller-John mounted a reprisal on Polish inhabitants in the town of Blonie after the Musikkorps bus came under fire. Yet no other source indicates any shooting of German troops within the incident. In any case, the killings were so heartless that the Wehrmacht immediately placed Müller-John under arrest. See special folder on investigation into war crimes of Müller-John, with wartime communications from von Reichenau and von Rundstedt as well as other documentary sources: BA-L, B162, 16610 (Müller-John; *Ermordung von Juden in Polen 1939*). In the final days of the war the Leibstandarte band leader committed suicide along with his wife and daughter in Austria.

27. The atrocities of the Leibstandarte during their march through Poland from September 1–17, 1939, are detailed in a contemporary account: Alexander B. Rossino, *Hitler Strikes Poland* (Lawrence: University of Kansas Press, 2003), 157–167. West German legal officials investigated these war crimes, taking depositions of scores of Polish witnesses: "Ermittlungsverfahren gegen Soldaten der SS Leibstandarte." BA-L, No. 7b Js 2679/82, March 12, 1986. In another incident Untersturmführer Alfred Lengenfeld with the 14th Company was court martialed, claiming to have been condemned (*wehrunwuerdig*) to Buchenwald concentration camp upon refusing orders by hot-headed commander Kurt Meyer, to shoot fifty Polish Jews in reprisal at Modlin at the end of the campaign. "Interrogation of Lt. Alfred

Lengenfeld," September 21, 1944, PWIS(H) LDC/358, NA RG 332, ETO Interrogations Reports, Box 30. The contemporary chronicle of the Leibstandarte covering this period says nothing of the incidents mentioned in the above other than the frequent claim by SS men of being fired upon by civilians in Polish villages: Lehmann, *The Leibstandarte*, Vol. 1, 91–104.

28. "Report on Information Obtained from Senior Officer PW on 2–4 August 1944," C.S.D.I.C. (U.K.), G.R.G.G. 169, PRO, WO 208/5017, Kew, London. The text is a conversation overheard by electronic eavesdropping between Genlt. Graf von Sponeck and Genmaj. Robert Sattler who had been captured in Tunisia and Cherbourg, respectively.

29. For Hitler's movements in Poland, see "KTB d. Kommandant d. FHQu: Darstellung der Ereignisse," NA RG 242, T-78, R-351, F6310623-6310642. For other details, Peter Hoffmann, *Hitler's Personal Security* (Cambridge, MA: MIT Press, 1979).

30. Otto Dietrich, *Auf den Strassen des Sieges*. Peiper is seen in the background on the photo insert at page 109. Peiper would later acknowledge his trips to the front with Hitler in Poland: "During the fighting, I was in the Führer Headquarters, where I had the opportunity to make car trips behind the front." "Vernehmung von Col. Joachim Peiper—Interrogation of Joachim Peiper," Landsberg/Lech, April 17, 1947. NA RG-238, M-1019, Roll 52, Frames 185–189.

31. J. Peiper, interview by John Toland, handwritten notes, October 10, 1963, Library of Congress, Toland Papers, Last Hundred Days, Box 15.

32. Guderian, *Panzer Leader*, 54.

33. Peiper's story regarding this episode to Whiting may be specious, but it clearly indicates that his family was politically well connected in prewar Berlin. See Whiting, *Massacre at Malmedy*, 16. The later Generalfeldmarschall Walter von Reichenau was one the Reichswehr officers who guaranteed the Reichswehr's loyalty to Chancellor Hitler prior to his seizure of power. Klaus-Jürgen Müller: *Armee und 3. Reich 1933–1939* (Paderborn: F. Schoeningh, 1987).

34. Dietrich, *Auf den Strassen des Sieges*, 107.

35. Ibid., 76. "The Jews in Poland are by no means poor," the Reich Press Chief scoffed, "but they live in such unimaginable dirt, in hovels in which no vagrant in Germany would stay overnight." The visit was one in which Dietrich accompanied Hitler on 10 September 1939. "We see the ghetto in Kielce, which is far dirtier than the Polish part of town. If we have ever thought we knew the Jews, we rapidly learned here, something else." Peiper was along on these travels as evidenced by photographic evidence.

36. Interview with Peiper from 1974. Transcript from Hans Kettgen and courtesy of Harvey T. Rowe; translation by Helmut Thiess.

37. "We are living ten beautiful days now on this train. . . . The chief leaves each morning with ten men in armored cars and we are left to wait." Letter of Hitler's secretary, Christa Schroeder to a friend on September 11, 1939. Christa Schroeder, *Er war mein Chef* (Coburg: Nation Europa Verlag, 1985), 98–99. For the locations and events describing Hitler's column in Poland: "K.T.B. d. Kommandant d. FHQu: Darstellung der Ereignisse," NA RG 242, T-78, R-351, F6310629-6310635.

38. Special thanks to Hanns Peter Frentz, son of Hitler's photographer, Walter Frentz, for calling the author's attention to this image: Bildarchiv Preußischer Kulturbesitz, Walter Frentz film, *Polen Feldzug*, September 13, 1939, Roll # 3918. Peiper's route of march with Hitler that date was SW of Łódź–Aleksandrow–Zgierz, Lucmirz–Bratoszewice–Dabrowka–Wielka to return to the airfield SW of Łódź.

39. See Heinrich Hoffmann, *Mit Hitler in Poland* (Berlin: Zeitgeschichte Verlag, 1939).

40. Locations are indicated by their German designation during the war. For instance, today "Danzig" is "Gdansk." Himmler's and Hitler's visit to Zoppot is described by Dr. Paul Schmidt in *Hitler's Interpreter* (New York: Macmillan, 1951), 162–163. For Peiper's presence, see "Fahrt ins Operationsgebiet and Quartierliste Kasino Hotel Zoppot," NA RG-242, T-78, R-351, F6310717–0722.

41. Domarus, *Hitler*, Vol. 3, 1807–1813.

42. As might be expected by potential propaganda value, Nazi investigations of the Polish atrocities against ethnic Germans were excruciatingly detailed. See "Polnische Greultaten in Bromberg und Pless," September 27, 1939, NA RG-242, T-77, R1492.

43. Breitman, *Architect of Genocide*, 70.

44. Heydrich's letter from September 21, 1939, to the SS commanders is given in IMT, EC-307 and PS-3362.

45. Each of the regiments of the newly organized Totenkopf Division had been originally created to guard specific concentration camps, a fact that contradicted any idea that these Waffen SS soldiers could be "soldiers like any others." These included Oberbayern for Dachau, Ostmark for Mauthausen, Thüringen for Buchenwald, and Brandenburg for Oranienburg. Georg Tessin and Norbert Kannapin, *Waffen SS und Ordnungspolizei* (Osnabrück: Biblio Verlag, 2000), 11. The transfer and exchange from KZ men to the front line was a normal procedure, as can be shown for every Waffen SS Division. Thus, the number of KZ guards having served with Waffen SS was over sixty thousand men. Miroslav Kárný, "Waffen-SS und Konzentrationslager," in *Die nationalsozialistischen Konzentrationslager*, Vol. 2, eds. Ulrich Herbert et al. (Frankfurt: Fischer-Taschenbuch Verlag, 2002), 787–799.

46. NCA, *op. cit.*, IMT, NO-3011, memorandum of Gen. Blaskowitz to Gen. von Brauchitsch, dated February 15, 1940. See Brauchitsch letter to der Oberbefehlshaber des Heeres dated January 15, 1940, NA RG 242, T-354, R614, 337–338. The original report to Blaskowitz came from Gen. Alfred Boehm-Tettlebach. See also "Interrogation of Johannes Blaskowitz," NA RG 238, M-1270, Roll 23. Upon learning of Blaskowitz's displeasure with the SS behavior in Poland, Hitler threatened to have him removed: Harold C. Deutsch, *The Conspiracy against Hitler in the Twilight War* (Minneapolis: University of Minnesota Press, 1968).

47. Irving, *War Path*, 14. That Hitler oversaw the pogrom in Poland was later revealed in a conversation with Foreign Minister von Ribbentrop on April 17, 1943. "Where the Jews were left to themselves, as for example in Poland, gruesome poverty and degeneracy ruled. They were just pure parasites. . . . If the Jews couldn't work, they were shot. If they couldn't work, they had to perish. They had to be treated like tuberculosis bacilli, from which a healthy body could be infected." Andreas Hillgruber, ed. *Staatsmänner und Diplomaten bei Hitler*, Vol. 2 (Frankfurt: Bernard & Graefe, 1970), 256–257.

48. IMT, PS-1980. In the Metz speech of September 1940, Himmler justifed to the Leibstandarte the need to field Totenkopf regiments as combat units.

49. See Alexander B. Rossino, *Hitler Strikes Poland: Blitzkrieg, Ideology and Atrocity* (Lawrence: University of Kansas, 2003).

50. Testimony of Joachim Peiper to State Prosecutor Filipiak, *Strafsache gegen Dr. Werner Best u. a. wegen Mordes*, January 19, 1967, 1 Js 12/65 (RSHA)-E16, Stuttgart.

51. For Peiper's presence at the Warsaw parade, See "Einteilung auf die Flugzeuge and Wageneinteilung Kolonne 1," NA, RG-242, T-78, R351, F6310754–0757. Peiper traveled in an automobile with Sepp Dietrich and Karl Wolff.

52. Domarus, *Hitler*, Vol. 3, 1827–1828. Hitler claimed the Lebensraum of Poland as rightfully a German state.

53. See Breitman, *Architect of Genocide*, 76. The Reichsführer considered cruelty a vital trait: "Himmler insisted that this reputation was his best capital, which he needed during the war. After the war, his friends would acquit him and it would be proved that accusations of his cruelty were untrue, but as long as the war lasted, he would have to keep his reputation." Interrogation of Ernst Schäfer, April 2, 1947, NA RG 238, M-1019, R62, 651–652.

54. William Schirer, *This Is Berlin* (New York: Random House, 2013).

55. For Peiper's autumn travels see "Programm des Reichsführers SS in Krakau am 28 Oktober 1939," NA RG 242, T-175, R112, 2637825–27. Along with Peiper were SS Obergruppenführer Krüger, Seyss-Inquart, Karl Wolff, and Zech. The intent of this journey through

Poland was to monitor the progress of deportation of Jews from the countryside into a mass concentration area near Lublin.

56. "Mein lieber Peiper!" Letter Oswald Pohl to Peiper, October 1, 1940, RG 242, T-175, R-112, 2637787.

57. Adolf Hitler, *My New Order*, ed. Raoul de Roussy de Sales (New York: Reynal and Hitchkock, 1941), 762.

58. Hitler aimed to rapidly seize northern France as a stepping stone to aerial domination of England. He chaffed over the delays to launch Operation "Yellow" before winter 1939 and hoped to coordinate a seaborne invasion of England by spring 1940. See Geoffrey P. Megargee, *Inside Hitler's High Command* (Lawrence: University of Kansas, 2000), 75–77.

59. "Kiermaier statement," *op. cit.*, PRO: WO-208/4474.

60. Hitler at the Bürgerbräukeller: Wünsche, taped interview by Toland, November 1971, LOC Sound Division, tapes C-36–39.

61. Walter Schellenberg, *Hitler's Secret Service* (New York: Harper and Row, 1956), 94.

62. These are unconfirmed rumors, as since the war claim plans by MI-6 in late 1938 of using a trained sniper, Col. F. Noel Mason-MacFarlane, with a high-powered hunting rifle to assassinate Hitler. The assassination was to come from the British embassy in Berlin as Hitler's motorcade proceeded down Wilhelmstrasse. Another shooting plan involved top British spy, William S. Stephenson. Alexander Cadogan, the permanent secretary of the Foreign Office, rejected both plans as "unsportsmanlike." However, with the dire progression of the war, a Special Operations Executive (SOE) evolved whose sole purpose to liquidate Hitler and top Nazi brass. Strangely, an argument within the British Intelligence against executing *Operation Foxley* late in the war arose from the perception that killing Hitler would eliminate his strategic blunders and set him up as a public martyr. See Anthony Cave Brown, *"C": The Secret Life of Sir Stewart Graham Menzies, Spymaster to Winston Churchill* (New York: Macmillan, 1987), 195. Also, "Plan to Kill Hitler was 'Unsporting,' *The Times*, London, August 5, 1969. *Operation Foxley: The Plan to Kill Hitler* (London: Public Records Office, 1998).

63. Hitler's rebuff to Himmler: *Der Stern*, May 17, 1964. The capture of British agents, Capt. S. Payne-Best and Maj. Richard H. Stevens, was a severe blow to British intelligence. Under torture and interrogation Payne-Best identified just about every MI-6 agent operating in Germany, even the identity of his supersecret boss, Stewart Menzies.

64. The Venlo incident remains shrouded in secrecy. Extant British records at the Public Records Office will not be released until 2015. Strangely, Elser was kept alive by Himmler at Sachsenhausen Concentration Camp up until the last week of the war. In captivity before his execution on April 9, 1945, Elser told British agent Payne-Best that he had installed the bomb on orders from Heydrich's underlings who had recruited him to do the deed while he was still captive at Dachau. He was to set the bomb to go off *after* Hitler had left to eliminate traitors to the National Socialist cause. Although hardly believable, the supposed motivation was to provide a pretext for the coming German attack in the West by attributing the attempted assassination of Hitler to Great Britain. Payne-Best and Stevens survived the war but are rumored to have been under an oath of secrecy. See S. Payne-Best, *The Venlo Incident* (London: Hutchinson, 1950), 130–132.

65. "I was myself only a member of the personal staff RFSS so I could take part with Himmler in the interrogation of the Burgerbraukeller assassins." *Strafsache gegen Dr. Werner Best u.a. wegen Mordes, Joachim Peiper*, January 19, 1967, 1 JS 12/65 Aussage Joachim Peiper vom 02.09.1970, ZSL.

66. "With wild curses Himmler drove his boots hard into the body of the handcuffed Elser. He then had him removed by a Gestapo official whom I do not know and taken to the lavatory leading off the head of the Gestapo Leitstelle's office where he was beaten up with a whip or some similar instrument until he howled with pain." Testimony of Dr. Albrecht

Böhme, "Attentat auf Hitler, 8.11.1939 in München im Bürgerbräukeller," IfZ, ZS-1939. Also, "Genmaj. d. Pol. Franz Josef Huber," ZS-735.

67. For Himmler's schedule during this trip: NA RG-242, Roll 112, 2637823–24. See also Breitman, *Architect of Genocide*, 89.

68. *Aussage Joachim Peiper vom 02.09.1970, op. cit.*

69. Volker Riess, *Die Anfänge der Vernichtung 'lebensunwerten Lebens' in den Reichsgauen Danzig-Westpreussen und Wartheland 1939/40* (Berlin, Frankfurt am Main: Peter Lang, 1995), 304–308. Mass carbon monoxide gassing of patients from the Tiegenhof asylum had begun three weeks earlier in a sealed bunker known as Fortress VII. These were among the earliest experiments within the Nazi regime using poison gas technology. Original citation is from testimony from Peiper investigation vs. Dr. Walter Best, *Strafsache gegen Dr. Werner Best u. a. wegen Mordes:* Joachim Peiper, January 19, 1967, 1 Js 12/65 (RSHA), ZSL. In author's possession. Peiper's admission of this damaging evidence was first elicited by the chief prosecutor in the Malmédy Trial, "Cross examination of Joachim Peiper," June 22, 1946, *United States vs. Valentine Bersin et al.*, Dachau, 1946, Case 6-24 (hereafter *NA: Case-24, US v. Bersin*), NA, RG 153, Roll 3, Frames 189–190. Also described by Peiper in his own handwritten statement: Testimony of Jochen Peiper, April 8, 1946. William R. Perl Papers, George Washington Library, Box 6, Folder 6. "I was present with the RFSS during the gassing of about twenty persons. There, the insane fell asleep without any fighting. The process may have taken ten to twelve minutes."

70. For Peiper's presence at the 16 December meeting with Hitler and the *Jungvolk*: Library of Congress, *"Pimpfe beim Führer," VB*, 17 December 1939 and Himmler's appointment calendar for 16 December 1939, T-581, R38A.

71. For the SS guide to the Julfest celebration: SS Oberabschnitt West, *Die Gestaltung der Feste im Jahres und Lebenslauf in der SS Familie* (Wuppertal: Völkischer Verlag, 1940). Walter Best, *Mit der Leibstandarte im Westen* (Munich: Zentralverlag der NSDAP, 1941), 70–72.

72. "Hitler exuded calmness and certainty. In the brief talk he made . . . he emphasized that the 1939 successes proved the superiority of the German Wehrmacht. The weather was very depressing, the thermometer hovering around 0°C, and a thin mist lay motionless over the whole landscape. Hitler recognized this and made a distinct attempt to raise the mood. It was dark when he returned to his railway coach." Nicolaus von Below, *At Hitler's Side* (London: Greenhill Books, 2001), 48.

73. "My dear parents": Peiper to Salmünster, December 2, 1946, Landsberg, NA, RG 153, Case 6-24, Box 83.

74. Today the Peiper home at Rüdesheimerplatz 7 is a pension bed and breakfast in the still-attractive neighborhood. The Woldemar Peiper home at Zähringerstrasse 17 no longer exists as it originally stood, the neighborhood having been razed by Allied bombing in 1943–1944. Thanks to my capable assistant, Ann Hamilton Shields, for delving into the Berlin neighborhood history.

75. For the shooting at Bromberg: "Vernehmung von Col. Joachim Peiper." Documentary evidence suggests the shooting actually took place during Himmler's visit to Poland from October 24–28, 1939, RG-242, T-175, Roll 112, F2637824–26. Peiper was clearly on the trip as evidenced by the travel manifest.

76. Horst Peiper was among members of Totenkopf Verbände sent to Danzig to reinforce SS troops, the so called Heimwehr Danzig, in the free city of Danzig prior to the outbreak of the war. BDC file for Horst Peiper, *op. cit.*

77. That Sigurd Peiper's brother, Kurt Hans Hinrichsen, was working for the SD is established by the letter he wrote to businessman Fritz Kranefuss then with Himmler on his command train in the Polish campaign. In the letter, he describes investigations of potential enemies of the Reich—and his opinions of the proper action. Hinrichsen to Kranefuss, September 5, 1939, NA, RG-242, T-175, Roll 57, 2572148. Kranefuss was in charge of

Himmler's Freundeskreis and had his finger in large industrial firms including Dresdner Bank, Deutsche Bank, and Mercedes while intending to create new firms to exploit enemy resources in conquered foreign countries.

78. "Petition for pardon of my son Joachim Peiper," Letter of Woldemar Peiper, August 30, 1946, Salmünster. Even at an age of sixty-one, father Peiper had rejoined the army when the war broke out in 1939 in a transportation replacement battalion as a major, then working for *Panzerwerkstatt Litzmannstadt* from September 1940 until April 1942, when he was released from service there on medical disability. WASt file for Woldemar Peiper. From April 24 to July 29, 1942, he was located at Res. Lazarett 112 in Austria.

79. January 1940 was the coldest month in Berlin in a century, a month-long ordeal with frigid temperatures (a record low of -8 degrees F was reached), deep snows, and frozen rivers. Most of rail traffic was even halted. The deep freeze did not let up until February and led to a shortage of heating coal, milk, and potatoes.

80. Manvell and Frankel, *Himmler*, 101. "Hard methods" meant inhumane and deadly: on January 18, 1940, Höss had forced eight hundred inmates claiming to be unfit for work to stand outside all day in subzero weather, leading to the death of dozens. Steven Paskuly, ed., *Death Dealer: The Memoirs of the SS Commandant at Auschwitz* (Buffalo, NY: Prometheus, 1992), 100.

81. For the photo of Peiper with Himmler at KZ Neungamme in January 1940, author's visit to the museum, April 2009, with thanks to Dr. Reimer Möller and the KZ-Gedenkstätte Neuengamme. For background on Himmler's visit: Hermann Kaienburg: '*Vernichtung durch Arbeit*': *Der Fall Neuengamme* (Bonn: J. H. W. Dietz, 1990), 152. Today, as one of the few completely preserved concentration camps in Germany, the impressive exhibits at Neuengamme should be seen to appreciate the perverse suffering inflicted by Himmler's KZ system. From 1938–1945 over half of the camp's one hundred thousand inmates perished, many from starvation and disease.

82. A photograph in the Hoffman Collection shows Peiper and Himmler escorting Schäfer after his return from an air field on that date: Bildarchiv Preussicher Kulturbesitz, BPK, Nr. 50057878.

83. See Alex McKay, "Hitler and the Himalayas: The SS Mission to Tibet," *Tricycle: The Buddhist Review* (Spring 2001). The term 'Aryan' comes from the Sanskrit word 'arya', meaning noble. In the Vedas, the most ancient of Hindu scriptures, the term described a race of light-colored people from Central Asia who conquered and dominated a race of darker-skinned people from the Indian continent. Although linguistic evidence supports migration of these people into what is now Europe, the facts were twisted into a fantastic myth of supernatural Nordic beings. The Aryan attribution to Germany can be traced to archaeologist Gustav Kossina, who, in 1902, identified that country as the Aryan homeland. The Thule society, to which Himmler belonged, promoted the myth of a mythical island in the frozen north by the same name which had been the home of Earth's master race. The supernatural inhabitants of Thule—which Himmler believed were the Atlanteans—had been forced to flee due to an extreme calamity which destroyed their world. To believers, the lofty Atlanteans, a tall, blonde blue-eyed race, were both the source of all art and science and were incomparable warriors. The survivors exiled themselves to Tibet, to hide in waiting for their modern descendants to reclaim their secret knowledge and powers.

84. The detailed itinerary for the January trip to Poland including Peiper's participation is given in NA RG-242, T-175, Roll 112, Frames 2637820–2637822. For Peiper's recollections of the trip: "Vernehmung von Col. Joachim Peiper—Interrogation of Joachim Peiper," Landsberg/Lech, April 17, 1947. NA RG-238, M-1019, Roll 52. For the broader story of this episode: Breitman, *Architect of Genocide*, 80–81. Also, Christian Gerlach, *Kalkulierte Morde. Die deutsche Wirtschafts und Vernichtungspolitik in Weissrussland 1941–1944* (Hamburg: Hamburger Edition, 1999).

85. Himmler's comment came later on May 4, 1940, near Łódź, but reflected well the problems with his idealistic resettlement program: BA-K R49/20.

86. "The Activities of Dr. Ernst Schäfer," Third Army Interrogation Center, OI-FIR Report, No. 32, February 12, 1946, NA RG-238, M-1070. Schäfer was a member of the Ahnenerbe, the SS pseudo-scientific ancestral organization. Himmler admired Schäfer for his successful expeditions to Tibet, which the Reichsführer considered the cradle of the last great civilization of conquest (Genghis Khan). Schäfer, who looked upon himself as purely an academic, was unable to stay out of trouble with his new master. In October 1941 Wolfram Sievers, the head of *Das Ahnenerbe* brought Schäfer to Dachau concentration camp to photograph diabolical high-altitude experiments on inmates carried out by a Luftwaffe officer, Dr. Sigmund Rascher. Schäfer claimed to have feigned illness to avoid the duty, but indicated that Wolfram Sievers became an eager participant in Rascher's infamous work. While Sievers was tried and hanged after the war, Ernst Schäfer successfully returned to academia in postwar Germany.

87. See Himmler's discussion of the *Wehrbauern*: Kersten, *The Kersten Memoirs: 1940–1945*, 132.

88. Christopher R. Browning and Jürgen Matthäus, *The Origins of the Final Solution: The Evolution of Nazi Jewish Policy, September 1939–March 1942* (Lincoln: University of Nebraska Press, 2004).

89. The photo, taken in Berlin on March 20, 1941, of "Construction and Planning in the East" can be found in Ackermann, *Heinrich Himmler als Ideologe*, 209.

90. "All lines [of responsibility for the program] led to [Ulrich] Greifelt; he was responsible. I had nothing to do with these things, because, as a soldier, I was, so to speak, forced into it. I do not say that because of fear. I would like to clarify that I merely set up the calendar for Himmler. Greifelt had a good career in the general SS because of these activities." For two quotes including, "I cannot tell you more." "Vernehmung von Col. Joachim Peiper." Ulrich Greifelt was the installed deputy for Himmler's new RKF (*Reichskommissariat für die Festigung des deutschen Volkstums*—the Reichs Commissariat for the Strengthening of the German People).

91. "Interrogation of Ernst Schäfer, February 12, 1946," NA RG 238, M-1270, Roll 27, Frame 192; also, NA RG 338, US Third Army Interrogation Center, OI-FIR/32. Globocnik almost certainly referred to the killing of 300 inmates of an insane asylum at Hordyszcze on January 12, 1940. See Breitman, *Architect of Genocide*, 95. Also, Declaration of Dr. Ernst Schäfer to Lloyd M. Rausch, Freising, Germany, August 16, 1945.

92. "Vernehmung von Col. Joachim Peiper," *loc cit.* For an illuminating account of the Nazi expedition to Tibet: Christopher Hale, *Himmler's Crusade* (London: Bantam Press, 2003).

93. "Vernehmung von Col. Joachim Peiper,"After witnessing the executions, according to Peiper, Himmler, told those present that he "regrets it, but it must be done. . . . Even for Himmler this is a painful matter, because most of them are German in origin." Declaration of Dr. Ernst Schäfer to Lloyd M. Rausch, Freising, Germany, August 16, 1945.

94. It was typical for those in Himmler's entourage to claim that he was shaken by the executions. A later example comes from Erich Bach-Zelewski and Karl Wolff, who, after the war claimed that Himmler was horrified to witness a mass killing at Minsk on August 15, 1941. If true (there is contradictory testimony of Otto Bradfisch), it would call into question why Himmler could place himself into this position after having witnessed another repulsive execution with Peiper two years before. However, it was Himmler's stated opinion that the necessarily cruel actions should be carried out with "decency" while "fulfilling one's duty." The Reichsführer was concerned that his SS men be able to dispassionately kill opponents to National Socialism rather than to fall prey to sadistic impulses. Himmler even had a favored term for this: *Anständigkeit*—to be tough, but decent. "Most of you know what it means when 100 corpses are laid out along with each other, or when 500 or a 1000 are laid out. To have gone through that and—aside from exceptions of human weakness—remain decent, that is what makes us

tough." Himmler's Posen speech, October 4, 1943. IMT 1919-PS. Ernst Schäfer indicated that Peiper had told him that Himmler had hardly spoken a word for days. Declaration of Dr. Ernst Schäfer, August 16, 1945.

95. For von Alvensleben's remark quoted by Ernst Schäfer: NA RG 242, M1019, Roll 62, Frame 638. There is powerful evidence for the hard-hearted nature of von Alvensleben. For instance, Peiper himself reported that when several Polish saboteurs were executed in Himmler's presence on the outskirts of Bromberg, and one survived wounded, von Alvensleben pulled out a pistol to finish the job (IfZ, ZS-1299). Further, von Alvensleben admitted to shooting Count von Alvensleben-Schönborn, who had married a Pole against the family wishes and educated his family with Jewish tutors. Von Alvensleben justified his action in a letter to Karl Wolff dated December 12, 1939 (see NA RG 242, T-175, Roll 112, Frames 2636602–604). The SS officer bragged widely of the deed as evidenced by the fact that both Karl Wolff and Ernst Schäfer reported the incident after the war. Lang, *Top Nazi*, 138. In April 1945 the British captured and held Alvensleben. Not surprisingly, at the end of 1945, he made an escape from the internment camp at Neuengamme. After a few months as a fugitive, he fled with his family to Peron's Argentina in early 1946 where he hid for the rest of his life.

96. Peiper's callous remark to Schäfer is contained in NA, RG 238, Microfilm 1019, "Interrogations of Ernst Schäfer," April 1, 1947, and February 12, 1946, Microfilm 1270. It is also quoted in an early interrogation of Schäfer where he offers another colleague as a witness: Declaration of Schäfer to Lloyd M. Rausch, Freising, Germany, August 16, 1945: "Peiper remarked that the Polish intelligentsia is now 'looking at the potatoes from below.' Peiper made the same or similar remark to my expedition comrade Krause in Berlin."

Chapter Five

1. For Peiper's presence at the dinner with Eicke: "Reiseplan des Reichsführer SS für die Fahrt vom 4.-7. März 1940," NA, T-175, R112, F2637817.

2. Sydnor, *Soldiers of Destruction*, 76–78.

3. "Reiseplan des Reichsführer SS für die Fahrt vom March 11–15, 1940," NA RG 242, T-175, Roll 112, Frame 2637813–815. Himmler's notes on his speech from March 13 are found on NA RG 242, T-380, Roll 37. See also, "Interrogation of Rudolf Brandt, December 16, 1946," NA RG 238, M-1019, Roll 9, Frame 714.

4. "SS Totenkopfdivision Kommandeur: Bezeichnung der s. Art. Abt, z. Zt. Wewelsburg," March 29, 1940, NA, T-175, Roll 106, F 000002. Peiper makes the notes for "R. F." in this document.

5. "Reiseprogramm des Reichsführer SS vom 4.-7, April 1940," NA RG 242, T-175, Roll 112, Frame 2637802–809. Only a very limited circle of individuals was allowed to visit the concentration camps of which Peiper was one as his superior's personal aide. For instance, Himmler emphatically turned down a request of Maj. Gerhard Engel, the army adjutant of Hitler to visit a KZ. See Engel, *Heeresadjutant bei Hitler 1938–1939, Die Aufzeichnungen des Major Engel* (Stuttgart: Vierteljahrshefte fur Zeitgeschichte (VfZG), 1974), 97.

6. For photographs showing Peiper's presence and data on KZ Ravensbrück, thanks to Britta Pawelke from the KZ Ravensbrück Memorial for helping Jens Westemeier obtain the sources. As of this date, there were some 4,353 women there. Since the camp had been established two years before, a hundred inmates at the camp had died.

7. Letter Himmler to Dr. Ernst Grawitz on March 2, 1941: Helmut Heiber, ed., *Reichsführer!* (Stuttgart: Deutsche Verlags-Anstalt, 1968), 84. Surrounded in Berlin at the end of the war, Dr. Grawitz blew himself and his family up with hand grenades rather than be taken prisoner. Gebhardt, the boyhood friend of Himmler and his head physician at the Hohenlychen Hospital, was hanged at Landsberg on June 2, 1948, after being found guilty of medical war crimes.

8. Peiper was present with Himmler at Dachau on January 20, 1941. French L. McLean, *The Camp Men* (Falls Church, VA: Schiffer, 1998) shows Peiper with Himmler at Dachau on January 20, 1941, 344. (Also available at the USHMM photographic archive: Photo No. 55743. Moreover, from photographic research at the KZ Gedenkstätte Dachau, an image clearly shows Peiper with Himmler as well (Photo F591 in the album covering this visit: "Besichtigung des Konzentrationslagers Dachau am 20.1.1941 durch Reichsführer SS in Beleitung des Herrn A.A. Mussert,"). For information showing eight died on January 20, 1941, *SS Sterbebuch Dachau*, courtesy Albert Knoll and museum director, Barbara Distel. From 1933–1941, 2,500 inmates had died at the camp—by the end of the war nearly thirty thousand human beings. Also present during the KZ visit with Peiper was SS Gruf. Oswald Pohl, "Himmler's brain" behind the growing SS empire, SS Gruf. Arthur Seyss-Inquart, Rost van Tonningen from the Netherlands, and SS Brigf. Richard Glücks, the inspector of the concentration camp system.

9. Statement of Jochen Peiper, April 8, 1946. William R. Perl Papers, George Washington Library, Box 6, Folder 6. This original handwritten statement prepared by Peiper had been lost within the investigative records until appearing within the William Perl papers at the Gelman Library. Peiper's testimony was never entered into the trial records, likely due to his exculpatory statement that likely did not meet with approval from Perl.

10. Helmut Krausnick, Hans Buchheim, Martin Broszat, and Hans Adolf Jacobsen, *Anatomy of the SS State* (New York: Walker and Co., 1965), 482 and 500.

11. Konnillyn G. Feig, *Hitler's Death Camps* (New York: Holmes and Meiers, 1979), 116.

12. Peiper can be seen just behind Werner Grothmann in an image taken at Mauthausen on April 27, 1941 (Bundesarchiv Bild BA-192–195), where Himmler was in conversation with August Eigruber, Gauleiter in Oberdonau/Ostmark in Austria, and KZ commandants Franz Ziereis and Georg Bachmayer.

13. For Himmler's visit to Buchenwald: NA RG 242, T-175, R112, Frames 2637752–53. For the retribution against Dutch Jews in progress during this time: Jacob Presser, *The Destruction of the Dutch Jews* (New York: Dutton, 1969).

14. Breitman, *Architect of Genocide*, 113–114.

15. Statement Josef Hubauer as quoted Anton Joachimsthaler, *Hitlers Liste* (Munich: Herbig Verlag, 2003), 236.

16. For Peiper's fidget with the ring, see photo of Peiper's conversation with Standartenführer "Teddi" Wisch on March 6, 1943, Rudolf Lehmann, *Die Leibstandarte im Bild* (Osnarbrück: Munin-Verlag, 1983), 181.

17. "Betrifft: Besichtigungsfahrt des Reichsführers SS am 27. und 28.4.1940 durch Südostpreußen," NA RG 242, T-175, R112, 2637799–801.

18. "Testimony of Otto Rausch," June 16, 1943, NA RG 238, NO-1073. Also, see Breitman, *Architect of Genocide*, 102–103.

19. Lang, *Top Nazi*, 153. For confirmation of the itinerary and Peiper's presence, see "Der Höhere SS und Polizei Führer," NA RG 242, T-175, R112, F2637798–803.

20. Franz Lucas, Himmler's driver, said he was aware of the annihilation camps in the east but had not been to any of them nor had the Reichsführer talked to him about them. However, in his testimony at the trial of Karl Wolff he implied that Wolff and the others such as Peiper in Himmler's closest circle would have to know about the Endlösung. Lucas did say that Jochen Peiper himself first told the driver about the birth of Himmler's son born with Hedwig Potthast. According to Lucas, Wolff made all the arrangements for the birth as well as the accommodations for quarters for Potthast near Berchtesgaden. Testimony of Franz Lucas in trial of Karl Wolff, BA-L, Z-Prot. II, 10a Js 39/60. The personnel file for Lucas (NA, RG-242, BDC A3343-SSO-279A) clearly shows that proximity to Himmler was a huge plus for promotion.

21. Witte et al., *Dienstkalender Heinrich Himmlers*. For Himmler's meeting with Peiper, Fegelein, Karl von Treunenfeld and Kurt Knoblauch on June 30, 1941, to discuss "serious

discipline problems—theft and mistreatment of subordinates—in the *14th SS Infantry Regiment*." see 181. Unearthed in archives in the former Soviet Union, this important source shows Himmler's appointments for his office through 1941–1942, copies can be seen at USHMM.

22. Regarding Globoknik's scheme to use Jewish labor to dig a massive antitank ditch on the Russian border, Peiper was defensive in his testimony in the postwar trial of Dr. Werner Best: "I never heard anything about Jews that were killed by this plan." *Strafsache gegen Dr. Werner Best u.a. wegen Mordes, Joachim Peiper*, January 19, 1967, 1 JS 12/65 Aussage Joachim Peiper vom 02.09.1970, ZSL. In separate testimony Peiper also mentioned "an enormous double anti-tank ditch" under construction east of Lublin in testimony he gave earlier at Dachau before his trial. "Thousands worked on that." he told interrogators. "Testimony of Joachim Peiper," April 8, 1946, William R. Perl Papers, George Washington University, Box 6, Folder 6.

23. Browning and Matthäus, *Origins of the Final Solution*, 144–151.

24. That the men of the Leibstandarte were unaware of the impending attack seems certain as evidenced by the extensive plans for competitive handball training in Neunkirchen, just three days prior. "Tagesbefehl Nr. 101, May 7, 1940," NA RG-242, T-354, Roll-235, F3902194.

25. "My relationship with Hitler was like that of a son and father. . . . I experienced this when I told him I wanted to go to the front in France and be released from headquarters." "'I really regret to grant your wish,'" Hitler told him, "'but I give you permission because I don't want you to say after the war that you did not fight because you had to stay at Hitler's headquarters during the war.'" Wünsche was wounded during the campaign in France and promoted to SS Hauptsturmführer on May 25.

26. For a vivid, if expunged, Waffen SS account of the 1940 campaign, see Kurt Meyer, *Grenadiere* (Munich: Schild Verlag, 1957). For original German records of the fighting: "Armeeoberkommando 18, Abt, Ia., 10.5.40–14.5.40," NA, T-354, Rolls 610 and 614.

27. Himmler was correct, at least to a limited extent. Germanic tribesmen had first driven the Romans out of the Low Countries in AD 400 and by 870 controlled the northern part of the region now known as the Netherlands.

28. For the propaganda march through Holland: NA RG 242, T-354, Roll 610, F0053, "Besondere Anordnungen für die Versorgung," May 16, 1940. "Impeccable attitude, marching discipline, flawless uniforms and well maintained vehicles will give the population the proper impression of the German army . . . smoking, decorations of vehicles with flowers or markings or waving is strictly prohibited."

29. "Darstellung der Ereignisse," NA RG-242, T-78, Roll 351, F631640–643. May 10–14, 1940.

30. Von Schröder would eventually become an SS Oberführer in the SS. Peter Ferdinand Koch, *Himmlers Graue Eminenz-Oswald Pohl und das Wirtschaftsverwaltungshauptamt der SS* (Hamburg: Verlag Facta Oblita, 1988), 189.

31. According to Frau Himmler, their relationship changed to a nonromantic one prior to the war—coinciding with her husband's taking up with Hedwig Potthast. Interrogation of Margarete Himmler, Nürnberg, December 6, 1945, IfZ, RG 260, 3/71–3/5/2.

32. Katrin Himmler, *The Himmler Brothers: A German Family History* (New York: Macmillan, 2007), 140. Not only was Marga Himmler much older than Heinrich, she was less educated and a divorcée—a fact that made her unpopular with Himmler's parents.

33. The family adopted a foster son, Gerhard, of a fallen SS officer in 1934, but Heinrich Himmler and his wife were always cool to that addition to the family, so much so that the son was almost ignored within any of the family outings and correspondence, and he was sent off to a boarding school.

34. See Himmler's intentions for SS polygamy on May 4, 1943: Kersten, *Totenkopf und Treue*, 223–224.

35. Himmler had bought his wife, Marga, and daughter, Gudrun, a house named Lindenfycht nestled among the gloomy firs at Gmund on the Tegernsee. Although Himmler dutifully sent his wife flowers on the last day of each month, after taking a mistress in 1940 he seldom visited. When he did, his wife made it a frosty affair: "I never met a man so hen-pecked as Heinrich Himmler. He oozed amicability, but the more amiably he behaved, the worse he was treated. At home, the head of the police and the SS, was a zero." Baldur von Schirach, *Ich glaubte an Hitler* (Hamburg: Mosaik Verlag, 1967), 213.

36. A diary of the trip survives: "Schriftgutverwaltung, Persönlicher Stab RFSS," T-175, Roll 119, Frames 264437–264449. Also, "Am Freitag den 17.V.1940: Tour Report of Heinrich Himmler from 17 May to 19 May 1940," IfZ, MA 407/26 44347. For the composition of the fellow travelers: letter Himmler to Heydrich, May 15, 1940: Heiber, *Reichsführer!*, 80.

37. James J. Weingartner, *Hitler's Guard: The Story of the Leibstandarte SS Adolf Hitler, 1933–1945* (Carbondale: Southern Illinois University Press, 1974), 50. Actions of the Leibstandarte on May 24 and 25 can be found in NA, "Marschbefehl für den 24.5.1940" and "Aufträge für die Leibstandarte am 25.5.1940," NA, T-354, Roll 610, Frames 547–548.

38. Guderian's meeting with Dietrich on May 25, 1940, is taken from Guderian, *Panzer Leader*, 104.

39. Weingartner, *Hitler's Guard*, 50. "Regimentsbefehl," NA, T-354, Roll 610, Frames 549–551. Also, "II/LSSAH, Bataillonsbefehl: 18.5.1940," T-534, Roll 622, F508–509.

40. Wünsche had recently been assigned from the 15th Motorcycle Battalion to function directly as Dietrich's personal adjutant.

41. "Fortunately, the ditch was deep," remembered Max Wünsche, "but they literally shot the edge of the ditch away with machine guns." Letter Wünsche to Charles Messenger February 19, 1986. Messenger, *Hitler's Gladiator: The Life and Times of Oberstgruppenführer and Panzergeneral-Oberst der Waffen-ss Sepp Dietrich* (Washington, DC: London: Brasseys, 1988), 83.

42. Guderian, *Panzer Leader*, 106.

43. Public Records Office (hereafter PRO), "2nd Royal Warwicks' War Diary," also, "Intelligence Summary of the 2nd Battalion," WO 167/839, Kew, London.

44. A cursory description of the Leibstandarte actions before Wormhoudt can be found in Weingartner, *Hitler's Guard*, 51, with the original source (with no mention of improprieties) from NA, RG 242, T-354, R610, Frames 000462–557. For the British version isolating the war crimes and particularly following the deeds of Wilhelm Mohnke: Ian Sayer and Douglas Botting, *Hitler's Last General* (London: Transworld Publishers, 1989), 32–112.

45. Leslie Aitken, *Massacre on the Road to Dunkirk: Wormhout, 1940* (Wellingborough: Stephens, 1988).

46. Weingartner, *Hitler's Guard*, 51. Original source: "Vorbefehl für den Angriff auf Dünkirchen," May 30, 1940, NA, T354, Roll 610, Frames 552–557.

47. Letter of Arthur R. Baxter to Tom H. Nicholls, December 14, 1979, as cited in Ian Sayer and Douglas Botting, *Hitler's Last General* (London: Bantam, 1989), 40–41.

48. Evans's letter is from Aitken, *Massacre on the Road to Dunkirk*, 73.

49. The principal source for the events at Wormhoudt from the British perspective are two reports prepared by the War Crimes Interrogation Unit at the London District Cage in 1947: WCIV/LDC/1500 and WCIV/LDC/1650, courtesy Ian Sayer. Parry's account of the overheard conversation at the SS headquarters is taken from the later of the two reports.

50. WCIU: WCIV /LDC/1650, "Wormhoudt, 2nd Report."

51. Rodenbücher's testimony is contained in WCIU: WCIV/LDC/1650. Along with it a total of nine of seventeen SS men interrogated by the WCIU after the war had "heard the [British] prisoners had been shot." Contrary to the accusations, the Regimental Adjutant, Fritz Beutler testified that Mohnke himself had ordered that a group of thirty prisoners be taken to the rear rather than be shot. Also, the commander of the 7th Company, Otto Baum, similarly

denied that any massacre had taken place in 1946 when he was interrogated in a POW cage in London. Not surprisingly, the "official" history of the Leibstandarte also denied any wrongdoing at Wormhoudt by completely omitting any mention at all! Lehmann, *Leibstandarte*, Vol. 1. For the more recent investigation of Mohnke, see, *Welt am Sonntag*, May 1, 1988. "Der Fall des SS-Generalmajors Wilhelm Mohnke." Meanwhile, HIAG remained fully committed to defending Mohnke. Their annual *Treffen* had come the week when Mohnke was accused. "We spoke a lot about you. We remained convinced that the accusations against you are not based on fact. Please know we will support you in every way." Hubert Meyer to Mohnke, May 18, 1988. BA-MA, HIAG Records, RS 7/ v. 509.

52. Wormhoudt was not the only blemish on the Waffen SS in France. Worse, was the behavior of Eicke's Totenkopf SS Infanterie Regiment 2, which on May 27 shot down ninety-nine soldiers of the Royal Norfolk Regiment after they surrendered in the small village of Le Paradis, just west of Béthune. Even though survivors of the machine gun fire were bayoneted or shot at close range by pistols, two men amazingly managed to survive. Interestingly, Peiper's brother, Horst, was regimental adjutant with the regiment under Obersturmbannführer Heinz Bertling at the time—many of the regimental members had been recently culled out of Eicke's concentration camps. Episodes like Wormhoudt and La Paradis—what the Waffen SS called "horror stories from the war"—continually dogged the troop during and after the conflict. Denials of wrongdoing by the SS remain a perennial occupation of sympathetic buffs and writers. Contemporary repudiation of the many charges can be found in the monthly publication of the HIAG, *Der Freiwillige*, as well as a spate of recent revisionist works, many published by Munin Verlag. Perhaps the most interesting postscript on this discussion is that fully 43 percent of all officers serving at the concentration camps had also served in the Waffen SS. Indeed, sixteen officers of the Leibstandarte Adolf Hitler held posts at the concentration camps: French L. McLean, *The Camp Men*, 278–285.

53. "Regimentsbefehl: Rgt. Gef. Stand, den 1.6.40: Beförderung," NA RG-242, T-354, R-235, F3902211.

54. Hitler's return to his old battlefield at Wervicq: BA-MA RW 47/6, "Kriegstagebuch des Kommandanten Führerhauptquartier," Entry for June 1, 1940. Hospitalized and hysterical after the Kaiser's humiliating defeat in November 1918, Hitler, according to some theorists, entered a Faustian pact with Providence to devote himself to reverse the course of German history. See Robert G. L. Waite, *The Psychopathic God: Adolf Hitler* (New York: Basic Books, 1977). For Hitler's remark about England: Karl Klee, *Das Unternehmen 'Seelöwe'* (Göttingen: Musterschmidt, 1958), 189. For Wünsche's fanciful remembrance of the episode, his November 3, 1971, interview by John Toland, LOC, Toland Collection, Tapes C-36–C-37. Hitler, Wünsche claimed, wasn't enthusiastic about the invasion. "If we don't make the invasion, we can make a bid for peace with England." In reality, Hitler would devote huge resources to the V-weapons aimed at total destruction of England's cities.

55. Source of this episode: Lehmann, *Leibstandarte*, Vol. 1, 157–161.

56. "Bericht: Brandt," NA, T-175, Roll 108, F2629803.

57. Peiper's action on June 19, 1940: "Der Soldat: Jochen Peiper's militärischer Werdegang," *Der Freiwillige*, November 9, 1976, 4; also Meyer, *Grenadiere*, 36. Confirmation of Peiper's wounds from the action are contained in a report signed by Hans Gruhle, January 30, 1945, from Peiper's soldbuch, given by Sigurd Peiper to Roger Lavaux. Copy courtesy Neill Thomson.

58. *Stuttgarter Illustrierte*, January 8, 1941.

59. Dietrich's tribute to his men in June 1940 can be found in "Regimentsbefehl," NA T-354, Roll 610, Frame 247.

60. For Hitler's endorsement of the Leibstandarte at the conclusion on December 26, 1940: Max Domarus, *Hitler*, Vol. 3, 2173.

61. Peiper's BDC file, letter to SS Gruppenführer Wolff at the Führer's headquarters, June 29, 1940. The car later broke down in December of that year to be replaced by a Hudson,

also of American make, memorandum to files for December 12, 1940. T-175, Roll 26, F2531997–2000.

62. Peiper was in the process of returning to Himmler's service immediately after his action on June 19, 1940, as there is period document signed by SS Gruf. Walter Schmitt on that date addressed to the adjutant on the field train, "Sonderzug Heinrich," asking when he will be promoted to SS Hauptsturmführer. Himmler had been angry when he found Wünsche still in France after the end of the fighting there, and ordered him to back to Hitler.

63. *New York Times*, July 7, 1940.

64. Before the war approximately one third of the 665,000 inhabitants of Łódź, Poland, were Jewish. After its capture on September 8, 1939, the Germans renamed the city Litzmannstadt and in early 1940 a ghetto in the city was formed with barbed wire and wooden fences where sixty thousand Jews were packed into a square kilometer of the ghetto. The ghetto within the city, within sight of the panzer repair shop, became a slave labor camp for Hitler's regime, producing textiles, furniture, and other goods. During the time when Woldemar was in Łódź starvation and disease killed many of the Jews there, but beginning in 1942 many of the Jews in the camp were sent to the death camp at Chelmno on the Ner River.

65. Breitman, *Architect of Genocide*, 126 and note 60 for that chapter.

66. Peter Fleming, *Operation Sea Lion* (New York: Pan Macmillan, 1957), 290–295; Schellenberg, *The Labyrinth*, 107–124.

67. The group departed at 1 p.m. by air to Freiburg. NA, RG-242, T-581, Roll 38A, handwritten entry for July 13, 1940.

68. "Reiseprogramm des Reichsführer vom 13.–15.7.1940," NA, RG 242, T-175, Roll 112, 2637795–96. Peiper had no idea when he drove from Vesoul to Gray on July 13, 1940, the eve of Bastille Day, that thirty-six years later he would end his days there.

69. Paul Kluke, "Nationalsozialistische Europaideologie," Vierteljahrshefte für Zeitgeschichte, No. 3, 1955. Said Hitler himself: "We must not forget that the old Kingdom of Burgundy played a prominent role in German history, and that it is for time immemorial German soil, which the French grabbed from us in times of our weakness." *Hitler's Table Talk*, 442, April 25, 1942.

70. Photo of Peiper and Max Wünsche at the Kroll Opera house on July 19, 1940, is from BA-K photographic archives for Hitler. Thanks to Frau Kuhl at BA-Koblenz for the photographic research help.

71. For Hitler's speech and a vivid description of the scene during the speech: William L. Shirer, *Berlin Diary* (New York: Galahad Books, 1941), 452–457.

72. This event is clearly illustrated in the photos of Walter Frentz taken during July 1940, which show Himmler, Wolff, and Peiper at the Berghof. By matching the guests seen in the film rolls against Himmler's known schedule in his diary, this must have been on July 29 where they show traveling from Gmund to the Obersalzberg: Himmler Diary for 1940, BA-K, N 1126/42. For the photo research, Hanns-Peter Frentz with the Bildarchiv Preußischer Kulturbesitz.

73. For "I would have put my head on the gallows," and other details, J. Peiper, interview by Toland, October 10, 1963.

74. In the summer of 1942, while in Himmler's company, Peiper became aware of Operation Bernhard—the idea to use Jewish inmates who were printing artisans from Sachsenhausen, Buchenwald, and Ravensbrück Concentration Camps to create millions of pounds of phony English currency, ostensibly to wreck the British economy. Peiper's account of Hitler's uncanny ability to sense the forgeries is from his interview with John Toland, October 10, 1963. For background: Richard Breitman, "Follow the Money," in *U.S. Intelligence and the Nazis* (Cambridge: Cambridge University Press, 2005). For a popular version: Lawrence Malkin, *Krueger's Men: The Secret Nazi Counterfeit Plot* (New York: Little, Brown, 2006), 76–78, and also a cinematic depiction: *The Counterfeiters* (Best foreign film of 2008).

75. J. Peiper, interview with John Toland, October 10, 1963, LOC, Last Hundred Days.

76. William L. Shirer, *Berlin Diary* (New York: Alfred A. Knopf, 1941), 486–487. As retribution, Hitler ordered London attacked without mercy. From September through mid-November 1940 two hundred Luftwaffe bombers hit London almost every night.

77. Throughout the autumn of 1940 Berlin was the target of British bombers, striking, on average, four times per week. Although the bombardment was only modestly effective, the psychological impact was greater as much of the city remained bleary-eyed after staying awake for much of the night when the air raids were in progress.

78. With the continued British bombing, there must have been some apprehension for the safety of Jochen's family in Berlin, however. In September and October 1940, the German capital was bombed more than two dozen times. Some of the strikes were not far away; the Palace at Charlottenburg was hit as well as the Berlin Zoo. Moreover, the bombing campaign moved to the industrial works at Schönefeld (Henschel), Babelsberg (Arado) and Genshagen (Daimler-Benz).

79. "I was on Himmler's staff since 1940. . . . In all this time the Reichsführer SS, as a superior and human being, displayed towards me a great kindness and camaraderie which greatly impressed me. . . . [I] was always, and still am, in debt to the Reichsführer SS." Werner Grothmann, "Zur Person Himmler's," Dachau, 1946, Toland Papers, FDR Library, Box 46.

80. Peiper was photographed with Himmler and others in the event: "Spanischer Polizeiführer zu Besuch in Berlin," *Das Schwarze Korps*, September 5, 1940. Also, "Der Chef der spanischen Polizei bei der Leibstandarte," *VB*, September 5, 1940.

81. Not counting the Republican soldiers killed in the fight, the number of executions carried out by Franco was in the vicinity of 2 million! In a lingering historical scandal, the Catholic Church did not make any effort to stop the genocide. Even Himmler professed to be dismayed by Franco's plan of action, although compassion played no part in his logic: why not get useful work from such political prisoners rather than just executing them?

82. Kersten, *The Kersten Memoirs: 1940*–1945, entry for August 20, 1940, 43–46.

83. Archive of the Memorial Site of the KZ Sachsenhausen: R 54/38, Erinnerungsbericht des Häftlings Dr. Franz Nowak.

84. William Shirer, *Berlin Diary, 1934–1941* (New York: A. A. Knopf, 1941), 461.

85. See L. V. Thompson, "'Lebensborn' and the Eugenics Policy of the Reichsführer SS," *Central European History* 4 (1971): 54–77. The impact of the institution became an inescapable economic fact for every SS man who paid a monthly contribution to Lebensborn in direct proportion to their number of offspring. Bachelors paid a substantial fraction of their monthly pay to the fund, while someone with a large family would pay almost nothing. Children outside of marriage was seen as a good thing—even polygamy. In a letter from Himmler to Sepp Dietrich on July 23, 1943, Himmler openly expressed his delight with the fact "that the men of the Leibstandarte have an encouraging number of children born out of wedlock." BA-K, Sammlung Shumacker/441.

86. Himmler had a large contingent of scholars under his Ahnenerbe studying Tibet and its influence on German affairs. As to the contradiction as to how Genghis Khan could be at the same time from an inferior Eastern race yet nearly come to rule the world, Himmler had ready a fantastic explanation: Khan and some other Mongols were descendants from Nordic emigrants from the lost continent of Atlantis. With Teutonic blood flowing through their veins, such people were the most dangerous of all! One of Himmler's chief experts on the *Welteislehre* (Ice Age Lore), was SS Brigadeführer Karl-Maria Wiligut (who immodestly referred to himself as "Weisthor") who believed himself a direct descendent of the Teutonic god, Thor. Himmler saw Weisthor as the Nazi-Irminist version of Merlin, with himself, of course, as King Arthur, and Wewelsburg as his Camelot. See "Interrogation of Ernst Schäfer," July 16, 1945, NA RG 238, Microfilm M-1270, Roll 27. For an in-depth study of Himmler's ancestral and racial offices, see Michael H. Kater, *Das 'Ahnenerbe' der SS, 1935–1945: Ein Beitrag zur Kulturpolitik des Dritten Reiches* (Stuttgart: Deutsche Verlags Anstalt, 1974).

87. HSSPF Theodor Berkelmann was assigned by Himmler in September of 1940 to help resettle "Germanic elements" from the French Alsace to the Ukraine based on the "suitability of their racial characteristics." Gauleiter Josef Bürkel argued that "inferior beings" [read Jews] would be sent to unoccupied France—or sent to concentration camps. See Longerich, *Heinrich Himmler*, 588–589. For photograph of Peiper and Himmler meeting with Berkelmann in September 1940, Jens Westemeier, *Joachim Peiper: A Biography of Himmler's SS Commander*, (Atglen: Schiffer, 2007), photo insert following 128.

88. "Reiseprogramm des Reichsführer SS, 6.9.1940–8.9.1940," NA RG 242, T-175, R112, 2637788–89. On the way to Metz, Himmler, Peiper and the others stopped in Semois at the Hotel Bartel on September 6 to meet with Gruppenführer Pohl on undisclosed business. Sepp Dietrich's orders for the day is found in "Sonderbefehl für die Übergabe der neuen Standarte durch R.F. SS," Metz, September 6, 1940, NA RG 242, T-175, R112, 2637794–95.

89. This and other quotes from the Day of Metz: Best, *Mit der Leibstandarte im Westen*, 51–54.

90. Best, *Mit der Leibstandarte im Westen*.

91. "Himmler's address to officers of the SS-Leibstandarte Adolf Hitler on the Day of Metz," NA RG-238, USA Exhibits 304, NM-66, Entry 2A, Box 18. IMT Document 1918-PS.

92. Old German saying: "Wer mit dem Teufel speist, braucht eine lange Gabel."

Chapter Six

1. Peiper's handwritten notes detailing the three thousand–kilometer journey (Fountainbleau–Le Havre–Cherbourg–Rennes–Brest–Bordeaux–Biarritz–Madrid) is seen on NA RG 242, T-175, R112, 2637644–45.

2. "Kiermaier statement," *op. cit.*, PRO: WO208/4474.

3. For Himmler's schedule and Peiper presence, see NA RG 242, T-175, Roll 112, 2637780–83. For details on Himmler's visit to Eicke birthday celebration and review of the Totenkopf Division: IFZ, *Das Schwarze Korps*, issue for October 31, 1940.

4. Primary source for Peiper's October travels is Public Records Office (hereafter PRO), "Interrogation of Werner Grothmann," WO208/4474, RC190054, Kew, London. Also, "Himmler: 1940 Visit to Spain," C10370, 10370/41, FO/371/24529.

5. Unternehmen Feuerzauber—Operation Fire Magic: German military aid to the Spanish Fascists began in the summer of 1936 with Hitler's response to a request from Franco for assistance with the civil war. One man, who would later fight alongside Peiper as a tough tank driver, August Tonk, had been a member of the crews operating with 1st Panzer light tanks of the Condor Legion in Spain under Wilhelm Ritter von Thoma.

6. For the story of Himmler's search for the Holy Grail in Barcelona: Montserrat Rico Góngora, *The Desecrated Abbey* (Madrid: Planeta, 2007). None other than Karl Wolff, who was along with Himmler and Peiper in Barcelona indicated that the story is true: "We had at that time Wewelsburg next to Paderdorn that was the predecessor of the *Deutscher Ritterorden* in Western Prussia and Himmler decreed that King Arthur's round table should be reborn there. . . . In the saga, the Knights of the Round Table were looking for the Holy Grail and we really were! We were searching for the holy grail in Spain and France." Wolff said their trip to Barcelona was at least partly to hunt for the grail. While searching they had on black SS uniforms and the monks passed them uneasily at the monastery. Letter Karl Wolff to Gerd Heidemann, March 23, 1982: "They made the sign of the cross when they passed us as they thought they were seeing the devil."

7. Wagner may have been inspired by the writing of the thirteenth-century bard, Wolfram von Eschenbach who claimed to know where the chalice was located. Others, however, ventured that the Holy Grail was stashed away in Montségur, France—another place Himmler had already sent his men looking into after the conquest that summer.

8. Photos of Peiper with Himmler during the trip to Spain appear in *Das Schwarze Korps*, October 31, 1940, PRO: WO208/4474.

9. Joseph Goebbels on October 26, 1940. Jana Richter, ed., *Die Tagebücher von Joseph Goebbels*/Teil 1, 1923–1941. Band 8, April–Nov. 1940, (Munich, K. G. Saur, 1998).

10. Staatsarchiv München, Spruchkammerverfahren, K 856 Josef Woldemar Keller-Kühne.

11. "Programm für den Besuch des Reichsführer SS in Norwegen," NA RG 242, T-175, Roll 112, 2637759–763.

12. For Peiper's comment: "But it was valuable blood," RG-238, M1019, Roll 52, 185–189: "Vernehmung von Col. Joachim Peiper," April 17, 1947. On the meeting with Terboven and the Norwegians: Witte et al., *Dienstkalender Heinrich Himmlers*, 159. Himmler's view of mixed races can be gleaned from his speech to commanding officers at Bad Schachen on October 14, 1943: "Obviously in such a mixture of peoples, there will always be some racially good types. Therefore, I think it is your duty to take their children with us, to remove them from their environment, if necessary by robbing or stealing them. This may seem strange to our European minds and many people will say: 'How can you be so cruel as to take a child from its mother?' I would say: 'How can you be so cruel as to leave on the other side a brilliant future enemy who will later on kill your son and your grandson?' Either we win over any good blood that we may use for ourselves and give it a place in our people, or gentlemen—you may call this cruel, but nature is cruel—we destroy this blood." NA RG 319, Investigative Repository Records (IRR), Himmler files, XE-000632.

13. "Kameraden aus dem Norden," *Das Schwarze Korps*, 1941. Also, "Persönlicher Stab Reichsführer SS," BA-K, NS 19/4008, 39–45.

14. Witte et al., *Dienstkalender Heinrich Himmlers*, entry for May 4, 1941. Photos by Heinrich Hoffmann.

15. Westemeier, *Himmlers Krieger*, 105.

16. Witte et al., *Dienstkalender Heinrich Himmlers*, entry for May 31, 1941, 165.

17. Jochen Peiper, statement, April 8, 1946. William R. Perl Papers, George Washington Library, Box 6, Folder 6.

18. Staff RFSS at celebration at Oppeln, Upper Silesia. Photographic source: BA-BA: 146-1969-052-27. The caption from Koblenz is in error. However, given the content and context, it is possible with the *Himmler Dienstkalendar* (166–167) to isolate the date to June 4 or 5, 1941.

19. Peiper was photographed in Łódź along with Himmler on June 6, 1941: Witte et al., *Dienstkalender Heinrich Himmlers*, 167, 168. Also, other photos courtesy of Peter Witte. For Himmler's presence at Łódź, see Brandt's log: NA RG 242, T-175, R39A, and handwritten entry for June 6, 1941. During Himmler's visit, Jews were forbidden to leave their homes. Conditions inside the ghetto were so terrible and hopeless that suicides among its enslaved population were an everyday event. See Lucjan Dobroszycki, *The Chronicle of the Łódź Ghetto* (New Haven, CT: Yale University Press, 1984), 58–61.

20. Christopher Browning, "Nazi Ghettoization Policy in Poland," *Central European History* No. 19 (1986): 355–366.

21. Statement of Jochen Peiper, April 8, 1946. William R. Perl Papers, George Washington Library, Box 6, Folder 6. In actuality, there is not a single document or independent source that would support Peiper's claim that a German police officer was killed, while in reality the Jewish population in Łódź was in such miserable conditions under the German occupation that any observer would everywhere see people starving to death.

22. Bach-Zelewski's statement as cited by Gerald Reitlinger, *Die SS: Tragödie einer deutschen Epoche* (Munich: Verlag Kurt Desch, 1957), 163. The footnote identifying Peiper appears only in the German imprint and not in the abridged Viking edition in English. For the recollection of the inhabitants of Wewelsburg, see Schneider letter as cited by Westemeier, *Himmlers Krieger*, 105. "Older inhabitants of Wewelsburg . . . fondly remember the handsome young

SS officer, who worked as HH's adjutant—and after working long hours always went along to one of the two inns."

23. Entry in Rudolf Brandt's office log for Thursday, June 12, 1941. NA RG 242, T581, R39A.

24. Himmler, "Und wieder reiten die Goten," *SS Leitheft*, NA, RG 242, T-611, Jg.7/Nr. 9B, 2.

25. For Himmler's Berlin schedule and appointments during this time with Kersten: Witte et al., *Dienstkalender Heinrich Himmlers*, 114–115. "We can't permit such a danger to our country; the homosexuals must be entirely eliminated. . . . Our forefathers knew what they were doing when they had their own homosexuals drowned in a bog," Kersten, *The Kersten Memoirs: 1940–1945*, 56–57.

26. Martin Sandberger's postwar recollection of Bruno Steckenbach's description of Heydrich's speech as cited by Breitman, *Architect of Genocide*, 163–164, and detailed in associated endnotes. Understanding that a secondhand recollection is less compelling, there is corroboration for Sandberger's paraphrasing of Steckenbach. Another SD man present, Walter Blume, recalled that "the Führer and the leadership of the state held the view that it [Eastern Jewry and the "reservoir of intellectuals for Bolshevism"] must be destroyed."

27. Himmler was so preoccupied with the notion that his SS not lower itself to kill in bloodlust that he would later order an internal investigation within his "Black Guards"of those who went on brutal killing rampages without orders. Ironically, the first investigations into the Holocaust came from the SS examining the actions of their own people. Jürgen Matthäus has effectively singled out the case of SS Ustuf. Max Täubner in this regard who killed hundreds of Jews in October 1941 in Scholochowo in the Ukraine in a horrifying brutal manner. Thanks to Dr. Matthäus for sharing a prepublication of a paper on this topic: "The First Holocaust Trials: SS Investigations into the Murder of Jews," USHMM, draft from autumn 2009. Documentation of the SS case against Täubner can be seen in NARA, BDC file A 3343-SSO, Roll B-171.

28. Mario R. Dederichs, *Heydrich: The Face of Evil* (London: Greenhill Books, 2006), 108.

29. Koch, *Himmlers Graue Eminenz*, 184.

30. The court certificate of her renunciation of the church is dated June 2, 1939: Nachlass Heinrich Himmler, BA-K, N 1126 / 38.

31. "Himmler's Girl Friend Left with Two Little SS Souvenirs," *Stars and Stripes*, September 6, 1945.

32. Established in 1841, the Forsthaus Valepp is still in operation above Tegernsee, a popular destination with bicyclists and *Bergwanderungen*—mountain wanderers.

33. Himmler Family Photos: "Shepperdess" Album: USHMMU, Photographic Archives. This is Himmler's daughter's souvenir album from the war in Russia which includes photos sent to "Puppi" (Gudrun Himmler) from the war front from summer 1941 as well as photos taken just days before the war started. Many of these are from Himmler's official photographer: Friedrich Franz Bauer. Courtesy of helpful archivists, Judith Cohen and Nancy Hartman, the author was able to examine the rear of the photographs for the first time, showing that many were dated with the locations indicated. See photos of Gudrun, Heinrich and Margarete Himmler picking flowers (e.g., #60455) taken in the fields around Valepp, and dated June 19, 1941.

34. Diary of Gudrun Himmler, June 21, 1941, *NSDAP Hauptarchiv*, Himmler Collection, Microfilm Roll #99, Hoover Institution, Stanford University. That Himmler's relationship with Marga was on ice seems clear through the eyes of the daughter: "Things are very tight in the household," she related after her father left. And then on July 19, 1941: "Mutti almost always has something the matter with her stomach."

35. Wilhelm Wulff, *Zodiac and Swastika* (New York: Coward, McCann and McGeoghegan, 1973), 81; first published in German as *Tierkreis und Hakenkreuz* (Gütersloh: Bertelsmann Sachbuchverlag Reinhard Mohn, 1968).

36. Schellenberg, *The Labyrinth*, 185. Heydrich said of Hitler and Himmler, "One is worried about the stars on the epaulettes. The other about the stars in the heavens. It's a question as to who is more difficult to work with."

37. "The people go to the people, and the flame to the flame. Rise to the sky sacred pyre, leap roaring from tree to tree," Reider, *The Order of the SS*, 180–181.

38. When asked why Hitler felt he could succeed where Napoleon did not, the German leader countered that the French emperor did not have airplanes to support his marching grenadiers, nor did he have fast tanks in place of horse and cannon.

39. Himmler's last minute hard sell to Hitler on using poison gas in the East likely reflected anxiety relative to the entire Barbarossa endeavor. Himmler's Aktenvermerk, June 21, 1941, NA RG 242, T-175, R 106, F2629109. Originally cited by Breitman, *Architect of Genocide*, 166.

40. For "the world will hold its breath," Joachim C. Fest, *Hitler* (New York: Random House, 1974), 648.

41. For record of the tennis match, see Rudolf Brandt's handwritten office log: NA RG 242, T-581, R 39A, and handwritten entry for June 23, 1941.

42. Alan Bullock, *Hitler: A Study in Tyranny* (New York: Bantam, 1961), 587.

43. "Rede des Reichsführers SS anläßlich der Gruppenführerbesprechung in Tölz," February 18, 1937, T-175, R190, F2611881. Hitler's opinion was identical: "A member of the SS and police who commits immoral acts will be punished by death," "Erlaß des Führers zur Reinerhaltung von SS und Polizei," November 15, 1941, T-175, R161, F2693487.

44. Although typically detailed, the divisional daily orders for the Totenkopf Division between June 11 and 14, 1941, makes no mention of Horst Peiper's death. BA-MA, RS 3-3/24.

45. Details of the career of Horst Peiper taken from his BDC RuSHA file at the NA (A-3343–RS-E508). The SS Heimwehr Danzig battalion with which Horst fought in Poland was implicated in atrocities against Poles in Pomerania on September 8, 1939. In France Horst served as adjutant for SS Obersturmbannführer Heinz Bertling who, along with SS Obersturmführer Fritz Knöchlein, was charged in the massacre of British troops at La Paradis on May 27, 1940. See Sydnor, *Soldiers of Destruction*, 41, 49, and 103–108. This episode of Horst Peiper's death was described by witness Alfred Roßdeutscher (then an SS Uscha. with the Totkenkopf Infantry Regiment 2), who said that Eicke had made the accusation in the summer of 1940: Charles Trank, *Totenkopf* (Bayeux: Editions Heimdal, 2006), 175. That Horst was homosexual was flatly denied by Roßdeutscher and others who knew him. For his part, Jochen Peiper believed his brother had witnessed the homosexual behavior of others and had been killed as a cover up. "It is possible that it was a suicide, but the circumstances of my uncle's death remains unclear." H Peiper, interview, May 21, 1999.

46. Letter Jochen Peiper to Häschen Potthast, September 23, 1941, BA K: Nachlass Heinrich Himmler, Bestand No. 1126, Folder 39. Thanks to Katrin Himmler and Gregor Pickro for assistance in locating the originals and assisting with questions regarding transcription.

47. "Himmler's field headquarters was in a barracks two hundred feet long, where he possessed an office, 18 x 25, with four windows and tastefully, but simply decorated. His daughter's photograph stood on his desk. Himmler took his evening meal at 8 p.m., which consisted of a hot meat dish or pea soup with a single glass of red wine. An evening cigar followed. During meals, service matters were not discussed, but nor was there any small talk. Himmler loved to discuss on these occasions the kingdoms of the Goths, Genghis Khan, the new SS state to be established in Burgundy or King Henry the First." Kersten, *The Kersten Memoirs: 1940–1945*, 303.

48. See Franz W. Seidler and Dieter Zeigert, *Hitler's Secret Headquarters* (London: Greenhill Books, 2004), 96–103.

49. The photograph of Himmler greeting Hitler with Peiper at his side at the Wolfschanze on June 29, 1941, is courtesy the research of Hanns Peter Frentz. Photographs of Walter

Frentz, Film N-4113, Frame 20. Also in the photo with Himmler and Peiper was Maj. Rudolf Schmundt Hitler's chief military adjutant, Reichsleiter Martin Bormann and Hitler's overweight physician, Dr. Theo Morrell.

50. Below in a letter to a friend from *Wolfsschanze* on June 28, 1941. Von Below, *At Hitler's Side*, 107.

51. Ian Kershaw, *Hitler: Nemesis 1936–1945* (New York: W. W. Norton, 2000), 298.

52. Adolf Hitler's table conversation taken on July 5–6, 1941, taken down by Heinrich Heim on Bormann's staff. *Hitler's Table Talk*, 3–4.

53. Dederichs, *Heydrich*, 108.

54. Browning and Matthäus, *Origins of the Final Solution*, 255, Breitman, *Architect of Genocide*, 170. For Peiper's presence with Himmler on June 30, 1941: Witte et al., *Dienstkalender Heinrich Himmlers*, 181. By July 18 Böhme's unit would claim 3,302 victims killed in the area with an increasing number of them women and children.

55. Peiper is seen in Grodno with Himmler talking to a Russian peasant woman in a photograph obtained from Karl Wolff by Peter Witte.

56. Peter Longerich, *Der ungeschriebene Befehl: Hitler und der Weg zur Endlösung* (Munich: Piper Verlag, 2001), 101.

57. Himmler's activities on the afternoon of June 30, 1941: NA RG 242, T-581, R39A. Peiper's presence for discussions that morning: Witte et al., *Dienstkalender Heinrich Himmlers*, 181. Heydrich's presence and reaction to Grodno: Helmut Krausnick and Hans-Heinrich Wilhelm, *Die Truppe des Weltanschauungskrieges* (Stuttgart: Deutsch Verlags Anstalt, 1981), 534.

58. Matthäus et al., *Ausbildungsziel Judenmord?*, 223.

59. Longerich, *Politik der Vernichtung*, 353.

60. Breitman, *Architect of Genocide*, 173; Matthäus et al., *Ausbildungsziel Judenmord?*, 223–224. Note that Breitman, without the benefit of more recently available data, was somewhat confused on the correct chronology for the proceedings in Bialystok.

61. Matthäus et al., *Ausbildungsziel Judenmord?*, 225.

62. Martin Cüppers, *Wegbereiter der Shoah: Die Kommandostab Reichsführer SS und die Judenvernichtung 1939–1945* (Darmstadt: Wissenschaftliche Buchgesellschaft, 2005), 98–107. as cited in Matthäus et al., *Ausbildungsziel Judenmord?*, 225.

63. For the morning routine within Himmler's command train, Peter Witte, interview by author, April 23, 2009. Also, SS-Stubaf. Tiefenbacher, "Kdt. D. Sonderzuges 'Heinrich'," NA RG-242, T-175, Roll 129/2. Contains the files of the RF-SS Persönlicher Stab (Karl Wolff). For the map "Säuberungsaktion der 1. SS Brigade vom 28.7.41," appendix of *Unsere Ehre heisst Treue: Kriegstagebuch des Kommandostabes Reichsführer SS, Tätigkeitsberichte der 1. und 2. SS-Infanterie-Brigade, der SS Kavallerie Brigade und von Sonderkommands der SS* (Wien: Europa Verlag, 1965). Grothmann also testified that "All orders issued by Himmler passed through the hands of his adjutant." "Summary of Evidence of Werner Grothmann: Witness for the SS taken before a Commission on June 25, 1946," Toland Papers, FDR Library, Box 46.

64. "Der Reichsführer SS zu den Ersatzmannschaften für die Kampfgruppe Nord am Sonntag, den 13. Juli 1941 in Stettin," NA, T-175, "Records of the Reich Leader of the SS and Chief on the German Police," Roll 9, Frame 263268. In the speech, Himmler continued, "These animals that torture and ill treat every prisoner from our side, every wounded man that they come across and do not treat them the way decent soldiers would, you will see for yourself. These people have been welded by the Jews into one religion, one ideology, that is called Bolshevism. . . . When you, my men, fight there in the East, you are carrying on the same struggle, against the same sub-humanity, the same inferior races, that at one time appeared under the name of Huns . . . and still another time under the name of Genghis Khan and the Mongols."

65. For photo of Peiper in Lublin on July 20, see Witte et al., *Dienstkalender Heinrich Himmlers*, 187. Seen in front of the forced labor camp on Lipowa Street with Peiper are

Himmler, Wolff, Globocnik, Friedrich-Wilhelm Krüger, and Dr. Hans Kammler. Krüger was an early proponent for establishment of large-scale Jewish forced labor camps. Kammler would soon draw up construction and engineering plans for the first death camps. Globocnik or "Globus" as Himmler called him, was given the job of not only building large new concentration camps, but also of creating new SS settlements—complete with homes—in Lublin and nearby Zamosc. For the significance of the unrecorded conversation between Himmler and Globocnik on July 20, see Breitman, *Architect of Genocide*, 184–187.

66. Witte et al., *Dienstkalender Heinrich Himmlers*, 188: July 24, 1941. 22.30. "Unterhaltung RF, d'Alquen, Peiper, Dohna, Grothmann, Brandt."

67. Himmler did not realize that radio communications to his train in East Prussia from SS Gruppenführer Erich von dem Bach-Zelewski, coordinating the execution squads in the field, were steadily intercepted and deciphered by Allied code breakers. Much of this information has just recently been declassified, largely due to the effort of Dr. Richard Breitman at American University. For example, on August 3, the SS Cavalry Brigade reported that through that date it had liquidated 3,274 partisans and "Jewish Bolsheviks" without any losses of their own—a telling indicator of the nature of their operation. See Breitman, *Official Secrets*, 41. Source: "Summary of German Police Decodes, July 3 to August 14, 1941," PRO, HW 16/6, Pt. 1, Kew, UK.

68. Given the birth of Himmler's son, Helge, on February 15, 1942, it seems likely that Hedwig Potthast became pregnant in late May 1941, just after Himmler and Peiper returned from Greece to Berlin.

69. Hedwig's brother, Dr. Walter Potthast, was a lawyer and Wehrmacht Lieutenant in the 2nd Panzer Division in the Polish, French, and Russian Campaigns. An NSDAP member since 1937, he personally met Heinrich Himmler early in the war. As evidenced by his frequent correspondence, Walter approved of their affair. However, Hedwig's sister, Thilde, and her parents in Trier were strongly opposed. Thilde taught young girls at an NSDAP Napola school in Kolmar-Berg, Luxembourg, and enthusiastically embraced Hitler and Himmler's ideas but drew the line at marital infidelity. In the fall of 1941 she wrote, "I fear Hedwig, that there can be no reconciliation with the parents. They would forgive everything at once if you would break it off with him. . . . He is already married and they see the whole matter as cheating on his wife and also disregard for you. Mother asks me whether his wife knows about it now, and unfortunately I have to say that up until now, so much as I know, that is not the case. They see that as cowardice. Our parents are suffering terribly over this." Nachlass Heinrich Himmler, Bestand N 1126, Folder 37. Katrin Himmler provided the author as translation of a letter from Heinrich Himmler to Hedwig Potthast dated June 20, 1944, in which the SS Reichsführer notes that they were now "celebrating their engagement" which had produced "two sweet *Lütten*," now exactly five years later. As other material discovered by the author showed that Potthast and Heinrich professed their romance in December 1938 in a meeting in Gmund, this would mean that Himmler and Hedwig consummated their relationship by the summer solstice of June 21, 1939, or at least made their sexual liaison official.

70. "Mein liebes gutes Häslein, Since 1600 I am sitting in my office in my bunker at the FHQ and now you get a letter," Letter Himmler to Hedwig Potthast, July 27–28, 1941, transcribed letter with a reproduction of the handwritten original in author's possession. Transcription and translation by Edith Umbert. The letter indicates clear apprehension by Potthast of her pregnancy as well as anxiety regarding the legal status of the baby to be born.

71. "Mein liebes gutes Häslein," Himmler to Hedwig Potthast, July 28/29, 1941.

72. For Fegelein's orders: "SS Kav Rgt. 1 1a, Regimentsbefehl Nr. 42," July 27, 1941, NA, T-175, Roll 109; for Himmler's clarification the following day: "Kommandosonderbefehl," Heinrich Himmler, July 28, 1941; reproduced in Norbert Müller, ed. *Die faschistische Okkupationspolitik in den zeitweilig besetzten Gebieten der Sowjetunion, 1941–1944* (Berlin: Akademie Verlag, 1991), 175–177.

73. "Programm für die Reise des Reichsführer SS nach Kowno, Riga, Minsk," NA RG 242, T-175, R 112, 2637747–48. Although the "Teilnehmer" does not show Peiper, his presence is established beyond a doubt by the photographic evidence. Given the nature of the mission—driving by car with Franz Lucas at the wheel, the itinerary would indicate Peiper was along August 29–31, with the photograph taken the first day.

74. The photograph taken by Friedrich Franz Bauer, Himmler's official photographer, clearly shows Himmler, Karl Wolff, Prützmann, Peiper, Himmler's doctor, Dr. Karl Gebhardt, Franz Lucas (Himmler's driver) and two others unidentified having a road picnic during the Latvian tour at the end of the month. The photo, likely taken on July 29, 1941, near Riga, is in a commemorative photo collection provided Bauer to Karl Wolff of the tour at the end of July and beginning of August 1941.

75. Richard Rhodes, *Masters of Death: The SS Einsatzgruppen and the Invention of the Holocaust* (New York: Knopf, 2002), 113.

76. Browning and Matthäus, *Origins of the Final Solution*, 191–293. Most of the killings came from two companies of auxiliary police with Latvian and Lithuanian volunteers under Karl Jäger's *Einsatzkommando 3*, which killed hundreds each day in the area between Kowno and Wilna from July onward.

77. The planned itinerary is given in "Programm für die Reise des Reichsführer SS nach Kowno, Riga, Minsk," NA RG 242, T-175, R 112, 2637747–48. The actual impending meeting is revealed in the summaries of German Police Decodes, July 29, 1941, PRO HW 16/32. The photo of Peiper looking into the KV-2 tank in Minsk is from the same Karl Wolff photo album made available to the author by Gerd Heidemann. (also Bildarchiv Preussicher Kulturbesitz: BPK No. 30023435). Its caption reads, "Heinrich Himmler besichtigt einen erbeuteten russischen Panzer Neben ihm auf dem Panzer stehend SS-Gruppenführer Karl Wolff." The number of KV-2 tanks captured in the July battle culminating in the Bialystok-Minsk pocket can be seen in the German wartime propaganda newsreel: *Deutsche Wochenschau*, No. 567, July 16, 1941.

78. Matthäus et al., *Ausbildungsziel Judenmord?*, 226.

79. *Unsere Ehre heisst Treue*, 16. Photos of Himmler's inspection of the cavalry brigade with Peiper in attendance can be seen in the photographic collection at the BA-K on the operations of the SS Cavalry Brigade in Russia in 1941 taken by SS Kriegsberichter Büschel.

80. Information on Hermann Fegelein during this period from BDC Files, NA, A-3343-SSO, Roll 198, Frames 709–715. Lombard was in charge of SS Kav. Rgt.1 under Fegelein. For visit of Peiper with RFSS on July 5 see *Unsere Ehre heisst Treue*, 16. In a postwar interview Hitler's SS driver, Erich Kempka, derided the promiscuous Fegelein as having his "brains in his scrotum."

81. "SS Kav. Rgt 2, Aug. 1, 1941," NA RG 242, T-354, Roll 168. Himmler's order to drive the women into the swamps was likely not a provision to spare them, but rather to spare his cavalrymen the experience of having to coldly murder women. That Hitler himself came to know of this incident is borne out in a speech he gave on October 25, 1941: "In the Reichstag, I prophesied to Jewry that the Jews will disappear from Europe if war is not avoided. This race of criminals has two million dead [of World War I] on its conscience, and now hundreds of thousands more. *Nobody can tell me we can't send them into the marshes!* For who bothers about our people? It is good if the terror [*der Schrecken*] goes before us that we are exterminating Jewry." Werner Jochmann, ed., *Adolf Hitler: Monologe im Führerhauptquartier: Aufzeichnungen Heinrich Heims, 1941–44* (Hamburg: A. Knaus, 1980), 106–108.

82. During this time Kurt Daluege, the Chief of the Order Police who was instrumental in the expanding execution of Jews in Russia, was becoming quite sensitive to the potential harm done from any of their numerous radio transmissions should their contents be revealed to their enemy. On September 13, 1941, he sent the following message to his militarized police battalions: "The danger of decipherment by the enemy of wireless messages is great. For this

reason only such matters are to be transmitted by wireless as can be considered open. . . . State secrets, calls for especially secret treatment. Into this category fall exact figure of executions." GC and CS, History of the German Police Section, 1939–1945," PRO HW 3/155.

83. Lombard's reports: "SS-Kav. Rgt. 1 Reit. Abt. Abteilungsbefehl Nr. 28," August 1, 1941, BA-MA, RS/4/441. Also Cüppers, 278–280.

84. This synopsis is taken from Matthäus et al., *Ausbildungsziel Judenmord?*, 266. By the end of 1941 Cüppers estimated that the Waffen SS Kommandostab units had killed forty thousand Jews.

85. Much of this damning evidence has only recently been declassified as part of records of the National Security Agency in the United States or the PRO in Great Britain. For instance, on July 14 Police Battalion 309 signaled that they had eliminated 1,153 Jews in Slonim west of Baranowicze while other battalions carried out "pacification" activities in the same area. See PRO HW 16/31 and 16/32; also NA RG 457, "National Security Agency: History of the Cryptographic Services," Box 1386.

86. Quotation of conversation with Peiper in Poland in 1940 while on Himmler's train. "Interrogation of Dr. Ernst Schäfer," April 1, 1947, NA RG 242, T-175, Roll 62, Frame 636. Asked if the Tibet expert believed that Peiper was referring to himself, Schäfer replied, "That was my impression—that he did not want to know of these things." That the mass killings of Jews had deleterious effect on the killers has been convincingly covered by Richard Breitman, "Himmler and the 'Terrible Secret' Among the Executioners," *Journal of Contemporary History* 26 (1991): 431–451.

87. "Programm für die Reise des Reichsführer SS nach Kowno, Riga, Minsk, 29.7.–31.7.1941," RG 242, T-175, R112, 2637747–46. Accompanied by Wolff and Grothmann, Himmler met with Gen. Daluege and Gruppenführer Bach-Zelewski, who were directly involved in the killings going on behind the German front lines.

88. There are many versions of Himmler's trip to Minsk on August 15, 1941, and his revulsion at the executions. According to Bach-Zelewski, Himmler's discomfort with the event propelled the idea for gas chambers. Not surprisingly, in an interview with Peiper's replacement, Werner Grothmann, after the war, Grothmann did speak of what he saw at Minsk on that day. However, Bach-Zelewski, Karl Wolff, and even Walter Frentz (along as a photographer) would later tell of the event. A recent summary including many sources is found in Breitman, *Official Secrets*, 61. Actually, Himmler's revulsion was likely invented as a postwar myth by the two greatest creative storytellers of the period: Bach-Zelewski and Karl Wolff. Wolff even repeated the story before cameras leading to widespread acceptance of this exaggeration. Peter Witte, interview by author, April 23, 2009. For Himmler's plan to support the mental health of the shooters through recreation after mass killings: "Geheimer SS Befehl des RFSS vom 12. December 1941 über Truppenbetreuung nach Massenerschießungen mit Schreiben des SSPF Lettland," ZSA Riga, R83-1-80, fol. 4f.; Copy in the archives of the USHMM, RG 18.002M, Roll 11. Thanks for Jürgen Matthäus for pointing out this document.

89. "Interrogation of Werner Grothmann," June 13, 1945, NA RG 319, Investigative Repository Records (IRR), Himmler files, XE-000632.

90. In the spring of 2009 the author communicated with Hinrich Peiper about the death of his uncle Horst. The episode had remained a disturbing family mystery, he related, with his grandmother unwilling to discuss the matter. In conversation with his father, Jochen Peiper indicated his closeness to his brother, but never offered a satisfactory explanation for what happened. Further, nowhere in the records of the Totenkopf Division is any mention made of the death of Horst Peiper. The author carefully examined the intact records at the BA-MA, RS 3-3/24 where Eicke's Division faithfully reported any of the infrequent noncombat deaths in May and early June 1941. Given the extent of the records (showing how another SS man died in May from an automobile accident), it becomes very strange (and seemingly deliberate) that no record is found of an SS officer who killed himself on June 11, 1941—not even an obituary.

91. For Himmler's "angry reaction," see letter of Joachim Peiper to Modifications Board/ Heidelberg, October 5, 1950, NA Case 6-24, RG 549, Case 6-24, Box 61.

92. Ibid. One can argue that if Peiper had really been affronted by the crimes and wickedness developing toward the elimination camps, he would have asked for a transfer as soon as he was witness to the shootings in Poland with Himmler and von Alvensleben as early as 1940. Himmler learned of Potthast's pregnancy by July 28 when he wrote to his mistress [See notes 69–70 above]. Yet in spite of spending Tuesday through Thursday, July 29–31, together in the field, Himmler neglected to tell his unhappy adjutant about the news. Only in Peiper's letter to Potthast in December of 1941 does he give an indication of having learned of the news of her pregnancy. His intervening communication (September 23) laments having been forgotten and asks Hedwig why she is no longer writing. See Peiper's letters: September 23 and December 10, 1941, BA-K, Nachlass Heinrich Himmler, Bestand N-1126, Folder 39.

93. Given the birth of Peiper's son in mid-April 1942, it seems likely Sigurd Peiper became pregnant during this short leave.

94. Later Sigurd Peiper would write to Hedwig Potthast about the change: "Too bad, that Jochen went his own way and left K H. . . . Jochen will forever regret it. You know, how he loves K. H., appreciates him, and honors him. . . . When Jochen took his leave from K H in July 1941, he must have said something like: 'In three years I am going to get you back to me.' Deep inside, Jochen seems to have counted on that. He indicated it variously at times." Letter Sigurd Peiper to Hedwig Potthast, November 11, 1944, *NSDAP Hauptarchiv*, Himmler Collection, Microfilm Roll #99, Hoover Institution, Stanford University.

95. Peiper's retrospective view of this time: "The German Army was intoxicated with success and the necessity to state a preventative war . . . we thought we would be able to force the military decision in three months time. Our arrogance, as well as the underestimation of our adversary, was typical, as well as tremendous." Jochen Peiper, "Brief Review and Reflections about the Battle in the Russian Theater of Operations," April 7, 1946, Burton Ellis Archives. That many in the German high command felt that Barbarossa was already won was clearly expressed in the war diary Gen. Franz Halder, the chief of the General Staff, "It is thus probably not saying too much," he presumptuously recorded on July 3, "if I maintain this campaign in Russia was won in the first fourteen days." *Kriegstagebuch*, Vol. 3 (Stuttgart: Kohlhammer, 1964). Hitler saw things the same way, remarking five days later of his intention to soon "level" Leningrad and Moscow "otherwise we will have to feed them through the winter." Percy E. Schramm, ed., *Kriegstagebuch des Oberkommandos der Wehrmacht*, Vol. 1 (Herrshing: Pawlak, 1982), 1021.

Chapter Seven

1. The impact of Peiper's connections with Himmler is clear in the manifest of office of the Reichsführer SS showing Sigurd Peiper receiving special allotments of coffee and other unavailable foodstuffs from Himmler's private black market cache to "Frau Peiper" Entries by Erika Lorenz, RG 242, T-175, R112, F2637504, Berlin, July 21, 1942.

2. Most menu items at Berlin's restaurants were typically unavailable: red cabbage, potatoes, and a mystery cut of meat was often the best one could do. The widely unpopular ersatz coffee was made from roasted malt or chicory and, worse yet, was caffeine free.

3. In fact, in spite of Goering's assurances, the Soviet air force struck Berlin in a small, but highly publicized bombing raid in August 1941. For other background, see detailed account of Berlin life in the summer of 1941 by a Berlin correspondent, *Life Magazine,* Stephen Laird, "Nazi Germany After Two Years of War," August 18, 1941, 72–81.

4. "Frau Peiper-1 Tortenheber z. Geb. v. RFSS geschenkt," August 13, 1941, BDC file Heinrich Himmler, NA, RG-242, A3343-SSO-099A, F 082.

5. Photo of Peiper in steel helmet near Cherson (Kherson) on August 19, 1941, seen in photo insert. See *Kampf zum Cherson*, August 19, 1941, BA-MA, N-756-107a.

6. Erich Kern, "Der Rotwein von Cherson," Autumn 1941, BA-MA, N756-107a.

7. For Peiper's command in Cherson: see Lehmann, *Leibstandarte*, Vol. 2, 83. Kurt Meyer's description of the action: Meyer, *Grenadiere*, 104. And James Weingartner's objective account: *Hitler's Guard*, 69–70. Combat actions are described in the divisional record: "Bericht über den Einsatz der LSSAH vom 8.8-22.9.41," NA T-354, R213, F860–876.

8. "Fast" Meyer had a reputation for speed since the campaign in France.

9. Michael Prawdin, *Tschingis-Chan, der Sturm aus Asien* (Stuttgart: Deutsche Verlagsanstalt, 1934).

10. The village of Greigova is in the area of Neu Danzig in the Ingul Valley in the Black Sea area. Erich Kern (alias Erich Kernmayr), *The Dance of Death* (London: Collins, 1951). Previously published in German: *Der Grosse Rausch* (Zurich: Thomas Verlag, 1948). As this incident constituted a potential blemish on the Leibstandarte record during the war, Rudolf Lehmann, the unit historian, made a concerted effort to discount the story. His repudiation was based primarily on the lack of Bundesarchiv records of the executions or orders to perform them. Yet Erich Kernmayr, who had served as an SS war reporter at the time, stood by his story. He had assisted Otto Skorzeny in Budapest after his stint with the Leibstandarte, later working as an informant to the US Counterintelligence Corps operating out of Salzburg—all with the intent to pass on intelligence information to help usurp Soviet influence in post-1945 Austria. See Richard Breitman, N. J. W. Goda, T. Naftali and R. Wolfe, *U.S. Intelligence and the Nazis* (Cambridge: Cambridge University Press, 2005), 276. Hardly a Nazi-turncoat after the war, Kernmayr became a leading postwar pro-Nazi propagandist for the right-wing monthly, *Nation Europa*. Wellington Long, *The New Nazis of Germany* (Philadelphia: Chilton Books, 1968). Most importantly, in the letter to Hubert Meyer, May 10, 1979, Lehmann discussed the supposed shooting of four thousand Russians by members of 4th Battalion (Anhalt) in August 1941. "I have made no progress with Kernmayr in changing his mind," Lehmann advised Meyer, "and he said that he stood next to where the shooting of 4,000 took place." BA-MA, RS7/ v.509.

11. Records of the atrocity at Greigova (Greigowo): "Nikolajew, den 19. August 1941: OKW: 'Kriegsverbrechen der russischen Wehrmacht 1941," NA RG-242, T-77, Roll 1492, F080–086. The report of Dr. Heinrich Schaffert of the 16th Panzer Division shows that the actual number murdered on August 15 was forty-one soldiers including one Hungarian. The executed German soldiers were unarmed when discovered with many killed in a circle. "The majority of the bodies had shattered faces and heads. . . . They were butchered in a beastly manner."

12. Heinz von Westernhagen to family, August 26, 1941. Westernhagen was at the time with the division staff of the Leibstandarte, Dörte von Westernhagen, *Die Kinder der Täter* (Munich: DTV Sachbuch, 1991), 43.

13. Nuremberg statement of Erwin Bingel, NO-5301, as cited by Breitman, *Architect of Genocide*, 174.

14. The official date of Hedwig's move to Caspar Theyss Str. 33 can be determined to have taken place between August 3 and 13 as seen by the marked forwarded mail on the later date as marked by the Berlin postmaster. Letters of Dr. Walter Potthast, N 1126, *op. cit.* However, it is very likely that Potthast had unofficially moved to the Caspar Theyss address more than a year earlier to continue her affair with Himmler in greater privacy.

15. Letter of Heinrich Himmler to Hedwig Potthast on June 20, 1944, in which Himmler notes that it has been five years since they consummated their relationship at their love nest (*späteren Nestchen*) at Caspar Theyss Strasse. This handwritten letter was discovered for sale on the Internet, transcribed and translated.

16. Beginning in September 1941, after leaving Himmler's services, Peiper received a secret payment (*Geheimszahlung*) from the Waffen SS central office of 366 Reichsmarks—the equivalent of another complete monthly salary—which was paid twice a year. This can be seen in Peiper's BDC file (*op. cit.*). Exactly what these monies were compensating is unknown.

17. "Er hat seine Soldaten verheizt!" Albert Frey, interview by Charles Whiting, as related to author on August 19, 2001, York, UK.

18. Concrete evidence of intimate knowledge of the ongoing pogram comes from one of Peiper's tough contemporaries. Sturmbannführer Jakob Hanreich, who fell into Allied hands in August 1944. In the autumn of 1941 he joined the Leibstandarte in Russia, where he learned of the brutal dimensions of the warfare there: "During the time Hanreich had first seen action in Russia in November of 1941, he was told by the commander of 3rd Battalion, Hauptsturmführer Albert Frey, that thousands of Jews had been murdered south of Mariupol and in Taganrog by the SD Einsatzkommandos. They were brought out of towns by being told that they were to be transferred, but were brought in front of some anti-tank ditches. There they had to undress, descend into the ditch and were shot. The anti-tank ditches were afterwards covered with earth." "Report on interrogation of PW KP 49359 Sturmbannführer Jakob Hanreich," August 19, 1944, PWIS(H)/LDC/299, NA RG 332, Box 30, 290/56/1/5. This source is extremely important as Hanreich, an "old fighter" from Hitler's early days, was captured in August 1944 south of Falaise in France and ventured this information well before any of the facts were widely known. Moreover, he ventured much of this information before there was any reason for coercion by his interrogators. Describing Peiper's tenure in Russia: he was"particularly eager to execute the order to burn villages."

19. Meanwhile Dietrich had personally requested his own SD team from Himmler in their meeting earlier that month and readily approved when Seetzen—a close friend (*Dutzfreund*)of Heydrich—agreed to follow his division toward Mariupol. For Dietrich's and the Leibstandarte's direct involvement: account of Lothar Heimbach, BA-L B162/125 and Rupert Hirmer, BA-L B162/1227. There are several hundred pages on this action at the Bundesarchiv in Ludwigsburg. Thus, similar killings began in the village Mariupol with over eight thousand killed over the following days, a pogrom in which some members of the Leibstandarte took part as Albert Frey's account suggests. Andrej Angrick, *Besatzungspolitik und Massenmord. Die Einsatzgruppe D in der südlichen Sowjetunion 1941–1943* (Hamburg: Hamburger Edition, 2003), 313. For Albert Frey's account of the shooting at Mariupol, "Interrogation of Jakob Hanreich," *op. cit.* Not surprisingly, after the war Frey would go to great lengths to leave Europe for Argentina, likely worried about the Taganrog-Mariupol episode. Frey had just been awarded command of the 3rd Battalion of the Leibstandarte on October 4 with Peiper assuming command of his 11th Company on the same day. See Lehmann, *Leibstandarte*, Vol. 2, 122.

20. Angrick, *Besatzungspolitik und Massenmord*, 311–315.

21. Born in 1906, Gestapo Officer Heinz Otto Seetzen by 1939 had become a *Dutzfreunden* of Reinhard Heydrich. Later, in 1944, he became the commander of the Security Police at Minsk where he would order the killing of over twelve thousand individuals. After the Nazi capitulation in May 1945, Seetzen hid for a time, eventually killing himself in August 1945. See Lawrence D. Stokes, Heinz Seetzen-Chef des Sonderkommmandos 10a," in *Karrieren der Gewalt. Nationalsozialistische Täterbiographien*, eds. Klaus Michael Mallmann and Gerhard Paul (Darmstadt: Wissenschaftliche Buchgesellschaft, 2004), 196–206.

22. "As far as the *Kommando* is concerned, proceeding in the direction of the northern Caucasus, the Jewish problem has been solved. . . . In Taganrog 20 Communist officials were liquidated. Ten of them were shot publicly in accordance with martial law." See "Operational Situation Report USSR No. 136: Activities of Einsatzgruppen A and D," Chief of the Security Police and Security Service (SD), November 21, 1941 in Yitzak Arad, Shmuel Karkwoski and Shmuel Spector, eds, *The Einsatzgruppen Reports* (New York: Macmillan, 1990).

23. Peiper, "Brief Review." *op. cit.*

24. Letter Jochen Peiper to Häschen Potthast, December 30, 1941, BA-K, Nachlass Heinrich Himmler, Bestand N-1126, Folder 39.

25. Himmler to Sigurd Peiper, December 29, 1941, "Greetings from Jochen," Witte et al., *Dienstkalender Heinrich Himmlers*, 299.

26. "Meine Herzlichen Glückwünsche zum Weihnachtsfest und für das Kriegsjahr 1942, Heil Hitler!" signed personally by Himmler and distributed with the Julleuchter. Both Sigurd and Jochen Peiper were shown on Himmler's meticulous manifest as receiving the candle holders. (NA, RG-242, T-175, Roll 112).

27. The total number of Jewish victims evicted from Berlin and sent to their death at the ghettos, concentration or elimination camps to the East totaled 55,896. Roger Moorhouse, *Berlin at War: Life and Death in Hitler's Capital, 1939–45* (New York: Basic Books, 2010), 160–183.

28. Ibid, 184–190. It is interesting to note that the British had evacuated children too, during the Battle of Britain.

29. There were but nine air alerts in Berlin in 1942 with none of them serious, as the RAF moved from attacking inland German cities to concentrating on bombing the German U-boat ports near Bremen.

30. Himmler's son, Helge, was born to Hedwig Potthast on February 15, 1942, in a difficult forceps delivery with the medical help of the SS Reichsführer's personal physician, Dr. Karl Gebhardt (Gebhardt then became Helge's godfather). The boy's name was chosen by the RuSHA for its Viking qualities: "The pure, strong, healthy one," but the actual child was challenged by chronic physical and emotional difficulties. Katrin Himmler, *Die Brüder Himmler: Eine deutsche Familiengeschichte* (Frankfurt: S. Fischer Verlag, 2005), 240.

31. Ibid., Thilde Potthast to Hedwig Potthast, November 7, 1941.

32. Thilde Potthast to Hedwig, letter, February 2, 1942. BA-K, N-1126.

33. Thilde Potthast to Hedwig, letter, February 2, 1942. The letter from Walter to Hilde had been received on January 27. BA-K, Nachlass Heinrich Himmler, Bestand N-1126, Folder 39, BA-K.

34. Jochen Peiper to Häschen Potthast, letter, January 10, 1942, BA-K, Nachlass Heinrich Himmler, Bestand N-1126, Folder 39, BA-K.

35. Hedwig's sister-in-law, Hilde, had informed Thilde about Walter's death in a letter from a comrade in March 1942, Ibid. "Hedwig, Walter is dead. I can't believe we will never see him again." Walter had been an attorney before the war and had been fighting on the Central Front with the antitank battalion of the 52nd Infantry Division. He became a casualty on December 22 with a stomach wound, finally succumbing two weeks later. Hilde Potthast to Hedwig, March 26, 1942, N-1126, *op. cit.*

36. "Petition for pardon for my son Joachim Peiper," Woldemar Peiper, August 30, 1946, NA, RG-153, Case 6-24, Box 83.

37. Jochen Peiper to Häschen Potthast, letter. October 19, 1942, *BA-K,* Nachlass Heinrich Himmler, Bestand N-1126, Folder 39. At that time, Potthast suffered loneliness, being estranged from her family after the birth of Himmler's illegitimate son and deeply pained by the death of her brother earlier that year. For the other personalities in Himmler's office to which the letter refers: Rudi Brandt was Himmler's office manager and someone with whom Peiper and his wife had grown acquainted (BDC A3343-SSO-099); Franz Lucas was Himmler's driver (A3343-SSO-279A), Sepp Kiermaier was Himmler's bodyguard (A3343-SSO-167A) and Werner Grothmann was Peiper's replacement as 1st Adjutant (A3343-SSO-038A). Herman Dörner was another older SS officer (born in 1908; BDC File A3343-SSO-159.) also on Himmler's staff having been reassigned after serving as an SS Untersturmführer and platoon leader of the engineer company with the SS Totenkopf Division.

38. Dr. Franz Neundorff, Agte, *Jochen Peiper*, 53.

39. For the orchestral show at the Trocadero: Lehmann, *Leibstandarte*, 233–234.

40. Walter Naasner, *SS-Wirtschaft und SS-Verwaltung*, Droste Verlag, Düsseldorf, 1998, 175. The "Institute for Food and Feeding"—*Versuchsanstalt für Ernährung und Verpflegung GmbH*—had served as a palatial estate for Pohl since 1940. By 1944 Pohl controlled 75 percent of national mineral water production—*Apollinaris*—being a coveted prize. For his part, Himmler condemned market practices in which the price of *mineral wasser* remained higher than beer.

41. Heilweg Weger, interview by author, July 12, 2012.

42. Dorothee Schmitz-Köster, *Kind L 364: Eine Lebensborn Familiengeschichte* (Berlin: Rowohlt, 2007), 104–134. Other details from Weger, interview by author, July 14, 2012.

43. Later Gebhardt would be tried and sentenced to death at Nuremberg in 1947 in the infamous "Doctors' Trial." He was hanged at Landsberg prison on June 2, 1948.

44. "Report on interrogation of PW Kp 186988 Rottenfuehrer. Otto Sierk, SS Vers. Kp. III/2 SS Pz Gren. Rgt." November 17, 1944. NA, RG 226, Entry 109, Box 698, Folder 6160. Also, PRO: WO 208/4295. Note that this intelligence appeared a month before Allied investigators knew anything about Peiper. Thanks to Dr. Richard Breitman for bringing this recently declassified document to my attention. Sources for the rescue of the 320th: 320th Infanterie Division, KTB for February 1943, RH 26 320/8–10, BA-MA, "Bericht Erhard Gührs, III gep. Btl.," Gührs Diary for February 1943, in author's possession. "KR. Fernschreiben An SS-Panzerkorps: Armeeabteilung Lanz, 12.2.43," NA, T-312, Roll 1620. For Dietrich's summary of Peiper's action and his recommendation for the German Cross in Gold," see "Vorschlag Nr. für die Verleihung des Deutschen Kreuzes in Gold," Peiper BDC file, March 1943. For "parade of misery," and the butchery of his men in Krasnaja Poljana, see Peiper's own account, April 10, 1976, Lehmann, Vol. III, op.cit., 63–64.

45. Letter Jochen Peiper to Hedwig Potthast, March 24, 1943. *Nachlass Heinrich Himmler: B-AK* N 1126/39. This letter is extremely significant to an understanding of Peiper view of fighting. "Aber auch ein schlechter Ruf verpflichtet—But a bad reputation (*schlechter Ruf*) has its obligations." Peiper reveals that his favorite wartime motto was taken from Nazi wartime cinematic diva Zarah Leander. The lyric is from the catchy and suggestive tune, "Yes Sir!" from the film "zu neuen Ufern." Hitler, like Peiper, loved the smoky-voiced Leander, but Himmler investigated her allegiances, given she had Jewish grandparents, jealously guarded Swedish citizenship, a love of Aquavit, and her insistence on payment in Swedish Kroner.

46. Heinz von Westernhagen letters, March 24, April 18, 1943, Westernhagen, *Die Kinder der Täter*, 46.

47. Peiper to Weingartner, April 9, 1976. "The Kharkov story is freely invented. Probably a colleague of Mr. Ellis was in charge of the prosecution, together with Ilja Ehrenburg."

48. In his personal memoirs, it is not surprising that Frey made no mention of this knowledge. See Albert Frey, *Ich wollte die Freiheit* (Osnabrück: Munin Verlag, 1990).

49. The entire description of the incident is contained in NA RG 549, Case 6-24, Box 33 under a file describing the handwritten description of Erich Rumpf: "Jefremowka (Russia)." The account was not strictly connected to the Malmédy incident and was never repudiated after the trial. Peiper remembered this episode: "I remember during the trial, a "testimony" of the commanding officer of the *9th Panzer Pionier Kompanie* was read, according to which we reduced a village to ashes after we had herded the people into a church à la Oradour. That referred to the Panzer Regiment to which he belonged at the time. I cannot say anything about that, because at the time I did not belong to the panzer regiment, but to the 2nd Panzer Grenadier Regiment." Peiper to Weingartner, March 1976.

50. There was some evidence that Meyer ordered all the inhabitants killed in Jefremowka in response to the Russian atrocity in the Ukraine near Broniki: Tony Foster to Hubert Meyer, letter, February 11, 1985, BA-MA, HIAG Records, RS7/483.

51. This Ukrainian village is now known as Yefremovka (with other phonetic spellings as well), and is about eighty kilometers due south of Kharkov. There are Ukrainian articles about the killing of civilians in the town (in Russian) which supposedly took place on

February 17, 1943. On February 12, 1943 German troops occupied villages. Five days later they killed 872 men. Some 240 of these were killed and burned in the church of Yefremovka village. Two surviving witnesses, Ivan Vasil'yevich Kiselev and Grigoriy Alekseevich Buznyka, claimed the killings were orchestrated by the half-tracked battalion of the Leibstandarte Adolf Hitler commanded by SS officer Jochen Peiper. www.vecherniy.kharkov.ua/print.php?Division=history&id=3621.

52. Hanreich interrogation, *op. cit.*

53. Peiper BDC file, *Funkspruch an SS Sturmbannführer Jochen Peiper*, March 9, 1943.

54. "Eier, Butter, Zucker und Mehl," Office ledger of Rudolf Brandt, May 1943, NA, T-175, Roll 43, Frame 2555116–7. It is significant that other than Peiper, almost all of the other households receiving black market goods from Himmler were high ranking SS generals.

55. Richard Bessel, ed, *Life in the Third Reich* (London: Oxford University Press, 1987); For Berliners listening to forbidden BBC broadcasts; Moorhouse, *Berlin at War*.

56. Guido Knopp, *Hitler's Women* (London: Routledge, 2003), 209.

57. The Allied bombers struck Berlin on August 23, 1943, but the result was quite different from that at Hamburg. The Germans had developed new night fighter defenses that rapidly crippled the British raids. Having lost many bombers, by September 3, the British called off the raids.

58. David M. Glanz and Jonthan M. House, *The Battle of Kursk*, University of Kansas Press, Lawrence, KS, 341. The 6th Guards Tank Army had about 680 tanks total.

59. BDC file for Werner Wolff, "Vorschlag Nr. 1 für die Nennung im Ehrenblatt des Deutschen Herres," November 2, 1944, signed by Jupp Diefenthal and Jochen Peiper, NA RG-242, SSOA-011C.

60. "Der siebente Tag," Hermann Schramm, *Das Schwarze Korps*, January 20, 1944.

Chapter Eight

1. Sigurd Peiper to Rudi Brandt, August 25, 1943, NA, T-175, Roll 117, Frames 2641931–32. Vera Hinrichsen had married Sigurd's brother, Dr. Rolf Hinrichsen who died on the *Bismarck* on May 27, 1941. She had then remarried Sigurd's other brother in the SD, Kurt Hans Hinrichsen, who had taken up residence in the resettled area of Poland known in the Reich as the Warthegau.

2. Dr. R. Brandt to Frau Sigurd Peiper, August 28, 1943, NA, T-175, Roll 117, Frame 2641924.

3. "Töchter und Väter," *Stern*, No. 2, January 6, 1983, 60.

4. Lang, *Top Nazi*, 41.

5. Thanks to Dr. Michael Heim for the photograph showing the wartime entrance to Rottach Egern in 1938: "Juden betreten den Ort auf eigene Gefahr." Hitler had visited Rottach on June 30, 1939.

6. The place was known throughout Hitler's Germany as "Lago di bonzo," *bonze* being a popular wartime expression for a party member of the NSDAP who had come into a leadership position and had enriched themselves through that position.

7. Information on the Peiper family's residence in Rottach-Egern from its municipal office and discussion with Birgit Mitchell of the Nathan family in Rottach-Egern on July 22, 2002.

8. Diary of Gudrun Himmler, November 1, 1943," *NSDAP Hauptarchiv*, Himmler Collection, Microfilm Roll #99, Hoover Institution, Stanford University. Married as Gudrun Burwitz after the war, Himmler's daughter dismissed her father's critics: "Whatever is said about my Papi, what has been written or shall be written in the future about him—he was my father, the best father I could have and I loved him and still love him." Gudrun Burwitz, interview by Gillich, January 22, 1974, Toland Collection, FDR Library, Box 46. Burwitz still lives in

nearby Bad Tölz, rousing old SS annually at a meeting in Schliersee, but otherwise keeping a low profile.

9. Himmler's damning Posen speech of October 4, 1943, has been detailed by many scholars, e.g., IMT, *op. cit.*, PS-1919. For a particularly telling evaluation: Richard Breitman, *Architect of Genocide*, 242–243. For nuances in the translation: *Skeptic Magazine*, Vol. 2, No. 4, 64–67.

10. Even though Karl Wolff was in Italy when Himmler's speech was given at Posen on 4 October, he was given a copy upon visiting the Reichsführer SS headquarters in East Prussia. Jochen von Lang, *Top Nazi*, 232–233. Given Peiper's close relationship to Himmler, it seems likely he would also be given a copy of the speech—of which Himmler was very proud—when he visited Hochwald in February 1944.

11. Rudolf Höss, *Commandant of Auschwitz: The Autobiography of Rudolf Höss* (New York: World Publishing, 1960), 205. Peiper was not present during the fateful conversation Höss had with the Reichsführer, but seems to have requested him to come to Himmler's headquarters. Although Breitman has theorized that the fateful meeting with Höss took place midsummer 1941 (by evaluation of possible times for the meeting), other scholars contend it took place months later. Breitman, *Architect of Genocide*, 189 and footnotes. However, if it was Peiper who requested Höss come to visit Himmler, then the visit must have come in June or July of the summer. It is also significant that Höss mentions that it was normally Himmler's custom to have his adjutant present for his discussions. For recent scholarship on this critical question of timing, see Longerich, *Politik der Vernichtung*, 423ff and 696, and Browning and Matthäus, *Origins of the Final Solution*, 526f207.

12. Westemeier, *Himmlers Krieger*, 600, and Dinse, interview by Westemeier, May 27, 1994.

13. BDC file for Otto Dinse. NA, BDC file, A3343-SSO-154. Also, Dinse, interview, May 21, 1996. Dinse was one of the few SS men, the author interviewed who did not deny SS war crimes. "Anyone who denies the existence of the elimination camps," he told me in the presence of other veterans, "He is not a comrade."

14. Rolf Reiser, interview by author, May 15, 1997.

15. Rolf Ehrhardt, as quoted, in Ralf Tiemann, *Chronicle of the 7. Panzer Kompanie* (Atglen, PA: Schiffer Publishing, 1998), 65.

16. The wartime German sources for the Leibstandarte guerrilla operations in Italy: "Anlage zum Tätigkeitsbericht der Abt. Ic, Abschlussbericht der Entwaffnungsaktion in Nord Italien," Heeresgruppe B, September 19, 1943, NA RG 242, T-311, R276, F65–67. Also, "Besonderes Feindnachrichtenblatt," September 22, 1943, F84–86 and "Stellungsnahme des Einheitsführer," T-354, R654, F363. For perspectives from a contemporary historian who has weighted both sides with the Italian and German evidence: Carlo Gentile, "September 1943: Documenti sull' attività della divisione 'Leibstandarte Adolf Hitler' in Piemonte," Michele Calandri, ed., in *Il Presente E La Storia 47* (Cuneo: Giugno, 1995).

17. Records of II SS Panzer Corps, from the Bundesarchiv contain indications that Peiper's battalion was actively involved in the arrests of the Jews near Cuneo. In the morning of September 20, the corps passed on the following message to the Army Group: "*In Borgo S. Dalmazzo 216 Juden festgesetzt. SD wird erwartet*—216 Jews detained in Boro San Dalmazzo. Waiting for SD," BA-MA, Freiburg/Br., RS 2-2/21 Teil 2, "Generalkommando II SS Panzerkorps, Tgb. Nr. 1087/43 gdh, Ic morning report of 20.9.1943 to Herregruppe B/Ic." A key point: at the time of the report there were no other German troops near Cuneo aside from Peiper's battalion. For the transportation of the Jews to Auschwitz from Borgo San Dalmazzo, where Peiper's battalion had moved them, see the detailed accounting in Alberto Cavaglion's *Nella Notte Stranier*, L'Arciere, Viale Sarrea, 1981.

18. Peiper to Weingartner, March 13, 1976. Dinse's denial: "Interrogation transcript for Otto Heinrich Dinse," State Criminal Office, Bad Würtemberg, October 9, 1964.

19. The author extensively interviewed witnesses in Boves in July 2002 who experienced firsthand the burning of the town by SS men in September 1943. Italian historians, who have studied the events, hotly dispute the claim that civilians fired on Peiper on September 19. "It is quite impossible that civilians fired guns," Michele Calandri insisted. "This is the great alibi of Peiper. It is false." Instituto Storico Della Resistenza, July 16, 2002.

20. On November 3, 1943, the division had a ration strength of 373 officers, 2,365 NCOs and 15,639 enlisted men. "Leibstandarte SS Adolf Hitler: Gefechts und Verpflegungsstärke, 3.11.1943," T-314, R1172, F000610. Peiper was awarded the bronze and silver close combat badges the first week in September. Peiper BDC file.

21. Letter Jochen Peiper to Hedwig Potthast, October 17, 1943, *Nachlass Heinrich Himmler: BA-K* N 1126/39. The passage: "Because of K.Hs new office, there will be even less time available than before" refers Himmler's new appointment as Minister of the Interior on August 25, 1943: Padfield, *Himmler*, 426. Days before, Himmler met with Albert Speer and his shadowy chief engineer, Heinz Kammler, after Hitler embraced a crash program to manufacture parts for five thousand V-2 rockets in the concentration camps. Albert Speer, *The Slave State: Heinrich Himmler's Masterplan for SS Supremacy* (London: Weidenfield and Nicholson, 1981), 206. Peiper's admonition to give regards to "you and your two men" refers to Himmler himself and their male son, Helge.

22. Moorhouse, *Berlin at War*, 320–321.

23. Peiper, overheard after tank losses on the radio, Agte, *Jochen Peiper*, 261.

24. Albert Frey to Jens Westemeier, February 28, 1994, as cited in *Himmler's Krieger*, 599.

25. Frey interview with Charles Whiting, as related to author on August 19, 2001.

26. "Ich weiss nichts davon dass, er mich verheizt hat. Peiper war ein Draufgänger und hat so auch das Regiment geführt." Hans Siptrott statement, October 21, 2010, courtesy Mike Smeets.

27. Letter Jochen Peiper to Hedwig Potthast, December 15, 1943, *Nachlass Heinrich Himmler: BA-K*, N 1126/39.

28. Arndt Fischer, interview by author, May 15, 1997. "I met Peiper in November 1943. We did not have a favorable impression of Peiper at first. We tank people didn't want an infantry person in charge. A tank officer has a different tactical view than the infantry including that on Pekartschina. The SPWs that Peiper commanded earlier operated more like cavalry. They were fast and mobile. Meanwhile, our panzers were very powerful, but also a little clumsy. . . . With Peiper, we were frequently far behind the Russian front and if a panzer broke down it was a death sentence."

29. The entire account of Peiper's attack on December 5–7, 1943, including that on Pekartschina is taken from his personal records in support of his nomination for the Oak Leaf Cluster of the Iron Cross, dated January 24, 1944, by the divisional commander, Oberführer Theodor Wisch. NA, Peiper's BDC file, *op. cit.*

30. "Tagesmeldung an Pz. A.O.K. 4," December 6, 1943, T-314, R1173, F000078.

31. BA-MA RS 4/1411, *KTB SS Panzergrenadier Regiment 2*, entry for December 6, 1943.

32. Quotations from radio conversation with Peiper cited in Lehmann, *Leibstandarte*, Vol. 3, 350.

33. For "We are frying potatoes": Müller, interview, May 19, 1999. Story as related to Benno Müller by Peiper after the war.

34. BA-MA RS 4/1411, *KTB SS Panzergrenadier Regiment 2*, entry for December 6–8, 1943.

35. Peiper to Everett, July 14, 1946, Everett Papers.

36. Peiper's letter to Woldemar Peiper, recalling various Christmas times in the war, December 2, 1946, NA, Case 6-24, RG-153, Box 83.

37. Ordered to take a rest, on February 11 and 12, 1944, SS doctors at Dachau Concentration Camp's "SS Health and Fitness Center" examined Jochen Peiper. They pronounced him ailing from low blood pressure—the reason for recent fainting spells. He was also suffering

nervous exhaustion—a Waffen SS euphemism for battle fatigue. The SS health center was just outside its electrified barbed-wire fence, amid the botanical gardens and greenhouses that fed Himmler's obsession with herbs. In winter 1944, eighteen thousand inmates were incarcerated there and, on the two days Peiper was treated, seven inmates died. How would Jochen Peiper not hear of rumors of the treatment of those at the camp? Beyond that were the medical experiments: Some inmates were subjected to high altitude tests and died in the agony from near vacuum. For an SS officer, it was also easy to learn how Dr. Sigmund Rascher was performing tests on some of those incarcerated to see how Luftwaffe pilots might survive hypothermia in the North Sea. Himmler's driver, Franz Lucas—who was on a friendly basis with Peiper since 1938—knew of these diabolical experiments first hand. After the war, Lucas recalled how he and Himmler personally witnessed Polish prisoners at Dachau being immersed in icy water to see if they could remain alive for extended periods. Amazingly, after the experiments, Lucas related how he and Himmler had lunch at the Dachau commissary with some of the prisoners who survived! "Vernehmungsniederschrift Franz Lucas," Trial of Karl Wolff, BA-L, Z-Prot. II, 10a Js 39/60, November 8, 1962. Telegram from the SS hospital in Berlin describing Peiper's status on March 30, 1944, was sent to the Leibstandarte Adolf Hitler. BA-MA, RS/4/1241. "Extensive nerve dysfunction in hands and legs, so that further treatment in a recuperation hospital is ordered . . . classified as currently unfit for duty."

38. For Léon Degrelle's march through Belgium, see Martin Conway, *Collaboration in Belgium: Léon Degrelle and the Rexist Movement* (New Haven, CT: Yale University Press, 1993), 244–247. For Peiper's participation in the event: his April 1967 interview reproduced in *La Libre Belgique*, July 19, 1976, "L'Affaire Peiper: une interview posthume de l'ex colonel SS," 4.

39. BDC file for Heinrich Himmler (NA, RG-242, A3343-SSOI-099A, F096) showing Peiper picking up flowers on the account of the RFSS to give to "Frau Peiper" on April 17, 1944. Later there are photos showing Sigurd with Jochen at Hasselt during a football game later that month.

40. "An SS Military Crime and its Punishment: Report on information obtained from PW SS-Man Langer, 6th Co., SS Pz Gren. 26," CSDIC (UK) SIR 681, RG 338, 290/56/1/1–2, Box 3. Langer was captured near Caen on June 27, 1944.

41. Original source: "1. SS Panzer Division 'LSSAH', Divisions Tagesbefehl Nr. 17: Kriegsgerichtliche Urteile," Those executed were SS Oschtz. Anton Müller, SS Schtz. Werner Wutke, SS Schtz. Hugo Triebke, SS Schtz. Günther Dettlaff and SS Schtz. Johann Riedinger. BA-MA, RS 3-1/77. Execution for chicken theft according to Arndt Fischer: "This type of thing had happened before, but we were shocked at the severity of the sentence," letter to author, January 9, 2002.

42. The date of the trial of the thieves from the diary of Benoni Junker, *op. cit.* Also, Reiser, interview, March 2006. Winston L. Field, Col. JAGC, Deputy Judge Advocate: to Der Oberstaatsanwalt bei dem Bayerischen Landgericht regarding Case No. 7 Js 562/57," July 12, 1956, NA: RG 338, War Crimes Tried, Landsberg: "Stayback" files, Box 6, (290/59/17/3–4).

43. Staatsanwaltschaft Flensburg 2 Js 437/56 AR 491/66. Now on file at Bundesarchiv Ludwigsburg 124 AR 491/1966. Peiper was interrogated at Landsberg on July 30, 1956, about the shooting near Beverloo, Belgium.

44. "Wir haben es für völlig richtig gehalten, gestehe ich, ja." Jochen Peiper, interview, provided to author by journalist Harvey T. Rowe, who obtained the interview of Peiper from Hans Kettgen, 5, no date, but 1971 or 1972, based on mentioned events.

45. Ian Kershaw, *Hitler 1936–1945 Nemesis* (New York: W. W. Norton, 2000), 639–640.

46. For the Klessheim episode: Toland, *Adolf Hitler*, 785; Joachim Fest, *Hitler* (New York: Harcourt, Brace and Company, 1974), 705; and Walter Warlimont, *Inside Hitler's Headquarters, 1939–1945* (Santa Barbara, CA: Praeger Press, 1964), 427.

47. The property at Schönau am Königsee required a secret payment from Bormann to Himmler of 80,000 Reichsmarks. The payment was made in August 1944.

48. Ulrich Chaussy, *Nachbar Hitler: Führerkult und Heimatzerstörung am Obersalzberg*, Ch. Links Verlag, Berlin, 2001.

49. Himmler's second daughter out of that relationship, Nanette Dorothea Potthast, was born June 3, 1944. *Nachlass Heinrich Himmler:* BA-K N 1126/39. Improbably, Sepp Dietrich was made the child's godfather as revealed in a letter from his wife, Ursula, to Himmler on July 25, 1944, ibid., "May I ask you, dear Reichsführer, to bring the small package to your lovely little Nanette, Sepp's godchild, with our heartfelt wishes. . . . After the terrible attempted assassination of the Führer, a new huge burden has been put on your shoulders." For further details see Katrin Himmler and Michael Wildt, eds., *Himmler privat. Briefe des Massenmörders* (Munich: Piper, 2014), 317. In all the literature the birth date is wrongly given as July 20, 1944. Thanks to Katrin Himmler for pointing this out.

50. C. P. Stacey, *Official History of the Canadian Army in the Second World War*, Vol. 3 (Ottawa, Canada: Queen's Printer, 1956), 189–190. The Highlanders suffered 139 casualties and reported that its opponent, "the Leibstandarte Adolf Hitler had fought with genuinely fanatical determination and much skill."

51. German account of the action on July 21 in Tilly: BDC file for Werner Wolff, *op.cit.*, "Vorschlag Nr. 1 für die Nennung im Ehrenblatt des Deutschen Heeres," Joachim Peiper, November 2, 1944.

52. Reiser, interview, May 15, 1997.

53. For background, see author's account: *Fatal Crossroads* (Cambridge, MA: Da Capo Press, 2012), 13–36.

54. Testimony of 2nd Lt. Kurt Kramm by Col. Lamar Tooze, Inspector General U.S. First Army," December 25, 1944, NA RG 153, Case 6-24, Box 70, Kramm had been wounded and captured in the Ardennes and then interviewed of the US Inspector General for the First Army on Christmas Day at the 77th Evacuation Hospital. Kramm served as ordnance officer for the 1st Panzer Battalion. He followed directly behind the tanks of the spearhead in a Kübelwagen.

55. For Hedwig Potthast's move to the Obersalzberg, see Gerda Bormann's descriptions of her new neighbor on September 21, 1944: "Did I tell you of my visit with Häschen. . . . It was very cozy yesterday at Schneewinkellehen." H. R. Trevor Roper, ed., *The Bormann Letters* (London: Weidenfeld and Nichols, 1954), 82 and 119.

56. Letter Sigurd Peiper to Hedwig Potthast, November 11, 1944, *Nachlass Heinrich Himmler:* BA-K N 1126/39.

57. *Nachlass Eleonore Pohl*, describing the November 1944 dinner with Himmler and Potthast, as cited in Peter Ferdinand Koch, *Geheim-Depot Schweiz* (Munich: List Verlag, 1997), 48–49.

58. Freya Klier, *Die Kaninchen von Ravensbrück: medizinische Versuche an Frauen in der NS-Zeit* (Munich: Knauer, 1994).

59. "Häschen, I want to send to you with the letter my little Christmas presents for your children. Helge may have fun with the little shopping bag. My little kids happily carry rolls or butter home in one. For Nanette, the doll actually is not yet a toy. But I wanted to see, if I could make such a doll. You will recognize in the *dirndl* the leftover material from shortening my own *dirndl* and recall some of the nice time we had together in Tegernsee. . . . It is just too bad, that we cannot telephone at least on the 24th. We both, again, shall light up the Christmas tree for the children without Pappi. My thoughts shall be with you and yours heartily." Sigurd Peiper to Hedwig Potthast, letter, December 11, 1944, *Nachlass Heinrich Himmler: BA-K,* N 1126/39.

60. For details, Parker, *Fatal Crossroads*, 235, 281.

61. Peiper's direct testimony on June 22, 1946, told of a conversation with his Tiger battalion commander, Heinz von Westernhagen, just outside Trois Ponts on December 18, 1944: "He told me in this conference that a 'mix-up' had happened at Ligneuville and that a rather large number of prisoners had been shot there. He did not know any details nor who had given the order to do that." Part of the Tiger battalion had come upon the scene well after it

had taken place, and von Westernhagen had communicated word to Peiper later the next day. RG 153, Case 6-24, *US v. Bersin*, Roll 3, Frame 000160, 1939, of courtroom proceedings.

62. BDC File on Joachim Peiper, NA RG-242, A 3343-SSO-348A. Vorschlag Nr. 1 für die Verleihung der Schwerter zum Eichenlaub das Ritterkreuzes de E.K, December 26, 1945.

63. Parker, *Fatal Crossroads*, 237–239.

64. Heinz von Westernhagen to family, December 29, 1944. Copy of original letter graciously provided by Dörte von Westernhagen.

65. Interview with Ralf Tiemann, Untergruppenbach, October 21, 1995.

Chapter Nine

1. Hedwig Potthast to Himmler ("Mein Teurer"), letter, January 20, 1945, Nachlass Heinrich Himmler, Bestand N-1126, Folder 39.

2. "Weihnachtspäckchen: Vermerk für SS Standartenführer Baumert," with distribution list including Jochen Peiper, December 27, 1944, T-175, Roll 25, F2531231–7. The distribution was exclusively for SS generals, but with a penciled exception by Himmler to include Peiper.

3. Roger Moorehouse, *Berlin at War* (New York: Basic Books, 2010), 356. Thanks to Ann Shields for personal investigation of the circumstances from the bombing that destroyed 8 Prinz Albrechtstrasse as well as the former building where Peiper grew up in Wilmersdorf.

4. "Request of SS Hstuf. Ludwig Pemsel to Frl. Erika Lorzenz," NA, RG-242, T-175, Roll 112, F2637306. This newly discovered communique shows that on January 29 Peiper was requesting that a pair of fur-lined boots (*Peltzstiefel*) be sent to Himmler's Birkenwald headquarters; he knew the cold weather he would soon face in the coming commitment to the east. It is unclear as to whether Peiper was already at Himmler's field headquarters at that point, but it seems likely as SS Captain Pemsel was assigned to the SS Reichsführer's field headquarters on January 1, 1945.

5. "Beförderung des SS Oberführers Wilhelm Mohnke," January 31, 1945, BDC file on Wilhelm Mohnke, NA (A3343-SSO-322A). For Peiper's presence with Mohnke earlier in January 1945: Ralf Tiemman, interview by author, May 1997. A recently located document suggests that Werner Grothmann reported on February 5, 1945 that Mohnke was suffering "morphine illness" and would be soon removed of command of the Leibstandarte. "Minutes of the Meeting of Werner Grothmann," NS 34, SS Personalhauptamt, BA-Lichterfelde.

6. For a description of Himmler's quarters at Birkenwald in the first days of February 1945: Hans-Georg Eismann, *Under Himmler's Command* (West Midlands, UK: Helion, 2010), 34–37.

7. Himmler's "miracle" is dated in his orders of February 1, 1945. "Now, we'll have time to build up the Oder defense after all." NA, RG242, T78, R304, F5774.

8. Antony Beevor, *The Fall of Berlin 1945* (London: Penguin Putnam, 2002), 72.

9. "Termine des Reichsführer SS am 4.2.1945," NA RG-242, T-175, R112, 2637562.

10. Even in Italy in April 1945 Genflm. Albert Kesselring told SS Gen. Karl Wolff he knew of "a last specific secret weapon which they call the *Verzweiflungswaffen*—Desperation Weapon. . . . Kesselring believed this weapon can prolong the war, but not decide it, but might cause a terrible bloodbath on both sides. Kesselring said if [the] Führer gave him an order to use the weapon, he would surrender his command." "Operation Sunrise," April 4, 1945, NA, Records of the Central Intelligence Agency, RG 263, File: CIA-RDP78T03194A000200010001-2, 90, declassified April 13, 2005.

11. In 1940 Dr. Hans Kammler joined the SS in which from 1942 he worked on various projects, showing no scruples in applying his engineering talents: designing gas chambers and crematoria for the extermination camps and helping with the explosive demolition of the Warsaw Ghetto. Later he was charged with constructing underground facilities for the various

secret weapons projects with slave labor including an enlarged version of the V-2 rocket (precursor to the ICBM), nuclear weapons research, and expanded jet fighter production. In April 1945 Kammler disappeared. Most likely, he was killed by a member of his staff, acting on orders from Himmler that persons with detailed knowledge of the secret weapons programs not fall into Allied hands. Yet the fact that his exact fate is unknown and his body was never found provided convenient fodder for postwar conspiracy theorists that had Kammler escaping to the United States to convey top-secret antigravity propulsion. A more recent example: Nick Cook, *The Hunt for the Zero Point* (New York: Broadway Books, 2001).

12. Speer, *Infiltration*, 148–150; assorted communication of Himmler with Oswald Pohl, Rudi Brandt and others on the subject of producing gasoline from fir tree roots in January and February 1945 is found in BA-K, NS 19/ 758. For Himmler's suggestion in 1945 that Chinese rickshaws be incorporated into the German army's logistical system, see his correspondence: T-175, Roll 48, Folder 235.

13. Speer, *Infiltration*, 146–147.

14. For Peiper's tour with Himmler and his adjutant of devastated Berlin, Werner Grothmann, interview, May 13, 1998, Agte, *Jochen Peiper*, 510. For the date of the tour, thanks to Peter Witte, who isolated the likely timing from the *Himmler Dienstkalendar* for 1945. Himmler's diary clearly shows a meeting with Peiper on February 4 with the SS Reichsführer remaining in Birkenwald until the morning of February 7, when he motored to the Reichskanzlei in Berlin arriving for at 2:20 p.m. for conferences with Hitler.

15. H. R. Trevor Roper, ed., *The Bormann Letters* (London: Weidenfeld and Nichols, 1954), 167–168.

16. "Himmler's Girl Friend Left with 2 Little SS Souvenirs," *Stars and Stripes*, September 6, 1945.

17. For the fatal battle for Veszprém the personal remembrances of Rolf Reiser who was Poetschke's adjutant: Ralf Tiemann, *Die Leibstandarte*, Vol. IV/2, 255-256. For Hitler on Himmler at the end of March: "The Führer now takes the view that Himmler has no operational capability. He is a punctilious person (*Tüftler*) but no commander. He totally lacks the divine spark." Goebbels Diaries, BA-K, N 1118/59, entry for March 31, 1945. For Peiper's account of his last meeting with Himmler: Toland interview with Peiper, October 10, 1963, *op. cit.*

18. Thilde Potthast to Hedwig Potthast, letter, April 4, 1945, *Nachlass Heinrich Himmler:* BA-K N 1126/39. "The front is now approaching, although we're not in a combat zone. It's impossible to find joy in beauty now, although my kids at least seem untouched. What will become of us?"

19. Thilde Potthast survived the war and continued in her role as a teacher, but never married. Relations between Hedwig and her parents were never favorably reestablished. The entire subject of Hedwig became a forbidden topic of conversation with most of the rest of the family. Jürgen Potthast, interview by author, March 12, 2010.

20. Werwolf did exist, although most of its actions seemed as imaginary as its shadowy namesake, appropriately enough under SS mystery man Otto Skorzeny. When the US 3rd Armored Division was closing on Paderborn on March 30, 1945, its commander, Gen. Maurice Rose, was taken prisoner by tanks of SS Ersatzbrigade Westfalen some two kilometers from Wewelsburg Castle, which Himmler had unsuccessfully attempted to have blown up at the last minute. As Rose attempted to drop his gun belt, he was shot by a tanker with a submachine gun. Later a Nazi radio communication, purporting to be Werwolf, claimed responsibility for his death because Rose was a Jew. Stuart Russell, interview with author, Wewelsburg, December 18, 2004. Also, Belton Y. Cooper, *Death Traps: The Survival of an American Armored Division in World War II* (Novato, CA:Presidio Press, 1998), 252–253. For a more thorough treatment: Alexander Perry Biddiscombe, *Werwolf: The History of the National Socialist Guerrilla Movement 1944–1946* (Toronto: University of Toronto Press, 1998).

21. "Hedwig Potthast: Reichsfuehrer Himmler's Mistress," Seventh Army Interrogation Center, SAIC/15, May 22, 1945, NA RG 319, Investigative Repository Records (IRR), Himmler files, XE-00632. At the time Potthast claimed she was at her home near Berchtesgaden.

22. Werner Poetschke, who had led Peiper's 1st Panzer Battalion, died on March 24 from wounds near Veszprem, Hungary. Werner Wolff, who had been a favorite of Peiper's, died on March 19 in the same actions and Heinz von Westernhagen on the same day. Later in his life Peiper would often claim, "The best of my command died in the war." H. Peiper, interview, May 21, 1999.

23. Peiper would later tell his former prisoner, Maj. Hal D. McCown that Hitler had personally phoned him with the promotion—or maybe more. "Late in the war, he was fighting with the *1st SS Panzer Division* in Austria against the Russians around Vienna. Hitler, in the last stages of the Third Reich, telephoned a verbal promotion for him for his heroism. . . . Peiper filled me in on this bit when I saw him in his cell after my testimony at the Dachau trials." McCown to John S. D. Eisenhower, March 18, 1966, John S. D. Eisenhower Papers, Abilene, KS, Bitter Woods, Box 2.

24. Peiper's rescue of his wounded in Rohrbach: Tiemann, *Chronicle of the 7. Panzer Kompanie*, 304.

25. Meldeschein: Woldemar Peiper, April 15, 1945, Village of Bad Gastein, Sammlung Westemeier. One must realistically ponder in what kind of business would Woldemar Peiper engage from 1942–1944 in the embattled city of Warsaw with its ghetto of suffering and death. By May 1943, all the visible Jews in Warsaw had essentially been eliminated. For a more complete treatment of this horrific episode: Norman Davies, *Rising '44: The Battle for Warsaw* (New York: Viking-Penguin, 2004).

26. Beevor, *The Fall of Berlin 1945*, 249.

27. "Interrogation of Reichmarschall Hermann Goering," SAIC /X/5, May 24, 1945, Seventh Army Interrogation Center, NA, RG 338, ETOUSA, ETO-MIS-Y, Seventh Army, Box 73.

28. Albert Speer, *Inside the Third Reich: Memoirs* (New York: Macmillan, 1970), 599.

29. Peiper, interview by Toland, October 10, 1963. Dr. Karl Gebhardt had described his final encounter with Hitler on April 23, 1945. As he and Dr. Stumpfegger emerged from Hitler's bunker to Goering Strasse, they found themselves in a surreal city hideous and scarred from continuous Russian artillery bombardment. Gebhardt offered an epitaph for Hitler's Reich "This is the end," he said. He was leaving Berlin. Dr. Stumpfegger turned in surprise before heading back to Hitler's bunker. "Karl, are you crazy? How dare you speak such a thing. . . . Only he who is faithful to Hitler at the end will get the spoils of victory." Gebhardt was dumbstruck and departed. Stumpfegger was later killed with Martin Borman while trying to escape from Hitler's bunker after his suicide.

30. "Interrogation of Reichsmarschall Hermann Goering," *op. cit.* Himmler: "I have undeniable proof that I am considered abroad to be the only person who can maintain peace and order." In fact, in May 1945 Winston Churchill wondered aloud in a war cabinet meeting whether they should negotiate with Himmler "and bump him off later" after peace terms had been reached. Jamie Doward, "Hitler Must Die Without Trial," *The Observer*, January 1, 2006. The revelations came from the War Cabinet notes of Norman Brook which were declassified by the PRO in 2005.

31. Otto Günsche interrogation, quoted by Beevor, *The Fall of Berlin 1945*, 262.

32. SS Adjutant Hermann Fegelein would suffer the fate of a deserter, having disappeared on the afternoon of April 27, 1945. Shortly thereafter he was captured on the outskirts of Berlin disguised in civilian clothes, claiming to be a refugee. In fact, he had been on a mission to help Himmler with his negotiations with Count Bernadotte. News of his capture was immediately brought to Hitler's attention, who did not hesitate to order him brought back and court martialed for treason. In spite of being the brother-in-law of Eva Braun, he was then gunned down in the Reich Chancellery garden. "Summary Interrogation: The Last Days in Hitler's Air Raid Shelter, Fraulein Hanna Reitsch," AIU/IS/1, October 8, 1945, NA, RG-407,

US First Army G-2, 101-2.13, PWI Files, Box 1511. Fegelein was not the only one leaving. Arming themselves with pistols, Alfred Jodl and some fifty other officers left Hitler on April 23 and moved through Krampnitz and crossed the Teltow canal to reach Nauen only half an hour ahead of the Russians. Eventually, on May 2, Jodl and his small group made their way to Flensburg, where he was later made captive by the British. "Interview with Generaloberst Alfred Jodl," August 2, 1945, John S. D. Eisenhower Papers, Box 41, The Supreme Command.

33. Interrogation of Otto Ohlendorf, December 15, 1945, IfZ, RG 260 3/71–3/5/4. What became of the large bags of foreign currency was never determined.

34. In a plot right out of a Sunday matinee Werner Baumbach had been advised by Hitler's personal pilot, Hans Baur, that he might be needed to fly away the top Nazi brass to continue the struggle outside of Germany. The plan was to use three gigantic BV-222 "Wiking" flying boats with a 3,800-mile range and take the top thirty Nazi leaders wherever he was ordered. The initial plan was to fly off Hitler, Speer, Himmler, Göring, and Jodl to Greenland after they had been picked up just north of Kiel. (The air crew had experience in the war flying between Germany and the weather station in Greenland to maintain its supplies.) As the planes used diesel fuel and a number of submarines operated in Greenland's waters, it would be possible to refuel and easily reach Argentina or even Japan. Yet Hitler elected to stay on in Berlin and end his life and in mid-April. Albert Speer, also told Baumbach he was not interested in the Greenland escapade. Two of the BV-222s were destroyed in an Allied bombing raid on the night of April 8, but the last huge aircraft was then readied and fully equipped with food, tents, weapons, and even arctic gear. However, Himmler, who spoke with Baumbach on April 28, waited too long. Four days later, as the British forces approached the port at Travemünde, the last of the giant sea planes was scuttled. Story of Hauptmann Ernst Koenig: Nick Fielding, "How I Prepared the Nazis' Plan for a Great Escape to Greenland," *Sunday Times* (London), December 28, 2003. Also Speer, *Inside the Third Reich*, 622–623.

35. Diary of Gen. Mummert, Andrew Tully, *Berlin: Story of a Battle* (New York: Simon and Schuster, 1963), 196.

36. Tully, *Berlin*, 8, 259.

37. Robert Payne, *The Life and Death of Adolf Hitler* (New York: Praeger Press, 1973), 549. In his postwar memoirs Heinz Linge placed this meeting two days later on April 27, having been ordered by Hitler to "hold in readiness woolen blankets and enough petrol for two cremations." Heinz Linge, *With Hitler to the End: The Memoirs of Hitler's Valet* (Yorkshire: Frontline Books, 2009), 192.

38. Vaisili I. Chuikov, *The Fall of Berlin* (New York: Holt Rinehart and Winston, 1967), 204.

39. "Special Interrogation Series, No. 10: Miss Johanna Wolf," PWB/SAIC/10, May 31, 1945, HQ 7th Army, RG 332, ETO-MIS-Y, Box 116.

40. "Hitler's Letze Lagebesprechungen," *Der Spiegel*, January 10, 1966, 42–45.

41. Roschus Misch, an SS Leibstandarte switchboard operator in Hitler's bunker remembered the scene: See Nicholas Best, *Five Days That Shocked the World: Eyewitness Accounts from Europe at the End of World War II* (New York: Thomas Dunne Books, 2012), 29.

42. First-person accounts of Hitler's death are many and often conflicting. I chose quotes from Erich Kempka, interview by John Toland, LOC, John Toland Papers, Last Hundred Days, Box 16. Also, "Testimony of Erich Kempka on the last days of Hitler," NCA Document 3735-PS, June 20, 1945, Otto Günsche, PRO, WO208 /3791. Also, Heinz Linge, *Bis zum Untergang: als Chef des persönlichen Dienstes bei Hitler* (Munich: Herbig, 1980). For factual matters I leaned heavily on the evaluation of these events by Anton Joachimsthaler, *The Last Days of Hitler* (London: Arms and Armor Press, 1996). For clarifications on several matters I was fortunate to be able to interview Herr Joachimsthaler on December 20, 2004.

43. "Historical Interrogation Report: Obersturmführer Erich Kempka," September 26, 1945, NA, RG-338, "Records of the War Department General Staff," 290/56/3/3, Box 116. Also, Kempka, interview by Toland, October 1963, LOC, Toland Papers, Last Hundred Days, Box 6.

44. Mohnke and Günsche were cornered by the Soviets in Berlin's Schultheiss-Patzenhofer brewery, surrendering in the last hours of May 2, 1945. Strangely both SS men were later invited to an improbable vodka celebration of the Soviet victory by inebriated Red soldiers. Soon, however, NKVD personnel arrived with different ideas. See James P. O'Donnell, *The Bunker* (New York: Houghton Mifflin, 1978), 321–335. Mohnke's conversations with Heidemann of these events are related in Heidemann, interview by author, April 20, 2009. The Germans having surrendered the day before, Mohnke had come close to shooting himself on May 9 before he was shipped off to Moscow. Otto Günsche persuaded him to put his service pistol away. "Look, General, we survived the Führerbunker together. We lived through the breakout; perhaps we can pull through whatever lies before us too."

45. Mohnke and Gunsche to Gerd Heidemann in joint interview, related to author, April 20, 2009.

46. Jupp Steinbüchel of the 1st SS Panzer Reconnaissance Battalion, as cited by Tiemann, *Chronicle of the 7. Panzer Kompanie*, 317.

47. Jochen Peiper to Willis Everett, July 14, 1946, Everett Papers.

48. "Second statement of Otto Wichmann," January 23, 1946, Prosecution Exhibit P-128-A, NA RG 549, Case 6-24, *op. cit.*, Box 9.

49. J. Peiper, interview by Toland, October 10, 1963.

50. "Wehrwolf . . . Sepp Dietrich: MFIU No. 5, 20 May 1945," NA, RG 338, 7th Army Interrogation Center, Unit #5, Box 76, 290/56/2.

51. Reinhold Kyriss, interview by author, May 20, 1997.

52. "The Dream of the Reich Is Finished!" Recollection of the panzer regimental surgeon, Dr. Herbert Knoll, on May 7, 1945, as recounted in Tiemann, *Chronicle of the 7. Panzer Kompanie*, 320. Peiper's final instructions to his men near Stiermark: Horst Schumann, interview by author, March 8, 2006.

Chapter Ten

1. "Vicinity Rottach . . . the 1st Battalion captured high German officers including Maj. Gen. Gehlen, Lt. Gen. Paul Winter and 33 high ranking SS officers who were brought to Regimental S-2," NA RG 407, 42nd Infantry Division, 222 Infantry Regiment, "Report of Operations," May 23, 1945.

2. Peiper direct trial testimony, June 22, 1946, *US v. Bersin*, Case 6-24, 1968.

3. Fritz Kosmehl's recollection of Peiper's feeling upon being captured. Fritz Kosmehl, interview with author, December 17, 2004.

4. Arthur N. Lee Jr. to N. Thomson, letter. August 19, 1997, Rainbow Division Veterans Association. The 1st Battalion of the infantry regiment captured 33 high-ranking SS officers on May 23, 1945 in the vicinity of Schliersee.

5. For the nearly forgotten blemish on the 42nd Infantry Division: "The Webling Incident," *After the Battle*, No. 27, 1980, 30–33.

6. AAR of the 431 AAA AW Battalion shows that the unit was guarding many SS troopers captured from May 20–23, all kept in an enclosure near Rottach. Moreover, the battalion reported that there were over five thousand convalescent German soldiers in the hospitals around Tegernsee. On May 25: "Captain Woefler reported that 1400 POWs had been evacuated by 40 trucks from the 4th Infantry Division to Ansbach," RG 407, 431 AAA Bn, Operations Journal, May 22–25, 1945.

7. For Himmler's end: Peter Longerich, *Heinrich Himmler* (Oxford: Oxford University Press, 2012), 735–736. Also, Peter Witte and Stephen Tyas, *Himmler's Diary 1945* (Stroud, UK: Fonthill Media, 2014).

8. Herbert J. Strong to Enemy Prisoner of War Information Bureau, April 21, 1952, RG 549, Peiper Prison File, "War Criminal Prison Nr. 1: Records Relating to Parolee 1945–48," Box 94, 290/59/30-31/2-1.

9. Sanders later learned from Peiper that his assistant at Dinkelsbühl was Paul Guhl with whom he had long fought on the Russian front.

10. Sanders, interview, January 21–22, 1999. Also, letters to Joachim Peiper, June 23, 1969. Hal McCown had previously been with the 22nd Regiment while it was still in Ft. Benning up until 1942.

11. Unless otherwise noted, Peiper's quotes are from Sanders interview. His morose assessment of SS prospects in US Army hands may not have been far off the mark. See "All SS Men May Be Tried as Criminals," Richard Lewis, *Stars and Stripes*, June 11, 1945, 5.

12. J. Peiper to Stephen Sanders, Stuttgart, August 2, 1969.

13. *Kommentar zum Buch Massacre at Malmedy vom Charles Whiting*, in author's possession.

14. Sanders interview.

Chapter Eleven

1. Simon Bourgin, "What Will They Do with the War Criminals?" *Stars and Stripes*, April 25, 1945, and "U.S. Now Insists Things Be Made Tough on the Nazis," *Stars and Stripes*, May 30, 1945.

2. "Nazis to Face Trial Soon for Mass Killing of Yanks at Malmédy in December," *Stars and Stripes*, May 29, 1945.

3. "Investigation of the Malmédy Massacre by War Crimes Branch, USFET," NA, Case 6-24, RG-549, Box 11. "Report of the Supreme Headquarters Allied Expeditionary Force Court of Inquiry re Shooting of Allied Prisoners of War near Malmédy, Belgium, 17 December 1944," National Archives, RG 331, Entry 56, Box 127.

4. Ellis to his wife, letter, May 24, 1945, Ellis Papers.

5. "MP Looks in PW Cage and Finds a Nazi General," *Stars and Stripes*, May 15, 1945.

6. For Dietrich's description of his capture and Peiper's surrender: "Testimony of Genobst. Josef Dietrich to Burton Ellis, Wiesbaden, 31 July 1945," NA, Case 6-24, RG-549, Box 33. For the intention to escape to Switzerland: Gerald Reitlinger, *The SS: Alibi of a Nation* (New York: Viking Press, 1957), 371n.

7. "This is not a comic session," warned Dietrich's interrogator, E. E. Minskoff. "Interrogation of Josef Dietrich," November 27, 1945, Nürnberg, BA-K, OMGUS 3/71–3/4.

8. Correspondence with the son, George Katsiaficas at Institute Chonnam National University, Korea, March 14, 2001. Also, letter of Jochen Peiper to Stephen Sanders, August 2, 1969. "I do remember Feuchtwangen and the fair treatment received by our custodians, and I also recall you and 1st Lt. Nicolaus Kaziaficas [sic], the camp commander, who was of Greek origin."

9. Peiper gave his word to the Greek American that he would return to the POW enclosure at Feuchtwangen if he would give him only an afternoon to see his family for a few hours. Whether, or how this took place is unclear as Katsiaficas is deceased and the son could only repeat the story his father had told him. However, that such things did happen is undeniable as a driver with the 26th Infantry Division complained to the army: "Today I took an SS major to Bad Ischil and Wiesbach from Steyr, Austria for the simple reason that he wanted to see his wife. The trip ticket said 'official business.' Since when does the American Army condescend to the whims of SS PWs?" "The B Bag," *Stars and Stripes*, November 17, 1945.

10. Theodore A. Thompson to Nicolas Katsiaficas, August 2, 1951, Records of War Criminal Prison No. 1., NA, RG-549, Records of War Criminal Prison No. 1, "Stayback."

11. "Flood of German Prisoners Poses Problem for Allies," *Stars and Stripes*, May 7, 1945.

12. John M. Centner, "Copy for Wolfgang Trees," March 30, 1998.

13. Special Agent Richard C. Lang, interview by author, 1st CIC Detachment, US 1st Infantry Division, February 3, 1999.

14. "10,000 SSers Clean Streets of Nuremberg," Frank Waters, *Stars and Stripes*, August 7, 1945.

15. John Marie Centner to author, December 25, 2001.

16. Richard Lang, interview by author, February 3, 1999.

17. "GI's No. 1 War Criminal Seized—CO of Malmédy Murders," *Stars and Stripes*, August 20, 1945.

18. "Headquarters, U.S. Forces European Theater: Evacuation of SS O/Stubf. Joachim Peiper," August 20, 1945, NA, RG-319, IRR Files for J. Peiper.

19. See Peter Schrijvers, *The Unknown Dead: Civilians in the Battle of the Bulge* (Lexington: University of Kentucky, 2005), 39–49.

20. Centner to author.

21. Lang, interview, 1999.

22. JA File, "Dear Editor," August 20, 1945, signed T/5 Ernest W. Bechtel, T/5 Louis H. Groth and Pvt. Joseph F. De Paulo, NA: RG 549, Case 6-24, *op. cit.*, Box 13.

23. "Preliminary Interrogation Report: Peiper, Joachim, AIC 1807," Headquarters Third US Army Intelligence Center, August 24, 1945, NA, RG 319, CIC Files, Records on J. Peiper.

24. Peiper direct testimony during the trial in his own defense, paper copy of trial record, R1885, NA, Case 6-24, *US v. Bersin*, RG 153, Box 73. Also, RG 153, Roll 2, Frame 000107-88.

25. "Affidavit: Joachim Peiper," June 5, 1948, Landsberg/Lech, Case 6-24, NA, RG-549, Box 60.

26. "In Freising, Mr. Paul informed me as follows:" Peiper, testimony, Ellis Papers, no date. "In view of the hopeless situation, I am prepared to admit all charges. It is my duty to save decent fellows by taking the blame of the incident upon myself. Otherwise to save face and die as a soldier."

27. Paul Guth, interview by author, May 28, 2001.

28. Dwight Fanton, interview by author, January 27, 1997; also Fanton, testimony, on May 5, 1949, MMIH, 279.

29. "An Interview with Joachim Peiper, 1 SS Pz Regt: ETHINT-10," September 7, 1945, Freising, Germany, NA, RG-238, Foreign Military Studies. Burton Ellis would later claim that Peiper prepared a seventy-page operations analysis of his participation in the Ardennes Offensive at Freising on August 25 and 26, 1945, although this document was never found even during later deliberations for the Senate investigations and numerous trial reviews (see Royce L. Thompson, "The ETO Ardennes Campaign, Operations of the Combat Group Peiper, 16–26 December 1944," OCMH, Washington, DC, July 24, 1952). The Freising interrogation, was however, extensively quoted within the trial itself: *US v. Bersin*, 1946, Case 6-24, NA, RG-549, 2532–47.

30. Ken Hechler, interview by author, December 15, 1994. Hechler would later become a congressman and secretary of state for West Virginia.

31. "Prisoner: Peiper, Joachim, AIC 1807: Results of Detailed Interrogation," September 7, 1945, ibid.

32. Col. H. G. Sheen to Assistant Chief of Staff, G-2, CIB, September 19, 1945, NA, RG 319, CIC Files, Records on J. Peiper. McCown's report is "Annex 3 to XVIII Corps (AB), G-2 Periodic Report No. 11: Observations of an American Field Officer who Escaped from the 1st SS Panzer Division "Adolf Hitler," January 6, 1945, 3.

33. Ellis to wife, August 29, 1945, Ellis Papers.

34. Ellis to wife, letter, September 13, 1945, Ellis Papers.

35. "Military Intelligence Service Center: Report of Operations," Records of US Forces in the European Theater (USFET), NA, RG-338, Box 3, 290/57/22/3.

36. "Handling of Prisoners: Headquarters U.S. Forces European Theater, Military Intelligence Service Center," June 24, 1945, NA, RG-338, Box 3, 290/57/22/3.

37. Observations of an American Field Officer Who Escaped from the 1st SS Panzer Division "Adolf Hitler," RG-407, 330-2.2 G-2 Records 30th Infantry Division Box 7569: 330-2.1, Operations Reports, December 1944, McCown's testimony was first reproduced in Annex 1

of "Headquarters 30th Infantry Division G-2 Periodic Report," No. 192, December 26, 1944. Given its unique perspective McCown's report was repeated by American intelligence officers at virtually all command echelons from SHAEF down to divisional level.

38. "Statements by Prisoner SS Standf. Joachim Peiper," September 15, 1945, by Leroy Vogel, Oberursel, within "General Correspondence: 1939–1947, 333.9 Personnel: McCown Hal D.: Interrogation of Col. Joachim Peiper, 30 October 1946," NA, RG 159, Entry 26E, Box 531.

39. In a statement made on October 30, 1946, from Landsberg, Peiper told Col. F. J. Pearson that although McCown had divulged no American tactical information during his captivity, they had discussed the Russians and the Jews in a derogatory fashion: Peiper: "This conversation was more along the line of a joke to keep our spirits up. I recall he said, 'Well, I guess the war is over on this front for me, so I'll help you fight the Russians. . . . We had a long conversation about the Jews. . . . He wanted to know why we persecuted the Jews and so I tried to explain to him the Jewish situation in Germany, how it came about. I told him we see America only though the eyes of propaganda and you do the same about Germany. . . . I asked him if all influential positions in the States were held by Jewish people. He told me something about the strong financial interest they had and I believe I said, 'OK, when this war is over, I'll pay back your support against the Russians and help you hang the Jews.' These remarks were made in a joking manner."

40. Peiper can be seen just behind Werner Grothmann in an image taken at Mauthausen on April 27, 1941 (Bundesarchiv Bild BA-192–195), where Himmler was in conversation with August Eigruber, Gauleiter in Oberdonau/Ostmark in Austria, and KZ commandants Franz Ziereis and Georg Bachmayer.

41. "Als Chaplain im Waffen-SS Gefangenen und Sonderlagern zu Ebensee 1945/46," Dr. Franz Loidl, document courtesy Dr. Wolfgang Quatember, KZ Gedenkstätte und Zeitgeschichte Museum Ebensee, Austria. Loidl described his nine months at Ebensee as "the collision of two extreme worlds: the SS and the Catholic church." Still, "many were glad to unburden their hearts in confession"—particularly youths drafted into the SS who felt particularly unlucky.

42. "I remember I visited Ebensee for a couple of days in September or October of 1945. I took a jeep down there with Shumacker. There were a lot of SS men there. It was a really wild place. We got lists from various camps of men there were held there and culled through lists of thousands. . . . It was a beautiful mountain site on the lake in Austria, but we only stayed a couple of days. We were trying to get a comprehensive list of suspects to put together in one place." Dwight Fanton, interview by author, April 5, 2010.

43. Hans Hennecke, previously unknown extended handwritten statement, of no date, NA, RG-549, Case 6-24, Box 36.

44. Peiper describes Ellis's early attempt at implicating him in his affidavit, dated June 5, 1948, from Landsberg Lech, NA, RG-549, Case 6-24, Box 60.

45. Ellis to wife, letter, September 30, 1945, Ellis Papers. "These newspaper reporters chill my blood. They have no principles, no morals, no nothing as far as I can see. Absolutely anything for a sensational story. The whole thing sickens me beyond words. . . . If we want revenge, let us say so. Not pretend to be such God-damned moralists. This is no way to prevent future wars. It's the way to insure them."

46. "JA War Crimes Branch to G-2 CIB," October 11, 1945, NA, RG 319, Investigative Repository Reports, "Records on J. Peiper," no box.

Chapter Twelve

1. MMIH, 270–271.
2. "Investigation of the Malmédy Massacre." *op. cit.*

3. For suspicion of Peiper's collusion with his men at Zuffenhausen: Fanton's memorandum to Ellis, February 19, 1946, MMIH, 294. Also, Ellis affidavit of October 1948, MMIH, 1217.

4. Testimony of Morris Ellowitz on April 22, 1949, MMIH, 132–133.

5. Ellis to wife, letter, December 9, 1945. Ellis would have been at Schwäbisch Hall for the first time on December 12–13, 1945. Quote and underline of "wants to tell all" in original.

6. "Extract Taken from Direct Testimony of Peiper, Joachim when Questioned by Dr. Terry," September 8, 1949. Records of the US Senate, 81st Congress, Committee on Armed Services, Malmédy Investigation," NA, Records of the US Senate, RG 46, Stack 12e3/7/26/3-4, Box 148.

7. MMIH, 483. Calvin Unterseher, testimony, MMIH, 651–652 and Fanton, testimony, 483.

8. Fanton, interview by author, April 5, 2010.

9. Rolf Reiser recalled that Sigurd Peiper was there in the courtroom for almost every day of the proceedings, sitting in the back with Frau Dietrich, who wore oversized hats. Reiser noted this fact in reviewing the Malmédy trial film with the author in an interview on March 16, 2006.

10. The extensive testimony of Peiper before the court is found in the trial record, 1885–2045.

11. As previously covered, in spite of claiming to never have been a member of the National Socialists, Peiper was actually given a party number in spite of his attempts to emphasize his career as a nonpolitical professional soldier.

12. The statement made by SS Hstuf. Gruhle with which Peiper was so distraught was one he gave on March 18, 1946, to Ralph Shumacker. In that statement he said on the late afternoon on December 15 he was personally approached by Peiper, who then took him to a large room after a tactical discussion to go over the supply situation. He then briefed Gruhle, Ustuf. Arndt Fischer, Ustuf. Kalinosky (adjutant 2nd SS Pz Battalion), Stubaf. Dr. Sickel, Ostuf. Maule (Weapons and ammunition officer) and Obstuf. Goelden (Transportation Officer) and company commanders: Kremser, Christ, Junker, Klingelhoefer, Sievers, Rumpf and also Maj. Wolf with the 84th AA Rgt and Stubaf. Diefenthal, Stubaf. Poetschke and Ostubaf. von Westernhagen. As Gruhle recalled Peiper's rendition of a new order: "The German nation has lined up for its last big fight. The objective is Antwerp and to break up the Allied forces that have lined up in the Aachen area. The German nation expects from its soldiers the greatest preparedness for action, courage and sacrifice. The people will not welcome our advance in whose territory we carry out the fight. Any resistance from this quarter and any acts of terror will be countered with the greatest ruthlessness. This fight will be conducted stubbornly with no regard for Allied prisoners of war who will have to be shot if the situation makes it necessary." Gruhle claimed the order was signed by Dietrich himself. NA, Case 6-24, RG-549, Box 9.

13. "Peiper Pleads He Was Beaten," *Stars and Stripes*, June 25, 1946.

14. See Parker, *Fatal Crossroads*, 115 and 132.

15. After the war Peiper maintained that the jeep also carried an American Lt. colonel from whom he learned that there was an American general in Engelsdorf. The author has determined that this officer was Lt. Col. John Ray with the HQ of the US First Army who had been sent out to warn US artillery installations of the enemy breakthrough. John Ray, interview by author, May 15 and 18, 1998, Natick, MA.

16. This was by House #10 in the original trial maps, the home of Benoit Lejoly. Just before the road enters the forest to the southwest.

17. Peiper continued (p. 1934), "I should like to mention that the concentrated fire of my spearhead, which amounts to a total of 25 machine guns and five cannons must have necessarily caused a lot of casualties." However, clear evidence shows that only two Americans were wounded in the original encounter with the German spearhead: Parker, *Fatal Crossroads*, 275.

18. Several American survivors of the eventual shooting at Baugnez recalled a German officer passing by on an armored vehicle call out to them, "It's a long way to Tipperary, boys!" Al Valenzi, interview, September 26, 1995.

19. Peiper: "Our conversation about this matter was not comprehensive at all because the importance of the technical problems would not permit that. . . . My road of advance from Trois Ponts on west could not be maintained and I had to find another crossing somewhere." Ibid., 1939–1940.

20. Peiper's important admission is on pages 1960–1961 of the trial transcript.

21. "A violent heart attack" is likely an error in translation or Peiper's colloquial characterization of his medical condition. He likely collapsed in nervous exhaustion.

22. "I offered him a cigarette and a cup of coffee, but the man was in no condition to smoke or drink. I established from him that he had been hiding in the woods near here for two weeks and he had been a first gunner on a machine gun. I asked him where the machine gun was, but the man was barely able to talk, it was more like barking than like talking. I then asked the regimental surgeon who was present, what we should do with poor fellow, whether we should put him in the hospital, which was located in the same house. My regimental surgeon cast a brief glance at his hands which were wounded—and shook his head and said, 'There's not much sense in that anymore.'" Ibid., 1964.

23. "Secret Weapons Nazi Bluff, Speer Says," and "Forced to Talk, Peiper Pleads," *Stars and Stripes*, June 22, 1946; "Use War Criminals as 'Guinea Pigs in A-Tests, League Asks," *Stars and Stripes*, June 23, 1946.

Chapter Thirteen

1. Karl Hollander, interview by Agte, as cited in Agte, *Jochen Peiper*, 14. SS Scharführer Hollander, the company clerk, had typed up Peiper's Genghis Khan manuscript while with him at Berlin's Lichterfelde barracks in 1936.

2. "*Our reputation precedes us as a wave of terror and is one of our best weapons*. Even old Genghis Khan would gladly have hired us as assistants." Letter Jochen Peiper to Hedwig Potthast from just after the Kharkov battles, March 24, 1943, Bundesarchiv Koblenz, "Nachlass Heinrich Himmler: Korrespondenz Hedwig Potthast," Bestand N 1126/37.

3. Himmler saw to it that young SS officers who were detailed for military and advanced education were given a written assignment to help them to think like the Mongol lord: "By what means did Genghis Khan win his battles?" Presentation by SS Oberführer Cummerow at the *Haus der Flieger* in Berlin: *Militärische und wissenschaftliche Weiterbildung der jungen SS-Führer, Vorträge anläßlich der SS-Gruppenführerbesprechung vom 25.1.1939*, Persönlicher Stab Reichsführer SS, Bundesarchiv NS 19/29. "The first attack, according to Genghis Khan's tactics, had to carry terror and panic to the remotest part of the country. The invaded country was to be paralyzed with fear; the inhabitants would be made to believe that resistance would be a futility."

4. Peiper said the first was in September 1944 when he was interrogated in Freising by three officers including one by Paul Guth, another at Oberursel (Ken Hechler) and still another at Schwäbisch Hall, William Perl.

5. This potentially important sixty-seven-page document has been lost since the trial (the author has looked for it for years in the catacombs of the National Archives). Its cover bears the description, "Investigation, Malmedy Case, W.C.B. File No. 6-24, Examination of Joachim Peiper, prisoner of war, August 25–26, 1945, in Freising, Germany." See trial record, *US v. Bersin*, 1946.

6. Ellis wanted to know how Peiper could take notes in Zuffenhausen if his cell was as dark as he claimed. "It was not that dark that I couldn't see at all. There was a hole in the door through which light from the outside could enter the room and I would write in front of this hole or play chess," 1981.

7. Peiper refers to a German saying, which indicates matters in a court of law appear different than they do on the spot. The aphorism comes from the 1932 masterpiece of ballet choreographer Kurt Jooss, *The Green Table,* which depicted the futility of peace negotiations in war.

8. "Peiper Denies Ordering Death of Children," *Stars and Stripes*, June 23, 1946.

9. The incident Ellis refers to is the killing of members of the Company A of the 27th Armored Infantry Battalion of the US Ninth Armored Division and three civilians by the little hamlet of Vaulx Richard. A poignant monument to those executed there is found just off the road near La Vaulx Richard today. See William C. C. Cavanagh, *A Tour of the Bulge Battlefield* (South Yorkshire: Leo Cooper, 2001), 87–88.

10. Everett to family, June 22, 1946, Everett Papers.

11. Ibid.

12. Peiper's testimony on the crossroads is from 2025 of the trial record.

13. Ellis's handwritten diary, in the author's possession, says on March 21, 1946: "Tex [Cain] brought in Dietrich before dinner. . . . Bill Perl got Peiper to confess on the orders—says they came down from the 6th Army signed by Dietrich." Ellis Papers. Also, notes by Perl with Dietrich's Schwäbisch Hall statement dated March 22, 1946, make it clear that he confessed the preceding night. "Was first interrogated by Col. Ellis while I acted as interpreter. This was the same evening he arrived, about 8 p.m. After about twenty minutes, still while Col. Ellis was interrogating, he confessed to having issued orders that a wave of terror and fright should precede the troops." NA, Case 6-24, RG-549, Box 33.

14. Paul Zwigart, statement, February 11, 1946, NA, War Crimes Cases Tried, Case 6-24, RG-338, Box 9.

15. Peiper's testimony: MMIH, 606. Trial testimony from 2045.

16. "That was one of the finest dissertations of a regimental commander that I ever heard. . . . Of course, he skipped over those little incidents." Rosenfeld, testimony, MMIH, 1431.

17. Everett to family, June 24, 1946, Everett Papers.

Chapter Fourteen

1. "Fear of the prosecution still lingers on.": Willis Everett on July 11, 1946. *Stars and Stripes*, Vol. 2, No. 191, July 12, 1946.

2. Ellis, interview. "They had reason to be fearful. We really cut them up."

3. Everett to family, June 29, 1946, Everett Papers.

4. Dwinell, MMIH, 421. "There was a set of rules for the prosecution and a set for the defense."

5. Handwritten Letter Jochen Peiper to Willis Everett, July 4, 1946, Everett Papers.

6. Testimony of Georg Freitag, *US v. Bersin*, 2769–2774.

7. Testimony of Albert Braun, 2783–2787.

8. In Braun's original Schwäbisch Hall statement he checked in with his company commander, Obstuf. Junker, prior to being moved off in an ambulance, rather than Poetschke, so the statement is probably correct on this point.

9. Statement of Rottenführer Albert Braun, January 7, 1946, NA, Case 6-24, RG-549, Box 37.

10. Testimony of Rolf Möbius, 2854–2864.

11. Testimony of Gerhard Walla, 2865–2876.

12. Testimony of William Perl, 2928–2939.

13. See Peiper's full courtroom testimony on p. 2041 of the proceedings.

14. Testimony of Harry Thon, 2939–2952.

15. "Decided to fight to the last man," 3052.

16. See courtroom testimony by Ebeling and Landfried about Hillig, Peiper and the shooting in Stoumont; 156 of Chapter 12.

17. In his closing argument Shumacker did point out that Hillig, being with "Kommandeur," could have hardly avoided shooting the prisoners in Stoumont without himself being executed. But Wichmann, the prosecution contended, could have left Peiper and Dr. Sickel with the frozen man, told him to run and fired shots into the air and pretended an execution. But this idea conveniently ignored that the frost-bitten American at Petit Thier was so weak that he could hardly have run away. Should Wichmann have abandoned him, he could have fallen nearby or wandered back, to be found once more and then brought back before Peiper.

18. For Peiper's orders to Hillig to shoot the American prisoner in Stoumont, see Hillig's statement and two other SS witnesses, Walter Landfried and Georg Ebeling: pp. 1363–1377 of trial record.

19. For Sickel's damning confession: "Now and then, against my will and on order of my superiors I had to deliver to the *Vernichtungslager* (Extermination) Camp Maideneck persons who had been working for me in the orthropedic workshops. It was known to me that gassings took place there and these people got gassed. However, I have not conducted myself any gassings." "Statement of Dr. Kurt Sickel," April 9, 1946, witnessed by Homer B. Crawford, NA, RG-549, Case 6-24, Box 9, trial record, *U.S. v. Bersin*, 1558–1562. Moreover, his SS records showed identical occupation of Dr. Sickel: "health" of the Jews in Lublin, BDC personnel file." Personal-Antrag," July 7, 1944, NA A 3343 SSO-134B. Sickel had been a member of SS Totenkopf Cavalry Regiment 2 in 1940 and later served in the 2nd SS Division before being assigned to the Leibstandarte Adolf Hitler.

20. Testimony of Dr. Leer defending Peiper, 3179–3193.

21. For Kramm's testimony, trial proceedings, 158–191.

22. For the jeep incident, see trial testimony of various witnesses: 1263–1293. After the trial Diefenthal, Karl Heinz Flacke, and Paul Fackelmeyer made strenuous legal efforts in statements and affidavits from 1947–1949 to establish that neither Diefenthal nor Peiper had been in the HQ SPW at Cheneux, which they claimed was driven by Zwigart alone. Diefenthal had moved to another tank and Peiper pedaled along on a bicycle! When the author interviewed Paul Zwigart May 20, 1997, the jeep incident was off the table, but the ex-SS man nervously made it clear that he resented Josef Diefenthal. He had been expected to take the rap for the entire affair. "I liked Peiper," he told the author, "but Diefenthal, we cannot talk about him."

23. Appeals for mitigation of sentences on the afternoon of July 11, 1946, 3209–3217. Those with pleas were: Freidel Bode, Willi Braun, Kurt Briesemeister, Willi von Chamier, Roman Clotten, Fritz Eckmann, Georg Fleps, and Heinz Friedrichs.

24. Siptrott's plea for mitigation of sentence on July 12, 1946, 3238–3239.

25. Ellis, handwritten supplemental affidavit, October 27, 1948, Ellis Papers.

26. Hans Hillig's personal plea before the court and verification of his statement on shooting an American soldier on Peiper's orders: 3224. On September 18, 1947, Gerald Coates, a US civilian investigator with Ellis's 7708 War Crimes Group, interviewed Hans Hillig, then held at Landsberg Prison to obtain clarification of Hillig's perspective on his plea for mitigation and his other statements. The signed and witnessed statement of Hillig revealed crafty influence by the German attorneys. "Dr. Leer tried repeatedly to change my first statement for the benefit of another defendant [Peiper], but I stressed that I was acting to the best of my knowledge and conscience and stated only the truth." Signed copy in of Hillig's statement of September 18, 1947, in author's possession, Ellis Papers.

27. "All 73 Malmédy Defendants Guilty," *Stars and Strips*, European Edition, July 12, 1946. The story was front-page news in the armed forces newspaper with a photo of Peiper under the headline.

28. Twenty-two of the defendants received sentences of life in prison, including Sepp Dietrich. Gruhle and Priess had twenty-year sentences, Arndt Fischer had a fifteen-year sentence; and Clotten, Hillig, Krämer, Reiser, and Wichmann had ten-year sentences. Even though admitting shooting American soldiers, Hillig and Wichmann received lesser sentences because they had acted on direct order of their superior, Jochen Peiper. Forty-three, including Peiper, were sentenced to death.

29. "43 Germans Doomed, 22 Get Life for Bulge Killing of Americans," *New York Times*, July 17, 1946. For Peiper's smile at his sentence: "43 Malmédy Butchers Get Death Sentence," *Stars and Stripes*, July 17, 1946. For appearance of the courtroom during sentencing: archival films of the Malmédy trial from July 16.

30. "Wanton in Bulge," *Kansas City Star*, August 8, 1946.

31. Peiper to Ellis, Dachau, July 13, 1946, Ellis Papers.

32. Peiper to Everett, July 14, 1946, Everett Papers.

33. Everett to family, July 17, 1946, Everett Papers.

34. Benjamin Narvid to Weingartner, November 19, 1976. Courtesy of James Weingartner.

Chapter Fifteen

1. The author has written extensively on the post-trial extrajudicial reviews of the Malmédy case as well as the Senate investigation, although space does not allow more than a summary here. For an expert synopsis, Weingartner, *Crossroads*, op. cit, 166–238.

2. Willi Schaefer to Everett, June 6, 1951, Everett Papers.

3. Everett to Sen. William Langer, February 28, 1951, Langer Papers, Box 483, Folder 6.

4. Peiper to Kosmehl, August 11, 1951.

5. Peiper's letter to the Race and Settlement Office from Himmler's staff headquarters in Berlin, RuSHA file for Kurt Hans Hinrichsen, letter to Reichsführer SS dated July 11, 1942, NA, RG-242, A-3343-RS-C0383.

6. Letter Sigurd Peiper to Landsberg Prison, September 23, 1951. NA Peiper Parole Files, *op. cit.*

7. Reiser, interview.

8. Ann Shields, interview with Roesch, February 18, 2009.

9. Woldemar Peiper to Gustav Süßmann, March 7, 1951, as cited by Agte, *Jochen Peiper*, 580.

10. "Letter R. Brüstle to Landsberg," Ravensburg, July 7, 1952, NA, Peiper Parole Files.

11. "Galgenhumor—Peiper schreibt aus Landsberg," reproduced letter to an unknown person from Peiper, *Die Strasse*, January 21, 1951, 9. NA, RG 338, Landsberg: "Records Relating to Post Trial Activities," Box 3.

12. Lina Heydrich, *Leben mit einem Kriegsverbrecher* (Pfaffenhofen: Verlag W. Ludwig, 1976), 140–141.

13. NARA, RG 260, OMGUS, Records of the Executive Office, Military Detachment Reports from Bavaria, Box 426: Landkreis Miesbach, Detachment G-232: July 29, 1945 and December 15, 1945: A secret organization of former party members, deposed from public and business life, is supposed to exist and has the code phrase: *alter Deutscher*. December 15: "There is a growing anti-Semitic attitude among the peasants and conservative Catholic element of the communities of this area. . . . Good deal of excited talk and resentment of the death sentence of [Dr. Klaus] Schilling in the Dachau trial."

14. "Weihnachtsveranstaltungen: Die HIAG Tegernsee/Miesbach," *Wiking Ruf*, No. 14, December 1952, Hannover.

15. For Adenauer's comment: *Die Zeit*, February 8, 1951.

16. Robert E. Conot, *Justice at Nuremberg* (New York: Harper and Row, 1983), 232–238. Ohlendorf described how he met with Himmler at Nikolayev on October 4, 1941, and being

told of his mission. "He [Himmler] assembled the leaders and men of the *Einsatzkommando*, repeated to them the liquidation order, and pointed out that the leaders and men who were taking part in the liquidation bore no personal responsibility for the execution of his order. The responsibility was his alone, and the Führer's."

17. Joseph Borkin, *The Crime and Punishment of I. G. Farben* (New York: Free Press, 1978). Ellis Oral History, 29, 44. Burton Ellis went off to Korea, where he was finally made full colonel, the thing he had sought for so long. But that experience with the 2nd Division did little to increase his comfort with the Malmédy verdict. "I've seen some things over there that aren't too nice," he said, "But you know if you're up in the line and your buddy gets killed and you think a lot of him and you get a chance for vengeance, you'll do it."

18. Christopher Simpson, *Blowback: America's Recruitment of Nazis and Its Effects on the Cold War* (London: Wiedenfeld and Nichols, 1988), 64–65.

19. "Denial of War Crimes," *The Times* (London), October 26, 1952; "Gehöre nicht zu Euch," *Der Spiegel*, November 5, 1952.

20. Adenauer to Hausser, letter, December 17, 1952, reproduced in Tiemann, *Chronicle of the 7. Panzer Kompanie*, 250.

21. *Frankfurter Allgemeine*, January 7, 1952.

22. Others released in 1952: Hans Hendel, Arnold Mikolascheck, Erich Münkemer, Hans Pletz, Heinz Tomhardt, Erich Werner and Otto Wichmann.

23. "Joachim Peiper to the Interim Mixed Parole and Clemency Board," Landsberg on Lech, December 28, 1952, Case 6-24, RG 549, Box 59.

24. Peiper to Fritz Kosmehl, April 11, 1951. Peiper worried about his children and the new generation: "The young ones have no understanding of their elders. . . . The world has come off its hinges."

25. "Installation Diary, War Criminal Prison No. 1," December 25, 1952, NA, RG-338, Entry 37042, Unit Histories, War Criminal Prison Detachment, Box 4939.

26. Ibid., War Criminal Prison No. 1, Statistics: As of 1 July 1953. A total of 1,645 inmates had been processed and screened through WCP No. 1.

27. Joachim Peiper, "Words from Landsberg," in Paul Hauser, *Waffen-SS im Einsatz* (Göttingen: Plesse Verlag K. W. Schütz, 1953), 262–269.

28. Paul Krellmann to Wolfgang Vorpersal, letter, January 24, 1976, BA-MA, Sammlung Vorpersal.

29. "Inmates Record of Visits and Visitors, Joachim Peiper, 1952–1956," NA Parole Files.

30. Hans Rudel visited Peiper on December 22, 1954, accompanied by Werner Roesch, who was the local spokesperson for Kameradenwerk near Landsberg. During the visit they saw both Peiper and Sepp Dietrich each for a period of thirty minutes. Roesch delivered Christmas gifts from Kameradenwerk, which were all carefully examined by the prison staff before being passed along. If Rudel had any shady proposals, they could hardly be discussed there, for right by the long table in the common room in which the meeting occurred, the discussion was monitored by a guard. Werner Roesch, letter to Ann Shields, January 12, 2009, and interview, February 18, 2009.

31. Investigative Repository Records, "Hans Ulrich Rudel," NA RG-319, File XE153440. Also, NA, Civil Records Division, US State Department Document, 762A.00/3-1555, "Rudel Launches DRP Campaign in Oldenburg." For Rudel's sponsorship of Josef Mengle: Gerald L. Posner and John Ware, *Mengele* (New York; McGraw Hill, 1986). Also, "Prison Break Plot Revealed," *New York Times*, March 21, 1953. Peiper also received several packages and letters from a variety of individuals in Argentina, most going by assumed names. Records of Rudel's visit in NA and correspondence, Peiper Parole files. A persona non-grata in Germany, Rudel later became a ski instructor after retiring to Kufstein, Tirol, in Austria in the 1960s. He remained unrepentant, speaking at Neo-Nazi gatherings and making appearances at SS Treffen

until his death in December 1982. His funeral was attended by over two thousand sympathizers, including many who stretched out arms in the forbidden Nazi salute while belting out the shunned verses of *Deutschland über Alles*. "Nazi Sympathizers at Funeral of German Ace," *New York Times*, December 22, 1982.

32. "Adolf and Eva," State Journal, Lansing, MI, 19 July 1945. Also, "Argentina: U-530," *Time Magazine*, July 23, 1945. The alarm came from a reporter in Montevideo who claimed that Hitler and Eva had landed on the foggy Argentinian shoreline earlier that summer in U-boat 530.

33. Brig. Gen. P. E. Peabody, "The Inner Fortress and Post War Nazi Underground," CSC, Military Intelligence Service, April 28, 1945, NA, RG-65, Records of the Federal Bureau of Investigation, 65-47826, World War II Files, "German Underground Movement," Box 204. In the fanciful German plans revealed by a captured SS officer in Cologne on March 7, 1945, after Germany reestablished its position there would be an eventual Third World War led by Himmler to eliminate the "yellow and brown peoples."

34. Frederic Forsythe, *The Odessa File* (New York: Viking Press, 1972).

35. The main Odessa escape routes were through Austria and Italy to Franco's Spain, and then to South America and particularly to Argentina and Paraguay, then under the right wing regimes of Juan Perón and Alfredo Stroessner. See "Odessa Organization," NA: RG 319, IRR Files, Box 64, File No. ZF015116. Naujocks had been a leading gangster-like secret agent in Heydrich's SD, the security service of the SS. A boxer and street ruffian, Naujocks was notorious for his operation faking a "Polish" attack on the German radio station at Gleiwitz, Upper Silesia on August 31, 1939—the incident serving as a pretense for the German invasion of Poland. Naujocks was imprisoned after surrendering to the British in 1944 but escaped captivity before he could be tried. Within Odessa Naujocks was responsible for fabricating false papers and passports while Skorzeny arranged funding and "tourism" travel to smuggle Nazis to South America. Naujocks ended his days as a one-eyed bouncer at a brothel in Hamburg's red-light district—the *Reeperbahn*.

36. BDC file for Herbert Kuhlmann, BDC SSO-A3343-SSO-070. Kuhlmann had joined the Nazi party in 1933 and the SS in 1934, After Peiper left the panzer regiment in early 1944 Kuhlmann led the tanks in Russia. Later, in Normandy, he was awarded the German cross in gold for his exploits as the Leibstandarte tank leader who had replaced Peiper during the failed Argenten offensive. "Vorschlag Nr. 357 für die Verleihung des Deutsches Kreuzes in Gold, 1. SS Panzer Division Leibstandarte Adolf Hitler," November 8, 1944, with the endorsement signed by Wilhelm Mohnke. By later fall 1944 Kuhlmann transferred to the 12th SS "Hitler Jugend" Panzer Division to serve as its tank regiment leader (Max Wünsche having been captured in Normandy). Kampfgruppe Kuhlmann was to advance in parallel to Kampfgruppe Peiper in the Ardennes.

37. Uki Goñi, *The Real Odessa: Smuggling the Nazis to Perón's Argentina* (New York: Granta Books, 2002), 298–303. At first Eichmann and Kuhlmann maintained an uneasy relationship in Argentina, both employed by CAPRI, one of Perón's pet hydroelectric projects. As Kuhlmann struck it rich, their relationship soured with the panzer commander striking off for Brazil in 1953, leaving Eichmann increasingly destitute and ripe for eventual arrest. See interview of Klaus Eichmann in the German magazine *Quick*, 1966, No. 1. Goñi's research firmly establishes the roles of the Vatican in helping the old Nazi to reach a South American safe haven.

38. See Martin Lee, *The Beast Reawakens* (Boston: Little Brown, 1997), 111–112. Courtesy of forged papers arranged by Rudel, Mengele once briefly visited Otto Skorzeny in Spain in 1965.

39. Peiper to Robert Sell, July 7, 1951. Peiper's other correspondence from Argentina remains mysterious: Dr. E. Dangel was very likely Dr. Rolf Dangl. However, J. Zaunmüller, O. Higging, and Gerda Susanna Vogel are unknown. Peiper's preference of the use of the word "Diaspora"—a dispersion of an original homogenous people—to describe postwar German

culture is likely anti-Semitic, for Diaspora's primary meaning is "the aggregate of Jewish communities living outside of Palestine."

40. Prison escape was synonymous with the name Otto Skorzeny. Organizing a bold "swat team" in 1947, the towering Viennese commando freed a German war criminal, SS Dr. Hans Eisele, during transfer from Nuremberg to Landsberg prison. Eisele later lived in exile in Egypt. The other escapee, Hermann Noack, was the only inmate to successfully flee Landsberg prison during its postwar operation. A skilled commando paratrooper, Noack lead Skorzeny's audacious 1943 operation to snatch Benito Mussolini from his captors at a nearly inaccessible mountain-top prison in the Dolomite Mountains. Even though plotting an ingenious escape from Landsberg (during which he ran naked from the prison!), Noack was later apprehended on the East German border and executed. Skorzeny himself escaped from Darmstadt Interrogation Center in 1948.

41. Also released in 1953: Ernst Goldschmidt, Oskar Klingelhoefer, Axel Rodenburg, Willi Schäfer, Oswald Siegmund, and Günther Weiss. NA, RG549 Records of Headquarters, US Army Europe, Records Related to Parolee Case Files, 1945–1958.

42. RG 549, Parole Files, *op. cit.* "Joachim Peiper: Work Assignment," Gardening section March 24, 1952–February 19, 1953, civilian motor pool February 19, 1953–May 7, 1954, school section May 7, 1954 and carpentry on November 6, 1956.

43. NA, RG 549, Case File 6-24, Box 59.

44. "Clemency Application of Joachim Peiper," January 6, 1954, NA Parole Files.

45. Letter from Sinzheim Bürgermeisteramt in Baden-Baden to author, August 8, 2001. Upon first moving to town, both Potthast and Sigurd Peiper shared quarters at Hauptstrasse 65. Potthast had moved to Sinzheim in February 1953, supposedly in a panic after American journalists discovered her in Teisendorf near Traunstein. In any case, Potthast's identification supposedly precipitated a series of moves for her and her family beginning in 1953: Koch, *Geheim Depot Schweiz*, 58. The author filed a Freedom of Information Act request with the US CIA for further information on Potthast, with no results. Frau Potthast gave her only interview to journalist Koch in 1987 at the age of seventy-five. Numerous attempts to contact Koch for better descriptions of his sources produced no results, and their veracity must be viewed critically. In fact, Potthast had officially been in Teisendorf from May 24, 1945, until February 24, 1953. City office of Teisendorf to Jens Westemeier, October 13, 2008.

46. Sigurd and her children first moved to Hauptstrasse 65 on April 15, 1953, and then to Bergstr. 32. Hedwig Potthast moved to Sinzheim in 1954. There she remained a neighbor of the Peipers until February 1957 when Sigurd and her children moved to Stuttgart after Jochen was released from prison. Elke Maierl to anonymous, December 25, 2001. "Frau Potthast was a close friend of my mother. Potthast then relocated to an expensive home in Baden-Baden. She remarried and took the last name of her husband, Hans-Adolf Staeck (forty years old in 1954), who, according to Koch, was also an ex-SS man. The Staeck family remained in the Sinzheim area until April of 1959 when they moved to Baden-Baden. Courtesy Alois Huck, the local historial of Sinzheim, December 2009.

47. NA RG 549, War Criminal Prison No. 1: "Records Relating to Parolees 1945–1948, Joachim Peiper," Box 94, 290/59/30/2-1.

48. Dr. Karl-Heinrich Wolman provided his home in the fashionable Berlin district of Grunewald in 1933 for secret negotiations by Hitler with an English diplomat after assuming power. Wolman to Lammers, letter, November 6, 1941, Bundesarchiv Berlin Lichterfelde, BA-B, R 43/4106. Born in 1876, Wolman considered himself a "personal friend of the Führer." He died on August 9, 1953.

49. Information on Dr. Wolman GmbH and Sinzheim courtesy of interviews with local historian Alois Huck and Fritz Scheif, interviews by author, August 21, 2003. Also, Dr. Hans Joachim von Kruedener, September 27, 2003. Wolman GmbH, now part of the industrial giant, *BASF*, claimed to possess no employment records.

50. Although Sinzheim factory workers knew nothing of their intimate SS connections, their status was not forgotten, a fact made obvious when SS General Sepp Dietrich, the godfather to Hedwig's children, paid a visit after his release from prison.

51. Koch, *Himmlers Graue Eminenz*, 194.

52. Koch, *Himmlers Graue Eminenz*, 190. The notary for the dissolution of Himmler's paternity over the Potthast children was a former SS Sturmbannführer, Wilhelm Schneider, the former head of the Third Reich's bar association (!), then living in Berlin and allegedly involved in laundering money from Swiss bank accounts to SS men after the war. Raul Teitelbaum and Moshe Sanbar, *Holocaust Gold: From the Victims to Switzerland* (Tel Aviv: Moreshet, 2001), 22.

53. After 1955 Hedwig Potthast sought to cut ties with her past, ostensibly for her children's sake. She remarried to Hans Staeck in Baden, giving her children that innocuous surname.

54. Immediately after the war Eleonore Pohl fled from Comthurey to Halfing (Brünings-Au) near Rosenheim in Upper Bavaria. Anticipating the location as a postwar refuge in November 1944, the SS had transferred eight Jehovah Witness prisoners with masonry and carpentry skills from KZ Dachau to repair the property that was still in the family. After the end of hostilities five former prisoners from KZ Ravensbrück were still working for Pohl as servants. Wolfgang Benz, Barbara Distel and Angelika Königseder, *Der Ort des Terrors: Geschichte der nationalsozialistischen Konzentrationslager* (Munich: C. H. Beck, 2005), 340. Potthast, meanwhile, had come from Schneewinkeln. In late May 1945 Hedwig Potthast and children were living with Eleonore Pohl at Brünings-Au when interrogated by US Seventh Army interrogators, likely Walter M. Baum. Landsberg record files for Oswald Pohl, RG 549 Records of Headquarters, US Army Europe (USAREUR), Records Related to Executee Case Files, 1945–1958 (290/59/30/2), Box 10. The area was just twenty-five miles south of Rottach Egern.

55. Dr. Guennel, interview by author, November 3, 2009, and followup letter to author on November 10. Guennel remembered Potthast being "attractive, but nervous and a live wire." The confiscated letters were in an envelope that was placed before Potthast during the interview, during which she admitted that she could not bring herself to destroy the letters from her former paramour. Guennel indicated the letters were confiscated and placed in Maj. Kubala's safe—standard operating procedure. "What happened to them after that," Guennel indicated, "I have no idea." As the letters now appear to be scattered all over auction houses around the United States, it is not surprising the Kubala (who is deceased) has been implicated in the disappearance of other Nazi-era documents and medals. At the time Guennel took little notice of Hedwig Potthast. "Kubala told me it was Himmler's mistress, but we were interviewing so many people in those weeks, that we were just overwhelmed. . . . She didn't make a big impression and claimed not to know much."

56. "Himmler's Girl Friend Left with Two Little SS Souvenirs," *Stars and Stripes*, September 6, 1945.

57. Hedwig Potthast to Karl Brandt, telegram, June 4, 1938. Helmut Heiber, *Reichsführer!* For weeks before the incident Himmler had been arguing with Dr. Franz Gürtner, the justice minister. "For some two months, you have been telling me that in your view too many people in the concentration camps have been shot while trying to escape. . . . I instructed Eicke to impress on the Death's Head troops who do guard duty, that they should only shoot in the most extreme necessity. The outcome has shocked me! The day before yesterday, I was in camp Buchenwald and was shown the body of a worthy 24 year old SS man whose skull had been smashed by two criminals with shovels. Both the criminals escaped . . . Two further criminals who knew of the break out attempt were shot in flight after the SS man had been killed—in the camp at a distance of 50 to 60 meters.. . . .when the court has pronounced the death sentence on the two, it should not be carried out in the courtyard of the Justice buildings, but in the camp before the assembled 3,000 prisoners—preferably with the rope on the gallows." Himmler to Dr. Gürtner on May 16, 1938. Imperial War Museum, H13/48.

58. Koch, *Geheim Depot Schweiz*, 48–57.

59. Statement from Martin Bormann Jr.: "Berliner Begegnungen," ARD, January 24, 2000. Also, Gitta Sereny, *Albert Speer: His Battle with Truth* (New York: Vintage Press, 1995), 309–310. Although many today question the story of the human furniture, according to Sereny, his siblings did not doubt Martin Bormann Jr.'s story. Stephan and Norbert Lebert, *My Father's Keeper* (Boston: Little, Brown and Co., 2001), 106–121 (although Lebert incorrectly located the Potthast home in Tegernsee). Also, Dan Bar-On, *Legacy of Silence* (Cambridge, MA: Harvard University Press, 1989), 179–199. Finally, at the author's behest, Martin Bormann Jr. confirmed his story in a telephone interview with the author on February 17, 2006. He verified the account with additional details and correction, professing surprise there was any doubt about his story.

60. "Bankier des Holocaust: Die geheime Ein-Mann Filiale der Deutschen Bank in Zürich," Gian Trepp, *Die Zeit*, No. 25, 1998. In July 1944 Hungarian Jew August Wild transferred his fortune to the SS Economics and Main Office in order to escape the gas chamber. For a fat fee, Kurzmeyer orchestrated the transfer from the Schweizerische Kreditanstalt in Zurich. Regardless of the arrangement, August Wild was subsequently shot on orders of Oswald Pohl in order to cover up the transaction.

61. "Report of Charlotte van Berckel about people with whom Himmler regularly contracted," Netherlands Military Mission to the Allied Control Council in Germany, 28.2.1946, NA RG 319, Investigative Repository Records (IRR), Himmler files, XE-00632.

62. "Pohl, SS Chief of Staff, Captured While Toiling as a Farm Laborer," *New York Times*, May 29, 1946. When British operatives approached Pohl tilling a garden, he was attired in a greasy laborer's suit, claiming his name was Ludwig Gniss (the name of the actual father of his adopted daughter, Heilweg!). Dorothee Schmitz-Köster, *Kind L 364: Eine Lebensborn Familiengeschichte* (Berlin: Rowohlt, 2007), 57–66. Challenging that his real name was Pohl, the disguised farmhand reached in his vest pocket to find two vials of cyanide. Only a short scuffle prevented his suicide. "Report of Capt. Harry Schweiger," dated June 20, 1946, WO 32 /12202, PRO, Kew, UK. "Secret Special Interrogation Report on SS Ogruf. SS Oswald Pohl," CDSIC(WEA) SIR 38, June 4, 1946, NA, RG 65, Records of the Federal Bureau of Investigation, Box 25, FBI Case Files, File 65-57260 (230/86/6/2).

63. Allied investigators were keen on learning whether Himmler's wealth had been transferred out of Germany. "I am interested in that too," Frau Himmler retorted. "You know the woman he lived with. She should be able to give you some information." Margarete Himmler, December 6, 1945, RG-260, OMGUS 3/71-3/5/2, Institut für Zeitgeschichte, Munich.

64. During the time when Eleonore Pohl stayed at the Brünings-Au estate in Halfing she was supported by monies and gifts from Das Kameradenwerk-Hilfswerk, with frequent contact from Hans Ulrich Rudel: Pohl Executee File, records of letters received, National Archives, RG-238, "Records of War Criminal Prison Nr. 1." After Pohl's death in June, Hedwig Potthast wrote Pohl's widow for the last time the following autumn, later telling her that she was ending their connection completely so she could start a new life for the sake of her children. Schmitz-Köster, *Kind L 364*, 187–199.

65. Koch, *Himmlers Graue Eminenz*, 194.

66. Heilweg Weger, interview by author, July 12, 2012.

67. Hedwig maintained her distance from the rest of the entire Potthast family after the war, only being seen by her sister's son at their father's funeral (Potthast, interview, March 12, 2010). Frau Potthast died on September 22, 1994, at the age of eighty-two of Alzheimer's. Son, Helge, and daughter, Nanette Dorothea (who became a doctor), were still living as of 2012.

68. RG 549, Peiper Parole Files, Box 94, *op. cit.*, letter of Dr. Günther Zimmermann, November 5, 1953.

69. Perhaps more importantly Willi Bittrich had led the SS Cavalry Division for a time in 1943, a formation that was implicated in numerous war crimes in the war.

70. Peiper to Lehmann, May 18, 1954, Klink Papers, BA-MA.

71. Letter Theodor Knapp to Dr. Emil Lersch, December 6, 1956, BA-K, Parole Akte Peiper, B305/762–763.

72. US parole officer, Deforest A. Barton, reviewed Peiper's parole application with a favorable, if ironic, outlook. "As a former tank officer, the applicant has considerable mechanical training which he hopes to utilize with the firm of Porsche." "Re-submission for 2nd Parole Application-Joachim Peiper," August 1, 1956, NA RG 549, Parole Files.

73. T. Knapp to D. A. Barton, July 24 and November 1, 1956, RG 549, Parole Records, *op. cit.* "His future life will, in any case, be difficult."

74. Helmut Seidenglanz, the divisional pharmacist of the Leibstandarte, visited Peiper at Landsberg on the following dates: January 3, 1953 (with SS Ustuf. Wilhelm Blume of *12.SS Pz Div*), December 20, 1954 (with Hans Sender), and on December 19, 1955. Seidenglanz played an important role during the investigation of the execution of the Leibstandarte recruits in Belgium in May 1944. RG 549, "Records Related to Parolees, Joachim Peiper," Box 94 (290/59/30-31/2-1). The BDC file of Leibstandarte jurist Christian Jochum (A3343-SSO-139A) made no mention of the incident, although it did show that he had been with the Totenkopf before coming to the Leibstandarte.

75. The article, "Die Mörder sind immer noch unter uns," appeared in the *Neue Illustrierte* in December 1955. Peiper was interrogated at Landsberg on July 30, 1956, about the shootings of the young SS recruits in Belgium. Staatsanwaltschaft Flensburg 2 Js 437/56 AR 491/66. Now on file at Bundesarchiv Ludwigsburg 124 AR 491/1966.

76. Letter Oberstaatsanwalt to Dr. Emil Lersch, November 7, 1956, BA-K, Parole Akte Peiper, B305/762–763.

77. Like Peiper, Preuss was stonewalled in years of applications for clemency. In 1955 Preuss wrote to Wilhelm Mohnke, also a native of Hamburg, after the former head of the Leibstandarte had been released by the Russians. Upon release, Preuss began office work with Bran & Luebbe in Hamburg but found it unsuitable. From 1957 to 1958 he unsuccessfully petitioned his parole board to allow him to attempt to enter the new *Bundeswehr* as a 1st Lt. or Captain. NA, RG549 Records of Headquarters, US Army Europe, Records Related to Parolee Case Files, 1945–1958, Box 98 and 99.

78. Letter Theodor Knapp to Dr. Emil Lersch, December 6, 1956, BA-K, Parole Akte Peiper, B305/762–763.

79. "HQ US Army, Europe, Secret, Staff Message Control: From USAREAUR to DA FOR JAGW, CINFO, TPMG," NA RG 549, *op. cit.*, December 21, 1956. The actual army order for Peiper's parole had come on December 19, 1956. "Cases Tried, Miscellaneous Orders of Parole," RG 549, Box 507, USAREUR Records.

80. Although sentenced to death, Jochen Peiper had been in prison for just over eleven years. "We should have hung him," Ellis later said. "The courts sentenced him to hang and his troops did things that he should have been accountable for," Ellis Oral History, *op. cit.*, 44. But not all of the prosecution saw it that way. Ralph Shumacker, Ellis's right hand man told the author: "Today, fifty years later, I am pleased that the men we sentenced to death were not killed and had their sentences commuted. . . . At the time, I had no sympathy for their situation, but time changes things and I feel differently about it today." Ralph Shumacker, interview by author, November 2, 1996.

Chapter Sixteen

1. Archiv des Erzbistums München und Freising, Munich, NL Morgenschweis, File 32.

2. Wieselmann, interview, May 13, 1999. "Jochen Peiper became a close friend of my father, Heinz-Ulrich Wieselmann. . . . Peiper always told a story of his release." The two men who approached Peiper were likely Capt. Wilson Morris and 1st Lt. William J. Miller, who

then witnessed his parole release before Maj. Stubbs. Peiper was met by Helmut Meng and Deforest Barton and then took the train to Stuttgart to meet his landlord, Mr. Hartmann. Story as related by Peiper, interview by Stutterecker, February 28, 2009.

3. "Morning Report 22 December 1956, War Criminal Prison Nr. 1," NA RG 549, "Records Relating to War Criminal Prison No. 1," 290/59/18/1-2. Box 2. Also, "Control Visit Report-December 22, 23 and 24, 1956," American Embassy in Germany, Bad Godesberg, January 15, 1958 (same location). Contrary to the postwar myth, Peiper was not the last of the Malmédy men freed. That distinction went to Hubert Huber, who confessed to brutally executing an American prisoner at the Baugnez crossroads in an act witnessed by several others. Huber was released on January 22, 1957, Landsberg, Box 2

4. "Control Visit Report: 22 December 1956," Helmut Meng, Records of Office of the US Parole Officer, Bad Godesberg, RG 549, Parole Files. Meng was the overall office head for the parole officers, which included Dr. Knapp who was directly charged with supervising Peiper.

5. All quotes in this section from H. Peiper, interviews, May 5, 1999, and May 21, 1999.

6. Elke Peiper to Whiting, in *Jochen Peiper*, 171.

7. Peiper visited his family on January 5 for three hours and again on January 11, when he stayed in Sinzheim for the weekend, RG 549, Peiper Parole files.

8. "Monthly Report of the Parolee," January 16, 1957, NA RG 338, *op. cit.*, Box 94, For Peiper's claim of first job washing cars for Porsche, H. Peiper, interview. It was an oft repeated story at home, even if likely exaggerated.

9. "Malmédy Figure Freed," *New York Times*, December 23, 1956. Also, "Malmédy Col Wins Release" and "Kefauver Irate at Freeing of Malmédy Colonel," *Stars and Stripes*, December 23 and 24, 1956. Kefauver, the Democratic vice presidential candidate in 1956, wrote Secretary of State John Foster Dulles, complaining that the parole of Peiper "would destroy any hope we might have that the proper punishment of war criminals would deter similar atrocities in the future."

10. "Peiper's Release Assailed by Clark," *Stars and Stripes*, January 1, 1957. The members of the mixed boards included Spencer Phenix of the United States, Sir Edward Jackson of Great Britain, Henri Eschback of France and Gottfried Kuhnt, Emil Lersch, and Helmuth von Weber of West Germany.

11. "Victim wants Malmédy Col kept in Jail," *United Press*, January 3, 1956.

12. "Jochen Peiper dankt, and Jochen Peiper endlich Frei!" *Der Freiwillige*, January 1957.

13. Ferry Porsche and Günther Molter, *Ferry Porsche: Autos sind Mein Leben* (Stuttgart: Motorbuch Verlag, 1994), 124–125.

14. BDC file for Ferdinand Porsche (A3343-SSO-389A) born September 19, 1909, in Vienna and SS member No. 346167 and made SS officer (Untersturmführer) on August 1, 1941.

15. Peiper received DM6,000 when he was released from Landsberg, a fact that was decried by the Deutsche Gewerkschaftsbund (German Federation of Trades Unions) in its 1958 newsletter *Feinde der Demokratie* (Enemies of Democracy) 7, no. 9 (1958), 9A and 9B.

16. Other Waffen SS contemporaries of Peiper's time could not have agreed more. While in captivity Kurt Meyer told those around him there would be a big war between Russia and the West within five years, with Germany likely falling victim. HIAG, "Sonderbeilage zum Informationsbrief Nr. 20 vom 20. Dez.1958," Sammlung Vorpersal, BA-MA, N756/413.

17. John Dornberg, *Schizophrenic Germany* (New York: Macmillan, 1961), 121. In a debate before the Bundestag on October 23, 1952, Adenauer admitted that 66 percent of his diplomats in higher positions were former Nazis.

18. For an interesting discussion of this question, see David J. Bercuson, "War and War Crime: A Historian's Perspective," Center for Military and Strategic Studies, University of Calgary, 2001.

19. Dornberg, *Schizophrenic Germany*, 113. Meyer was speaking of SS Sturmbannführer Adolf Diekmann, who had become scapegoat for the atrocity at Oradour-sur-Glane. He

had been killed by artillery fire shortly after the incident. "He was scheduled to go before a court-martial," Meyer claimed, "but he died a hero's death before he could be tried."

20. "Deutschland, Deutschland über alles" was not a Nazi creation but rather was introduced in 1922 by the social-democratic president with words by German poet Hoffmann von Fallersleben and set to a melody composed by Joseph Haydn in 1797 in honor of the Austrian Emperor Franz Joseph. So popular was the anthem that the Germans did not dare abolish it but instead added their own creation in 1933, the so-called Horst Wessel Lied, so that at all official functions during the Hitler years there were two anthems to be played.

21. Kurt Meyer, *Grenadiers*, 392. However, when asked during his captivity about his knowledge of the concentration camps, Meyer said he knew nothing about them. He had been too busy fighting at the front. MacDonald, *Trial of Kurt Meyer*, 79.

22. H. Peiper, interview, May 19, 1999. It must be noted that Peiper repeated this story to everyone around him and the tale took on a life of its own. See letter of Benno Müller to Willis Everett (Müller to Everett, September 10, 1959, Everett Papers) and Wieselmann, interview, for other instances.

23. Peiper was to earn DM477 when he began to work for Porsche in 1957. RG 549, "Records Relating to Parolees 1945–1948, Joachim Peiper," Box 94, 290/59/30/2-1. Letter of Dr. Ferdinand Porsche dated October 24, 1955.

24. Elke Maierl to author through anonymous source, May 2001.

25. H. Peiper, interview, May 5, 1997.

26. Westemeier, *Himmlers Krieger*, 533.

27. "Steeple chase for money." J. Peiper, interview by Whiting, as cited in Whiting, *Massacre at Malmédy*, 240.

28. Wieselmann, interview, May 13, 1999.

29. Müller, interview, May 18–19, 1999. "The relationship with the children was difficult. The children learned what had happened to their father after the war. The propaganda against the Nazis turned everything around."

30. Peiper on January 30, 1960. As cited in Agte, *Jochen Peiper*, 583. Also, H. Peiper, interview.

31. On August 5, 1960, Jochen's father, Woldemar, passed away.

32. Peiper to Toland, December 1, 1957, LOC, Toland Papers, general correspondence, Box 108. Toland would go on to write the best-seller *Battle: The Story of the Bulge* (New York: Random House, 1959), in which he would lean heavily on an interview with Hal D. McCown.

33. See numerous pieces or correspondence showing Skorzeny's cover name (O.S. = Otto Skorzeny) for correspondence going all over the world: Österreichisches Staatsarchiv, Vienna, Nachlass Otto Skorzeny, B 2158. Relative to the Skorzeny archives in Vienna, it must be said that the collection has limited value to what might otherwise have been a fantastic treasure to modern-day researchers of covert espionage operations after the war. When Skorzeny's wife, Ilse, died in 2002, only five boxes of material remained. Within this limited archive there is no correspondence with SS men, John Toland, or others that are known to exist in multitude from examination of *their* respective *Nachlässe*. Within the Skorzeny collection all such material has been purposefully removed or destroyed, and the remainder largely consists of legal and financial documents. There are some notable exceptions to the document destruction, but the sensitive letters and correspondence—which must have been truly massive—are conspicuous by their absence. Regardless, the author is appreciative to Skorzeny's daughter, Dr. Waltraut Riess, for providing access to the material.

34. Separating truth from myth is particularly difficult for Otto Skorzeny's postwar activities as the subject actively encouraged obfuscation. For a well-researched appraisal see Martin A. Lee, *The Beast Reawakens* (Boston: Little Brown, 1997). Also, Stuart Christie, "Otto Skorzeny and the 'Circle of Friends'," in *General Franco Made Me a Terrorist* (London: Christie Books,

2003), 211–212; Richard Breitman, Norman J. W. Goda, Timothy Naftali, and Robert Wolfe, *U.S. Intelligence and the Nazis* (Cambridge: Cambridge University Press, 2004), 417.

35. In February 1973 Skorzeny also met American writer Glenn Infield for an interview, during which he made clear his disdain for Albert Speer, whom he, like Peiper, viewed as a turncoat. Glenn B. Infield, *Skorzeny: Hitler's Commando* (New York: Military Heritage Press, 1981), 3–5.

36. For Toland's tempered admiration of Skorzeny, discussion with his daughter Tamiko on September 17, 1997. Skorzeny quoted soon after his escape. "A Token from Der Fuehrer," *Time*, August 9, 1948. Skorzeny had come to Spain in November 1950 but took pains ten years later in an intercepted letter dated November 15, 1960, to disassociate himself from the intrigue that conveyed war criminal Adolf Eichmann to Argentina in 1948. However, the same recently declassified CIA file shows that Skorzeny was at the same time working with the Egyptian Intelligence Service and, later in 1962, attempted to obtain legal help to defend Eichmann. See NA, RG-263, Records of the Central Intelligence Agency, Adolf Eichmann Name Files, Directorate of Operations, Vol. 2, "Skorzeny, Otto," Documents 116 and 117. Also, Vol. 3, "Efforts on Behalf of Eichmann by Otto Skorzeny," Letter recommending the services of Dr. Robert Jacovella, February 23, 1962, Document 77. In interview with Martin Lee, Ilse Skorzeny insisted that her husband's training of Egyptian forces in 1953 was with the sponsorship of the Reinhard Gehlen intelligence organization, which was working in turn for the CIA. In fact, declassified documents reveal that Skorzeny was a *person-nongrata* with the German intellligence services and never worked for them.

37. Skorzeny to *Der Freiwillige* in Osnabruck, letter, Madrid, October 11, 1957, BA-MA, HIAG Archives, B-438 v/394. "I have spoken for a day to the American author, John Toland. He has the intention to write a book about the Ardennes Offensive. In our sense, it will be a correct book. I was able to by researching the different explanations that he has, he absolutely has good expectations intention for justice for both sides. I urgently need the address of Ziemssen and Jochen Peiper and also Panzer Meyer."

38. Skorzeny to HIAG, October 11, 1957, BA-MA, RS 7/ v. 394.

39. Skorzeny to Toland, February 20, 1959, LOC, Toland Papers, General Correspondence arranged alphabetically, Box 108.

40. Peiper to Toland, February 22 and April 1959, LOC, Toland Papers, General Correspondence: 'P', Box 108.

41. Toland to Everett, February 18, 1958, Everett Papers.

42. Freda Utley to Everett, November 8, 1954. Utley, the Nazi sympathetic right-wing social commentator who had written essays herself about Malmédy, implored Everett to write a book on his experiences in defending Peiper and the others she concluded were victimized innocents. Freda Utley Papers, Hoover Institution, Stanford University, Palo Alto, Box 5.

43. Everett to Toland, February 17, 1958, Everett Papers.

44. Toland to Everett, March 3, 1958.

45. Peiper to Toland, April 5, 1959. Library of Congress, Toland Papers, Box 108.

46. Hilfsgemeinschaft auf Gegenseitigkeit der Soldaten der ehemaligen Waffen SS (HIAG)—Landesverband Baden-Württemberg e.V., July 1, 1958, BA-MA, RS7, v. 588.

47. Evi Butz Gurney to author, April 3, 2006. Peiper's office had been next to hers at Porsche.

48. Benno Müller, born January 24, 1912, had been a physician with the 5th SS Division "Wiking." Müller's BDC file (NA, RG-242, A3343-SSO-327A. Müller became an NSDAP member in May 1, 1937. His promotion on the division list to SS Obersturmführer of February 16, 1942 Beförderungen an die SS-Division "Wiking"shows the name of infamous Dr. Josef Mengele just above that of Dr. Müller on the division. Mengele had fought with the division for two years as a standard medic, being awarded the Iron Cross for his effort in saving two men wounded severely in combat. Wounded himself, Mengele went on to become

the notorious doctor at Auschwitz who presided over perverse medical experiments involving genetically similar twins in hopes of finding methods to create a race of blue-eyed Aryans that might realize dreams of Himmler's racial pseudo-science. Mengele, although in hiding in South America, remained proud of combat service with Wiking. After his terrible career at Auschwitz became widely known, SS veterans toiled to disassociate his name from the rolls of their service. Yet with Müller and Mengele both being doctors in the division, the two men would have known each other at least informally. Peiper and Müller met after the war as the latter was a photographer for the racing circuit with Uli Wieselmann. At the very least, with the Israeli capture of Adolf Eichmann in 1960 and the worldwide manhunt for Mengele by the Bonn government after 1962, it would be surprising if these topics were not ardently discussed by Peiper and Müller. Both men embraced the old Nazi racial ideas. Indeed, the author's interview with Müller's second wife, Uta, on May 18, 1999, was exceedingly strained, as she inquired about the author's racial heritage, seemingly worried by brown eyes or any skin with nonfair pigment.

49. See Benno Müller, *Beim Pferderennen* (Karlesruhe: G. Braun Buchverlag, 1999). An indication of the political sympathies of Müller is contained in the photographs of the book itself where carefully crafted images of the beautiful people at the horse races are contrasted with snapshots of obese and poorly clothed German immigrants.

50. Müller to Everett, September 10, 1959, Everett Papers.

51. Everett to Müller, October 19, 1959, Everett Papers.

52. Müller to Everett, October 25, 1959, Everett Papers.

53. For a very detailed account of the Peiper-Porsche affair using original sources: Westemeier, *Himmlers Krieger*, 533–536.

54. In fact, Huschke von Hanstein had become a member of the Allgemeine SS and before the war was chosen by Himmler himself as the designated SS race driver in 1938. During the war Germany competed in the grueling endurance automotive race in Northern Italy, the Mille Miglia (Thousand Miles) to show that, in spite of the war, life was going on as usual. His assistant from 1960 to 1964 at the company told the author she knew nothing of the intrigue between von Hanstein and the former SS colonel. "I was only vaguely aware of his past and I never met anybody at Porsche at that time who talked about it. . . . No one talked about the past. We talked about racing." Evi Gurney to author, April 2, 2006.

55. William Sholar to Everett, November 2, 1959, Everett Papers.

56. William Sholar to Willis Everett, November 2, 1959; also, Everett to Peiper, November 24, 1959, Everett Papers. For Sholar and Ferry Porsche at the 1960 gathering: "History of the Porsche Club of America," Porsche Club of America.

57. Everett to Peiper, November 24, 1959, Everett Papers.

58. Peiper to Everett, December 13, 1959, Everett Papers.

59. Everett to Peiper, December 22, 1959. Everett indicated that he had never received a letter from Peiper immediately after his release, a fact that seemed to trouble him.

60. Everett to Peiper, December 22, 1959, Everett Papers.

61. See James J. Weingartner, "Unconventional Allies: Colonel Willis Everett and SS Obersturmbannführer Joachim Peiper," *The Historian* 60, no. 1 (Fall 1999).

62. Everett to Peiper, February 5, 1960, Everett Papers.

63. Everett to Peiper, November 24, 1959, Everett Papers.

64. Peiper to Everett, February 6, 1951, Everett Papers.

65. Peiper to Mary Everett, December 1975, Everett Papers. In the letter Peiper outlined a plan to write his own book about Malmédy and requested papers, photographs, and documents.

66. "Meine Begegnungen mit Joachim Peiper [My Encounters with Joachim Peiper]," unpublished manuscript by Fritz Kosmehl provided to the author; also *Fritz Kosmehl Selbstbiographie*,(Oldenburg: self-published biography) 902. Kosmehl lost his eyesight from severe

wounds he received on August 20, 1944, while in the command tank of Herbert Kuhlmann of the 1st Panzer Battalion in the Falaise Pocket. Kuhlmann, who was commanding 1st SS Panzer Regiment due to Peiper's absence, pulled Kosmehl from his burning tank. Their radio operator, Helmut Jahn, remained in contact with Peiper for years, although suffering severe illness eventually that led him to suicide on March 26, 1976. Otto Becker and Horst Schumann, the other members of the crew, also remained in periodic contact.

67. Fritz Kosmehl, interview by author, December 17, 2004.

68. Kosmehl, "Meine Begegnungen mit Joachim Peiper": "he never liked 'chummy' situations. Despite that, he was still very relaxed amongst us."

69. A sum of 2000 deutsche marks a month in 1960 would be approximately US$3,700 in 2014—big money in post war Germany. For background on the Porsche trial: Landesarchiv Baden-Württemberg, Staatsarchiv Ludwigsburg (StAL) FL 700/13II, Az: 1 Ca 411961, Arbeitsgericht Stuttgart Joachim Peiper gegen Firma Porsche KG.

70. See George Arnaud, interview by M. Blank of Porsche Automotive, *L'Affaire Peiper*, Antenne 2, January 1979. "Personalien: Jochen Peiper," *Der Spiegel*, June 7, 1961. Blank was the union representative with Porsche at the time. It is noteworthy than Erich Kempka, Hitler's personal driver, was also employed by Porsche and, unlike Peiper took essentially the same deal of more money without extra promotion. Kempka, who remained a convinced Nazi after the war, had been close to Porsche during the National Socialist period.

71. Klaus Jelonneck, "Welt der Arbeit," *Deutscher Gewerkschaftsbund*, May 19, 1961; "Der Fall Porsche," *Der Freiwillige*, 1961, originally in *Deutsche Soldatenzeitung*, No. 11.

72. See Ulrich Herbert, *Best: Biographische Studien über Radikalismus, Weltanschauung und Vernunft* (Bonn: J. H. W. Dietz, 1999).

73. Günter Grass, *Katze und Maus* (Darmstadt: Hermann Luchterhand Verlag, 1961). Since the internationally acclaimed publication of *Die Blechtommel* (*The Tin Drum*) in 1959, Grass had been judged by many of his countrymen as a merciless judge and heavy-handed moral authority over postwar Germany. In fact, in calling for Germany's atonement, Grass was concealing his own guilt; he had been a member of the Waffen SS at the end of the war for the 10th SS Panzer Division, a fact only revealed in 2006. See Günter Grass, *Peeling the Onion* (New York: Harcourt, 2007).

74. Hans Stutterecker, interview by author, February 28, 2009. (Schomstein: Chimney) Stutterecker had occasion to visit the Peiper family several times where he overheard arguments between the father and son. This friction was also observed by another anonymous witness.

Chapter Seventeen

1. In fact, statistical surveys by Dr. F. W. William of Princeton University in 1946, found that the majority of the German public (53 percent) approved of Hitler's ideas but concluded that he carried them out badly. However, the same survey found that 85 percent of those surveyed believed that all war criminals on trial at Nuremberg were guilty. "Survey Finds Germans Liked Hitler's Ideas," *Stars and Stripes*, July 1, 1946. Even today, in interviews conducted for this book, the author found some of the wartime generation expressing this view: Hitler was right in his ideas, but too extreme.

2. H. Peiper, interview. "It was not that he was opposed to these meetings, he just did not prefer that. He was more interested in his life after the war." Although Peiper was not a formal member of HIAG, he maintained very close contact with a number of members of the organization including Rudolf Lehmann, who would serve as the chonicler for the 1st SS Panzer Division. "Peiper was not officially within the HIAG, but he was very active in its 'underground.'" Stutterecker, interview, February 28, 2009. This perception is keenly verified by examination of Peiper's communication with the HIAG during the 1960s seeking to expunge

the reputation of the Waffen SS. For example see, Peiper to Kurt "Panzer" Meyer, November 28, 1959, and response; also, Peiper to Karl Cerff, March 8, 1969, and June 17, 1969, BA-MA, B-438, Records of the HIAG, Folder 320.

3. "For the short trip Harzer drove with me to Regensburg for the meeting of the Knight Cross Holders. I had hoped to meet you there, but you didn't show up." Peiper to Kurt Meyer, November 28, 1959, BA-MA, RS 7/v 282.

4. After the war Lammerding moved back to the British zone in Düsseldorf to resume his profession as a civil engineer, despite that a 1951 French tribunal in Bordeaux sentenced him to death in absentia for his complicity of the hangings at Tulle. Predictably, Lammerding declined to attend the proceedings and the British refused to hand him over. Some said it was because the French were unreliable in witch hunts, but others maintained he was protected from extradition due to his help to British intelligence on knowledge of Soviet fighting tactics. Regardless, a German court found Lammerding guilty of war crimes, and he later served a prison sentence. Subsequently he was automatically immune to extradition under the Bonn constitution. Yet Lammerding continued to blame Tulle and Oradour on subordinates Aurel Kowatsch and Adolf Diekmann, both conveniently deceased. "It was necessary to provoke terror among the *macquisards* to deprive them support of the civilian population," he told a colleague. "The remedial method was cruel, but this was war. . . . I assume that it is useless to recall that the Geneva Convention formally forbids the actions of frac-tireurs, and warns all will be shot." Max Hastings, *Das Reich: The March of the Second SS Panzer Division Through France* (New York: Henry Holt and Company, 1982), 224. In the meantime the French threatened to take matters into their own hands to seize him in a commando raid as the Israelis had Adolf Eichmann. Before any of this developed, Eicke's old protege died of cancer in 1971. "The Lammerding Affair," *Time*, January 11, 1971.

5. For a photo of Peiper at the *Ordensgemeinschaft der Ritterkreuzträger* dinner: see photo insert.

6. Kurt Meyer, *Grenadiere* (Munich: Schild Verlag, 1957).

7. For Otto Günsche's flaming disposal of Hitler's and Eva Braun's bodies just outside the bombed out Reich's Chancellery: Toland, *Hitler*, 888–890.

8. Karl Wolff was convicted on September 30, 1964, by a West German court in Munich to fifteen years imprisonment for the mass murders of Jews at Vinnitza and sending off some three hundred thousand Jews to their deaths at Treblinka. *New York Times*, October 1, 1964, 1.

9. In 1949 Karl Wolff and Hedwig Potthast cooperated with German journalist Melitta Wiedemann, attempting to create a more "appropriate" biography of Heinrich Himmler, a collaboration that ultimately backfired. See Katrin Himmler, *The Himmler Brothers* (New York: Macmillan, 2007), 276–277.

10. *Stern* journalist Gerd Heidemann had extensive interviews with Karl Wolff before his disastrous association with the forged Hitler diaries. In those conversations Wolff indicated that he did not look favorably upon Peiper. The feeling seems to have been mutual. Letter Heidemann to author, March 24, 2007. Heidemann, interview, April 20, 2009.

11. Prosecutor: "Did you have any doubt that Aktion Reinhard happened?" Wolff: "No, I don't doubt these facts." Prosecutor: "We do know exactly by documents what happened to the Jews near Lublin under Globoknik. So we know from your previous statements that Himmler must have nakedly lied to you if what you say is true. What do you say to this?" Wolff: "Yes, for sure Himmler did lie to me at that time. Himmler knew me from nine years of close cooperation that he knew that I would have refused to help with this horrible Jew annihilation plan . . . For sure he would have driven me into suicide if he told me." Wolff testimony, "Fortsetzung der Vernehmung am 2. Februar 1962," Ermittlungssache gegen Karl Wolff," BA-Ludwigsburg, 8 AR-Z 203-59.

12. Lang, *Top Nazi*. 189–190. Wolff was released from prison due to health reasons in August 1969, retiring to Prien on the Chiemsee. There, he continued to grant interviews and

pumping up his vain stature within the Third Reich. To the public, he presented himself as the savior of Pope Pius XII! Unabashedly unreconstructed—"a Zeitgeist of the Nazi era"—Wolff died in a Rosenheim hospital in 1984.

13. Lang, *Top Nazi.*, 346. Jochen von Lang, the *Stern* journalist, was actually Joachim Piechocki, an SS man in the service of Joseph Goebbels who had made the famous final broadcast from Berlin announcing that Hitler "had fallen in battle."

14. "Staatsannswaltschaft bei dem Landgericht München II: Ermittlungssache gegen Karl Wolff," BA-Ludwigsburg, 8 AR-Z 203-59, 10a Js 39/60, January 26, 1962, Peiper was mentioned twice during the trial by Wolff himself (February 8, 1962) and once by Himmler's driver, Franz Lucas, on November 8, 1962. According to the German press both Lucas and Grothmann made "sorry figures by all they could not remember."

15. "Himmler war Hitler sklavisch ergeben," *Stuttgarter Nachrichten*, August 8, 1964. To believe Grothmann's alibis required fantastic naivete of those in the Wolff trial: "I believed during the war that the Final Solution was only the Madagascar plan or the resettlement of Jews to the East. I only learned what is known about it today after the war." "Das Landgericht Untersuchungsrichter II: Ermittlungssache gegen Karl Wolff," BA-Ludwidgsburg, 8 AR-Z 203-59, 4a Js 586/56, Frankfurt am Main, January 2, 1961, Protokoll C.

16. "Bach Zelewski belastet Wolff," *Frankfurter Rundschau*, July 25, 1964.

17. After the war, in the 1960s, Himmler's bodyguard, Kiermaier, and office security director, Sepp Tiefenbacher, remained close in the Gmund am Tegernsee community. That Peiper remained in touch with each is made clear from his prison correspondence prior to release. Also, NA, RG-319, Investigative Repository Reports, Paul Baumert, Box 660, File XE 159216. Baumert and family lived at Wiesseerstr. 72 Gmund/Tegernsee.

18. See Tiefenbacher's SS officer file (BDC A3343-SSO-183B) and NA, RG-263, Records of the Central Intelligence Agency, CIA Names Files Released under the Nazi War Crimes Disclosure Act: Josef Tiefenbacher, Box 128. Tiefenbacher became acquainted with Haj Amin al-Musayni, the Grand Mufti of Jerusalem, when the latter was a refugee in Germany during the war, and parlayed his contact into a two-year assignment with Egyptian military officials from 1951–1953.

19. Walter Harzer to Ernst Klink, May 13, 1963, BA-MA, Klink Papers.

20. Although Ernst Klink pretended to be a politically neutral historian at the MGFA in Freiburg, he was often at odds with others there, particularly in matters concerning the Waffen SS. The real bias became evident to the author in reviewing his personal papers. There was no question about the sympathies of Klink's mother, Frau Gertrud Scholtz-Klink, whom had been the chief of all Nazi women's organizations. Hiding after the war, Scholtz-Klink was arrested in Tübingen in the winter of 1948, saying that she had no idea whether Adolf Hitler was still alive but that "as long as he lives in the hearts of his followers, he cannot die." "Princess Indicted for Helping Nazis," Kathleen McLaughlin, *New York Times*, March 4, 1948. She remained unreformed. See Scholtz-Klink, interview by Claudia Koonz, *Mothers of the Fatherland* (New York: St. Martin's Press, 1987).

21. See letter Trudi Aschenauer to Hubert Meyer, January 27, 1985. In the letter Frau Aschenauer implies that she counts on the help of Dr. Klink to help "screen them"—*erst sichten*—documents and letters in the donations of her husband's papers to the Bundesarchiv in Freiburg. Rudolf Aschenauer was an attorney at the center of the Malmédy investigation. BA-MA, RS/7 v. 480.

22. *Unsere Ehre heisst Treue*, 16. There are multiple sources: For declassified radio transmissions showing executions of "Jews and Bolshevists" by the SS Kav. Brigade: Breitman, *Official Secrets*, 59–62. For Lombard's participation in the Pripet actions, where "10,412 plunders were shot by 8 August 1941": NA: T-175, Roll 129, F 2655958. Like Lombard, Göhler had fought under Hermann Fegelein in SS Kav. Rgt 1 in its unsavory campaigns until October 1943. Göhler had joined Eicke's SS Totenkopf Verbände Oberbayern in April 1937; see

Göhler's BDC file: NA, BDC, Roll A3343-SSO-18A. Johannes Göhler was also involved in grand intrigue over Hitler's final possessions in the closing days of the war. This occurred near Zell am See (Schloss Fischorn) in a convoluted affair that has never been satisfactorily resolved. NA: RG-319, IRR, "Apprehension and Interrogation of Hauptsturmführer Franz Konrad," August 26, 1945, Box 31A. Also, "Interrogation of Johannes Göhler," document August 6, 1945, John Toland Collection, FDR Library, Box 49. "On 1 May 1945, Göhler was at the Berghof at Berchtesgaden, and encountered Gretl Braun Fegelein with a friend, one Frau Schneider who said she would like him to take charge of the safe-keeping of a large chest of letters which. . . . between her sister Eva Braun and Hitler . . . When Göhler was in Fischorn on 8 May, he said Haufler told him that the contents of the chest had been burned." Yet it appears that the burned documents were, in fact, a truckload of Himmler's secret documents which obedient secretary Erika Lorenz had dutifully cast into a blast furnace. The author attempted on several occasions to interview Göhler, who proved evasive. However, he was able to review and use some of Göhler's letters written to his wife that exist within the Irving Collection: Microform, Hitler's War, Reel 4, Section 15. Until the end of his life Göhler was a firebrand for revisionists, denying the gassing of the Jews and the killings done by the SS cavalry division and denigrating any who questioned Hitler's leadership.

23. Hausser defended himself against a flurry of accusations at Nuremberg, including several lodged at Peiper's troop. NMT, Vol. 20, August 6, 1946. Q: Did you hear the speech of Himmler to his three Waffen SS divisions in spring 1943 near Kharkov?" Hausser agreed that he had. Said Himmler: "We will never let that excellent weapon fade, the dread and terrible reputation which preceded us in the battle for Kharkov, but will constantly add new meaning to it." The prosecutor then asked if Hausser knew the 2. SS Panzergrenadier Regiment had burned down the villages of Staroverovka, Stanitchnoye, and Jefremowka. Hausser said no, complaining that "the prosecution chains the Waffen SS to the fate of Heinrich Himmler and a small circle of criminals around him." Ironically, the prosecution had no clear idea that the head of the 2nd SS Panzergrenadier Regiment that burned down the named villages was then Teddi Wisch and his subordinate, Jochen Peiper, in charge of the SPW armed 3rd Battalion.

24. Müller, interview.

25. Paul Hausser and Jochen Peiper, trans., *Wenn alle Brüder schweigen* (Osnabrück: Bundesverband der Soldaten der ehemaligen Waffen-SS e.V, Munin-Verlag, 1973). The book was later published in English in 1977 in which Hubert Meyer, Walter Harzer and Richard Schulze-Kossens had a press conference for the book in England in which David Irving helped defend the old SS men. This led to big trouble in the UK, with Meyer being thrown out of the country. Meyer to Günsche, January 12, 1984, BA-MA, RS7, v. 485. The following year, in an editorial to *Der Spiegel*, Schulze-Kossens claimed the the SS Junkerschule were apolitical. Journalist Heinz Höhne wrote back, "And we should believe you who hasn't the slightest sensibility for the war crimes of the Third Reich while arranging annual reunions of SS veterans forty years after the war? . . . I'm sorry to have to tell you that you are an example of the unwilling people in your circles to come to terms with your past in a critical way. . . . Your book about the Junkerschulen is the best proof." Höhne to Schulze-Kossens, June 11, 1985, BA-MA, RS7, v. 488.

26. Wilhelm Friedrich Mayr was an old SS member before 1933 and a leader on the 1. SS Motor Standarte. In 1935 Himmler forbade him to have further children due to his Danish wife's partial Jewish ancestry. Himmler to Mayr, September 13, 1939. T-175, Roll 23, Extensive letter file in Folder 784. Later, by 1935, Mayr was assigned to Himmler's personal staff. NA, RG-242, BDC File for Wilhelm Mayr, A3343-SSO-304A.

27. After 1929 the ownership of the paper was split between Mayr and M. Müller & Sohn and the Völkischer Beobachter out of Munich. After that time Mayr became the printer of the newspaper and gave up all editorial responsibilities.

28. See the Denazification file for Wilhelm Friedrich Mayr, Staatsarchiv München, SpKa Karton: Mayr, Wilhelm Friedrich. By 1942 Mayr was earning more than 350,000 Reichsmarks annually from his publishing business, with a net worth of more than 30 million RM at the end of the war.

29. Astrid Nathan and Charlotte Zimmermann, interview by author, Tegernsee, August 17, 2003.

30. Permission for the visit to see the Mayrs in early 1957 is given in Peiper's parole file at the National Archives, *op. cit.*

31. Brigitte B., Miesbach, interview with author, June 19, 2004. "He was an intellectual Prussian, not much humor and serious." Sigrid Mayr née Magnussen was of North German and Danish ancestry, her great grandfather being a famous painter. Sigrid had been one-quarter Jewish, although marrying an important SS man, SS-Obersturmführer Wilhelm Friedrich Mayr in 1933. Even though at an advanced age in 2004, Sigrid Mayr remained upright, attractive, and proud, continuing an impressive presence in Miesbacher scene and society. The author was taken aback, however, when being told that it would be best not to mention that the aging matron was one-quarter Jewish—the clear implication that people in the region saw the revelation of Jewish blood being worse than disclosing a Nazi past! Thanks to Dr. Michael Heim for assistance with the interview.

32. Born on February 11, 1912, Moritz became a member of the National Socialist Party on January 5, 1933 (Partei No. 2,338,625), with his occupation listed as an auto mechanic from Reutlingen. Wartime service confirmed by Deutsche Dienstelle in Berlin in letter to author, September 16, 2002. His WASt file shows Moritz ended his wartime career with the staff of Panzer Battalion Norwegen before becoming a French prisoner of war on May 10, 1945.

33. As head of sales promotion, Peiper designed the logo for Autohaus Max Moritz, which is still in use, and held training seminars for the sales force. Letter from Hinrich Peiper, May 2001.

34. Only months before, Dietrich had been greeted by "thunderous cheers" at a meeting of a thousand Waffen SS veterans in Rendsburg, "Nazi SS Veterans Cheer Former General at Meeting," Philip Shabecoff, *New York Times*, October 25, 1965.

35. Dietrich on Peiper as an "arrogantes Schwein": Whiting recollection of 1970 interview with Albert Frey: Whiting, August 19, 2001. For "his narrow face": Heinrich Springer to Jens Westemeier, March 11, 1993. The tall and strapping Albert Frey had escaped to Argentina after the war, disguised as an American soldier! He was likely worried about what he witnessed with the Einsatzgruppen near Taganrog in 1941 (see Chapter 4). His wife was a ballerina. Albert Frey, *Ich wollte die Freiheit: Erinnerungen des Kommandeurs des 1. Panzergrenadierregiments der ehemaligen Waffen-SS* (Osnabrück, 1990).

36. Peiper interview with John Toland, October 10, 1963, LOC, Toland Papers, The Last Hundred Days, Box 15. Of Dietrich: "As an army commander, he was a good Joe. He behaved like a man of lower rank, but he had a good nose for the situation. He had a much more primitive experience than generals who had never smelled powder. . . . He was more popular with rank and file than staff. He was a soldier's soldier."

37. Karl Heinz Steidle to Kameraden, January 3, 1968, BA-MA, RS 7, v.511.

38. Eventually the HIAG celebrations grew so large and bold that they created enormous problems for the old vets. In 1985 Walter Krüger, the spokesperson (Geschäftsführer) for the 1st SS Panzerkorps, attended one of the largest meetings with Otto Remer, an affair that translated into a big public relations disaster in Nesselwang/Ostallgäu. There was singing of forbidden Nazi songs, inappropriate jewelry, clashes with demonstrators in the streets, and even Waffen SS reenactors who looked astonishingly like the real thing. A *Stern* reporter, Gerhard Kromschröder, disguised in a beard, attended the meeting posing as a war buff. The Hotel Krone, where the Treffen took place, was run by Rolf Buchheister, an SS officer himself. In a cigarette smoke–filled room, Remer and Krüger guffawed over their beers, fawning over young

attractive women who looked eager to be with the old Nazis. In the table conversation the disguised *Stern* reporter dropped bombs. What about the photos of the death camps in Poland? "The photos shown to you showing reported gas chambers are false," Krüger retorted. "And if six million Jews had been killed, as the Jewish propaganda says, they would still be burning." Krüger was the former signals leader and SS Oscharführer of the 3rd Battalion, Leibstandarte, and had fought with Peiper at Kharkov. Even at seventy-two, he was still jovial, saying that he had been at the KZ Oranienburg near Berlin and had seen the real concentration camp situation himself: "In the morning I was woken up by beautiful singing. The songs were coming from prisoners in clean uniforms who were going off to work. They were singing like birds." An early National Socialist street fighter, having fought in the streets of Berlin in 1932, Krüger created a media firestorm with such comments. In 1988 a film about the life of the outspoken SS man (*Kamerad Krüger*) resulted in wide condemnation by fellow veterans. "I was and still am an SS man and I was a political soldier who started in 1930 to go through the fire for the National Socialist idea and to fight for Adolf Hitler. Somebody may smile about this and say it is old fashioned. I am not smiling. Has the oath to Hitler died with him? For me, it has never gone away. . . . We are and will remain the SS." Krüger to Hubert Meyer, BA-MA, RS7/ v.508, March 27, 1989. Krüger died on May 17, 1991, in Hamburg. For the extensive records on the Krüger affair: BA-MA, HIAG Records, RS7, v. 373, 435 and 620.

39. For the coordination to write a favorable history of the Leibstandarte, see correspondence in BA-MA RS 7/ v 511.

40. Rudi Lehmann to Hubert Meyer, letter, August 28, 1979, BA-MA, RS 7/ v. 509.

41. Dietrich Ziemssen, *Der Malmedy Prozess*, Munich, Deschler, 1952. The five men are identified in the book by Oswald Siegmund, (*Meine Ehre heißt Treue: Von der Leibstandarte ins Landsberger Kriegsverbrechergefängnis* [Essen, 1992]), which includes a letter dated November 16, 1951, to the Landsberg Malmédy men that "we are all still working for the left behinds." The letter is signed by Dietrich Ziemssen, Rolf Reiser, Arndt Fischer, Rudi Woch, and Gerd Walter. The Ziemssen booklet eventually morphed into the similar apologist tract by Lothar Greil, *Oberst der Waffen SS Jochen Peiper und der Malmedy Prozess* (Munich, 1977), which was the precursor for the later Tiemann (see endnote 54). In an interview with Rolf Reiser in March 2006 he admitted to the author that he had assisted Ziemssen in writing the original booklet on the trial. Even today the aging survivors of this tiny group maintain frequent communication "im kleinen Freudenskreis" to prop up the official Waffen SS version. Beyond that, in 1986 he provided many of his personal papers on the Malmédy case to the Bundesarchiv in Freiburg with a content that is pointedly designed to support the HIAG version of the events and refutation of the trial. See Reiser to Helmuth Thöle, October 26, 1986, BA-MA, RS/7 HIAG Records, v. 510.

42. "Treffen für die Lötlampen Abteilung," announcement of Walter Malek for summer 1973 in BA-MA, Sammlung Vorpersal, NS 756/ 414.

43. Peiper to Walter Malek, April 7, 1973.

44. Managing an industrial plant in Wuppertal after the war, Wünsche became a successful businessman, maintaining close contact with the old SS veterans. In his interview with John Toland on November 3 and 19, 1971, (LO, Toland, Tapes C-36–C-39) Toland pointedly asked Wünsche about the Final Solution. "I can swear that [while I was with Hitler] I never heard about this. . . . I learned of the extermination of the Jews when I was a POW in England. I couldn't believe it. No one had any idea of it. When we were POWs, we thought things were exaggerated. But I can't tell you that it did not happen. Now, it is a shame for the German people that this happened." Toland: "Did Hitler know?" Wünsche: "I think it came to this [the extermination] which was not really wanted. It was out of control. . . . I can't believe that he ordered it, but Hitler must know. . . . It is still a shock to me today. The kids see this on TV and ask us how we did not know. . . . It will always be on the conscience of the German people." Max Wünsche died on April 17, 1995.

45. This and all quotes of Uli Wieselmann and Jochen Peiper from Judith Mutke, interview by author, October 6 and 7, 2003. Mutke saw Peiper twice more with Wieselmann on other trips to Germany.

46. "Strafanzeige gegen SS-Führer" *Stuttgarter Nachrichten*, July 1, 1964. Also, "Joachim Peiper—der SS Mordbrenner von Boves," *Die Tat*, No. 32, August 8, 1964. The latter article mentioned that Peiper headed advertising for Max Moritz Motors in Reutlingen that summer but also charged, in error, that he was the head of the Baden-Württemberg section of the HIAG—former members of the Waffen SS.

47. "Vernehmung Sepp Dietrich am 27.11.1945," Nuremberg, OMGUS 3/71, IfZ, Munich.

48. Peiper interview with Toland, *op. cit.*, October 10, 1963.

49. A loyal Nazi, Warlimont had worked in Hitler's field headquarters as deputy chief of operations under Alfred Jodl. Like Peiper, Gen. Warlimont was imprisoned after the war at Landsberg and was not released until 1954. Warlimont was another citizen in the Peiper family neighborhood around Rottach-Egern. He was known to be a good friend to Peiper as disclosed by Weller, interview. "High Ranking German Army Personalities," SAIC/3, April 11, 1945, 7th Army Interrogation Center, MIS-Y, RG 338, 290/56/2/4-5, Box 72.

50. Information on Dr. Hanns Dietrich Ahrens and his activities with right-wing circles and attempts to influence US industrialists and politicians. Letters Hanns Dietrich Ahrens to Freda Utley, 1953–1967, Freda Utley Papers, Hoovers Institution, Stanford, Box 2.

51. Suspicious of illegal collusion, German police made a raid on the house of Dr. Werner Best on March 20, 1969, and found the intention to fake evidence and coordinate favorable testimony from a number of witnesses including Jochen Peiper. The state attorney discovered letters in the home of Best indicating that he had been in contact with other important witnesses in his case, prior to their testimony, including Peiper and Streckenbach as well as many others. The letter mentioning Weller and her movements with Dr. Ahrens and in SS circles was in a letter from Dr. Best to the state attorney dated, July 3, 1969. Generalstaatsanwalt Filipiak to Herrn Untersuchungsrichter II bei dem Landgericht Berlin, (1 Js 12/65 (RSHA), Landesarchiv Berlin, B Rep. 057-01, No. 633. The letter of Best to Peiper is DoKo XXIV B 9f in the same series.

52. There is more evidence that Peiper sought to distance himself from the actions of his men. At Landsberg, he wrote a piece entitled, "*Über die Verantwortung eines Panzerführers—* [The Responsibility of a Tank Commander]," which bore his signature and described how a panzer leader could not be expected to control his fast moving, far-flung armored forces. This became controversial, as it was planned for publication in the *Der Freiwillige* before Ralf Tiemann put the kibosh on the piece. "We advise you not to publish this as it could confuse matters, given the tendency of this report to suggest to some of the old tankers of the Leibstandarte that Peiper sought to shift responsibility and whitewash (*Persilschein*) himself, imparting a bad reflection on the people in the spearhead." Tiemann to Helmuth Thöle, March 17, 1985, BA-MA, RS 7, v.361.

53. All quotes from Weller, interview. "My opinion," Weller said, "is that the American soldiers brought the whole thing on themselves." Of Ellis, Weller was shocked to find him living. "He is a liar. You can't believe anything he says."

54. Ralf Tiemann, *Der Malmedy Prozess: Ein Ringen um Gerechtigkeit* (Osnabrück: Munin Verlag, 1990). Carefully orchestrated by Leibstandarte veterans, the book is typical of SS apologist literature, in which footnotes and narrowly selected sources cover for a pseudo-academic approach. The text consists largely of right-wing essays originally composed during the 1950s by lawyers Rudolf Aschenauer and Eugen Leer with the intention to free Peiper and the other Malmédy men at Landsberg. A key source was a pointedly biased essay written by American Judith Weller, who was a college equestrian riding instructor. See Prof. Judith Ann Weller, "Das Geschehen an der Malmedy Kreuzung," and Ralf Tiemann 3.4.85, BA-MA, HIAG Papers, RS/7 v. 56b. Even without relevant training and espousing strong pro-Nazi sympathies,

Weller was elevated to the rank of "Professor of History"! In Weller's decidedly biased account of the incident at Malmédy, "a large part of the prosecution material is forged and based on extorted confessions," while "the prosecution witnesses, frequently committed perjury, especially American soldiers." Much was made of the fact that the testimony of Ken Ahrens and Virgil Lary did not agree in all respects. To Weller, this was a sure indication of dishonesty rather than difference in recall. In reviewing the voluminous records on the Malmédy investigation at the National Archives, the author found Weller's pull slips still present in the first few boxes and dated January 1968.

55. "Apparently some of her connections were known if not appreciated by her colleagues during her brief stay here." J. Lance Kramer, Vice President of Academic Affairs, William Woods College, October 10, 1997.

56. Tiemann, *Chronicle of the 7. Panzer Kompanie*, 51.

57. Peiper to Charles Whiting, September 29, 1970. "I would like to draw your attention to Miss Judith Ann Weller. Last year she wrote, equipped with the analytical mind of a history professor and the reliable documents of the Pentagon, a study of the Malmédy incident."

58. Burton Ellis to Peiper, letter, April 10, 1966, Ellis papers.

59. Peiper to Burton Ellis, letter, April 20, 1966, Ellis papers.

60. Peiper: "The tone of the interrogation [with Perl] was polite and correct and aimed at a gentleman's agreement. Sign anything we desire and we shall find an honorable end." "Sworn Statement of Joachim Peiper," January 15, 1948, Landsberg/Lech W.C.P., NA, Case 6-24, RG 153, Box 81.

61. "Senator McCarthy claimed that the '1939ers' hated the Germans and therefore tortured them. To prove that fact wrong, I referred to things which I did for gentile Germans." Perl to Joe Kirschbaum, July 16, 1949, George Washington University, William R. Perl Papers, Box 6, Folder 57.

62. "Director, FBI, SAC, WFO, Confidential, William R. Perl, Departmental Applicant, Psychological Interne, Federal Detention Headquarters, New York," May 7, 1951, Declassified by Army letter, June 29, 1977, Perl Papers, Box 8, Folder 2. Potential witnesses to Perl's alleged indiscretion were Capt. Henry P. Schardt and 1st. Lt. Peter Salz who had been with the 15th Army Interrogation Center in Rheinbach, southwest of Bonn.

63. SAC, WFO (185-378): Dr. William R. Perl, Revue Lev-tov, PFO-Subversive Conspiracy," August 11, 1976, Perl Papers, Box 8, Folder 2. Perl died on December 24, 1998, the previous year again denying to the author any wrong doing in the Malmédy investigation: "I just want to reiterate that it would have been idiotic on my part to try to obtain confessions by the use of violence. My strength was knowledge of the psychological makeup of the prisoners. . . . These were tough men, hardened by their education in the SS. . . . The approach varied with the individual, but in most cases I also used an appeal to their pride. . . . I told the prisoners after being confronted by the evidence, 'Do you want to act like a little '*Hühnerdieb*—chicken thief—or do you have the courage to stand up as an SS man?'" Letter to author, March 7, 1997.

64. *"Zeige mir Deine Freunde, und ich sage Dir, wer du bist."*

Chapter Eighteen

1. Martin Cüppers, *Wegbereiter der Shoah* (Darmstadt: Meidenbauer Martin Verlag, 2006), 332.

2. ZSL B 162/ 6370–6371, Interrogation of Joachim Peiper, September 7, 1964.

3. Jens Westemeier, interview by Otto Dinse, May 28, 1994.

4. For a description of coordination of the Boves story: Statement of Dr. Friedrich Breme, BAL N 1470/ 1178, October 1, 1965.

5. BA-MA, B438/287, "Eugen Wittmann to Karl Cerff," July 23, 1968. At the time Göhler was under investigation in the SS Reiter case agains Gustav Lombard and others.

6. Gustav Lombard, on receiving an order to liquidate the Jews in the Pripret Marshes on August 1, 1941, advised his battalion that "In future not one male Jew is to remain alive and not one family in the villages." Browning and Matthäus, *Origins of the Final Solution*, 281.

7. For Peiper's whereabouts, Toland, *Hitler*, 352. For the charges brought forth by the Italians: BA-K, N 1470/1175, Letter Dr. Adalbert Rückerl, ZSL 8 AR 1007/64 to G. Biancani und G. Prunotto from June 24, 1964: "Therefore I confirm the receipt of your charge brought against Peiper dated June 23, 1964. The Central Court will start the investigation against the former SS Sturmbannführer Peiper and in case the proceedings go forward the state attorney responsible for the execution of the procedure will be forwarded."

8. Contrary to the view stated elsewhere, there was no attempt by the Italians to kidnap Peiper and return him to Italy or to harass his wife. H. Peiper, interview. Recognition of Peiper by Biancani in Toland's book: "Peiper Était Bien L'Auteur du Martyre de la Petite Ville Piémontaise de Boves," *La Montagne*, July 23, 1976. For filed charges against Peiper: BA-L, 8 AR 1007/64, Vermerk: Giuseppe Biancani and Giuseppe Prunotto, June 23, 1964. The photographs had been given to Italians in Cuneo to develop from Peiper's battalion. Somehow the Italians retained the prints that turned out to contain a number of photos of Peiper in the Boves action. Peiper himself identified himself in the photographs. "I am with the binoculars and on my left is my ordnance officer Möhrlin and next to him is Dinse." Peiper to the State Prosecutor in Stuttgart, September 17, 1964.

9. See "Strafanzeige gegen ehemaligen SS-Führer," *Allgemeine Wochenzeitung der Juden in Deutschland*, July 10, 1964, IfZ, MZ-161/12, Munich. Robert M. W. Kempner was a German-born lawyer who had been an early opponent of the Nazis having attempted in 1931 to drag Hitler before the courts on charges of treason and perjury. In 1933, after the Nazis took power, Kempner had been fired by Goering and fled to the United States although his future wife who survived the concentration camps. Thirteen years later he was chief of the war crimes division preparing the case against Goering and the other defendants at the Nuremberg trial.

10. Joachim Peiper to the State Prosecutor in Stuttgart, personal Statement, September 17, 1964, BA-L, 13 Ja 161/64.

11. Article from the *Gazzetta del Popolo*, October 6, 1965. See documentation for 13 Js 161/64, BA-L. He spent more than a week in the Cuneo area developing evidence for the trial.

12. See Otto and Ilse Skorzeny's letters with Freda Utley from 1954–1958. Freda Utley Papers, Hoover Institution, Stanford University, Palo Alto, Box 11. In spite of working with Utley on coordinating deals between US steel interests, Skorzeny's foreign scrap metal firm and Krupp Industries in Peron's Argentina, the political writer was unable to help secure a visa for Skorzeny to visit the United States.

13. Nachlass Otto Skorzeny, B 2158, Österreichisches Staatsarchiv, Vienna.

14. In his interview with John Toland on September 28, 1957, Skorzeny, having established that Toland seemed sympathetic, launched into a diatribe against the Polish Jews: "Our most deadly enemy is the Jews," he said. "They are destructive sexually. They were coming so strongly into power. After the war, they are back again in the press, TV and business." John Toland Papers, Battle: Story of the Bulge, LOC, Box 8.

15. Skorzeny to Toland, July 7, 1965, John Toland Papers, Last Hundred Days, Box 17, Library of Congress. Largely filmed in Ultra-Panavision in Spain, with tank battles depicted in the desert-like Yakima firing range in western Washington, *Battle of the Bulge* depicted the Malmédy Massacre as an organized execution rather than a battlefield event. Arguably one of the worst of Hollywood war films, it premiered on December 16, 1965 to round denouncement by nearly all participants—even Dwight D. Eisenhower!

16. Otto Dinse interview with author, May 21, 1996. When Peiper was needing character witnesses during the proceedings, he was disturbed to find that some of those who could have helped him would not come forward. His battalion surgeon, Dr. Robert Brüstle, whom Peiper

often referred to as "Don Roberto" and for whom "he would have thrust both hands in the fire" was unwilling to assist.

17. Westemeier, *Himmlers Krieger*, 600.

18. Otto Dinse, interview with author, May 21, 1996. Skorzeny's ODESSA operations (actually called *Die Spinne*) ceased in 1952 to be replaced by another organization called *Kameradenwerk* (Comrade Workshop), which over the following score years aided former Nazis overseas to avoid capture and to maintain concealment. Whereas ODESSA's less than dramatic subversive operations were centered in Coburg, Germany, Kameradenwerk functioned mainly in Spain and South American countries where governments were sympathetic to ultra-right-wing causes. The US CIA closely watched Skorzeny while tracking Neo-Nazi developments in South America. CIA, "German Nationalist and Neo-Nazi Activities in Argentina," WH Division, July 8, 1953, NA, CIA-RDP62-00865R000300030004-4, Declassified in April 2000. Also, NA, RG-319, Records of the Army Staff, Investigative Interrogation Reports, "Organization Odessa," 15 July 1947, (XE 180023), in Box 39.

19. *Cuneo am Morgengrauen des Faschismus*: "Torture of Boves" ("Das Martyrium von Boves").

20. Dinse testimony, *op. cit.*, "I was the one, who, first in a peaceful manner, attempted to get the two prisoners back. . . . I can now see where this investigation is going."

21. Other than the postwar Boves investigation, the main sources for the Italian version of the events consulted are: Renato Aimo, *Il Presso Della Pace: La gente bovesana e la Resistenza 1943–45* (Cuneo: Edizioni L'Archiere Cuneo, 1989). Also, Carlo Gentile, "Settembre 1943: Documenti sull'attività della divisione "Leibstandarte SS Adolf Hitler" in Piemonte, *Il Presente e la Storia rivista dell'Instituto Storico della Resistenzia in Cuneo e Provincia* (Cuneo: Giugno, 1995), 75–130. And Faustino Dalmazzo on the trial: "La ricostruzione dei fatti di Boves attraverso il processo in Germania," *La Guerra sul Fronte Russo: La provincia di Cuneo dalla guerra alla liberazione*, Instituto Storico della Resistenza, Cuneo.

22. Faustino Dalmazzo (Boves), interview by Georges Arnaud and Roger Kahane, *L'Affaire Peiper*, Antenne 2, 1977.

23. Wiesenthal to Staatsanwalt Rückerl, December 3, 1964. BA-L, 8 AR-Z 17/64.

24. Affidavit of Joachim Peiper as provided by his Stuttgart attorney Dr. Arthur Fischer, November 29, 1965, Nachlass Robert M. Kempner, BA-K, N 1470/ 1170 and Affidavit of Otto Dinse, February 9, 1966, Nachlass Kempner, *op. cit.*, Band 1171, 2–3. The original handwritten notice and its typed-up version (both in Italian) by SS Captain Müller on September 18, 1943, is in the later folder in Kempner's personal papers. In spite of considerable effort the author was unable to locate such a personality and rank in Italy either in the SD or the LAH. Not surprisingly, in the author's interview with Erhard Gührs on December 17, 2006, he denied that he and the rest of Peiper's battalion had anything to do with the apprehension of the Jews for the concentration camp. Yet a key point arises from the records of the German field commands in Italy: here we learn that Peiper's command was the *only* German unit in the Cuneo area at the time. Who else could have helped round up the Jews? For more details, Westemeier, *Himmlers Krieger*, 257–273.

25. Landgericht Stuttgart, I.gr.Strafkammer," I Ars 62/68, 309–312, *ZSL*.

26. Peiper described this episode in a 1969 speech to old SS veterans: Recollection of Erhard Liss, *op. cit.*, March 28, 1969. He also described the same to his editor Wolfgang Schilling: "The Italian Boves investigation was going on while I knew him at work. Peiper told me at one time that 'I have been three times interrogated by attorneys in Stuttgart and one time the Italian TV showed up in front of my house.'" Wolfgang Schilling, interview by author, June 22, 2007.

27. "Scharfe Angriffe aus Italien gegen die Stuttgarter Justiz," *Stuttgarter Nachrichten*, September 19, 1968.

28. "Durchführung der 'Endlösung' an den gefluechteten Juden," Nachlass Robert M. Kempner, BA-K, N 1470/1178.

29. Kempner was bitter with the result of the investigation—a smudge on his career: "From a legal standpoint, the result of the trial [*sic*] was unconvincing. The Massacre of Boves recalled the ugly incidents at the French village of Oradour and the Czech town of Lidice." Robert M. W. Kempner, *SS im Kreuzverhör* (Nördlingen: Delphi Politik, Franz Greno, 1987). In his own memoirs he wrote that Peiper's command had looted the whole village of Boves and the judgement of the investigation "seemed totally fishy." Robert M. Kempner, *Ankläger einer Epoche. Lebenserinnerungen* (Frankfurt: Jörg Friedrich, 1983), 428.

30. Simon Wiesenthal, "L'affaire Defregger et les tabous de la justice allemande: Le massacre de Boves," *Le Monde*, September 17, 1969, 7.

31. Peiper to Weingartner, letter from March 1976, courtesy James Weingartner. The author was never able to find evidence of a press conference as alluded to by Peiper.

32. BA-Ludwigsburg, AZ/Ars 62/68, "Landgericht Stuttgart." December 23, 1968. Also, Stuttgarter Zeitung, September 25, 1968.

33. Westemeier, interview by Dinse.

34. BAL, B 162/3145, Statement of Josef Diefenthal, August 17, 1965.

35. BA-MA, 756/2b, Declaration of Rudolf Lehmann, July 11, 1950.

36. BAL, B 162/ 3142, Statement of Herbert Gerretz, November 17, 1964. "At the Waldforest they had to leave and were to follow a path. Then they were shot. I have clearly in my memory that all three leaders were shot with pistols. They shot for a long time until all the Jews were lying down. The German speaking woman was a very athletic and attractive. She tried to escape and was nearly lucky, but then she bought it. Some victims of the massacre were thrown into the lake. The other bodies were buried at a mass grave near a small forest."

37. BA-Ludwigsburg, Az 5 Str 218/G9. Also, "1943 am Lago Maggoiore: 'Privater Judenmord," *Westdeutsche Allgemeine Zeitung*, Ausgabe No. 154, July 5, 1968.

38. "All we say about this is that we distance ourselves from it," Lehmann wrote. "We must be ashamed of it." Lehmann, *Leibstandarte*, vol. 3, 294.

39. On April 28, 1969, Best admitted writing an official document on September 21, 1939, summarizing the impact of orders to kill Polish intelligensia: "Only 3% of the Polish priests, teachers, nobles and goverment officials remain in place." Landesarchiv Berlin, B Rep 057-01, No. 633.

40. Testimony of Joachim Peiper: "Der Generalstaatsanwalt bei dem Kammergericht," Stuttgart, January 19, 1967, 1 Js 12/65 (RSHA)-E16. "After the end of the Poland campaign, Himmler considered the war to have been won. He wanted, by all means, to create new Germanic eastern provinces and was possessed by the idea of settling the newly won eastern provinces with Germanic elements. Accompanying Himmler, I even had to visit the resettlement camps. But it did not become known to me, that in this resettlement that Poles of value category 4 were destroyed in order to make room for Baltic or Wolhynia Germans. As far as it had been known to me, there was no plan to kill the resettled Poles. Rather, they were to be gained as workers for the Reich."

41. Testimony of Joachim Peiper, *op. cit.*, January 19, 1967.

42. Ibid.

43. "Report on interrogation of PW KP 49359 Sturmbannführer Jakob Hanreich," August 19, 1944, PWIS(H)/LDC/299, NA RG 332, Box 30, 290/56/1/5. Hanreich was captured in August 1944 in France and ventured the information before Peiper was even known to Allied intelligence.

44. "We had better win this war," Peiper told Dinse, "or we'll be in deep trouble because of these things." Westemeier, *Himmlers* Krieger, 600. Otto Dinse, author's interview, May 27, 1994.

45. Testimony of Joachim Peiper, "Strafsache gegen Dr. Werner Best wegen Mordes," Landgericht Berlin, 1 Js 12/65 (RSHA) (E16), z. Zt. Stuttgart, September 2, 1970.

46. Declaration of Dr. Ernst Schäfer to Lloyd M. Rausch, Freising, Germany, August 16, 1945.

47. Himmler's detailed itinerary for the January trip to Poland including Peiper's participation and Schäfer's presence is given in NA RG-242, T-175, Roll 112, Frames 2637820–2637822. Additional corroboration comes from Brandt's handwritten office journal: NA RG-242, T-581, R38A. Ernst Schäfer, Nazi Indiana Jones, later became entangled in trouble himself. At first he planned further expeditions, but one to the Caucuses to Russia was suspended in 1942 when the Germans lost possession of that region. Later he published a book, *Geheimnis Tibet,* whose publication Himmler himself ordered suspended for giving too favorable an impression of the British. In 1943 Schäfer was moved to Dachau Concentration Camp to assist with filming of terrible medical experiments being carried out there by Dr. Sigmund Rascher. That assignment haunted Schäfer for the rest of his days. Although repeatedly questioned at Nuremberg, Schäfer managed to narrowly exonerate himself, and fled for several years to Venezuela. He was lucky that aspects of his time at Mittersill, Austria, had not come up. There, in the lush Salzach valley, from summer 1943 until the end of the war, Schäfer coordinated the work for the *Ahnenerbe* by conscripts from nearby Mauthausen concentration camp. Worse, there were rumors from Baron Hubert von Pantz who returned to Schloss Mittersill in Austria in 1945, and claimed to have found shelves of Asian skulls in storage on his property. In the end Schäfer was able to resume an academic career, ending his days as a curator for the State Museum of Lower Saxony in Hannover. Email from Michel Kater, University of Toronto, May 2000. For his wartime career, BDC File for Ernst Schäfer, NA A3343-SSO-066B. Also Christopher Hale, *Himmler's Crusade* (Hoboken, NJ: John Wiley and Sons, 2003), 325–332, and Heather Pringle, *The Master Plan* (New York: Hyperion, 2006), 307–309.

48. Testimony of Joachim Peiper, "Strafsache gegen Dr. Werner Best wegen Mordes," Landgericht Berlin, 1 Js 12/65 (RSHA) (E16), z. Zt. Stuttgart, September 2, 1970. Sworn statement of Dr. Ernst Schäfer, August 15, 1945, Freising, Germany. Karl Wolff's testimony on the shootings of Polish saboteurs: Jochen von Lang, *Der Adjutant, Karl Wolff: Der Mann zwischen Hitler und Himmler* (Munich: Herbig, 1985), 138. For Peiper's previous version, admitting witness to the Bromberg shootings: "Vernehmung von Col. Joachim Peiper—Interrogation of Joachim Peiper," Landsberg/Lech, April 17, 1947. NA RG-238, M-1019, Roll 52, F185–189.

49. Harald von Saucken, who became an officer with the Waffen SS with the Totenkopf Verbände, appears next to Peiper in one of the earliest photos with Himmler. After the war von Saucken as a private driver racing a Porsche, placed fourteenth in the 1958 thousand-kilometer Nürburgring race.

50. Norman Cobb, correspondence, and Rudolf Launer, interview. "After the war, Porsche ran things his own way. He gathered all of the SS after the war. Mr. Kempka was chosen for Porsche to handle the hand-over of cars to customers. He gave them the final polish. But these men did not speak about the past. If you asked them anything, they knew nothing."

51. Launer, interview, VW Zentrum Max Moritz, Reutlingen, May 17, 2001, and October 20, 2002.

52. Anonymous, interview, October 2002. The woman in question knew nothing about Peiper's past at the time she met him.

53. Launer, interview.

54. Bez, interview.

55. Not all employees had good things to say about Peiper: "On the surface he was very friendly," recalled Lothaire Junghans, "while he made scathing reports to the management. . . . He did not seek to hide the fact that he had been a Colonel in the Waffen SS, but he continued to be a proponent of Nazi propaganda. He teased incessantly those who professed, as I,

democratic views. And he made fun of those who do not have blonde hair and blue eyes, telling them that they did not belong to the Aryan race. He remained a Nazi fanatic." Source: "Ja'ai Bien Connu le SS Peiper il etait Reste un Nazi Fanatique," Paul Dreyfuss communication with Lothaire Junghans, *L'Echo Liberté*, July 24, 1976, BA-MA, RS 7, V320. Junghans had met Peiper in the sales department at *Autohaus Moritz* in 1962 where he worked for three years.

56. "*Wessen Brot ich esse, dessen Lied ich singe!*" and "*Judenschule!*" Siegfried Bez, interview by author, October 20, 2002. Bez was a nineteen-year-old apprentice mechanic at Moritz Autohaus when he met Peiper in 1963. The author's inquiry of the cafeteria head woman produced only the opinion that Peiper had been arrogant and she had as little to do with him as possible.

57. "*J'étais Nazi et je le suis resté!*" J. Peiper, April 1967 interview, reproduced in *La Libre Belgique*, July 19, 1976, "L'Affaire Peiper: une interview posthume de l'ex colonel SS," 4. Although Peiper agreed to questions, he did not allow a photographer.

58. *La Libre Belgique, op. cit.*

59. Peiper, speech, as recorded by Erhard Liss, *op. cit.*, March 28, 1969.

60. In December 1969 Peiper had met with still another American, former US Infantry Major, John H. Hill, who discussed Malmédy with him. "He did not order the guards to kill the American prisoners. They acted on their own prerogative." Or so he told Maj. Hill. Letters of John H. Hill II to author: May 2 and May 19, 1995. Hill, formerly with Company I of the US 394th Regiment of the 99th Division met with Peiper in Stuttgart in December 1969 after several failed attempts.

61. *La Libre Belgique, op. cit.*

62. Later in the interview the Belgian journalist asked Peiper about the exculpating manifesto written by Lothar Greil, entitled "The Truth of Malmedy." Lothar Greil, *Oberst der Waffen SS Joachim Peiper und der Malmedy Prozeß* (Munich: Schild Verlag, 1958).

63. Peiper to Klink, April 25, 1964, December 31, 1966, January 6, 1967, BA-MA, Klink Papers. *Towaritsch* was Russian for "comrade." In 1967: "Please respond soon. Among others, the following died in the last year: Sepp Dietrich, Steiner, Keppler and Gille."

64. Peiper to Klink, January 25, 1970, BA-MA, Klink Papers. In responding to Peiper's move to France, Klink addressed his former superior as "Dear Hermit."

65. Schulz to Hubert Meyer, letter, February 27, 1968. BA-MA B 438, 69/2. Thanks for Jens Westemeier for this recent finding.

66. As an example: "Die 1. SS Panzer-Division 'LAH' in Einsatz in der Ardennen-Offensive 1944," Der Freiwillige, March 1965, Pt. 3 of 4.

67. Peiper to Fuchs, January 10, 1967, BA-MA, RS 7/v. 282. Dr. Herbert Fuchs had been an SS Ustuf. with the LAH, joining the division in 1939 and wounded while fighting with the 7th Panzer Grenadier Company in Russia in the summer of 1943. After the war Dr. Fuchs was the president of the Baden-Würtemberg court for administrative law and a legal friend to the Leibstandarte in the Bonn government.

68. Peiper to Toland, September 1, 1970, Toland Papers, FDR Library, Box 54.

69. Peiper to Richard Schulze Kossens, Stuttgart, November 8, 1970, BA-MA, NA-475, Papers of Nikolaus von Below, correspondence file. Thanks to Dr. Andreas Kunz at the Bundesarchiv Freiburg for helping me reach this important source.

70. Just a year before, Albert Speer, the industrial minister of Hitler's empire, published *Erinnerungen* (Frankfurt/M, Ullstein: Siedler Verlag, 1969), *Inside the Third Reich* (English translation) (New York: Macmillan, 1970), which became a worldwide best-seller, although controversial with Hitler's inner circle as it was very critical.

71. J. Peiper, interview by Whiting, 1969, cited in Whiting, *Massacre at Malmedy*, 242. Whiting's letter to author, April 9, 2001. Whiting's notes from his interview with Peiper are quoted in "Wer kennt die Wahrheit über Peiper?" *Aachener Volkszeitung*, July 1976.

72. The Denazification files for Schwarz van Berk show him taken into custody on January 11, 1946, at Kornwestheim and then escaping from Camp 74 on April 11, 1947. Spruchkammerakte Hans Schwarz van Berk, Baden-Würtetemberg Landesarchiv, Staatsarchiv Ludwigsburg.

73. Hans Schwarz van Berk was a journalist and SS Obersturmführer for the wartime weekly *Das Reich* and a protégé of Joseph Goebbels. "Interrogation of Hans Schwarz van Berk," Records of the War Department General Staff, Interrogation Reports," NA RG 338, Box 116. After the war van Berk was implicated by Albert Speer at Nuremberg as the source for forlorn German hopes in miracle weapons during the last phase of the war. In testimony to the prosecution staff of the International Military Tribunal he said the source for his article on "wonder weapons" on December 3, 1943 ("Die ungeahnten Folgen des Bombenkrieges") had come straight from Speer himself. Thomas J. Dodd Papers, University of Connecticut, Nuremberg Trial Series, Box 298. Schwartz van Berk, whose enthusiasm for Hitler's cause seems to have never waned, visited Peiper while he was incarcerated at Landsberg on October 8, 1953. After the war Schwarz van Berk was quite wealthy and funneled his fortune into an opulent lifestyle. Peiper and Schwarz van Berk maintained a lively communication in 1972 prior to his death the following year. Nachlass Hans Schwarz van Berk, BA-K, Bestand, N 1373, Band 6.

74. "Reiseprogramm des Reichsführer vom 13.-15.7.1940," NA, RG 242, T-175, Roll 112, 2637795–96.

75. Joachim Peiper to Jean Michel Besina, June 23, 1976, *RTL Radio*. "I think it is very important that Germans and French people should meet and talk and help to understand that the future is only possible if we become friends and if the political grudges are now forgotten."

Chapter Nineteen

1. Heinz-Ulrich Wieselmann was born on April 16, 1913, and in the Polish campaign fought with Panzerabwehr Ersatz Company 208 and later with 2nd Company Panzerabwehr Abt. 24 in France. In August 1941 he received a cushy post to the Army weapons office (*Heereswaffenamt*) in Paris until he was later assigned to workshop crew of the s. Panzerjäger Battalion 519 in May 1944, where he finished out the war as a *Feldwebel*—technical sergeant. Source: WAst file for Wieselmann. Interestingly, the assault guns and Jagdpanthers of s. Panzerjäger Abt. 519 were attached to the 3rd Fallschirmjäger Division in the Ardennes on December 21, 1944, and fought in the vicinity of Waimes-Thirimont, nearby to where the Malmédy Massacre had taken place. "OB West, Tagesmeldung vom 21.12.44," BA-MA, RH IV/85. NA, RG-242, T-314, Roll-1594, F1046.

2. Heinz-Ulrich Wieselmann, *Unsterbliches Berlin* (Berlin-Bielefeld: Verlag Klasing, 1948).

3. Launer, interview.

4. "I have recently sent a photo of Peiper. . . . Our government is a mishmash of humanitarians, Christian ideas, militarism, East Zone sentimentalists, corruption and greed. Intellectuals are lost. We have lost our fundamental fountain and drink through all possible water taps, which contaminates us." Ursula Müller to *Swatt*, May 6, 1964, Nachlass Schwarz van Berk, BA-K, N 1363/6.

5. Heinz-Ulrich Wieselmann, *Pedro, Gedanken eines Hundes* (Berlin/Bielefeld: Verlag Klasing, 1948), and *Als gäbe es kein Morgen* (Stuttgart: Motorbuch Verlag, 1969).

6. When Peiper had known Sepp Dietrich before the war, dapper Dietrich would often don his all-white racing togs, goggles, and strap himself into one of the Auto Union racers for a well-publicized zip about Berlin Blaine Taylor, *Guarding the Führer* (Missoula, MT: Pictorial Histories, 1993).

7. Wieselmann, interview, May 13, 1999.

8. Wolfgang Schilling, interview by author, June 22, 2007.

9. Ursula Müller to *Swatt*, May 6, 1964.

10. Wieselmann could not help but notice that some of the books Peiper passed on for her to read were lettered in blue ink on the end pages—"Passed by the Censor." They had come from Landsberg. Wieselmann, interview, June 17, 2004.

11. Wieselmann, interviews, October 20, 2002, and June 23, 2007. "I knew he had this past," she said, "but even today, I have not looked into it, preferring my memories."

12. Peiper later related all this to his editor, Wolfgang Schilling, who also smoked like a fiend, but wished to stop. Peiper said he too had a tough smoking habit but had devised a surefire system to quit, ideally suited to his personality. How so? Schilling wanted to know. "By plan, I smoked one cigarette after another all day," Peiper pronounced, "and by night, I was so fed up with cigarettes that I had to quit." Schilling, interview, June 22, 2007.

13. Wieselmann, interview, June 17, 2004.

14. Peiper to Karl Wortmann, November 28, 1974. On Peiper's eulogy: Wieselmann, interview, June 17, 2004.

15. Benno Müller, *Mit offenem Visier* (Stuttgart: Motorbuch Verlag, 1978), text by Rainer Buschmann. Peiper translated a number of projects through his relationship with Wolfgang Schilling. As Peiper was the public relations chief at *Auto, Motor und Sport*, Schilling asked whether he knew of any good English translators for military books. Peiper told Schilling that he could do that. The working connection began in 1968 and was "very professional, not *Duzen*." After Peiper's move to France the former SS colonel and now translator came to Stuttgart two or three times a year as book projects were finished and was put up near the airport at the Hotel Schinderbuckel, where the two had dinner together. Schilling visited Peiper once in Traves.Schilling, interview, February 22, 2006.

16. Peiper to Schwarz van Berk, May 7, 1972, Nachlass Schwarz van Berk, BA-K, N 1363/6.

17. "Die Reise nach Traves," Nachlaß Hans Schwarz van Berk, BA-K, N 1373. "Fragmente für die 'Erinnerungen,' 946–949.

18. Peiper to Hans Schwarz van Berk, November 9, 1972, BA-K, Bestand, N 1373, Band 6.

19. Müller, interview, May 18, 1999. "Peiper was very happy in France . . . [but]One has to say that Mrs. Peiper has to be admired. For her, life would have been better elsewhere. Naturally, Traves was very lonely place, and . . . she was jealous of Benno Müller because Mrs. Peiper was a northern German and very proper. My husband was an uncomplicated German man from Baden. . . . She was not so excited by the influence of my husband and his easy going ways on Mr. Peiper. She was Northern German and tolerant, but without much humor. She was fairly strict."

20. That Peiper remained attractive to women, even later in his life, became obvious to the author through a number of interviews, including two sources who wished to remain anonymous.

21. "Die Wahrheit über Malmedy," *Das Ritterkreuz*, No. 2 (Wiesbaden: Mitteilungsblatt der OdR, Orden vom Militär-Verdientst-Kreuz, 1976), 2.

22. Martin, *L'Affaire Peiper* (Paris: Editions Dagorno, 1994), 136; H. Peiper, interview. West German chancellor Konrad Adenauer and French president Charles de Gaulle signed the Franco-German Treaty of Cooperation in 1963, an event hailed as a major reconciliation between France and Germany, traditional enemies for centuries.

23. Ernst Wiechert's *Das einfache Leben* (*The Simple Life*) was written after his return from Buchenwald prison camp in 1939. Peiper may have been subconsciously drawn to the book, for Himmler's SS house organ, *Das Schwarze Korps*, had featured an article embracing many of the same themes in an article by same name ("Das einfache Leben") on December 30, 1943. "The simple life is a life out of one's power, uniting oneself only with genuine and lasting values."

24. Over four hundred innocent Vietnamese villagers were shot down that day. See Seymour Hersch, *My Lai 4: A Report on the Massacre and Its Aftermath* (New York: Random House, 1970).

25. From the introduction of Peiper's fragmentary manuscript he wrote in 1976 about the Ardennes operation. Agte, *Jochen Peiper*, 620; translation of the original German by Helmut Thiess. Also, Peiper's opinion on the Southeast Asian conflict as revealed to Heinz Stuttecker: "I am sure the U.S. boys will not win. I know how partisans fight. And the North Vietnamese are fighting like that. I know something about fighting them." Peiper told Stuttecker he hated guerrillas, seeing himself as a strict soldier: "Please put on your uniform, mount your tank and fight." That was the way is should be done. Stuttecker, interview, February 28, 2009.

26. Jochen Peiper to James Weingartner, February 19, 1976. Nor was the blemish for the US Army confined to Vietnam. In World War II the massacre of thirty-six Italian and German solders in Sicily near Biscari on July 14, 1943, was a worrisome event for George S. Patton and the 45th Infantry Division. (See James J. Weingartner, "Massacre at Biscari: Patton and an American War Crime," *The Historian*, November 1989.) The surviving guilty American soldiers in that episode would serve only a six-month sentence. Declaring the whole matter secret, the War Department was careful to suggest that "no publicity be given to this case because to do so would give aid and comfort to the enemy and would arouse a segment of our own citizens who are so distant from combat that they do not understand the savagery that is war." However, the frequency of the transgressions of the US Army in World War II can in no way be compared with that of the Waffen SS.

27. Peiper to Karl Wortmann, November 28, 1974.

28. "Besuch im Schicksalsdorf La Gleize," *Der Freiwillige*, August 1976, 11. The group of LAH veterans met in Losheim on May 27–30, 1976, and then traveled throughout the Ardennes making the Hotel Au Bienvenue their base in Coo.

29. One of the author's most telling interviews was with Peiper's old comrade, Fritz Kosmehl, who fought with Peiper in tanks from the time he took over the panzer arm in Russia in 1943. Kosmehl had been almost completely blinded after a hit against his Panther in Normandy. Kosmehl spent years dropping the war and all with it, embracing the unlikely hobby of sport and engaging Peiper in lengthy correspondence. Kosmehl found Peiper somewhat relaxed in 1961 in Stuttgart, but in Traves, he found him tense and worried. "Even there—cutting trees and doing work—Peiper was somehow still a soldier. He was not fitting into the modern world. . . . It was a false quiet time." Later, the two men spoke on the phone, but Kosmehl found him paranoid that others were listening. On most occasions, we carefully avoided speaking of the war, but once he told me on the phone. 'I walked 1,200 kilometers from the Enns River to my home, but we managed to not be taken prisoner until the end. Now, after the war, I am not sure what we accomplished.'" Asked whether Peiper was really reformed after 1945, Kosmehl considered the question carefully. Peiper had been totally obsessed by the war in prison, he told me. After the war he read a lot and struggled to become an intellectual. Years passed. "He really wanted to change," the now blind panzer man said, "but in the end he could not. . . . The weight of the past was too much." Kosmehl, interview by author, December 17, 2004, Oldenburg.

30. Peiper to Kosmehl, February 18, 1973.

31. Stutterecker, interview, February 28, 2009. Also Peiper's active communication with HIAG after his release from prison: Peiper to Kurt "Panzer" Meyer, November 28, 1959, and response; Also, Peiper to Karl Cerff, March 8, 1969, and June 17, 1969. BA-MA, B-438, Records of the HIAG, Folders 320.

32. Peiper to Ernst Klink, June 9, 1975, BA-MA, Nachlass Ernst Klink. Underline and exclamation point are Peiper's own. The book by Venner was titled *Söldner ohne Sold. Die deutschen Freikorps* 1918–1923 [*Mercenaries Without Pay*] (Wien: Paul Neff Verlag, 1974). Today the same book is published by the right-wing publishing house, Arndt Verlag, under the title *Ein deutscher Heldenkampf*. The book worships those who fought with the Freikorps, saying they sought to save Germany from the worst, even though their own government disowned them.

33. Peiper to Whiting: "The Americans personify me as an Al Capone with a tommy gun in each hand," Peiper said. Whiting had the feeling that Peiper was defeated by peace. He

had been let down by his regimental comrades and despised the postwar generation and their self-centered "*ohne mich*—only me" focus.

34. J. Peiper, interview by Whiting, 1969, as cited in Whiting, *Massacre at Malmedy*, 242. Charles Whiting, interview by author, August 19 and 20, 2001.

Chapter Twenty

1. "He loved the French. Unfortunately, the French go crazy on their national holidays." Dinse, interview, May 21, 1996. In actuality, while enjoying living in France, he was not living in the typical manner in which French people were accustomed, which was a very public lifestyle of dining and socializing.

2. Like many other things, the BMW 3.0 had been provided by his accommodating friend, Dr. Benno Müller. Being a doctor, Müller became very popular during his visits to France as he would bring along birth control pills that were now the rage. Müller jokingly called himself, "Dr. Pill." Müller, interview, May 18–19, 1999. Merchants at the bakery in Traves remembered that the man's wife would come to the shop and, although polite, ventured little more than "Good morning . . . Good evening." "Joachim Peiper Avait Reçu de Nouvelles Menaces La Veille de sa Mort," Grande Region, *RL*, July 15, 1976, Maurice Delaval Papers, US Army Military History Institute, Carlisle, PA.

3. NA, BDC File for Erwin Ketelhut (A3343-SSO-166A). Born in Essen in 1918 and son of a blacksmith, Ketelhut had joined the SS in 1936. Ketelhut became a Nazi party member in 1938 and was with the Leibstandarte Adolf Hitler from October 1936 until 1943. As a motorcycle rifleman, he participated with the campaigns in Austria, Czechoslovakia, and Poland. In February of 1940 Ketelhut transferred to the SS officers school at Braunschweig and returned to the combat unit of the Leibstandarte in September of 1940 as an officer. He fought with the division in Greece and Russia, meeting Peiper, who would be his neighbor during the campaign in the East in 1942. Later, Ketelhut became commanding officer of a battery of the 9th SS Division, "*Hohenstaufen.*" He followed this with a stint in the artillery in the division *Reichsführer SS* where he became a captain in January 1945.

4. Ketelhut was made prisoner by the US Army in Austria at the end of the war. Dominique Leroy, "Un singulier témoin," *L'Lorrain*, February 17, 1987. Ketelhut bought the mill property for ₣110,000 and then invested ₣1.5 million into its restoration and expansion, Lavaux Police Report, 28.

5. Müller, interview.

6. Schilling, interview, June 22, 2007. "I said we wanted a dog when it seemed convenient. He said, 'If you think I will get dog later, then you never will. You just get one now or you won't.'"a

7. "Although I went to Traves several times, Frau Peiper was only there once. But we never talked about their relationship. I knew her and we had some conversations, but she was not really a warm woman. The atmosphere was cool when she was in the house; she was not *gemütlich* [warm]." Anonymous, interview. Another source that preferred not to be identified hinted more to the author: "She was cold as a stone," he said. And for Jochen's view? "Like all men, he had an eye for beautiful women."

8. "Die Reise nach Traves," Nachlaß Hans Schwarz van Berk, BA-K, N 1373. "Fragmente für die 'Erinnerungen,' 946–949.

9. For clarification of the relationship with Mayor Rigoulot, thanks to Hinrich Peiper. Letter of May 7, 2000. For "French friendly": Wieselmann, interview.

10. "Die Reise nach Traves," *op. cit.*

11. Kosmehl, "Meine Begegnungen mit Joachim Peiper," and *Kosmehl Selbstbiographie*, 1393. "Peiper never mentioned that he felt pursued," Kosmehl recalled. "He had no reason to worry in this village."

12. Jochen Peiper to Arndt Fischer, letter, December 1, 1974.

13. Jochen Peiper in Traves to Hinrich Peiper, undated letter. Source: Nachlaß Ernst Klink, BA-MA, Zur Trauerfeier am 17.4.1979.

14. "Pech für Ihn," *Der Spiegel*, No. 30, July 19, 1976, 56.

15. Sigurd Peiper to Hinrich Peiper, no date, but late 1978 or early 1979. Nachlaß Ernst Klink, BA-MA, Zur Trauerfeier am 17.4.1979. The love story of Philemon and Baucis is appropriate: elderly, kind peasants living in a humble hut in the country of Phrygia are befriended by Zeus and invited to live in splendor on Mt. Olympus. In the end, however, both long for the simple impoverished life they enjoyed before. At that instant, each sprouts leaves and their skin changes to bark. Embracing each other, Philemon turns into an oak and Baucis into a linden tree.

16. Jochen Peiper to Arndt Fischer, letter, December 1, 1974.

17. Letter of last testament from Jochen Peiper to Sigurd Peiper, June 22, 1976.

18. "You completely forget," Peiper wrote, "that Europe in general and Germany in particular are still completely torn apart as far as the recent past is concerned and that persecution, trials and slander go on incessantly." Letter, Peiper to Toland, September 5, 1964, Library of Congress, Manuscript Division, John Toland Papers.

19. Jochen Peiper to Otto Dinse, letter, December 24, 1973.

20. Joachim Peiper in Traves to Hinrich Peiper, undated letter. Source: Nachlaß Ernst Klink, BA-M, Zur Trauerfeier am 17.4.1979. With "on this island" Peiper alludes directly to the terminology for isolation and sanctuary used in *The Simple Life*.

21. H. Peiper: "In Traves, the dream of my father for safety, quiet and security was fulfilled. He had always dreamed of this in his death cell of the war crimes prison at Landsberg, but considered it completely impossible ever to own a house under trees and on his own soil and ground.""Der Mann, dem nicht verziehen wurde," Constanze Knitter and Günter Stiller, *Bild am Sonntag*, August 1, 1976.

22. *Der Spiegel*, "Pech für Ihn."

23. Peiper, in Traves, to his son, Hinrich, letter, undated. Source: Nachlaß Ernst Klink, BA-MA, Zur Trauerfeier am 17.4.1979. Hans Klink had been SS Untersturmführer with SS Heavy Panzer Battalion 102, which fought in Normandy until he was taken captive during the fighting in the Falaise Pocket on August 12, 1944. NA: BDC File, A3343-SSO-180A, F1384–8.

24. Jochen Peiper to Fritz Kosmehl, November 29, 1974.

25. Peiper to Towaritsch—Ernst Klink, January 1, 1975, BA-MA, Klink Papers.

26. Jochen Peiper to Fritz Kosmehl, August 2, 1971, referring to the recent visit of Stephen Sanders: "I am sort of like an old American colonel, who once told me that every morning at 76 years, he jumps with both feet out of bed and says to himself—'Oh boy! Oh boy, this is another great day!'"

27. "My path ends in a forest." Jochen Peiper to Fritz Kosmehl, August 2, 1971.

Chapter Twenty-One

1. Cacheux's description of his meeting and conversation with Peiper, interview by Craig Unger, as described in "Les Mystères de l'Affaire Peiper," *French Playboy*, June 1979.

2. For "Cacheux, you see SS everywhere!" and "He is just an ordinary German," Martin, *L'Affaire Peiper*, 25.

3. Peiper to Fritz Kosmehl, November 29, 1974.

4. Although not named, Otto Dinse, Erhard Gührs, Ernst Klink, Benno Müller, and Arndt Fischer frequently visited Peiper.

5. Kosmehl, "Meine Begegnungen mit Joachim Peiper"; *Kosmehl Selbstbiographie*, 1431.

6. Born in August 1923, résistant Pierre Durand had been held at the Buchenwald Concentration Camp. Later during the war, he worked in the caves at the KZ Dora assembling parts

for German V2 rockets. After the war, Durand was an outspoken French Communist, working as a journalist for *L'Humanité* and serving as the president of the International Buchenwald-Dora Commission. Pierre Durand, *La chienne de Buchenwald*, (Paris: Temps actuels, 1985).

7. "I do not know to what extent mail and telephone are monitored. Even in war, however, mail was not discontinued because of possible enemy interference." Letter to Rudolf Lehmann, July 4, 1976.

8. The French Communist manifesto *L'Humanité* accused the French government of sympathy for war criminals, calling the Traves problem the result of "a favor made by Giscard, Poniatowski and Chirac to Peiper." "Untergrundorganisation droht mit Tötung deutscher Kriegsverbrecher," *Frankfurter Allgemeine*, July 16, 1976, 5.

9. *Der Spiegel*, "Pech für Ihn."

10. According to Lavaux's police report, those involved in distributing the leaflets were Roger B., Michel H., Alain H., Gérard D., Marc H., Fabrice R., and Raphaël M., all coordinated by Paul Cacheux and André Vuillien's Communist Federation of the Haute Saône. Lavaux Police Report, 17; last names purposely withheld.

11. André Moissé, interview by author, March 29, 2014.

12. Pierre Durand, "Un membre de l'tat-maj de Himmler en Haute Saône," *L'Humanité*, Paris, June 22, 1976.

13. Robert Daley, "Last Stand in a War that Ended Long Ago," *San Francisco Chronicle*, November 14, 1976, B-7.

14. All details in this section from Moissé, interview, March 29, 2014.

15. Moissé, "Dix ans de prison j'ai payé."

16. Kosmehl, "Meine Begegnungen mit Joachim Peiper."

17. Werner Kahl, "In München wird das Rätsel um Joachim Peiper gelöst," *Die Welt*, July 24, 1976.

18. Former *Stasi* chief Markus Wolf to Neill Thomson, letter, April 1, 1997. The *Stasi* file clearly shows that the East German police kept only loose records on Peiper's activities from the 1960s onward. Pierre Durand had actually been in East Berlin to check on other survivors from the *Dora Mittelwerk* concentration camp where he had been captive, and likely checked on Peiper only to see if there was substance to Cacheux's accusation.

19. Martin, *L'Affaire Peiper*, 22. Pélagey's claim is not entirely true, as an interview the year before in a regional newspaper of SS Colonel Otto Skorzeny as mentioning that his old comrade of the battle of the Ardennes, Joachim Peiper, was now living in the Alsace in Eastern France.

20. Both quotations are from Kai Hövelmann, "Das tödliche Ende eines Kesselteibens," *Quick*, No. 32, July 1976. Hinrich Peiper, sent a letter of correction to the Munich magazine which was published on August 26, 1976. Peiper told *Quick* that "at no time was my father a member of HIAG, much less the head of Baden-Württemberg HIAG."

21. On July 23, 1976, *France Soir* reported that Peiper had confided his telephone number to the baker in Traves to give him a call when he had available fresh loaves of country rye bread.

22. Kahl, "In München wird das Rätsel um Joachim Peiper gelöst."

23. *Les Mystères de L'Est*, André Moissé, Collection "Reflets et Racines," ed. *L'Est Républicain*, 1988.

24. Remiot Andrée to Rigoulot, July 1, 1976. Rigoulot papers, provided to the author.

25. Michele Cotta, "L'Enigme Peiper," *L'Express*, July 19–25, 1976.

26. According to Roger Martin the "Peiper SS" black-top graffiti was painted by Paul Cacheux himself—an event observed by local police who chose not to intervene. *L'Affaire Peiper*, 27.

27. "A photographer took position a few days ago on the opposite bank of the Saône with a telephoto lens and steadily, like an Indian sneaks from cover to cover, observing my

movements." Letter Jochen Peiper to Rudolf Lehmann, July 4, 1976, also cited in *Der Stern*, No. 31, August 1976. "I hardly will get to the book I planned," Peiper said of his interrupted writing on Malmédy. "I bury this project without too much grief as much too much garbage has been put to paper."

28. Klaus-Peter Schmid, "Hexenjagd auf französisch," *Die Zeit*, July 23, 1976.

29. Joachim Peiper, interview by Jean Michel Bezzina, *RTL Radio interview*, June 23, 1976, recording in author's possession.

30. Check Cotta, "L'Enigme Peiper." "The most troublesome thing about this affair," Cotta concluded, "was that Peiper had already paid for his crimes, even if his punishment appeared too light for some."

31. Peiper to Rudolf Lehmann, letter, June 30, 1976. "Jochen Peiper—zum Gedächtnis," *Der Freiwillige*, July/August 1986. Peiper's dogs, the Drahthaar, are a mix of the German Braque and Griffon and are pointers. They were neither "ferocious" as the press insinuated, nor simply "calm and affectionate," as Peiper and his friends maintained. Raymond Louette, who saw Peiper with Timm and Tamm nearly everyday, told the author, "They really were nice dogs—very friendly." Louette, interview.

32. Robert Daley, "The Case of the SS Hero," *New York Times Magazine*, November 7, 1976.

33. Peiper's declaration to gendarmerie in Vesoul on June 22, 1976.

34. Jochen Peiper to John Toland, letter, April 5, 1959, Library of Congress (LOC), Manuscript Division, Box 108.

35. Kahl, "In München wird das Rätsel um Joachim Peiper gelöst."

36. For Rigoulot's visit to Peiper on July 6, 1976 and his recollection of their conversation, Lavaux Police Report, 18.

37. Louette, interview, August 16, 2001. "Peiper was a man of his word," Louette said, "but had it been me, I would have shot at them."

38. That the siege wore on Peiper seems undeniable. One villager in Traves recalled, "'L'Allemand had changed a lot. Suddenly, he seemed to have gotten old—his wife too. Visibly, they were anxious. Before when we met them, they were polite. Those last times, they barely answered our greeting." "Peiper ne sera pas identifié avant plusieurs jours," *France Soir*, July 16, 1976. "He was older in his mind than in his years," mentioned his son to the author in one interview. "He was not willing to go through this again."

39. Albert Camus wrote the theatrical adaptation of Faulker's *Requiem for a Nun* in 1956.

Chapter Twenty-Two

1. Jochen Peiper to Rudolf Lehmann, June 30, 1976. Peiper again appealed for help in lobbying the head of the prefect of Vesoul: "So when the French-Italian Communists and Simon Wiesenthal describe me only as an 'Oradour' type and Eichmann deputy; the German side should point out that I was only a soldier and had less to do with the dirt than some others."

2. Jochen Peiper to Arndt Fischer, December 1, 1974. "I can imagine that in these disquieting time there are other people who also dream of a few more years away from questionable society in a mostly sane world."

3. Jochen Peiper to Arndt Fischer, letter, July 9, 1976 in author's possession.

4. Peiper received DM3,000–4,000 (the equivalent of US$1,200–$1,600 at the time) to translate books for Motorbuch Verlag. Interview.

5. Schilling, interview, June 22, 2007.

6. "Brandanschlag auf das Haus eines Waffen-SS-Offiziers in Frankreich: Peiper tot," *Die Welt*, July 15, 1976.

7. Jochen Peiper to Rudi Lehmann, letter, July 12, 1976, in author's possession. At that time, Peiper was already working on his book about Malmédy, having written Lehmann about progress in other letters dated March 25 and May 24, 1976. With the July letter Peiper enclosed a copy of his correspondence sent the same day imploring the German ambassador in Paris for assistance with his harassment.

8. Peiper to Lehmann, March 25, 1976, Klink Papers, BA-MA. The preceding autumn Peiper told Karl Wortmann that he was interested in: "a sober and realistic description of the Kampgruppe Peiper from Losheimergraben to Landsberg. Above all I am interested in repaying a debt of gratitude to my old comrades, whom until today, the victors have burdened with a 'typical' war crime that never happened." Peiper to Wortmann, November 29, 1975.

9. Peiper to Klink, April 1, 1975. "Thank you for the Engel breviary. . . . I shall return the trashy book to you during your next visit." BA-MA, Klink Papers.

10. Peiper to Klink, December 27, 1975, BA-MA, Klink Papers. Peiper had written to Ernst Klink on the same subject on December 14. "Thirty years of silence is really enough."

11. "Soldiers of the Sixth Panzer Armee! We stand before the greatest decision of the war. The Führer has given us a particularly important mission. We have the mission of quickly attacking across the Meuse River without looking left or right. . . . We aim to be the first German panzer troops to cross the Meuse." Sepp Dietrich.

12. Peiper to Mary Everett, December 14, 1975 Everett papers.

13. Peiper to Kosmehl, February 4, 1976. "My life here revolves around three focal points: typewriter, dogs and forest work."

14. Dietrich Ziemssen to Peiper, May 2, 1976, BA-MA, RS 7/v. 320. Ziemssen had been the divisional operations officer. His previous book on the irregularities of the Malmédy trial had been composed while Peiper and the others were awaiting execution in Landsberg and was ostensibly composed to save their necks. Dietrich Ziemssen, *Der Malmédy Prozess*, Josef Deschler, Munich, no date, but 1949–1950. On Peiper's reference to Gaeta: also in prison at Gaeta, Italy was Waffen SS war criminal, Walter Reder.

15. From the introduction of Peiper's fragmentary manuscript he wrote in 1976 about the Ardennes operation. Agte, *Jochen Peiper*, 620. Translation of the original German by Helmut Thiess. Aeschylus was the earliest writer of Greek tragedy and one who knew the ethos of war, having fought at the Battle of Marathon.

16. Jochen Peiper to German Ambassador, letter, Paris, July 12, 1976.

17. In 1941 Peiper had met Klink in Russia, where the two men fought together for two years. Klink to Wortmann, October 12, 1976, BA-MA, Klink Papers. Like Peiper, Klink's brother Hans had also retired to France to Vedene near Avignon. He was a former Waffen SS officer in Heavy SS Panzer Battalion 102, fighting in Normandy alongside the Hitler Jugend Division and captured in France on August 12, 1944 (BDC File for Hans Klink, NA, RG-242, A3343-SSO-180A). After the war he later rose to an executive position with the Porsche company in charge of sales in France. Klink remained defiant after the war, unwilling to be interviewed.

18. Klink to Peiper, July 12, 1976.

19. "Rain Mars Bastille Day Parade, but Delights Farmers," *New York Times*, July 15, 1976, 3.

20. Clarification of her trip to Basel and the surrounding circumstances: Sigurd Peiper to Kosmehl, November 1, 1978. Kosmehl Papers. Also Wieselmann, interview, June 23, 2007.

21. Account of Madame Louette: Unger, "Les Mystères de l'Affaire Peiper." Clarification of Sigurd's travels: Hinrich Peiper to author, May 7, 2000. Peiper's daughter Silke and Katja also left Traves at the same time.

22. Peiper to Ernst Klink, July 13, 1976; the last letter Peiper wrote, Klink Papers, BA-MA.

23. Paul Martin, "SS Man May Have Survived Murder Attempt," *The Times,* July 17, 1976.

24. Müller, interview, May 19, 1999. Sigurd Peiper told Mrs. Müller that she would be back by their home on the return to Traves. The Müllers were already aware of Jochen Peiper's plight, having been at his home in late May of 1976.

25. Lavaux Police Report, 14: "qu'on allait bruler sa maison, le tuer ainsi que ses chiens le 14 juilllet. Il était précisé que "ce jour là sera chaud." (P.V. 44).

26. *Bild am Sonntag*, *op. cit.*

27. *Les Mystères de l' Est*, *op. cit.*

28. "Un Vésulien, M. Paul Cacheux affirme avoir 'déniché' Peiper," *L'Est Républicain*, July 17, 1976.

29. Arnaud and Kahane, *L'Affaire Peiper*. The television documentary by the same name aired from *Antenne 2* aired on Sunday, January 21, 1978; videotape copy in author's possession. Roger Kahane and Georges Arnaud interviewed Jacques Delaval ("Riquette") in their documentary on the Peiper affair prepared for Antenne 2. The day after the incident two of the firefighters who fought the blaze at Traves visited Riquette's bar and noted his placard. Where had Riquette been? He did not answer them directly, "Even with a drought, that's what the police commission gets for forbidding fireworks!" he laughed. The owner thought little of it until eight days later, when he was visited by the police inspectors of Dijon, who questioned him for three hours. Only witnesses who could place Riquette in Vesoul at midnight during the Bastille celebration were able to get him off the suspicion list. The restaurant owner received death threats from neo-Nazi groups as late as two years after the fire.

30. Peiper may have determined from the previous harassing encounters with French youths on Friday, June 25 and Thursday, July 1, 1976, that his troublemakers with rocks and dirt clods could easily come from the east or west of Traves.

31. Regarding the planned book, see Peiper letter to Rudolf Lehman, December 6, 1975. The incomplete surviving manuscript was published as an appendix in Patrick Agte's biography, *Jochen Peiper*.

32. For Klink's conversation with Peiper: *Der Spiegel*, "Pech für Ihn." For Klink's last-minute decision not to join Peiper on July 13, 1976, letter Eckart Klink to author, March 16, 2003. For events of July 12, 1943, interview, August 19, 2003, and Peiper to Klink, letter, January 6, 1967, Klink papers, *op. cit.*

Chapter Twenty-Three

1. Peiper had also left the front south window (SE) of the kitchen in a half-open position, in addition to the window from the west terrace to his library that was in a full open position. Inspector Lavaux would later call it, "Peiper's great mistake. . . . One cannot understand that Peiper, an old fighter that he was, with his intelligence and his understanding of his defensive position, had not tightly closed the wooden shutters of his house. He wanted, no doubt, to have a good view on the field from his enclosure, but he had to run from top to bottom and from left to right to keep a watch on as he knew they were coming." Lavaux to author, April 28, 2000.

2. The location of the binoculars and Peiper's likely movements during the night of July 13, 1976, is from the police report, provided to the author by Inspector Lavaux, 5.

3. On both July 13 and 14, 1976 at 5 p.m. France Meteo Vesoul recorded sunny conditions with a cloudless sky and a temperature of 29 degrees Centigrade (84 degrees F)—unusually hot for Eastern France even at midsummer. "Le Temps: Région," *L'Est Républicain*, July 15, 1976.

4. Unger, "Les Mystères de L'Affaire Peiper." An ambulance did pass through the village that night, but its intention was above board, coming from Echenoz-la-Meline to fetch a sick Frenchman in Chantes. "Traves, village traumatisé," *L'Est Républicain*, July 16, 1976. The author spoke to Mme Guyot again on August 16, 2001. She recalled seeing cars come through

the town that night but could no longer remember what type. "Later, I heard loud sounds. I thought it was fireworks."

5. "Joachim Peiper avait reçu de nouvelles menaces la veille de sa mort," Grande Region, *RL*, July 15, 1976, Maurice Delaval Papers, US Army Military History Institute, Carlisle, PA.

6. Gérard Sebille and André Moissé, "Un cadavre carbonisé découvert dans la maison incendiée de Joachim Peiper," *L'Est Républicain*, July 15, 1976.

7. Dominique Leroy, "Un singulier témoin." *Le Républicain Lorrain*, February 17, 1987. Ketelhut first denied hearing any gunshots when first interrogated by police on July 15, 1976. He altered his story when testifying again on January 26, 1977, although claiming not to have heard any dogs barking nor to have noticed any sign of fire when he went to sleep.

8. The scenario of the attack given here is taken directly from the lengthy police inspector's report from Roger Lavaux as given to the author. Service Régional de Police Judiciaire à Dijon, No. 2 400/SC, le commandement du Capitaine Pierre Marchal.

9. Indications are that Peiper fired in the direction of his assailants, although with the blasts sent into the treetops, he did not likely intend harm but rather wished to frighten off his attackers. Letter Roger Lavaux to author, November 15, 1999. "He fired shot in the air, hoping that like sparrows they would fly." Louette. interview. The trajectories and ballistics of Peiper's shots were traced by French ballistics expert Roland Thuillier, Lavaux Report, 6.

10. The weapon was a US-made 1940 Remington model 11 Sportsman semi-automatic 12-gauge shotgun.

11. From the police report, the revolver was a .38 Special Colt PTFA-MFG CO with a three-inch-long barrel and designed for police work. The lightweight hunting carbine was a 22 LR J. G. Anschütz, which was found with its single chambered cartridge expended.

12. Associated Press, "Avengers kill SS colonel in France," *The Times*, July 15, 1976. "The police said it was strange that he made no effort to telephone for help when the attack began in the early hours of the morning, for no attempt had been made to cut his telephone line."

13. Peiper's telephone was in his library on the ground floor. Charles Garreau, "A Traves, on ressort les fusils," *L'Est Républicain*, November 24, 1976.

14. One unburned Molotov cocktail with a singed Dacron wick was found about ten meters from the house on the southwest side at the base of an oak tree, close by where Peiper had fired shorts with the pistol. One of the .38 caliber rounds was recovered from the ground nearby. The Molotov cocktail that set the house afire appears to have been tossed through the open window from the west veranda to the library.

15. The police report was uncertain on this point. Peiper may have fired the pistol and rifle until the attacker left or may have fired each time into the darkness when he came down to take out possessions to the wood shed. Lavaux Police Report, 3.

16. Lavaux Police Report, 3. Investigation of the manner in which the fire spread was examined by experts Henri Teisseyre of Marseille and René Pouillande of Lyon. Chief among the factors was the staircase linking the ground floor with the upper one, which acted as a chimney to accelerate the combustion.

17. "Peiper's Own Book," from an appendix in the book of Agte, *Jochen Peiper*.

18. The two wooden drawers are still in possession of Neill Thomson and show no signs of burning or smell of smoke. Thus, they must have been either moved to the woodshed before the fire or very soon after it started.

19. Contrary to some reports, some of the papers and materials that Peiper saved were strewn about on the yard, leading one to believe that they had been hastily moved during the fire. "I have seen this with my own eyes." Police inspector Roger Lavaux to author: April 28, 2000. The piles of clothing can also be seen in photographs taken the day after the fire that appeared in *L'Est Républicain*.

20. Lavaux Police Report, 7.

21. For particulars of the fire, Lavaux Police Report, 3.

22. The youths were from Velle-le-Châtel and stopped in Traves to wake the mayor. Later they reported the incident to the police: "Les policiers recherchent une R 16 blanche," *L'Est Républicain*, July 22, 1976.

23. *RL*, July 15, 1976, *op. cit.* Years later the author could not get Farque to speak. "He is just a simple farmer," a nervous go-between told us. "He won't talk to you."

24. On July 29 the twelve firemen from Traves were detained and then extensively questioned. A lingering suspicion was that the men had sabotaged their firefighting equipment and let Le Renfort burn to the ground. The last member of the group was released at 11 a.m. on July 30. This angered the head of the volunteers, Monsieur Raymond Obriot. Yet the press continued accusations as did the police. Obriot offered his resignation and the volunteer firefighters of Traves quit for a time. The real problem, they said, was a lack of maintenance and rust. The late arrival of the other firefighters from Vesoul likely had to do with the confounding festivities (e.g., drinking) on Bastille eve. Even today, however, the possibility of sabotage of the fire fighting equipment remains controversial in the official police report. Lavaux Police Report, 19–20. This was based on an inspection of the equipment by the Fire Department of the Haute-Saône: M. Francis Courtejoie and Jean Bernard on July 29, 1976. In the end Lavaux did not suspect complicity of the Traves firemen. Interview, July 12, 2002.

25. Louette, interview, August 16, 2001.

26. "Deux heures pour capturer les chiens," *L'Est Républicain*, July 16, 1976. The two Drahthaar dogs were captured by the animal shelter at St. Adrian, where the wounded hound was treated by a veterinarian. Timm and Tamm had been chased for two hours all the way from Cubry-Chantes to Traves. Ironically, they were captured about five hundred meters from their master's burned-out ruin at about 3 p.m. on July 15 by M. Hubert Viscardi. Peiper's wife did not want possession of the dogs after July 14; she bequeathed Peiper's beloved dogs to the police.

27. Inspector Lavaux, interview by author, May 15, 1999.

28. At first Sigurd Peiper refused the copy of *Mein Kampf* and the police retained possession until she reconsidered and asked for its return on July 16, 1976. The dedication from Hitler was "on the occasion of the Peipers' wedding day." Hinrich Peiper to author, May 7, 2000.

29. Lavaux Police Report, 7.

30. Details from at the scene of the crime are taken from the description of Police Inspector Roger Lavaux, interview by author, Dijon, May 15, 1999. Also, letters to author, July 20 and November 15, 1999. Comparison of the 6.35mm shell casings with other similar weapons did not yield any matches: evidence of Ceccaldi, Lavaux Report, 9. Ketelhut's initial statement to police: "He was a fighter. He knew well his situation. If he had wanted he would have otherwise defended himself. But, I am persuaded that he did not want to kill anyone. He was tired of all this drama. He told me that it was an affair that had arisen because of a coordinated effort between Paris and East Germany." *France Soir*, "Ce soir, je serai mort." July 17, 1976.

31. Today Lavaux laments the unavailability of DNA testing in 1976, which would have allowed timely identification of the corpse and abbreviation of the ensuing controversy. Location of the body: Lavaux to author, April 28, 2000.

32. The village priest arrived along with everyone else, but became convinced that the charred shape was not even human. "The police asked me if I was squeamish. I said 'no'. They allowed me to look in the house. The body had been dropped into a wheel barrow. I wasn't affected by it. It was like a charred piece of wood with no arms. The bottoms of the legs were missing. I thought it looked like a tailor's mannequin rather than a person. It looked artificial. They picked it up like a piece of burned cordwood and put it in a sheet. . . . I don't think it was a body. It looked like a dummy." Louis Ducros, interview by author, August 16, 2001.

33. Louette, interview.

34. Lavaux, interview, May 15, 1999.

35. Lavaux Police Report, 7. The Heuer watch that Peiper possessed was an expensive model (~US$5,000), which must have been given to him as a gift, or otherwise purchased back in Germany during his high-earnings days with Max Moritz.

36. Based on the times that the watch and clock had stopped, and when the first shots were heard, it would seem that Peiper had died between 12:40 and 1:00 a.m. on July 14, 1976, before the fire consumed the timepieces and caused them to stop working.

37. Dominique Leroy, "La mise en scène," *Le Républicain Lorrain*, February 16, 1987. Also, Lavaux to author, November 15, 1999. Also, Lavaux Police Report, 5.

38. Curé Louis Ducros, interview by author, August 16, 2001. "I've never believed he was killed, because when I got to the spot, I saw Peiper clothes on one side and the police dogs running off in the direction that Peiper had escaped. There were some Gauloise cigarettes at the foot of the barbed wire fence which should have helped explain Peiper's escape. Someone helped him escape. . . . I've always said that. . . . I told the police, I told everyone." Asked why his story was never published, Ducros expressed a negative opinion of the Vesoul newspaper, *L'Est Républicain.* "It's crooked." That autumn Ducros was quoted by a reporter claiming that Peiper still lived: "Traves: un village à l'heure allemande," Marianne Lohse, n.p., September 17, 1976.

39. Conclusion of Dr. Michel Durignon, Lavaux Police Report, 10.

40. Martin, *L'Affaire Peiper*, 14. One interviewed local witness, who wished to remain anonymous, told the author that a boat or boats from the River Sâone was the certain origin of several of the attackers, a claim that cannot be verified but one that the police never eliminated as a possibility.

41. Inspector Lavaux, interview by author, Dijon, November 16, 2013.

42. "En attendant des expertises approfondies Le mystère 'Peiper' jette le trouble in Haute-Saône," *L'Est Républicain*, July 19, 1976.

43. Moissé, interview. Moissé had been planning a holiday trip to the Îl de Ré, off the west coast of France for July 14, but due to the needed coverage on the Peiper affair, would not leave until three days later.

44. "Le mystère du SS Peiper reste entier," and "L'ancien lieutenant de Peiper menacé de mort," *L'Est Républicain*, July 17 and 18, 1976.

45. Inspector Lavaux found one of the bullets fired from the revolver by the woodshed. Letter to author, July 20, 1999. Also, Lavaux Police Report, 4.

46. "Die Mörder von Oberst Peiper," *National Zeitung*, No. 30, July 23, 1976.

47. *Bild am Sonntag, op. cit.* Hinrich Peiper disputed Rigoulot's simplistic characterization of his father as one shooting until the end. See "Greuelmärchen aus dem Krieg," No. 34, *Der Spiegel*, August 16, 1976.

48. BA-MA, HIAG Archives, B 438, V/320 Letter Kernmayr to Lehmann, July 15, 1976. For background on Kernmayr's postwar intrigue with US intelligence while continuing his brand of Austrian right-wing extremist journalism glorifying a Nazi past: NA, RG 319, Investigative Interrogation Reports, IRR Erich Kernmayr, XE 189259.

49. "Has the SS killer escaped his avengers again?" Michael Brown, Paris, *Daily Express*, July 16, 1976. Part of the problem came from a civilian who falsely claimed to be part of the official investigation: "We cannot be sure yet, but there are indications that the body was not that of Peiper."

50. Yves Maréchal and René Guillois, "Peiper n'a pas éte assassiné il s'est suicidé," *Ici Paris Hebdo*, July 1976. The journalistic theory exposed by the Paris weekly was quickly discounted when the initial autopsy revealed that the blow in the middle of the victim's chest was caused, not by a bullet wound but rather by a falling heavy object such as a roofing tile or wooden beam. Lavaux to author, April 28, 2000.

51. Müller, interview, May 18, 1999. "On 12 July, Peiper informed us of his wife's visit to us the next day. She wanted to visit a lady-friend in Basel and passed us on the way. She came

to us by car on the morning of 13 July. We had a serious conversation. She said she would not have driven, given the situation, but her husband had urged her insistently."

52. Hinrich Peiper had learned of the tragedy while at his law office when his sister-in-law said the story was on the news. With his father-in-law, he journeyed down to meet his mother in Bad Krozingen at the home of Benno Müller. They stayed there the night before driving to Traves the following morning with his mother. H. Peiper, interview, May 5, 1999. Also, letter to author, May 7, 2000. Sigurd had traveled on July 13 to stay with the sister of a close friend, Artur 'Kaj' Keser, the legendary press chief within the Mercedes Automotive Company who had made his home in Stuttgart. Wieselmann, interview, June 17, 2004.

53. *Bild am Sonntag, op. cit.* "The Death of Joachim Peiper," For details on the autopsy, *After the Battle*, No. 40, 1983, 47–53. The investigation revealed traces of smoke in the lungs of the body, indicating that the victim had been alive when the fire began. There were no visible bullet wounds, although the body was so badly incinerated that it was impossible to determine whether there were other wounds. A section of the lower jaw was available to allow limited comparison with Peiper's dental records. Would Peiper have fled or fought back? "I believe that if my husband was attacked," Sigurd Peiper declared to Vesoul investigation judge Daniel Clerget on July 15, "he would have defended himself." Dominique Leroy, "La Mise en scène," *Le Républicain Lorrain*, February 16, 1987. Although Sigurd Peiper was unable to confirm the identity of the remains, she obviously suspected it to be her husband, a fact made obvious by her immediate steps to repatriate the corpse to Germany. Gérard Sebille, André Moissé and Hubert Paruit, "L'épouse de l'ancien colonel SS ń a pas pu indentifier le corps calciné de la maison de Traves," *L'Est Républicain*, July 16, 1976.

54. For Sigurd Peiper's statement in French—"Je ne peux absolument pas dire s'il s'agit de mon mari"—and her composure in Traves, see Jacques Buob, Richard Cannavo, Charles Garreau, and Lucien Pinchon, "Ce soir, je serai mort," *France Soir*, July 17, 1976.

55. Sigurd Peiper to Fritz Kosmehl, November 1, 1978. "I feared that you too believed I had deserted Jochen or let him send me away, as the press reported all over. That, however, was not the case. I had informed my sister [sic] about my planned trip to Basel on 13/14 July already at the beginning of the month. If I had myself sent away, I certainly would have taken with me documents and papers important to us and would not traveled only with a traveling bag with overnight stuff."

56. J. Peiper to Willis Everett, July 14, 1946, *Willis Everett Papers*, Atlanta.

57. Jochen Peiper to Sigurd Peiper, June 22, 1976. "Jo" was Sigurd Peiper's affectionate term for her husband. Copy of this important letter provided by Neill Thomson. The letter was saved by Peiper and placed in the wooden drawers with other papers and was recovered by the police the following day. Lavaux, interview, May 15, 1999. Peiper's wife was grateful for the local police's effort in the confusing affair; she made a gift of all the remaining wine in the cellar of the burned-out house to the local gendarmes along with a number of other scorched items of no particular value. The letter was dated one day after the antagonistic notices were circulated about Traves in June 1976.

58. James Goldsborough, "Body in Ruins of Ex-SS Officer's Home Puzzles French," Associated Press, Paris, July 16, 1976.

59. As example of the extreme scenarios, see *Express*, "The Secret Life of Hitler's Guard," July 16, 1976, Paris and "Affaire Peiper," *New Society*, July 22, 1976. These articles had Peiper, a Nazi James Bond, killing one of the would-be assassins who is then burned beyond recognition. Peiper then escaping to assume control of an elaborate international SS network called the "Mannheim Connection" funded by wartime loot locked away in Switzerland and run by SS Hauptmann Hans-Alfred Zimmer. Other information had Peiper a part of a shadowy group of retired SS officers: *Die Spinne*—the Spider, which was organized by Nazi commando extraordinaire, Otto Skorzeny.

60. "French Study Apparent Slaying of Former Nazi," *New York Times*, Sunday, July 18, 1976, also "Pech für Ihn," *Der Spiegel*, No. 30, July 19, 1976. However, the police investigation in Vesoul was quick to discount the Avengers and members of the resistance as those responsible for the burning of Peiper's estate. The attack, they maintained, was much too clumsy to have been the work of members of the French resistance. Years later, a member of the Parisian police confided in journalist Roger Martin that one of the hooded members had been recognized and later told him that the press conference on the third floor of the Grand Hôtel had been staged. Martin, *L'Affaire Peiper*, 63.

61. Goldsborough, "Body in Ruins of Ex-SS Officer's Home Puzzles French." "Peiper was one of those rare Nazis who paid for his crimes with ten years in prison," said Klarsfeld.

62. Michael Brown, "Is Colonel Peiper of the SS dead or alive?" *Daily Express*, August 1976.

63. Robert Daley, "Aftermath: A Mystery and a Symbol," *San Francisco Chronicle*, November 14, 1976, B-7. Ironically, Paul Cacheux would die exactly twenty years after Peiper's departure, on July 14, 1996.

64. "Untergrundorganisation droht mit Tötung deutscher Kriegsverbrecher," *Frankfurter Allgemeine*, July 16, 1976, 5. "The communists naturally condemn the murder, verbally, but they forget that they had started the smear campaign."

65. Karl Jetter, "Der Mord an Joachim Peiper und sein politisches Ziel," *Frankfurter Allgemeine*, July 19, 1976, 2. "The instigation for expelling Peiper can be documented step-by-step to have begun with hints from East Berlin. Members of the Union CGT in the Postal Service handled his correspondence with Germany and his secret telephone number."

66. "Le mystère du SS Peiper reste entier," *L'Est Républicain*, July 17, 1976.

67. Roger Lavaux to author, April 28, 2000.

68. For Peiper in hand-to-hand combat with his assailants: Gérard Sebille and André Moissé, "Identification difficile du cadavre de la maison Peiper," *L'Est Républicain*, July 17, 1976.

69. Autopsy records provided to author by anonymous source. The records show that the corpse was burned so severely that it was impossible to determine if it had been injured from inflicted or traumatic wounds associated with death. The only real evidence was a small section of the upper jaw. The Dijon police inspector, Roger Lavaux, did reveal to the author that there was no evidence of any gunshot to the head. Interview by author, May 15, 1999. See also, "L'ancien colonel SS Joachim Peiper est mort asphyxié," *L'Est Républicain*, September 3, 1977. One theory regarding the missing gold tooth was that it had melted away in the fire—gold melting at 1000 degrees C and the fire having approached 1400 degrees. André Moissé, *L'Est Républicain*, July 6, 1986.

70. Arndt Fischer, interview by author, May 15, 1997. Years later the events associated with the autopsy still puzzled Fischer. He noted the many unusual circumstances. "The body was so cut up. In the first autopsy, the head was missing. Only one molar was present and it was cut in half." The German autopsy was performed by the court forensic, Professor Wolfgang Spann at the Institut für Rechtsmedizin. Spann wrote a book entitled *Cold Surgery*, but it did not mention the case and has never said anything publically about the matter. When the cadaver arrived from France, it was missing the head. Later this was provided, but had been split up; the single tooth provided to Fischer for identification had been cut in half. "It has never been convincingly proven that the body was that of Peiper."

71. Suicide was also a theory put forth within the early investigation. Certainly a number of others of the SS had ended their lives in this fashion in May 1945, and some postulated that Peiper ended his life in the flaming ruins of his home rather than face another move. Gérard Sebille, André Moissé, and Hubert Paruit, "L'épouse de l'ancien colonel SS ń a pas pu identifier le corps calciné de la maison de Traves," *L'Est Républicain*, July 16, 1976.

72. Kahl, "In München wird das Rätsel um Joachim Peiper gelöst."

73. Lavaux, Müller, and H. Peiper, interviews. Hinrich completely dismisses the possibility that his father sought his death in Traves. "In the beginning I talked of the murder of my father," his son told the author, "now I would rather say he was killed (manslaughter: *Mord/Totschlag*)."

74. Nachlaß Ernst Klink, BA-MA, Letter Hinrich Peiper to Klink, June 25, 1979.

75. Michael Brown, *Daily Express*, July 16, 1976.

76. Unidentified newspaper clipping, Neill Thomson archives, copy in author's possession.

Chapter Twenty-Four

1. Charles Hargrove, "Sightseers Flock to Look at SS Man's Wrecked Home," *The Times*, July 19, 1976. "Cars full of sightseers converged this weekend on the small village of Traves, in the Haute Saône to get a glimpse of the the burnt out house of Joachim Peiper, the former SS colonel who is perhaps not dead." See also, "La maison incendiée transformée en lieu d'excursion dominicale," *Dernière Nouvelles d'Alsace*, July 19, 1976. Martial Rigoulot, interview by author, August 15, 2001. "No one could get through the village the day after."

2. *Der Spiegel*, "Trauriges Nachspiel," July 15, 1977. Rigoulot: "The whole affair has ruined the village, opening up old sores and causing misery . . . There are people who think that it was some of the villagers who wanted to settle accounts, but I don't believe it. I believe the Communists were behind it all—it was they who exposed his record—because they want to wreck the political understanding between France and Germany and overturn the Common Market."

3. Letters courtesy Martial Rigoulot, received by his father on August 23, 1976 and typical of many others (Rigoulot papers). As late as March 1980 they were still receiving threats: "Men live for a long time and we will have patience. Traves will be marked with a red stone. You have been warned."

4. "A lot of garbage.
All we've paid
And your going to pay
You French!"

5. J. M. Bourget, "La Fin Mystérieuse de Joachim Peiper," *L'Aurore*, July 16, 1976. The day after the fire the priest received a truly odd request from a group of Frenchmen, who expressed the desire to come to Peiper's home to pay homage to the fallen SS leader. Gérard Sebille and André Moissé, "Un cadavre carbonisé découvert dans la maison incendiée de Joachim Peiper," *L'Est Républicain*, July 15, 1976.

6. J. P. Van Geirt, "Trente ans après La Vengeance Foundie Peiper L'Officer SS," *Paris Match*, July 24, 1976. Strangely some of the resistance fighters against the Germans in the area around Vesoul came from a battalion of Ukrainians that had been located there during the war. Gaston Laroche, "La vengeance frappe Peiper l'officier SS: On les nommait des éstrangers," *Les émigrés dans la Résistance*, 1965. And the European Parliament: "The Chirac government, which is otherwise so quick in expelling immigrant workers from Morocco or Tunisia, could have done better by denying this SS man residence within their jurisdiction." Tod eines SS-Mannes, Europäisches Parlament: Schriftliche Anfrage No. 551/76 von Herrn Dondelinger, 20 October 1976, BA-MA, Sammlung Vorpersal, N 756/405.

7. "Tout le monde condamne l'attentat mais," *L'Aurore*, July 16, 1976.

8. Lavaux Police Report, 17. French Communist reports to the police were confined to the reportage of mailed threats that had received in August of 1976. Nothing was helpful to solution of the Peiper case. "Whoever may be the perpetrators of this expeditious justice, the Communist Party carries a serious part of the responsibility having been the instigator." "En marge de l'affaire Peiper," *L'Est Républicain*, July 27, 1976.

9. Charles Garreau, "A la kermesse du curé soudain un cri: 'Au feu!': Six mois après la mort du Waffen SS Peiper, la haine et la peur pèsent encore sur Traves," *France Soir*, January 26, 1977.

10. Karl Jetter, "Der Mord an Joachim Peiper und sein politisches Ziel," *Der Freiwillige*, August 1976. Peiper himself had seen the Soviet Communist party as the source of his troubles before his death. "The communist group [after me] comes from Moscow, is coordinated with Italy and France and is aimed against the French-German friendship." Letter Peiper to Arndt Fischer, July 9, 1976.

11. Karl Jetter, "das Resultat einer Kommunistischen Kampagne," *Frankfurter Allgemeine Zeitung*, July 19, 1976.

12. Ibid.

13. "Affaire Peiper: Un journaliste et un commerçant de Vesoul portent plainte pour menaces de mort," *Le Bien Public*, July 27, 1976.

14. "Bomb Diffused at Synagogue," *Los Angeles Times*, July 19, 1976; Guy Walters, *Hunting Evil: The Nazi War Criminal Who Escaped and the Quest to Bring Them to Justice* (New York: Broadway Books, 2009), 373–375. Even if Groupe Joachim Peiper was bluffing, there was no questioning that at midnight, July 5–6, 1979, Klarsfeld's red Renault 5 was blown to bits not far from their apartment in southwest Paris. Three days later, a typed message addressed to Serge Klarsfeld claimed responsibility for the bombing. Even if improbable, the letter—with ten centime stamps arranged as a swastika—asserted that ODESSA was responsible for the action.

15. "Mystérieux attentat contre la maison d'un militant communiste à Vesoul" and "Après l'incendie de la rue des Prunus: information ouverte par le parquet," *L'Est Républicain*, August 20 and 21, 1976. "Un magsasin de Vesoul plastiqué par les 'Vengeurs' du SS Peiper," *L'Est Républicain*, September 4, 1976. At the time Cacheux was not even any longer with the shattered store. The graffiti threatened "Cacheux Criminal of the PCF"—the French Communist Party—with the mysterious signature of responsibility: O.N.R.

16. "L'attentat de Vesoul: aucun lien avec l'affaire Peiper affirme le parti communiste," *L'Est Républicain*, August 21, 1976.

17. Louba Schirman to Burton Ellis, letter, December 3, 1979, Burton Ellis Papers. "No one was injured, but some wreckage of his apartment. Both Nordman and Cacheux are members of the French Communist Party. . . . One is really fed up with all these extremist groups."

18. Garreau, "A la kermesse du curé soudain un cri."

19. Pierre Dornier, "Pas de représailles à Traves pas de progrès dans l'enquête," *L'Est Républicain*, August 1, 1976.

20. Garreau, "A Traves, on ressort les fusils."

21. Ducros wrote to the both the French Ministry of the Interior, as well as President Valéry Giscard d'Estaing to ask for funds to help with their losses, but without response. Letter of Louis Ducros to the French Minister of the Interior, February 25, 1977, and Letter of Ducros to D'Estaing, February 4, 1978, Rigoulot papers.

22. Garreau, "A la kermesse du curé soudain un cri." The priest in Traves worked for years with the French national lottery to make up the money lost in the canceled kermesse, a financial blow, from which his parish never recovered. "We've been the victim of this . . . The state promised they would pay us for what we lost in the kermesse, but they didn't." Ducros, interview, August 16, 2001.

23. "Rache für Peiper," *Die Welt*, December 18, 1976. Also among the graffiti in Vesoul: "Nichts für uns—alles für Deutschland"—"Nothing for us; all for Germany." Also, "'Nous vengerons Peiper' inscriptions noctures sur les murs de Traves," *L'Est Républicain*, November 1976.

24. Lavaux to author, November 15, 1999.

25. Lavaux, interview, July 12, 2002.

26. Louette, interview, August 16, 2001. Louette thought Peiper's attackers had come by boat and used the car to get away.

27. "L'enquête centrée sur Traves," *L'Est Républicain*, July 22, 1976.

28. Lavaux Police Report, 21. (P.V. 2, 3, 4, 5, 20 and 21).

29. Jacques Gauthier, interview by author, August 16, 2001. "I had the number because when we made the rye bread he wanted, I would be able to ring him up to come and pick it up. When the incident happened, the police interrogated this reporter [*sic*, photographer], [Marc] Paygnard and asked him where he had gotten the unlisted number. He told them he had gotten it from me. And then the police came to see me and it was straightaway a case of handcuffs. Eventually they let me go."

30. Garreau, "A Traves, on ressort les fusils." The priest's statement in defense of the two boys: "Les flics se croient bien malins: ils ne trouveront rien. Les gens de Traves sont plus forts qu'eux." Also, statement by Ducros in September, "Traves: un village à l'heure allemande," Marianne Lohse, September 17, 1976.

31. "Après la disparition de Joachim Peiper," *L'Est Républicain*, July 19, 1976. The priest had become something of a thorn in the sides of the police investigating. "He was always trying to steal the limelight as if he knew everything," Lavaux remembered. "He went around spreading fantastic stories." Letter to author, September 26, 2001.

32. "SS Peiper: la clé de l'énigme à Traves," *L'Est Républicain*, July 23, 1976. "The police wish to end the investigation rapidly because the anonymous letters are multiplying and resulting in fear in the village. The situation is creating the most incredible rumors. . . . Several persons already questioned that live in Traves are being questioned again." Also, "Tandis qu'un movement 'autonomiste' revendique à son tour l'attentat le Renfort est passé au peigne fin," *L'Est Républicain*, July 19, 1976.

33. Martin, *L'Affaire Peiper*, 94.

34. Anonymous witness, interview by author, August 2001. "Since this happened, this place has been messed up. . . . This village is prettier than it is nice [*Ce village est plus beau que bon!*]"

35. Daley, *The Case of the SS Hero*. Marc Dreyfus was the attorney general in Vesoul working with Daniel Clerget, the examining magistrate.

36. Asphyxiation was listed in the autopsy as the official cause of death. Examination of the remains had found traces of carbon monoxide in the lungs ("*Dose Toxique—60ml par litre*"), indicating that Peiper had likely been overcome by smoke. This conclusion was reached on January 19, 1977, by a panel of doctors and forensics. Autopsy report, *op. cit.*; also, "L'ancien colonel SS Joachim Peiper est mort asphyxié," *L'Est Républicain*, September 3, 1977. The three experts performing the autopsy were Professors Michon, Campana, and Ceccaldi, flown in by the French Justice Ministry when the Giscard government perceived developing controversy with the identification. See Lavaux Report, 10.

37. After long study of the event Police Inspector Lavaux says today that he is confident that Peiper's death was the work of kids and not that of professionals. "It was done by people in the local area and had support of people in the local area. If it was not the four individuals we identified," he said laconically. "It was several others very similar to them. It was definitely local because of the methods used—a little pistol and poorly made firebombs." Further he does not believe that Peiper's assailants intended his death. "They only looked to warm up the situation." Today the police inspector terms speculation of a well-organized conspiracy "a complete fantasy." Lavaux, interview and correspondence with author. Also, Lavaux Police Report, 30.

38. The rumor that Italian revengers were responsible for the fire arose repeatedly. Yet this speculation was readily rebuffed by the Chief Police Commissioner Henri Bernard-de-Pelagey of Vesoul, who observed that "all of the threats received by him [Peiper], be by letter or by telephone, were always in excellent French!" Martin, *L'Affaire Peiper*, 65.

39. For the television documentary, see, "L'affaire Peiper sur le petit écran mais Traves veut le silence," *L'Est Républicain*, September 22, 1976. For Peiper as a Red spy: Robert Caron, "L'ex-officier SS Peiper serait devenu un agent du KGB, *France Soir*, September 1976. Members of the extreme right [*Deutsche Volksunion*] met in Cologne to deny the allegations that had appeared in *France Soir*: it is "a lot more likely that the KGB. had ordered and organized

the murder of Peiper for disturbing the French-German friendship and the unification of Europe."

40. "L'Inspecteur Divisionnaire Roger Lavaux à Monsieur le Directeur du Service Régional de Police Judiciaire à Dijon: Service Régional de Police Judicaire à Dijon: No. 2 400/SC" no date. This official report prepared for Daniel Clerget, the examining magistrate of Vesoul, was provided to the author, hereafter: Lavaux Police Report. The report clearly laid the blame: "The fire was a result of an intense campaign led by several weeks by the Communist Party and the members of the Resistance," 2.

41. "L'Histoire de quatre suspects," *L'Est Républicain*, February 1997.

42. Charles Garreau, "La mort du SS Peiper: le filet se resserre sur quatre suspects," *France Soir*, August 7, 1976.

43. Dominique Leroy, "Pistes suivies . . . et oubliées," *Le Républicain Lorrain*, February 18, 1987. Lavaux Police Report, 25.

44. Information on the police investigation and findings associated with the Peiper case are primarily based on Lavaux, interview, May 15, 1999. Lavaux has a copy of the official police summary report, which was also provided to the author (Lavaux Police Report).

45. The other three suspects: Rémy R., Jean-Michel E., and André G. Last names withheld.

46. "Les suspects de l'agression 'Nous étions au bal avec des files'," *L'Est Républicain*, February 17, 1987.

47. Lavaux Police Report, 26 (P.V. 133).

48. Martin, *L'Affaire Peiper*, 95.

49. In January 1988 André Moissé made an effort to track down Daniel D. in Gray. After a considerable hunt, he located the youth, whose parents at first refused to allow him to speak to the journalist. Eventually Moissé did convince him to talk, but Daniel maintained that a head injury sustained in the intervening years made it impossible to remember what happened on the night of July 13, 1976. Moissé, interviews, March 29, 2014, and April 22, 2014.

50. Lavaux, interview. An anonymous person in Traves echoed the thoughts of many. "If it was a member of the old resistance," they ventured, "or young people from around the corner, then it is better that we never know their identity." Domininque Leroy, "Un cadavre qui arrange tout le monde," *L'Est Républicain*, February 19, 1987.

51. Ducros, interview. "I chased the police out of my house because they persecute me over it [the Peiper affair]. They did that because I maintained Peiper had escaped. They wanted me to say the exact opposite of what I believe. I couldn't do that. 'No,' I told them, 'he escaped.' I believe they were under orders to shut me up because I wanted to tell the truth. The orders were coming from above . . . I wrote to Giscard d'Estaing to complain about it and the cancellation of the Kermesse. I never got a response from him."

52. Letter Roger Lavaux to author, April 20, 2000. Years after the affair Ketelhut lived in a small village near Besançon some fifty kilometers from Traves, "where he endeavored to be forgotten."

53. How was Ketelhut so certain it was Peiper when seeing a charred mummy reduced to only twenty inches? "I have some knowledge of anatomy being a sculptor of human figures. It was his shoulders and his head." "Traves: Un village à l'heure allemande," Marianne Lohse, n.p., September 17, 1976.

54. "Le voisin de J. Peiper met en vente sa Propriété," *L'Est Républicain*, July 27, 1976. Was Ketelhut worried for his welfare? "Ketelhut certainly knows much more than he wants to say. Perhaps his life depends on his silence . . . Under the pretense of illness, he carries out some frequent travels to Germany." Garreau, "A Traves, on ressort les fusils." Even the priest, who thought Ketelhut "a nice man," said there "are many questions about him. He lived only a 100 meters [*sic*] from Peiper's house and claimed to have never heard a damned thing. He was a clever and cunning chap. Now, he is dead and the whole thing will never be understood." Ducros, interview, August 16, 2001.

55. Lavaux Police Report, 29. "What is unthinkable is the fact, as claimed by the witness, that he heard neither the detonations of shotgun shells, bullets from other guns and pistols, nor the roaring of the fire." (P.V. 44).

56. Lavaux, interview, July 12, 2002.

57. Garreau, "La mort du SS Peiper: le filet se resserre sur quatre suspects." Judge Nannini was convinced that the youths had done the deed, but no one was changing their story. They claimed to have been at a dance—an alibi friendly witnesses readily embraced. Nannini was convinced that in setting fire to the dump later that night, the youths were merely attempting to throw the firemen off track in responding to their incendiary mission against Le Renfort. Only the reexamined Ketelhut told anything different, admitting that he vaguely remembered hearing gunshots yet insisting that he did not rise to investigate until the firemen woke him. Today Lavaux still regards Ketelhut with suspicion, noting that the German citizen moved a number of times since the death—to Germany and then back to France. Of his "old friend" Peiper: "He knows much more than he told us." Lavaux to author, November 15, 1999.

58. "Il y a trois ans l'affaire Peiper," *L'Est Républicain*, July 17, 1979.

59. Quotation of Ketelhut: Martin, *L'Affaire Peiper*, 142. Veterans from the Leibstandarte Adolf Hitler from the war, the two became friends at Volkswagen, and Peiper invited him to visit his vacation home in Traves. Upon looking for himself, Ketelhut found the region "beautiful and friendly." One day Peiper called Ketelhut in Germany to let him know that the old mill at the edge of town was for sale. With little hesitation, Ketelhut moved to Traves.

60. Lavaux Police Report, 29.

61. "Il y a trois ans l'affaire Peiper," *L'Est Républicain*, July 17, 1979.

62. R. Lavaux to author, July 20, 1999. André Moissé spoke to one of the suspects in 1987. "When one is young, one doesn't fear anything," he told the reporter refusing further discourse. "Now it is time to bury this terrible affair." André Moissé, "L'histoire de quatre suspects . . . ," *L'Est Républicain*. To the reporter the youth's words amounted to an implicit confession. Later attempts by Inspector Lavaux to contact the youth were fruitless. Soon after the missed telephone call Daniel D. left his employer, with no information as to his destination. Strangely the same is true for the other three youths—all have disappeared from the region with no available information on their whereabouts.

63. In August 1976 Hinrich Peiper wrote a scathing condemnation of the reporting on his father's murder in the July 19 issue of *Der Spiegel*. The article was flippantly titled, "Pech für ihn"—"Tough Break for Him"—after the remark of the Traves mayor, Ernest Rigoulot. "This was not a case where one had a tough break. This was the end of a postwar tragedy, a fate that the man did not deserve. The man who was killed carried the personified personal guilt of others for overcoming the past and died because the Communists fanned up existing resentments using horror tales from the war." "Greuelmärchen aus dem Kriege," *Der Spiegel*, No. 34, August 16, 1976, 10.

64. Sigurd Peiper to Hinrich Peiper, letter, 1976. Source: Nachlaß Ernst Klink, BA-MA, Zur Trauerfeier am 17.4.1979.

65. "Traves: un village à l'heure allemande," Marianne Lohse, n.p., September 17, 1976.

66. Lavaux Report, 9–10. As a follow-up on October 26, 1976, Professors P. Cernea and C. Brocheriou of the hospital in Salpétrière conducted an autopsy of the second molar on the cadaver with the X-ray records provided by Arndt Fischer, confirming that the examined tooth and those in Peiper's records look to have "come from the same person."

67. Hubert Meyer's speech from Peiper's memorial service is taken from *Der Freiwillige*, November 1976, 5. The quote from Peiper's open letter from Landsberg, "Worte aus Landsberg," is taken from Paul Hausser, *Waffen-SS im Einsatz* (Göttingen: Plesse Verlag, 1953), 262–269.

68. "Der Fall Jochen Peiper—ein halbes Jahr danach," Letter, Hinrich Peiper to *Die Welt*, January 10, 1977, 6. That same year Hinrich also naïvely defended his father's past to the

newspaper *France Soir*: "Do not confuse the SS and the Waffen SS," he wrote, "The SS were, in general, were some terrible and famous torturers. On the contrary, the Waffen SS were soldiers who fought in the war in uniform, like my father."

69. Gerhard Frey to Hinrich Peiper, August 27, 1976; H. Peiper to Frey, August 29, 1976, and Dietrich Ziemssen to Frey, October 19, 1976, BA-MA, RS 7/v. 282.

70. "L'Affair Peiper au jour le Jour," *France Soir*, January 26, 1977.

71. H. Peiper, interview, May 1999. Also, see "La famille de Peiper s'oppose aux manifestations de l'extrème-droite allemande," *L'Est Républicain*, September 11, 1976. The right-wing group meeting in Cologne had the intention of inaugurating a monument emblazoned with the iron cross with the inscription: "Joachim Peiper: Born 30-1-1915, assassinated 14-7-1976." The monument was to be transported to Dachau to be installed a few hundred meters from the old concentration camp. The principal organizer was Dr. Gerhard Frey, the outspoken editor of the *National Zeitung*, a right-wing publication within Germany, who had written for weeks after the incident (see, e.g., "Oberst Peiper—Held und Märtyrer [Hero and Martyr]," *National Zeitung*, July 23, 1976).

72. "Neither during the Third Reich was he a member of the NSDAP—nor after the end of the Second World War was my father politically active." Hinrich Peiper's pledge under oath to stop the effort of Gerhard Frey as recounted in H. Peiper to Ernst Klink, April 29, 1977.

73. Klink to Hinrich Peiper, May 2, 1977. "The Reiter-SS clearly was part of the general SS; your father had an SS number. Membership in these political organizations did not expire upon joining the Readiness Troops. . . . In your declaration, you primarily denied him the right to take action in any manner about your father, and—so to speak beyond personal matters—also a formal membership in the circle of persons occupied by Frey. As Mr. Frey also does not have the authority to speak on behalf of a collective of persons by membership in a former political organization, at most, he can sue on behalf of persons in his party, specifically, your declaration deals with the post-war period. Your father neither joined the HIAG nor an association for the protection of the rights of internees, above all not any right-leaning party. So, nobody can claim him . . . On the other hand, the Readiness Troops had a guards status; at least that feeling was developing. In any event, he and the overwhelming number of his age group did not see joining the SS as a declaration of a political belief. On the other hand, one can not go as far as denying any membership in the Waffen SS. Especially, with your father's career until the war." Klink's last point almost certainly alluded to Klink's knowledge that Peiper had been adjutant to Heinrich Himmler.

74. Dorothee Peiper-Riegraf to Ernst Klink, May 6, 1977, BA-MA, Klink Papers. Regarding the book by Höhne, *Der Orden unter dem Totenkopf*. "I am just getting sick from reading the subjects of the examinations at the Junkerschule. . . . In the case of my father-in-law, I must appeal to the paragraph on page 408 [441 of the English translation] 'The chief of the SS is therefore forced to camouflage the real purpose of the *Verfügungstruppe* [readiness troops] . . . there can be no other explanation for the fact that even today senior Waffen SS commanders seriously believe that from the outset they were serving in a normal military force."

75. Harvey T. Rowe, "Wehe den Besiegten!" *Quick*, February 10, 1977.

76. Hinrich Peiper to Klink, December 7 and 20, 1976, BA-MA, Klink Papers. Peiper's son put Rowe in contact with Dietrich Ziemssen, who had long defended the Waffen SS point of view in the Malmédy affair for Leibstandarte veterans and had appeared as a witness for the defense at the trial. See, for example, Dietrich Ziemssen, *Der Malmedy Prozeß* (Munich: privately published, 1952), English translation by the Institute for Historical Review, Torrance, CA, 1981, a press infamous for its revisionist views.

77. Hinrich Peiper to Klink, December 31, 1976, BA-MA, Klink Papers. Also Harvey Rowe, interview by author, June 18, 2004. Rowe met Ernst Klink and later Dietrich Ziemssen, "who seemed to be a typical old SS officer, but somehow seemed to be involved with Odessa." Even though Rowe had some question about his developing associations, Ziemssen

later introduced him to another SS officer, Hans Kettgen, who produced a transcript of a two-and-a-half-hour interview he had with Peiper that he forwarded to him on February 10, 1977. Rowe also attended, with some trepidation, a meeting of the old Leibstandarte men in the early spring of 1977 at the Lenggries resort near Bad Tölz. Soon afterward, however, he gave up after learning the family disapproved of his project.

78. Walter Harzer to a HIAG gathering in Stuttgart on September 4, 1976. "This project must be done in the form of a book. . . . The bad rumors on the person of Peiper must be taken away. We must steadfastly remain behind the wheel and direct this book ourselves, otherwise [Erich] Kern of *Schildverlag* will do it. Then we can only complain about the outcome." BA/MA RS 7/v. 320. Herbert Reinecker was a Waffen SS correspondent during the war, writing the leading article for the very last issue for the *Das Schwarze Korps* in 1945, but went on to author numerous movie scripts and books including, ironically, the *Von Trapp Family in America*. Reinecker maintained a periodic communication with SS veterans such a Hubert Meyer after the war (see d'Alquen correspondence: BA/MA RS 7/v. 480. See Erich Kern (alias Kernmayr) was an SS Stubf. who took over the position in charge of press for the NSDAP in Vienna and had followed behind reporting on the Leibstandarte in Russia in the summer of 1941. After the war he composed countless essays with anti-Semitic overtones, expunging the Waffen SS, claiming that the Allies were responsible for the real crimes against the German people.

79. Klink to Hinrich Peiper, February 21, 1977, BA-MA, Klink Papers.

80. Brigitte B., Miesbach, interview by author, June 19, 2004.

81. Raymond Daniell, "Nazis in Bavaria Regaining Position," *New York Times*, April 24, 1946.

82. Sigurd Peiper to Klink, February 18, 1977, BA-MA, Klink Papers. For the letter forbidding Sigrid Mayr nee Magnussen to have more children in her marriage to an SS officer: Himmler to Mayr, September 13, 1939. Helmut Heiber, *Reichsführer!*. "SS Obersturmführer Mayr gave his word to have no further kids with his wife and knows that the three already living children will never get permission to marry a member of the SS."

83. Sigurd Peiper to Fritz Kosmehl, November 1, 1978. "Unfortunately my health is not good and I just spent three months in a Munich hospital."

84. "Trauriges Nachspiel," *Der Spiegel*, July 15, 1977. In late 1976 Sigurd Peiper announced not only her intention not to sell Traves, but to eventually rebuild it. Paul Cacheux cautioned against that: "It would be extremely tactless for Mrs. Peiper to rebuild the destroyed cottage as she had said she intends. . . . We cannot forget what our generation has known in the prisons and the concentration camps." *France Soir*, January 26, 1977. By that time the insurance companies had paid ₣300,000 for the house and another ₣20,000 for a life insurance policy. *L'Est Républicain*, November 13, 1976. (*France Soir* claimed the insurance policy was worth ₣260,000 but that the adjusters were hesitant to fully pay, given doubt regarding the identity of the identified corpse).

85. Proceedings of the German Bundestag [Lower House] 8th Election Period, Stenographic Vol, 100, Answer of Dr. Hamm-Brücher to question by Count Stauffenberg, March 2, 1977, Bonn. Stauffenberg petitioned the government of Bonn to help both with apprehending those responsible for Peiper's death and to expedite the return of his body to the family: Peiper's corpse was first held at the mortuary of the Paul Morel hospital in Vesoul and then later sent to Paris for further inspection.

86. "Peiper est Bien Vivant!: Simon Wiesenthal Rèvéle la Méthode Utilisée par les Nazis Démasqués," n.p., n.d., Rigoulot Papers.

87. For Wiesenthal's statement, "Is Colonel Peiper of the SS dead or alive?" *Daily Express*, Michael Brown, Paris, no date on clipping, but late August 1976. See also Ernst Klink to James Weingartner, letter, June 22, 1977. "The rumor of Wiesenthal was that the corpse was not that of Peiper, but that Peiper carried the body of a stranger into the house and escaped.

Plain crazy!" Klink also decried the supposition, which still persists today, that the head of the body was never returned to the family.

88. Two Berlin journalists, Jost von Moor and Bengt von zur Mühlen, produced the series for Chronos Film for ARD (the official goverment network). Their view of Malmédy: "Perhaps among the accused there were a few perpetrators. What was their motives? Was it all a mistake, or did they shoot, as can be assumed, because prisoners tried to flee?" They attempted an objective view of the Peiper affair: "An innocent victim of coincidental circumstances. . . . The death of Peiper was painted as "the consequence of a press campaign led by the Communists with the intention to upset the improving relations of France and Germany."

89. Bengt von zur Mühlen to Hinrich Peiper, December 29, 1976, Klink to Hinrich Peiper, February 21, 1977, and Jost von Morr to Klink, March 2, 1977, Klink Papers, BA-MA.

90. "Conclusions des experts: le corps carbonisé de Traves est celui de Joachim Peiper," *L'Est Républicain*, March 1977. "The presence of carbon monoxide at a toxic dose level in the superior region of the respiratory systems suggests that death was a consequence of asphyxia." The most significant proof of the identity of the corpse: "The study of the remains of the jawbones along with one intact tooth could be compared by radiography to one from Peiper's dental records. Those two negatives superimposed on each other perfectly."

91. One of the most fantastic stories circulated in late 1977 in a book entited *Dossier Néo Nazisme*, by Patrice Chairoff (aka Dominique Calzi), which claimed that Peiper had indeed survived the fire through help in staging the event with the help of the Odessa network. Unlike other stories, that of Chairoff contained a luxury of details: Peiper had arranged passage through Italy in the region of Brixen and then embarked on a cargo boat at Trieste, which put in at Barcelona in the first week of October 1976. Since then the Waffen SS colonel had settled in the Balmes section of Barcelona. To the priest of Traves, these stories might as well have been true. Of Peiper's charred corpse in the burned-out ruin, he remained skeptical: "Not a lot of people saw it like me. It didn't look real . . . Why was the body in Vesoul so long? I think it was because they needed time to find a proper body to send back to Germany." Ducros, interview.

92. When the body was returned to the family on April 1, the Munich district attorney's office confiscated the casket due to the inflamed controversy surrounding the certainty of Peiper's death. The casket was then brought to the Forensic Institute in the City of Munich, where it was opened for examination three days later by Dr. Wolfgang Spann. Peiper's former dentist and friend Arndt Fischer was also present. To the everyone's great dismay, the head of the corpse was missing, making it impossible to conduct a postmortem investigation. And even the attempt in France to bring a close to the chapter by Marc Dreyfus was frustrated when, in May 1977, the Supreme Court of Vesoul refused to make definitive pronouncement: "Absolute proof does not exist that the corpse discovered at Traves is that of Peiper . . . however, there is a strong likelihood of it." In spite of this, on May 24 Dreyfus declared that Peiper was officially deceased on July 14, 1976 at 1 a.m. It was only after further tedious negotiations with French officials on September 27, 1978, that the head was returned to the Forensic Institute; it had somehow been sent separately to Paris. And then only a single molar, sawed in half, was available for examination. To both Fischer and Spann, this was less than satisfactory for determination of identity of the corpse. Meanwhile, the Munich District Attorney's office would not release the body until February 19, just seven weeks before Sigurd Peiper died. As a result, a simple private service was held for both Sigurd and Jochen Peiper before their bodies were jointly cremated. Fischer, interviews, May 17, 1997, and April 7, 2000. Also, Agte, *Jochen Peiper*, 602, and Martin, *L'Affaire Peiper*, 116. Dr. Spann, who also presided over the controversial autopsy of the Rudolf Hess, never responded to the author's letters.

93. "Affaire Peiper: Le cadavre (sans nom) de Traves transféré hier à Munich," *L'Est Républicain*, April 2, 1978. "Am 14. Juli 1976 ist in Traves in dem Le Renfort." For a detailed description of the transfer of Peiper's body to Germany, letter Dorothee Peiper-Riegraf to Harvey T. Rowe, April 1977.

94. "L'Affaire Peiper," Antenne 2, January 21, 1979. Also, Arnaud and Kahane, *L'Affaire Peiper*. The fervid headline "J'ai la preuve que Peiper est vivant!" appeared in a Sunday supplement of *L'Est Républicain*, May 21, 1978.

95. "Peiper vivant? Arnaud témoin à Vesoul," *L'Est Républicain*, June 1978. Christian Nannini had replaced Daniel Clerget as the magistrate in Vesoul. For his view of Arnaud's claims, see *Le Monde*, June 6, 1978. "His book on Peiper has been seen as a sham by officials in the investigation." On June 12, 1978, Arnaud responded to newspaper's editors decrying the investigation. "The officials have already used the word 'sham' to pass judgement on the issue, something that seems imprudent. Why would they want to hear from me when they have already made up their minds."

96. For the hearing of Arnaud and its aftermath, see Martin, *L'Affaire Peiper*, 127–128.

97. André Moisse, "L'affaire Peiper entre dans la légende," *L'Est Républicain*, July 17, 1979.

98. Letter alleging bodies were moved to the massacre field from Peiper postwar attorney: Eugen Leer to Klink, November 20, 1984, based on speculation from a German paratrooper in Honfeld. For "known and untenable." Klink to Leer, November 22, 1984. As both a Leibstandarte veteran and historian, Klink was in frequent contact with Peiper, Dietrich, Hausser, and others. As such, his statement that "even the inner circle does not know" is of particular relevance. "After Peiper had been murdered, I received his sparse estate of notes and occasionally made myself available as a provider of information. . . . From the very long and good personal relationship with Peiper and his family, additional contacts developed with Hinrich Peiper. Subsequently, a few years ago, I turned all of the material over to him, because a historical treatment by Rudolf Lehmann was planned. Neither the Peiper family, nor the since deceased widow Peiper, nor myself considered a new scientific study of these matters."

99. Gerd Cuppens to Charles Hammer, June 10, 1986, USAMHI, Charles Hammer Papers, 285th FAOB, Box: Overseas Correspondence.

100. Ducros, interview, August 16, 2001. "You have to discount whatever the police says. Everything is being hidden. It was political. It was the President Giscard d' Estaing and the Minister of the Interior Michael Poniatowski. He is still alive. . . . The police had to find someone who set the fire. You can discount whatever the police said as they had a mission. I think Peiper set fire to the place himself. This fire was planned for that night. I don't even believe it was a body. I think it was a plastic dummy." From the other side, Police Inspector Lavaux says "the priest [of Traves] was never for me, a valid witness. During all our work before the media, he was always looking to put himself in the limelight like he was the center of the entire affair. . . . to quiet him, we were forced to solicit the cooperation of the Bishop of Besancon, Lord Lallier." Letter to author, September 26, 2001.

101. "I think the men that killed him . . . it was a deliberate attack to get him. I don't want to say more." Louette, interview, August 16, 2001.

102. Jacques Gauthier, interview by author, Vesoul, August 16, 2001.

103. Erwin Ketelhut, conversation from 1996, as quoted by Ducros, interview, August 16, 2001. Unfounded rumors that Peiper escaped remain in circulation. For weeks in 2002 participants on a Third Reich history website debated the authenticity of a fabled letter sent on February 20, 1985, written to US Army Lt. Stephen Rusiecki supposedly from "J. Peiper" with a South American postmark. At the time Rusiecki was working on a history of the pitched battle for the Losheimergraben crossroads. The author contacted Rusiecki in April 2004, who verified that there was no such letter; the allegation was a shameless hoax by an acquaintance. "Who Killed Peiper?" forum.axishistory.com, post of April 5, 2002.

104. Letter Lavaux to author, November 15, 1999. Erwin Ketelhut died in 1998, taking whatever he knew about the Peiper affair to his grave.

105. See Kersten, *The Kersten Memoirs: 1940–1945*, 184–186. Himmler quoted on March 6, 1943: "I'll see to it that Burgundy is permeated by the philosophy of the SS so that the model state of the Führer's dream will come into being."

106. "Mort de Peiper un mystère qui alimente la rumeur," *L'Est Républicain*, February 17, 1987.

Epilogue

1. Rigoulot, interview, August 15, 2001, and Ducros, interview, August 16, 2001.

2. Sigurd Peiper to Fritz Kosmehl, Advent 1978.

3. Hinrich Peiper to Fritz Kosmehl, June 17, 1979.

4. A year before his death Peiper had worried to his friend Arndt Fischer that people might falsely martyr his life—a reasonable concern. He asked Fischer to help him locate some secret place for his burial. With the attendant confusion of the circumstances surrounding his death, nothing came of his request. Fischer, interview, May 11, 1997.

5. Nachlaß Ernst Klink, BA-M, Letter Hinrich Peiper to Klink, June 25, 1979.

6. In early 1976 an unnamed French official warned American author John Toland that there would be an attempt to "assassinate the SS man living in Eastern France" Although they had a stormy correspondence at first, Toland and Peiper had become friends over the years through Toland's Japanese wife, Toshiko, and her relationship with Sigurd. Toland visited Peiper in Traves and found his place of retirement a strange choice. Eastern France seemed "hostile and crooked." Afterward Toland telephoned Peiper, but he dismissed leaving. "I will not retreat," he told Toland. "I have nowhere else to go." Later in July the author learned of his death. Toland thought Peiper "gutsy, but a strange man. I have always been convinced that he sought his death there." Toland told the author he could not reveal the French official who provided the warning, as "I gave my word to not reveal from whom I learned this, and he is still living. If I told you, his life or that of his family could be endangered." John Toland, interview by author, September 18, 1997. Toland died on January 4, 2004.

7. Nachlaß Ernst Klink, BA-M, Letter Hinrich Peiper to Klink, June 25, 1979, and Hinrich Peiper to Karl Heinz Schmitt, September 27, 1981. Hinrich Peiper moved to the United States in November 1980 and remained there for a number of years before returning to Germany. Currently he has retired in Germany after returning from New York as a successful executive with Dresdner Bank.

8. Hinrich Peiper to author, March 11, 2012.

9. That a generational chasm, covered by secrecy, still pervades many families in Germany is periodically disclosed anew before the press.

10. Understandably Hinrich Peiper initially chose to see his father's past in a favorable light: "He had much sorrow in understanding and admitting all the atrocities that happened under Hitler during the war," he once said. "Yet he has made the war of a soldier. For him the atrocities of the Nazi camps belonged to another universe." Martin, *L'Affaire Peiper*, 113. Yet, when writing those words, Hinrich Peiper was not aware of the extent of his father's participation in Himmler's SS organization, reflecting the elder's communication to his son. From his time with Himmler, Peiper had known quite well of the concentration camps and all involved but never shared that with his children—a common situation in postwar Germany.

11. Ducros, interview; also anonymous French local, interview by author.

12. Six years after Peiper death, on Thursday, August 11, 1982, the new magistrate in Vesoul, John Marie Depommier, quietly closed the file for L'Affaire Peiper, releasing a statement that the case was "unsolved." "Affaire Peiper; Non-lieu prononcé," *L'Est Républicain*, August 12, 1982, Vesoul. Even so, many living in that region of France remained dubious of Peiper's death. "Le fantôme de Traves," *L'Est Républicain*, February 16, 1987: "No thesis can explain all the contradictions . . . ten years after," pondered the local newspaper. "Many declare him still alive."

ACKNOWLEDGMENTS

HISTORICAL RESEARCH SPANNING TWO DECADES NECESSARILY DEPENDS ON MANY institutions and individuals. Peiper's story owes a great deal to many who helped me.

I was greatly assisted by Dr. Jens Westemeier, whose PhD dissertation on Peiper at the University of Potsdam towers over supposition and myth. Although we have approached our subject very differently, Jens was instrumental in making many contacts and interviews and was always helpful. Indeed, we did ten years of research in parallel and developed a friendship over that time. One day we shall write of the hunt itself. That is another interesting story.

One person to whom I owe an exceptionally heavy debt is my very professional Austrian interpreter, Helmut Thiess. More than a professor with interest in languages, Helmut became a close friend, only to die tragically in the midst of the long research. Helmut performed a very difficult job in assisting me during three trips to Germany, with many interviews, as well as the translation of hundreds of pages of key documents relative to this story. I miss his warm wit and wise counsel and like to think he would be proud of what he helped me create.

In France André Moissé, formerly with *L'Est Républicain*, was instrumental in helping me with many of the nuances of the events of summer 1976 through an interview and detailed follow-up. He knows how much he helped. His companion, Marc Paygnard, assisted with photographs. In Dijon the chief police inspector into Peiper's death, Inspector Roger Lavaux, made a crucial difference in my understanding of those convoluted events. Inspector Lavaux also shared with me his own otherwise secret personal report to the head of police in Dijon, which greatly assisted in penetrating the cloudy circumstances surrounding Peiper's death. This aided other interviews I conducted in the little village of Traves itself, a number of which had to be anonymous. In many ways I learned more than I wanted to.

Will C. C. Cavanagh helped me interview some of the civilian witnesses in Traves, France. We also spoke with dozens of civilian witnesses in the Ardennes, but that's another book. My many Belgian helpers and friends in the Ardennes over the years will also forgive me if their story still must wait.

Neill Thomson, an expert on Jochen Peiper, was always enthusiastic in assisting with various documents and matters important to the puzzle. In Holland, Mike Smeets was helpful with the many tidbits and interviews he has collected over the years. For translation of French documents and correspondence I am indebted to Angela Ackerman and my daughter, Sarah.

Although the Peiper family has long suffered the curious, Hinrich Peiper was helpful with two interviews and clarification in a long correspondence on a number of points. In the end our relationship matured, largely as both of us came to terms with the realities of his father's past. Such a reckoning is difficult for any son, and I am impressed by his candor at the end of my work. On the other side, Peiper's eldest daughter, Elke, provided useful, if reluctant, review of the translation of some very important wartime letters but has otherwise remained unhappy with the probing depth of my research. If not observing her wishes, I respect her opinion.

Appreciation also to Dr. Hans-Juergen Peiper and Dr. Matthias Peiper for further information on the larger family.

Other close friends to the family, Ms. Bettina Wieselmann and Dr. Uta Müller, provided key insight. Dr. Volker Daum provided several useful introductions. Others who knew the Peipers provided additional information, although the author respected their wishes to keep sources confidential. Luckily an author can know what they know.

In Germany Col. Eckart Klink provided important access to his father's papers containing a voluminous correspondence with Jochen Peiper. Astrid Homert and Birgit Mitchell (née Nathan) were very helpful in describing the Peiper family days in Rottach Egern. The *Quick* journalist Harvey T. Rowe shared documents collected in his own research into the Peiper affair.

Near the end of my project, it became important to carefully evaluate crucial handwritten letters from Peiper to Hedwig Potthast by careful transcription of old script into German and then accurate English translation considering nuances of period language. Thanks to Ann Shields and Edith and Sarah Ulbert for their layered and diligent attention in this process.

The hospitality of tiny Boves, Italy, was touching during our extended interviews in the summer of 2002. Thanks to Dr. Daniela Silvestrin and particularly Laura Cavallera, our incomparable guide to the Piedmontese region. In Cuneo Michele Calandri and Marco Ruzzi and the Insituto Storico della Resistenza in Cuneo e Provincia were instrumental in helping me reach a balanced perspective regarding the events of September 19, 1943. Also thanks to a specialist on German war crimes in Italy who helped greatly with this episode, Carlo Gentile.

At the US National Archives I had much help. For over a decade Richard Boylan and the late John E. Taylor at the US National Archives have been instrumental in helping me to wade through the mountain of documents and papers dealing with the Malmédy trial, Peiper, and the multitude of records involved. Jim Kelling and Niels Cordes assisted with long hours reviewing microfilm records. Richard Raiber helped with archival sources on Peiper's trip with Himmler to Danzig. Other thanks to Patricia Spayd, an industrious historian in her own right, for her unselfish willingness to help at NARA as well as sharing work in one research trip to Germany. At the US Holocaust Memorial Museum I am indebted to Dr. Jürgen Matthäus and also Judith Cohen and Nancy Hartman for their help with documentary and photographic archives revealing more about Himmler and Peiper's travels and motives than I would have otherwise not discovered.

Spending many weeks in Washington, I am indebted to the staff at the Tabard Inn, my home away from home. There I always felt welcome each evening after long hours with old documents. Simple acts of kindness combined with the revelry from regulars—wonderful.

Thanks to the late John Toland and his daughter Tamiko for making all of his private papers and taped interviews available to me at both the Franklin D. Roosevelt Library and the Library of Congress. In Hyde Park Karen Burtis ably assisted me, and at the Library of Congress I had assistance from Ronald E. Cogan, Jeff Flannery, and Bryan Cornell. Linda Wheeler guided me through the NSDAP Hauptarchiv at the Hoover Institution at Stanford University, where we unearthed critical letters that Peiper wrote to Himmler's mistress during wartime. We located the originals at the BA-Koblenz. Thanks also to Nancy Richards at George Washington University for assistance with the important William R. Perl papers.

In England I had the considerable assistance of Vivienne Bales and Bruno Derrick as well as the other capable staff at the Public Records Office at Kew Gardens. Special thanks to Carl Shilleto for his assistance and friendship. Also there, the late Charles Whiting made a number of documents and letters available to me from his association with Peiper and was kind enough to cover his recollections at his home in York. Similarly Gen. Michael Reynolds, the author of his own important account of the Kampfgruppe Peiper, always lent a hand when asked. Finally, although embracing views rejected by the author, David Irving assisted in making available a number of obscure documents, diaries, and letters. Those were appreciated.

The late John S. D. Eisenhower graciously made available his personal papers at the Eisenhower Library as well as agreed to a pleasurable afternoon interview covering his father's remembrances on the Malmédy episode. At the Eisenhower Library in Abilene, Kansas, James Leyerzapf helped me wade through the collections there.

At the Institut für Zeitgeschite in Munich I was ably assisted by Eva Rimmele and Petra Mörtl. And at the Bundesarchiv-Koblenz I was guided through important personal papers by Gregor Pickro and photographic collections by Frau Brigitte Kuhl. Similar help was rendered by Dr. Günther Montfort and Carina Notzke at the Bundesarchiv-Freiburg and by Dr. Heinz-Luger Borgert at the Bundesarchiv Ludwigsburg. Dr. Michael Heim and local historian Benno Eisenburg assisted with information on the Peiper family days in Tegernsee. Dr. Robert Rill at the Österreichisches Staatsarchiv assisted with access to the Skorzeny Papers in Vienna.

Knowledge of Heinrich Himmler and Peiper's stint under the Reichsführer SS benefited from material provided by noted scholar Peter Witte in Hemer. Peter was kind enough to help share reproductions of Himmler's daily appointment book, where entries in Peiper's hand could be readily recognized. Similarly, Katrin Himmler in Berlin, the great niece of Heinrich Himmler (who is decidedly condemnatory of the Nazis), was very helpful with pointing me to archival sources and transcribing cryptic written entries in her great-uncle's day calendar. Noted Third Reich scholar Anton Joachimsthaler transcribed handwritten German documents written in the old script and suggested profitable research avenues. At the KZ Gedenkstätte in Dachau I was ably assisted by Albert Knoll and director Dr. Barbara Distel, who helped me locate photographs verifying Peiper's presence at the concentration camp on at least two occasions.

From the side of the trial prosecution, the late Burton Ellis consented to an interview and made all of his personal papers and documents available for the work before his passing. Similarly, from the defense, Willis Everett III made similar material available from his late father's papers. Melvin Bielawski provided background perspective on the conditions at Zuffenhausen when Peiper was held there in December 1945.

Of particular note also must be Dr. James Weingartner at Southern Illinois University, the author of the best single work on the trial: *Crossroads of Death*. Jim always shared from the Everett Papers and other resources to support my own project. Similarly, Dr. Richard Breitman at the American University helped locate materials from Peiper's time with Heinrich Himmler: several breakthrough papers declassified under the Nazi War Crimes Disclosure Act of 1999.

In Germany many faced me with openness even when our views did not match. Although many veterans were hesitant to speak, others were forthcoming: Hans Siptrott, Arndt Fischer, Rolf Reiser, Paul Fröhlich, Erhard Gührs, Ralf Tiemann, and Manfred Thorn. In particular, Fritz Kosmehl graced me with his insight from his lengthy correspondence with Peiper after the war. I am also grateful to him for much archival material. Werner Ackermann consented to three extensive interviews concerning his experiences in the tank regiment of the Leibstandarte and particularly over key insights relative to the Malmédy incident and the postwar cover-up. I also acknowledge several unmentioned who were willing to speak only a condition of anonymity. Appreciation also to the late Hubert Meyer for allowing me access to the previously closed HIAG archives at BA-MA Freiburg, which made a pivotal difference in my research. Finally, Dörte von Westernhagen assisted with important letters from her father, who fought alongside Peiper during the war, as well as providing historical context.

I made a special effort to present each side of the story. As such, there is certain to be material in the book that will affront both camps. To this I remain unapologetic; the story of this personality has long suffered from biased coverage. Still, please know that I approached the story with as much objectivity as I could muster and let facts speak for themselves.

Within the project I benefited from helpful readers. First and foremost would be Ann Hamilton Shields, who helped review the writing with critical comment throughout. During my last five years of work Ann really became the project research assistant in Germany and contributed hundreds of selfless hours with her husband, Mo. Also assisting: Terry Hirsch and Carol Byrne

Early on, Clyde Taylor, my literary agent with Curtis Brown Ltd., professed confidence in this project. He was convinced that the story of Peiper, particularly at the end of his life, was one the world needed to know. Tragically, Clyde died suddenly in early 2001. Fortunately Kirsten Manges and, later, Katherine Fausset, also with Curtis Brown, stepped in with a conscientious manner. Given the glacial pace of my research and writing, I appreciate their patience.

At Da Capo Press, thanks to Andrea Schultz for the vision to take the project on and, with Robert Pigeon, my editor, who helped slice up a sprawling opus into something readable. Thank you also to my meticulous copy editor, Josephine Mariea, as well as Lori Hobkirk at the Book Factory.

At home, my family endured my years of work with Jochen Peiper. Lisa critiqued, translated, and served as my devoted companion and French interpreter for some of my European jaunts. My daughter, Sarah, a formidable writer in her own right, cheerily helped with questions of literary judgment. And my son, Wade, distracted me with sport and other facets of life when I needed it. That means a lot.

Danny S. Parker
Cocoa Beach, July 2014

INDEX

Abbeville, France, 58
Adenauer, Konrad, 190–191, 203
Adolescents, relocation of to rural areas, 90
L'Affaire Peiper (Arnaud & Kahane), 300, 301
Ahrens, Hanns Dietrich, 220
Alber, Johanna, 93
Alessandria, Italy, 103
Alpine Redoubt, 196
Alsace, France, 68
Alvensleben, Ludolf von, 47, 50, 225, 336–337n95
Amann, Max, 37
Amsterdam, Netherlands, 57
Andrejew, 105
Annakin, Ken, 225
Anschluss, 22
Anti-Semitism, 9, 10, 27, 189, 190, 194
Apenburg, Otto von, 48
Ardennes Offensive, 109–111
Arnaud, Georges, 300
Arras, France, 58
Aryans, 335n83
Assenmacher, Hans, 179
Augustowo, Poland, 77
L'Aurore, on identity of Peiper's body, 280, 287
Auschwitz Concentration Camp, 102, 226
Axmann, Artur, 123, 127

Bach-Zelewski, Erich von dem, 72, 73, 78, 81, 214
Bachmayer, Georg, 145
Bad Gastein, Austria, 122
Bad Polzin, Germany, 40
Barkmann, Ernst, 213
Barton, Deforest, 200
Battle: Story of the Bulge (Toland), 209
Battle of Britain, 66, 68
Battle of the Bulge, film about, 225
Baugnez, Belgium. *See* Malmédy Massacre
Baum, Otto, 340n51
Baum, Walter M., 196
Baumbach, Werner, 125–126, 364n34
Baumert, Paul, 122, 215
Baur, Hans, 125
Baxter, Arthur, 60
Beer Hall Putsch, 5, 27
Beger, Bruno, 48, 50
Belgium, invasion of by Germany, 56
Below, Nicholaus von, 71, 76, 123
Berchtesgaden, Germany, 20, 108, 110, 120–122
Berger, Gottlob, 38, 64, 119, 122, 124, 160
Berkelmann, Theodor, 67
Berlin
- bombing of, 89–90, 100, 117, 120, 124–125
- in 1930s, 7, 17, 43–44
- in wartime, 48, 84, 89–90, 96–97, 100, 104, 335n79, 343nn77–78

Bernadotte, Folke, 122, 124
Bernardi, 224, 226
Bertram, Erik, 41
Best, Werner, 34, 220, 229–230
Betts, T. J., 137
Beverloo, Belgium, 198
Bialystok, Poland, 77, 78
Biancani, Giuseppe, 224
Binder, William E., 140–142
Birkenwald, Germany, 118
Bismarck (battleship), 31, 75
Bittrich, Willi, 197
Blaskowitz, Johannes, 41, 42, 43

Blitzkrieg (lightning war), 39, 56, 75
"Blowtorch Battalion," 169, 226
Blutkitt (blood cement), 102
Bocchini, Arturo, 27, 33
Bock, Feodor von, 40
Böhme, Albrecht, 45
Böhme, Hans-Joachim, 77
Boleslawiec, Poland, 39
Bolshevism, 10, 31, 61, 72, 75, 79, 203, 348n64
Boltz, Marcel, 172, 177
Börchers, Günther, 15
Borgo San Dalmazzo, Italy, 226–227
Bormann, Martin, 46, 49, 108, 120, 127, 193, 211
Bormann, Martin Jr., 196
Bouhler, Philipp, 46
Bournon, Robert, 271
Boves, Italy, 102–103, 219, 223, 225–228, 253, 286
Bracht, Fritz, 72
Bracht, Werner, 33
Brandt, Rudolf "Rudi," 25, 69, 79, 100, 230
Bratoszewice, Poland, 41
Brauchitsch, Walther von, 42, 53
Braun, Albert, 174
Braun, Eva, 65, 120, 126
Braunschweig, 24, 320n10
Breme, Friedrich, 223
Briesemeister, Kurt, 180
Britain, military units of
  48th Infantry Division, 59
  Royal Norfolk Regiment, 341n52
Brohl, Karl-Heinz, 15
Bromberg, Poland, 42, 47
Brûly de Pesche, Belgium, 62
Brüstle, Robert, 189, 223
Buchenwald Concentration Camp, 54, 196
Buenos Aires, Argentina, 194
Büllingen, Belgium, 152–153, 163–164, 174
Burckhardt, Carl, 37
Burgdorf, Wilhelm, 123
Burgundy-Franche-Compté region of France, 310n20
Buschmann, Rainer (Peiper's pen name), 238, 249
Butenhoff, Kurt, 228
Butz, Evi, 207
Bzura, Poland, 39

Cacheux, Paul, 251–253, 281, 287–288, 294
Calley, William, 240
Canada, 3rd Division, 108
Canada, Nova Scotia Highlanders, 108
Cavallera, Anselmo, 286
Ceccaldi, Pierre-Fernand, 281
Centner, Jean Marie, 139–140
Chappaz, Pierre, 255
Charleroi, Belgium, 106
Cheneux, Belgium, 166, 179, 181
Chenogne, Belgium, 206
Cherson, Soviet Union, 85
Chicken theft, execution of soldiers for, 107
Christ, Frederich, 172
Clark, William, 202
Clay, Lucius, 187
Clerget, Daniel, 279, 281, 292
Clisson, Henry "Red," 140
Clotten, Roman, 180
Cold War, 190, 203, 223
Collins, "Hollywood" Harry, 130
Communists, French, 251, 253, 254, 258, 266, 270, 280, 287
Communists, Italian, 223
Communists, Soviet, 76, 88, 136, 223
Comthurey, Germany, 93
Concentration camps, 16–17, 32–33, 48, 54–56, 72, 90, 102, 144–145, 253
Cosmic Ice Theory (Welteislehre), 36
Counterfeit British pounds, 65–66
Cracow, Poland, 49, 50
Cuneo, Italy, 102–103, 219, 224, 226
Cuppens, Gerd, 301
Czech Republich, takeover of by Germany, 32

D-Day (June 6, 1944), 107
Dachau Concentration Camp, 16–17, 32, 54, 106, 359–360n37
Dalbey, Josiah T., 163, 165, 169, 170, 179, 181–182
Dalmazzo, Faustino, 226
D'Alquen, Günther, 69, 220
Daluege, Kurt, 27, 33, 66, 73, 350n82

Daniel D., 291–292, 294–295, 416n62
Danzig, Poland, 41
Darré, Richard Walther, 9
Degrelle, Leon, 106
Delaval, Jacques, 268
D'Estaing, Valéry Giscard, 254, 288
"Deutschland, Deutschland über alles," 381n20
Diebitsch, Karl, 26, 34, 55, 326–327n72
Diefenthal, Jupp, 151, 152, 153, 154, 156, 157, 165, 167, 179, 228
Dietrich, Josef "Sepp"
  birthday celebration for, 21
  capture by Americans, 138
  at Christmas festival, 47
  death of, 216
  at Esquelbecq, France, 59–61
  fighting style of, 39
  Holland, invasion of, 56
  Knight's Cross, award of, 62
  Lago Maggiore, incident at, 228
  Mount Watten, capture of, 58
  in Munich with Hitler, 44
  order of to surrender to Americans, 128
  position of in Hitler's hierarchy, 13, 20
  sentence at Malmédy Massacre trial, 182
  at SS veterans' gatherings, 210, 213, 215, 233
  at Taganrog, Soviet Union, 88, 354n19
  testimony about, 168
  on trial, 148
  victory tour of Dutch countryside, 56–57
  visit to Himmler's Birkenwald headquarters, 118
Dietrich, Otto, 41
Dinkelsbühl, Germany, 132, 134
Dinse, Otto, 102, 223, 225, 226, 228, 230, 247
Dirkson, Viktoria von, 34
Dollmann, Eugen, 27, 69, 192
Dönitz, Karl, 123, 127, 144, 210
Dora-Mittelbau Concentration Camp, 253
Dörner, Hermann, 84, 98, 123
Dr. Wolman GmbH, 195
Dreyfus, Marc, 290, 293, 299, 300
Ducros, Curé Louis, 277, 286, 289, 290, 301, 302, 420n100
Dulles, Allen, 190
Dunkirk, France, 59, 61
Durand, Pierre, 253, 255, 258
Dürr, Eduard, 132–133
Dwinell, John, 149, 151–158, 163, 176
Dwinger, Edwin, Erich, 26

Ebeling, Georg, 156, 177, 179
Ebensee, Austria, 144–145
Ebensee Concentration Camp, 144–145
Ehrhardt, Rolf, 240
Eichmann, Adolf (aka Riccardo Klement), 193–194, 211, 376n35
Eicke, Theodor, 17, 32, 33, 39, 53, 69, 75
Einsatzgruppen (killing squads), 39, 64
Eisele, Hans, 376n38
Eisenhower, Dwight D., 141
Ellis, Burton F., 138, 143–146, 148, 159–170, 172, 181, 182, 221
Ellowitz, Morris, 147
Elser, Georg, 45, 333n64
Engeldorf (Ligneuville), Belgium, 164
England, plan for invasion of, 64
Esquelbecq, France, 59–61
L'Est Républicain, interview with Peiper, 255–258, 290
Etrépilly, France, 61
Eugenics, 25, 328n9
Europe, map of, x–xi
Euthanasia of institutionalized patients, 46
Evans, Bert, 60
Everett, Willis M., 148, 151, 165–166, 171, 172–173, 177, 180, 183–184, 187–188, 206–210
Eysell, Otto, 15

Fanton, Dwight, 137–138, 140–142, 147, 148
Farben, I. G., 190
Farque, Jean-Michel, 271, 273, 282
Fegelein, Hermann, 55, 80, 81, 120, 124, 126
Feldherrnhalle, 311n1
Felsenest headquarters, 57
Feuchtwangen, Germany, 131–134, 138
Finielz, Robert, 276

Fischer, Arndt, 107, 145, 154–155, 160, 192, 217, 247, 262, 282, 284
Fleps, Georg, 180
Flossenbürg Concentration Camp, 54
Forster, Albert, 43
France, 58–62, 341n52
  See also Traves, France
France Soir, on Peiper's disappearance, 291
Franco, Francisco, 69, 343n81, 344n5
Frank, Hans, 49, 50
Frankfurter Allgemeine, on identity of Peiper's body, 281
Franz, Gerhard, 198
Franz Joseph, Archduke, 213
Freikorps Deutschland, 193
Freising, Germany, 140–142, 144
Freitag, Georg, 173
Der Freiwillige, on Peiper's release, 202
Frey, Albert, 85, 104, 217, 389n36
Frey, Gerhard, 296
Freya von Moltke Stiftung, 306
Frings, Josef, 191
Fuhmann, Ernst, 204

Garcelles, France, 108
Gauthier, Albert, xix, 235, 310n26
Gauthier, Jacques "Jacky," 290, 301, 413n29
Gebhardt, Karl, 54, 57, 94, 190, 337n7
Gehlen, Reinhard, 190
Geller, Pedro (Herbert Kulmann), 194
General Anzeiger, on Peiper, 287
Genghis Khan, 38, 80, 85, 94, 157, 159–160, 167, 329n16, 343n86
Genghis Khan: Storm Out of Asia (Prawdin), 38
Genocide. *See* Jews, elimination of
Gerbino, Ettore, 219
Germany, military units of
  Armeegruppe Vistula, 119
  Armeegruppe Wenck, 125
  Army Detachment Steiner, 124
  Company Rumpf, 156
  Death's Head Division (SS Totenkopf), 53, 54
  Eighth Army, 42, 43
  Einsatzgruppen D, 190
  Leibstandarte, 1st Battalion, 2nd Company 59
  Leibstandarte, 2nd Battalion, 59–60
  Leibstandarte, 3rd Battalion, 11th Company, 58, 61
  Leibstandarte, 4th Battalion, 86
  Leibstandarte, 5th Company, 60
  Leibstandarte, 7th Company, 60
  Leibstandarte, 13th Company, 98
  Leibstandarte, 15th Company, 59
  Sixth Army, 93
  15th Motorcycle Company, 59, 62
  32nd SS Division, 118
  320th Infanterie Division, 94
  SS Cavalry Brigade, 78
  SS Heavy Panzer Battalion 501, 155
  SS Infantry Regiment 2, 341n52
  SS Kampfgruppe Nord, 71
  SS Regiment Duetschland, 33
  SS Wiking Division, 72
  I SS Panzer Corps, 120
  II SS Panzer Corps, 120
  1st Panzer Division, 94, 109
  2nd Panzer Division, 59
  2nd SS Panzergrenadier Regiment, 1st Battalion, 228
  3rd Panzer Company, 107
  3rd Panzer Division, 40
  5th SS Panzer Division Wiking, 207
  6th Panzer Army, 111, 117–118
  7th Panzer Company, 108, 128
  9th Panzer Division, 56
  9th Panzer Engineer Company, 145
  12th Panzer Grenadier Company, 226–227
  12th SS Panzer Division, 152
  1st SS Brigade, 78
  1st SS Cavalry Regiment, 80, 82
  2nd SS Cavalry Regiment, 82
  1st SS Panzer Division, 135
  1st SS Panzer Grenadier Training and Replacement Battalion 12, 180
  1st SS Panzer Regiment, 128, 148
  12th Volksgrenadier Division, 152
  XIX Panzer Corps, 58
  See also Leibstandarte
Germany, postwar, 202–204, 211–213, 225–231, 346n27
Gerretz, Herbert, 229
Gerullis, Michael, 13
Gestapo, 25, 45

Ghent, Belgium, 58
Ghettos, 55, 72, 90, 342n64, 345n19
Gille, Herbert O., 191
Glasl, Ernst, 29, 323n45
Glasl, Max, 131
Globocnik, Odilio, 49, 50, 79
Glücks, Richard, 72
Goebbels, Joseph, 27, 44, 47, 70, 98, 124, 125, 127
Göhler, Johannes, 215, 223
Goldschmidt, Ernst, 163
Göring, Hermann, 66, 84, 98, 123, 124
Görlitz, Germany, 76
Gottgläubigkeit, 34
Grass, Günter, 212
Graudenz, Poland, 40
Grawitz, Ernst, 54, 337n7
Greece, subjugation of, 71
Gregoire, Gerard, 240
Greifelt, Ulrich, 53
Greigova, Soviet Union, 86–87
Grodno, Poland, 77
Gronau, Germany, 56
Grothmann, Werner, 54, 66, 69, 76, 78, 82, 92, 101, 118, 120, 214–215
Gruhle, Hans, 150, 163, 177, 191, 198, 369–370n12
Guderian, Heinz, 37, 40, 58, 59
Guennel, G. K. "Joe," 196
Gührs, Ehrhard, 223, 225, 228
Günsche, Otto, 124, 128, 213
Gut Staren, Germany, 100
Guth, Paul C., 130, 141–142, 161, 169
Guyot, Maria Thérèse, 271, 301
Gypsies, 73, 88

Hácha, Emil, 32
Hadeln, Hajo von, 27
Haefner, Paul, 140
Halder, Franz, 40
Hamburg, Germany, 97
Hammerer, Max, 163
Handy, Thomas T., 191
Hanreich, Jakob, 95, 230, 354n18
Hansen, Max, 85
Hanstein, Huschke von, 202, 207, 208, 383–384n54
Hardieck, 160–161
Harris, Arthur, 104
Hartmann, August, 200
Harzer, Walter, 213, 215, 233, 298
Hausser, Paul, 15, 34, 53, 191, 192, 215, 233, 316n8
Hechler, Kenneth W., 143, 368n30
Henley, Clifford M. "Swede," 132
Hennecke, Hans, 145, 150, 158, 172, 176, 194
Hess, Rudolf, 47, 49
Heydrich, Lina von Osten, 28–29, 189
Heydrich, Reinhard, 25, 27, 32, 33, 39, 42, 64, 66, 73, 77
HIAG (Hilfsgemeinschaft auf Gegenseitigkeit), 190, 202, 205–206, 207, 213, 215, 217, 223, 258, 278, 295, 298, 389n39
Hillig, Hans, 150, 151, 156, 165, 177–178, 180–181, 372n17
Himmler, Gebhard, 57
Himmler, Gudrun (daughter), 74, 101, 357n8
Himmler, Heinrich
  apology for actions in Poland, 53–54
  astrology, obsession with, 24
  background of, 311n5
  at Birkenwald headquarters, 118–119
  birth of daughter, Nanette Dorothea, 108
  birth of son, Helge, 91
  on Christianity, 326n69
  combat methods, demonstration of, 33
  crackpot science, love of, 119
  daily schedule, 25–26
  Dutch, impression of, 57
  Elser, interrogation of, 45
  family life, 57, 74, 101, 339n33, 339n35
  Franco, visit to, 69–70
  Genghis Khan, obsession with, 38, 343n86
  genocide, announcement of need for, 73
  goals of, 38
  Hedwig Potthast, affair with, 30, 57, 74, 80, 93, 324n50
  Holy Grail, search for, 19, 29, 70, 344nn6–7
  homophobia of, 20, 73, 75
  at Joachim Peiper's wedding, 35

Himmler, Heinrich (*continued*)
killing, philosophy of, 73, 346n27
lost Aryan tribe, search for, 48
on marriage, 325n52
medical experiments, 54
metaphysical interests, 26, 38, 70, 328n6
Mussolini, visit to, 27
Nordic mysticism, 18–19, 36–37
peace with Allies, plans for, 119, 122, 125–126
plan to establish racial paradise in France, 64
plans for repopulation of Poland with illegitimate SS offspring, 49
racial engineering, 9, 25
as Reichskommissar for Consolidation of German Nationhood, 43
as reincarnation of King Heinrich I, 18, 24–25, 36
resettlement program, 49
responsibilities of, 67
Spanish police chief, visit from, 66–67
speech on genocide, 101–102
speech to motorcycle battalion, 67–68
SS ideology, indoctrination of, 10
SS Race and Settlement Office, establishment of, 9
at SS swearing-in ceremony, 4–5
suicide of, 131
Tegernsee, homes near, 28
tours of conquered areas, 31–32, 44–46, 48–50, 53–55, 57, 64, 77–78, 80–81, 349n67
trip to Italy to look for buried treasure, 32–33, 325n63
Himmler, Helge (son), 91, 94, 103, 195
Himmler, Margarete Boden "Marga" (wife), 23–24, 57, 74, 197
Himmler, Nanette Dorothea (daughter), 108, 117, 195
Hinrichsen, Kurt Hans, 47, 188
Hinrichsen, Rolf, 31, 75, 188
Hinrichsen, Sigurd Anna, 28–30, 34–35
Hinrichsen, Vera, 100
Hiroshi Oshima, 77
Hirsch, Erich, 204
Hitler, Adolf
astrology, disapproval of, 74
Bolshevism, desire to eliminate, 61, 72, 75
Christmas in Berlin (1939), 46–47
combat methods, demonstration of, 33
D-Day invasion, response to report of, 107–108
Greece, speech on success in, 71
Jews, threat to annihilate, 30–31, 321n30, 350n81
last days of, 120, 123–125, 126
at Leibstandarte swearing-in ceremony, 4–6
living space *(lebensraum),* acquisition of, 38
Munich, assassination attempt in, 44–45
Poland, conquest of, 39–41
political support for, 10, 314n37
rise to power of, 8, 11
Russians, contempt for, 77
Soviet Union, order for liquidation of undesirables, 73
victory parades, 43, 64
Hitler Youth, 10, 32
Hochwald (High Woods), 76, 86, 106
Hohenlychen medical facility, 54, 93, 94, 120
Holland, invasion of by Germany, 56, 339n27
Hollander, Karl, 22
Honsfeld, Belgium, 152, 163
Hoppe, Paul Werner, 315n1
Hörbiger, Hans, 36
Horst Wessel song, 6, 312n13, 381n20
Höss, Rudolf, 48, 102
L'Humanité, French Communist newspaper, 253, 255, 288
Hungary, 117, 120
Huy, Belgium, 58

Isenburg, Princess, 190

Jackson, Robert H., 137
Jaeckel, Siegfried, 164
Japan, capitulation of, 140
Jeckeln, Friedrich, 78
Jefremowka, Soviet Union, destruction of, 95

Jewish Defense League, 222
Jews
  anti-Semitism, in Germany, 9
  elimination of, 30–31, 42, 43, 63, 67, 68, 77–82, 88, 90, 226
  persecution of, 27, 55
Jochum, Christian, 198, 228
Jochum, Markus, 107
Jodl, Alfred, 124
Johst, Hanns, 20, 48
Jünger, Ernst, 9
Junghans, Lothaire, 396n55
Junker, Benoni, 188, 192

Kahane, Roger, 300
Kaltenbrunner, Ernst, 123
Kammler, Hans, 119, 362n11
Kameradenwerk, 193, 194
Katsiaficas, Nicolas, 138
Kefauver, Estes, 202
Keitel, Wilhelm, 76, 123
Keller-Kühne, Josef, 71
Kempka, Erich, 41, 44, 126–127, 203
Kempner, Robert, 224, 227
Kern, Erich, 298
Kernmayr, Erich, 86, 278, 353n10
Kersten, Felix, 39, 74, 119, 124
Kesselring, Albert, 210
Ketelhut, Erwin, xv, 245, 253, 268, 271, 276–277, 288, 293–295, 302
KG 200 (Bomber Wing 200), 125
Kharkov, Soviet Union, 94–95, 97, 170
Kielce, Poland, 41
Kiermaier, Josef "Sepp," 92, 214–215
Kiewit, Belgium, 107
King, Edmund L., 141, 143
Klarsfeld, Beate, 280, 288
Klarsfeld, Serge, 280
Kleinheisterkamp, Matthias, 15
Klement, Riccardo (Adolf Eichmann), 194
Klingelhöfer, Oskar, 150
Klink, Ernst, 207, 215, 233, 241, 264, 266, 269, 296–297, 298, 301, 417n73
Klink, Hans, 202
Knapp, Theodor, 198, 200, 201–202
Knittel, Gustav, 111, 156, 162, 194
Koegel, Max, 54
Kortschiwka, Soviet Union, 105–106
Kosmehl, Fritz, 194, 210–211, 247, 253, 400n29
Kraas, Hugo, 228
Kraemer, Fritz, 180
Krag, Ernst-August, 213
Kramm, Kurt, 109, 150, 178
Krasnaja Poljana, 94, 356n44
Krätschmer, Ernst-Günther, 16
Kraus, Herbert, 138
Krebs, Hans, 126
Kristallnacht, 27, 321n27
Krottingen, Poland, 77
Kruedener, Hans Joachim Freiherr, 195
Krüger, Fredrich-Wilhelm, 49, 63
Krupp, Alfried, 219
Kubala, Paul, 196
Kuhlmann, Herbert (aka Pedro Geller), 107, 193–194, 376n35
Kühn, Werner, 158
Kumm, Otto, 118, 215
Künstler, Karl, 13, 315n2
Kurzmeyer, Alfred, 197
Kyriss, Reinhold, 128

La Gleize, Belgium, 111, 135, 148, 155, 156, 157, 162, 166, 174–176, 177, 240
La Vaulx Richard, Belgium, 165
Lago Maggiore, Italy, 228–229
Lammerding, Heinz, 213, 385n5
Landfried, Walter, 156, 177, 179
Landsberg Prison, 187–99
Lang, Richard C., 139–140
Langefeld, Johanna, 54
Langer, William, 188
Langwasser, Germany, 139
Lary, Virgil Jr., 164, 202
Lauchert, Meinrad von, 225
Lavaux, Roger, 274–277, 284, 288–290, 292–294, 414n37, 416n62
Le Meriot, France, 62
Le Paradis, France, 341n52
Le Renfort, xv, xx–xxi, 247, 310n12
League of German Girls, 318n45
Leander, Zarah, 95–97, 356n44
Lebensborn program, 67, 343n85
Lebensraum (living space), 38

Lechler, Paul, 198
Leer, Eugen, 166–170, 172–175, 178, 184, 197
Lehmann, Rudolf, 13, 93, 105, 106, 197, 217, 229, 233, 263, 278
Leibstandarte
Anschluss, 22
atrocities of, 330n27
defense of Berlin by, 125
designation as Panzer Division, 103
at the Eastern Front, 85–88, 93, 95, 97–99, 117, 118, 120, 121
in France, 58–62, 91–93, 108–109
in Greece, 71
in Hungary, 117, 120
in Italy, 100, 102–103
Night of the Long Knives, 17–18
physical requirements for, 11–12, 315n45
surrender of, 128–129
swearing-in ceremony, 4–6
training, 9–10, 14–17, 107
See also Germany, military units of
Lęki Duże, Poland, 39
Lengenfeld, Alfred, 330n27
Ligneuville, Belgium, 154, 164–165
Lindenfycht, 28, 100–101
Linge, Heinz, 125, 126–127
Linz, Austria, 54
Lithuania, mass murder in, 81
Living space *(lebensraum),* 38
Lochmüller, Rolf, 16
Łodż, Poland (Litzmannstadt), 41, 45, 47, 63, 72, 90, 102, 342n64
Loidl, Franz, 145
Lombard, Gustav, 11, 81, 82, 214, 215, 224
Löns, Hermann, 7
Lorenz, Erika, 89, 90
Louette, Raymond, xxi, 274, 276, 289, 301
Lublin, Poland, 42, 49, 55
Lucas, Franz, 55, 57, 338n20
Ludwigsburg, Germany, 216, 217, 223, 234
Luftwaffe, 56, 61, 66, 97
Lutrebois, Belgium, 158
Luxembourg, 67
Madagascar, 63
Magill, Franz, 15, 82
Maight, Alfred de, 198, 201
Malmédy Massacre, 111–112, 135, 137, 198, 206, 217, 220–221, 232–234, 257, 263–265, 301
Malmédy Massacre, investigation and trial
closing statements, 177–179
German officers, testimony of, 172–176
interrogation of witnesses, 141–145, 147–148
investigations of trial, 187–188
pleas from accused, 180–181
sentencing, 182, 373n28
US Supreme Court, appeal to, 187
See also Peiper, Joachim, on trial
Der Malmédy Prozess (Weller), 221, 391n55
Marchal, Pierre, 255, 274–275, 277, 288, 289, 295
Mariupol, 87, 88, 354n18–19
Marks, Carl, 19, 62
Masur, Norbert, 122
Mauthausen Concentration Camp, 54–55, 72
Mayalde, Conde de, 66
Mayr, Friedrich Wilhelm, 215–216
Mayr, Sigrid, 215–216, 298, 388n32
McCarthy, Joseph, 187
McCloy, John J., 190
McCown, Hal, 135, 142–143, 144, 148, 157, 165–166, 175, 179
Medical experiments, 94, 110
Meng, Helmuth, 200
Mengele, Josef, 194, 211, 383n48
Mével, Roland, 255
Meyer, Hubert, 295
Meyer, Kurt ("Panzermeyer"), 56, 62, 68, 85, 95, 96, 108, 203, 213, 330n27
MI-6, 45
Michel, Emile, 259
Mickelwaite, Claude B., 137, 140
Mielezyn, Poland, 39
Miesbacher Anzeiger (National Socialist newspaper), 216
Military units. *See* Canada; Germany; Soviet Union; United States

Minsk, Soviet Union, 214, 215, 351n88
Mittersill, Austria, 395n47
Möbius, Rolf, 174–175, 179
Mohnke, Wilhelm, 60, 110–112, 118, 125, 126, 127, 143, 151, 152, 157, 340n51
Moissé, André, 254–258, 277
Le Monde, on Peiper documentary, 301
Monserrat Abbey, Barcelona, 70
Monthiers, France, 61
Moritz, Max, xviii, 216, 231, 232, 234–235, 236, 245
Moritz Autohaus, 216, 231, 388n34, 396
Motzheim, Anton "Tony," 156, 177, 192
Müller, Benno, xiv, 207–208, 215, 236, 237, 245, 267, 279, 284, 383n48
Müller, Käte, 74, 93, 120
Müller, Uta, 240
Müller-John, Hermann, 39, 330n26
Mussert, Anton, 54
Mussolini, Benito, 21, 27
Mutke, Judith, 218–220
Mutke, Peter, 218, 219

Nannini, Christian, 293, 300
Narvid, Ben, 184
National Socialism, 4, 6, 9, 10, 17, 18, 30, 79, 316n12
Naujocks, Alfred, 45, 65, 193, 375n33
Nazi underground movement, 193–194
Nebe, Arthur, 33
Netherlands, 339n27
Neue Illustrierte, on execution at Beverloo, Belgium, 198
Nieder Ellguth, Poland, 41
Nietzsche, Friedrich Wilhelm, 317n27
Night of the Long Knives, 11, 17–18, 317n28
Nijmegen, Netherlands, 57
Noack, Hermann, 376n38
Noble, Andreu Ripol, 70
Nordhausen, Germany, 253
Nordman, Joe, 288
Nowo Danzig, massacre at, 86, 353n10
Nuremberg, Germany, 139, 190
Nüske, Gerhard, 95–96, 152, 163, 198

Oberursel, Germany, 144, 166
Obriot, Michel, xix, 289
Oder Front, 118–119
ODESSA (Organization of Former SS Members), 193, 375n33
OdR, 232
Ohlendorf, Otto, 190
Ohlendorf, Werner, 33
Oliva, Poland, 41
Olympic Games, Berlin, 1936, 20–21
Operation Barbarossa, 72–73, 75–77
Operation Bernhard, 65
Operation *Frühlingserwachen* (Spring Awakening), 120
Operation Werwolf, 122
Operation Wüste, 195
Operation Zitadelle, 98
Oradour-sur-Glane, France, 203
Oranienburg Concentration Camp, 33
Ostwall Panzergraben (East Wall anti-tank ditch), 56
Otto, Martin H., 137–138, 141

Paine, Thomas, 179
Panzermeyer (Kurt Meyer), 108
Paris, France, 62
Parry, Richard, 60
Parsifal (opera), 70
Pawlosiow, Poland, 41
Paygnard, Marc, 255–256, 258, 277
Peiper, Charlotte (mother), 6, 14, 83, 91, 122
Peiper, Elke (daughter), 63, 83, 84, 89, 91, 96, 201, 204, 211, 239, 307
Peiper, Hans Hasso (brother), 6, 8, 83, 313n24
Peiper, Hinrich (son), 96, 201, 204, 235, 239, 279, 284, 295–300, 306–307
Peiper, Horst (brother), 6, 17, 47, 63, 73, 75, 317n26, 347n45, 351n90
Peiper, Joachim "Jochen," early years and training
  allegiance sworn to Adolf Hitler, 3–6
  childhood and adolescence, 6–8
  evaluation of as officer candidate, 14
  full name of, 6
  Himmler, invitation by to join SS Verfügungstruppe, 12

Peiper, Joachim "Jochen," early years and training (*continued*)
Hitler, presentation to, 21
Hitler Youth, membership in, 10
leisure activities, 20
as National Socialist Party member, 28, 322n32
as 2nd Lieutenant of Leibstandarte Adolf Hitler, 17
at Officer's Candidate school, 13–14
at platoon leader course, 16–17
at SS Junkerschule in Braunschweig, 14–16
SS Reitersturm, membership in, 10–11
Peiper, Joachim "Jochen," with Himmler
as adjutant to Himmler, 23, 33
birth of daughter, Elke, 63
Christmas in Berlin (1939), 46–47
concentration camps, visits to, 32, 33, 48, 54, 72, 337n5
death's head ring, receipt of, 55
denial of knowledge of fate of Poles, 45–46, 50
description of Peiper, 37
euthanasia of institutionalized patients, account of, 46
as First Adjutant under Himmler, 33
genocide, knowledge of, 78, 82
German treatment of Poles, view of, 43
Himmler, relationship with, 36
at Hitler's Berghof headquarters, 65
Lodz ghetto, visit to, 72
marriage to Sigurd Hinrichsen, 34–35
Munich, with Hitler in, 44–45
National Socialist party, membership in, 28
Poland, tour of with Himmler, 39–43
promotions, 33
re-settlement camps, visit to, 46
reassignment as First Military Adjutant to Himmler, 62
resettlement program, view of, 49
significant meeting with Hitler, 65
travels with Himmler, 31–32, 44–46, 48–50, 53–55, 57, 64, 69–72, 80–81
ethnic German children, on placement of, 71
Zauberkreis (magic circle), as part of, 73
Peiper, Joachim "Jochen," Leibstandarte career of
in Austria, 121, 127–129
at Baugnez, 112, 153–154, 164, 167
Boves, massacre at, 102–103
in command of 11th Company, 62
comparison of Western and Eastern Fronts, 136
on concentration camps, 128
on cover of *Stuttgarter Illustrierte,* 62
at Eastern Front, 85–88, 93, 95, 97–99, 104–106
in France, 91–92
Hedwig Potthast, correspondance with, 82, 87, 88–89, 90–92, 94, 103–105, 323–324n46
at Himmler's Birkenwald headquarters, 118–119
last days of war, 127–129
medals, 58, 62, 96, 103, 106
medical leave, 106
Poles and Jews, opinion of, 135
as prisoner of war, 130–136, 147–148
promotions, 58, 106, 122
on suicide as option for soldiers, 129
Peiper, Joachim "Jochen," in Landsberg prison
commutation of sentences, 188, 198
friends, visits from, 192
parole board, appeals to, 191, 195
prison break plan, 188–189
release on parole, 199–204
Sigurd, visits from, 191–192
Peiper, Joachim "Jochen," on trial
at Baugnez crossroad, 153–154, 164, 167
on Büllingen, POWs in, 152–153
on conversation with Ellis, 169–170
on frozen POW at Petit Thier, 151, 157–158
Himmler, association with, 159–160
on Honfeld, presence in, 152
on killing of flier, 162
letters to Ellis and Everett, 182–184
at Ligneuville, 154–155

military career, description of, 149
on orders to kill POWs, 162–163, 169
pre-trial interrogation of, 141–144, 147–148, 149
on pre-trial statements, 160–161, 166
on prisoners of war, 148, 150–152, 154–158, 165, 168
sentence of, 182
on yellow/tan jacket, owner of, 152, 163

Peiper, Joachim "Jochen," return to civilian life
Americans, assessment of, 240
as book translator, xiv, xxi, 249
Borgo San Dalmazzo, charges regarding, 226–227
Boves massacre trial, 225–228
decorations, return of, 221
discovery of in France, 251–255
expulsion from France, call for, 258–259
family, adjustment to, 201, 204, 212
interview by Whiting, 241
love of fast cars, 236
Malmédy, work on book about, 263–265
Moritz Autohaus, employment by, 216
Motorbuch Verlag, work at, 238
newspaper interview in Traves, 255–258
plans to leave Traves, 262–263
with Porsche automotive company, 201–204, 208, 211
preparation to defend home at Traves, 268–269
press campaign against, 260–261
on quitting smoking, 398n12
retirement in Traves, France, xiii–ii, 238–239, 245–250
SS veterans, involvement with, 213–217, 232–233
testimony in war crime trials, 229–231
threats against, 259, 261, 268, 270
Toland's book, reaction to, 206–207
war books, concern about, 233–234
women friends, 218–221
working for *Auto, Motor, und Sport,* 236–237

Peiper, Joachim "Jochen," death of
burial of, 305–306
cause of death, 418n90
Daniel D., confession and retraction of, 291–292, 294–295, 416n62
delay of burial, 295–296, 299–300
exploitation of, 296–300
house, attack on, 272
house, destruction of, 272–274
identity of body, investigation of, 281–284
identity of body, speculation about, 276–278, 280
investigation of, 289–295, 407n24, 413n29, 414nn36–37
Ketelhut, police interest in, 293–294
public reaction to, 286–288
speculation about, 301–303

Peiper, Sigurd Hinrichsen (wife)
in Baden, Germany, 195, 197
brother Rolf, death of, 75
death of, 305
gifts from Himmler, 85, 89
health of, 204, 247–248, 295
Hedwig Potthast, friendship with, 109–111, 195
as Himmler's secretary, 28–29, 323n42
Jochen's death, 279, 295
Jochen's release from prison, 201
in Kiewitt, Germany, with Jochen, 107
at Malmédy trial, 149, 182, 184
marriage to Joachim Peiper, 34–35
in Miesbach, Germany, 298, 299
political perspective of family members, 322n35
in Rottach-Egern, Germany, 101, 188, 189
in Traves, France, 238
visit to friend in Switzerland, 267
visits from Jochen, 63, 73, 83, 84, 96, 106
visits to Jochen in prison, 191–192
in the Wartheland, 97, 100
in wartime Berlin, 84, 96

Peiper, Silke (daughter), 106, 195, 239, 307

Peiper, Woldemar (father), 6–7, 14, 47, 63, 89, 123, 189, 312n16, 313n19, 334–335n78
Peiper-Riegraf, Dorothee (daughter-in-law), 297
Peiper's House, map of, 283
Pekartschina, Soviet Union, 105, 359n29
Pélagy, Henri Bernard, 258, 266
Perl, William R., 149–150, 158, 159–160, 161, 162, 167, 169, 176, 221–222, 392n64
Perón, Evita, 193
Perón, Juan, 193–194
Petit Thier, Belgium, 151, 157–158, 179
Pfister, Dr., 178, 228
Piaski, Poland, 39
Pietsch, Paul, 236, 238
Piorkowski, Alexander, 54
Plenow, Poland, 40
Plock, Poland, 55
Poetschke, Werner, 107, 122, 147, 153–155, 157, 162, 167, 168, 175
Pohl, Eleonore von Brüning, 93, 110, 120, 196, 197
Pohl, Oswald, 32, 33, 44, 54, 55, 72, 93, 110, 120, 190, 197
Poland, 39–41, 42, 43, 45–48, 49
Polangen, Poland, 77
Porsche, Ferdinand, 202, 204
Porsche, Ferry, 202, 208
Porsche automotive company, 200–203
Posen, Poland, 46, 101–102
Postel, Georg-Wilhelm, 94
Potthast, Hedwig
  background of, 323n40
  birth of daughter, 108
  birth of son, 91
  end-of-war advice from Himmler, 120
  Himmler, affair with, 30, 57, 74, 80, 87, 93
  Himmler, correspondance with, 80, 324n50
  interrogation by US Army, 196
  interview by journalist, 196
  Jochen Peiper, correspondance with, 82, 87, 90–92, 94, 103–105, 323–324n46
  parents, reaction of to affair with Himmler, 80, 90, 349n69
  postwar life, 197
  at Schneewinkellehen, 117
  Sigurd Peiper, friendship with, 29, 90, 109–111, 195, 323n40
Potthast, Hilde, 90
Potthast, Karl, 90
Potthast, Thilde, 90, 117, 121, 362n19
Potthast, Walter, 80, 90, 91
Potthast, Wilhelmina, 90
Pouillaude, René, 276, 281
Prochorowka, Soviet Union, 98–99
Prawdin, Michael, 38, 160, 329n16
Preuss, Georg, 162, 199, 227
Priess, Hermann, 160
Prinzing, Albert, 198
Pripet Marshes, 78, 81–82, 350n81
Pruchtnow, Richard, 29
Pruneto, Giuseppe, 224
Prützmann, Hans-Adolf, 81, 122
Przemyśl, Poland, 48, 49

Racial engineering (eugenics), 25, 328n9
Racial superiority, 9, 37, 328n8
Raeder, Erich, 64
RAF air raids, 70, 97, 100, 104
Rahn, Otto, 29
Ramcke, Bernhard, 191
Rasch, Otto, 55
Ravensbrück Concentration Camp, 54, 93, 110
Ray, John, 370n15
Rediess, Wilhelm, 55
Reich Chancellery, 65, 120, 122, 127
Reichenau, Walther von, 10, 40, 42, 43, 314n39
Reinecker, Herbert, 298
Reiser, Rolf, 108, 109, 145, 150, 188, 217
Reitsch, Hanna, 144
Remer, Otto, 210
Resettlement program, 49, 395n40
Reuchet, Colonel, 287, 291
Ribbentrop, Joachim von, 39, 44, 64, 98, 99, 122
Riccardo Klement, 193–194
Riefenstahl, Leni, 11
Riemer, Otto, 145
Riga, Latvia, 80–81
Rigoulot, Ernest, xvii, xx, 239, 246, 259, 261, 277, 285, 286, 301

Rigoulot, Martial, 310n14
Rineck, Hans, 179
Ritzer, Rolf, 175
Rodenbücher, Alfred, 61, 340n51
Roermond, Netherlands, 57
Roesch, Werner, 189
Röhm, Ernst, 17
Rohrbach, Austria, 122
Röhwer, Hans, 228, 229
Rollin, Madeleine, 271, 273
Rommel, Erwin, 40, 41, 96, 97, 232
Roßdeutscher, Alfred, 75
Rosenfeld, Abraham, 163, 165, 170–171
Rosenstock, Herbert, 159
Rostov, Soviet Union, 87–88
Rottach-Egern, Germany, 110, 117, 131, 138, 188
Rotterdam, Holland, 56
Rowe, Harvey T., 297
Royall, Kenneth, 187
RSHA (Reich Main Security Office), 34
Rudel, Hans Ulrich, 192–193
Ruggles, John F., 132, 135
Rumkowski, Chaim, 72
Rumpf, Erich, 95, 96, 150, 169, 175–176
Rundstedt, Gerd von, 43, 57

Sachsenhausen Concentration Camp, 33, 48
Sanders, Stephen J. Jr., 132–136
Sator, Emil Adolf, 13, 14, 315n1
Säuberungsaktion (cleansing action), 79
Saucken, Harald von, 231
Schäfer, Ernst, 48, 49, 50, 229–231, 395n47
Schellenberg, Walter, 45, 64, 122
Schilling, Klaus, 190
Schilling, Wolfgang, 237, 238, 246, 263, 297
Schinkel, Kark Friedrich, 25
Schleswig-Holstein (battleship), 47
Schmidt, Wilhelm, 93
Schneewinkellehen, 108, 117
Schneider, Egon, 227
Scholtz-Klink, Gertrud, 387n21
Schönau, Germany, 108, 117
Schönfelder, Manfred, 239
Schörner, Ferdinand, 210
Schröder, Kurt von, 57
Schulze, Captain, 128
Schulze, Karl-Heinz, 233
Schulze-Kossens, Richard, 16, 233
Schützeck, Ernst, 60
Schwäbisch Hall, 147, 148, 149, 150, 160, 162, 171, 174, 177, 232
Schwarz van Berk, Hans, xviii, 192, 234, 237–238, 239, 246–247
Sebille, Gérard, 255, 277
Seetzen, Heinz Otto, 88, 354n21
Seidenglanz, Helmut, 198, 202
Selbstschutz (protectors of expatriate Germans), 47
Sell, Robert, 194
Senate Committee on Armed Services, 187
Sholar, William J., 208
Shumacker, Ralph, 174–175, 177–178
Sickel, Kurt, 113, 151, 158, 177–178
Sierk, Otto, 94, 356n44
Sievers, Franz, 157, 165, 172, 177
Sievers, Wolfram, 190
Simon, Gustav, 67
The Simple Life (Wiechert), 240
Simpson, Gordon A., 187
Siptrott, Hans, 104, 180, 207
Six, Franz, 64
Skorzeny, Otto (aka Rolf O. S. Steinbauer), 189, 193, 194, 205–206, 224–225, 376n38
Smijew, Soviet Union, 94
Smith, Carter, 210
Soldau, Poland, 55
Soviet Union
  assault on Berlin by, 118–119, 123–125
  Jews, gypsies, and political functionaries in, planned liquidation of, 73, 79–82
  Operation Barbarossa, 72–73, 75–77
  Stalingrad, defeat of Germans at, 93
  Vienna Woods, battle in, 121
Soviet Union, military units of
  5th Guard Tanks Corps, 98
  9th Guards tank army, 128
  29th Tank Corps, 98
  79th Guards Division, 125
  121st Rifle Division, 105
  148th Rifle Division, 105
  322nd Rifle Division, 105

Speer, Albert, 123, 158
Sprenger, Gustav, 148, 165
SS Race and Settlement Office, 9
SS (Schutzstaffel), 3, 9, 311n3, 316n12, 316–317n17
St. Momelin, France, 58
St. Pourçain, France, 62
Stalin, Joseph, 86
Stalingrad, Soviet Union, 93
La Stampa magazine, on Boves memorial, 223
Stars and Stripes, on Joachim Peiper, 140, 141, 145, 202
Stasi (East German Communist secret police), 253, 258
Stavelot, Belgium, 111, 155, 165
Steinbauer, Rolf O. S. (Otto Skorzeny), 205
Steiner, Felix, 33, 124, 218
Steininger, Herbert, 175
Sternebeck, Werner, 128, 145, 164
Stettin, Poland, 79
Steyr, Austria, 128
Stoumont, Belgium, 151, 156, 158, 165, 173, 177, 179
Straight, Clio E., 137
Streicher, Julius, 135
Strong, Herbert, 175
Stubbs, Daniel W., 199
Student, Kurt, 56
Stumpfegger, Ludwig, 57, 124, 128
Stuttgarter Nachrichten, on massacre at Boves, Italy, 219
Styrty, Soviet Union, 105
Sudetenland, annexation to Germany, 31
Swastika, 3, 36, 311n3, 327n2

Taganrog, Soviet Union, 87–88
Tank, Willi, 193
Die Tat, on Peiper's role in Boves massacre, 219
Tegernsee, 28–30, 74, 100–101, 106, 109, 117, 215
Teisseire, Henri, 281
Temme, Günther, 11
Terboven, Josef, 71
Theresienstadt Concentration Camp, 90
Thiele, Jochen, 152
Third Reich, 5, 312n8
Thon, Harry W., 148, 176–177, 181
Tiefenbacher, Sepp "Tüpferl," 215
Tiemann, Rolf, 113
Tilly, France, 108
Tilsit, Einsatzkommando, 77
Toland, John, 205–207, 209–210, 233, 420–421(Epilogue)n6
Tomhardt, Heinz, 172, 177
Tonk, August, 145, 344n5
Tortschin, Soviet Union, 106
Totenkopf Infantry Regiment 2, 63
Traves, France
  map of, xvi
  Peiper's death, consequences of, 286, 288, 289, 303
  Peiper's retirement in, xxi–xxii
  present-day, 307
Triumph of the Will (film), 11
Truman, Harry S., 137, 190
Tzschoppe, Erwin, 16

Ukrainians, welcome of German troops, 86–87, 88
United States, military units of
  1st Infantry Division, 136, 138, 139
  1st Infantry Division, 1st Counterintelligence Corps Detachment, 139
  1st Infantry Division, 26th Infantry Regiment, 139
  4th Infantry Division, 135, 136
  30th Infantry Division, 135, 179
  36th Infantry Division, 138
  80th Infantry Division, 145
  2nd Battalion S-2, 135
  3rd Army, 141
  7th Army, 141
  11th Armored Division, 206
  12th Army, 135, 137
  22nd Infantry Regiment, 2nd Battalion, 132, 135
  42nd "Rainbow" Division, 222nd Infantry Regiment, 130
  49th Anti-Aircraft Brigade, 112
  285th Field Artillery Observation Battalion, 141, 157
  431st AAA AW (Anti-Aircraft Artillery Automatic Weapons Battalion), 131

Counterintelligence Corps, 190
Eighth Air Force, 117
Untermenchen (subhumans), 73
Utrecht, Netherlands, 57

Van Roden, Edward L., 187
Vasallo, 224, 226
Venlo, Netherlands, 45, 57, 333n64
Verneuil, France, 93
Vesoul, France, 251, 254, 279, 288–289
Veterans, SS
meetings of, 203, 213–214, 223
organizations and journals, 217–218
rewriting of Leibstandarte history, 217
war crimes trials, 214–215
Vietnam, 240
Vogel, Leroy, 144
Vuillien, André, 254, 258–259, 280, 287

Waffen SS, 39, 42, 53, 71, 78, 107, 130–131, 190–192
Wagner, Eduard, 42
Wagner, Richard, 70
Wahler, Lt., 181
Walla, Gerhard, 175
Walter, Gerd, 217
Wandervögel movement, 131n21, 313n12
Wandt, Siegfried, 98
Wanne, Belgium, 111, 113
Warlimont, Walter, 220
Warsaw, Poland, 43, 49
Wattenberg, France, 58
Webling, Germany, 131
Weibgen, Georg, 9
Weidenhaupt, Wilhelm, 85
Weidinger, Otto, 233
Weller, Judith Ann, 220–221
Die Welt
letter by Hinrich Peiper, 296
on Peiper's death, 284
Werwolf, 193, 362–363n20
Westernhagen, Heinz von, 16, 94, 111, 113, 122, 155, 163, 167, 174, 317n22
Wewelsburg castle, 18–19, 54
When All Our Brothers Are Silent (Hausser & Peiper, eds.), 215
Whiting, Charles, 221, 234, 241
Wichmann, Otto, 128, 177
Wiechert, Ernst, 240, 309n9
Wieruszów, Poland, 39
Wieselmann, Bettina, 236–237, 260, 307
Wieselmann, Heinz-Ulrich "Uli," xviii, xix, 218–219, 236–238
Wiesenthal, Simon, xix, 226, 227, 299
Wiligut, Karl Maria, 87, 343n86
Wisch, Teddi, 98, 198, 228
Wittman, Michael, 105
Wlocalawek, Poland, 42
Woch, Rudi, 217
Wolf, Johanna, 126
Wolff, Karl
after release from prison, 386n13
arrest and trial of, 214, 386n9, 386n12
in Himmler's entourage, 25, 27, 39, 50, 54–55, 58, 65, 79, 80–81, 119, 214
house at Tegernsee, 101, 115
Wolff, Werner, 98, 108, 122
Wolfsschanze (Wolf's Lair), 76, 106
Wormhoudt, France, 59, 61, 340–341n51
Wortmann, Karl, 240
Wünsche, Max, 13, 23, 44, 56, 59, 60, 61, 62, 65, 108, 188, 218, 319nn3–4, 390n45

Żdżary, Poland, 39
Zhitomir, Soviet Union, 104, 105
Ziemssen, Dietrich, 217, 265, 296
Zimmermann, Günther, 197
Zloczew, Poland, 39
Zoppot, Poland
Zuffenhausen, Germany, 147, 149, 158
Zwigart, Paul, 170, 179, 181